Garden Insects of North America

Garden Insects

of North America

THE ULTIMATE GUIDE TO BACKYARD BUGS

Whitney Cranshaw

PRINCETON UNIVERSITY PRESS
PRINCETON AND OXFORD

Copyright © 2004 by Princeton University Press

Published by Princeton University Press, 41 William Street, Princeton, New Jersey 08540

In the United Kingdom: Princeton University Press, 3 Market Place, Woodstock,

Oxfordshire OX20 1SY

Library of Congress Cataloging-in-Publication Data
Cranshaw, Whitney.
   Garden insects of North America: the ultimate guide to backyard bugs / Whitney Cranshaw.
     p. cm.
   Includes bibliographical references (p.) and index.
   ISBN 0-691-09560-4 (cl. : alk. paper) — ISBN 0-691-09561-2 (pbk. : alk. paper)
    1. Garden pests—North America—Identification.   I. Title.

SB605.N7C73   2004
635′.0497—dc21   2003056330

British Library Cataloging-in-Publication Data is available

This book has been composed in Times

Printed on acid-free paper. ∞

www.nathist.princeton.edu

Printed in the United States of America

10 9 8 7 6 5 4 3

ISBN-13: 978-0-691-09560-8 (cloth)

ISBN-10: 0-691-09560-4 (cloth)

ISBN-13: 978-0-691-09561-5 (paperback)

ISBN-10: 0-691-09561-2 (paperback)

To entomology educators and to the Cooperative Extension system which so well fosters the spirit of shared learning

---

Contents

PREFACE   xi

ACKNOWLEDGMENTS   xiii

PHOTOGRAPHIC CREDITS   xv

CHAPTER ONE
Introduction to Garden Insects and Their Relatives   1
   Metamorphosis   2
   Hexapod Orders   4
   Identification of Immature Stages of Arthropods   6
   Excreted and Secreted Products Useful in Diagnosing Garden Arthropods and Slugs   12
   Body Parts Useful in Diagnosing Garden Arthropods   14
   Fruit and Foliage Injuries Produced by Arthropods and Slugs   16
   Plant Pathogens Transmitted by Arthropods   24

CHAPTER TWO
Management Principles for Some Garden Pests   26
   Leaf Chewers and Leafminers   26
   Flower, Fruit, and Seed Feeders   31
   Sap Suckers   35
   Gall Makers   41
   Stem, Twig, Branch, and Trunk Damagers   41
   Root, Tuber, and Bulb Feeders   43
   Miscellaneous Garden Insects   45

CHAPTER THREE
Leaf Chewers   48
   Slugs and Snails   48
   Grasshoppers   52
   Crickets and Katydids   56
   Walkingsticks   60
   Earwigs   62
   Ants   64
   Leafcutter Bees   70
   Conifer Sawflies   72
   Common Sawflies   76
   Slug Sawflies   82
   Other Sawflies   84
   Webworms   86
   Sod Webworms   92
   Diamondback Moth   94
   Leafrollers   96
   Spruce Budworms   104
   Skippers   106
   Webspinning Sawflies   108
   Skeletonizers   110
   Tent Caterpillars   112
   Gypsy Moth   116
   Fall Webworm   118
   Tussock Moths and Tiger Moths   120

Woollybears   126
Cankerworms, Spanworms, and Inchworms   128
Cutworms and Armyworms   134
Loopers   144
Hornworms/Sphinx Moths   146
Prominent Moths   150
Giant Silkworms/Royal Moths   154
Slug Caterpillars/Flannel Moths   158
Bagworms   160
Casebearers   162
Whites and Sulfurs   166
Swallowtails   168
Brushfooted Butterflies   172
Blister Beetles   176
Leaf Beetles   178
Flea Beetles   198
Mexican Bean Beetle   202

CHAPTER FOUR
Leafminers   204
Leafmining Flies   204
Leafmining Sawflies   210
Leafmining Moths   212
Leafmining Beetles   220

CHAPTER FIVE
Flower, Fruit, and Seed Feeders   222
Flower Thrips   222
True Bugs That Feed on Flowers, Fruits, and Seeds   224
Stink Bugs   228
Other Seed-Feeding Bugs   230
Fruit Flies   234
Yellowjackets and Hornets   242
Caterpillars That Damage Flowers, Fruits, and Seeds   246
Fruit-Infesting Sawflies   266
Fruit- and Flower-Infesting Beetles   268
Sap Beetles and Other Fruit-Damaging Beetles   272
Fruit, Flower, and Seed Weevils   276

CHAPTER SIX
Sap Suckers   284
Whiteflies   284
Psyllids   290
Aphids   296
"Woolly" Aphids   310
Adelgids   314
Mealybugs   316
Eriococcids, or Feltlike Scales   324
Cochineal Scales   326
Soft Scales   328
Margarodid Scales   340
Kermes, Pit, and Falsepit Scales   342
Armored Scales   344
Leafhoppers   356
Treehoppers   366
Spittlebugs   368

Squash Bug   372
Plant Bugs   374
Chinch Bugs   378
Stink Bugs   382
Lace Bugs   384
Thrips   386
Spider Mites   392
Tarsonemid Mites   402
False Spider Mites   404
Rust Mites   404

CHAPTER SEVEN
Gall Makers   408
Aphid Galls   408
Adelgid Galls   410
Phylloxeran Galls   412
Psyllid Galls   414
Gall-Making Flies   418
Gall Wasps   424
Eriophyid Mite Galls   430

CHAPTER EIGHT
Stem and Twig Damagers   434
Cicadas   434
Pine Tip Moths   438
Other Conifer-Tip-Boring Moths   440
Stem-Boring Moths of Deciduous Trees and Shrubs   442
Stem-Boring Sawflies   446
Pith-Nesting Bees and Wasps   448
Weevil Borers of Terminal Growth   450
Twig-Feeding Beetles   452
Twig-Boring Flies   458

CHAPTER NINE
Trunk and Branch Borers   460
Horntails   460
Clearwing Borers   462
Carpenterworms   468
Pyralid Borers   470
Noctuid Borers   472
Metallic Wood Borers/Flatheaded Borers   474
Longhorned Beetles/Roundheaded Borers   480
Weevil Borers   488
Bark Beetles   490

CHAPTER TEN
Root, Tuber, and Bulb Feeders   500
Pillbug and Sowbugs   500
Millipedes   502
Symphylans   502
Springtails   504
Root Aphids and Other Sucking Insects   506
Bulb Mites   508
Termites   510
Mole Crickets   512
Root Maggots and Bulb Flies   514

White Grubs   524
Root Weevils   532
Billbugs   540
Wireworms   542

CHAPTER ELEVEN
Beneficial Garden Arthropods   544
Predators   544
Parasites   564
Pathogens   568
Pollinators   572

APPENDIX OF HOST PLANT GENERA AND ASSOCIATED INSECTS AND MITES   577
GLOSSARY   629
SELECTED REFERENCES   637
INDEX   639

Preface

There are well over 100,000 insects and other arthropods in North America, and the scope of this book is necessarily limited. Emphasis is on those species most likely to be encountered in a yard and garden, particularly those that injure plants. This excludes many that are primarily restricted to forests, grasslands, or waters—although there certainly can be much overlap among species in these environments and those that occur in yards.

To establish what to include, the first step was to peruse myriad gardener-oriented books to see what they mentioned. This was then supplemented by reviewing standard entomology references (see Selected References). A review of Cooperative Extension entomology publications was used as a late-stage criterion for inclusion; if a species or group of species was worthy enough for a Cooperative Extension colleague to have written it up fairly recently, it was included. To further check for insects that may have been overlooked, and to produce the appendix of host plant associations, databases of samples received by diagnostic clinics were reviewed. The lists provided by Texas A&M and Virginia Polytechnic Institute and State University were particularly useful in this regard.

ORGANIZATION

The organization of this book is a hybrid of the ways many entomology texts are organized. The broadest groupings involve host plant associations, i.e., the area of the plant and type of injury produced. Therefore, insects that chew leaves are separated from those that suck sap from leaves, as well as from those that chew on a different part of the plant (e.g., roots, fruits, stems). The purpose of this organization is that the part of the plant where an insect is encountered is likely to be how a gardener most strongly associates the insect.

Within these main sections, the associated insects (and other garden "bugs") are organized by taxa, to the genus level whenever appropriate. Furthermore, an effort is made to place together in the text insects of somewhat similar appearance or habit. For example, mealybugs are placed near related groups such as "woolly" aphids and soft scales. Also, the caterpillars of many families of moths and skippers form protective shelters of silk, frass, and/or leaf fragments, and these are grouped. At the end of a section, classification to the order and family level is noted. For example, following discussion of the peach tree borer there is the notation Lepidoptera: Sesiidae to indicate that the peach tree borer is in the order Lepidoptera (moths and butterflies) and the family Sesiidae (clearwing borers).

The diversity of insect habits clearly defies any such easy grouping. For example, western corn rootworm develops as a root-feeding larva on corn plants, then feeds on leaves and flowers of a wide variety of plants as an adult. Japanese beetle is a first-class problem both in turfgrass, where it develops as a white grub, and later when it feeds on leaves and flowers of many garden plants. Such "crossover" species are primarily treated in one section (western corn rootworm as a leaf chewer, Japanese beetle as a flower feeder), but there are cross-references within the text.

COMMON NAMES

Throughout the book the use of common names, defined by scientific names, has been attempted. If a common name has been established by the Entomological Society of America (M. B. Stoetzel, *Com-

mon Names of Insects and Related Organisms), that takes precedence. For many insects and their relatives, however, there is not yet an officially recognized common name. Where this occurs, often one or more names have been proposed in other publications, and I have used those where appropriate. For a few insects and mites I propose common names in this book. Ultimately I hope all such common names will be formally proposed and, where acceptable, recognized by the Entomological Society of America and Entomological Society of Canada.

APPENDIX AND INDEX

The Appendix of Host Plant Genera and Associated Insects and Mites attempts to group all of the insects and mites associated with a plant genus. (In a small number of cases, it also includes slugs, snails, millipedes, and symphylans, where these four groups do notable damage.) This organization was a compromise that may be overly broad for some purposes. For example, all insects associated with any type of maple are grouped under the genus *Acer*. However, many insects found on red maple are specific to that species (*Acer rubrum*), whereas others are specific to sugar maple (*A. saccarhum*) or to boxelder (*A. negundo*). Also, some insect species that are extremely broad in host range, such as some grasshoppers, are generally excluded. Regardless, it is hoped that this appendix may help identify insects based on the plant(s) on which they are encountered.

The standard index at the end of the book is arranged by both scientific and common names.

Acknowledgments

Going into this project, I was perhaps naive in my understanding of what was involved and the effort it would take. So many fine entomology publications have been produced over the years, and this book is in large measure merely a compilation and synthesis of what has already been done. The variety of North American garden insects is awe inspiring, however, and this project has proved to be a challenge, although an enjoyable and ongoing one. I hope that all the time I have had to focus on this project has not taken too great a toll on my family, friends, and work associates. Sue, Sam, and Bill, you are wonderful.

I have read and reread many times the entomology references I have long found useful as a Cooperative Extension entomologist, and these are listed at the back of the book under Selected References. However, a few of these I would like to specifically mention. I have used *Insects That Feed on Trees and Shrubs* by Warren T. Johnson and Howard H. Lyon as the standard of a great entomology reference, and it is one I have always tried to emulate in my own Extension publications. In my estimation, no single work now approaches John Capinera's *Handbook of Vegetable Insects* as a definitive treatment for this area of entomology. Its publication in 2001 was a godsend. My understanding of vegetable and fruit problems in California has been greatly deepened by the outstanding series of publications put out by the University of California Statewide Integrated Pest Management Program. I remain always in awe of E. O. Essig's 1929 *Insects of Western North America*, written at a time when entomologists had a small fraction of the support available to them that they have today. Cynthia Westcott's *The Gardener's Bug Book* (1964) also remains an outstanding reference.

The availability of the internet to check details and locate materials has been critical to this project. I have looked over the Cooperative Extension publications of every state and have drawn heavily on many. I have particularly enjoyed and learned most from those produced by Ohio, Texas, Washington, North Carolina, New York, and Virginia. The work that James Baker and his colleagues in North Carolina did on ornamental insects is particularly good and so very accessible. The University of Florida merits special mention for the excellence of their myriad web sites.

Several people have provided special expertise on groups I found difficult. Susan Halbert has been invaluable in assistance with aphids and several related groups. Rayanne Lehman provided a wonderful edit of my mite sections, and Sharon Collman has straightened me out on root weevils. Boris Kondratieff keeps me straight on *everything*.

Actually getting this project completed would have been impossible without the outstanding, highly professional assistance of Princeton University Press. Robert Kirk guided me in developing the original ideas behind this book, and Linny Schenck kept me going to the end. Dimitri Karetnikov and Lorraine Doneker actually made it real with their design and illustration. And Liz Pierson gave me a wonderful lesson in editing that I will always remember.

I would also like to acknowledge the energy I have been able to draw on for this project from the work and example of so many colleagues. At Colorado State University I have long enjoyed the privilege of having Frank Peairs as my Extension entomology cohort. Dave Leatherman and I have long worked together on projects, and his zest for and abilities in natural history are inspirational. There are also many entomologists around the country who work hard and do so well in the area of bringing information on insects to the public. I wish especially to acknowledge the contributions to this project that have been made by three: James Baker, John Capinera, and David Shetlar.

This book is intended primarily for identification. As such it often provides little detail on the fascinating habits of the many, many insect species that surround us. Partly this is a limitation of the scope of this book, but it is partly because we humans remain so ignorant about these all-important life forms that surround us. To make up this deficiency in part, I urge all readers to pick up a copy of *Life on a Little Known Planet* by Howard Ensign Evans, which remains the best introduction ever to how insects live. Howard has long been an inspiration, and his recent passing, while this book was being written, was a real loss to all who knew him.

Photographic Credits

The illustration of this book has involved the generous assistance of so many. I have drawn particularly heavily on some individuals and organizations. IPM Images, a joint project of the National Science Foundation Center for Integrated Pest Management and the Bugwood Network coordinated out of The University of Georgia provides an outstanding resource of slides taken by scores of entomologists. Their work helped invaluably to showcase and ultimately get in contact with several individuals, all of whom granted permission to use their work. The Pacific Agri-Food Research Centre in British Columbia has great public-access information on fruit insects. Several U.S. Department of Agriculture agencies allowed access to images, notably the Agricultural Research Service (ARS), Forest Service (FS), and Animal and Plant Health Inspection Service, Plant Protection and Quarantine (APHIS PPQ). The University of California Statewide Integrated Pest Management Program and New York Agricultural Experiment Station also provided valuable assistance both in images and resource materials. Individually, David Shetlar has provided hundreds of slides for this project. Other major contributors who have donated use of a dozen or more images include Robert L. Anderson, Art Antonelli, James Baker, Ric Bessin, Doug Caldwell, John Capinera, John Davidson, Bastiaan Drees, H. C. Ellis, Dan Herms, Lacy L. Hyche, Bruce Kauffman, David Leatherman, Gerald J. Lenhard, Herbert A. "Joe" Pase III, Frank Peairs, Lance Risley, J. D. Solomon, and E. Bradford Walker.

And may there be a special place in heaven for Ken Gray and all those at Oregon State University who have made his collection available to all.

Contributing photographers and institutions include the following.

Mohammed Al-Doghairi, King Saud University
A. D. Ali, Davey Tree Expert Company
Robert L. Anderson, USDA Forest Service
Art Antonelli, Washington State University
James E. Appleby, University of Illinois
Mark E. Ascerno, University of Minnesota
James Baker, North Carolina State University
Scott Bauer, USDA-ARS
Ricardo Bessin, University of Kentucky
Ronald F. Billings, Texas Forest Service, Forest Health
Louis Bjostad, Colorado State University
J. Wayne Brewer, Auburn University
Ralph Byther, Washington State University
David Caeppert, Michigan State University
Doug Caldwell, Collier County, Florida, Cooperative Extension
R. Scott Cameron, International Paper, Forest Resources Research
John Capinera, University of Florida
Robert Childs, University of Massachusetts

William Ciesla, Forest Health Management International
Jack Kelly Clark, University of California Statewide Integrated Pest Management Program
Clemson University Archives
Sharon Collman, University of Washington
Connecticut Agricultural Experiment Station Archives
David Cook, University of Tennessee
John A. Davidson, University of Maryland
Eric Day, Virginia Polytechnic Institute and State University
Terry DelValle, Duval County, Florida, Cooperative Extension
Nihat Demirel, Colorado State University
Jerald E. Dewey, USDA Forest Service
G. Keith Douce, The University of Georgia
Bastiaan Drees, Texas A&M University
Arnold T. Drooz, USDA Forest Service
H. C. Ellis, The University of Georgia
Howard Ensign Evans, Colorado State University

CHAPTER ONE

Introduction to Garden Insects and Their Relatives

With few exceptions, the animals covered in this book are all members of the phylum Arthropoda—the arthropods. As such, all share certain physical features, including:

- division of the body into segments;
- an external skeleton (exoskeleton) and growth that requires periodic shedding of the exoskeleton (molting);
- jointed appendages;
- internal structures that include a heart running along the upper (dorsal) part of the body and a nerve cord running along the lower (ventral) part of the body; and
- bilateral symmetry in body organization, i.e., similar on both sides.

Within the phylum Arthropoda are several subdivisions known as classes. Although this book concerns itself primarily with the class Hexapoda, which includes the insects, five other arthropod classes can also be found in yards and gardens—crustaceans, millipedes, centipedes, symphylans, and arachnids.

The primary exception to arthropods included in this book are the slugs and snails. These are mollusks, more closely related to clams and mussels than to insects. They are often included in the broad purview of "garden bugs," however, and thus are discussed here.

The classification of the animals in this book, to the order level, is summarized as follows.

Phylum MOLLUSCA - *Mollusks*
Class GASTROPODA - *Slugs* and *Snails*
  Stylommatophora
Phylum ARTHOPODA - *Arthropods*
Class CRUSTACEA - *Crustaceans*
  Isopoda - *Pillbugs* and *Sowbugs*
Class DIPLOPODA - *Millipedes*
  Julida
  Spirostreptida
  Spirobolida
Class CHILOPODA - *Centipedes*
  Lithobiomorpha - *Stone Centipedes*
  Scolopendromorpha - *Tropical Centipedes*
Class SYMPHYLA - *Symphylans*
  Scutigerellidae - *Symphylans*
Class ARACHNIDA - *Arachnids*
  Opiliones – *Daddylonglegs,* or *Harvestmen*
  Aranae - *Spiders*
  Acari - *Mites and Ticks*
Class HEXAPODA - *Hexapods* (includes *Insects*)

METAMORPHOSIS

Because arthropods possess an external skeleton, they grow in distinct stages, each punctuated by a molting of the old exoskeleton and formation of a new, usually larger one. The stages between episodes of molting are known as instars.

During this growth process arthropods often undergo changes in form, a process known as metamorphosis. Sometimes these changes are minor, primarily involving an increase in size perhaps combined with changes in coloring or patterning. These changes can be more dramatic, however, particularly in insects as they approach the ultimate, adult form.

Broadly speaking, insects follow one of two general patterns of metamorphosis: simple metamorphosis or complete metamorphosis. Earwigs, grasshoppers, and aphids are examples of those that have a simple type of metamorphosis (see Figure 1). They have immature stages, known as nymphs or larvae, that generally resemble the adult and share many habits. In addition to a change in size, the nymphs may develop external features, such as wing pads, in transition to the adult. Adult insects differ from nymphs by being sexually mature and, if they are winged, have functional wings.

Much more specialization of function—and difference in form—occurs among the insects that undergo complete metamorphosis. The immature stages are collectively known as larvae, although larvae of many insects are so recognizable that they commonly go by another name such as grub, caterpillar, or maggot. Several larval instars often are similar in appearance, although they get progressively larger in size. At the end of the last larval stage they often move to some protected site and become inactive in preparation for transition to a unique stage known as the pupa. Tremendous changes take place during the pupal stage as larval features dissolve and are transformed into those of the adult. Among insects with complete metamorphosis, the appearance and habits of the adult may be very different from those of larvae. The overwhelming number of insects species are those that undergo complete metamorphosis and include beetles, moths and butterflies, flies, bees, ants, and wasps (see Figure 2).

Regardless of the type of metamorphosis, further development of external structures ceases once insects reach the adult form. Therefore a little fly is not a "baby" big fly or a tiny ant a "baby" ant. They are merely adults of a small species or were stressed through poor diet or some other factor during larval development.

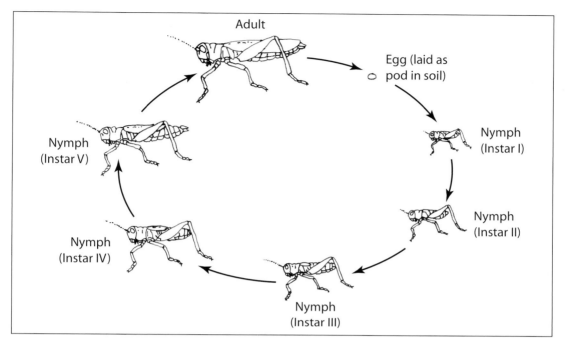

Figure 1. Simple metamorphosis of a grasshopper. *Figure by L. Mannix.*

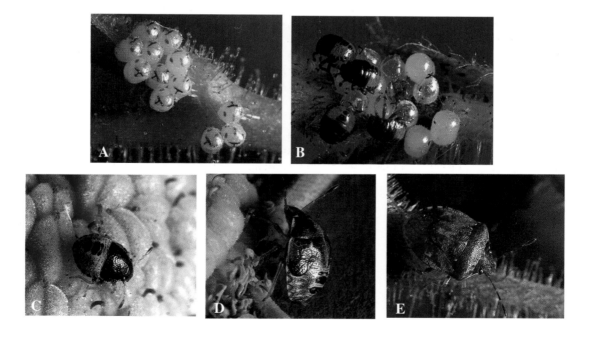

A. Egg mass of stink bug *Cosmopepla intergressus*. *K. Gray*. **B.** Egg mass at time of hatch. *K. Gray*. **C**. Nymph of *Cosmopepla intergressus*. *K. Gray*. **D**. Nymph of *Cosmopepla intergressus*. *K. Gray*. **E**. Adult of *Cosmopepla intergressus*. *K. Gray*.

HEXAPOD ORDERS

The hexapods share several features that separate them from the other arthropod classes. These include:

- division of the body into three main regions (head, thorax, abdomen);
- three pairs of legs, located on the thorax; and
- one pair of antennae.

Many also develop wings in the adult stage and thus are the only winged arthropods.

Two subdivisions (subclasses) of the hexapods are generally recognized. The overwhelming majority are Insecta, the insects. A small number of hexapod species are in the subclass Entognatha, which includes most prominently the springtails. Entognatha share many features more characteristic of crustaceans and thus are now commonly considered separate from the insects.

Currently, approximately 30 different orders of insects are recognized. Several are infrequently encountered in the yard and garden because of their small size, scarcity, or habits that restrict them to different environments, as in the aquatic insects. The orders and type of metamorphosis of the insects most likely to be seen in yards and gardens include the following.

Order (Common Name)	Type of Metamorphosis
Coleoptera (beetles)	Complete
Diptera (flies, gnats, mosquitoes, and relatives)	Complete
Lepidoptera (butterflies, moths, skippers)	Complete
Hymenoptera (ants, bees, wasps, sawflies, and relatives)	Complete
Neuroptera (lacewings, antlions, and relatives)	Complete
Thysanoptera (thrips)	Variation on simple metamorphosis including nonfeeding stages prior to adult emergence
Orthoptera (grasshoppers, crickets, katydids)	Simple
Mantodea (mantids)	Simple
Phasmatodea (walkingsticks)	Simple
Isoptera (termites)	Simple
Dermaptera (earwigs)	Simple
Hemiptera (true bugs)	Simple
Homoptera (aphids, psyllids, whiteflies, scale, cicadas, leafhoppers, and relatives)	Simple, but some species have nonfeeding stages that share features intermediate with complete metamorphosis
Collembola (springtails)[1]	Primitive type with little change in features, other than size, between immature and mature stages

[1] Classified in the subclass Entognatha; all other orders here are in the subclass Insecta.

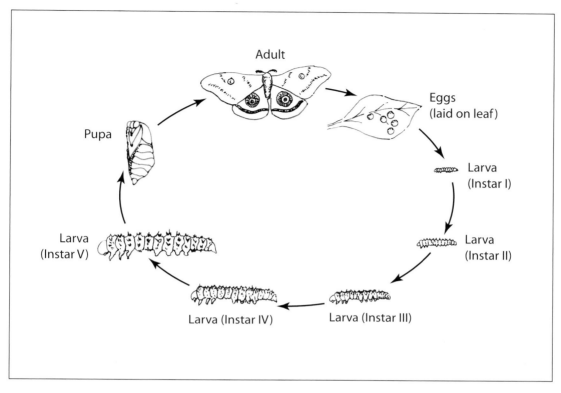

Figure 2. Complete metamorphosis of a moth. *Figure by L. Mannix.*

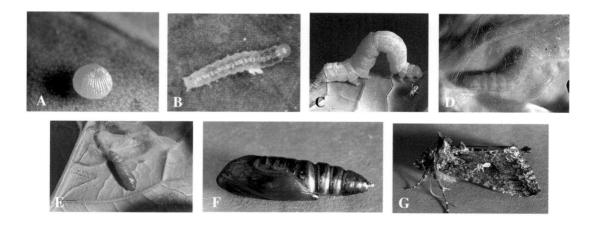

A. Cabbage looper egg. *K. Gray.* **B.** Newly hatched cabbage looper larva. *W. Cranshaw.* **C.** Cabbage looper larva. *K. Gray.* **D.** Cabbage looper larva spinning cocoon prior to pupation. *K. Gray.* **E.** Early-stage cabbage looper pupa. *K. Gray.* **F.** Later-stage cabbage looper pupa, after darkening. *K. Gray.* **G.** Cabbage looper adult. *K. Gray.*

IDENTIFICATION OF IMMATURE STAGES OF ARTHROPODS

Because of the changes that occur during development, arthropods change in appearance at different life stages. These changes are particularly dramatic in insects that undergo complete metamorphosis (e.g., beetles, moths and butterflies, flies). Often it is the immature stage (e.g., caterpillars, grubs) that causes most plant injury, as many larvae are specialized feeding machines. Adults may have very different form and functions (e.g., reproduction, dispersal). Thus, it can be difficult when observing insect activity to associate the adult and immature stages of the same insect.

The arthropod orders whose immature stages are most likely to be seen in yards and gardens are discussed below.

Coleoptera (Beetles)

Beetle larvae are often known as grubs. All possess strong jaws designed to chew, and the jaws may be quite prominent in species that chew wood or capture prey. The larval form is often elongated. Three pairs of legs on the thorax are clearly present among those species that actively move about aboveground or on the surface of plants (e.g., lady beetles, leaf beetles).

Grubs that develop belowground or within plants typically lose pigmentation and are pale colored, usually creamy white. For those that actively dig in soil, such as the white grubs, the front legs are well developed and may be used in digging. Many important groups of beetles develop within plants, however, and their larvae have lost all legs, leaving only the darkly colored head capsule as a conspicuous feature. The bodies of bark beetles and weevil larvae somewhat resemble pieces of puffed rice with a dark head. Flatheaded borers, larvae of metallic wood borers, are quite elongated and have a broad area on the first segment of the thorax. Roundheaded borers, larvae of longhorned beetles, are also quite elongated, with the dark prominent jaws distinguishing the head region.

Lepidoptera (Butterflies, Moths, Skippers)

Immature stages of lepidopterans are known as caterpillars. They possess three pairs of clawlike true legs on the thorax. Unlike most immature insects, however, they also possess fleshy leglike extensions, known as prolegs, on several segments of the abdomen. Each proleg is tipped with minute hooks, known as crochets, arranged in patterns characteristic of each family. All lepidopteran caterpillars can be distinguished from other insect larvae by the presence of two to five pairs of prolegs, each of which is tipped with crochets (see Figure 3).

The legs and prolegs of caterpillars that bore into plants (e.g., clearwing borers) may be very reduced. However, the presence of crochets always distinguishes them from other wood-boring insects.

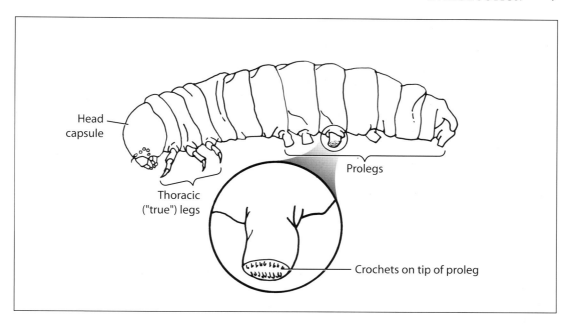

Figure 3. Features of larval insects. *Figure by L. Mannix.*

A. Lady beetle larva with prey. *K. Gray.* **B.** Colorado potato beetle larva. *W. Cranshaw.* **C.** Weevil larva. *F. Peairs.* **D.** Typical flatheaded borer, larva of a metallic wood borer. *K. Gray.* **E.** Roundheaded borer, larva of longhorned beetle. *F. Peairs.* **F.** Tomato hornworm larva, a typical caterpillar with five pairs of prolegs. *W. Cranshaw.* **G.** Cabbage looper, a caterpillar with three pairs of prolegs. *K. Gray.* **H.** Underside of a peach tree borer larva showing hooklike crochets at base of each proleg. *W. Cranshaw.*

Neuroptera (Lacewings, Antlions, and Relatives)

All neuropteran larvae are predators. Curved, lancelike jaws project prominently from the head. Larvae are active and possess legs on the thorax but no prolegs on the abdomen.

Hymenoptera (Ants, Bees, Wasps, Sawflies, and Relatives)

Rarely do gardeners encounter the larval stages of Hymenoptera. This is because they occur in colonies (e.g., social wasps, honey bees, ants), develop in specialized nest cells (e.g., hunting wasps, leafcutter bees), or are in plants (e.g., gall wasps). These larvae are usually very pale colored and have little pigmentation except around the mouthparts. A distinct head region is present but can be difficult to distinguish since there is little color difference.

Larval features are very different among some of the active leaf-feeding larvae, notably the sawflies. Sawfly larvae look quite similar to moth and butterfly larvae and similarly are often termed caterpillars. Like Lepidoptera larvae, sawfly larvae have prolegs on the abdomen, but the number is significantly different. Sawflies possess six to eight pairs of prolegs, and none have the hooklike crochets at the tip that characterize moth and butterfly larvae.

Diptera (Flies, Gnats, Mosquitoes, and Relatives)

Larvae of the "true flies" completely lack legs. Furthermore, many lack any distinct head area. Instead the head end is often tapered to a point and surrounds a pair of tiny hooks that are normally retracted. A pair of eyelike spiracles are commonly present on the hind end. This larval form is known as a maggot and is produced by flies in the suborder Brachycera (e.g., root maggots, house flies, flower flies).

Larvae in the suborder Nematocera (e.g., gnats, midges, mosquitoes) also lack legs but have a distinctly visible head capsule which often is darker than the rest of the body.

Thysanoptera (Thrips)

Most immature thrips (larvae) roughly resemble adults in body form, and the first stages often are found together with the adults on plants. (Late-stage larvae usually drop to the soil and undergo a non-feeding period where they experience some physical changes.) However, immature thrips lack wings and often have different coloration.

Hemiptera (True Bugs)

True bugs have a simple type of metamorphosis, and thus immature stages (nymphs) feed in a manner similar to the adults and share many other habits with them. Body form is generally similar, but nymphs lack the fully developed wings of the adults and are not sexually mature. Wing pads become increasingly prominent as the nymphs approach maturity.

A. Larva of a yellowjacket wasp. *K. Gray.* **B.** Larva of mountain-ash sawfly. *D. Herms.* **C.** Typical maggot-form larva of many dipterans. *K. Gray.* **D.** Mosquito larvae. *K. Gray.* **E.** Immature gladioulus thrips. *K. Gray.* **F.** Life stages of house fly. *Courtesy Clemson University.* **G.** Larva of an ant lion, a neuropteran. *K. Gray.* **H.** Squash bug nymph. *K. Gray.* **I.** Head of damsel bug showing prominent piercing-sucking mouthparts of Hemiptera. *W. Cranshaw.*

Homoptera (Aphids, Psyllids, Whiteflies, Scales, Cicadas, Leafhoppers, and Relatives)

Homopteras undergo simple metamorphosis. In most families, immature stages roughly resemble adults except they lack wings. In some families, however, there can be unusual forms. In whiteflies and psyllids, nymphs are quite flattened and look very different than the winged adults. This is particularly true in whiteflies where there is a special nonfeeding transition stage (sometimes referred to as a pupa) immediately preceding the adult. The first stage following egg hatch among scale insects, known as the crawler, is highly mobile and little resembles the more sedentary later stages which produce a waxy cover. Similarly, the nymphs of cicadas are specialized for life belowground, whereas adults are winged and look substantially different.

Orthoptera (Grasshoppers, Crickets, Katydids)

Most features of immature and adult Orthoptera are similar. Only the adult has fully developed wings, however. Coloration and patterning among nymphs also commonly change with age. Wing pads are present on immature stages and become more prominent as maturity approaches.

Mantodea (Mantids)

Most external features of immature and adult mantids are similar except the wings. As mantids develop, the wing pads become increasingly prominent, with the wings becoming fully developed and functional only in the adult stage.

Dermaptera (Earwigs)

Most features of immature and adult earwigs are similar. The tail-like cerci on the tip of the abdomen and the wing pads increase in size as the insects mature.

Isoptera (Termites)

Features of almost all immature and adult termites are similar, differing only in size. Metamorphosis can be more flexible among these social insects, and some may develop into different castes (e.g., soldiers, reproductives) as colony needs determine. Reproductive forms possess large, functional wings in the adult stage and distinct wing buds in the early stages of development.

Collembola (Springtails)

All stages of springtails have similar external features and differ only in size.

Acari (Mites and Ticks)

Following egg hatch, all mites (except eriophyid mites) and ticks are minute and six legged, a stage known as a larva. After the first molt they transform into eight-legged immature stages and possess the general body form of the adult for the remainder of their development. Among spider mites there are two additional molts as they transform through the protonymph and deutonymph, ultimately reaching the adult form. Other mites may have an additional nymphal stage (tritonymph). Special inactive "resting stages" may occur with these groups of mites.

An unusual mite family is the eriophyid mites. These are minute, with an elongate, carrot-shaped form, and they possess only two pairs of legs in all life stages.

A. Adult aphid and nymphs. *K. Gray*. **B.** Eggs and immature whiteflies. *K. Gray*. **C.** Psyllid nymphs. *K. Gray*.
D. Crawler stage of soft scale. *K. Gray*. **E.** Grasshopper nymph. *W. Cranshaw*. **F.** Termite worker. *K. Gray*. **G.** Mantid nymph. *W. Cranshaw*. **H.** Mother earwig and young nymphs. *K. Gray*. **I.** Spider mite colony with different life stages. *K. Gray*. **J.** Springtails. *W. Cranshaw*.

EXCRETED AND SECRETED PRODUCTS USEFUL IN DIAGNOSING GARDEN ARTHROPODS AND SLUGS

Honeydew. This is a sticky, largely sugary liquid excreted by certain insects that feed on the phloem of plants. It is produced by certain insects in the order Homoptera, including aphids, soft scales, whiteflies, mealybugs, and some leafhoppers. Because of its high sugar content, honeydew is highly attractive to ants, wasps, bees, and other insects. On surfaces where honeydew persists for long periods, it supports sooty molds; fungi similarly use honeydew for growth.

Fecal, or Tar, Spots. Dark fecal spots on foliage are associated with many plant-feeding insects that suck sap from the mesophyll of plants. These include thrips, lace bugs, and some leafhoppers, spider mites, and plant bugs. Because of the nature of the feeding, there is usually associated leaf spotting. The size of the tar spots is related to the size of the insects.

Spotting is also produced by most moths shortly after they emerge from the pupal stage. It is usually pale brown or reddish brown and is known as meconium. Syrphid flies, a common family of aphid predators, also leave dark smears of excrement on plants.

Frass. The solid excrement produced by insects that feed on solid foods is known as frass. Texture and consistency largely depend on diet; insects feeding on high-moisture foods produce soft and watery frass, whereas those feeding on dried wood or grain produce granular frass. In some species the frass may have a highly characteristic pattern or texture and can be a useful identification aid.

Silk. The silk found around plants is most characteristic of caterpillars such as leafrollers, tent caterpillars, and fall webworms which use silk to create shelters and tie together foliage. The webspinning sawflies also construct shelters of silk. Silk, formed into a cocoon, also surrounds the pupal stage of many moth larvae, sawflies, lacewings, and other insects.

Most spider mites produce visible silk, particularly when their populations are high. Spiders also use silk for many purposes. Most obvious are the webs some species use to snare prey. Other spiders use silk to form a "retreat" in which they hide when not foraging for prey. Also, almost all spiders use silk to cover egg masses.

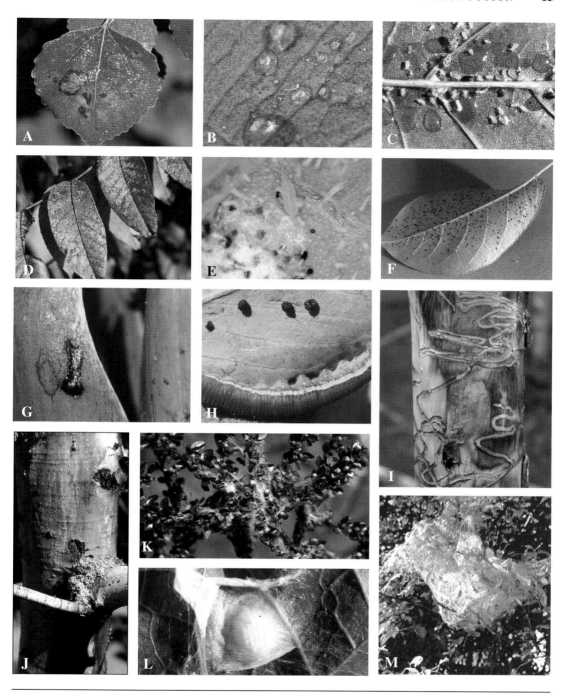

A. Honeydew and fungal leafspotting on aspen leaf. *W. Cranshaw*. **B.** Honeydew droplets. *W. Cranshaw*. **C.** Norway maple aphids and excreted honeydew. *W. Cranshaw*. **D.** Sooty mold growing on honeydew-contaminated walnut leaves. *W. Cranshaw*. **E.** Thrips nymph with associated scarring and fecal spotting. *W. Cranshaw*. **F.** Tar spots characteristically excreted by lace bugs. *K. Gray*. **G.** Fecal smear produced by syrphid fly larva. *W. Cranshaw*. **H.** Frass produced by alfalfa caterpillar. *W. Cranshaw*. **I.** Tunneling under bark characteristic of flatheaded borers. *D. Leatherman*. **J.** Sawdust-like frass and oozing at wound made by poplar borer larva. *D. Leatherman*. **K.** Webbing produced by cotoneaster webworm. *S. Collman*. **L.** Spider egg sac and surrounding silk. *W. Cranshaw*. **M.** Tent produced by fall webworm. *K. Gray*.

Wax. Many bees produce wax, to line or form cells used to rear young and store fluids. On plants, waxy material may be present as excreted products of some sap-feeding insects, particularly psyllids. This excreta may take the form of small pellets or waxy threads.

Wax also covers the body of the "woolly" aphids, mealybugs, and some scale insects. It is often quite conspicuous when produced to cover egg sacs. All of these insects typically occur in groups.

Mucous Trails. Slugs and snails produce a mucous covering that appears as a "slime trail" on surfaces they contact. It disappears rapidly with drying and is best observed early in the morning or in humid sites.

BODY PARTS USEFUL IN DIAGNOSING GARDEN ARTHROPODS

Cast Skin (Exuvium). All arthropods shed their exoskeleton several times in the process of developing. Insects with chewing mouthparts usually consume the old cast skin, or exuvium, shortly after molting. Insects with sucking mouthparts, however, such as aphids, leafhoppers, and spider mites, cannot feed on the exuvium, which subsequently persists.

Scale Cover. The waxy cover of a scale insect, also known as the exuvium, is usually distinctive enough to distinguish species. It often persists on plants for a year or more after the insect has died, ultimately weathering and flaking off. The scale cover also can identify the stage of the insect, as the covering often appears as a series of rings, each produced following a molt.

Egg Shells. Following egg hatch, many insects with chewing mouthparts consume the old egg shells. However, spider mites and insects with mouthparts designed to suck fluids leave the old egg shells intact. These may persist on foliage for a considerable period. Even when the insects or spider mites are no longer present, the old egg shells can be useful for diagnosis.

A. Wax frames produced by honey bees establishing colony on tree branch. *W. Cranshaw.* **B.** Waxy strands (lerps) excreted by boxwood psyllid. *J. Capinera.* **C.** Colony of "woolly" apple aphids on branch. *W. Cranshaw.* **D.** Mealybugs with egg sac. *K. Gray.* **E.** Cottony maple scale with waxy egg sac. *K. Gray.* **F.** Aphids with cast skins following molt. *W. Cranshaw.* **G.** Cast skin of a dog-day cicada. *W. Cranshaw.* **H.** Recently emerged lady beetle and old pupal skins. *T. J. Weissling.* **I.** Scale covering of armored scale. *K. Gray.* **J.** Spider mites with old cast skins and eggs. *W. Cranshaw.* **K.** Scale covering of soft scale. *K. Gray.*

FRUIT AND FOLIAGE INJURIES PRODUCED BY ARTHROPODS AND SLUGS

Bronzing/Russeting. A generalized bronzing or graying of leaf and needle surfaces results from sustained feeding by large numbers of spider mites or rust mites. Often there is an associated thickening or increased leatheriness of the leaf. When such an injury occurs on fruit, it is often termed russeting and may also show some slight scarring.

Catfacing of Fruit. Distortion of the normal shape of fruit can result from a wide range of injuries to young fruit. Insects with sucking mouthparts, notably plant bugs and stink bugs, kill areas around the feeding site, resulting in deep dimples as the fruit expands. Smaller dimpling may result from egg-laying wounds or chewing injuries of adult weevils. Surface feeding on expanding fruit by caterpillars (fruitworms, leafrollers) typically results in large sunken areas, often with a scabby texture. Collectively these types of fruit distortions induced by insects are known as catfacing injuries.

Defoliation. Strictly, defoliation relates to any leaf loss. However, it can be effected in many different ways. Most commonly it is caused by chewing insects that remove sections of tissue from individual leaves. Entire leaves may be consumed in this manner or may subsequently drop (abscise) in response to injury. Defoliating insects that chew leaves include caterpillars, adults and larvae of many beetles, sawfly larvae, grasshoppers, earwigs, and leafcutting ants. Some insects defoliate plants in a characteristic manner and produce injuries described by such terms as *notching, shotholing, skeletonizing,* and *windowpaning* (see below). Slugs cause characteristic injuries because of their rasping mouthparts.

Leaves may also drop prematurely in response to various stresses including drought and nutrient deficiencies. High populations of spider mites and sap-sucking insects (aphids, leafhoppers, scales) also may induce premature leaf drop.

Flagging. Wilting of leaves that remain attached results when water movement has been restricted to the terminal. This can be caused by various pathogens that girdle twigs, such as fire blight, or those that restrict water movement by plugging the xylem, such as Dutch elm disease. However, many insects can produce flagging by chewing twigs. Twig girdlers, certain grasshoppers, and European hornets are examples of insects that may chew on the outside of bark. Tip moths cause dieback of twigs, and other twig-boring caterpillars cause similar injuries to deciduous trees and shrubs. Flagging may occur on just the terminal growth, as occurs with white pine weevil.

A less common cause of flagging is wounding produced during egg-laying. These oviposition injuries are most prominent with cicadas, whose wounds often cause twigs to break.

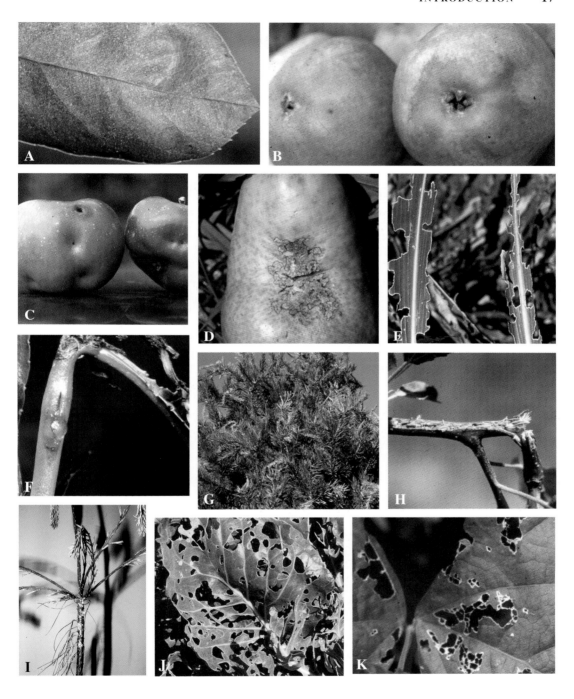

A. Leaf rusting symptom following infestation by southern red mite. *W. Cranshaw.* **B.** Russeting at end of pear fruit by pear russet mite. *E. Nelson.* **C.** Catfacing injury caused by plant bug feeding. *W. Cranshaw.* **D.** Catfacing injury caused by a chewing insect, obliquebanded leafroller. *R. Zimmerman.* **E.** Leaf chewing injuries by grass-hoppers. *W. Hantsbarger.* **F.** Flagging at tip caused by infestation of oriental fruit moth. *Courtesy Clemson University.* **G.** Tip dieback caused by pine tip moths. *W. Cranshaw.* **H.** Twig break (flagging) caused by egg-laying wounds of Putnam's cicada. *W. Cranshaw.* **I.** Flagging of terminal caused by white pine weevil feeding injury. *E. B. Walker.* **J.** Leaf-chewing injuries by caterpillars on cabbage. *W. Cranshaw.* **K.** Irregular chewing injuries typical of slug feeding. *W. Cranshaw.*

Leaf Cupping. Leaves may cup in response to removal of tissue or to feeding by sucking insects during leaf expansion. This kind of injury is most characteristic of certain thrips, plant bugs, aphids, and psyllids. There are many other causes of leaf cupping, including exposure to some herbicides and cold injury.

Leaf Curling. This typically results from injuries caused during leaf expansion. Aphids developing on new growth are a common cause of leaf curling in spring and early summer. Thrips and plant bugs also cause certain types of leaf curling. Leaves may also curl after leaf expansion by leafrollers and leaftiers. These are caterpillars that pull together leaves and fasten them with silk to form shelters in which they feed.

Mining of Leaves and Needles. Certain insects, known as leafminers and needleminers, develop by tunneling between the upper and lower surfaces of leaves and needles, respectively. External evidence of these insects is characteristically patterned tunnels, often in a blotch or serpentine form. Leafminers can be separated from other causes of leaf spotting (e.g., fungi, bacteria, chemical injuries) by the leaf surfaces being easily separated and by the presence of the larvae and/or excrement. Leaf- and needleminers include larvae of various caterpillars, sawflies, flies, and leaf beetles.

Notching of Leaf Margins. Chewing along the edge of leaves is characteristic of many insects such as certain adult weevils, caterpillars, sawflies, and grasshoppers. Only a few limit feeding to the margin, however, and some make regular, angular cuts. This is particularly common among adult root weevils, such as the black vine weevil. Notching is also used to describe the semicircular cuts characteristic of leafcutter bees and leafcutting ants.

Oviposition Scars. Some insects damage plants in the process of laying eggs (oviposition). Small puncture wounds in leaves or needles are characteristic of sawflies. Leafmining flies also puncture leaves. Less conspicuously, eggs are inserted into leaf tissues by several other insects such as leafhoppers, plant bugs, lace bugs, and thrips.

Egg-laying scars also occur on other parts of the plant. Twig scars are produced when cicadas, treehoppers, and certain leafhoppers insert eggs into young twigs. (Seriously damaged twigs may break, producing flagging.) Fruit may be damaged when flower thrips or fruit flies insert eggs into developing fruit or when weevils chew the fruit surface prior to egg-laying.

Pansy Spotting of Fruit. Diffuse cloudy areas on the surface of maturing fruit result from injuries by some insects. This is a common result of stink bugs feeding on maturing fruit. Egg punctures of thrips can also result in halo-shaped "pansy spots" on seed pods and fruit surfaces.

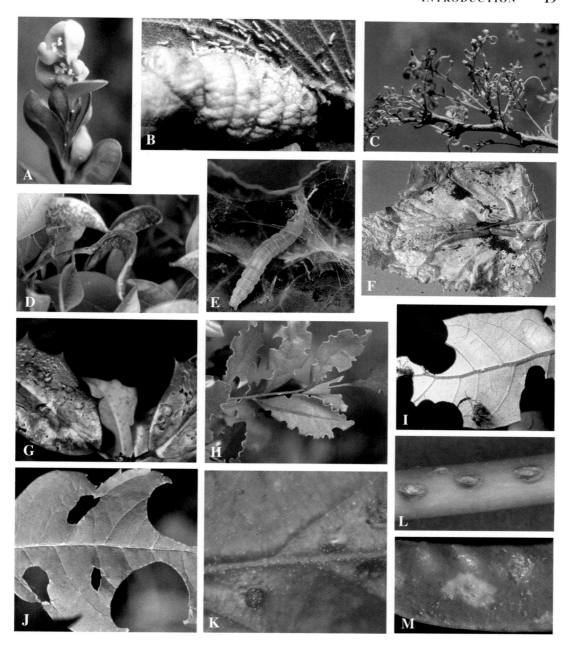

A. Leaf cupping by boxwood psyllid. *D. Herms.* **B.** Leaf curling by aphids on elm. *W. Cranshaw.* **C.** Leaf curling associated with plant bug injury to honeylocust. *W. Cranshaw.* **D.** Leaf curling caused by Cuban laurel thrips. *D. Shetlar.* **E.** Fruittree leafroller webbing together a leaf shelter. *W. Cranshaw.* **F.** Birch leafminer injury. *E. B. Walker.* **G.** Holly leafminer damage. *D. Shetlar.* **H.** Angular leaf margin notching characteristic of many root weevils. *W. Cranshaw.* **I.** Texas leafcutting ant. *R. S. Cameron.* **J.** Circular leaf notching characteristic of leafcutter bees. *W. Cranshaw.* **K.** Leaf scars made during egg-laying by elm leafminer. *W. Cranshaw.* **L.** Oviposition scars on young twig produced by treehopper. *W. Cranshaw.* **M.** Scarring of pod and surrounding "pansy spot" from egg-laying wound of western flower thrips. *W. Cranshaw.*

Reddening. Leaf reddening can be a plant response to saliva introduced by certain aphids, scales, and spider mites. This reaction is often plant specific; i.e., it may occur on some species or cultivars but not on others. Color changes also can occur in evergreens when branches die. For example, certain bark beetles that affect conifers can cause foliage to turn reddish brown. The process of color change from the original green is often called "fading."

Scarring. Leaf scarring can result from the reaction of a plant to many insects that suck sap from the mesophyll and destroy cells as they feed. Scarring injuries are most commonly associated with thrips, however. Initial thrips injuries typically appear silvery but often darken later to produce streaky scars on the affected leaves, fruit, and flowers. A hypersensitive response in some plants to thrips feeding may produce small wartlike growths.

Shotholing. Shothole injuries are small, generally round holes cut into leaves. One leaf surface is usually left intact, but it typically dries, allowing a hole to form. Insects that produce shotholes include adult flea beetles, young stages of some caterpillars, and some young sawfly larvae. Large holes are typical of feeding by some adult leaf beetles and older sawflies.

Leaf tissues may drop out in response to the puncture wounds some insects make when laying eggs. Damage of tissues by plant bug feeding sometimes results in irregular areas that later die and drop. Some fungi also cause shotholes to form on foliage in areas where infected tissue drops out. The term *shothole* is also applied to exit holes produced by various small wood-boring bark beetles and weevils.

Skeletonization. This involves a pattern of selective feeding on leaves where chewing insects avoid main veins and usually one leaf surface. This kind of injury is characteristic of insects such as Japanese beetle, larvae of certain leaf beetles, slug sawflies, and caterpillars known as skeletonizers. This feeding habit may be restricted to younger stages of caterpillars that later feed more generally on plants. The leaf surface that is skeletonized (upper vs. lower) can also be characteristic of an insect's feeding habit.

A. Leaf damage by adult elm leaf beetle. *W. Cranshaw*. B. Leaf reddening resulting from feeding injury by spider mites. *W. Cranshaw*. C. Reddening of pines killed by mountain pine beetle. *R. Stevens*. D. Shothole wounds produced by young stages of brownheaded ash sawfly. *W. Cranshaw*. E. Foliage reddening of currant caused by infestation of currant aphid. *W. Cranshaw*. F. Thrips scarring of flower. *W. Cranshaw*. G. Emergence holes of shothole borer. *Courtesy Clemson University*. H. Silvery wounding with dark fecal spots characteristic of onion thrips feeding. *W. Cranshaw*. I. Skeletonizing of leaf caused by feeding group of scarlet oak sawfly. *R. L. Anderson*. J. Skeletonizing injury by elm leaf beetle larvae. *W. Hantsbarger*.

Stippling. Whitish or yellowish spots, known as stippling, are produced when insects or mites remove cell sap from leaves. Mesophyll-feeding insects such as certain leafhoppers, plant bugs, and lace bugs characteristically produce very visible stippling. The affected leaf surface can differ between species, and often there is some associated dark fecal spotting around the injury. Smaller wounds result from feeding by thrips and spider mites. When damage is extensive, injuries may coalesce to produce silvery patches or a bronzing color change on the leaves.

Stippling is also used to describe the small punctures produced by some insects with their ovipositor. Many types of flies in particular use their ovipositor not only to insert eggs but to puncture plant cells so fluids will be released, on which the flies feed. This type of injury may result in small sunken areas.

Streaking. Streaking of leaves and stems occurs from feeding by some aphids, scales, mealybugs, and other sucking insects, particularly those that develop on grasses.

Tunneling of Fruit. Many kinds of insects develop in fruits and nuts, including weevils, fruit flies, and certain caterpillars and sawflies. They chew characteristic tunnels, and many concentrate damage around the developing seeds. The size of the tunnels varies largely in relation to the size of the insect, with thin meandering tunnels produced by fruit flies and large gouging wounds caused by fruit-feeding caterpillars such as codling moth.

Windowpaning. This injury is associated with chewing insects that leave a surface (usually the upper surface) of foliage intact, producing a translucent hole covered by a thin fill of leaf epidermis. Windowpaning is typical of many kinds of young caterpillars; some slug sawflies also produce it. This type of injury intergrades with shotholing (see above).

Yellowing. Yellowing (chlorosis) is a generalized plant response to a wide variety of stresses, including nutrient deficiencies, drought, and infection by certain pathogens. It can also be induced by heavy infestations of certain sap-sucking insects such as aphids, soft scales, and psyllids. Yellowing may also result from feeding by spider mites and eriophyid mites (rust mites).

A. Stippling injuries produced by leafhopper. *W. Cranshaw*. B. Stippling injury caused by lace bug feeding. *J. Capinera*. C. Leaf stippling caused by spider mite feeding. *W. Cranshaw*. D. Leaf striping resulting from feeding of Russian wheat aphid. *W. Cranshaw*. E. Seed damage by weevil larvae. *K. Gray*. F. Fruit tunneling by caterpillar. *K. Gray*. G. Leaf curling and yellowing by green peach aphid. *E. Nelson*. H. Diamondback moth with associated area of windowpane feeding injury. *W. Cranshaw*. I. Small windowpane feeding wounds made by caterpillars. *W. Cranshaw*. J. Yellowing caused by infestation of potato/tomato psyllid. *W. Cranshaw*. K. Premature foliage yellowing resulting from heavy scale infestation. *W. Cranshaw*.

PLANT PATHOGENS TRANSMITTED BY ARTHROPODS

Many arthropods, particularly insects and some eriophyid mites, are involved in spreading plant diseases. The greatest involvement is by those species that act as vectors, providing the sole means of disease spread. Other species may have a more casual relationship with the pathogen, moving it around as an external contaminant. In a few situations the relationship between the plant pathogen and its arthropod vector benefits the arthropod, a situation known as a *mutualistic relationship*. Some of the plant diseases most commonly transmitted by arthropod groups in North America are summarized below.

Plant Disease	Arthropod Group
Viruses	
Many viruses of various classes, including cucumber mosaic, potato virus Y, potato leafroll	Aphids
Beet curly top	Leafhoppers
Lettuce infectious yellows, tomato yellow leaf curl, many geminiviruses	Whiteflies
Tomato spotted wilt, impatiens necrotic spot, iris yellow spot (tospoviruses)	Thrips
Wheat streak mosaic, peach mosaic, rose rosette	Eriophyid mites
Phytoplasmas	
Aster yellows, ash yellows, elm phloem necrosis	Leafhoppers
Pear decline	Psyllids
Xylem-Limited Bacteria	
Pierce's disease of grape, bacterial leaf scorch	Leafhoppers (sharpshooters)
Other Bacteria	
Various soft-rotting bacteria	Root maggots
Bacterial wilt of cucurbits, Stewart's wilt of corn	Leaf beetles
Many bacteria, as external contaminants	Vinegar flies
Fungi	
Dutch elm disease, blue stain of conifers	Bark beetles
Ambrosia fungi	Ambrosia beetles
White rots	Horntails
Oak wilt; many other fungi, as external contaminants	Sap beetles
Many fungi, as external contaminants	Vinegar flies
Many root-rotting fungi, as external contaminants	Bulb mites
Many root-rotting fungi, as external contaminants	Fungus gnats
Nematodes	
Pine wilt	Longhorned beetles (pine sawyers)

A. Symptoms of bean common mosaic (left), a virus disease that can be spread by aphids. *W. Cranshaw.* B. Wilting of foliage symptomatic of Dutch elm disease, a fungal disease vectored by bark beetles. *Courtesy Minnesota Dept. Natural Resources.* C. Plants dying from infection with bacterial wilt, transmitted by a beetle. *R. Bessin.* D. Distortion of flowers (phyllody) of cosmos due to infection by aster yellows, a phytoplasma transmitted by leafhopper. *W. Cranshaw.* E. Twisting of head leaves of lettuce due to infection by aster yellows, a phytoplasma transmitted by leafhopper. *W. Cranshaw.* F. Ringspot symptoms on tomato fruit, characteristic of tomato spotted wilt virus, transmitted by thrips. *W. Cranshaw.* G. Symptoms of bacterial leaf scorch, which is a xylem-limited bacteria transmitted by leafhopper, on northern pin oak. *J. Hartman.* H. Symptoms of beet curly top, a virus transmitted by a leafhopper, in bean. *H. Schwartz.*

CHAPTER TWO

Management Principles for Some Garden Pests

The overwhelming majority of arthropods encountered in the yard and garden are of innocuous habit or may even be beneficial. When sufficiently abundant, however, some species rise to the level where they become pests. Management may be considered when this occurs.

When managing garden pests, identification is always the required first step—and this book is designed to assist in this. Finding additional information on the life history and habits of the pests is also critical to understand their potential to cause injury and to identify when in their life history they may be vulnerable to control.

Once controls are considered, it is almost always best to use a variety of methods. Typically the management approaches available for garden pest control are described as cultural controls (e.g., growing plants in a manner to avoid injury), physical or mechanical controls (e.g., trapping, handpicking), biological controls (e.g., manipulation of natural enemies), and chemical controls. These are best used in a complementary manner, in what is commonly recognized as Integrated Pest Management.

In the U.S. there is no better source than the state and county Cooperative Extension offices to start finding information on the best means of controlling garden pests. Cooperative Extensions are found in all states and are associated with the state land grant university. In Canada, Agriculture Canada also provides some outstanding materials on pest management.

As an initial reference, the following sections summarize some general principles for managing certain types of arthropods. Supplement this with locally derived information sources. Also, whenever using pesticides, always check to ensure that the intended use is specifically labeled on the product. *The label is the law,* and all pesticides can be used only in a manner consistent with label directions.

LEAF CHEWERS AND LEAFMINERS

Slugs and Snails

Natural controls of slugs and snails include predators such as fireflies, certain ground beetles, and slugs and snails that are predatory. Some birds, particularly ducks, readily feed on slugs.

Slugs are also highly sensitive to drying and reproduce poorly under hot, dry conditions. Any garden modifications that can be done to reduce humidity—changes in irrigation, mulching, etc.—can affect slug problems. Also, since slugs seek out moist, sheltered areas to spend the day, they may collect under certain materials placed about the garden. Old citrus rinds, moistened newspapers, and boards can all be used to concentrate slugs for collection and destruction.

Salty materials are actively avoided by slugs, and direct application of salts to slugs is often lethal. Wood ashes and certain soaps can be effective slug repellents because of their high salt content.

Copper is also avoided by slugs and snails. Copper foil barriers can be used to restrict snails and slugs from moving into new areas in a yard or greenhouse.

Insecticides have little, if any, effect on slugs and snails, which are very different types of animals than insects. However, direct application of dilute ammonia (as well as salt) is an effective contact slug killer.

Pesticides used for slug and snail control include as an active ingredient metaldehyde or iron phosphate. When these are used, the garden should not be irrigated since high moisture can negate the effects of these products. Metaldehyde also breaks down rapidly in light and should be applied late in the day, just before slugs feed.

Fermenting materials of many kinds can be used to lure slugs and snails. Fermenting sugar water and beer are commonly poured in shallow dishes to serve as slug and snail traps.

Grasshoppers

Grasshopper resting on vegetation. *W. Cranshaw*

In areas where they are common, grasshoppers can be among the most difficult insects to control because of their great mobility. Many natural controls act on grasshopper populations, however, so outbreaks are usually short-lived. Grasshoppers are common prey for birds, many other vertebrates, blister beetle larvae, and some other insect predators and succumb to diseases produced by fungi, protozoa, and nematodes. Weather conditions, particularly surrounding the period of egg hatch, are also critical to grasshopper survival, as adverse weather can inhibit egg hatch and kill young nymphs. Tilling of garden beds disturbs grasshopper egg pods and usually kills them.

In many areas where grasshoppers affect gardens, the source of grasshoppers is outside the garden. Areas of undisturbed soil such as fields, roadside ditches, and empty lots commonly serve as grasshopper breeding sites. Treating these areas with insecticides to kill grasshoppers can prevent more serious problems later, when grasshoppers may have spread over a much wider area. Breeding sites can be treated with several insecticides (e.g., permethrin, carbaryl), but bait formulations are particularly effective. A biological control is a bait containing spores of the protozoan parasite *Nosema locustae*, sold under trade names such as Semaspore or NoLo Bait. *Nosema locustae* is fairly slow acting and is only effective against developing grasshoppers, so it needs to be applied early in the season, shortly after egg hatch.

If possible, poultry can be used as excellent controls for grasshoppers. Their use usually requires some screening of the garden area to prevent injury by scratching birds.

In extreme situations, plants need to be covered to prevent injury, as even repeated applications of insecticides fail to adequately control migrating grasshoppers. However, grasshoppers can chew through thin fabrics.

Although grasshoppers may have wide tastes, some plants are less favored. Tomato and squash are usually little damaged by grasshoppers.

Sawflies

The most important biological controls affecting most sawflies are various parasitic wasps. Viruses are important with some sawfly species, and general insect predators, such as predatory stink bugs, will feed on some. Weather, including strong winds or heavy rains, may also limit sawfly outbreaks.

In small plots, sawflies can be dislodged with a vigorous jet of water. Slug sawflies, such as pear slug, can be killed by dusting with wood ashes.

Sawflies are easily controlled with most garden insecticides, although not by *Bacillus thuringiensis* products. As sawfly injury often occurs very rapidly, effective use of insecticides requires detecting outbreaks at early stages.

Leaf-feeding Caterpillars

Damage by leaf-feeding caterpillars (cabbageworms, loopers, inchworms, hornworms, gypsy moth, tent caterpillars, fall webworm, tussock moths, climbing cutworms, leafrollers, etc.) can be conspicuous, particularly if silken tents or other structures are produced. These injuries may have little effect on established and rapidly growing plants, however. Defoliation typically must exceed at least 20% before effects on a plant's health or growth can be observed. On deciduous trees, injuries tend to be more important if they occur early in the season and reoccur at high populations levels. Damage to conifers tends to be more serious than to deciduous trees. Where direct injury to the marketed or valued part of a plant is important, as when cabbageworms feed on broccoli heads, control of leaf-feeding caterpillars is particularly important.

Natural controls affecting almost all leaf-feeding caterpillars include a complex of parasitic wasps and tachinid flies. Eggs may be parasitized by *Trichogramma* wasps and other egg parasitoids. General predators, particularly predatory bugs and spiders, may kill many larvae. Hunting wasps and paper wasps often are important predators in yards and gardens, as are some birds. Handpicking can effectively supplement these natural controls, particularly with larger species such as hornworms.

Caterpillars often succumb to many diseases. Viruses, such as those that produce wilt diseases, can be devastating to some species. Some fungi, such as *Entomophaga maimaiga* which affects gypsy moth, can be extremely important when environmental conditions are suitable. Bacteria and protozoans parasitize some caterpillars.

Hand picking can be used to control larger insects.
W. Cranshaw

Tillage can control insects that winter in soils. *W. Cranshaw*

Most garden insecticides—particularly the various pyrethroids, spinosad, and carbaryl—are highly effective against leaf-feeding caterpillars. Insecticide preparations containing the bacterium *Bacillus thuringiensis* (*kurstaki* or *aizawi* strains) are specific against leaf-feeding caterpillars, and their use integrates well with existing natural controls. Some cutworms are inherently less susceptible to *B. thuringiensis,* and older caterpillars of most species are less well controlled than are young caterpillars.

Cutworms

Cutworms are subject to natural enemies that include parasitic wasps, tachinid flies, and general predators that occur around the soil surface such as ground beetles.

Cutworms that damage plants in the spring overwinter in the garden as eggs or small larvae. Many overwintering cutworms can be killed by tilling gardens before spring planting. Keeping gardens free of dense weedy vegetation in late summer can make gardens less attractive to egg-laying moths.

Individual plants can be protected from cutworms by various collars or similar physical barriers placed around the plants.

Several garden insecticides can control cutworms. Pyrethroids are most commonly used for this purpose, but spinosad and carbaryl can also be used. A *Bacillus thuringiensis*–based insecticide is often less effective than for control of leaf-feeding caterpillars; cutworms may be insensitive to its effects, and coverage of actively growing seedlings on which cutworms feed is difficult. Insect parasitic nematodes in the genus *Steinernema* have been used for cutworm control but require soil temperatures greater than 50° F.

Leaf Beetles and Mexican Bean Beetle

Foliage damage by leaf beetles (Colorado potato beetle, elm leaf beetle, and relatives) and Mexicaan bean beetle is conspicuous but may have little effect on established and rapidly growing plants. Defoliation typically must exceed at least 20% before effects on a plant's health or growth can be observed.

Natural controls usually include parasitic wasps and, for some species, tachinid flies. Certain predatory stink bugs are leaf beetle larvae specialists, and other general predators (e.g., earwigs, lady beetles) can kill some leaf beetle eggs and larvae. The fungi *Beauveria bassiana* and *Metarhizium anisopliae* can be important natural controls if environmental conditions are suitable for infection.

Many leaf beetles can be fairly easily dislodged by a strong jet of water. Crop rotations within a yard usually have minimal effect since adult leaf beetles are usually good fliers. Not growing a suitable host of a pest leaf beetle (e.g., of Colorado potato beetle) for an entire season, however, can suppress local numbers for a year or so. Crop rotation can also be important in managing western corn rootworm and northern corn rootworm, two leaf beetle larvae which only develop high populations where corn is grown in the same location in successive years.

As the eggs of leaf beetles are conspicuous, they can be easily found and crushed in small plantings. Care should be given to avoid inadvertently destroying egg masses of beneficial species of lady beetles, which produce egg masses that look fairly similar.

Most garden insecticides are highly effective against leaf beetles, although some strains of Colorado potato beetle in the eastern U.S. may be fairly resistant. The *tenebrionis* (aka *san diego*) strain of *Bacillus thuringiensis* is active against younger leaf beetle larvae, as is neem.

Controls for Mexican bean beetle, a type of lady beetle, are generally similar to those for leaf beetles. Mexican bean beetle is not well controlled by the strain of *B. thuringiensis* that is used against leaf beetles, however, nor is neem particularly effective. Natural enemies that are commercially available for Mexican bean beetle include a wasp that parasitizes larvae (*Pediobius foveolatus*) and predatory stink bugs (e.g., spined soldier bug).

Flea Beetles

Parasitic wasps and nematodes affect many flea beetles, causing overall regulation of their numbers. Flea beetles are quite mobile, however, and those that have rapidly colonized plantings often are little affected by biological controls. Because of the flea beetles' mobility, crop rotations also may have relatively little effect on managing them in gardens.

Effects of flea beetle damage to seedlings can often be reduced by overseeding to diffuse the attacks and then thinning to select the most vigorous survivors. Any cultural conditions that favor rapid plant growth also can limit effects of flea beetle injury during stand establishment, and well-established plants usually well outgrow flea beetle damage to foliage. Floating row covers can be used to exclude beetles if infestations are extreme.

Several insecticides can be used for flea beetles (e.g., carbaryl, permethrin), and diatomaceous earth is somewhat repellent. Insecticide control of flea beetles on seedlings, however, often is difficult since the plants are small and actively growing, and reinvasion by flea beetles is rapid.

Leafminers

Leafmining injuries are conspicuous but can be well tolerated by plants unless infestations precipitate a high percentage of defoliation. Furthermore, most leafminers have numerous natural enemies which usually regulate populations quite effectively. Some species, however, regularly occur in outbreak numbers (e.g., locust leafminer) or occur at unacceptable levels on leafy vegetables (e.g., spinach leafminer).

Insecticide controls are most effective if applied before or during egg-laying and egg hatch. This timing differs for each leafminer species. After leafminers have entered the leaves, insecticide control becomes more difficult. Insecticides with some systemic activity (acephate, imidacloprid) can be used effectively against some types of leafminers on ornamental plants. When using these materials, applications can be timed to coincide with the first appearance of egg-laying scars and the first signs of tunneling.

Insecticides are not normally recommended for leafminer control on vegetables and sometimes can aggravate problems by having detrimental effects on natural enemies. With spinach leafminer, the eggs are conspicuous and can be crushed. Infested leaves and larvae can be handpicked and destroyed.

FLOWER, FRUIT, AND SEED FEEDERS

Fruit-Infesting Flies and Apple Maggot

Fruit flies (cherry fruit flies, currant fruit fly, blueberry maggot, etc.) are all attracted to yellow, which can be coated with sticky material to trap many adults. In the case of apple maggot, traps can be an effect control. In the first few weeks after the adults emerge, they are strongly attracted to yellow sticky traps. Females with matured eggs can be trapped by sticky red spheres—"super apples"—which are highly attractive to them. In many cases, the use of only a few such traps per tree can adequately control this insect.

Apple maggot is most damaging to soft, early-maturing fruit varieties. Survival is reduced in firm-fleshed late varieties. A cover of vegetation under trees has been shown to reduce survival of the insects moving from trees to pupate in soil, presumably by encouraging predators that frequent the soil surface. Fruit that is obviously infested by apple maggot or other fruit flies can be picked and destroyed to assist in management, but larvae often have exited fruit before their damage is highly visible.

Red sticky sphere trap in apple tree. *E. Nelson*

Fruit flies can be well controlled by cover sprays of several insecticides. As with the fruit-infesting moths, timing is critical and should coincide with peak periods of egg-laying. The use of yellow sticky cards is useful for making this determination, and the dark bands on the flies' wings are distinctive.

Codling Moth and Other Fruit-Infesting Caterpillars

Codling moth and all the other fruit-infesting caterpillars have numerous natural enemies, although these biological controls often are inadequate. Birds sometimes feed on the mature larvae and pupae in cocoons. Perhaps most important, codling moth larvae and pupae are often killed by several types of parasitic wasps. The activity of these wasps has been improved in some areas by the presence of

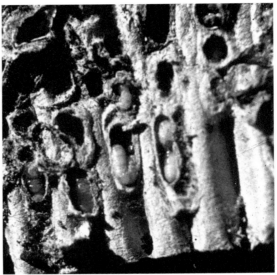

Cardboard tree band to concentrate pupating codling moths for destruction. *R. Zimmerman*

Codling moth larvae and pupae in carboard tree band. *W. Hantsbarger*

nearby flowering plants which provide alternative food sources. Codling moth larvae also are attacked by several general predators such as ground beetles and earwigs.

Keeping loose bark scraped from trees and removing debris from around trees can eliminate shelter used by the insects when they pupate. This causes them to be more exposed to birds and other natural controls. Pupae of the codling moth and other species that pupate on the trunk or at the base of trees can be concentrated by placing bands of corrugated cardboard or burlap around the trunk; the pupae can then be easily collected and destroyed.

Since caterpillars often need some leverage to help them cut into fruit, many larvae enter where two fruits are touching. Thinning apples to prevent this can reduce the survival of the delicate young larvae.

Traps that contain the sex pheromone used by the female to attract males are useful in monitoring many fruit pests. These can help determine periods of adult activity, allowing insecticides to be better timed to coincide with egg-laying and egg hatch, when the insecticides are most effective. Since only male moths are attracted, pheromone traps cannot control the insects where migration of mated females from nearby areas occurs. In many species, however, adult moths of both sexes can be attracted to fermenting sugary solutions and trapped. A typical design is a gallon jug baited with a pool of dilute fermenting molasses and water (ca. 1:10 to 1:15 dilution with water).

Insecticides should be applied during periods of peak egg-laying by the adult moths. Two damaging generations of codling moth are common, one in late spring (after petal fall) and the other in midsummer. The latter causes most fruit damage.

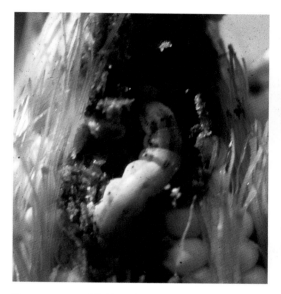

Corn earworm. *W. Cranshaw*

The ear tip is the location of egg-laying and larval entry by corn earworm. *W. Cranshaw*

Corn Earworm

Usually only a single corn earworm larva is present in a fruit or ear tip of sweet corn as these larvae are quite cannibalistic. Many general predators common in gardens feed on corn earworm eggs and young larvae before they tunnel into and damage plants.

Sweet corn becomes attractive to egg-laying moths almost immediately after silks appear and remains attractive until silks turn brown. Covering the ear tips with repeated insecticide applications during this period can kill larvae before they enter the ear. Regular releases of *Trichogramma* wasps during this period may also kill many eggs before larvae hatch and move into the ear.

Larvae within the ear cannot be killed with surface-applied insecticides. Young larvae, however, may be killed by injecting the ear tip with parasitic nematodes (*Steinernema carpocapsae*) or mineral oil.

In sweet corn, damage is limited to the tip, which can be cut off without affecting the quality of the remaining ear.

Tobacco Budworm

Tobacco budworm eggs and larvae are subject to numerous natural enemies including general predators such as stink bugs, green lacewing larvae, and lady beetles. Parasitic wasps and tachinid flies kill older larvae.

Larvae usually feed at night and hide around the base of plants during the day. They may be most easily located for handpicking around dusk.

Flowers vary in susceptibility to tobacco budworm, and less susceptible plants should be used where damage is common. For example, ivy geraniums are much less commonly damaged than are standard geraniums. Some colors of petunias seem to be less commonly damaged.

Some cultivars, such as ivy geranium, resist tobacco budworm injury.
W. Cranshaw

Although traps can capture Japanese beetles, they are
ineffective for control of plant damage as they usually draw
more beetles into the vicinity. *W. Cranshaw*

Pyrethroid are currently the most effective insecticides for control. *Bacillus thuringiensis* can be used with fair effect on flowers where petals are eaten (e.g., petunias) but not on those where bud tunneling predominates (e.g., geraniums).

Japanese Beetle

Natural enemies of Japanese beetle include parasitic wasps and various diseases. One of the latter, known as milky spore (*Bacillus popilliae*), is commercially available and infects the white grub stage of Japanese beetle, which occurs as a turfgrass pest. There is considerable debate as to the effectiveness of this treatment, however, particularly when applied to a limited area. Other controls of the white grub stage are discussed on p. 44. Optimal timing for larval treatments is just after the majority of eggs have been laid, which typically occurs in early August. In addition to several insecticides, nematodes in the genus *Heterorhabditis* can also be used for larval control.

Several traps are sold for control of Japanese beetle adults. These contain an attractant floral-base lure that can draw large numbers of Japanese beetles into a trap. Unfortunately use of the traps has no effect on incidence of adult beetles in the vicinity. Instead, increased problems with Japanese beetles around traps are reported since many beetles are drawn into the area of the floral lure but are not trapped.

Insecticides may be needed to protect highly susceptible plants from feeding by adult Japanese beetles. Several garden insecticides can be effective but usually require reapplication during peak periods. Alternatively, many states produce Cooperative Extension publications listing landscape plants that are generally avoided and not damaged by Japanese beetles.

Weevils Affecting Flowers, Fruits, and Seeds

Most adult weevils drop readily when disturbed, a behavior that can be used in their control in small plantings. Many weevils can be dislodged and collected by shaking plants over a sheet. (Note: Weevils typically draw in their legs and may be difficult to detect.)

Most fruit- or seed-infesting weevils (plum curculio, rose curculio, hollyhock weevil, pecan weevil, etc.) develop for an extended period within the plant. Therefore removing infested fruit or seeds before adults emerge can be useful in control.

Insecticides applied for control of fruit- or seed-infesting weevils are most effective when timed for periods when adults are present on plants just before egg-laying.

SAP SUCKERS

Whiteflies

Where whiteflies persist outdoors, there can be many effective natural controls. The most important are parasitic wasps in the genera *Encarsia* and *Eretomocerus*. These whitefly parasites are also widely available from commercial sources and are commonly used to control whiteflies in greenhouses.

Breaking the life cycle of whiteflies by having a host-free period can be very useful for controlling whiteflies. In southern states, where whiteflies may occur outdoors year-round, planned planting of crops so that favorable host plants are not present for a period can cause local populations to crash. In the north, freezing winter temperatures kill greenhouse and silverleaf whiteflies, and new infestations outdoors are de-

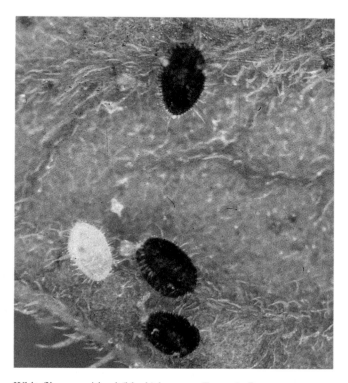

Whiteflies parasitized (black) by wasp *Encarsia formosa*. *W. Cranshaw.*

pendent on annually introduced sources from plants grown in greenhouses where whiteflies can survive winters.

To prevent infestations of indoor plants, new plants should be carefully inspected for whiteflies to prevent their introduction. It is best to further quarantine new plants that may host whiteflies in a separate area for a few weeks and inspect them again before introducing them into areas where other plants are grown.

Yellow and white are attractive to adult whiteflies and can be incorporated into traps with sticky surfaces. These are effective in monitoring whitefly abundance but have only modest effect on suppression. Such traps do not affect eggs and immature stages, which occur on plants.

Some insecticides can control whiteflies. Pyrethroid insecticides are usually effective against adults. Horticultural oils, insecticidal soaps, and neem can be effective against the nymphs on leaves. Some soil-applied systemic insecticides (e.g., imidacloprid) may also control whiteflies.

Aphids

Natural controls, including natural enemies (lady beetles, lacewings, syrphid flies, parasitic wasps), usually bring aphid populations under control shortly after they become noticeable. Before any insecticide treatments are contemplated, a search of the aphid colonies for these natural enemies should be made. High numbers of beneficial insects usually indicate that aphid problems are being controlled without any need for intervention.

Aphids exposed on plants often can be controlled simply by hosing them with a strong jet of water. Injured aphids often succumb, and those that are dislodged rarely make it back onto plants. Aphids washed onto adjacent plants will not feed on those plants if they are not hosts for the aphid.

Sprays of dilute preparations of soap can be effective against many aphids that are exposed on plants. A few other garden insecticides can control aphids, although selection can sometimes be complicated by several factors. For example, insecticide-resistant strains of some aphids (e.g., cotton/melon aphid, green peach aphid) are common. Also, some insecticides that have only minimal effectiveness may ac-

Cabbage aphid colony. *W. Cranshaw*

tually aggravate problems by being more injurious to natural enemies of aphids. Furthermore, different kinds of aphids may respond differently to insecticides. Carbaryl, for example, is a poor insecticide for most aphids and may aggravate problems, but it can be used successfully against some of the "woolly" aphids. When applying any contact insecticide, complete spray coverage is essential for good aphid control.

Aphids that have already produced a leaf curl or similar protective structure can only be controlled with systemic insecticides. Presently there are some insecticides with systemic activity that can be used as foliar sprays (acephate, imidacloprid) or as soil treatments (imidacloprid) which are effective against aphids.

Some aphids, particularly those that cause early-season leaf curls, often overwinter as eggs on the plant. Dormant oil sprays can help control these aphids. Aphids that winter as eggs on herbaceous perennial plants and cause leaf curls in spring can usually be managed by cleaning out old plant debris, which contains overwintering eggs, before the new spring growth emerges.

Numerous natural enemies of aphids are commercially available and are widely used in greenhouses. These include several parasitic wasps, aphid predator midges, green lacewings, and the fungus *Beauveria bassiana*. Mass release of field-collected adult lady beetles is a popular practice but is generally considered marginally effective for aphid control. Methods of encouraging existing natural enemies by providing alternate foods and protection from adverse practices can be more productive for managing aphids in outdoor settings.

Mealybugs

Many natural enemies of mealybugs occur and may be present in outdoor populations where mealybugs survive year-round. Several biological control organisms are commercially available, including parasitic wasps and certain lady beetles, which are used primarily for controlling citrus mealybug on indoor plants.

Insecticide sprays applied for mealybugs can give variable results because of the mealybugs' protective covering of wax and occurrence of life stages in various locations, including soil, where they are difficult to reach. Alcohol sprays can be useful for controlling exposed stages of mealybugs on houseplants that can tolerate such treatment. Mealybugs can be controlled by several insecticides used as sprays, including certain insect growth regulators. Soil-applied systemic treatments may also be effective, although some mealybug species respond poorly to systemic insecticide applications.

Soft Scales

Soft scales have a diverse complex of natural controls, and most species are usually well controlled by them. Parasitic wasps and general predators (predatory bugs, predatory mites, green lacewing larvae) are most important. Many birds prey heavily on soft scales, particularly when birds are fledging young and seeking protein-rich foods. Rainfall (or strong hosing) can be destructive to the newly hatched crawlers.

Horticultural oils are among the most useful of all treatments for soft scales, both on outdoor and indoor-grown plants. Soft scales remain susceptible to oils during much of their life and are particularly susceptible when young.

The newly hatched crawlers are susceptible to almost any garden insecticide and are the stage most consistently well controlled. Timing of these "crawler sprays" is critical since applications made too late may not control scales and may interfere with natural enemies, aggravating problems.

Some soil-applied systemic insecticides (e.g., imidacloprid) can be effective for control of soft scales.

Armored Scales

Armored scales frequently succumb to numerous natural controls, and many species are usually well controlled by them. Parasitic wasps, predatory mites, and certain lady beetles that specialize in armored scales are most important. Rainfall during periods when newly hatch scales are present can be very detrimental to armored scales.

Proper tree care, including pruning of heavily scale-infested branches, can assist control of some scales on outdoor plants. Many armored scales can also be scrubbed off with a plastic kitchen scrub pad or similar object.

Overwintering armored scales on trees and shrubs often can be killed by oil sprays applied as dormant treatments in spring before bud break. Control of armored scales using dormant-season applications of oils is more erratic than with soft scales, however, because of the armored scales' protective covering.

Horticultural oils are also useful for scale control on many plants after new growth emerges. Armored scales remain susceptible to oils during the first few weeks after egg hatch, when their covering is relatively thin.

The protective waxy covering produced by armored scales affords considerable protection from many insecticides. However, the newly hatched, first-stage nymphs known as crawlers lack this covering and are susceptible to almost any garden insecticide. Timing of these "crawler sprays" is critical since applications made too late may not control scales and may interfere with natural enemies, aggravating problems.

Crawlers, the stage present after egg hatch of a scale insect, are easily controlled by many methods. *F. Peairs*

Scale crawler activity can be monitored in many ways. Branches known to be infested can be shaken over a collecting surface (e.g., paper, trays) and examined for the presence of the tiny crawlers. Often it helps to use a surface that is smooth and contrasts with the color of the crawler, i.e., light-colored surfaces for detecting dark crawlers such as pine needle scale and darker surfaces for detecting light crawlers such as oystershell scale. Alternatively, crawlers can be trapped on double-sided sticky tape which, if examined regularly, can also be used to sample relative scale activity.

Soil-applied systemic insecticides provide poor control of armored scales. This is because insecticides move little to the site in the plant (mesophyll cells) where armored scales typically feed.

Thrips

The most important predators that feed on thrips are minute pirate bugs and predatory mites. Some of these are commercially available and may be useful for thrips control in greenhouses. The entomopathogenic nematode *Steinernema feltiae* applied as a soil drench can also assist in thrips control in greenhouses.

Rainfall is an important natural control which washes thrips from plants and seals pupal stages in the soil, preventing emergence. Where scarring of seedling plants and foliage is a concern, thrips may be temporarily suppressed by vigorously washing plants with a jet of water. Plants will usually outgrow thrips injury to foliage if other cultural conditions are favorable for plant growth.

Certain colors are attractive to thrips, something commonly observed when thrips occur among differently colored flowers. Sticky traps incorporating these attractive colors can be used to control adult thrips on indoor plantings; such traps have little effect outdoors, however, because of the tremendous number of thrips present. Yellow and pale blue are most often used for thrips traps.

Gladiolus thrips can be controlled by ensuring that noninfested corms are planted, as gladiolus thrips do not survive winter outdoors. Corms that are stored can be disinfested by briefly placing them in a hot-water bath.

Colored sticky traps are attractive to winged stages of many insects. *W. Cranshaw*

Control of thrips with insecticides poses many serious challenges and is rarely successful. Problems include difficulty reaching thrips in flowers and other protected sites; occurrence of thrips in different sites as they develop (eggs in leaves, feeding stages on plants, and transition "pupal" stages in soil); and resistance to insecticides.

Where the primary issue involving thrips is their importance in transmitting virus diseases (e.g., tomato spotted wilt, impatiens necrotic spot), a vigorous program of sanitation is fundamental. All plants showing symptoms of these diseases should be removed immediately. In the absence of a strict sanitation program, these diseases cannot be controlled no matter how intensive are the controls directed at the thrips vectors.

Squash Bug

Although natural enemies of squash bug do occur, notably the tachinid fly *Trichopodes pennipes*, squash bug can be a chronic problem in areas where lethally harsh winter conditions do not occur. Problems are particularly severe on hard winter-types of squash. Summer squash, melons, and cucumbers may avoid more serious infestations.

Mulches should be avoided when growing plants susceptible to squash bug. During hot periods, squash bugs seek shelter around the base of the plant, and mulches can provide more suitable cover for them.

Effectively using insecticides to control squash bugs can be tricky as the species is relatively resistant to most insecticides and coverage is difficult on large plants. Insecticides are most effectively used early in the season, shortly after eggs are laid. Attention to early-season control usually allows for minimal problems close to harvest. Treatment around the base of plants, where squash bugs often aggregate, is particularly important.

As squash bug eggs are distinctive, they can easily be found and crushed in small plantings.

Spider Mites

Among the most important predators of spider mites are minute pirate bugs, predatory thrips, dustywings, predatory mites, and the "spider mite destroyer" group of lady beetles (*Stethorus* spp.).

Spider mite populations typically develop rapidly under dry conditions, since their feeding rate is partly dependent on how rapidly excess water evaporates. Plants under stress are particularly susceptible to injury. Spider mite problems can also be induced through the use of certain insecticides (e.g., carbaryl, permethrin) that destroy natural insect enemies of spider mites.

Proper watering and fertilization of plants are primary means of limiting spider mite injury. Forceful hosing of foliage can be particularly useful since this can crush and dislodge many mites.

Certain broad-spectrum insecticides with some mite activity are available, although such treatments devastate natural enemies. (Effectiveness of these treatments can vary considerably between the different mite species.) Horticultural oils also can be effective spider mite treatments. During outbreaks, however, it may be difficult to get control with any pesticide, particularly when pesticide-resistant strains of twospotted spider mite are present.

Treatments applied for spider mites are most effective during the early stage of outbreaks. This differs among spider mite species, with some more active during warm months and others in spring and/or fall.

Leaf bronzing by spider mites. *W. Cranshaw*

GALL MAKERS

Galls (e.g., horned oak gall, oak rough bulletgall) can cause problems for trees when they occur on twigs and branches and interfere with transport of food and water. However, little if any significant injury to the plant results from the great majority of galls, although the bizarre growths often attract attention and concern. Most controls are directed at preventing these aesthetic injuries.

Since only actively growing tissues are susceptible to the gall-making stimuli, most galls are produced solely during the rapid growth period of late spring. Once galls are initiated, their formation is irreversible. Although the galls are often conspicuous and may be unattractive, rarely does any real plant damage occur. Under most circumstances, control of galls is not recommended.

A few gall-making insects and mites (e.g., Cooley spruce gall adelgid) overwinter on trees and may be controlled by dormant oil applications. Most galls, however, are produced by insects that move to new growth as it develops in spring and can only be controlled by insecticides that cover the leaves during the egg-laying period. Because the quality of the insecticide coverage diminishes as leaves expand, repeat applications may be necessary.

Timing treatments for gall wasps can be a little more difficult because of their complex life cycles. Furthermore, several important species lay eggs into dormant buds in fall and winter, months before the new growth that is galled begins to noticeably grow.

STEM, TWIG, BRANCH, AND TRUNK DAMAGERS

Tip Moths and Other Twig or Terminal Feeders

Tip moth injuries are typically much more conspicuous than they are damaging. As the plants recover, there is often little long-term injury other than a slightly increased bushiness at the injury site or a curve in the stem as it continues to grow. Tip moths can be serious pests of landscape plants, however. Also, white pine weevil damage to the top leader of white pine or blue spruce can seriously affect the form of these plants.

Tip moth populations tend to be highly cyclic. Several natural enemies, primarily parasites, reduce survival of tip moth larvae and can be highly effective in reducing their numbers to non-injurious levels.

Tip moth control requires that an insecticide cover susceptible terminals at the time of egg-laying and egg hatch. Often this coincides with shoot elongation, although it varies with different insect–host plant combinations. For example, overwintered white pine weevil may begin to move to terminals and feed following a warm sunny period in midspring.

Some measure of control can be gained by mechanically destroying larvae in tips or terminals. Timing of this removal is critical as it has no effect after the insects have left the plant. Where white pine weevil has damaged the top leader, training one of the side shoots to become the dominant new leader can largely recover the desired growth form of pine and spruce.

Bark Beetles

Most bark beetle species successfully breed only in trees that are severely stressed or dying. Newly transplanted trees may be particularly susceptible to attack by some species, such as ips beetles affecting pines. Proper cultural practices to promote tree vigor are the most important means of preventing most bark beetle problems. This may include pruning to eliminate damaged, shaded, or infested branches. Pruned wood should be removed from the area around susceptible trees, as many bark beetles can develop in prunings. Often, such cultural techniques are sufficient for control.

A few bark beetles are capable of killing healthy trees, either through coordinated mass attacks (mountain pine beetle, for example) and/or through introduction of disease-causing fungi into healthy trees (elm bark beetles). Sanitation and insecticide applications are of great importance in managing these pest situations. For example, the single most important method to control Dutch elm disease, spread by the smaller European elm bark beetle, is to immediately remove all trees that are infected, before the beetles emerge from the diseased tree.

Once bark beetles have initiated tunneling, no insecticides are effective. Bark beetle preventive insecticide applications involve a thorough wetting of the bark to the point of run-off before the egg-laying period. Carbaryl and permethrin are currently used for control of bark beetles.

Lilac/ash borer entering pheromone-baited trap. *W. Cranshaw*

Wood Borers

Most borers (roundheaded borers, flatheaded borers, clearwing borers, etc.) are only capable of successfully attacking dying or stressed trees. This is particularly true of roundheaded and flatheaded borers. Proper watering and care are the first-line approaches for preventing all borer injuries, allowing plants to better resist attacks. Good cultural practices can also allow an infested tree to better tolerate borer injuries by producing callous tissues over wounds and to recover energy losses.

Pruning can assist in borer management. Removing over-shaded and damaged limbs denies borers favorable sites

Small raised areas on canes indicate location of larval tunneling by borers. *W. Cranshaw*

for developing. In small fruits and shrubs, borer-infested canes should be pruned and removed from the site before borers emerge.

Insecticide controls are usually targeted at the egg-laying adults or newly hatched larvae. This requires well-timed applications just before egg-laying and egg hatch. The occurrence of these life stages varies with different borer species and often lasts a month or longer. Consequently, repeat applications are often necessary for control. After the eggs hatch and the young borers have moved underneath the bark, insecticide treatments are ineffective. Traps containing a lure of the sex pheromone females use to attract mates are available to aid in the timing of treatments for control of clearwing moth borers (peach crown borer, lilac/ash borer, etc.).

These insecticides are used as coarse sprays applied to the trunk until the point of run-off. Lower branches and the crown area may need to be sprayed, depending on the habits of the borer. Spray deposits typically last for several weeks to months; insecticide degradation is much slower on coarse bark (e.g., elm) than on smooth bark (e.g., birch). Currently carbaryl and permethrin are most commonly used to control wood borers.

Squash Vine Borer

Squash vine borer survives winter as a pupa among the debris of previously infested plants. Removing and destroying old vines and tilling the garden can prevent production of new infestations that originate from the garden. The adult moths are quite mobile, however, and fly over an extensive area.

Trap crops can be used to divert the attack. This involves planting a highly favored plant (e.g., Hubbard squash) early in the season. Egg-laying and damage may be concentrated on this plant, which should then be destroyed.

If larval tunneling is observed, stems can be individually "dewormed" by puncturing the larvae or using some similar method to destroy them. Burying vines can allow rooting at several points, which may allow plants to partially recover.

Insecticides are only effective if applied at the time eggs are being laid and are hatching.

ROOT, TUBER, AND BULB FEEDERS

Root Maggots, Bulb Flies, and Carrot Rust Fly

Numerous natural enemies of root maggots and bulb flies are reported, including rove beetles, parasitic wasps, ground beetles, and ants. Root maggots also often succumb to a fungus disease, *Ento-*

mophthora musca, that causes infected adult insects to die stuck near the top of plants or attached to other high points in the garden.

For maggots that are host specific, such as onion maggot, having a season without suitable hosts can break the life cycle and suppress populations until they recover from reinvasion. Onions, carrots, and other hosts of root-feeding flies should be destroyed at the end of the season to kill overwintering stages associated with plants. Root maggots and carrot rust fly injury also can be largely avoided by planting at times that allow growing crops to avoid peak egg-laying periods.

Some pest insects can be introduced in transplants and thus may become established in new sites. This is a particularly common way that narcissus bulb fly and other bulb flies become established in new gardens. Carefully checking transplants, bulbs, and other plant materials can identify and destroy infestations. Narcissus bulb fly may also be detected and destroyed while examining bulbs whenever digging and separating them in the fall.

Planting into a warmed, well-prepared seed bed is particularly important in reducing infestations of seedcorn maggot. Damage is greatly increased if soil temperatures prevent rapid germination of corn, bean, melon, and other hosts of this insect. Adults may be attracted to areas where fresh and incompletely decayed animal manures have been applied.

Insecticide options, applied in the soil at planting, are currently limited. Most previously used treatments (diazinon, chlorpyrifos) for vegetable crops have been banned or greatly curtailed. Parasitic nematodes (*Steinernema* spp.) generally provide only marginal control.

White Grubs of Turfgrass

Natural controls affecting white grubs include parasitic wasps (tiphiids) and flies, certain microbial diseases, and large vertebrate predators such as skunks. The last sometimes aggravate turf injury through their digging for white grubs.

Since white grubs injure plants through root injuries, improving other cultural conditions often allows plants to substantially tolerate and eventually outgrow root pruning. Providing sufficient water is particularly important.

Insecticides can provide erratic results with white grubs for several reasons. Larger white grubs tend to be quite resistant to insecticides, and applications are best applied against young larvae. These are present shortly after the peak period when adults lay eggs in the soil. The most commonly used insecticides at present (imidacloprid, halofenizide) move slowly into the soil and usually take a few weeks before effects are evident.

Moving surface-applied insecticides to the root zone where grubs are present also provides problems. Larvae are best controlled when they are feeding near the surface; irrigating lightly before applying insecticides can cause larvae to migrate high in the soil. Interference with the movement of insecticides to the root zone can be a serious problem if a thick layer of thatch occurs, as most turfgrass insecticides readily bind to organic matter.

Entomopathogenic nematodes in the genus *Heterorhabditis* can be effective for white grub control.

White grub (top) killed by insect parasitic nematodes (*Heterorhabditis* sp.).
W. Cranshaw

Root Weevils

Root weevils are considerably more difficult to control since much of their life cycle is spent underground or off the plants. Adults are usually active at night, and searching plants at this time can confirm active infestations. Certain insecticides, mostly pyrethroids at present, can provide some control of adult root weevils. Soil drenches of entomopathogenic nematodes in the genus *Heterorhabditis* can control larvae.

Most root-infesting weevils of vegetables and ornamentals do not fly or fly poorly. Arranging plantings for a period so suitable host plants are not present for a season, a form of crop rotation, may starve out local populations.

MISCELLANEOUS GARDEN INSECTS

Ants

Control of ants always gives temporary results at best and should only be applied to individual colonies that are specifically producing problems. Whenever ants are eliminated, other ants rapidly move into the site and recolonize it. Indeed, maintenance of native ants can inhibit the movement of some introduced species, such as red imported fire ant.

Ant colonies are best controlled by use of baits. These are designed to be fed on by the workers and returned to the colony where the bait is fed to others, including young. A slow-acting toxicant is used,

Ants visiting mint-apple-jelly bait. *W. Cranshaw*

often an insecticide that disrupts insect growth or subtly depletes energy. Boric acid is also a popular toxicant in ant baits; it is mixed with whatever foods the ants favor. Some ants favor sweets (e.g., apple jelly, honey), others greasy foods (e.g., peanut butter, Crisco) or proteins. Furthermore, the foods favored by ants may shift during the season, depending on colony needs. The insecticide is usually mixed in low concentration (under 5% by volume) with the bait.

Fire ant baits consist of corn grits coated with soybean oil and combined with a slow-acting insecticide. The insecticide is meant to be taken into and distributed within the colony. Effects from such treatments may include gradual decline in activity or disruption of egg production by the queen and typically take 5 to 10 weeks before colonies are destroyed. Treatments should be made during periods when ants are actively foraging. This can be determined by placing a small amount of bait near mounds and observing whether ants shortly begin to remove the bait.

Control of individual mounds can be attempted, although ants colonies may be extensive with multiple entrances. Insecticides in dust form are usually best for use on an ant mound as these formulations allow the ants to better track the insecticide into the colony. If liquid insecticides or granular formulations are used on a mound, they need to be diluted with sufficient water (1 to 2 gallons per mound) to allow colony penetration. Boiling water, used at about 3 gallons per mound, can eliminate some ant colonies; it is most effective when ants are near the soil surface, as on a cool, sunny morning.

Yellowjackets

With few exceptions, yellowjacket colonies are abandoned at the end of the year and are not recolonized. If the location of the colony is known and is not in an area causing serious risk of stinging, it can be avoided until it has naturally eliminated itself.

Several brands of yellowjacket traps exist that can successfully attract some species of yellowjackets, notably western yellowjacket. These traps are most effectively used early in the season, when colonies are small and survival still problematic. Traps used late in the season, when colonies include hundreds of individuals, may capture many individuals but have little effect on overall numbers. Yellowjacket traps do not attract other paper-producing wasps (e.g., *Polistes* spp., baldfaced hornet, European hornet).

To avoid having yellowjackets forage in an area, attractive foods should be eliminated as best possible. This includes overripe fruit, garbage, and plants supporting high populations of honeydew-producing insects. In dry climates, moisture sources also may be attractive and similarly should be eliminated.

If the entrance to a colony is known, it can usually be eliminated with insecticides. Several products are available for this purpose and typically contain a fast-acting pyrethroid for rapid "knock-down" (e.g., resmethrin, pyrethrins) and an insecticide with more persistence. Insecticides should be applied in a manner to penetrate as best possible into the colony, which is almost always below ground. Repeat applications often are needed as the colony is difficult to reach and control is based on residual activity of insecticides applied around the nest entrance. To reduce the chance of being stung, treat the nest after dark.

CHAPTER THREE

Leaf Chewers

SLUGS AND SNAILS

Slugs and snails are types of animals known as gastropods, fairly close relatives of clams, mussels, and other mollusks. As such they have several different features than the arthropods (insects, mites, spiders, etc.) and lack distinct segmentation or an external skeleton. The body is soft and moves by means of a broad, muscular "foot" that covers the underside. On slugs, a large lobe called the mantle is present on the front half of the back; this is covered by a hard shell in snails. Two pairs of tentacles are present in the front, a short pair for sensing odors and a longer pair tipped with eyes. Many slugs and snails are hermaphrodites, possessing both sex organs, but these mature at different times, producing male and female phases.

Slugs and snails typically feed at night or during heavily overcast periods, avoiding sunny, drying conditions. During the day most slugs migrate to sheltered areas under debris and in soil cracks.

Milky Garden Slug (*Deroceras reticulatum*)[1]

Hosts: Almost all garden plants, although lettuce, bean, corn, and hosta are among those particularly favored.

Damage: Slugs feed by rasping the plant surface with numerous fine "teeth." They typically produce irregular damaged areas on foliage and leave slime trails on areas where they have been active.

Distribution: Of European origin; found throughout North America but most common in temperate areas.

Appearance: Generally light brown or gray, sometimes almost creamy. There are small concentric folds on the mantle. A milky slime is characteristically produced.

Life History and Habits: Milky garden slug is quite tolerant of low temperatures and may be active at fairly cool temperatures. Most activity occurs during spring and fall, with masses of clear eggs laid in soil cracks. Development may be suspended during very warm temperatures. The slugs develop rapidly, becoming full grown in 3 to 6 months. Life span rarely exceeds 1 year.

Other Garden Slugs

Midget milky garden slug (*Deroceras agreste*) is much less common than milky garden slug but can be a serious pest. The mucuous slime it produces is clear. **Marsh slug** (*D. laeve*) is a native species common in the Gulf states.

Great gray garden slug (*Limax maximus*),[2] also known as **spotted garden slug,** is an introduced species now widespread in the northern half of the U.S. and southern Canada. It is a moderately large, "fast-moving" species that may feed on other slugs, including members of its own species. **Tawny garden slug** (*L. flavus*) is another common introduced species now found in most of the continent.

A. Milky garden slug feeding on broccoli. *W. Cranshaw.* **B.** Slug damage to lupine. *J. R. Baker.* **C.** Milky garden slugs. *W. Cranshaw.* **D.** Eggs of milky garden slug. *W. Cranshaw.* **E.** Marsh slug. *J. Capinera.* **F.** Great gray garden slug. *K. Gray.* **G.** Great gray garden slug feeding at tomato. *K. Gray.* **H.** Tawny garden slug. *J. Capinera.*

Black slug (*Arion ater*)[3] is a large species, about 5¾ inches, found in moist regions along the Pacific Coast. Both black and red forms exist, each with a striped red-orange "skirt." Despite its size, black slug is rarely a garden problem, although it sometimes feeds on strawberries. One generation is produced annually. Three to four clutches, of 30 to 60 eggs each, are laid in fall. Related species are minor garden pests, including **banded slug** (*A. circumscriptus*) and **garden slug** (*A. subfuscus*).

The large **banana slugs** (*Ariolimax* spp.) are native to the Pacific Northwest. They are associated with forested areas and are not garden pests, but their extreme size and odd color definitely attract attention.

Brown Garden Snail (*Helix aspersa*)[4]

Hosts: Fairly wide range, with boxwood, rose, hibiscus, peach, magnolia, and citrus among those most commonly damaged.

Damage: Brown garden snail primarily feeds on leaves but may rasp the bark of twigs and small branches. It is an edible species, said to taste best in spring when levels of calcium salts are lowest.

Distribution: Purposefully introduced as a potentially edible species in the San Francisco area in the 1850s and currently common throughout the Pacific states. It is found in localized infestations elsewhere, particularly in the southern U.S., although it has been eradicated from Florida.

Appearance: The globular brown shell is flecked with yellow. Full-grown, the shell may be 1½ inches in diameter with four to five whorls.

Life History and Habits: Brown garden snail remains dormant in winter, sealing itself in the shell with a thin membrane (epiphragm). Activity resumes in spring, and adults lay masses of eggs, about two dozen at a time, in soil. Eggs hatch in a few weeks, and the snails grow slowly, becoming full grown in about 2 to 3 years.

Other Garden Snails

Bulimula alternatus mariae is a tree-climbing snail found in southeastern Texas. It feeds on legumes, notably acacia. Like most tree-climbing snails, it is never abundant enough to cause significant injury.

Decollate snail (*Rumina decollata*) is a predator of brown garden snail. It is sometimes sold for use for biological control, although its distribution is limited in some areas because of its potential to damage native species.

[1] Stylommatophora: Agriolimacidae; [2] Stylommatophora: Limacidae;
[3] Stylommatophora: Arionidae; [4] Stylommatophora: Helicidae

A. Reddish form of black slug. *W. Cranshaw.* **B.** Black slug. *K. Gray.* **C.** Brown garden snail. *W. Cranshaw.*
D. Brown garden snail. *K. Gray.* **E.** Brown garden snail laying eggs. *K. Gray.* **F.** Brown garden snail at egg hatch.
K. Gray.

GRASSHOPPERS

Grasshoppers are some of the most familiar of all insects, and more than 550 species occur in North America. Only a small number regularly damage gardens, however, and almost all of these are in the genus *Melanoplus*.[1] Species particularly injurious include the following four.

Twostriped Grasshopper (*Melanoplus bivittatus*)
Differential Grasshopper (*Melanoplus differentialis*)
Migratory Grasshopper (*Melanoplus sanguinipes*)
Redlegged Grasshopper (*Melanoplus femurrubrum*)

Hosts: Although grasses are particularly favored, most all garden plants can be damaged. Bean, leafy vegetables, iris, and corn are among the more commonly injured garden plants.

Damage: Grasshoppers damage plants by chewing. Most feeding occurs on foliage, although immature pods and fruit may also be eaten. Bark from twigs is sometimes gnawed, causing girdling wounds.

Distribution: Redlegged grasshopper is found throughout the U.S. and southern Canada but is most common in the upper Midwest. Migratory grasshopper has an almost equally broad range but is absent in extreme southern Texas and Florida. Twostriped grasshopper is found everywhere except the Deep South. Differential grasshopper is present throughout the U.S. except in the extreme northeast, southeast and northwest. It is most abundant between the Rocky Mountains and Mississippi River.

Appearance: The largest grasshoppers in this group are the differential and twostriped grasshoppers, with some adults more than 1½ inches long. A dark herringbone pattern on the hind femur characterizes differential grasshopper, although very dark forms also are produced sometimes. Two pale yellow stripes run along the back of the thorax and wings of twostriped grasshopper. Redlegged grasshoppers range from ¾ to 1 inch long with a bright yellow underside and red tibia on the hind leg. Migratory grasshopper is also medium sized, with a blue-green or reddish hind tibia.

Life History and Habits: As a generalized life history, *Melanoplus* grasshoppers spend the winter as eggs, in elongate egg pods containing 20 to 120 eggs. The eggs hatch in mid- to late spring, depending on temperature, location of the eggs, and species characteristics. Twostriped is a very early hatching species, as some embryonic development occurs the previous season. Egg hatch of migratory grasshopper typically follows about 2 to 3 weeks later, and differential grasshopper eggs often hatch shortly after this. Redlegged grasshopper eggs hatch in late spring or early summer. In all four species, the period of egg hatch can extend over a considerable period if eggs are laid in scattered sites, or hatch may occur over a short period.

Development of the nymphs typically takes 5 to 7 weeks, during which time they pass through five or six nymphal stages. Females feed for about 2 weeks before laying eggs. Eggs are laid as pods, often containing 50 or more eggs, and several pods may be produced. Each species has preferences as to where it lays eggs, with some preferring sun-exposed sites with compacted soil. Egg pods are typically inserted around the crown area or roots of plants.

A. Migratory grasshopper, female. *K. Gray.* **B.** Migratory grasshopper, male. *K. Gray.* **C.** Differential grasshopper. *J. Capinera.* **D.** Redlegged grasshopper. *J. Capinera.* **E.** Twostriped grasshopper. *W. Cranshaw.* **F.** Grasshopper egg pod. *W. Cranshaw.* **G.** Early instar nymph of redlegged grasshopper. *K. Gray.* **H.** Egg pod of redlegged grasshopper. *K. Gray.* **I.** Late instar nymph of redlegged grasshopper. *K. Gray.* **J.** Grasshoppers resting on vegetation. *W. Cranshaw.*

Grasshoppers can show migratory behaviors. Nymphs sometimes march considerable distances in bands during outbreaks. Adults are capable of flight and may fly for several miles, often at elevations of several hundred feet. Modest physical changes may sometimes occur in populations that become more migratory. For example, thinner body size and longer wings are produced by twostriped and migratory grasshoppers that go into the more migratory phase.

Other Garden Grasshoppers

Clearwinged grasshopper (*Camnula pellucida*)[1] has had several historical outbreaks in the Rocky Mountain/High Plains region. It is a fairly common species, found in most of North America except the southeastern states. Adults are medium sized and yellow to brown with mottled forewings and transparent hindwings. Grasses are favored, and the species can be a severe pest of small grains, but it occasionally damages onions, lettuce, cabbage, and peas in gardens. Clearwinged grasshopper eggs hatch quite early in the season, following a few warm days in early spring, and most eggs hatch over a brief period. During the summer, when eggs are being laid, the females alternately move from feeding sites in fields to egg-laying beds where soil conditions are favorable.

Carolina grasshopper (*Dissosteira carolina*)[1] is a common, large grasshopper usually seen flying over areas of bare ground. The hind wings, exposed in flight, are colorfully marked with black and have a yellow border. However, the overall color of the grasshopper, and of the covering forewings, is tannish to gray brown. Carolina grasshopper feeds on a wide variety of plants but is rarely abundant enough to cause serious damage. It is apparently fairly tolerant of cold temperatures as adults may persist well into fall.

Eastern lubber grasshopper (*Romalea guttata*)[2] is the largest grasshopper found in North America. Heavy bodied and reaching a length of 2 to almost 3 inches, it is a colorful insect of variable patterning, primarily black in young stages with more yellow in the adults. The short, nonfunctioning wings are pinkish or reddish. Eastern lubber is found in the southeastern states, from South Carolina to east Texas. It is most abundant in slightly moist habitats where it feeds on a wide range of weedy plants, but it does occasionally invade vegetable and flower gardens. Eggs hatch in March and April. In much of the High Plains and Rocky Mountain region, **western lubber** (*Brachystola magna*) is present and rivals eastern lubber in size. Also known as "plains lubber" or "homesteader," it feeds primarily on wild sunflower, kochia, hoary vervain, and other rangeland plants, rarely damaging cultivated plants.

[1] Orthoptera: Acrididae; [2] Orthoptera: Romaleidae

A. Clearwinged grasshopper. *K. Gray.* **B.** Carolina grasshopper. *W. Cranshaw.* **C.** Eastern lubber grasshopper, adult female. *J. Capinera.* **D.** Eastern lubber grasshopper feeding on holly. *Courtesy University of Georgia.* **E.** Western lubber grasshopper. *W. Cranshaw.* **F.** Clearwing grasshopper. *W. Cranshaw.*

CRICKETS AND KATYDIDS

Field Crickets (*Gryllus spp.*)

Damage: Field crickets eat a wide variety of plant materials. They occasionally damage crops such as alfalfa, tomato, and bean. They also enter homes, where their chirping may be considered annoying and where they occasionally chew holes in fabrics.

Distribution: Throughout North America. It is difficult to distinguish species; some can be separated only by behavior, including the type of song they produce. **Fall field cricket** (*G. pennsylvanicus*) and **spring field cricket** (*G. veletis*) tend to predominate in most of North America. **Southeastern field cricket** (*G. rubens*) is restricted to the southeastern U.S.

Appearance: Field crickets are predominantly black, often shiny, but may have some brown on the front wing. When full grown they are about ¾ inch long. Males and females can be easily separated by the presence or absence of the prominent ovipositor, used by the females to lay eggs. Field crickets are also well known among the "singing" insects, producing the familiar *chirp, chirp, chirp* noises of the night. Only the males sing, by scraping special ridges along their wings margins. Songs are used to attract mates and defend territories.

Life History and Habits: Overwintering stages may vary; fall field crickets winter as eggs in soil, spring field cricket as nearly full-grown nymphs. Eggs are laid in small groups in slightly damp soil. After egg hatch, nymphs take 2 to 3 months to develop, during which time they molt eight or nine times. Most field crickets have a single generation per year, but southeastern field cricket has two.

Other Crickets and Katydids

Tree crickets (*Oecanthus* spp.)[1] are similar in length to field crickets but more slender bodied. Typical species are green or yellow green; some have dark markings and black appendages. They are most commonly associated with trees and shrubs, particularly tree fruits and caneberries.

Although tree crickets may feed on leaves, they do little damage. Plants are injured primarily during late summer when eggs are laid. Females insert eggs into stems and canes, which may result in rough calloused areas around the wound, increased susceptibility to stem breakage, the entry of canker-producing fungi into the plant.

One species of tree cricket, **snowy tree cricket** (*O. fultoni*) of the northeastern U.S., can be used as a type of thermometer. Its rate of chirping varies reliably with temperature in a manner that has been quantified. The formula for determining temperature by its chirping rate is known as Dolbear's Law, after A. E. Dolbear, who first published on the phenomenon in 1897. The formula is $T = 50 + (N - 40)/4$, where T is temperature and N is chirps per minute.

A. Field cricket. *W. Cranshaw.* **B.** Field cricket damage to tomato. *J. L. Hoerner.* **C.** Tree cricket. *W. Cranshaw.* **D.** Tree cricket. *K. Gray.* **E.** Tree cricket eggs inserted into stem. *K. Gray.* **F.** Egg-laying punctures made by tree cricket. *K. Gray.*

Katydids[2] are usually large grasshoppers with long antennae and thin jumping hind legs. Most are green and associated with trees and shrubs. They are more commonly heard than seen as they call during evening and night. These calls may range in form from the loud rasping noises, repeated lisps, or "tics," such as those produced by **broadwinged katydid** (*Microcentrum rhombifolium*), to the *katydid, katy-didn't* song of **true katydid** (*Pterophylla carnellifolia*). Most katydids lay distinctive flattened eggs on twigs in late spring or early summer. Both the nymphs and adults chew leaves, rarely causing noticeable injuries.

Mormon cricket (*Anabrus simplex*)[2] is a wingless katydid, native to rangeland of many western states and particularly abundant in areas of Nevada and Utah. Rarely damaging to garden plants, it occasionally occurs in outbreak numbers during which it bands together in large groups and migrates. During these outbreak phases, Mormon crickets are very dark. Their normal appearance, in the solitary phase, is green or light brown.

Mormon crickets spend the winter as eggs in the soil. Eggs are laid in midsummer, inserted singly into firm soil that is free of roots (e.g., barren hillsides). Eggs hatch in mid- to late spring. Mormon cricket is a general feeder, being particularly fond of various shrubs and broadleaf plants, especially flowers. It is also highly cannibalistic and readily feeds on other Mormon crickets that are wounded, killed, or vulnerable during molting.

Jerusalem Crickets

Jerusalem crickets (*Stenopelmatus fuscus* and other species)[3] are odd-looking insects generally distributed in much of the western U.S., particularly the southwest. Sometimes locally called "children of the earth" or "potato bugs," they attract attention when encountered but cause little damage to gardens. They are primarily predators or scavengers of insects, spiders, and other small arthropods. Occasionally they also feed on plant material such as roots and tubers. Jerusalem crickets readily bite if handled carelessly, giving a painful pinch.

Jerusalem crickets are active at night, living in burrows constructed under rocks and other cover during the day. They may inadvertently enter homes, usually basements, or be encountered under porches. Both adult and immature (nymph) stages overwinter in the soil. They have a prolonged life cycle and take about 4 to 5 years to mature.

[1] Orthoptera: Gryllidae; [2] Orthoptera: Tettigoniidae; [3] Orthoptera: Stenopelmatidae (or subfamily Stenopelmatinae of the Gryllacrididae)

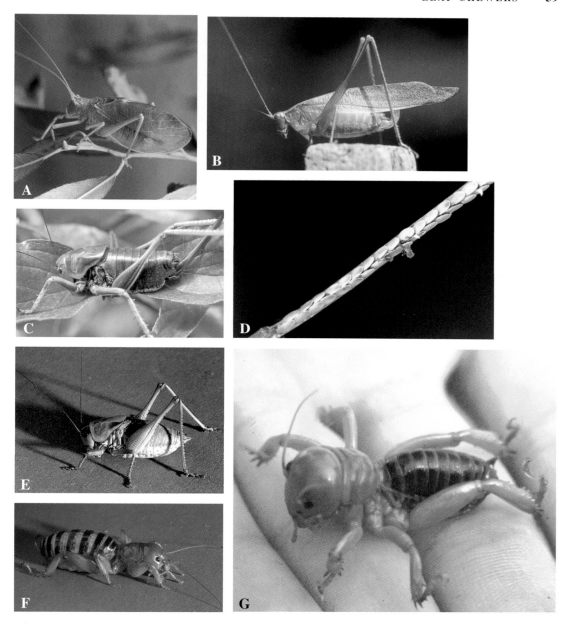

A. Katydid. *W. Cranshaw.* **B.** Broadwinged katydid. *W. Cranshaw.* **C.** Mormon cricket. *C. MacVean.* **D.** Katydid eggs hatching. *W. Cranshaw.* **E.** Male Mormon cricket. *K. Gray.* **F.** Jerusalem cricket. *K. Gray.* **G.** Jerusalem cricket. *W. Cranshaw.*

WALKINGSTICKS

The walkingsticks[1] are unusual insects most notable for their extremely elongate form. All develop by feeding on leaves, but their injuries rarely are serious. Walkingsticks mostly attract attention as curiousities.

Walkingstick (*Diapheromera femorata*)

Hosts: Oak, black cherry, elm, basswood, and black locust are favored plants. Paper birch, aspen, dogwood, and hickory are occasional hosts.

Damage: Nymphs and adults chew leaves. Damage is usually minor, but occasional outbreaks in forests cause significant defoliation.

Distribution: Over much of the area east of the Great Plains except the most southern states. It is most numerous around the Great Lakes.

Appearance: Full-grown adults reach a length of about 3 inches. They are highly variable in color and may be nearly pure green, gray or brown, or mottled.

Life History and Habits: Walkingstick hatches in late spring from eggs resting on soil. In forests the young nymphs usually feed first on the leaves of low-growing plants and later move to trees as they get older. Adults are present by midsummer, and the females drop their seedlike black eggs indiscriminately until frost. In southern areas of the range these eggs usually hatch the following spring, but in the northern states and Canada they remain dormant until the second season.

Related Species

Twenty-nine species of walkingsticks occur in North America, but most are rarely observed. The most common species in the Great Plains and Rocky Mountains states is **prairie walkingstick** (*D. velii*). **Twostriped walkingstick** (*Anisomorpha buprestoides*) occurs on oak in the Gulf states.

[1] Phasmatodea: Heteronemiidae

A. Prairie walkingstick. *W. Cranshaw.* **B.** Mating pair of walkingsticks. *G. K. Douce.* **C.** Walkingstick. *B. W. Kauffman.*

EARWIGS

Earwigs make up the insect order Dermaptera, a fairly small group that includes about 20 species in North America. A pair of pincers on the hind end, used during mating and to assist in manipulating food, is characteristic of earwigs. Adults of most species are winged, and the wings fold under short wing covers that do not extend to the abdomen.

European Earwig (*Forficula auricularia*)[1]

Hosts: European earwig is a true omnivore and feeds on a diet of insects and plant matter. Small, soft-bodied insects such as aphids and insect eggs are important protein sources; this is supplemented with soft plant matter from leaves and flower petals.

Damage: Adults and nymphs may feed on flower blossoms, corn silks (and some corn kernels), and tender vegetable seedlings. Their habit of crawling into tight, dark places to spend the day makes them an unwanted presence in harvested fruits, vegetables, and flowers.

Distribution: An introduced species. It has spread rapidly and is now found throughout almost all of North America except some southern states.

Appearance: Adults are approximately ½ inch long with prominent pincers. The general color is reddish brown, often with bronze tones. Short, pale brown wing covers are present on the thorax, and there are prominent pincers on the hind end; those of males are bowed, those of females fairly straight.

Life History and Habits: Earwigs overwinter in the adult stage. They become active on warm days in late winter, when females produce small nests dug beneath a rock or in some other protected site. A cluster of about 50 eggs is produced and is tended by the mother. After the eggs hatch, typically in April, the mother continues to guard and care for the young earwigs for several weeks until they have molted and are ready to leave the nest. The young forage on their own, becoming full grown in about 1 month. Often the mother lays a second, smaller egg mass in May or June. There is only one generation per year, but developing earwigs may be present throughout the growing season because of the double broods of overwintered females. Foraging occurs at night, with movement to dark, sheltered areas during the day. As the season progresses, the earwigs increasingly tend to aggregate in these shelter sites. Although the European earwig has wings, it very rarely flies.

Other Earwigs

Ringlegged earwig (*Euborellia annulipes*)[2] is primarily found in warmer areas but occasionally is found throughout much of the continent. It is somewhat darker than European earwig and wingless. It has omnivorous feeding habits, and although chewing injury to leafy plants can occur, ringlegged earwig is primarily a predator of other arthropods and can be an important biological control. Two generations are produced annually.

Earwigs in the genus *Doru*[1] occur in the southern U.S. They have wings and are marked with tan bands on the area behind the head (pronotum) and front wings. They are predators of caterpillars and other insects.

[1] Dermaptera: Forficulidae; [2] Dermaptera: Carcinophoridae

A. Pale, newly molted European earwig. *W. Cranshaw.* **B.** European earwig hiding in flower. *W. Cranshaw.*
C. European earwig female (top) and male (bottom). *W. Cranshaw.* **D.** Earwig damage to leaves of seedling. *K. Gray.*
E. European earwig female tending eggs. *K. Gray.* **F.** Ringlegged earwig. *J. Capinera.* **G.** Injury to cosmos flower by
European earwig. *W. Cranshaw.*

ANTS

Ants (Formicidae family)[1] are among the most commonly encountered insects in any yard and garden. All of the nearly 700 North American species are social insects that have different castes including a fertilized female queen, numerous infertile female wingless workers, and some winged reproductives. The reproductives include both males and females (potential queens) which leave the colony during mating flights.

Ants have a fantastic range in habits, and their effects on gardens can be highly variable. Most ants feed on other insects as at least part of their diet, and some are highly beneficial predators of plant pests. Others that use sweets as an important part of their diet may "tend" honeydew-producing insects such as aphids, whiteflies, and soft scales. In this process they may actively interfere with lady beetles, lacewings, and other biological control agents, indirectly contributing to plant problems.

A few ants directly damage plants. Some feed on seeds or soft plant tissues. The leafcutting ants occasionally defoliate shrubs and use the cut leaf fragments to culture special fungi, used for food, in their nests. Some ants damage plants by tunneling around the root system, excavating trunks for nesting, or killing tissues with toxic secretions such as formic acid. Finally, the painful stings of some ants, notably the imported fire ants, can cause serious nuisance and occasionally health problems.

Texas Leafcutting Ant (*Atta texana*)

Hosts: A wide variety of plants, including grasses, small fruit, plum and peach, nut trees, certain ornamentals, and weeds.

Damage: Leafcutting ants remove plant buds and cut leaf fragments, causing potentially serious foliage loss. Young plants are at particular risk and may be entirely defoliated in a short period.

Distribution: Western Louisiana, eastern Texas, and northern Mexico.

Appearance: Leafcutting ant workers are rusty brown or dark brown. On close inspection they have a characteristic pair of spines on the thorax and a spine on the head. Size varies considerably, from $\frac{1}{16}$ to $\frac{1}{2}$ inch long. Reproductive stages (males, potential queens) are larger and have dusky colored wings.

Life History and Habits: Leafcutting ants are fungus gardeners. The leaf fragments they cut from plants are not eaten but instead are used to cultivate a fungus that grows in special chambers deep in the colony. Parts of this fungus provide the sole food source of the leafcutting ant.

Crater shaped mounds around the nest entrance are external evidence of leafcutting ant colonies. These mounds may be from 5 to 14 inches high and 1 to $\frac{1}{2}$ feet in diameter. The belowground colony can be very large, extending 15 to 20 feet below the surface. The soil tunneling by leafcutting ants can cause great changes in surface mounding. Very large colonies may survive for several years and contain up to 2 million individuals.

Winged reproductive forms emerge for mating flights on clear, moonless nights in late spring following heavy rains. Females that mate during this flight subsequently attempt to establish new colonies, with little chance of success. They carry with them a small packet of the essential fungus that they use to establish fungal gardens.

Leafcutting ants may travel over 600 feet from the colony to locate forage. Activity usually occurs during nights when temperatures are very warm and during the day during cooler weather.

A. Field ant tending boxelder aphids. *F. Peairs.* **B.** Leaf injury by Texas leafcutting ant. *H. A. Pase III.* **C.** All adult forms of Texas leafcutting ant. *S. Cameron.* **D.** Texas leafcutting ant. *S. Cameron.* **E.** Mounds produced by Texas leafcutting ant. *S. Cameron.* **F.** Adult of Texas leafcutting ant. *B. Drees.* **G.** Texas leafcutting ant carrying leaf fragment. *R. F. Billings.* **H.** Trails produced by foraging Texas leafcutting ants. *D. Shetlar.*

Red Imported Fire Ant (*Solenopsis invicta*)

Damage: Fire ants are primarily predators of other insects and can be effective at controlling a wide range of plant pests. However, they occasionally directly damage plants by feeding on seedlings and the tender growth of many garden plants. Buds, pods, and fruits may occasionally be damaged, with okra particularly susceptible to injury. Fire ants may tunnel tubers, and in general their soil tunneling can disrupt the root system of plants, including citrus.

Red imported fire ant aggressively defends nests and produces a painful sting. Small whitish pustules typically develop at sting sites. Some people become sensitized to fire ant stings.

Distribution: From its original introduction in Mobile, Alabama, red imported fire ant has spread to currently infest some 260 million acres throughout eleven southeastern states, extending to the eastern two-thirds of Texas. Since the late 1990s it has been found in parts of New Mexico, Arizona, and California.

Appearance: Reddish brown and quite small, with individuals ranging in size from 1/16 to 1/4 inch.

Life History and Habits: Colonies are initiated by a single fertilized female (queen) shortly after the mating flight. She soon drops her wings, using her flight muscles to sustain her during colony establishment. The immature stages of development all take place in the nest and require about 2 to 3 weeks following egg hatch to complete. Colony size grows rapidly as new workers take over the chores of colony maintenance and foraging. Individual workers typically live for about 5 weeks after reaching the adult stage, but queens typically live 2 to 6 years. Winged reproductive forms (males and reproductive females) begin to be produced after a year or so and permanently leave the colony during mating flights. Mating flights usually take place in the afternoon following rains.

Some colonies have multiple queens. When this occurs, colonies may also be established by "budding," with individual queens moving with part of the colony to a new location. Single-queen colonies may also readily move, as a single intact colony, to a new location if conditions become unfavorable at the original nest site.

Red imported fire ants feed on a wide variety of materials. Mostly they eat living or dead insects, earthworms, or other materials of animal origin. Workers also collect honeydew and forage for sweets, proteins, and fats from various sources. Plant feeding is infrequent.

Related Species

Black imported fire ant (*Solenopsis richteri*) is currently restricted to parts of Alabama, Mississippi, Georgia, and Tennessee. Apparent hybrids of this species and red imported fire ant occur in some parts of this region. A few native *Solenopsis* species occur in the southern U.S., including **southern fire ant** (*S. xyloni*) and **native fire ant** (*S. geminata*). The latter is primarily a seed feeder.

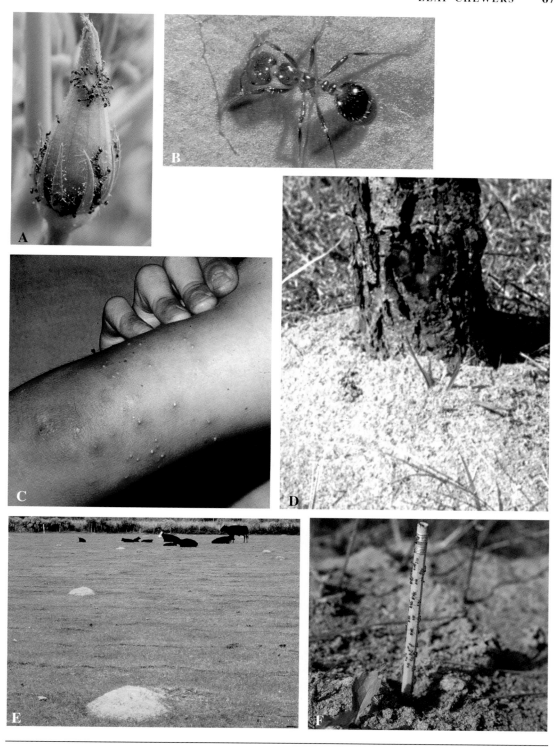

A. Red imported fire ant around bud of okra. *J. Capinera.* **B.** Red imported fire ant worker. *J. Capinera.* **C.** Typical pustules that develop from sting of red imported fire ant. *Courtesy USDA-PPQ and Bugwood Network.* **D.** Mound produced by imported fire ant nesting. *Courtesy Clemson University.* **E.** Red imported fire ant mounds in cattle pasture. *Courtesy USDA-PPQ and Bugwood Network.* **F.** Red imported fire ant on pencil to show relative size. *Courtesy USDA-PPQ and Bugwood Network.*

Miscellaneous Ants

Harvester ants (*Pogonomyrmex* spp.) are native to much of western North America and build large mounds. They are common in grasslands and rarely establish around a garden but clear an area of vegetation around the mound. Harvester ants are seed feeders. Although capable of producing painful stings, they are not aggressive and rarely sting unless their colony is directly disturbed.

Argentine ant (*Linepithema humile*) is now found throughout most of the southern states, in California, and in isolated infestations in many other areas. It has become a notorious household pest in many areas, readily nesting around the base of homes and commonly foraging indoors, particularly when the weather is cool and wet. It is highly aggressive to other surface-foraging ants and commonly displaces other species, resulting in some severe ecological impacts. In gardens, Argentine ant is often important as it tends and protect aphids, whiteflies, soft scales, and other honeydew-producing insects from natural enemies. Nests may honeycomb the soil around the base of aphid-infested plants, further stressing plants by exposing roots. Argentine ant is a relatively small ant, with workers ¹⁄₁₀ inch and light to shiny dark brown in color.

Carpenter ants (*Camponotus* spp.) are particularly common in wooded areas and are a diverse genus with 48 North American species. They are among the largest of all North American ants, but size of workers in individual colonies is highly variable. **Black carpenter ant** (*C. pennsylvanicus*), common in much of the eastern U.S., is black, as are many other carpenter ants. (Other black species of carpenter ants that commonly damage wood include *C. modoc* in the western states and *C. herculeanus* throughout the northern U.S. and southern Canada.) Other carpenter ants may be partially or almost completely reddish brown, such as **red carpenter ant** (*C. novaboracensis*), common in the upper Midwest and southern Canada, and **Florida carpenter ant** (*C. floridanus*), a bicolored species found in the southeastern states. The thorax of all carpenter ants in side view is broadly and smoothly arched, a diagnostic characteristic of that allows these ants to be separated from other large ants such as field ants.

Carpenter ants nest in wood, excavating an extensive system of tunnels that become smoothly polished. Shredded wood fragments are expelled from the openings. Initial nesting is confined to wood that is partially decayed, but as colonies expand they may enter sound wood of tree trunks. Structural weakening of old trees and occasional infestations of timbers in homes are the primary concerns with carpenter ants. Carpenter ants can produce a mildly painful bite but do not sting. Their diet is mixed and includes living and dead insects as well as honeydew. Protein-rich foods tend to be favored early in the season, with more sweets taken later.

Field ants (*Formica* spp.) are common throughout North America. Most are black, but many are reddish brown or of variable color. They are moderately large and sometimes mistaken for carpenter ants but can be distinguished by having an indentation on the back of the thorax. Field ants nest in soil, sometimes creating large mounds mixed with plant debris. When nesting adjacent to woody plants, they may injure them by secreting formic acid, which damages tender bark. Field ants actively seek sweets and readily tend aphids for their honeydew.

Pavement ant (*Tetramorium caespitum*) is an introduced species currently found in much of the northern half of the U.S. and southern Canada with a steadily expanding range. It attracts attention by the piles of fine soil and sand it commonly produces in sidewalk cracks, among patio stones, and near the base of buildings. On sunny afternoons following some rainfall, large numbers of winged reproductive stages may be pushed out of the nests for mating flights. Pavement ant feeds primarily on oily foods, sometimes sweets. Although abundant about yards, it does little to affect garden plants.

[1] Hymenoptera: Formicidae

A. Harvester ant worker. *K. Gray.* **B.** Harvester ants at nest entrance. *W. Cranshaw.* **C.** Mound produced by harvester ants. *K. Gray.* **D.** Tunnels produced by nesting carpenter ants. *D. Leatherman.* **E.** Winged male (top) and female (bottom) carpenter ants. *W. Cranshaw.* **F.** Carpenter ant worker. *Courtesy Clemson University.* **G.** Carpenter ant worker. *W. Cranshaw.* **H.** Larvae of carpenter ants. *W. Cranshaw.* **I.** Argentine ant tending scale insects. *J. K. Clark/UC Statewide IPM Program.* **J.** Winged female field ant. *K. Gray.* **K.** Winged male field ant. *K. Gray.* **L.** Small carpenter bee pupae in stem of plant. *J. Baker.* **M.** Colony of field ants with larvae, pupae, workers and a winged reproductive. *W. Cranshaw.* **N.** Mound produced by field ants (*Formica* sp.). *H. E. Evans.*

LEAFCUTTER BEES

The leafcutter bees (Megachilidae family) are solitary bees where the female does all rearing of young and colonies are not produced. Many species line nest cells with cut fragments of leaves and petals. Most are native, although one common species now well established in western North America, **alfalfa leafcutter bee** (*Megachile rotunda*), was introduced to assist with alfalfa pollination.

Note: Other common bees that are important pollinators and do not damage plants are discussed in chapter 11.

Leafcutter Bees (*Megachile* spp.)[1]

Hosts: Many broadleaf plants, particularly rose, ash, lilac, and Virginia creeper.

Damage: Leafcutter bees do not eat plants, but adults do cut semicircular notches along the edges of leaves and flowers. Damage is usually cosmetic, but serious defoliation is often reported on isolated plantings in many western states. Many leafcutter bees are important pollinators of flowering plants and are used commercially in the production of alfalfa seed.

Distribution: Throughout North America, common. More than 100 species occur, including some introduced species.

Appearance: Adults are usually black or gray and slightly smaller than a honey bee. Pollen is carried on hairs on the underside of the abdomen rather than in pollen baskets on the legs as in some other bees.

Life History and Habits: Winter is spent as a pupa in a cell lined with leaf fragments fashioned together by the adult females. In late spring and early summer the adults emerge. Females seek out natural hollows for nest sites or excavate tunnels in rotten wood or in the pith of plant stems. They then create nest cells from pieces of cut leaves or flower petals. When complete, these somewhat resemble a cigar butt, and individual cells may involve more than two dozen leaf fragments cemented together. The nest cells are then packed with a mixture of pollen and nectar, and an egg is laid in each one. Larvae develop in the cells. One generation is produced per year.

Leafcutter bees are nonaggressive and sting only when handled. The sting is only mildly painful.

[1] Hymenoptera: Megachilidae

A. Typical leaf cutting injury produced on wild rose by leafcutter bees. *W. Cranshaw.* **B.** Leafcutter bee injury to flower petal. *W. Cranshaw.* **C.** Leafcutter bee cutting lilac leaf. *W. Cranshaw.* **D.** Leafcutter bee visiting flower. *W. Cranshaw.* **E.** Rearing cells of cut leaf fragments made by leafcutter bees. *K. Gray.* **F.** Larvae of leafcutter bees exposed from rearing cells of cut leaf fragments. *K. Gray.* **G.** Leafcutter bee returning with leaf fragment. *W. Cranshaw.*

CONIFER SAWFLIES

More than three dozen species of conifer sawflies (Diprionidae family)[1] develop on needles of pines and other conifers. Eggs are inserted in the needles, and early-stage larvae often limit feeding to the surface, leaving a strawlike remnant. Later they consume entire needles, and defoliation by many species occurs on older foliage before new growth has emerged. Larvae often feed in groups and may have bizarre defensive behaviors such as mass twitching, arching, and disgorging of salivary fluids when disturbed. The adults are thick-bodied wasps, dark brown or black, with conspicuous antennae that are particularly well developed in the males. Sawflies do not sting.

European Pine Sawfly (*Neodiprion sertifer*)

Hosts: Pines, particularly mugho and table top pines.

Damage: Larvae consume the older foliage in spring, before bud break. Seriously affected plants have a tufted "bottle brush" appearance with only new needles present.

Distribution: Generally distributed throughout the Midwest, Northeast, and parts of southern Canada.

Appearance: Larvae are grayish green and about 1 inch when full grown. A light stripe runs down the back, and a light stripe followed by a dark green stripe runs along the sides. Adults are about ⅓ inch long. Males are nearly black and have highly feathered antennae. Females are reddish brown and somewhat larger.

Life History and Habits: European pine sawfly spends winter in the egg stage, inserted in needles. Eggs hatch in midspring and the larvae feed on needles, often in small groups, with three or four per needle being common. When disturbed, they raise both their head and tail in defense. In late spring or early summer, full-grown larvae move to soil or bark cracks where they form a cocoon and pupate. Adults emerge in late August and September. Females insert six to eight of the overwintering eggs per needle and may lay eggs in about a dozen individual needles. Egg-laying scars may be quite visible, particularly after frosts cause the wounded areas to yellow.

Related Species

Almost three dozen *Neodiprion* species develop on conifers in North America, mostly on various pines. **Redheaded pine sawfly** (*N. lecontei*) is an important species in parts of the midwestern U.S. and southeastern Canada. It feeds on two and three needle pines, including Scotch, jack, shortleaf, loblolly, slash, red, and mugho. It produces two generations over much of its range, with the spring generation stripping old needles before bud break and the summer generation consuming new needles. Redheaded pine sawfly is gregarious and may form feeding groups of 100 larvae which twitch in unison when disturbed. Winter is spent as a prepupa in the cocoon, which is formed among leaf litter or dug shallowly in soil. Redheaded pine sawfly may remain dormant for a few years in this stage. Adults lay eggs in slits in rows along the needle edge.

A. Eggs of pine sawfly at hatch. *D. Leatherman.* **B.** European pine sawflies. *D. Shetlar.* **C.** Egg scars of European pine sawfly. *D. Shetlar.* **D.** European pine sawflies. *E. B. Walker.* **E.** Feeding damage by European pine sawflies. *D. Herms.* **F.** Redheaded pine sawflies. *G. J. Lenhard.* **G.** Redheaded pine sawflies. *G. J. Lenhard.* **H.** European pine sawfly adults. Male is darker and has larger antennae. *D. Shetlar.*

Among the other *Neodiprion* species of importance are:

- *N. swainei,* **Swaine jack pine sawfly**, a common species in eastern Canada that develops primarily on Jack pine;
- *N. autumnalis,* a common "pine sawfly" of western forests, particularly damaging to ponderosa pine. Feeding damage occurs in mid- to late summer;
- *N. pinetum,* **white pine sawfly**, a species that occurs throughout the natural range of its primary host, eastern white pine. Both new and old needles are consumed by this species, which can be seriously damaging during outbreaks;
- *N. excitans,* **blackheaded pine sawfly**, common on loblolly and shortleaf pines in the southeastern and Gulf states. Three to four generations per year may occur in southern areas of its range;
- *N. edulicolis,* **pinyon sawfly**, a common and sometimes outbreak species of pinyon in the southwestern states; and
- *N. tsugae,* **hemlock sawfly**, found across the northern U.S. and Canada in association with the native range of either western or, possibly, eastern hemlock.

Introduced pine sawfly (*Diprion similis*) feeds primarily on white pine throughout the northeastern quadrant of the U.S. Scotch, jack, red, and Swiss mountain pines are less commonly infested. Adults lay about 10 eggs, in a row, on needles, and the young larvae feed gregariously in groups. The first-generation feeding occurs before bud break and confines feeding to the previous year's needles, but a midsummer generation consumes both old and newly produced needles. Pupation occurs in a cocoon, often on the host tree.

The most important sawfly affecting spruce is **yellowheaded spruce sawfly** (*Pikonema alaskensis*), a species restricted to western North America. Adults lay eggs in late spring on current-season needles or tender twigs, and the larvae consume the new growth. Larvae have a reddish yellow to chestnut brown head and an olive green body. A single generation is produced, with winter spent as a full-grown larva in a cocoon at the base of previously infested trees.

The genus *Monoctenus* contains several species that are minor pests of conifers. **Juniper sawfly** (*M. fulvus*) feeds on the tips of junipers, sometimes checking the new growth and causing a thinning of the shrub. However, the larvae do not appear to feed heavily on shrubs, even when in high populations. Larvae are generally gray-green with an orange head. **Arborvitae sawfly** (*M. melliceps*) occasionally damages arborvitae and juniper in the northeastern states.

Bull pine sawfly (*Zadiprion townsendi*) feeds on ponderosa pine needles in the western U.S. In an unusual life history, the larvae continue to feed on warm days throughout winter, becoming full grown in late spring. Adults appear in summer to lay eggs, and the newly hatched larvae begin to feed on needles by early fall.

[1] Hymenoptera: Diprionidae

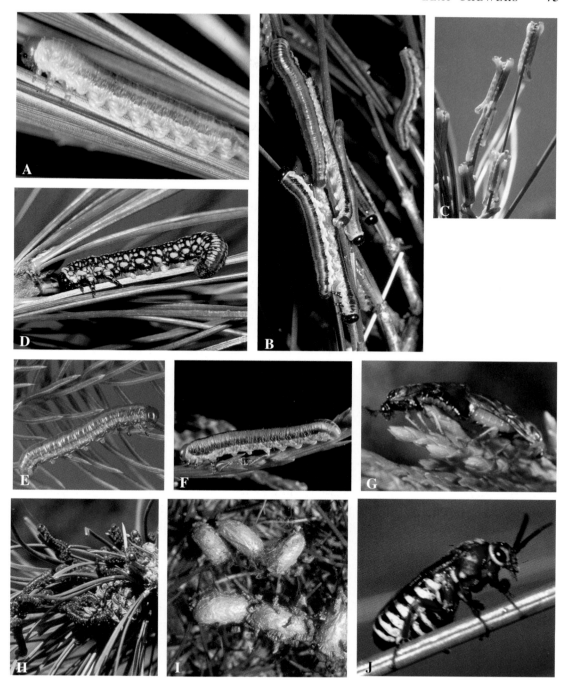

A. *Neodiprion autumnalis. Courtesy USDA-FS Rocky Mountain Research Station.* B. Blackheaded pine sawflies. *A. T. Drooz.* C. Larvae of *Neodiprion ventralis. D. Leatherman.* D. Introduced pine sawfly larva. *E. B. Walker.*
E. Yellowheaded spruce sawfly. *E. B. Walker.* F. Juniper sawfly. *J. Capinera.* G. Juniper sawfly adults, mating pair. *J. Capinera.* H. Bull pine sawfly larvae feeding in early spring. *W. Cranshaw.* I. Bull pine sawfly pupae. *W. Cranshaw.*
J. Bull pine sawfly adult. *W. Cranshaw.*

COMMON SAWFLIES

The common sawflies, or tenthredinids (Tenthredinidae family),[1] are a large insect family with more than 700 North American species. Larvae are usually similar to those of conifer sawflies and often resemble caterpillars. Most, however, can be distinguished by having six or more pairs of prolegs (vs. 2 to 5 pairs) which lack the terminal hooks of caterpillar prolegs. Adults are usually black or brownish, thick-waisted, nonstinging wasps with slender antennae.

Imported Currantworm/Currant Sawfly (*Nematus ribesii*)

Hosts: Currants, gooseberry.

Damage: The larvae chew the leaves of currants and gooseberries, often extensively defoliating plants early in the season. Foliage in the interior is damaged first, but all leaves may be eaten. Yield and quality of fruit can be affected by this injury.

Distribution: Northern half of U.S. and southern Canada.

Appearance: Larvae are generally light green-gray with numerous black spots; newly molted, they are uniformly light green. Adult females are thick-bodied wasps, about ⅓ inch long with a dark head and thorax and yellowish abdomen. Males are slightly smaller and more generally dark.

Life History and Habits: Imported currantworm spends the winter in a cocoon in the soil around previously infested currants and gooseberries. The adults usually emerge shortly after the first leaves have expanded, and females insert eggs into the main veins of the leaf underside. The larvae hatch about 7 to 10 days after eggs are laid and at first chew small shotholes in the leaf interior. Later they disperse throughout the plant and feed along the leaf margins, becoming full grown in about 3 weeks. Young larvae are pale green but develop distinctive dark spots as they grow and reach a size of about ¾ inch.

The full-grown larvae drop to the ground and form a cocoon. Some pupate and emerge in late June and July, producing a small second generation. The majority remain dormant and emerge the following year.

Other Tenthredinid Sawflies

Willow sawfly (*Nematus ventralis*) is occasionally abundant on willow in the central states and Prairie Provinces. Larvae are dark green and commonly feed in groups. Multiple generations may be produced. Larvae may remain dormant for two winters before completing development and emerging as adults in spring.

Two species of **azalea sawflies** (*Amauronematus azalae*, *Nematus lipvskyi*) are damaging to azaleas in much of the Midwest and Northeast. The larvae are green and feed along the leaf edge, often consuming the entire leaf except the larger veins. One generation is produced annually.

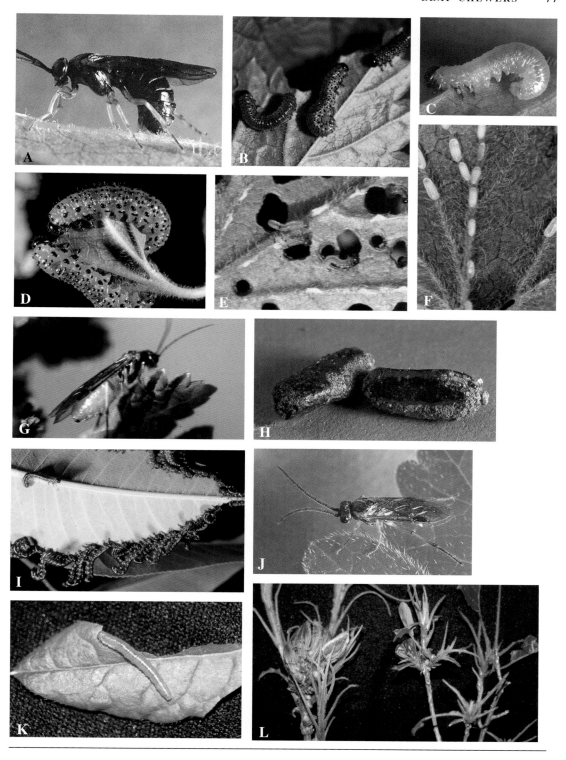

A. Adult of sawfly *Pristophora rufipes*. *K. Gray.* **B.** Imported currantworm larvae. *W. Cranshaw.* **C.** Larva of *Pristophora rufipes*. *K. Gray.* **D.** Imported currantworm larvae. *W. Cranshaw.* **E.** Imported currantworm at egg hatch. *W. Cranshaw.* **F.** Imported currantworm eggs inserted into leaf veins. *W. Cranshaw.* **G.** Imported currantworm, adult female. *W. Cranshaw.* **H.** Pupal cocoons of imported currantworm. *K. Gray.* **I.** Willow sawflies. *D. Shetlar.* **J.** Imported currantworm, male. *K. Gray.* **K.** Azalea sawfly. *R. Childs.* **L.** Azalea sawfly damage. *R. Childs.*

Brownheaded ash sawfly (*Tomostethus multicinctus*) is a sporadic but important early-season defoliator of ash in Colorado and many eastern states. Green ash is particularly damaged, but all species are susceptible.

Brownheaded ash sawfly spends the winter as a full-grown larva in a cocoon around the base of a previously infested ash tree. Pupation occurs in early spring. Adults are small, black wasps that emerge in April and sometimes can be found in swarms around the tree. Females insert eggs into young leaves, usually around the edge, resulting in a slight distortion of the leaves. Early-stage larvae feed on the interior of the leaf, producing small pinhole feeding wounds. Older larvae feed extensively on the leaf, avoiding only the main veins. Larval development and feeding occur throughout May, and by early June individuals are full grown. Full-grown larvae shed a papery larval skin that remains attached to the leaf and then crawl to the ground, where they form protective cocoons.

Blackheaded ash sawfly (*Tethida cordigera*) is associated with red, green, and white ash through much of the eastern U.S. It is also found in California. Habits are similar to those of brownheaded ash sawfly.

Mountain-ash sawfly (*Pristophora geniculata*) is a common sawfly on mountain-ash east of the Mississippi River. Adults emerge in late spring and insert eggs in small groups along the leaf edge. The larvae usually feed gregariously, clinging to the leaf edge and consuming the entire leaf except the mid rib before moving to the next leaf. Like many sawflies that feed as a group, they rear in unison in an S-shape when disturbed. Full-grown larvae drop to the soil and form a cocoon. Some complete pupation and produce a second generation in late summer. Others remain as prepupae in the cocoon and winter in this stage.

Columbine sawfly (*P. aquiligae*) defoliates columbine in late spring in areas of the Midwest, Rocky Mountain region, and some eastern states. Larvae are pale green and appear to produce only a single generation. **California pear sawfly** (*P. abbreviata*) makes a semicircular cut, somewhat resembling that of leafcutter bees, of pear leaves. The larvae lie along the cut and blend well. There is only one generation produced, with peak feeding in late April and May. **Chokecherry sawfly** (*P. serrula*) is a common species on chokecherry in the Rocky Mountain states.

Larvae of **raspberry sawfly** (*Monophadnoides geniculatus*) feed on the interior of raspberry leaves, cutting irregular holes between veins. When they are abundant, foliage may become very lacy, but raspberry sawflies develop rapidly and the full-grown larvae begin to crawl to the ground within about 2 weeks after the eggs hatch. They dig a small cell in the soil and spin a cocoon in which they remain until the following spring.

Dusky birch sawfly (*Croesus latitarsus*) is a common defoliator of birch and is found widely in North America. Gray birch is the favored host. Larvae strongly hold a rather unusual S-shaped form while they feed along the leaf margin. One or two generations may occur annually.

A. Brownheaded ash sawfly and pupal cocoon. *W. Cranshaw.* **B.** Leaf damage by brownheaded ash sawfly. *W. Cranshaw.*
C. Brownheaded ash sawfly eggs inserted into edge of young ash leaf. *W. Cranshaw.* **D.** Brownheaded ash sawfly larva.
W. Cranshaw. **E.** Young larvae and characteristic shotholes produced by brownheaded ash sawfly. *W. Cranshaw.*
F. Blackheaded ash sawfly larva. *D. Shetlar.* **G.** Mountain ash sawflies. *E. B. Walker.* **H.** Columbine sawfly. *W. Cranshaw.*
I. Chokecherry sawfly larva. *J. Capinera.* **J.** Chokecherry sawfly adult. *J. Capinera.* **K.** Dusky birch sawflies. *L. L.
Hyche.* **L.** Young larvae and damage by raspberry sawfly. *W. Cranshaw.* **M.** Raspberry sawfly. *W. Cranshaw.*
N. California pear sawfly. *W. Cranshaw.*

Grape sawfly (*Erythraspides vitis*) feeds on wild grape in the southern U.S. The larvae are distinctly marked with a double row of black tubercles on each segment and feed as groups on the leaf underside.

Violet sawfly (*Ametastegia pallipes*) feeds on wild and cultivated pansies and violets. The larvae are dark olive green with a black head. Several generations may occur, with injury most evident in late summer. Larvae skeletonize the underside of leaves, then feed more generally, later leaving the food host plant to pupate in the pith of larger nearby plants.

Young larvae of **poplar leaffolding sawfly** (*Phyllocolpa bozemani*) induce an unusual leaf fold along the edge of poplar, cottonwood, and willow. The young larvae wound the expanding leaf, causing it to curl around them. Later they move out and feed along the leaf edge. There is normally only one generation per year, completed by early summer.

Dogwood sawfly (*Macremphytus tarsatus*) feeds on leaves of various dogwood, particularly gray dogwood. It is most common in the northeastern U.S. and Great Lakes area but is known as far west as Colorado. Larvae are white in early stages and become prominently spotted in the last larval instar.

One of the most bizarre sawflies is **butternut woollyworm** (*Eriocampa juglandis*). Larvae are covered with long threads of whitish wax and develop on the foliage of nut trees in the southeastern states.

[1] Hymenoptera: Tenthredinidae

A. Grape sawfly larvae. *L. Risley.* **B.** Leaf fold produced by poplar leaffolding sawfly. *W. Cranshaw.* **C.** Young larva of poplar leaffolding sawfly. *W. Cranshaw.* **D.** Dogwood sawfly larva. *W. Cranshaw.* **E.** Dogwood sawfly larva. *W. Cranshaw.* **F.** Butternut woollyworm larva. *L. L. Hyche.*

SLUG SAWFLIES

The slug sawflies[1] are a group of tenthredinid sawflies of odd habit and appearance. Larvae are slug-like with legs that are greatly reduced in size. They feed on the leaf surface, characteristically producing skeletonizing injuries where leaf tissues are removed from between veins.

Pearslug (or Pear Sawfly or Cherry Slug) (*Caliroa cerasi*)

Hosts: Sweet and ornamental varieties of cherry, plum, hawthorn, pear, and cotoneaster.

Damage: Larvae feed on the upper surface of leaves, producing distinctive skeletonizing wounds. Heavily damaged leaves turn brown and drop early.

Distribution: Throughout most of the northern half of the U.S. and southern Canada.

Appearance: Pearslug larvae are shiny and sluglike in general appearance but can be somewhat variable in color. Many are a dark olive green, but later instars tend to be lighter and may even have orange tones. Adults are shiny black stout-bodied wasps, about ⅓ inch long.

Life History and Habits: Adults emerge in late June or early July. Females insert their eggs singly in circular slits on the upper surface of leaves. Eggs hatch in about 2 weeks, and larvae chew small pits in the upper surface of leaves during early development. Later they more extensively chew the leaves but always avoid feeding on the larger veins and lower leaf surface, producing a typical skeletonizing injury pattern.

When larvae are full grown they wander off the plant and dig a shallow cell in the soil to pupate. Pupation occurs in a small cocoon encrusted with soil particles. In about 2 weeks, many of the insects continue development and emerge as adults to produce a second generation. Larvae of these typically cause peak injury in early September. Populations of this second generation are usually smaller than those of the first generation, since many pearslugs remain dormant until the following spring. The full-grown larvae from the September generation drop to the soil and spin a cocoon in which they spend the winter. They pupate the following spring.

Other Slug Sawflies

Larvae of **roseslug** (*Endelomyia aethiops*) are smooth and pale green, largely lacking the shiny moist surface of the pearslug. They feed as skeletonizers on the underside of rose leaves, giving a window-pane appearance to leaves. Most injury is completed by late spring, as there is only one generation.

Multiple generations may be produced by **bristly roseslug** (*Cladius difformis*). Larvae can be distinguished by having the body covered with short bristles. Younger larvae feed in a similar skeletonizing manner but later become more general feeders and chew holes through leaves.

Scarlet oak sawfly (*Caliroa quercuscoccineae*) feeds on scarlet, pin, black, and white oak over a broad area east of the Mississippi River. Larvae feed primarily on the lower leaf surface in a skeletonizing pattern. Two generations may occur, and damage is more evident in late summer. Pin oak may be infested by two species, **pin oak sawfly** (*C. lineata*) and *C. petiolata*.

[1] Hymenoptera: Tenthredinidae

A. Pearslug larva. *K. Gray.* B. Egg scar and feeding by young pearslug larva. *W. Cranshaw.* C. Pear sawfly adult. *K. Gray.* D. Larvae and damage by pearslug. *W. Cranshaw.* E. Bristly roseslug larva. *K. Gray.* F. Roseslug and injury. *K. Gray.* G. Roseslug and injury. *K. Gray.* H. Scarlet oak sawfly larvae. *D. Shetlar.* I. Larvae of sawfly *Caliroa petiolata.* *R. L. Anderson.* J. Bristly roseslug pupal cocoon. *K. Gray.* K. Bristly roseslug adult. *K. Gray.*

OTHER SAWFLIES

Birch sawfly (*Arge pectoralis*)[1] is the most commonly encountered of the argid sawflies, a small family of sawflies marked by dusky wings, a dark body, and unusually developed antennae on the males. They are found in the northeastern U.S. and southern Canada where they primarily feed on birches, occasionally on alder and willow. Larvae feed during summer and are yellow with six dark spots along the side.

Hollyhock sawfly (*Neoptilia malvacearum*)[1] can be very damaging to hollyhock in Ohio and some mid-Atlantic states. Young larvae first feed on the leaf undersurface and produce windowpane injuries on the leaves. They later skeletonize extensively. The larvae are light green with dark spots. Adults are all black or black with an orange thorax. Two generations normally occur in Ohio, with a small third generation in warm seasons. **Hibiscus sawfly** (*Atomacerca decepta*)[1] has been reported to damage hibiscus, marshmallow, buttonbush, and some other perennial plants in the mid-Atlantic states.

Elm sawfly (*Cimbex americana*)[2] is a large sawfly, widely distributed with a host range that includes willow, elm, and occasionally basswood, birch, maple, poplar, and alder. When feeding, the larvae often coil the hind end around an adjacent twig. Elm sawfly larvae can be distinguished by their development of unusual pebbly skin when nearly full grown, pale yellow-green coloration, and dark stripe down the back. They feed during the summer and are rarely abundant enough to cause significant damage, although isolated outbreaks are reported. *Trichiosoma triangulum*[2] is a related species that feeds on ash, birch, poplar, willow, and wild cherry. *T. viminalis* is common on willow and poplar in the Midwest.

[1] Hymenoptera: Argidae; [2] Hymenoptera: Cimbicidae

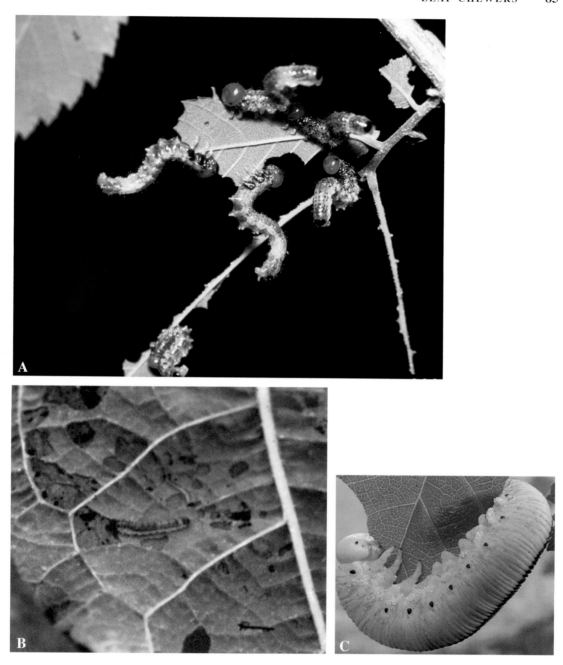

A. Elm sawfly larvae. *R. F. Billings.* **B.** Hollyhock sawflies. *D. Caldwell.* **C.** Elm sawfly, older larva. *H. A. Pase III.*

WEBWORMS

"Webworm" is a term loosely applied to some caterpillars that produce visible webbing over foliage as they feed. Caterpillars from several families and genera of insects that share this habit may be described as webworms. The amount of webbing produced can vary considerably, with some species producing fairly prominent webbed structures whereas others limit webbing to loosely tying leaves.

Mimosa Webworm (*Homadaula anisocentra*)[1]

Hosts: Honeylocust, mimosa.

Damage: Larvae feed on leaf surfaces of honeylocust, producing skeletonizing injuries that cause leaves to turn dull gray or appear scorched brown. Individual larvae web together several leaves and may feed together in groups, creating large areas of unsightly webs. Isolated trees, particularly adjacent to buildings, tend to be most consistently damaged.

Distribution: Mid-Atlantic and southeastern states west to eastern Kansas and Nebraska.

Appearance: Caterpillars are grayish to dark brown, sometimes tinged with rose or pink. Full grown they are about ⅝ inch and extremely active, wriggling and dropping on a silken strand when disturbed. Adults are undistinguished gray moths, rarely seen, with a wingspan of ½ inch, gray with silver sheen and black spots.

Life History and Habits: Adults begin to lay rosy colored eggs in late May to June on flowers and foliage. The young larvae produce silk and skeletonize adjacent foliage and flowers. As they get older, webbing is more extensive and may coalesce with that of adjacent larvae. By midsummer the larvae descend to the ground on silken threads and pupate in cocoons in bark cracks, on adjacent buildings, and among ground cover. A second generation with peak feeding injury in August is often more conspicuously damaging. A third generation is reported in the southeastern area of the range.

Other Webworms

Juniper webworm (*Dichomeris marginella*)[2] develops on most *Juniperus* species and occasionally on arborvitae. It has spread throughout much of the northern U.S. and southern Canada. Young larvae mine needles, and the brown dead needles become incorporated in webbed "nests." Older larvae feed on the outside of needles and may consume them entirely. The larvae are reddish brown caterpillars and are present in silken tubes they produce among the juniper foliage. One generation is produced per year.

Cotoneaster webworm (*Athrips rancidella*)[2] is a European species currently established in northern California and the Pacific Northwest. During spring it makes dense webs on cotoneaster that are filled with leaf fragments and frass. There is one generation per year.

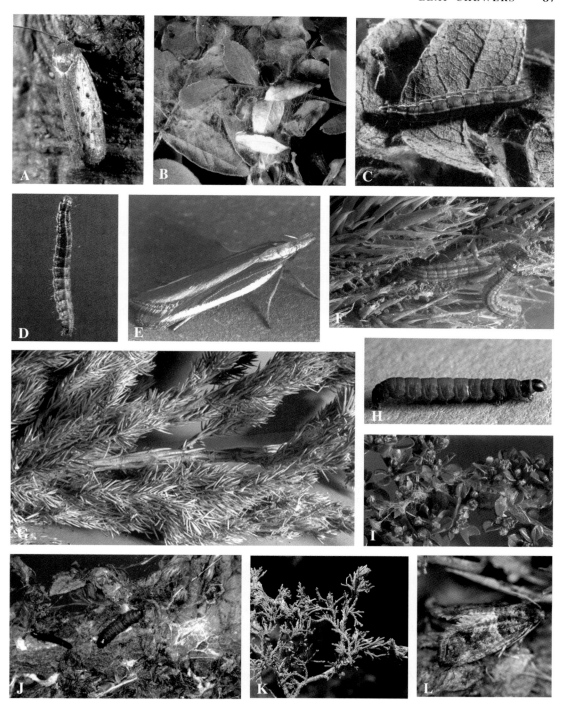

A. Mimosa webworm adult. *D. Shetlar.* **B.** Mimosa webworm damage. *D. Shetlar.* **C.** Mimosa webworm larva. *D. Shetlar.* **D.** Mimosa webworm larva spinning down from tree. *D. Shetlar.* **E.** Juniper webworm adult. *K. Gray.* **F.** Juniper webworm larvae and associated damage. *K. Gray.* **G.** Damage by juniper webworm. *K. Gray.* **H.** Cotoneaster webworm larva. *K. Gray.* **I.** Cotoneaster webworm injury. *S. Collman.* **J.** Cotoneaster webworm larva and associated webbing. *S. Collman.* **K.** Damage by juniper webworm. *D. Leatherman.* **L.** Cotoneaster webworm adult. *S. Collman.*

Uglynest caterpillar (*Archips cerasivorana*)[3] is found across the northern U.S. and southern Canada. It feeds on a wide range of trees and shrubs, although cherry and chokecherry are most commonly infested. Uglynest caterpillars feed in groups, creating large, loose silken shelters that cover foliage in a manner similar to that of fall webworms (p. 118). One generation is produced per year, with the olive green caterpillars present from the time of egg hatch in late spring through much of the summer.

Ailanthus webworm (*Atteva punctella*)[4] is one of the few insects commonly associated with tree-of-heaven. It feeds on leaves and loosely covers them with silk.

Pine webworm (*Pococerca robustella*)[5] feeds on several species of pines throughout the eastern U.S. and Canada. In northern areas young caterpillars are present in late spring and originally feed as needleminers. As they get older, they feed in groups, loosely webbing together needles of pine terminals. One generation is produced annually in northern states, with winter spent as a pupa in a cocoon in soil. In the southeast two generations may be produced.

Barberry webworm (*Omphalocerca dentosa*)[5] is an eastern species associated with mahonia and barberry. The larvae are black, about 1½ inches long when full grown, and feed on the leaves and new shoots in a loose silken shelter.

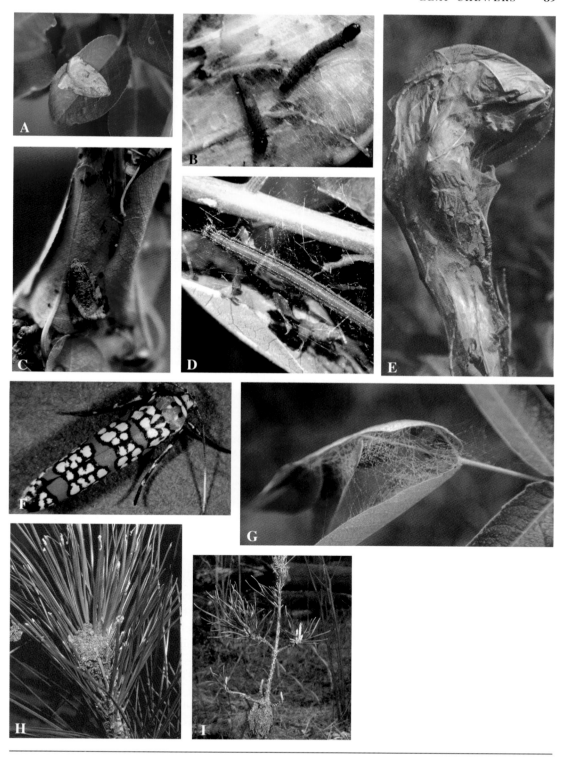

A. Uglynest caterpillar adult. *D. Leatherman.* **B.** Uglynest caterpillars. *W. Cranshaw.* **C.** Uglynest caterpillar moth and pupal skin. *D. Leatherman.* **D.** Ailanthus webworm. *J. Fengler.* **E.** Nest produced by uglynest caterpillar. *W. Cranshaw.* **F.** Ailanthus webworm adult. *D. Gilrein.* **G.** Ailanthus webworm tying leaf. *D. Gilrein.* **H.** Pine webworm injury. *R. F. Billings.* **I.** Pine webworm damage. *R. L. Anderson.*

"Garden Webworms"[5]

Two closely related species sometimes damaging to gardens are **alfalfa webworm** (*Loxostege cerealis*) and **beet webworm** (*L. sticticalis*). The caterpillars produce shelters of loose webbing and feed on adjacent leaves. Young larvae typically skeletonize leaves. These insects may occur on a wide range of garden vegetables including cabbage, beet, carrot, lettuce, and cucumber. They also occur on several weeds, including lambsquarter, pigweed, and dock. Both species are found primarily in western North America.

Caterpillars are about ¾ inch when full grown. They are green or yellowish green when young but darken as they get older. Larvae are found in silken tunnels spun among the foliage and wriggle vigorously when disturbed.

Alfalfa and beet webworms winter as mature larvae in soil. Adults are active in spring and lay eggs in a small mass that looks somewhat like overlapping fish scales. The newly hatched caterpillars make a small silk pad and skeletonize the leaf surface. Older larvae more extensively web together foliage and produce a silken tube where they rest and from which they emerge to feed. Pupation occurs in the upper soil in a silk-lined cell. Two to four generations may occur per year, depending on temperature and location.

Garden webworm (*Achyra rantalis*) can be found in the eastern U.S. and parts of California but is primarily damaging in the southern High Plains. It shares many habits with beet and alfalfa webworms and also produces webbing that ties together leaves and forms a loose shelter. Young larvae skeletonize, and older stages feed more generally on leaves. Larvae are generally yellow-green with prominent dark spots and a yellowish head.

Celery leaftier (*Udea rubigalis*), also known as greenhouse leaftier, is broadly distributed in North America and occurs both as a greenhouse and garden pest. Many vegetables are hosts, with celery being seriously damaged. Several weeds and garden flowers also support this insect. It feeds on the leaves, silking them together in a manner similar to that of "garden webworms." Eggs are laid in small groups on leaves, and both larval and pupal stages occur in the foliage. Generations can be completed in from 1 to 3 months, depending on temperature. In the northern half of California and the Pacific states, the closely related **false celery leaftier** (*U. profundalis*) is present and sometimes similarly damaging.

Cabbage webworm (*Hellula rogatalis*) is found throughout the southern U.S., occasionally dispersing into northern states. Larvae develop on cabbage and related crucifers and cause the most damage when older larvae web together leaves that they chew and damage the growing point. Younger caterpillars act as leafminers and may tunnel main veins, causing tip dieback. Cabbage webworm is yellowish gray with a dark head and is usually found in the loose webbing it produces.

Cross-striped cabbageworm (*Evergestis rimosalis*) is an occasional pest of collards, Brussels sprouts, and related vegetable plants. It can be found over much of the eastern U.S. but is common only in some of the southeastern states. Caterpillars have a distinctive patterning of thin black and white striping on the back and prominent yellow lines on the sides. Several generations are produced annually; in southern areas, the species can often be active and damaging by early spring. A related species, **purple-backed cabbageworm** (*E. pallidata*), is a northern species that occasionally damages cabbage family plants in eastern Canada. Mature caterpillars are olive green or purple-brown.

[1] Lepidoptera: Glyphipterygidae; [2] Lepidoptera: Gelechiidae; [3] Lepidoptera: Tortricidae; [4] Lepidoptera: Yponomeutidae; [5] Lepidoptera: Pyralidae

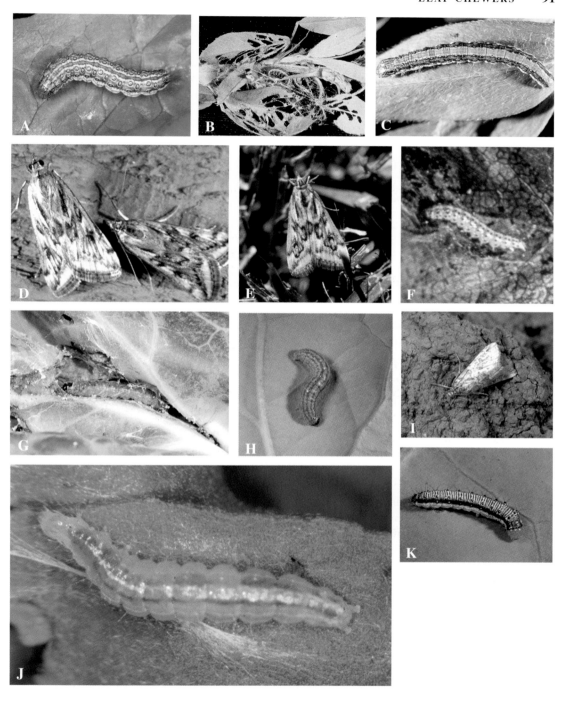

A. Beet webworm larva. *F. Peairs.* B. Alfalfa webworm larva and associated webbing. *J. Capinera.* C. Alfalfa webworm larva. *J. Capinera.* D. Alfalfa webworm adults. *J. Capinera.* E. Alfalfa webworm adult. *W. Cranshaw.* F. Apple and thorn skeletonizer. *A. Antonelli.* G. Cabbage webworm larva. *J. Capinera.* H. Cabbage webworm. *R. Bessin.* I. Cabbage webworm adult. *R. Bessin.* J. Celery leaftier. *D. Gilrein.* K. Cross-striped cabbageworm. *R. Bessin.*

SOD WEBWORMS

Sod webworm[1] is a general description for about two dozen species of caterpillars that develop on grasses. Larvae of most species produce tubes of webbing at the base of the plants in which they live. Adults are known as snout moths or lawn moths and are active at dusk, often seen hovering above grassy areas.

Larger Sod Webworm (*Pediasia trisecta*)

Hosts: Primarily bluegrass, but ryegrass and fescues may be eaten.

Damage: Larvae chew grass blades, producing thinning of lawns with a ragged appearance. Severely pruned plants may be killed.

Distribution: Northern U.S. and southern Canada.

Appearance: Adults are snout moths with a wingspan of about 1 inch. The wings are generally cream colored with light-colored veins and silvery scales on the tip. Larvae are yellowish or greenish yellow with chocolate brown spotting and a yellow-brown head.

Life History and Habits: Winter is spent as a partially grown larva in a silken shelter at the base of grass plants. It resumes feeding in spring and completes development in May. Pupation occurs in a cocoon adjacent to the feeding shelter. Adults from the first generation are usually most abundant in June.

After mating, females begin laying eggs, which they drop over the grass while in flight. Most egg-laying takes place for a few hours after sunset. Early-stage larvae locate within the leaf fold at the base of the plant and feed on the leaf surface. As they get older, they move to the base of the plant and form a silken tube used as a retreat. They emerge at night and clip grass blades which are dragged back to the the shelter and consumed. The silk tunnel often fills with fecal droppings (frass) and leaf fragments, forcing the larvae to initiate a new tunnel. Larval development following egg hatch may take 30 to 50 days to complete, after which a cocoon is formed in which to pupate. The second-generation adults subsequently emerge in midsummer and repeat the cycle. A third generation is sometimes observed in warmer areas.

Other Sod Webworms

Close to two dozen species of sod webworms have been reported to develop in lawns, and most have habits generally similar to those of the larger sod webworm. Among those developing on cool-season turfgrasses are **western lawn moth** (*Tehama bonifatella*), **bluegrass webworm** (*Parapediasia teterrella*), **western sod webworm** (*Pediasia bonifatellus*), **striped sod webworm** (*Fissicrambus mutabilis*), **elegant sod webworm** (*Microcrambus elegans*), **vagabond crambus** (*Agriphila vulgivagella*), *Agriphila ruricolella*, **yellow crambus** (*Crambus luteolellus*), **silver-striped webworm** (*C. praefectellus*), **corn root webworm** (*C. caliginosellus*), **silver-barred webworm** (*C. sperryellus*), **Leach's crambus** (*C. leachellus*), and *Thaumatopsis pexellus*. The most serious sod webworm pest of warm-season turfgrasses in the southern U.S. is **tropical sod webworm** (*Herpetogramma phaeopteralis*), which develops year-round on St. Augustinegrass, bermudagrass, and centipedegrass. Peak injury occurs in fall.

A. Sod webworm adult. *W. Cranshaw.* **B.** Sod webworm damage. *D. Shetlar.* **C.** Sod webworm larva. *J. Capinera.*
D. Sod webworm exposed in silken tunnel. *J. Capinera.* **E.** Adult of sod webworm *Pediasia trisecta. W. Cranshaw.*
F. Adult of sod webworm *Thaumatopsis pexellus. J. Capinera.* **G.** Sod webworm larva. *D. Shetlar.* **H.** Western lawn
moth adult. *K. Gray.* **I.** Leach's crambus adult. *K. Gray.*

Cranberry girdler (*Chrysoteuchia topiaria*) is a sod webworm of unusual habit. It feeds primarily in the crowns and upper root system rather than on leaves. Damage is not limited to grasses, and roots of cranberry and some woody plants may also be injured. Peak injury occurs much later in the season than is observed with other sod webworms, typically in September and October. Reflecting their subterranean feeding habit, the larvae lack the dark markings of most sod webworms and are instead pale colored with a light brown head.

[1] Lepidoptera: Crambidae

DIAMONDBACK MOTH

Diamondback Moth (*Plutella xylostella*)[1]

Hosts: A wide variety of plants in the mustard family, including cabbage, broccoli, mustard, watercress, and many related weeds.

Damage: Caterpillars feed on leaves. Although very small (individual caterpillars feed far less than cabbage looper or imported cabbageworm), they can be extremely abundant. Diamondback moth has increased in importance because of its ability to become resistant to many commonly used insecticides.

Distribution: Throughout North America.

Appearance: Larvae are small caterpillars, less than ½ inch when full grown, and are pale green with the hind pair of prolegs conspicuously protruding. They are very active and wriggle vigorously and drop from plants when disturbed. Adults have generally gray wings which, when folded over the body, show a series of white diamond patterns on the back.

Life History and Habits: In northern areas, diamondback moths winter as pupae, with adults emerging and becoming active in early spring. In southern areas, development may be continuous. Eggs are laid singly or in small groups on leaves of various mustard family plants. Young larvae typically feed on the underside of leaves and produce windowpane injuries. Older larvae feed more generally. Pupation occurs in a loose cocoon, usually attached to outer leaves. Three to four generations are typically produced annually in northern areas, with over a dozen possible in the south.

[1] Lepidoptera: Plutellidae

A. Cranberry girdler adult. *K. Gray.* **B.** Cranberry girdler larva. *J. Capinera.* **C.** Diamondback moth. *R. Bessin.*
D. Diamondback moth caterpillar. *W. Cranshaw.* **E.** Diamondbackmoth pupa. *W. Cranshaw.* **F.** Diamondback moth
caterpillar and associated damage. *W. Cranshaw.*

LEAFROLLERS

Leafrollers are caterpillars that are loosely related (Tortricidae family). Older larvae have the habit of curling over the edge of leaves and fastening with silk to create a rolled leaf shelter. This large family comprises more than 1,000 species in North America. A few species, particularly those that damage fruit, are considered pests.

Fruittree Leafroller (*Archips argyrospila*)[1]

Hosts: A wide variety of deciduous trees and shrubs, including apple, crabapple, honeylocust, ash, and linden.

Damage: Larvae chew leaves, producing skeletonizing wounds during early stages, and later feed more generally. On fruit trees, incidental feeding on young fruit may occur, inducing fruit abortion or distortion (cat facing).

Distribution: Throughout most of North America.

Appearance: Larvae are green with a black head and are found in the rolled leaves. When disturbed they wriggle vigorously and may escape the shelter by dropping on a strand of silk. Adults have rusty brown wings with silvery or pale gold patches. Wingspan is about ¾ inch.

Life History and Habits: Fruittree leafrollers winter as eggs in a flat gray-brown mass typically containing more than 100 eggs. Egg masses are glued to twigs and hatch in spring shortly after leaves emerge. Young larvae usually feed first around the tips and emerging leaves. Older larvae begin to tie up leaves with webbing and feed inside this shelter. When mature, larvae usually pupate in the rolled leaves but may disperse to bark cracks of the trunk and large branches. Adult moths appear 2 weeks later, mate, and lay the overwintering egg masses. There is one generation per year.

Other Leafrollers

Boxelder leafroller (*Archips negundanus*)[1] is found throughout most of the northern half of the U.S. and Canada, feeding on leaves of boxelder and, less commonly, honeysuckle and alder. **Oak leafroller** (*A. semiferana*) is primarily associated with oak, occasionally damaging maple. It is widely distributed throughout North America. **Oak webworm** (*A. fervidanus*) also feeds on oak, typically in small groups that produce small nests of webbing. **European leafroller** (*A. rosanus*), sometimes known as filbert leafroller, develops on filbert, apple, pear, hawthorn, cherry, currant, and privet in the northwestern U.S. and western Canada. The life histories of these other *Archips* species are similar to that of fruittree leafroller.

Eyespotted bud moth (*Spilonota ocellana*)[1] is a pest of tree fruits and caneberries in the Pacific states and British Columbia. Winter is spent as a young larva on bark in a cocoon (hibernaculum). Larvae emerge and begin to feed around bud break in spring, damaging newly opening buds and leaves. They may also tunnel in shoots of apple or cherry, causing twig dieback. By late spring they complete development, usually pupating on the plant. Eggs are laid during midsummer, and larvae active at this time feed on leaves, typically cutting them and rolling them together fastened with silken thread. Fruit damage occurs when leaves of feeding shelters include fruit, which then may be scarred by feeding larvae.

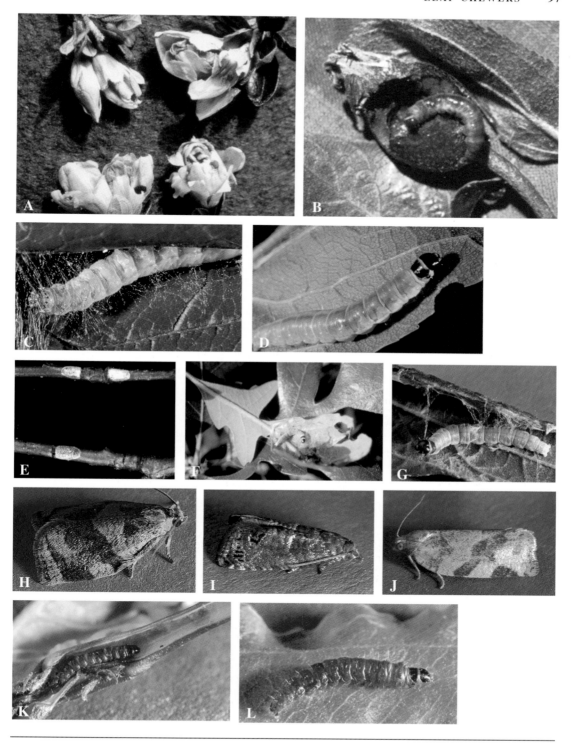

A. Blossom injury by leafroller. *A. Antonelli.* **B.** Fruittree leafroller larva and young apple fruit. *W. Hantsbarger.*
C. Fruittree leafroller larva. *J. Capinera.* **D.** Fruittree leafroller larva. *J. Capinera.* **E.** Fruittree leafroller egg masses. *W. Hantsbarger.* **F.** Oak leafroller larva. *W. Cranshaw.* **G.** European leafroller larva. *K. Gray.* **H.** European leafroller adult. *K. Gray.* **I.** Eyespotted bud moth adult. *K. Gray.* **J.** Fruittree leafroller adult. *K. Gray.* **K.** Eyespotted bud moth larva in shoot. *K. Gray.* **L.** Eyespotted bud moth larva. *K. Gray.*

Obliquebanded leafroller (*Choristoneura rosaceana*)[1] is one of the most common leafrollers, found throughout most of North America except arid areas of the southwestern U.S. It has an extremely wide host range but feeds primarily on azalea and various rosaceous plants, including fruit trees. Damage begins earlier than with some other leafrollers, as winter is spent as a partially grown larva in a protected cocoon (hibernaculum) on the bark, from which it emerges and tunnels buds during spring. Developing fruit may also be damaged at this time. First-generation adults are present in late spring, and eggs are laid as masses on leaves during June. The summer generation is completed by August. **Large aspen tortrix** (*C. conflictana*) is a forest species that feeds on aspen leaves, folding and tying them during the late stages of development.

Redbanded leafroller (*Argyotaenia velutinana*)[1] is an occasional pest of apple orchards in the northeastern and midwestern states. Both the body and head of larvae are uniformly colored green to pale yellow. The larvae live in a loose silken shelter they spin on leaves and among buds and emerging growth. Leaf-feeding injuries are insignificant, but serious fruit injury is caused when developing fruit is incorporated into the webbing and chewed. Young fruit fed on by the first-generation larvae often aborts or develops deep gouging wounds. Injuries by the summer generation produce more superficial fruit scarring.

Orange tortrix (*Argyrotaenia citrana*) is a western species that ties together and feeds on the leaves of tree fruits, citrus, willow, oak, goldenrod, geranium, begonia, black walnut, and many other plants. It usually does little damage, but may damage citrus when larvae incidentally chew into the peel of fruit tied among the leaves of the feeding shelter. A minor but commonly observed pest of eastern white pine is **pine tube moth** (*A. pinatubana*), which forms shelters of 5 to 20 needles. It chews the needles until they are about 1 inch long and then abandons the shelter to form a new one. Two generations occur per year in Pennsylvania, with adults emerging in early to mid-April and the second-generation adults present in July. A related forest species in western North America is **jack pine tube moth** (*A. tabulana*), which develops on jack, lodgepole, and whitebark pines.

Blackheaded fireworm (*Rhopobota naevana*),[1] sometimes known as **holly bud moth**, is a common insect in much of North America. Young larvae of the first generation feed on the opening buds of apple, cherry, blueberry, holly, and other woody ornamentals. Later stages act as leafrollers, tying together leaves in which they feed. Two generations occur, with moths from the second generation present in June in North Carolina. The wintering stage consists of eggs laid on the host plant.

Cherry bark tortrix (*Enarmonia formosana*)[1] may develop on most tree fruits and is presently found in parts of Washington and British Columbia. Larvae feed primarily on bark, causing some injuries to underlying cambium. Bark is loosened from these activities and may allow development of cankers. Older stone fruits (*Prunus* spp.) with preexisting wounds are most commonly attacked.

Several leafrollers in the genus *Platynota*[1] are minor pests of fruit crops in most areas of the U.S. In the eastern states, **variegated leafroller** (*P. flavedana*) is occasionally damaging to strawberry and apples when larvae chew fruit incorporated in the leaves they primarily consume. The host range is fairly wide and also includes rose, peach, azalea, begonia, and helianthus, although leaf-feeding injuries are minor. Variegated leafroller has two generations in the Midwest, with peak egg-laying in June and again in late August in Michigan. Winter is spent as a partially grown larva at the base of plants, and some spring feeding on low-growing plants occurs in spring before pupation. **Tufted apple bud moth** (*P. idaeusalis*) has become an increasingly important pest of apples in the upper Midwest and eastern states. It produces a unique leaf injury as larvae partially sever the petiole, causing the leaf to hang and wilt. The last-stage larva folds and ties the leaf and feeds in it. One generation is produced per year, with most eggs being laid in mid- to late June. Black haw, blackberry, osage orange, and goldenrod are other hosts.

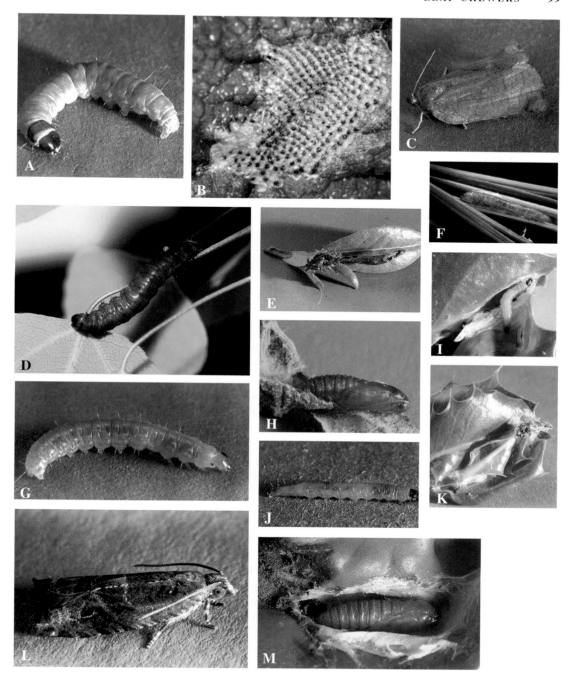

A. Obliquebanded leafroller larva. *K. Gray.* B. Egg mass of obliquebanded leafroller. *K. Gray.* C. Obliquebanded leaf-roller adult. *K. Gray.* D. Large aspen tortrix larva. *E. H. Holsten.* E. Orange tortrix damage to bud. *K. Gray.* F. Pine tube moth larva. *Courtesy Connecticut Agricultural Experiment Station Archives.* G. Orange tortrix larva. *K. Gray.* H. Orange tortrix pupa. *K. Gray.* I. Blackheaded fireworm (holly bud moth). *K. Gray.* J. Blackheaded fireworm larva. *K. Gray.* K. Blackheaded fireworm (holly bud moth) damage to holly. *K. Gray.* L. Blackheaded fireworm adult. *K. Gray.* M. Blackheaded fireworm pupa. *K. Gray.*

Omnivorous leafroller (*Platynota stultana*)[1] occurs throughout much of the southern half of the U.S. It has an extremely wide host range that includes most tree fruits, cotton, rose, chrysanthemum, and numerous weed hosts including lambsquarter, curly dock, little mallow, and many legumes. It typically ties together and feeds on new foliage. However, most damage occurs when these feeding shelters also include fruit that subsequently is scarred by shallow feeding grooves. Several generations may occur, with up to six per year reported from Arizona. A species of similar habits is *Sparganothis sulfureana*,[1] variously known as **sparganothis leafroller**, **blueberry leafroller**, or **cranberry leafroller**. It also has a wide range of hosts, as diverse as apple, clover, buttercup, strawberry, blueberry, cranberry, willow, and pine. Two generations are produced. Overwintering larvae mature during spring, and the adults appear in June. Eggs are laid in masses, and the larvae feed on foliage, flowers, and fruit. Fruits may be tunneled but also are chewed on the surface, a type of injury different from that produced by cranberry fruitworm. The second-generation adults are present in late August and September.

Apple pandemis (*Pandemis pyrusana*)[1] is a moderately important pest of apple, pear, cherry, and caneberries in the Pacific Coast states and British Columbia. Larvae are green with a straw- or gold-colored head and are very similar to obliquebanded leafroller and orange tortrix in the damage they produce. Although primarily a leaf feeder, apple pandemis may incidentally chew blossoms and the surface of young fruit during the spring generation. The summer generation limits feeding to leaves, producing windowpaning symptoms. A related species is **threelined leafroller** (*P. limitata*), which feeds on willow, aspen, ash, oak, apple, birch, and many hardwoods in much of the northern U.S. and Canada. *P. cerasana* is known to feed on oak and raspberry in British Columbia.

Several species of *Ancylis*[1] tie leaves and occasionally damage fruit of many species. **Sycamore leaffolder** (*A. platanana*) is a common species in the eastern states. It folds the leaves of sycamore and develops in a silken tube at the base of the fold. **Strawberry leafroller** (*A. comptana fragariae*) is widespread in the U.S. and occasionally damaging to strawberry, less commonly raspberry. Adults emerge in April and May and lay eggs singly on foliage. The larvae tie together the leaflets and skeletonize them from within. Two to three generations per year are reported to occur in Illinois. *A. discigerana* and *A. logiana* are two eastern species commonly associated with leaffolding of birch.

Omnivorous leaftier (*Cnephasia longana*)[1] is found throughout much of the U.S. It feeds on a wide range of plants including vetch, wild daisies, flax, strawberry, filbert, pear, hops, and many nursery crops. Winter is spent as a minute first-stage larva that becomes active during warm days in late winter and early spring. It then disperses, being wind-blown on silk threads, and crawls to suitable plants. The larvae first tunnel into the plant, creating small mines in leaves. Later stages feed on foliage, usually at the tips of plants which they tie loosely with silk. Fruit and flowers may also be incorporated in this loose shelter and be damaged. Feeding is usually completed by the end of May; adults are present in late May and early June in Oregon.

In the northeastern states, **sumac leafroller** (*Episimus argutanus*)[1] can be common on sumac, witch-hazel, and poison ivy. Two generations are produced annually.

Redbud leaves are folded and tied with silk by **redbud leaffolder** (*Fascista cercerisella*).[2] The larvae are highly active, similar to leafrollers, and marked with black and white bands. Two generations are produced annually.

Leaffolding of grape and some ornamentals can be produced by **grape leaffolder** (*Desmia funeralis*).[3] It is widespread but primarily a southern species, reportedly damaging in parts of Florida and California. Young larvae feed together as a group, between leaves tied together. Later they individually form shelters of folded or rolled leaves in which they feed. Three generations are produced annually. Later generations often produce leaf folds adjacent to previous areas of damage.

A. Tufted apple bud moth larvae. *J. R. Baker.* **B.** Threelined leafroller larva. *Courtesy Pacific Agri-Food Research Centre.* **C.** Omnivorous leafroller in cotton bud (square). *B. Freeman.* **D.** Omnivorous leafroller larva and damage to cotton bud. *R. Smith.* **E.** *Pandemis cerasana* larva. *Courtesy Pacific Agri-Food Research Centre.* **F.** Omnivorous leaftier in flower. *K. Gray.* **G.** Silken tube of sycamore leaffolder. *J. D. Solomon.* **H.** Sycamore leaffolder larva. *J. D. Solomon.* **I.** Omnivorous leaftier in strawberry. *K. Gray.* **J.** Strawberry leafroller larva. *K. Gray.* **K.** Strawberry leafroller adult. *K. Gray.*

New growth of canna may be fed on by **lesser canna leafroller** (*Geshna cannalis*).[4] Most feeding occurs on the surface of unfolded leaves, which may be loosely tied together. In Florida, adult moths may begin to lay eggs in late winter, and several generations can be completed at intervals of about 1½ months. Lesser canna leafroller is restricted to the southeastern U.S., where it commonly occurs in coinfestation with larger canna leafroller (p. 106).

Genista caterpillar (*Uresiphita reversalis*)[4] feeds on crape myrtle, Texas laurel, honeysuckle, goldenchain, and taxus in many areas in the southern half of the U.S. The caterpillars are about 1 inch when full grown, orange or green with small patches of white hairs emerging from dark spots. Eggs are laid as small masses, and early-stage larvae feed in groups, producing some associated webbing. Later stage larvae disperse throughout the plant, and after feeding is completed they frequently wander from the plant and may pupate on adjacent buildings. Two generations are produced annually.

China mark moth (*Nymphuiella daeckealis*)[4] is one of several pyralid moths that develop by feeding on aquatic plants. Larvae chew notches along the edges of water lilies, giving them a ragged appearance. The insect gets its name from the features of the adult moth, which has white forewings marked with dark gray. Eggs are laid on the leaf surface. The pale green larva then cuts two small leaf fragments, creating a tiny "boat" in which it remains protected, a habit leading to a common name "sandwich-man caterpillar." It then floats, settling along the edge of a leaf where it feeds. Older larvae leave the floating shelter to feed on the leaf surface or tunnel into leaf petioles. Pupation occurs in a cocoon on the leaf underside. **Waterlily leaf cutter** (*Synclita obliteralis*)[4] has somewhat similar habits and feeds on waterlily, pondweed, and duckweed.

American lotus borer (*Ostrinia penitalis*)[4] is a common insect associated with American lotus in eastern North America. Adults are first active in midspring, and eggs are laid as amber-colored masses on the leaf surface. The young caterpillars concentrate feeding at the edge of the leaf. Skeletonizing injuries are typical, and large amounts of webbing are produced to prevent larvae from being washed off plants and to afford protection. Late-stage caterpillars migrate to petioles where they excavate a tunnel. After feeding for a while in this protective retreat, they pupate. A midsummer generation is subsequently produced.

American lotus borer is capable of swimming, and there can be considerable movement among plants and migration to shoreline plants. Pupation is also reported to commonly occur in stems of various smartweeds and knotweeds and occasionally in other plants.

[1] Lepidoptera: Tortricidae; [2] Lepidoptera: Gelichiidae; [3] Lepidoptera: Pyraustidae; [4] Lepidoptera: Pyralidae

A. Genista caterpillar. *B. Drees.* **B.** Defoliation produced by larva of China mark moth. *S. Gill.* **C.** China mark moth. *S. Gill.* **D.** China mark moth larva on waterlily leaf. *S. Gill.*

SPRUCE BUDWORMS

Western Spruce Budworm (*Choristoneura occidentalis*)[1]

Hosts: Douglas-fir, spruce, and firs.

Damage: Larvae tunnel buds and chew needles, concentrating on the newly emerged current-season growth. During outbreaks, trees may be extensively defoliated. These injuries can cause serious stress that can directly kill the tree or make it susceptible to secondary pests such as Douglas-fir beetle. Western spruce budworm is the most serious defoliator of native forests in western North America.

Distribution: Coniferous forests from the Rocky Mountains and Black Hills through western North America.

Appearance: Larvae are olive brown or reddish brown caterpillars that can reach 1 to 1½ inches long at maturity. They have ivory-colored paired spots on each body segment and a chestnut brown head and collar. The adult moths have a wingspan of about 1 inch. They are highly variable in color and have mottled medium brown, dark brown, or orange brown forewings and tan hindwings.

Life History and Habits: Winter is spent as a minute caterpillar protected in a silken cocoon (hibernaculum) under bark flakes or among lichens. In late May or June, it begins to feed, mining old needles or tunneling into buds or developing cones. Following bud break, the larva moves to the new growth.

Larvae mature about 30 to 40 days after feeding begins in spring. Pupation occurs among foliage, and adults emerge in July and early August. Females are good fliers and may disperse considerable distances if favorable winds occur. Eggs are laid in shinglelike masses on the underside of needles. They hatch in about 10 days, and the resulting larvae immediately spin overwintering hibernaculae on the bark. There is one generation per year.

Related Species

Spruce budworm (*Choristoneura fumiferana*) is the most important pest of coniferous forests in eastern North America, particularly damaging to balsam fir and spruce. Its life cycle is very similar to that of the western spruce budworm.

Pine budworm (*C. lambertina*), also known as **sugar pine tortrix**, feeds on ponderosa pine and occasionally other pines in forests of the western U.S. **Jack pine budworm** (*C. pinus*) develops on Scotch and jack pine in the Great Lakes region. Life cycles parallel those of the spruce budworms.

[1] Lepidoptera: Tortricidae

A. Western spruce budworm adult. *W. Cranshaw.* **B.** Spruce budworm spinning down from tree. *J. E. Dewey.* **C.** Egg mass of western spruce budworm on needle. *D. Leatherman.* **D.** Defoliation pattern of western spruce budworm. *D. Leatherman.* **E.** Spruce budworm adult and pupa. *J. E. Dewey.* **F.** Needlemining by young western spruce budworm. *D. Leatherman.* **G.** Spruce budworm larva. *D. Leatherman.* **H.** Spruce budworm. *J. E. Dewey.* **I.** Pine budworm larva. *D. Leatherman.* **J.** Larval feeding damage to ponderosa pine by pine budworm. *D. Leatherman.* **K.** Pine budworm pupa in damaged terminal. *D. Leatherman.*

SKIPPERS

Skippers (Hesperiidae family)[1] share many features with the butterflies but are separately classified. Most are rather heavy bodied and possess antennae that are hooked at the tip. They fly during the day and are fast and often erratic fliers. Larvae are recognizable from other caterpillars by having a distinct constriction behind the head. Approximately 300 species occur in North America, most in the extreme south, but only a few cause significant plant injuries.

Larvae of **silverspotted skipper** (*Epargyreus clarus*) tie together several leaves and feed within these "nests." Wisteria and various leguminous plants such as black locust, honeylocust, and *Cassia* species are common hosts. Damage to alfalfa has been reported in the mid-Atlantic states. Silverspotted skipper is found throughout most of the U.S. and southern Canada. One generation occurs in northern areas, two in the south. Adults are light brown, heavy-bodied butterflies, known as skippers, with a distinct white spot on the underside of the hindwing.

Larger canna leafroller (*Calpodes ethlius*) chews the leaves of canna lily in the southern and parts of the eastern U.S. It also characteristically folds leaves, fastening them with silk. Several generations can be completed, with larval development taking about 2 weeks. Pupation occurs on a pad of silk in the folded leaf. Peak injury usually is observed in mid- to late summer.

Larvae of **fiery skipper** (*Hylephila phyleus*) chew blades of turfgrasses in much of the southern half of the U.S., being particularly common in the southeastern states. Bermudagrass seems to be preferred, but St. Augustinegrass, bentgrass, and some grassy weeds such as crabgrass are also eaten. Larvae have a black head with a distinct constriction just behind it. The body color is pale greenish yellow, but larvae darken with age. They construct a loosely webbed shelter among the base of grass plants from which they emerge to forage on nearby grass blades at night. Adults are orange, yellow, or brown heavy-bodied butterflies with a wingspan of about 1 inch. They are fast fliers but commonly visit low-growing flowers such as clover and alfalfa and flowering shrubs. Three to five generations may be produced in southern areas of the species' range.

Bean leafroller (*Urbanus proteus*) is a tropical species restricted to the extreme southeastern U.S. Adults are sometimes known as longtail skippers because they possess tail-like extensions of the wings. Females lay eggs singly or in small groups. The caterpillars cut a small patch at the leaf edge and fold and fashion it into a shelter. They emerge to feed at night on leaves and may cause extensive defoliation to beans late in the summer. As larvae get older, they construct a series of shelters, in the last stage webbing together two separate leaves. Pupation occurs in these folded leaves. A generation can be completed in about a month, and several generations are produced during the year. Bean leafroller is sensitive to cold temperatures and probably dies back in most years to southern Florida, dispersing northward the following year.

[1] Lepidoptera: Hesperiidae

A. Silverspotted skipper larva in curled leaf. *K. Gray.* B. Silverspotted skipper. *K. Gray.* C. Silverspotted skipper larva. *K. Gray.* D. Fiery skipper. *J. Fengler.* E. Fiery skipper larva. *J. Fengler.* F. Larger canna leafroller adult. *H. A. Pase III.* G. Larger canna leafroller larva. *H. A. Pase III.* H. Characteristic leaf folding produced by larger canna leafroller. *H. A. Pase III.* I. Bean leafroller larva. *A. Sparks.*

WEBSPINNING SAWFLIES

The webspinning sawflies (Pamphiliidae)[1] are sawflies of unusual habit and appearance. Larval stages of most have very reduced legs and prolegs, with restricted movement about the plant. Instead most construct shelters of webbing similar to those of leafroller moths or tent caterpillars and remain in these structures. Although some may attract attention and curiousity, none are considered serious pests, and most are rare.

Pine false webworm (*Acantholyda erythrocephala*) is found in much of the northern U.S. and southern Canada. Adults insert small groups of eggs into needles in spring, and the newly hatched larvae spin webs at the base of needles. They feed in this shelter, cutting adjacent needles which they draw and pull into the web. Often several feed in a loose group, creating a messy "nest" of silk incorporated with needle fragments and frass. When full grown they drop to the ground and spend winter as full-grown larvae in cocoons in the soil at the base of previously infested plants. Eastern white pine and red pine are favored hosts. Other species of *Acantholyda* also feed on pine.

Cephalcia species also feed on pines as well as spruce. Some feed gregariously, producing messy nests. Most have solitary habits and live inconspicuously in a silken tube at the base of needles.

Some sixteen species of webspinning sawflies in the genus *Pamphilius* occur in North America. Most are solitary leafrollers of various deciduous trees and shrubs, curling leaves and fastening them with silk. *P. phyllisae* feeds on northern red oak and curls a new leaf after each molt. Its life cycle my take over a year to complete under certain conditions. Larvae normally are present on plants for about 3 weeks, after which they move to the soil and produce overwintering cocoons. Other species include **peach sawfly** (*P. persicus*) and **blackberry sawfly** (*P. dentatus*).

Plum webspinning sawfly (*Neurotoma inconspicua*) is found in plum and sand cherry throughout much of the midwestern and northeastern U.S. and southern Canada. It feeds in groups, creating nests of large, loose webbing that enclose the tips of branches in a manner similar to that of uglynest caterpillar. Larvae are grayish yellow. One generation is produced annually. In the southern U.S. **cherry webspinning sawfly** (*N. fasciata*) has similar habits and is associated with black cherry.

[1] Hymenoptera: Pamphiliidae

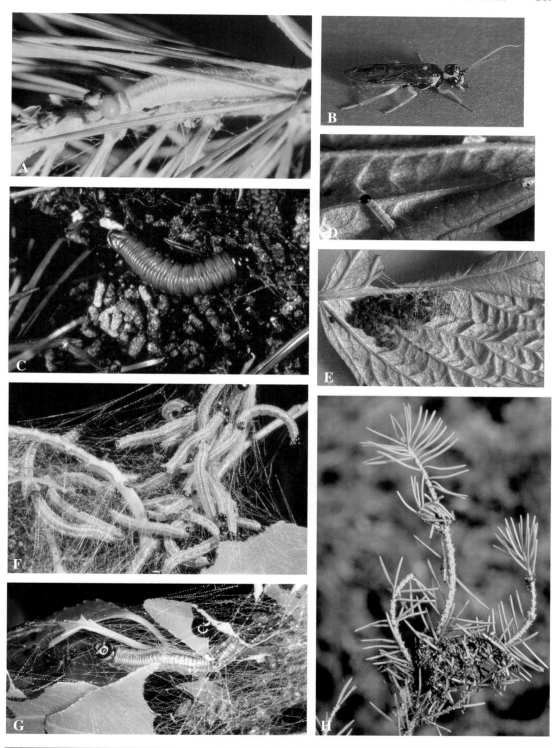

A. Pine false webworm. *D. Shetlar.* **B.** Adult of webspinning sawfly, *Pamphilius* sp. *K. Gray.* **C.** Webspinning sawfly larva. *A. Antonelli.* **D.** Webspinning sawfly larva in leaf curl. *K. Gray.* **E.** Webbing associated with sawfly *Pamphilius sitkensis. K. Gray.* **F.** Cherry webspinning sawfly larvae. *D. Shetlar.* **G.** Cherry webspinning sawfly larvae. *L. L. Hyche.* **H.** Web-spinning sawfly "nest" in spruce. *D. Leatherman.*

SKELETONIZERS

The term "skeletonizer" is broadly applied to caterpillars of several moth families that feed between veins of leaves, producing skeletonized appearance. Such a pattern of feeding may also be produced by some other insects (see p. 20).

Apple and thorn skeletonizer (*Choreutis pariana*)[1] is common in much of the northern U.S. and southern Canada, sometimes occuring in populations that flucuate greatly in abundance between seasons. It is primarily associated with fruit trees but has a wide host range that includes crabapple, apple, birch, cherry, hawthorn, willow, and mountain-ash. The overwintering moths lay eggs shortly after bud break. Larvae first feed on the underside of leaves under a covering of silk. They later migrate to the upper leaf surface and construct a new shelter tying together adjacent leaves. During the warm season, the life cycle can be completed in a month and up to four generations per year can be produced.

Oak ribbed skeletonizer (*Bucculatrix albertiella*)[2] occurs in the Pacific states. Young larvae feed as leafminers of oak leaves. As they get older, they skeletonize the surface. They produce characteristic cocoons that are strongly ribbed. Two generations are produced in Washington. **Oak skeletonizer** (*B. ainsliella*) is particularly common around the Great Lakes but ranges from New England to Mississippi. It feeds on oak and chestnut. Adults appear in late May and lay eggs on leaves. Initial feeding occurs as small mines, and later feeding skeletonizes the underside of leaves. Small patches of webbing are produced whenever oak skeletonizers molt, and they also pupate in white, ribbed cocoons.

Birch skeletonizer (*Bucculatrix canadensisella*) feeds on birch, particularly paper birch. It pupates off the tree, spinning down when full grown and producing a dark cocoon in leaf litter and other debris. **Apple bucculatrix** (*B. pomifoliella*) occurs in the northeastern U.S. and southeastern Canada where it feeds on hawthorn, apple, black cherry, and serviceberry. **Hollyhock leaf skeletonizer** (*B. thurnberiella*) skeletonizes hollyhock and malva in California.

Western grapeleaf skeletonizer (*Harrisina brillans*)[3] is found west of the Rockies where it develops on wild and cultivated grapes, Virginia creeper, and Boston ivy. Some fruit trees are occasionally infested. Adults are unusual bluish black or greenish black moths with a wingspan over 1 inch and first emerge from late April through mid-May. Females lay eggs in clustered groups on the underside of leaves, usually in shaded areas of the vines. The larvae feed together, often side by side, during most of their development, skeletonizing leaves from the underside. As the larvae get older, extensive defoliation can rapidly occur. The larvae are strikingly colored insects with brightly colored bands of yellow, white, blue, and black across the body. They also are covered with moderate-sized hairs that can be very irritating to people who are sensitive to them. In central California three generations are produced annually. Winter is spent as a pupa in a cocoon, often attached to loose bark of the vines.

In the eastern states, **grapeleaf skeletonizer** (*H. americana*) is present and similarly feeds on grape and Virginia creeper. Most of its habits parallel those of western grapeleaf skeletonizer. Larvae are yellowish with black banding and usually feed gregariously, although late-stage larvae chew holes in leaves. One generation is typically completed, sometimes a second.

Pryeria sinica is a newly established species in Virginia that develops on euonymus. Young larvae feed as a group and skeletonize but later disperse throughout the plant and cause more general defoliation, particularly around leaf edges. Injury occurs in April and May.

[1] Lepidoptera: Choreutidae; [2] Lepidoptera: Bucculatricidae; [3] Lepidoptera: Zygaenidae

A. Apple and thorn skeletonizer larvae. *A. Antonelli.* **B.** Apple and thorn skeletonizer adult. *K. Gray.* **C.** Apple and thorn skeletonizer larva. *K. Gray.* **D.** Birch skeletonizer larva. *E. B. Walker.* **E.** Cocoons and feeding of oak-ribbed skeletonizer. *A. Antonelli.* **F.** Feeding group of grapeleaf skeletonizers. *R. Bessin.* **G.** Oak skeletonizer larva. *G. K. Douce.* **H.** Mating pair of the western grapeleaf skeletonizer. *J. K. Clark/UC Statewide IPM Program.* **I.** *Pryeria sinica* feeding injury to euonymus. *E. Day.* **J.** *Pryeria sinica* larvae. *E. Day.* **K.** Oak skeletonizer larvae. *J. D. Solomon.*

TENT CATERPILLARS

Tent caterpillars[1] are a group of moderately large (ca. 2 inch) caterpillars in the genus *Malacosoma*. They usually "nest" in groups, at least during early stages, and most species construct conspicuous, tightly woven tents of silk where they rest during the day and molt. Tent caterpillars are among the earliest defoliators of shade trees and shrubs, often active by midspring. Outbreaks of cyclical occurrence are common with some species. All have a single generation per year.

Eastern Tent Caterpillar (*Malacosoma americanum*)

Hosts: Rosaceous plants including most fruit trees (apple, crabapple, plum, cherry, hawthorn); sometimes found on poplar, willow, ash, and birch.

Damage: Caterpillars chew leaves early in the season and can cause significant defoliation. Developing fruit may be chewed incidentally. Conspicuous tents of tightly woven silk in branch crotches attract attention and may be considered unsightly.

Distribution: Throughout the eastern U.S. and southern Canada, to the Rocky Mountains.

Appearance: Larvae are overall dark, primarily black, with a distinct light stripe on the back and a series of blue markings on the sides. Adults are rather stout moths with reddish brown wings marked with a pair of wavy light bands.

Life History and Habits: Eggs are laid on twigs as distinct masses, shiny black and covered with varnishlike material (spumaline). They hatch shortly after bud break, and the young larvae immediately begin to spin a silken mat in a branch crotch near the egg mass. The tent is gradually expanded as the caterpillars get older. Most often the caterpillars feed at night on nearby foliage, returning to rest together on or in the tent during the day. Late-stage caterpillars tend to disperse through the plant and feed in a more solitary manner. When full grown they migrate from plants and produce white or creamy white cocoons on nearby trunks or rocks, under eaves, or in other sheltered locations. Adults emerge in early summer, and after mating females lay the overwintering egg masses. One generation is produced per year.

Other Tent Caterpillars

Western tent caterpillar (*Malacosoma californicum*) is found in much of the U.S. from the Great Plains westward. It is rarely a pest of ornamental plantings but is common on wild hosts such as mountain-mahogany, wax currant, and aspen. Plum, other fruit trees, willow, and several other deciduous woody plants are less common hosts. The caterpillars can be distinguished from other species by being slightly hairy and having a typically light brown general coloration with powdery blue markings along the sides and a blue head. However, several races are recognized with slightly different appearances.

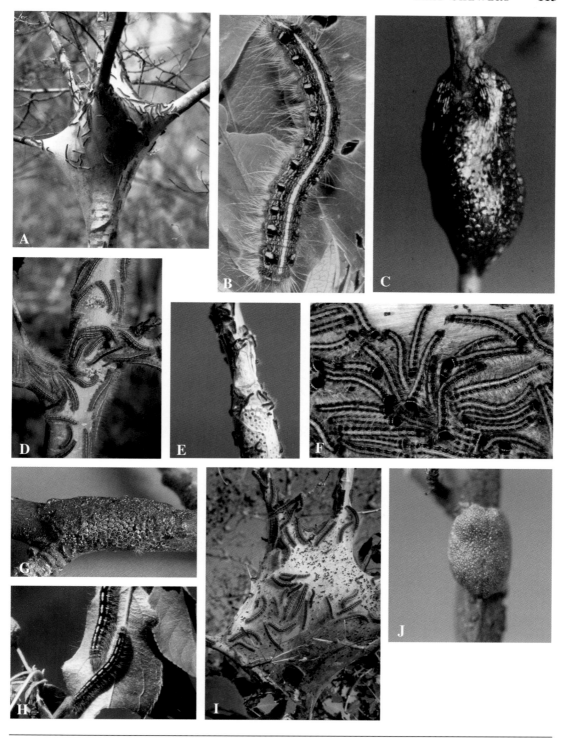

A. Eastern tent caterpillar colony. *R. L. Anderson.* B. Eastern tent caterpillar. *J. Capinera.* C. Egg mass of eastern tent caterpillar. *W. Cranshaw.* D. Western tent caterpillars. *D. Leatherman.* E. Egg mass of western tent caterpillar at egg hatch. *W. Cranshaw.* F. Young eastern tent caterpillars. *L. L. Hyche.* G. Egg mass of western tent caterpillar. *K. Gray.* H. Western tent caterpillars. *W. Cranshaw.* I. Western tent caterpillar in Aspen. *D. Leatherman.* J. Egg mass of western tent caterpillar. *W. Cranshaw.*

Southwestern tent caterpillar (*M. incurvum*) can be an important pest west of the Rockies, most commonly feeding on poplar and cottonwood along riverways. Eggs hatch very early, in late March or early April, and feeding is completed by mid-May. In the southwestern U.S., **Sonoran tent caterpillar** (*M. tigris*) feeds on native stands of oak, especially Gambel oak. In the Pacific states oak is the host for **Pacific tent caterpillar** (*M. constrictum*).

Forest tent caterpillar (*M. disstria*) is the most widespread and perhaps most frequently damaging tent caterpillar in North America. Ash, aspen, various fruit trees, poplar, and willow are among the many deciduous trees this insect may feed on. In many areas it has short-lived outbreaks during which there is extensive defoliation, particularly to aspen. At these times large numbers of wandering caterpillars may be present, leading to them locally (and erroneously) being called "armyworms."

Although this is the most common of the tent caterpillars (*Malacosoma* spp.), it does not make a permanent silken tent in branch crotches. Instead, colonies make several resting mats of lightly spun silk during a season on trunks and larger branches. The forest tent caterpillar is also distinctive in having an electric blue color and a series of yellow "keyhole" patterns along its back.

[1] Lepidoptera: Lasiocampidae

A. Eastern tent caterpillar tent in trunk crotch. *D. Shetlar.* **B.** Defoliation by southwestern tent caterpillar. *W. Cranshaw.*
C. Southwestern tent caterpillar. *W. Cranshaw.* **D.** Adult forest tent caterpillar. *W. Cranshaw.* **E.** Sonoran tent caterpillar.
W. Cranshaw. **F.** Forest tent caterpillar. *K. Gray.* **G.** Mass of forest tent caterpillars resting on tree trunk. *W. Cranshaw.*
H. Forest tent caterpillars. *G. J. Lenhard.* **I.** Forest tent caterpillars at egg hatch. *W. Cranshaw.* **J.** Forest tent caterpillar
egg mass. *W. Cranshaw.* **K.** Forest tent caterpillar pupa. *W. Cranshaw.*

GYPSY MOTH

Gypsy Moth (*Lymantria dispar*)[1]

Hosts: An extremely wide range, potentially including more than 200 species. Oak and aspen are often particularly favored, but plants as diverse as hemlock, white pine, and poison ivy also support development.

Damage: Larvae chew leaves of plants during late spring. Gypsy moth is a notorious outbreak species of forests and frequently causes extensive defoliation. Droppings (frass) and leaf fragments produced during outbreaks further contribute to nuisance problems.

Distribution: Since its original, accidental introduction outside Boston in 1868, gypsy moth has steadily extended its range. It is currently found in a broad swath over much of the northern U.S. as far west as parts of eastern Minnesota and southward into the Carolinas. Isolated infestations have been found in almost every state because of the movement of egg masses on plant materials and other infested items moved in commerce.

A strain of the gypsy moth native to parts of Russia, known as **Asian gypsy moth**, produces females that are capable of flight. This insect has on occasion been introduced into the Pacific Northwest. Strong efforts to limit its introduction and to eradicate known infestations are ongoing by government agencies in both the U.S. and Canada.

Appearance: Larvae are generally dark gray or blue but have many colored spots and tubercules that may be yellow or orange. They have numerous hairs on the body. Male moths are generally dark brown with wavy darker markings across the wings. Females have wings that are generally white with dark wavy stripes; however, they are incapable of flight.

Life History and Habits: Winter is spent as eggs laid in a mass covered with hairs from the body of the female. Eggs usually hatch in April, and the young larvae often move to the tips of branches where many may be dispersed by wind. Larval development typically involves six or seven caterpillar stages (instars) which are completed over the course of about 6 weeks. Most feeding occurs at night, with the larvae moving to trunks and branches during the day to rest and molt. Later stages often feed during the day, however, particularly during outbreaks.

The larvae may settle on plants for pupation or wander and pupate on rocks, adjacent vegetation, sides of buildings, and other upright surfaces in the vicinity. The pupa is naked and only loosely covered with and attached by silk. Adults emerge about 2 weeks later. The male adult is a strong flier, but females are flightless and lay eggs near where they pupate. After mating, females lay a single egg mass, typically containing more than 250 eggs and covered with pale yellow hairs from the female's abdomen. The eggs require an extended cold period for hatching and remain dormant until the following spring.

[1] Lepidoptera: Lymantriidae

A. Leaf fragments and frass from gypsy defoliation activities. *J. H. Ghent.* **B.** Gypsy moth defoliation. *W. Ciesla.* **C.** Gypsy moth egg masses at hatch. *W. Ciesla.* **D.** Gypsy moth female laying mass of eggs. *D. Herms.* **E.** Late stage gypsy moth larva. *E. B. Walker.* **F.** Gypsy moth, male. *J. Fengler.* **G.** Gypsy moth egg masses and pupae. *D. Herms.* **H.** Gypsy moth larvae, including some with signs of virus infection. *W. Cranshaw.* **I.** Gypsy moth larvae and pupae. *W. Cranshaw.*

FALL WEBWORM

Fall Webworm (*Hyphantria cunea*)[1]

Hosts: Fall webworm has one of the widest host ranges of any caterpillar and may feed on more than 100 species of deciduous trees and shrubs. Some plants tend to be preferred, e.g., cottonwood, chokecherry, mountain-ash, pecan, elm, willow, and various fruit and nut trees.

Damage: The larvae feed on leaves and build unsightly silken tents. Heavy infestations can defoliate trees. Wandering larvae are sometimes a serious nuisance. Fall webworm is the most common tent-making caterpillar in much of North America.

Distribution: Widely distributed through most of North America, extending from southern Canada to northern Mexico.

Appearance: Larvae of fall webworm are hairy caterpillars with distinct paired dark spots on each segment of the back. They can be variable in color, however, with both black- and red-headed races present, sometimes together. The general color of the caterpillars also is variable, with the black-headed form tending to be yellow or pale green with light-colored hairs. The red-headed form is usually darker with reddish brown hairs. Caterpillars are about 1 inch long when mature. The adults are attractive satiny white moths, sometimes with brown or black spots. The wingspan is about 1½ inches.

Life History and Habits: Fall webworm spends the winter as a pupa in a flimsy light-colored cocoon found in protected areas such as bark furrows, crevices along the sides of buildings, or mixed among debris around the soil surface. In southern areas of its distribution, adults begin to emerge in early spring, whereas emergence usually occurs in late June or July in northern areas. Eggs are laid in masses on the underside of leaves, and the young larvae feed together, first skeletonizing the leaf and then incorporating leaves and ultimately entire branches in their loosely spun tent of silk. Unlike in tent caterpillars (p. 112), all larval development and feeding occur in the tents, into which leaf fragments, droppings, and cast skins become incorporated. The caterpillars, when disturbed, often twitch in an effort to deter potential predators.

When full grown the larvae usually wander from the plant and search for a protected location to pupate. A single generation occurs in northern areas of the range; in southern states, there may be up to four generations per year.

[1] Lepidoptera: Arctiidae

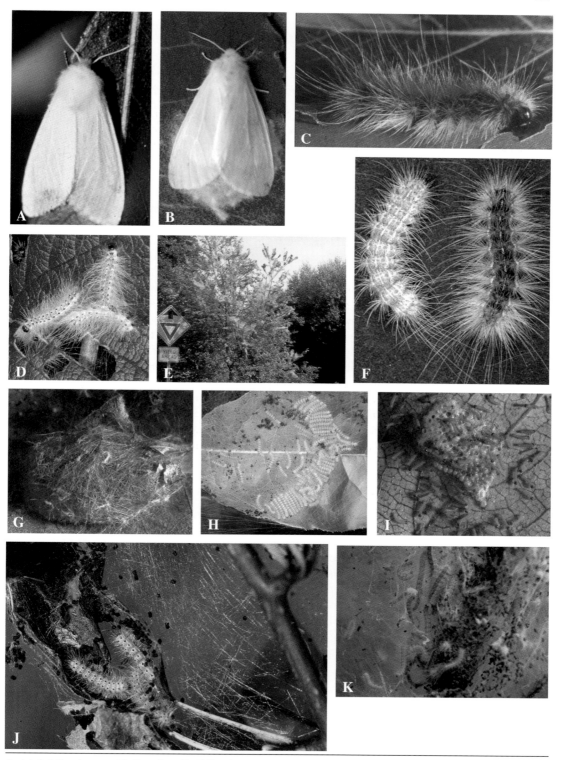

A. Adult fall webworm. *W. Cranshaw.* **B.** Fall webworm laying mass of eggs. *H. C. Ellis.* **C.** Fall webworm, black-headed form. *K. Gray.* **D.** Fall webworm, blackheaded form. *L. L. Hyche.* **E.** Fall webworm tents in chokecherry. *W. Cranshaw.* **F.** Fall webworms, orange head race. *L. L. Hyche.* **G.** Fall webworm pupa. *K. Gray.* **H.** Newly hatched egg mass of fall webworm. *L. L. Hyche.* **I.** Fall webworm egg mass hatching. *K. Gray.* **J.** Fall webworms. *W. Cranshaw.* **K.** Fall webworms. *K. Gray.*

TUSSOCK MOTHS AND TIGER MOTHS

The term "tussock moth" is loosely applied to certain caterpillars that are thickly covered with hairs, sometimes clumped together in dense tufts. "True" tussock moths are in the family Lymantriidae.[1] However, many hairy caterpillars in two other families (Arctiidae, Noctuidae) are similarly named. Certain hairy caterpillars that produce strikingly patterned adult moths are sometimes known as tiger moths. Those caterpillars that possess slender, dark tufts of hairs may be referred to as dagger moths.

Whitemarked Tussock Moth (*Orygia leucostigma*)

Hosts: A wide variety of trees and shrubs including apple, basswood, elm, sycamore, maple, birch, pyracantha, live oak, mimosa, and redbud. Some conifers are occasional hosts.

Damage: Larvae chew leaves, occasionally causing significant defoliation.

Distribution: Generally distributed east of the Great Plains. Also known from British Columbia.

Appearance: Larvae are cream colored overall with coral red heads. On four segments of the abdomen distinctive brushlike tufts of white or yellowish hairs are present, and there are pencil-like tufts of hairs at both the hind and front ends. Adult females are wingless, about ½ inch in length. Adult males are grayish brown with a wingspan of about 1⅓ inches and a distinctive white spot at the base of the forewing.

Life History and Habits: Winter is spent as eggs that were laid adjacent to wherever females previously pupated. Eggs hatch in mid- to late spring, and the early-stage larvae skeletonize leaves. Later-stage larvae feed more generally and become full grown 3 to 4 weeks after egg hatch. They often wander a considerable distance before pupating, and the pupal stage occurs in a cocoon mixed with hairs of the larvae. A second generation is common in much of the range, with peak feeding in midsummer.

Related Species

Douglas-fir tussock moth (*Orgyia pseudotsugata*) is a western species ranging from Colorado into the Pacific Northwest. It feeds on spruce, Douglas-fir, and white fir. Overwintered egg masses hatch shortly after bud break, and the young larvae first consume emergent new growth. Defoliation typically is concentrated on the upper areas of the plant, and serious defoliation can cause tree crowns to die and trees to become susceptible to bark beetles. Sensitization to the hairs of the caterpillars is reported in some people following outbreaks of this insect, particularly when the full-grown larvae wander off the tree in search of pupation sites. Males can fly but females are wingless, mating and laying eggs among the cocoon and pupal skin fragments in early summer. One generation is produced per year.

A. Whitemarked tussock moth caterpillar. *W. Cranshaw.* **B.** Whitemarked tussock moth pupae. *J. D. Solomon.* **C.** Cocoon containing pupa of Douglas-fir tussock moth. *D. Leatherman.* **D.** Rusty tussock moth larva. *Courtesy USDA-FS Missoula Archives.* **E.** Adult female whitemarked tussock moth laying mass of eggs. *D. Shetlar.* **F.** Douglas-fir tussock moth larvae feeding on new growth. *D. Leatherman.* **G.** Douglas-fir tussock moth egg masses on wall adjacent to infested tree. *D. Leatherman.* **H.** Douglas-fir tussock moth larva. *D. Leatherman.* **I.** Female Douglas-fir tussock moth laying egg mass. *K. Gray.*

Western tussock moth (*O. vetusta*) is found throughout the Pacific states. Larvae develop on various fruit and nut trees, hawthorn, manzanita, oak, pyracantha, toyon, walnut, and willow. Two cycles of feeding occur annually, in spring and in late summer/early fall. **Rusty tussock moth** (*O. antiqua*) is widely distributed and found throughout much of the northern U.S., southern Canada, and into northern California. It is rarely seriously damaging but has a wide host range including many hardwood trees and shrubs and conifers. The common name relates to the rusty color of the adult male moth.

Satin moth (*Leucoma salicis*) is a European species found in the northeastern and northwestern U.S. and adjacent areas of Canada. Several shade trees and shrubs are hosts including poplar, willow, aspen, and oak. The life history is unusual, with winter spent as a partially grown larva in a silken bag attached to a tree, a habit somewhat resembling that of bagworms (p. 160). Peak feeding occurs when the larvae emerge to feed on new growth in spring. The pupa is jet black and is produced in late spring, with adults active in early summer. Eggs are produced during this time. They later hatch and produce larvae that feed for a brief period as leaf skeletonizers, until they move to winter shelters.

The genus *Dasychira* contains several species that develop on trees, but none are considered seriously damaging. *D. grisefacta* is occasionally abundant in forests, where it feeds on a wide range of conifers including pinyon, ponderosa pine, Douglas-fir, and spruce. *D. vagans* feeds on birch, aspen, poplar, and willow, reportedly preferring the last.

A. Eggs laid by rusty tussock moth. *K. Gray.* **B.** Rusty tussock moth laying mass of eggs. *K. Gray.* **C.** Satin moth caterpillar. *K. Gray.* **D.** Rusty tussock moth larva. *K. Gray.* **E.** Satin moth larvae. *A. Antonelli.* **F.** Satin moth pupa. *K. Gray.* **G.** Satin moth adult male. *K. Gray.* **H.** Underside of satin moth egg mass. *K. Gray.* **I.** *Dasychira vagans* larva. *D. Leatherman.*

Silverspotted Tiger Moth (*Lophocampa argentata*)[2]

Hosts: Primarily Douglas-fir, but many conifers are occasional hosts.

Damage: Larvae feed on needles, sometimes causing serious defoliation. The hairs that cover the caterpillars and pupae are irritating to some people, and the conspicuous tents attract attention.

Distribution: Pacific states ranging into British Columbia. Two subspecies occur. *L. a. subalpina* feeds on pinyon and juniper in the Rocky Mountain region, and *L. a. sobrina* occurs on Monterey pine in California.

Appearance: Caterpillars are quite hairy, generally brown to reddish brown in color. Numerous tufts of yellow and black hairs are present along the back. Adults are brightly patterned moths with reddish brown wings marked by numerous silvery spots.

Life History and Habits: Eggs are laid in clusters on twigs and needles during midsummer. In about 3 weeks the larvae emerge and begin to produce loose webbing. They feed together and continue to expand the silken tent. They remain in the tent through the winter and resume feeding with the return of warm weather. Late-stage larvae then disperse and feed as individuals. Pupation occurs in late spring in a brown cocoon attached to plants or among debris on the ground. There is one generation per year.

Related and Similar Species

Hickory tussock moth (*Lophocampa caryae*)[2] feeds from July through September on a wide range of deciduous trees and shrubs, including nut trees, apple, basswood, and birch. Eggs are laid in masses, and subsequent early-stage caterpillars feed as a group, later dispersing. All stages of the caterpillars have a black head and are pale colored, often becoming whiter as they complete development. Pupation in a cocoon occurs around the base of plants and is the wintering stage. Hickory tussock moth occurs over the northeastern quarter of the U.S. and in southeastern Canada. **Sycamore tussock moth** (*L. harrisii*) develops on sycamore and plane tree in the eastern U.S. Eggs are laid in late spring with subsequent peak larval feeding in mid- to late summer.

Oleander caterpillar (*Syntomeida epilais*)[2] feeds on oleander in Florida and southern Georgia. Eggs are laid as masses, and the caterpillars feed in groups, moving up and down the plant as they get older. They are hairy caterpillars, bright orange with tufts of long black hairs. At pupation they continue to aggregate, pupating in a group. Adults are brightly colored, polka-dotted moths that fly during the day. A related species that feeds on oleander, **spotted oleander caterpillar** (*Empyreuma affinis*)[2] occurs in extreme southern Florida and the Florida Keys.

American dagger moth (*Acronicta americana*)[3] is a predominately yellow caterpillar with dark tufts of pencil-hairs. It feeds primarily on maple and boxelder, infrequently on apple, basswood, oak, and willow. The caterpillars feed at night and have the unusual habit of cutting the partially consumed leaf at the petiole before retreating to daytime shelter. This species is widely distributed east of the Rockies. Related species that feed on poplar, cottonwood, and willow are **cottonwood dagger moth** (*A. lepusculina*) and **poplar dagger moth** (*A. leporina*). Habits and general appearance of the caterpillars are similar to those of American dagger moth. Of similar appearance are caterpillars of **pale tussock moth** (*Halysidota tessellaris*)[2] which feed on various flowers as well as the foliage of sycamore, alder, and hickory.

[1] Lepidoptera: Lymantriidae; [2] Lepidoptera; Arctiidae; [3] Lepidoptera: Noctuidae

A. Silverspotted tiger moth larva. *K. Gray.* **B.** Silverspotted tiger moth pupa. *K. Gray.* **C.** Silverspotted tiger moth. *K. Gray.* **D.** Tent produced by silverspotted tiger moth caterpillars. *D. Leatherman.* **E.** Mass of silverspotted tiger moth caterpillars. *A. Antonelli.* **F.** Sycamore tussock moth. *J. Fengler.* **G.** Hickory tussock moth larva. *W. Cranshaw.* **H.** Oleander caterpillar. *J. Fengler.* **I.** Oleander caterpillar moth ovipositing. *D. Caldwell.* **J.** Characteristic petiole cutting of leaves damaged by American dagger moth. *D. Leatherman.* **K.** American dagger moth larva. *F. Peairs.* **L.** Oleander caterpillars. *D. Caldwell.*

WOOLLYBEARS

The term "woollybear" is loosely applied to some densely hairy caterpillars of the family Arctiidae.[1] Most are commonly observed wandering late in the season.

Yellow Woollybear (*Spilosoma virginica*)

Hosts: Yellow woollybear is a general feeder of almost all garden vegetables, small fruit, many flowers, and weeds.

Damage: Larvae chew foliage. Damage is rare and most commonly occurs late in the season when many hosts die, causing yellow woollybear to concentrate on remaining succulent crops.

Distribution: Throughout North America but most common in the western half of the continent.

Appearance: Caterpillars are covered with fine hairs of uniform color. Young stages are always quite pale, and yellowish coloration predominates throughout development. Brown forms sometimes occur. Adults have nearly pure white wings that span 1½ to 2 inches. One black spot occurs on the forewing, three spots on the hindwing.

Life History and Habits: Winter is spent as a pupa in a loose cocoon mixed with hairs from the larvae, under debris and other protected sites around the soil surface. First-generation adults emerge in midspring, and females lay eggs in masses on leaves. The newly hatched larvae originally feed as a group and skeletonize the undersurface of leaves. They disperse and feed more generally as they get older. They then pupate and produce a second generation. A third generation likely is also common, after which the overwintering pupae occur.

Other Woollybears

Saltmarsh caterpillar (*Estigmene acrea*) is the most common damaging species of woollybear, particularly in the southwestern U.S. Feeding habits are similar to those of yellow woollybear. Caterpillars are originally dark brown but later turn variable colors, including yellowish brown or black. Winter is spent as a mature larva in the cocoon, and pupation occurs in spring. The adult, known as the **acrea moth**, has white forewings marked with numerous dark spots. Hindwings of the male are yellow, of the female white. There may be three or four generations a year in southern areas, a single generation in the north.

Banded woollybear (*Pyrrharctia isabella*) rarely damages crops, limiting most feeding to a wide range of weeds. The caterpillar is well recognized, however, by its broad brown central band bordered by black. The central band does tend to widen as the caterpillars mature, but there is no basis for the folk legend that its widening predicts the severity of the upcoming winter. Winter is spent as a nearly full grown caterpillar that resumes feeding for a brief period the following spring before pupating. Adults are known as **Isabella moths**. One to two generations are produced annually.

[1] Lepidoptera: Arctiidae

A. Yellow woollybear caterpillar. *F. Peairs.* **B.** Yellow woollybear. *W. Cranshaw.* **C.** Yellow woollybear adult. *K. Gray.* **D.** Yellow woollybear egg mass. *J. Capinera.* **E.** Banded woollybear adult, known as Isabella moth. *K. Gray.* **F.** Banded woollybear. *D. Shetlar.* **G.** Saltmarsh caterpillar egg mass. *J. Capinera.* **H.** Adult saltmarsh caterpillar and egg masses. *L. Mannix.* **I.** Older-stage larva of saltmarsh caterpillar. *J. Capinera.* **J.** Young-stage larva of saltmarsh caterpillar. *J. Capinera.*

CANKERWORMS, SPANWORMS, AND INCHWORMS

Cankerworms, spanworms, and inchworms (Geometridae family)[1] develop as slender caterpillars marked by the absence of all but two (rarely three) pairs of prolegs. This causes them to walk in an unusual manner, in a series of loops and extensions of the body. "Inchworms," or "measuring worms," is a general term applied to the larvae, whereas adults are known as "geometers." Adults of most species are slender-bodied moths with a wingspan of about 1 inch. (Some species produce wingless females.) Both the hind- and forewing are broad and are usually patterned similarly. This is a large family of insects with more than 1,400 North American species, a handful of which may occur as pests of shade trees and shrubs in yards and gardens.

Fall Cankerworm (*Alsophila pometaria*)

Hosts: A wide range, including ash, basswood, beech, boxelder, black cherry, elm, red and sugar maples, and red and white oaks.

Damage: Larvae chew leaves, occasionally causing significant defoliation. During outbreaks there are minor nuisance issues involving the excreted droppings and numerous larvae that spin down from trees on silk threads.

Distribution: Widely distributed through southern Canada to Alberta and in the U.S. from North Carolina west to Colorado. Isolated populations are reported from Utah and California.

Appearance: Larvae vary from light green to dark brownish green and are about 1 inch when full grown. The light green form has white lines along the body; dark forms, which predominate during outbreaks, have a broad black stripe on the back. Unlike most inchworms, fall cankerworm has three pairs of prolegs because of the presence of a very small pair on the fifth segment. Male moths are brownish gray with a wingspan slightly greater than 1 inch. Females are wingless and brownish gray.

Life History and Habits: Most often fall cankerworm winters as eggs in a mass glued to small twigs. Eggs hatch in late April and early May. Young larvae feed on the lower leaf surface and produce skeletonizing wounds. As they get older, they feed in a more general manner and consume all of the leaf excepting the main veins. When full grown they spin down from the trees, enter the soil, and pupate in a cocoon.

Adults usually emerge after a hard freeze in fall. The flightless females climb the trees and, after mating, lay masses of about 100 eggs in a band around twigs. Occasionally emergence occurs in early spring, particularly in northern areas of the range.

Other Inchworms

Spring cankerworm (*Paleacrita vernata*) often occurs in coinfestations with fall cankerworm and shares much of its broad range of host plants. Caterpillars are green to reddish brown, have a single yellowish stripe on each side, and lack the third pair of prolegs of fall cankerworm. Spring cankerworm adults emerge in late winter, during warm spells in February and March. Females are flightless and climb trunks to lay eggs in masses under bark flakes and in trunk crevices. Peak feeding by larvae occurs in late spring, after which the larvae spin to the ground to pupate.

A. Winged male and female fall cankerworms. *D. Shetlar.* **B.** Fall cankerworm, dark form. *E. B. Walker.* **C.** Cankerworm spinning down from tree. *D. Shetlar.* **D.** Spring cankerworm moth laying egg mass. *D. Shetlar.* **E.** Fall cankerworm laying egg mass. *J. H. Ghent.* **F.** Spring cankerworm larva. *W. Cranshaw.* **G.** Spring cankerworm, dark form. *D. Shetlar.*

Elm spanworm (*Ennomos subsignaria*) feeds on elm, hickory, ash, oak, basswood, and birch and sometimes appears in large outbreak numbers similar to and coincident with cankerworms. Larvae may vary in color from slate black to light green, with darker forms predominating when populations are high. When full grown they usually pupate in a cocoon attached to the tree. Adults of both sexes are winged and nearly pure white. Females lay eggs in masses on twigs and small branches during midsummer.

Linden looper (*Erannis tiliaria*) is a common caterpillar of shade trees throughout much of the northern half of the U.S. and Canada, east of the Rockies. It has a broad host range, including basswood, apple, maple, and oak. Females are wingless and lay eggs in fall, in small clusters under loose bark. One generation is produced per year.

Barberry looper (*Coryphista meadii*) caterpillars feed on leaves of mahonia and barberry, sometimes seriously defoliating the plants. Winter is spent as a pupa in the ground, and the adults lay eggs in masses of about 100 on twigs in early spring. Larvae first skeletonize leaves and later consume the entire tough leaf except the larger veins. Three generations may be produced during a growing season.

Holly looper (*Thysanopyga intractata*) is found in the eastern U.S. wherever its primary host plant, American holly, is present. It is a highly migratory insect, and overwintering populations in the Gulf states may disperse long distances by midsummer. Caterpillars are light green. Typical injury to holly appears as deep notching cuts along the leaf margins.

Spear-marked black moth (*Rheumaptera hastata*) is found primarily in the northern U.S. and southern Canada, east of the Mississippi River. Birch and aspen are the most common hosts. Larvae fold leaves and then skeletonize the surface within the leaf fold. Adults are attractive, nearly black moths.

Currant spanworm (*Itame ribearia*) is generally distributed in the northern U.S. and southern Canada, east of the Rockies. Currants and gooseberry (*Ribes* spp.) are hosts. Larvae first feed on leaf tips and then become general defoliators. They are primarily white with yellow stripes that run along the back and sides. Numerous dark spots are also present, making larvae superficially resemble larvae of the more common currant sawfly. Dullish yellow-gray eggs that subsequently overwinter are laid in early summer on branches, usually in the lower canopy.

Bruce spanworm (*Operopthtera bruceata*) occurs throughout southern Canada and the upper midwestern and northeastern states. It develops on a wide variety of shade and forest trees including sugar maple, aspen, willow, and beech. It sometimes damages blueberry and raspberry as well. Overwintering eggs hatch in early spring, and most larval feeding occurs during May and June. Larvae vary from greenish to dark brown and have three light stripes. They may feed in small groups and sometimes loosely web together leaves as they feed. Pupation occurs in a cocoon around the base of plants. Adults emerge in fall and mate, and females lay numerous single eggs in various crevices on the plant. Females have rudimentary wings but are incapable of flight.

A. Elm spanworm. *D. Shetlar.* **B.** Elm spanworm, light form. *A. T. Drooz.* **C.** Currant spanworm. *W. Cranshaw.*
D. Linden looper. *W. Cranshaw.* **E.** Linden looper. *J. H. Ghent.* **F.** Bruce spanworm. *E. B. Walker.* **G.** Bruce spanworm
adult. *Courtesy Pacific Agri-Food Research Centre.* **H.** Bruce spanworm, mating pair. *A. T. Drooz.* **I.** Caterpillar of
spear-marked black moth. *E. H. Holsten.* **J.** Spear-marked black moth. *E. H. Holsten.*

Omnivorous loopers (*Sabulodes aegrotata, S. caberata*) are Pacific Coast species that feed on a wide range of trees and shrubs including acacia, boxelder, California buckeye, chestnut, citrus, elm, eucalyptus, fruit trees, ginkgo, magnolia, maple, pepper tree, and willow. Larvae feed in leaves that they tie together with silk. Early feeding primarily appears as skeletonizing but later becomes more generalized. Pupation also usually occurs in the rolled leaves. As many as five generations may be produced in a year.

Filament bearer (*Nematocampa limbata*) is an eastern species that has a rather bizarre appearance with long filaments on the second and third abdominal segments. It has a wide host range that includes hemlock and fir as well as various deciduous trees such as maple, oak, pin cherry, buckeye, and apple. **Horned spanworm** (*N. resistaria*), a minor pest of cranberry in the northeastern U.S., possesses similar fleshy filaments on the abdomen.

Several *Lambdina* species affect shade trees. **Hemlock looper** (*L. fiscellaria*) is an eastern species that has produced historical forest outbreaks, particularly involving Canada hemlock. Several other trees may also host this insect, however, including Douglas-fir, balsam fir, spruce, maple, basswood, birch, and cherry. **Eastern pine looper** (*L. pellucidaria*) also has occurred in outbreaks among native pines. In the western states, **oak looper** (*L. punctata*) can be common on oak, particularly scrub oak. All of the *Lambdina* species overwinter as eggs on trunks and among protective debris and have one generation with larval feeding in spring. When outbreaks occur, they are short-lived because of the effects of numerous natural enemies.

Striped grassworms (*Mocus* spp.), sometimes known as grass loopers, are occasionally observed feeding on warm-season turfgrasses in the southern U.S. Damaged turfgrass may appear ragged because of feeding on blades and growing tips, with peak injury often in late summer. Multiple generations occur, beginning in April. *M. latipes* is the most common species.

[1] Lepidoptera: Geometridae

A. Filament bearer. *J. Capinera.* **B.** Oak looper. *D. Leatherman.* **C.** Eastern pine looper, adults. *J. E. Dewey.* **D.** Eastern pine looper. *Courtesy Connecticut Agricultural Experiment Station.* **E.** Hemlock looper. *Courtesy Connecticut Agricultural Experiment Station.*

CUTWORMS AND ARMYWORMS

Many of the caterpillars in the family Noctuidae[1] that feed at or just below the soil and that cut plants are usually known as cutworms. In addition, there are many species of "climbing cutworms" that do not restrict feeding to the soil surface and that climb plants and chew leaves. Those that have the habit of feeding aboveground and that also become abundant at times and occur in large migrations may be known as "armyworms." Adult stages of cutworms are moderately large gray or brown moths, usually with indistinct markings.

Variegated Cutworm (*Peridroma saucia*)

Hosts: Arguably the widest range of any caterpillar that occurs in North America. Variegated cutworm has been reported damaging to vegetables, many fruit crops, and field crops and is also a turfgrass pest on occasion. Potato, pea, cabbage, lettuce, and tomato are among the garden crops most commonly damaged.

Damage: Larvae feed on foliage, buds, and shoots and may cut seedlings. Existing fruit may be tunneled. Potato tubers are gouged by feeding larvae.

Distribution: Throughout North America.

Appearance: Larvae are among the most recognizable of the cutworms, with a series of pale yellow spots on the back of most segments. A dark W mark is usually present on the eighth abdominal segment. Adult moths are ashy or light dirty brown with some dark brown mottling.

Life History and Habits: Variegated cutworm usually winters as a pupa in the soil, but it may be active year-round in extreme southern areas. Adults are strong fliers and may disperse over wide areas. Eggs are laid in batches of 60 or more on stems and leaves or on nearby inanimate objects such as fences and buildings. Larvae feed primarily at night but may be active during the day on occasion. The entire life cycle requires about 6 to 8 weeks to complete during the growing season, and two generations are usually completed in the northern U.S. In warmer areas of the south, as many as four generations are sometimes reported.

Fall Armyworm (*Spodoptera frugiperda*)

Hosts: Primarily grasses, including corn and bermudagrass. Legumes, some vegetables, fruit trees, and flowers are occasionally damaged.

Damage: In young corn, larvae tunnel into the whorl and shred the emerging leaves. As ears develop, they tunnel into ears, often entering from the sides as well as the tips. When turfgrass is chewed it has a ragged appearance.

Distribution: Fall armyworm is a tropical species that irregularly survives winter in the U.S., even in the Gulf states. It is highly dispersive, and migrations from Mexico and Central America annually occur, frequently reaching as far north as New England by early summer.

Appearance: Adults are similar to other cutworms, with a wingspan of about 1½ inches and dark gray forewings mottled with lighter and darker patches. There is a noticeable whitish spot near the wing tip. Larvae range from light tan to green or nearly black. A prominent inverted white Y on the head distinguishes this species from armyworm and some other cutworms.

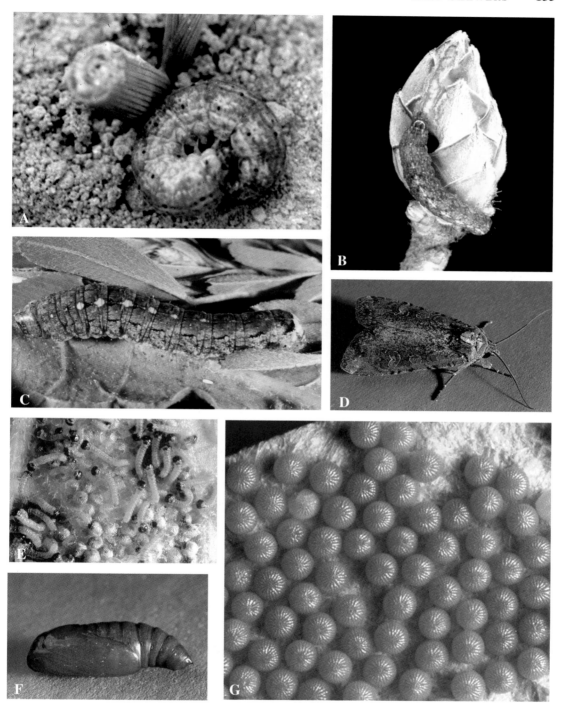

A. Surface cutting of corn by cutworm. *Courtesy Clemson University.* **B.** Variegated cutworm feeding on bud. *L. L. Hyche.* **C.** Variegated cutworm. *J. Capinera.* **D.** Variegated cutworm adult. *K. Gray.* **E.** Variegated cutworm egg mass hatching. *K. Gray.* **F.** Variegated cutworm pupa. *K. Gray.* **G.** Variegated cutworm egg mass. *K. Gray.*

Life History and Habits: Annual activity begins in spring when migrations reach the U.S. or when overwintering pupae emerge as adults. Migration can occur in huge swarms at times and cover long distances. Eggs are laid at night in masses of about 400 eggs, covered with hairs of the moth. Egg masses are laid directly on corn and other plants, but infestations of turfgrass often result from larvae dispersing from eggs laid on inanimate objects such as goal posts, flagging, and the underside of tree leaves. Younger stages often feed on only a single side of the leaf blade, leaving a transparent outer surface. Older larvae are more general feeders and consume entire areas of the leaf. When populations are abundant and food becomes limiting, fall armyworm larvae may move in masses in an armyworm-like manner. Larval development takes about 2 to 3 weeks to complete, and pupation occurs in the soil in a loose cocoon. Three or four generations per year are typical for the southern U.S. and one or two in the north.

Beet Armyworm (*Spodoptera exigua*)

Hosts: A wide range, including vegetables as diverse as lettuce, most crucifer crops, beet, tomato, bean, onion, and asparagus. Many herbaceous ornamentals and weeds are also hosts.

Damage: Caterpillars primarily chew foliage but may chew into stems and sometimes upper roots. Beet armyworm may bore into the head of leafy vegetables, characteristically from the base.

Distribution: Primarily found in the southern U.S. but occasionally disperses to northern states.

Appearance: Caterpillars are smooth and light olive green. Dark lateral stripes and fine wavy light stripes along the back are the primary markings. Adults have slightly mottled grayish brown forewings with a pale spot in the middle of the front margin.

Life History and Habits: Winter is usually spent as a pupa in a shallow earthen cell. Adults emerge in spring, and females lay eggs in masses. Approximately 80 eggs are laid in a mass, which is then covered with hairs, giving it a cottony appearance. Early-stage larvae feed as a group and skeletonize the leaves. Older larvae disperse and feed singly, often tunneling into plant parts. Beet armyworm larvae can be quite mobile and frequently move between plants. The life cycle can be completed in about a month under normal summer conditions, and four generations are commonly produced annually over much of the range.

Related Species

Yellowstriped armyworm (*Spodoptera ornithogalli*) and **western yellowstriped armyworm** (*S. praefica*) have a wide host range potentially including most vegetables and some flowers. They are sometimes important defoliators of commercial vegetable crops but rarely are serious pests in gardens, with caterpillars often preferring various weeds, including grasses such as foxtails. Yellowstriped armyworm is found over a broad area of the eastern U.S. east of the Rockies but also extends southwest into southern California. Western yellowstriped cutworm predominates in northern California and the Pacific Northwest. Life cycles of both species are similar to that of the beet armyworm.

Southern armyworm (*S. eridania*) is a common pest of vegetables in the southeastern states. The larvae are generally dark with prominent yellow stripes running the length of the body. Young larvae feed as a group, skeletonizing leaves. As they get older, they become solitary and may enter fruit, exposed tubers, and stems as well as feed on leaves. Four generations are thought to occur in Florida, with activity from March through October.

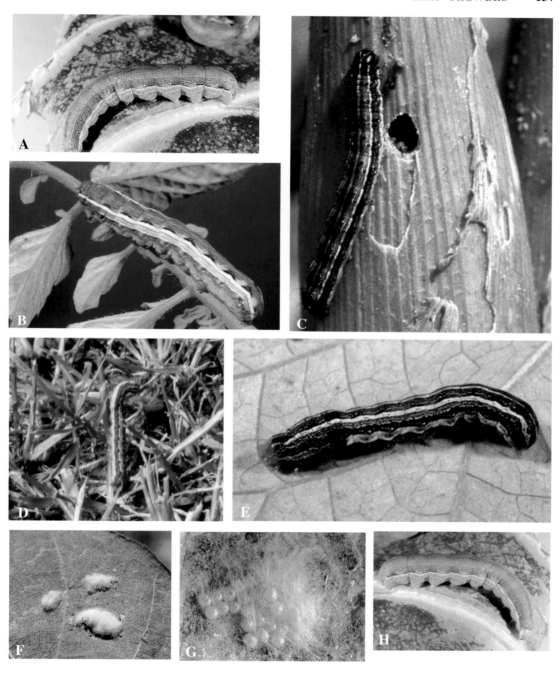

A. Beet armyworm larva. *J. Capinera.* **B.** Yellowstriped armyworm. *D. Shetlar.* **C.** Fall armyworm and ear damage. *Courtesy University of Georgia.* **D.** Fall armyworm in lawn. *D. Shetlar.* **E.** Yellowstriped armyworm. *D. Shetlar.* **F.** Egg masses of beet armyworm. *R. Smith.* **G.** Egg mass of beet armyworm. *K. Gray.* **H.** Beet armyworm larva. *J. Capinera.*

Other Cutworms and Armyworms

Armyworm (*Pseudaletia unipuncta*), sometimes known as the "true armyworm," is primarily a grass feeder. The adult moths are uniformly brown, distinguished by a small white dot in the center of the forewing. They are strong fliers and may migrate long distances. Eggs are laid in masses of more than 100 eggs, usually among dense grasses or other moist vegetation. Grasses are highly preferred, and armyworm is primarily a pest of small grains and, less commonly, turfgrasses. However, it feeds on a wide variety of plants and can damage most vegetable crops. When populations are abundant and available food has been consumed, armyworm caterpillars will migrate in large masses to seek new food sources.

Armyworm occurs throughout much of North America but is most common east of the Rocky Mountains. The overwintering stage can be variable—both pupae and larvae are reported. Four or five generations are produced annually. Outbreaks can be explosive but rapidly decline because of natural controls.

Bronzed cutworm (*Nephelodes minians*) occurs in the northern U.S. and southern Canada east of the Rockies. It is common in bluegrass and ryegrass lawns and may cause considerable thinning during peak feeding in late spring. Larvae have five white or yellow stripes running the length of a generally bronzy colored body. They are similar to armyworm, but their distinct metallic sheen distinguishes them, as does their habit of early spring feeding. Pupation occurs in the soil and persists through summer, with adults emerging in late August and September and laying eggs that overwinter among the grass.

Army cutworm (*Euxoa auxiliaris*) is the most important cutworm in the High Plains and Rocky Mountain region. Overwintering larvae resume feeding in spring and feed on a wide range of plants, preferring broadleaved plants over grasses. Emerging garden plants may be cut at this time, and army cutworm can contribute to spring lawn thinning when it occurs together with sod webworms and bronzed cutworm. Pupation occurs in the soil following the spring feeding peak.

The life cycle of the army cutworm exhibits an unusual feature after the adults begin to appear in late April and May. These are grayish brown moths with wings marked with numerous light spots and kidney-shaped markings that have a highly variable pattern. The adults become migratory at this time, but reproduction remains suspended. The adults seek out nectar and pollen sources on which to build fat reserves and follow flowering plants to high elevations. These migrations often cause them to pass through population centers, particularly near foothills, and the migratory army cutworm is well known as the miller moth in eastern Colorado, Wyoming, and New Mexico and adjacent regions. In summer army cutworm moths occur in mountainous areas where they alternately feed and rest in crevices, under rocks, and in other sheltered locations. In fall a reverse migration occurs back to the lower elevations, and eggs are laid at this time. Larvae feed in fall as conditions allow.

Redbacked cutworm (*Euxoa ochrogster*) is often the most abundant cutworm in the far northern U.S. and southern Canada. Larvae can be distinguished by their brick red stripes on the back, separated by a light line. They feed at night, cutting small plants and sometimes climbing. Broadleaf plants are most commonly damaged, including a wide variety of vegetables and even buds of some fruits. Outbreaks are cyclical and usually follow periods of dry weather. **Darksided cutworm** (*E. messoria*) also occurs through southern Canada and the northern U.S. but is rarely damaging. Larvae feed on leaves and stems of young plants in late spring, sometimes producing stand losses. Adults of both species are active in late summer and lay eggs in loose soil. Egg hatch occurs in spring.

A. Armyworm. *F. Peairs.* **B.** Armyworm. *F. Peairs.* **C.** Bronzed cutworm. *F. Peairs.* **D.** Army cutworm larva. *F. Peairs.*
E. Army cutworm pupa. *W. Cranshaw.* **F.** Army cutworm adult. *W. Cranshaw.* **G.** Redbacked cutworm. *K. Gray.*
H. Darksided cutworm adult. *K. Gray.* **I.** Darksided cutworm. *K. Gray.* **J.** Army cutworm adults aggregated in daytime
shelter. *W. Cranshaw.*

Bertha armyworm (*Mamestra configurata*) is primarily a pest in the Prairie Provinces and British Columbia but is occasionally damaging in the Pacific Northwest and northern High Plains. It has a wide host range but primarily feeds on crucifers and beet family plants, with wild mustard and lambsquarter being important weed hosts. Other commonly damaged plants include potato, beans, and several garden flowers such as hollyhock, petunia, and zinnia. Moths emerge in June and July, and females lay eggs as masses on the underside of leaves. Young stages are greenish with narrow pale stripes on the back and sides. Later stages become darker, sometimes brownish. Feeding occurs at night, when the larvae work as "climbing cutworms," chewing leaves and flower buds. Pupation occurs in the soil, in a cell often dug to a depth of 1 foot or more.

Spotted cutworm appears to be a complex of two species of similar habit, *Xestia adela* and *X. dolosa*. They are grayish brown or green with a series of distinct paired black triangular wedges along the back. Spotted cutworms climb foliage and have been reported damaging fruit buds as well as vegetables.

The name **dingy cutworm** also appears to be applied to a species complex of grayish brown caterpillars including *Feltia jaculifera*, *F. subgothica,* and others. Winter is spent as partially grown larvae that resume feeding in spring and are most damaging as surface cutters of seedling plants. Pupation occurs in the soil, and adults are present in late summer and early fall. Eggs are usually laid in areas of dense vegetation. The larvae feed for a while before going dormant for the winter. Dingy cutworm occurs throughout North America.

Western bean cutworm (*Loxagrotis albicosta*) is primarily an insect of the western Great Plains. Although beans and tomato are occasionally damaged, it most commonly damages corn. Larvae chew leaves and tunnel ears during late summer. Eggs are laid as masses in late July and August, and larvae may occur in small groups, unlike more solitary cutworms such as corn earworm. After feeding is completed, larvae tunnel into the soil to pupate. One generation is produced annually.

Black cutworm (*Agrotis ipsilon*) is a common surface cutter of garden plants and is the most important early-season cutworm throughout the eastern U.S. It also is found in turfgrass and is particularly damaging to bentgrass golf greens where it produces irregular chewed spots.

Black cutworm is primarily a subtropical and tropical species that fails to survive winter except in the warmest areas of the U.S. The adult moths, however, are strongly migratory and may fly from Central America to cover broad areas of the U.S. and southern Canada by summer. Black cutworm moths have a wingspan of about 2 inches with wings that are uniformly dark brown with a black daggerlike marking on the forewing. The caterpillars are fairly uniformly colored, from gray brown to nearly black with a somewhat greasy sheen. Black spots surround the spiracles along the sides.

Black cutworm lays eggs at night in small clusters on foliage. Caterpillars feed at night, with early stages feeding on foliage. They begin to cut plants after the second molt (3d instar), pulling the cut plant pieces into shelters of soil cracks or surface debris. The entire life cycle is completed in about 2 months. One or two generations commonly are completed in northern areas, three or four in the south.

Granulate cutworm (*Agrotis subterranea*) is the most important cutworm pest of vegetables in the Gulf states and ranges northward to Ohio. Adult females lay eggs directly on foliage, and the young larvae skeletonize leaves as they feed. Older larvae move to the soil during day and feed at night, becoming general feeders. Granulate cutworm may cut seedlings, consume leaves, and incidentally damage fruit of a wide range of vegetable crops. It may reproduce continually in southern areas, with all stages present year-round. In Tennessee there are three generations, with winter spent as a pupa.

A. Bertha armyworm adult. *K. Gray.* **B.** Bertha armyworm. *K. Gray.* **C.** Spotted cutworm adult. *K. Gray.* **D.** Spotted cutworm. *W. Cranshaw.* **E.** Spotted cutworm. *K. Gray.* **F.** Western bean cutworm. *K. Gray.* **G.** Dingy cutworm larva. *J. Capinera.* **H.** Dingy cutworm adult. *K. Gray.* **I.** Western bean cutworm egg mass at egg hatch. *K. Gray.* **J.** Surface cutting of seedling by black cutworm. *Courtesy Clemson University.* **K.** Western bean cutworm adult. *K. Gray.* **L.** Western bean cutworm pupa. *K. Gray.* **M.** Black cutworm larva. *J. Capinera.*

Zebra caterpillar (*Melanchra picta*) is one of the most distinctive garden caterpillars. Black, white, and yellow stripes run the length of the body and numerous small, alternating black and yellow bands run across the body. This species may feed on several vegetables as well as some flowers but is primarily damaging only to cabbage and related plants. Winter is spent as a pupa in the soil. The adults are chocolate brown moths that lay eggs as masses. The newly hatched larvae feed as a group, skeletonizing the leaf surface. Older larvae disperse and feed more generally on leaves and flowers. Two generations are normally completed annually.

Eightspotted forester (*Alypia octomaculata*) feeds on grape and Virginia creeper east of the Rockies. The common name refers to the features of the adult, a velvety black moth with paired light markings on each of the four wings. Moths fly during the day and often can be seen visiting flowers for nectar. The caterpillars are white or pale bluish, well patterned with rows of black spotting, orange banding along the side, and a rounded hump on the hind end. They chew leaves from early June through August. Apparently two generations are produced, with adults most common in May and early August. Winter is spent as a pupa in a cocoon in the soil.

Okra caterpillar (*Anomis erosa*) feeds on leaves of okra and related mallow family plants in the southeastern U.S. Although common, it is rarely abundant enough to cause serious injury. The caterpillars walk in a manner similar to loopers, but they do possess a fourth, albeit small, pair of prolegs. Okra caterpillars are yellowish green or green and have a dark stripe down the back.

One of the few chewing insects that damage ferns is **Florida fern caterpillar** (*Callopistria floridensis*), native to many southeastern and Gulf states. The caterpillars have two color phases, either pale green or velvety black, and are marked with two wavy light stripes.

[1] Lepidoptera: Noctuidae

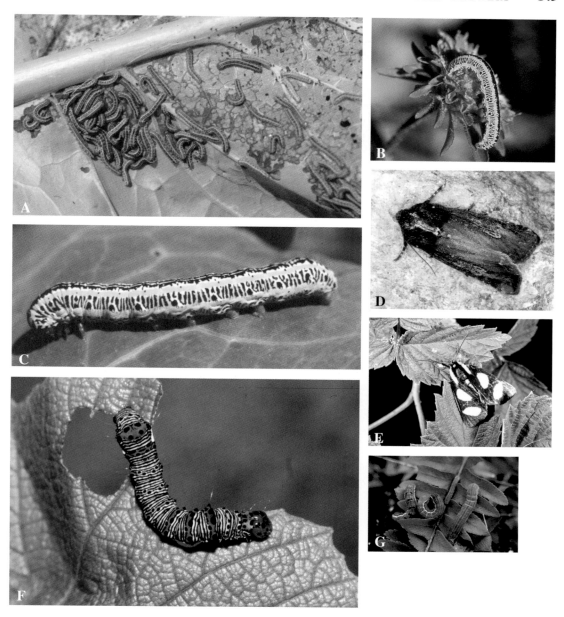

A. Young feeding group of zebra caterpillars. *W. Cranshaw.* **B.** Zebra caterpillar on flower. *W. Cranshaw.* **C.** Zebra caterpillar. *W. Cranshaw.* **D.** Zebra caterpillar adult. *Courtesy Pacific Agri-Food Research Centre.* **E.** Eightspotted forester adult. *J. Capinera.* **F.** Eightspotted forester larva. *J. Fengler.* **G.** Florida fern caterpillars. *J. Baker.*

LOOPERS

Many insects described as "loopers" are members of the cutworm subfamily Plusiinae.[1] These are characterized by having only three pair of prolegs on the abdomen, versus five pairs found among other members of the order. This causes them to walk in a looping fashion, somewhat like the inchworms (see p. 128).

Cabbage Looper (*Trichoplusia ni*)

Hosts: Despite its name, cabbage looper is not limited to mustard family plants but may also damage plants as diverse as potato, tomato, pea, lettuce, spinach, nasturtium, and carnation. It is sometimes found as a greenhouse pest on various ornamentals.

Damage: Larvae chew leaves of various plants, occasionally causing serious defoliation. Late stages tend to tunnel into heads of cabbage, lettuce, and other plants, causing additional injury.

Distribution: Throughout North America, common. Cabbage looper thrives best in warmer climates and survives poorly following winters in areas with extended freezing temperatures. Adults, however, are strong fliers and annually migrate long distances.

Appearance: Caterpillars are pale green, darkening somewhat as they get older. Faint white stripes run the length of the body. Adults are of moderate size (wingspan about 1½ inches) with mottled gray or brown forewings and a distinctively patterned silvery white central spot.

Life History and Habits: Eggs are hemispherical and glued singly to foliage, often in small groups. They hatch in a few days, and the first-stage larvae are creamy colored. They go through a series of molts as they develop, becoming full grown in about 3 weeks. Young larvae typically feed on outer leaves, producing windowpaning patterns on thick-leaved plants such as cabbage. Late stages feed more generally and tend to tunnel into heads. Pupation occurs on or in the nearby vicinity of host plants in a loose cocoon, and the pupal stage lasts 1 to 2 weeks. The number of generations produced annually is highly variable, and during the growing season generations greatly overlap and become indistinct.

Other Common Garden Loopers

Celery looper (*Anagrapha falcifera*) is found throughout most of North America and feeds on a wide range of broadleaf plants. However, it is rarely abundant enough to cause serious injury to gardens. Pea, lettuce, celery, and beet are among the more common hosts.

Alfalfa looper (*Autographa californica*) is a western species particularly abundant in the Pacific states. It develops on a wide range of vegetables and even some fruits but is most damaging to lettuce, beans, and cabbage family crops. Two or three generations may be completed annually, with winter spent as a pupa in a loose cocoon. **Plantain looper** (*A. precationis*) is an eastern species. It feeds on a wide variety of weeds and is rarely damaging to gardens but may occur on some vegetables (bean, cabbage, pea, parsnip) and several ornamental plants (hollyhock, sunflower). Larvae can be distinguished from other loopers by the presence of three thin light stripes on each side of the back and a white stripe along the side. Winter apparently is spent as a larva, with pupation in spring. Two or three generations may occur annually.

Soybean looper (*Pseudoplusia includens*) occurs primarily in the southern states where it may feed on leaves of many plants. In addition to tomato and some other vegetables, it commonly damages foliage of many flowers including aster, begonia, geranium, chrysanthemum, and poinsettia. Soybean looper may breed continually in extreme southern areas, producing up to five generations annually. Two generations are more commonly reported from the more northern areas where it occurs.

[1] Lepidoptera: Noctuidae

A. Cabbage looper adult. *W. Cranshaw.* **B.** Cocoon produced by cabbage looper pupa. *W. Cranshaw.* **C.** Eggs of cabbage looper on tomato. *W. Cranshaw.* **D.** Cabbage looper. *J. Capinera.* **E.** Celery looper. *J. Capinera.* **F.** Soybean looper. *Courtesy Clemson University.* **G.** Celery looper adult. *K. Gray.* **H.** Alfalfa looper adult. *J. Capinera.* **I.** Celery looper pupa. *K. Gray.* **J.** Alfalfa looper larva. *J. Capinera.*

HORNWORMS/SPHINX MOTHS

Hornworms (Sphingidae family)[1] are among the largest caterpillars found in North America. All are marked by having, at least in the first stages, a prominent "horn" on the hind end. More than 120 species occur on the continent, but only two (tobacco hornworm and tomato hornworm) are considered significant pests. The majority develop on shade trees and shrubs, where damage is rarely noticed. Adults are strong-flying, heavy-bodied moths known as sphinx moths or hawk moths. The moths feed on nectar from deep-lobed flowers. Those that are active during the day are sometimes known as "hummingbird moths."

Tomato Hornworm/Five-spotted Hawk Moth (*Manduca quinquemaculata*)
Tobacco Hornworm/Carolina Sphinx (*Manduca sexta*)

Hosts: Tomato and tobacco are particularly susceptible to injury. Pepper, potato, and certain nightshade family weeds are also hosts.

Damage: Caterpillars chew leaves and can defoliate plants rapidly. Fruits, particularly green fruit, may also be chewed.

Distribution: Both species are found widely throughout the U.S. and southern Canada. Tobacco hornworm tends to predominate in southern areas and tomato hornworm in the north, but distributions overlap considerably.

Appearance: Larvae develop into large caterpillars, with five pairs of prolegs and a "horn" on the last segment. Most are generally green. Seven diagonal white stripes are present along the side of the tobacco hornworm, and the horn is usually red. Tomato hornworm has a series of V-shaped white markings along the sides, and the horn is often black. Less common dark green or even black forms of tomato hornworm may be present. Adults of both are strong-flying, heavy-bodied moths. The forewings may have a span of up to 5 inches and are generally gray or grayish brown with light wavy markings.

Life History and Habits: Tomato and tobacco hornworms winter as pupae in a chamber approximately 4 to 6 inches deep in the soil. Adult moths emerge in mid- to late spring and may migrate long distances. Eggs resemble small pearls and are laid singly on foliage. The newly hatched caterpillars posses a horn that is nearly the same length as the body and subsequently pass through four to five additional larval stages over the course of about a month. Full-grown larvae burrow several inches into soil and create a cell in which pupation occurs. Two generations are usually produced per year.

A. Whitelined sphinx, the most common hummingbird moth. *W. Cranshaw.* **B.** Early-stage tomato hornworm larva. *W. Cranshaw.* **C.** Tobacco hornworm egg. *W. Cranshaw.* **D.** Tomato hornworm larva. *W. Cranshaw.* **E.** Tobacco hornworm adult. *J. Capinera.* **F.** Tomato hornworm adult. *J. Capinera.* **G.** Tobacco hornworm larva, full grown. *W. Cranshaw.* **H.** Tobacco hornworm feeding on tomato fruit. *W. Cranshaw.* **I.** Tobacco hornworm pupa. *W. Cranshaw.* **J.** Light and dark phases of tomato hornworm. *Photographer unknown.*

Other Common Hornworms

Whitelined sphinx (*Hyles lineata*) is the most widely distributed sphinx moth in North America. It is particularly common throughout western North America where it is familiar to gardeners as the most commonly encountered hummingbird moth, marked with a prominent white band on the forewing. Larvae develop on a wide variety of plants but rarely significantly damage those considered economically important. Portulaca, primrose, and wild grape are among the most common hosts for the larvae. Hornworms of whitelined sphinx can be highly variable in color. Most are predominately green, with some yellow, white, and/or black markings. Less common are predominately black forms with yellow markings. Two generations are produced annually, with overwintering occurring as a pupa in soil. Adults of **great ash sphinx** (*Sphinx chersis*) also are commonly observed as day-flying hummingbird moths. Larvae develop on ash, lilac, and privet.

Larvae of **achemon sphinx** (*Eumorpha achemon*) are unusual in that they lose the terminal horn after the first molt. Instead, subsequent larval stages are marked by a prominent eyespot at the hind end. The caterpillars develop on Virginia creeper, grape, and related vines. Apparently there is one generation per year, with full-grown caterpillars most commonly observed in late August and early September. In eastern North America another common species that feeds on Virginia creeper and grape is **Virginia-creeper sphinx** (*Darapsa myron*).

Catalpa sphinx (*Ceratomia catalpae*) occurs throughout most of the eastern U.S., being particularly abundant in the southern states where it may occur from Florida through parts of Texas. It develops on all species of catalpa and is sometimes abundant enough to defoliate isolated trees, usually in August and September. Up to four generations may be produced annually in southern parts of the range. The caterpillars, sometimes known as "catawba worms," are highly prized as fish bait in some locations. Related species include **elm sphinx** (*C. amyntor*), which feeds on elm and occasionally birch, basswood, and cherry, and **waved sphinx** (*C. undulosa*), which develops on ash, privet, oak, and hawthorn. **Walnut sphinx** (*Cressonia juglandis*) occurs on black walnut, hickory, beech, butternut, and pecan in eastern North America.

Sweetpotato hornworm (*Agrius cingulata*), also known as **pink-spotted hawk moth**, is a tropical and subtropical species that feeds on sweetpotato and some related weeds. It is common in the southern U.S., occasionally straying into the Midwest.

Hornworms in the genus *Hemaris* are among the smallest in the family. Adults, sometimes known as "**clearwings**," are unusual in that the wings have clear areas in the center, giving the insects the overall appearance of large bumble bees. Larvae develop on various shrubs including honeysuckle, snowberry, cherry, plum, and cranberry. **Hummingbird clearwing** (*H. thysbe*), found primarily in eastern North America, and the broadly distributed **snowberry clearwing** (*H. diffinis*) are the dominant species.

Poplar and willow host many kinds of hornworms. **Twinspot sphinx** (*Smerinthus jamaicensis*) and **one-eyed sphinx** (*S. cerisyi*) are both quite common in northern areas. Twinspot sphinx occurs primarily in the eastern half of the northern U.S. and southern Canada and one-eyed sphinx in the western half, although ranges overlap. One of the largest sphinx moths is **big poplar sphinx** (*Pachysphinx occidentalis*), restricted to the western half of North America.

[1] Lepidoptera: Sphingidae

A. Whitelined sphinx. *E. Nelson.* **B.** Larva of achemon sphinx. *J. Capinera.* **C.** Hummingbird clearwing. *D. Shetlar.* **D.** Larva of one-eyed sphinx. *K. Gray.* **E.** Sweetpotato hornworm, green form. *J. Capinera.* **F.** Snowberry clearwing. *W. Cranshaw.* **G.** Elm sphinx caterpillar. W. *W. Cranshaw.* **H.** Larva of great ash sphinx. *W. Cranshaw.* **I.** One-eyed sphinx. *K. Gray.* **J.** Big poplar sphinx larva. *D. Leatherman.* **K.** Big poplar sphinx. *W. Cranshaw.* **L.** Catalpa sphinx caterpillar. *J. H. Ghent.* **M.** Whitelined sphinx larva, green form. *W. Cranshaw.* **N.** Larva of snowberry clearwing. *W. Cranshaw.*

PROMINENT MOTHS

Several caterpillars of the prominent moth family (Notodontidae)[1] are associated with trees and shrubs. In general form, the caterpillars somewhat resemble climbing cutworms but often have distinct markings or fleshy projections. A few species are pests of trees and shrubs, and these usually are observed feeding in groups. In response to disturbance, members of the feeding group typically arch and twitch to deter predators.

Walnut Caterpillar (*Datana integerrina*)

Hosts: Walnut, butternut, pecan, and hickory.

Damage: Larvae chew leaves, originally skeletonizing and later consuming most of the leaf excepting main veins.

Distribution: Much of the eastern U.S. but particularly common in the central and southcentral states.

Appearance: Full-grown caterpillars are about 2 inches long with a dark gray body, some yellow stripes along the side, and a body generally clothed in long hairs. When disturbed, a group of larvae usually arches in a defensive posture. Adults are moderate-sized brown moths with a wingspan of about 2 inches and are marked with some dark lines.

Life History and Habits: Winter is spent as a pupa, in a cell constructed in soil in the vicinity of previously infested trees. Adults emerge in mid- to late spring, and females lay eggs in masses. Upon hatching, the caterpillars feed gregariously, first skeletonizing leaves and later feeding more generally. Larvae periodically migrate from foliage to large branches and trunks where they rest in masses and molt, often in synchrony. The full-grown caterpillars often wander considerable distances before pupating. Two generations are produced in the southern states, with adults emerging in midsummer. One generation is common in northern areas.

Other Notodontid Moths on Shade Trees

Yellownecked caterpillar (*Datana ministra*) is a common species in the Appalachian Mountains and occasionally is found in much of the eastern U.S. The caterpillars are marked with bright orange-yellow segments behind the head. They have a wide host range, including many deciduous fruit, nut, and shade trees. **Azalea caterpillar** (*D. major*) is often a serious defoliator of azalea in the southeastern U.S. The caterpillars are brightly patterned, yellow and black with a red head and legs. One generation is typical, with peak injury in mid- to late summer.

A. Walnut caterpillar adult. *H. C. Ellis.* **B.** Walnut caterpillars feeding in group. *J. D. Solomon.* **C.** Walnut caterpillars feeding in group. *L. L. Hyche.* **D.** Walnut caterpillar egg mass at hatch. *H. C. Ellis.* **E.** Yellownecked caterpillars feeding in group. *G. J. Lenhard.* **F.** Yellownecked caterpillar. *R. L. Anderson.*

Redhumped caterpillar (*Schizura concinna*) is probably the most commonly encountered and widespread of the prominent caterpillars in North America. Caterpillars are marked with a pronounced reddish hump behind the head, and during early development they feed gregariously, sometimes stripping individual branches. Apple and crabapple are among the more common hosts, although this species develops on many woody plants. One generation is produced per year. The closely related **unicorn caterpillar** (*S. unicornis*) is an unusual brown and green caterpillar with a large fleshy projection on the first segment of the abdomen. Of very similar appearance is **false unicorn caterpillar** (*S. ipomoeae*), sometimes known as "morning glory prominent." Dark markings on the head and abdomen absent on false unicorn caterpillar, can distinguish the larvae. Both species of unicorn caterpillars are found throughout most of North America and may feed on a wide range of deciduous trees and shrubs.

Orangehumped mapleworm (*Symmersia leucitys*) is a northern species that develops primarily on sugar maple. The caterpillars have an orange-red head and longitudinal black, yellow, and white striping with an orange marking on the hind end. Young stages feed gregariously and skeletonize the upper leaf surface. Older caterpillars are solitary and feed along the leaf margins. **Redhumped oakworm** (*S. canicosta*) also occurs in the northeastern U.S. and southeastern Canada where it develops primarily on white and bur oak. Basswood, sugar maple, paper birch, beech, and elm are less common hosts.

Saddled prominent (*Heterocampa guttivitta*) is a caterpillar of bizarre appearance. Early-stage larvae have black antlerlike horns behind the head, which are lost at the first molt. Full-grown caterpillars are about 1½ inches long, generally green with an orange-red "saddle marking" on the middle. The species is most common in New England. **Variable oakleaf caterpillar** (*H. manteo*) occurs over a broader area of eastern North America, from southern Ontario to northern Texas. White oak is the preferred host, but several other trees are occasionally infested. Damage is most common in the southern states, where two generations can occur. This caterpillar also can cause blistering of exposed skin from a formic acid mixture it can spray when disturbed.

Poplar tentmaker (*Clostera inclusa*) occurs over a wide area of southern Canada and the eastern half of the U.S., ranging south to Georgia. It develops on aspen, poplar, and willow. Larvae feed gregariously and construct a structure of leaves loosely tied with silk. Two generations are produced, with eggs from the overwintered generation laid in March and April, followed by a summer generation with eggs laid mostly in July and August. Winter is spent in a cocoon around the base of previously infested trees.

Although not a notodontid, the closely related **California oakworm** (*Phryganidia californica*)[2] is a common caterpillar along coastal areas of California and southern Oregon and is associated with coast live oak. Caterpillars survive the winter as early-stage larvae on the underside of leaves, causing minor skeletonizing. They rapidly develop during early spring and may defoliate trees during outbreaks. They then pupate on bark of trunks, suspended from limbs or on nearby vegetation. Adults, which are tan-gray moths with a wingspan of approximately 1¼ inches, are weak fliers and subsequently lay their eggs in the near vicinity of previously infested plants. Eggs are laid as small masses on twigs or leaves during late summer and early fall. Two generations per year are normally produced; a third generation is sometimes produced if favorable conditions occur.

[1] Lepidoptera: Notodontidae; [2] Lepidoptera: Dioptidae

A. Redhumped caterpillars. *S. Rachesky.* **B.** Redhumped caterpillar. *Courtesy Clemson University.* **C.** Unicorn caterpillar. *L. Risley.* **D.** Saddled prominent larva. *L. L. Hyche.* **E.** Redhumped oakworms. *Courtesy USDA-FS Rocky Mountain Experiment Station Archives.* **F.** Variable oakleaf caterpillars. *R. F. Billings.* **G.** Variable oakleaf caterpillar. *R. F. Billings.* **H.** False unicorn caterpillar. *D. Leatherman.* **I.** Variable oakleaf caterpillars at egg hatch. *R. F. Billings.* **J.** California oakworm larva. *J. K. Clark/UC Statewide IPM Program.* **K.** Poplar tentmaker larva. *R. L. Anderson.*

GIANT SILKWORMS/ROYAL MOTHS

The giant silkworms (Saturniidae family)[1] include the largest caterpillars that can be encountered, with some over 5 inches long. All feed on leaves of trees and shrubs, and individual caterpillars consume impressive amounts toward the end of their life cycle, usually in mid- to late summer. Rarely are they abundant enough to cause significant injury, however, and their presence is mostly a curiosity—or even a source of wonder—because of their unusual size and appearance. Furthermore, populations of several species have been in decline for many years, the reason for which is of considerable debate.

Adults, often known as **royal moths**, are large moths that may have a wingspan exceeding 6 inches. Adults do not feed and thus die a few days after emergence from the cocoon. Moths are usually present in late spring or early summer.

Cecropia Moth (*Hyalophora cecropia*)

Hosts: At least 50 species of deciduous trees and shrubs are hosts of larvae. Boxelder, sugar maple, wild cherry and plum, apple, alder, birch, dogwood, willow, lilac, ash, and viburnum are common hosts.

Damage: Cecropia moth caterpillars can be among the most conspicuous late-season defoliators of shrubs. Because the feeding occurs late in the season, however, there is little if any plant injury.

Distribution: Primarily east of the Rockies.

Appearance: The larvae are large, sluggish, sea green caterpillars, from 3 to 4 inches long. They possess numerous colored knoblike tubercles—pale blue along the sides, orange on the thorax, and yellow on the abdomen. Adults are large and colorful moths with a wingspan of 5½ to 6½ inches. They have brownish gray wings with white crescent-shaped eyespots, a dark spot near the tip of each forewing, and red-bordered crossbands. The pupa occurs in a tough cocoon which is attached along its entire length to a twig.

Life History and Habits: Winter is spent as a pupa in the cocoon, usually attached to a small branch. Adults emerge in late spring. They do not feed, but they mate and females lay eggs on twigs over the course of a few days before dying. The caterpillars then begin to feed on leaves and develop over a period of 2 to 3 months. All stages of cecropia moth caterpillars bear prominent tubercles on the body, but the caterpillars develop more intense coloration as they age. One generation is produced per year.

Other Giant Silkworms/Royal Moths

Hickory horned devil (*Citheronia regalis*) is a bizarre caterpillar that may be 5 inches long. Generally blue green, it has numerous spikes, particularly two long curving pairs on the thorax, giving it a rather dragonlike appearance. It is found in much of the eastern U.S., being more common in the southern states. Hickory, walnut, and a few other trees and shrubs may host the caterpillars.

Luna moth (*Actias luna*) is one of the most distinctive moths of North America, having pale green wings developed into an elongate "swallowtail" and marked with a yellow spot. Larvae are translucent pale green with a pale yellow line along the lower side and feed on a wide variety of nut, fruit, and shade trees. The species is known from parts of Texas and Nebraska eastward but has become considerably less abundant in recent decades.

A. Caterpillar of cecropia moth. *D. Leatherman.* **B.** Cecropia moths. *B. Drees.* **C.** Hickory horned devil adult. *R. F. Billings.* **D.** Cocoon of cecropia moth. *W. Cranshaw.* **E.** Young caterpillar of cecropia moth. *D. Leatherman.* **F.** Hickory horned devil larva. *G. J. Lenhard.* **G.** Luna moth. *G. J. Lenhard.* **H.** Luna moth caterpillar. *G. J. Lenhard.*

Larvae of **polyphemus moth** (*Antheraea polyphemus*) are stout bodied, apple green, and only sparsely marked by spines. This species is widely distributed throughout much of North America and feeds on many deciduous trees and shrubs in late summer. Dogwood, oak, willow, maple, and birch are among the more common plants on which the caterpillars develop.

Caterpillars of **promethea moth** (*Callosamia promethea*) are pale bluish green and possess four prominent red-orange spikes near the head and one yellow spike near the rear. They occur in the eastern U.S. and southeastern Canada. Hosts include cherry, magnolia, tuliptree, ash, and lilac.

Imperial moth (*Eacles imperialis*) develops on a wide range of shade trees, including some conifers as well as deciduous trees. The caterpillars are yellow-green and covered with short, light blue-green hairs.

Pandora moth (*Coloradia pandora*) is a western species associated with pines. It has had several historical outbreaks, and the caterpillars have sometimes been used as a food source by Native Americans. The life cycle requires 2 years to complete, with partially grown larvae wintering on the tree during the first year and then moving to the soil to pupate in a cocoon following the second year.

Greenstriped mapleworm (*Dryocampa rubicunda*) is associated with maple throughout the eastern U.S. and is particularly common in the southern half of its range where outbreaks sometimes are recorded. Caterpillars possess a cherry red head and yellow-green body with seven dark green lines running the length. The insect is also marked with two slender, flexible horns behind the head. **Orangestriped oakworm** (*Anisota senatoria*) occurs in much of the eastern half of the U.S., excluding some of the southeastern states. It feeds on oak and occasonally causes extensive defoliation in late summer. **Spiny oakworm** (*A. stigma*) is marked by two prominent spines on the thorax. It ranges east from southern Ontario to parts of Texas and develops on oak and hazel.

Io moth (*Automeris io*) is one of the smaller giant silkworms, reaching about 3 inches when mature. The larvae possess numerous stinging hairs that produce a painful reaction on touch. Io moth caterpillars are the most widespread and commonly encountered of the caterpillars in North America that can produce painful stings.

Larvae are large, pale green caterpillars with a lateral stripe of pink and creamy white down each side, covered with clusters of branching spines. They develop on a wide range of deciduous shade trees including willow, elm, apple, maple, hickory, and sycamore and are about 3 inches long at maturity. Pupation occurs in a cocoon, and the stinging hairs of the larvae coat the pupae. Adults have a wingspan of 2½ to 3 inches, the females with lightly patterned purplish red wings, the males smaller with yellowish wings, and both with a large circular black eyespot on the hindwings. One generation is produced in most areas, but two can occur in the more southern states.

A few species of *Hemileuca* species, sometimes known as "buck moths," are occasional tree pests. Older larvae are generally dark and possess numerous tufts of branched spines. The spines are attached to poison glands capable of producing a painful sting, although not as painful as that of io moth. The most common western species, **Nevada buck moth** (*H. nevadensis*), develops on poplar and willow. **Eastern buck moth** (*H. maia*) is an eastern species that feeds on scrub, live, blackjack, and dwarf chestnut oak. **New England buck moth** (*H. lucina*) is restricted to the New England states and feeds on oak, black cherry, willow, gray birch, and blueberry. Adults of all buck moths are fairly large, fly during the day, and have wings prominently patterned with white and black.

[1] Lepidoptera: Saturniidae

A. Polyphemus moth. *D. Leatherman.* **B.** Polyphemus moth caterpillar. *D. Leatherman.* **C.** Polyphemus moth cocoon, dissected to expose pupa. *W. Cranshaw.* **D.** Imperial moth. *B. Drees.* **E.** Greenstriped mapleworm larva. *G. J. Lenhard.* **F.** Io moth caterpillar. *W. Cranshaw.* **G.** Imperial moth caterpillar. *L. L. Hyche.* **H.** Io moth. *R. F. Billings.* **I.** Mass of early-stage Io moth caterpillars. *J. Capinera.* **J.** Orangestriped oakworms. *J. D. Solomon.* **K.** Greenstriped mapleworm adult. *L. L. Hyche.* **L.** Eastern buck moth larva. *J. D. Solomon.* **M.** Nevada buck moth larva. *W. Cranshaw.*

SLUG CATERPILLARS/FLANNEL MOTHS

The slug caterpillars (Limacodidae family) are often bizarre in appearance and attract attention but are rarely abundant. Most larvae possess prominent spines and bright coloration and may be an unusual shape. The spines are highly irritating upon contact and can produce a painful reaction. Because of the stinging hairs, some species are locally known as "asps."

Saddleback caterpillar (*Sibine stimulea*)[1] is among the most commonly encountered species, found in much of the eastern half of the U.S. and particularly abundant in the Atlantic states. Larvae are brown with a pronounced green saddle-shaped area over the center of the body. Colorful sharp spines, connected to poison gland cells, extend from both front and back and are extremely painful. Saddleback caterpillars feed on apple, pear, cherry, corn, canna, lily, dahlia, and many other plants but are never abundant enough to cause serious plant injury. The pupa occurs in a cocoon, and the stinging hairs are retained on the surface. Adults fly in July and August in the north and year-round in the extreme south. **Stinging rose caterpillar** (*Parasa indetermina*)[1] also has tufts of stinging hairs, but the general color is reddish or orange red with striping down the center of the back. Common hosts include wild rose, redbud, oak, hickory, bayberry, wild cherry, and sycamore.

Caterpillars of **hag moth** (*Phobetron pithecium*)[1] are bizarre insects with numerous long curved spines along the sides, particularly on the third, fifth, and seventh segments. The spines are also connected to poison glands and are painful on contact. Larvae feed on many deciduous trees and shrubs including wild rose, sassafras, alder, and spirea.

Other Stinging Caterpillars

Another species with stinging hairs that is common in parts of the southern U.S. is **puss caterpillar** (*Megalopyge opercularis*).[2] Larvae are densely covered in long hairs that may be yellowish, reddish brown, or mouse gray. The young larvae typically feed in groups, skeletonizing the leaf surfaces of many deciduous trees including oak, elm, hackberry, and sycamore. Two generations are produced annually.

A related species that occurs in the southeastern U.S. is **hackberry leaf slug** (*Norape ovina*).[2] Larvae have six small tufts of stinging hairs on each segment and feed on several woody plants, particularly redbud, red maple, and hackberry. The adult is known as the white flannel moth. A related species found in southwestern states that also has stinging hairs is **mesquite stinger** (*N. tenera*).

[1] Lepidoptera: Limacodidae; [2] Lepidoptera: Megalopygidae

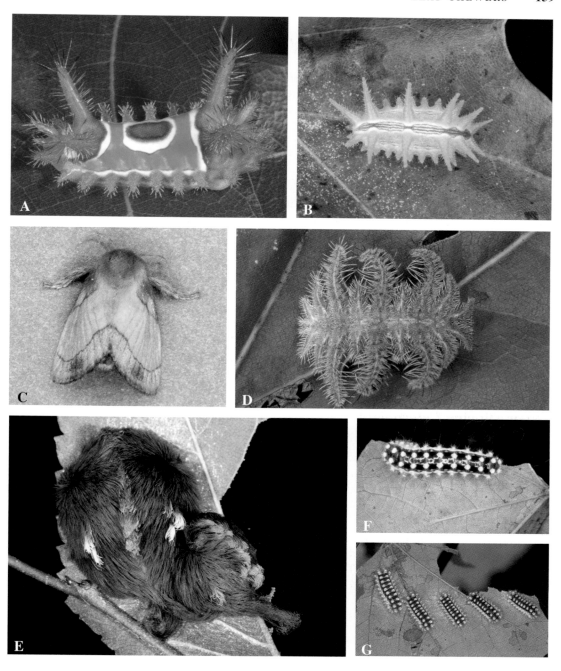

A. Saddleback caterpillar. *G. J. Lenhard.* **B.** Stinging rose caterpillar. *L. L. Hyche.* **C.** Adult of stinging rose caterpillar. *L. L. Hyche.* **D.** Caterpillar of hag moth. *Courtesy Clemson University.* **E.** Puss caterpillar. *L. L. Hyche.* **F.** Hackberry leaf slug. *L. L. Hyche.* **G.** Feeding group of hackberry leaf slugs. *L. L. Hyche.*

BAGWORMS

Bagworms (Psychidae family)[1] are unusual caterpillars that develop in a silken case covered with leaf fragments or other debris. Adult females are wingless moths that remain in the case. Adult males, if they are produced, are winged.

Bagworm (*Thyridopteryx ephemeraeformis*)

Hosts: Juniper, cedar, false cypress, and arborvitae are most commonly infested. Bagworm may feed on a wide variety of other woody plants including black locust, elm, pine, cabbage palmetto, honeylocust, buckeye, sycamore, and willow.

Damage: Caterpillars chew foliage and during outbreaks can seriously defoliate plants. Swellings on twigs sometimes occur around the site where bags were attached for pupation.

Distribution: Generally in the eastern U.S. from southern New England to parts of Nebraska and south to Texas and Florida.

Appearance: Bagworm is a bizarre caterpillar that develops in a silken bag with bits of interwoven twigs and foliage. When full sized the bag may be 1½ to 2 inches long. Females remain in the bag through all life stages. Males emerge from the bag and are black moths with clear wings that span about 1 inch.

Life History and Habits: Bagworm winters as eggs in the bag of the mother. In most areas eggs remain dormant until late spring, at which time the larvae emerge and disperse. They begin to feed and construct the case almost immediately, first being found on the upper leaf surface where they feed on surface tissues. Later they migrate to the underside of leaves and feed more generally, expanding the bag as they grow. When full grown they pupate in late summer. Mating and egg-laying typically occur in September. One generation is produced annually in most areas; bagworm may reproduce continually in parts of Florida.

Other Bagworms

Snailcase bagworm (*Apterona helix*), sometimes known as garden bagworm, is an odd insect that constructs a coiled case of silk covered with particles of soil and excrement. Larvae have a wide host range that includes broccoli, bean, squash, gypsophila, violet, alfalfa, vetch, rose, apple, pear, ponderosa pine, and Douglas-fir. Snailcase bagworm is found in localized areas throughout the western states and has become established in parts of New York, Pennsylvania, Massachusetts, and Michigan. The introduced insect is easily spread and can be expected to increase its range.

Winter is spent as a young larva in the case of the mother bagworm. Larvae emerge in spring to complete development, producing the typical case they carry and remain in throughout life. As they feed, larvae often chew the leaf interior, similar to a leafminer but with the bag remaining on the outside. Injuries result from windowpaning or from skeletonizing. Mature larvae have a migratory habit and move to a vertical surface where they fasten firmly for pupation. Adult females emerge in the case in August and lay eggs. Males are unknown for this species.

[1] Lepidoptera: Psychidae

A. Adult male bagworm. *G. J. Lenhard.* **B.** Bagworm larva feeding. *G. J. Lenhard.* **C.** Bagworm pupae. *G. J. Lenhard.*
D. Bagworm developing on pine. *R. L. Anderson.* **E.** Group of snailcase bagworms feeding. *G. J. Lenhard.*
F. Snailcase bagworms. *W. Cranshaw.* **G.** Snailcase bagworm larva exposed from case. *K. Gray.*

CASEBEARERS

Casebearers are larvae of small moths that produce a parchment-like case that the caterpillar carries throughout development.

Pistol casebearer (*Coleophora malivorella*)[1] is widespread east of the Rocky Mountains and feeds on leaves of most tree fruits. Larvae feed and destroy leaf and flower buds early in the season. Later they make shallow mines as they feed on maturing fruit and leaves.

Winter is spent as a partially grown larva in the case, which is dirty gray-brown. Larvae move to buds with warm days in spring, and as they grow they continue to enlarge the case with silk mixed with leaf fragments and excrement. The case becomes curved in later stages, somewhat resembling a pistol. Around mid-June the larvae secure the cases to twigs or leaves and pupate.

After about 2 weeks they emerge as adults and lay most eggs within a few days of emergence. Eggs are laid on the upper side of leaves. After egg hatch, larvae tunnel to the underside of leaves, feed until fall, and secure themselves to twigs for winter.

Cigar casebearer (*Coleophora serratella*)[1] has a similar life history and overlaps both in its range of hosts and in distribution. Larvae are dark orange with a black head and produce a cigar-shaped case of leaf fragments. Adults are small, steel gray moths with fringed wings and are present in early summer. **Elm casebearer** (*C. ulmifoliella*)[1] is an eastern U.S. species that produces brown patches between leaf veins of American, red, and slippery elm. **Pecan cigar casebearer** (*C. laticornella*) causes similar injury to pecan. The first generation of **pecan leaf casebearer** (*Acrobasis juglandis*)[2] also damages early-season growth of pecan. Later generations cause little damage to leaves. Older larvae live in a grayish case.

Larch casebearer (*Coleophora laricella*)[1] is an introduced species that now occurs throughout the range of native larch and occurs as a pest where larch is used in landscape plantings. Peak injury is caused shortly after bud break when the overwintered larvae resume feeding. They mine individual needles, as deeply as their bodies can extend beyond the case they carry. They become full grown and pupate by late spring, in the case that is constructed of silk and portions of damaged needles. Adults lay eggs in late spring and early summer. Early-stage larvae feed through the summer as needleminers and then create a case in which they winter. The case is located at the base of larch buds and resembles dead needles.

A. Pistol casebearer. *D. Caldwell.* **B.** Elm casebearer adult. *D. Shetlar.* **C.** Elm casebearer. *B. Childs.* **D.** Larch casebearer. *D. Shetlar.* **E.** Larch casebearer pupae. *D. Shetlar.* **F.** Needle feeding injuries by larch casebear. *B. Childs.* **G.** Pecan cigar casebearer. *H. C. Ellis.* **H.** Pecan leaf casebearer. *H. C. Ellis.* **I.** Cigar casebearer. *W. Cranshaw.*

Larvae of **maple trumpet skeletonizer** (*Calastega aceriella*)[3] make unusual trumpetlike tubes of silk and incorporate frass that covers their bodies. Adults lay eggs on leaves of sugar and red maples in June and early July, and the larvae develop as skeletonizers feeding between veins. They drop to the ground later in the summer when full grown and pupate in a cocoon. One generation is produced. Maple trumpet skeletonizer occurs in the northeastern U.S. and southeastern Canada.

Also feeding on maple in the northeastern U.S. and southern Canada is **maple leafcutter** (*Paraclemensia acerifoliella*).[4] Early larval feeding is as a leafminer and is initiated shortly after new leaves have emerged. Older larvae move outside and fashion a case out of round, cut leaf fragments. When feeding, the larva attaches the case to the leaf surface and feeds as far as it can reach, producing circular holes in the leaves. Feeding is usually completed by late spring, and the larva drops to the ground to pupate and overwinter.

A case of dried leaves and silk is produced by **leaf crumpler**[2] (*Acrobasis indigenella*). It feeds on leaves of a wide variety of rosaceous plants including crabapple, pyracantha, hawthorn, and pear. It occurs in most of North America east of the Mississippi River and in the Pacific states. In most areas two generations are produced. Winter is spent as a partially grown larva in the case. Larvae resume feeding in spring and may leave their cases to feed at night, returning with leaf fragments. Pupation occurs in May, and adults lay eggs on leaves a few weeks later. Peak feeding usually occurs with the subsequent generation, which is most active in late June and July. Adults from this generation are usually present in August and lay eggs that produce the overwintering larvae. In northern areas only a single generation may be produced.

[1] Lepidoptera: Coleophoridae; [2] Lepidoptera: Pyralidae; [3] Lepidoptera: Tortricidae; [4] Lepidoptera: Incurvariidae

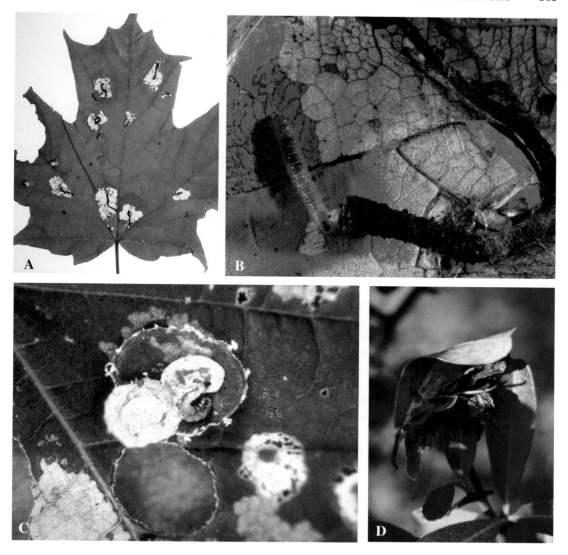

A. Maple trumpet skeletonizer damage to maple leaf. *E. B. Walker.* **B.** Maple trumpet skeletonizer larva. *J. H. Ghent.*
C. Maple leafcutter larva. *R. S. Kelley.* **D.** Leaf crumpler injury. *J. R. Baker.*

WHITES AND SULFURS

Whites and sulfurs (Pieridae family)[1] are moderate-sized butterflies with a wingspan typically about 2 inches. They are often the most commonly observed butterflies and are associated with a wide variety of plants. Few of the caterpillars are of concern to gardeners, but the "cabbageworms" can be very damaging.

Imported Cabbageworm/Cabbage Butterfly or Cabbage White (*Pieris rapae*)

Hosts: Essentially all cabbage family plants including cabbage, broccoli, Brussels sprouts, and many related weeds.

Damage: Larvae chew foliage. Most early feeding occurs on outer leaves, but older larvae tend to feed more intensively on the newer growth and can seriously tunnel the head of many plants.

Distribution: Common throughout North America.

Appearance: Caterpillars are rather sluggish, velvety green with five distinct pairs of prolegs. A faint yellow line runs along the back of older larvae. Upper wings of the adults are predominantly white with a dark tip. Males have a single black spot on the forewing, whereas females have two such spots. The underside of the wings is yellowish.

Life History and Habits: In the northern U.S. and Canada winter is spent as a pupa among plant debris in the vicinity of previously infested plants. The familiar adult butterflies may be active in mid-spring, and females lay yellow, bullet-shaped eggs on leaves. (The appearance of this insect in spring, coincident with when cows would again begin to produce milk, is the source of the English term "butterfly.")

Larvae hatch in 3 to 5 days and begin to feed on plants, often first remaining on the outer leaves. Later they tunnel into the head. Larvae are full grown in 2 to 3 weeks. Pupation occurs in the vicinity of the plant. Two to four generations are typically completed in much of the northern area of the range. In the southern U.S., however, breeding can be continual and as many as six to eight generations may occur.

Related Species

Southern cabbageworm (*Pontia protodice*) is found primarily in the southern U.S., but may disperse northward. Larvae are much more brightly colored than imported cabbageworm, with black spotting and yellow striping. Feeding habits are similar to that of imported cabbageworm, but southern cabbageworm tends to feed more often on buds and flowers. The adult stage is known as the checkered white butterfly and possesses more dark spotting on its white wings.

Alfalfa caterpillar (*Colias eurytheme*) feeds on legumes, including pea, most clovers, alfalfa, and bean. The caterpillars are dark green with a light line running along the side. Adults are orange-yellow butterflies that sometimes become abundant where alfalfa is grown. Closely related and of similar habit is **common sulfur** (*C. philodice*).

---

[1] Lepidoptera: Pieridae

A. Cabbage white, or cabbage butterfly, adult of imported cabbageworm. *W. Cranshaw.* B. Cabbage butterfly laying egg on broccoli. *W. Cranshaw.* C. Egg of imported cabbageworm. *W. Cranshaw.* D. Newly hatched imported cabbageworm larva. W. *Cranshaw.* E. Checkered white, adult of southern cabbageworm. *W. Cranshaw.* F. Larva of imported cabbageworm. *W. Cranshaw.* G. Southern cabbageworm larva. *W. Cranshaw.* H. Alfalfa butterfly. *W. Cranshaw.* I. Prepupa and pupa of imported cabbageworm. *W. Cranshaw.* J. Chrysalis (pupal stage) of alfalfa butterfly. *W. Cranshaw.* K. Alfalfa caterpillar larva. *J. Capinera.* L. Pupa and prepupa of southern cabbageworm, as an adult known as checkered white. *W. Cranshaw.*

SWALLOWTAILS

Swallowtails (Papilionidae family)[1] include some of the largest and most striking butterflies found in North America. Adults are common and are welcome visitors to garden flowers. The larvae are also unusual, with many having bright warning coloration, large eyespot, or sometimes a cryptic appearance resembling bird droppings. Larvae also have the unique habit of being able to evert a pair of fleshy "horns" (osmetaria) from behind the head when disturbed. These glands also secrete odors that may be distasteful to potential predators.

Parsleyworm/Black Swallowtail (*Papilio polyxenes*)

Hosts: Primarily dill, parsley, and fennel. Rarely on carrot, Queen Anne's lace, celery, and other plants in the family Apiaceae.

Damage: Parsleyworm primarily chews leaves. It may clip flower heads and feed on developing seeds.

Distribution: Primarily east of the Rockies, although occasionally it is found in southern California and Arizona.

Appearance: Adults are known as black swallowtails, large butterflies with a wingspan of 2¼ to 3¼ inches. The primary coloration is shiny black, sometimes with iridescent blue, marked with yellow bands or spots along the edge of the wings. Young caterpillars are mottled black and white, resembling bird droppings. Later stages dramatically transform to possess prominent banding of yellow, white, and black.

Life History and Habits: Parsleyworm spends the winter as a pupa (chrysalis) attached to tree bark, the sides of buildings, or other protected locations. Adults emerge in late May and early June and lay eggs singly on plants in the carrot family (Apiaceae). After hatching, the caterpillars feed for about 3 to 4 weeks, undergoing a series of color changes as they get older. When full grown they wander away from the plant to find a place to pupate. They then form the pupa in a grayish chrysalis that blends in color with the background. Adult butterflies emerge after about 2 weeks, feed on nectar, mate, and lay eggs to produce a second generation beginning in early August. There are typically two generations per year in northern areas and three in southern areas.

A. Black swallowtail at zinnia. *W. Cranshaw.* **B.** Parsleyworm everting osmeteria in defense. *W. Cranshaw.* **C.** Late-stage parsleyworm after molt. *W. Cranshaw.* **D.** Parsleyworm feeding on dill. *W. Cranshaw.* **E.** Parsleyworm prior to pupation (prepupa). *W. Cranshaw.* **F.** Chrysalis of parsleyworm, also known as black swallowtail. *W. Cranshaw.* **G.** Parsleyworms with early-stage coloration. *W. Cranshaw.*

Other Swallowtails

The closely related **anise swallowtail** (*Papilio zelicaon*) develops on fennel and some plants in the citrus family (Rutaceae). It is found primarily west of the Continental Divide, including the southwestern U.S., and its larvae are sometimes known as the **California orangedog. Shortailed swallowtail** (*P. brevicauda*) occurs in eastern Canada and occasionally damages the foliage of parsnip.

Tiger swallowtails are large yellow and black butterflies. In western North America two common species are **twotailed tiger swallowtail** *(Papilio multicaudatus)*, developing primarily on chokecherry and ash, and **western tiger swallowtail** (*P. rutulus*), associated with willow, cottonwood, and chokecherry. In eastern North America **eastern tiger swallowtail** (*P. glaucus*) develops on the foliage of various trees including wild cherry, sweetbay, basswood, tuliptree, birch, ash, cottonwood, mountain-ash, and willow. Young tiger swallowtail caterpillars are mottled black and white and resemble bird droppings. Older caterpillars may be brown or lime green with prominent eyespots.

Giant swallowtail (*P. cresphontes*) is common in much of the southwestern and southeastern U.S., commonly migrating northward. Caterpillars develop on citrus, and the conspicuous caterpillars are sometimes known as **orangedogs**.

[1] Lepidoptera: Papilionidae

A. Egg of twotailed tiger swallowtail. *W. Cranshaw.* **B.** Larva of twotailed tiger swallowtail. *J. Capinera.* **C.** Young larva of twotailed tiger swallowtail. *J. Capinera.* **D.** Twotailed tiger swallowtail. *W. Cranshaw.* **E.** Eastern tiger swallowtail. *D. Herms.* **F.** Giant swallowtail. *B. Drees.* **G.** Orangedog, caterpillar of giant swallowtail. *G. J. Lenhard.* **H.** Tiger swallowtail pupa (chrysalis). *W. Cranshaw.* **I.** Western tiger swallowtail. *W. Cranshaw.*

BRUSHFOOTED BUTTERFLIES

Brushfooted butterflies (Nymphalidae family)[1] are a common group of moderately large butterflies. The upper wings are often brightly colored, but the lower wings may be more camouflaged. The front pair of legs is greatly reduced. Although many brushfooted butterflies feed at flowers, others visit sap flows, fermenting fruit, and animal dung. Few species seriously damage plants in the caterpillar stage, and the brushfooted butterflies are welcome additions to almost any garden.

Painted Lady/Thistle Caterpillar (*Vanessa cardui*)

Hosts: A wide range of plants, with more than 100 species from several plant families reported. Common hosts include Canada thistle, other thistles, sunflower, Jerusalem artichoke, hollyhock, common mallow, and lupine.

Damage: Caterpillars chew foliage, sometimes causing significant defoliation.

Distribution: Painted lady is one of the most widely distributed butterflies in the world, found on almost every continent. It occurs throughout the U.S. and southern Canada as either a winter resident or seasonal migrant.

Appearance: The caterpillar stage, known as thistle caterpillar, is generally black with some lighter flecking and numerous fleshy dark spines. It is almost always associated with the loose silken shelter it constructs among leaves. The adult stage of the insect is known as painted lady. It is generally orange with irregular black and white spotting on the wings.

Life History and Habits: Painted lady is an annual migrant in much of North America, spending the winter in more southerly areas, including Mexico. In spring, migrations are northward; in fall, to the south. Females lay eggs singly on host plants. Caterpillars produce a shelter of loose webbing by tying leaves together. When abundant, they extensively defoliate plants, and once the food plant is destroyed, the caterpillars migrate. Pupation occurs in a silvery chrysalis, usually some distance from the food plant. Adults emerge about 1 week after pupation and usually disperse from the area. Several overlapping generations are produced annually, with return southward migrations observed in late summer.

Related Species

Species closely related to painted lady include **red admiral** (*Vanessa atalanta*) which develops primarily on nettles, **west coast lady** (*V. annabella*) which develops on mallows, and **American lady** (*V. virginiensis*) which favors sunflower family plants.

A. Red admiral. *D. Shetlar.* **B.** Painted lady, adult of thistle caterpillar. *W. Cranshaw.* **C.** Thistle caterpillar. *W. Cranshaw.* **D.** Painted lady, adult of thistle caterpillar. *W. Cranshaw.* **E.** Young thistle caterpillar. *W. Cranshaw.* **F.** Thistle caterpillar, light phase. *F. Peairs.* **G.** Thistle caterpillar chrysalis. *W. Cranshaw.*

Other Brushfooted Butterflies

Mourning cloak (*Nymphalis antiopa*) is a dark purple-black butterfly with a yellowish border on the wing. It is one of the few butterflies that winters in the adult stage. Eggs are laid in spring in masses on aspen, cottonwood, poplar, willow, birch, elm, or hackberry. Larvae, known as **spiny elm caterpillars**, are generally dark colored with purple markings and feed as a group during early stages. Often entire branches may be stripped by larval feeding. Caterpillars subsequently pupate, and the adults present in summer remain in a reproductively dormant state, although they periodically feed at flowers, sap flows, and on rotting fruit.

Variegated fritillary (*Euptoieta claudia*) produces brightly colored larvae covered with fleshy spines. They feed on pansy, violet, johnny-jump-up, wild flax, and occasionally sedum, *Passiflora*, alyssum, and purslane. This species can be common and damaging to gardens and is sometimes known as pansyworm. It is primarily a southern species, overwintering as a full-grown larva, but it frequently strays into northern states during summer.

Hackberry butterfly (*Asterocampa celtis*) and **tawny emperor** (*A. clyton*) are associated with hackberry and sugarberry throughout the range of these plants. **Question-mark** (*Polygonia interrogationis*) develops on succulent foliage of elm, basswood, and hackberry in the eastern states. **Viceroy** (*Limenitis archippus*) is an unusual and interesting butterfly found throughout much of North America. The adults closely mimic the appearance of the monarch (*Danaus plexippus*), a milkweed butterfly that is distasteful because of the toxins it acquires from its caterpillar host plant (milkweed). Viceroy larvae mostly feed on willow, and the caterpillars resemble bird droppings.

[1] Lepidoptera: Nymphalidae

A. Mourning cloak, adult of spiny elm caterpillar. *W. Cranshaw.* **B.** Chrysalis of mourning cloak. *W. Cranshaw.*
C. Feeding group of spiny elm caterpillars. *D. Leatherman.* **D.** Spiny elm caterpillar, larva of mourning cloak. *D. Leatherman.* **E.** Larva of variegated fritillary. *W. Cranshaw.* **F.** Larva of hackberry butterfly. *W. Cranshaw.* **G.** Monarch butterfly. *W. Cranshaw.* **H.** Monarch caterpillar. *W. Cranshaw.* **I.** Viceroy caterpillar. *W. Cranshaw.* **J.** Variegated fritillary. *W. Cranshaw.* **K.** Monarch (left) vs. viceroy. *W. Cranshaw.*

BLISTER BEETLES

Blister beetles (Meloidae family)[1] are elongated beetles of moderate size. They have relatively soft wing covers that do not cover the tip of the abdomen. More than 300 species occur in North America, but few are commonly associated with gardens. The common name of the family is related to a defensive oil, cantharidin, that the beetles produce. Cantharidin can be highly irritating and is capable of producing blisters in high concentration. (When concentrated as contaminants in alfalfa hay, blister beetles can be a serious poisoning threat to horses.) Fortunately, most blister beetles found in gardens contain relatively low amounts of cantharidin and pose little threat to gardeners who may handle them.

Blister Beetles (Meloidae family)

Hosts: A wide range of plants. Legumes, including lupine, caragana, and alfalfa, are often particularly favored, but blister beetles may feed on leaves and flowers of a wide range of garden plants. The former prominence of some species on potatoes—prior to the spread of the Colorado potato beetle—led to them sometimes being referred to as "old fashioned potato bugs."

Damage: Only the adult form damages plants, by chewing leaves and foliage. Large numbers may defoliate plants rapidly before dispersing. Adults leave dark, irregular fecal spots on remaining leaves and stems.

Distribution and Appearance: Blister beetles occur throughout North America. Many are uniform in color, such as **ashgray blister beetle** (*Epicauta fabricii*) and **black blister beetle** (*E. pensylvanica*), the latter often the most common blister beetle in gardens east of the Rockies. A slight striping at the margins of the wing covers distinguishes **margined blister beetle** (*E. pestifera*), a common species in much of the midwestern U.S. Some blister beetles are prominently striped, such as **striped blister beetle** (*E. vittata*) and **threelined blister beetle** (*E. lemniscata*); others are spotted, such as **spotted blister beetle** (*E. maculata*). Blister beetles in the genus *Lytta* are often quite brightly colored with a metallic sheen. One odd group of blister beetles found in the western U.S. is the "oil beetles" (*Meloe* spp.). These large, fat, black beetles have short wing covers and are incapable of flight.

Life History and Habits: Larvae of the most common blister beetles (*Epicauta* spp.) develop by feeding on the egg pods of grasshoppers. Adults lay eggs near ground depressions, and the newly emerged larvae actively dig to the shallowly buried grasshopper eggs. Some of the most attractive blister beetles are those in the genus *Lytta*, which usually are iridescent green or dark blue. *Lytta* and *Meloe* species develop as parasites of bumble bees and other ground-nesting bees.

Blister beetles usually overwinter in the form of full-fed larvae in the soil and transform to the pupal stage in late winter. Adults begin to emerge in late spring. The adult of many species are strong fliers and often occur suddenly in small swarms on plants. One generation is produced per year.

[1] Coleoptera: Meloidae

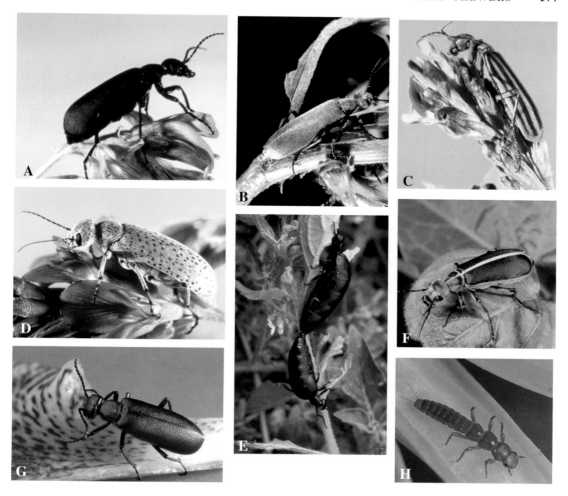

A. Black blister beetle. *J. Capinera.* **B.** Ashgray blister beetle. *J. Capinera.* **C.** Threelined blister beetle. *J. Capinera.*
D. Spotted blister beetle. *J. Capinera.* **E.** Mating pair of oil beetles. *W. Cranshaw.* **F.** Margined blister beetle. *R. Bessin.*
G. *Lytta* sp. blister beetle. *K. Gray.* **H.** First-stage larva of blister beetle. *K. Gray.*

LEAF BEETLES

Leaf beetles (Chrysomelidae family)[1] are one of the largest insect families in North America, containing about 1,500 species, several of which are serious plant pests. All species feed on plants in both adult and larval stages. Among the different species there is a wide range in the size of the adults ($\frac{1}{10}$ to nearly $\frac{1}{2}$ inch), and most are oval or elongate oval in form. Many leaf beetles are brightly colored, others have banded or striped patterning. Larvae possess a dark head and legs, but the legs are small in species that develop in plants or feed on roots, such as rootworms and some flea beetles.

Elm Leaf Beetle (*Pyrrhalta luteola*)

Hosts: Elm, particularly Siberian, rock, and English elm, but often American elm.

Damage: Both the adult and larval stages chew leaves. Adults chew circular holes in the leaf interior, whereas larvae skeletonize the lower leaf surface. In some areas an important secondary "damage" is the nuisance movement of overwintering adult beetles into homes.

Distribution: Now generally found throughout North America wherever elm hosts are grown.

Appearance: Larvae are generally black with some yellow striping and feed primarily on the underside of leaves. Overwintering adults are drab olive green. During the growing season, colors intensify and the beetles are marked with broad green and yellow bands.

Life History and Habits: Winter is spent in the adult stage in protected areas, including nearby buildings. In late April and early May the beetles emerge and move to elm trees to feed and mate. During this time their wing color changes to a yellow-green, signaling the end of the dormant winter condition (reproductive diapause). After a period of several weeks, females begin to lay masses of bright yellow eggs, typically attached to veins on the lower leaves. Larvae hatch after about 10 to 14 days and feed for about 3 weeks, molting three times in the course of development. They then crawl down the tree trunk in search of pupation sites. Most pupate at the base of the tree, but some rest in folds of bark furrows. Adults emerge in 10 to 15 days, and in most areas of the U.S. there is a second generation. In northern areas the beetles may feed briefly and then move to winter shelter without reproducing.

Other Leaf Beetles of Shade Trees, Shrubs, and Ornamentals

Larger elm leaf beetle (*Monocesta coryli*) is one of largest leaf beetles in North America, about $\frac{1}{2}$ inch in length. Much less damaging to elm than elm leaf beetle, it also feeds on foliage. It currently is found from Pennsylvania to Florida and west to Kansas.

A. Various life stages and injury of elm leaf beetle. *D. Leatherman.* **B.** Elm leaf beetle larvae. *W. Cranshaw.* **C.** Overwintering elm leaf beetles in diapause. Note change in color. *W. Cranshaw.* **D.** Larger elm leaf beetle. *G. J. Lenhard.* **E.** Elm leaf beetle. *W. Cranshaw.* **F.** Larger elm leaf beetle larvae. *G. J. Lenhard.* **G.** Pupae of elm leaf beetle. *W. Cranshaw.* **H.** Elm leaf beetle larva molting. *K. Gray.*

Pacific willow leaf beetle (*Pyrrhalta decora carbo*) develops on willow, poplar, and alder in the Pacific Northwest. Adults closely resemble elm leaf beetle but are dull black. A grayish or yellow-brown subspecies (*P. d. decora*) is present in the Prairie Provinces.

Viburnum leaf beetle (*Pyrrhalta viburni*) is a European species recently introduced into North America and currently found in New York, northern New England, and Ontario south to northeastern Pennsylvania. Larvae and adults feed on leaves of several types of viburnum and have been very damaging to some species; other viburnum species show resistance. Winter is spent as eggs glued to the underside of twigs. Larvae hatch in early May and initially feed in groups, skeletonizing the lower leaf surface. Older larvae feed more generally. Adults, which appear similar to drab-colored elm leaf beetles, appear in July and are present through September. Adult feeding produces oblong holes in the interior of leaves. One generation is produced annually.

Imported willow leaf beetle (*Plagiodera versicolor*) is a small species of leaf beetle (ca. ⅛ inch), metallic black to dark greenish blue. Eggs are laid in clusters on willow, particularly black and white willows. The young larvae feed as a group, skeletonizing the underside of leaves. Older larvae disperse, and adults may chew small holes in leaves. Two to three generations may occur through the range, which currently extends from New England to Virginia and west to Michigan.

Cottonwood leaf beetle (*Chrysomela scripta*) is found throughout much of North America and can be very damaging to cottonwood and poplar, particularly in the midwestern states. During early stages, larvae feed in groups and produce ragged skeletonizing injuries; later they feed more generally on leaves. Succulent new growth is favored. Adults feed on tender twigs and also skeletonize leaves, but they do much less damage than the larvae.

Cottonwood leaf beetle is a light tan, oval beetle about ⅜ inch long marked with elongate black spots. Widely distributed in North America, it is most common in the northern U.S. and southern Canada. Cottonwood leaf beetles winter as adults, scattered around previously infested trees in protected locations such as under leaf litter or clumps of grass. Shortly after leaves emerge, the adults begin to move back to trees and feed. After a few weeks females begin to lay eggs, which are deposited in clusters of a few dozen or more, on the undersurface of leaves. The larvae are black and grublike, with whitish spotting appearing as they age. When disturbed they can produce defensive chemicals that ooze from the light-colored glands on the body. Cottonwood leaf beetles pupate attached to the leaf, the old larval skin conspicuously present at the base of the black pupa. Adults from this first generation emerge in early summer and produce a second generation.

Several other *Chrysomela* species are found throughout North America, producing similar injuries to willow and aspen. All resemble cottonwood leaf beetle but have slightly different markings on the wing covers.

Elm calligrapha (*Calligrapha scalaris*), sometimes known as linden leaf beetle, is also similar in appearance. It feeds on foliage of elm, linden, alder, and willow in areas of the Midwest and Northeast. *C. bigsbayana* feeds on willow in the northeastern states.

A. Adult of Pacific willow leaf beetle. *K. Gray.* **B.** Cottonwood leaf beetle. *W. Cranshaw.* **C.** Viburnum beetle adult. *P. Weston.* **D.** Imported willow leaf beetles, mating pair. *D. Shetlar.* **E.** Cottonwood leaf beetle pupae. *W. Cranshaw.* **F.** Cottonwood leaf beetle egg mass. *W. Cranshaw.* **G.** Viburnum beetle larvae and damage. *P. Weston.* **H.** Cottonwood leaf beetle larvae and damage. *W. Cranshaw.* **I.** Cottonwood leaf beetle at egg hatch. *W. Cranshaw.* **J.** Cottonwood leaf beetle larvae. *W. Cranshaw.* **K.** Leaf beetle larvae (*Chrysomela* sp.) feeding on willow. *W. Cranshaw.* **L.** Imported willow leaf beetle larvae. *R. Childs.*

Coreopsis beetle (*C. californica coreopsivora*) skeletonizes foliage of coreopsis and ambrosia.

Strawberry rootworm (*Paria fragariae*) is a common insect associated with strawberry, and less commonly blueberry, in much of eastern North America and in California. Larvae feed on roots, but most damage is in the form of leaf chewing by adults, which feed at night. Feeding injuries may conspicuously riddle leaves, although effects on plant growth are usually minor.

Adults are about ⅛-inch-long, shiny black beetles with four light patches on the wing covers. They emerge from overwintering cover in spring and alternate between feeding and egg-laying at this time. Larvae develop during late spring and early summer. Adults are present again in late summer and also feed at this time before moving to winter shelters.

Adults of **cranberry rootworm** (*Rhabdopterus picipes*) produce conspicuous feeding injuries to rhododendron, camellia, photinia, and other shrubs. They feed at night on the emerging leaves, causing elongated, often crescent-shaped feeding holes in the mature leaves. Larvae develop on the roots of cranberry and blueberry but rarely cause much injury.

Leaf Beetles of Aquatic Plants

Waterlily leaf beetle (*Xanthogaleruca nymphaeae*) is associated with water lilies particularly yellow water lily, in eastern North America. Both larvae and adults feed on the upper leaf surface of floating lily leaves. Injuries by the insect also provide entry courts for leaf pathogens, contributing to decay. The overwintering stage is an adult that spends winter under protective debris in the vicinity of ponds. Adults are dark brown to yellow brown with a yellow underside. They become active in late spring and lay masses of eggs on the upper leaf surface. Eggs hatch in 4 to 5 days, and subsequent larval development is rapid, being completed in about 9 days. Younger larvae usually feed in small groups and skeletonize leaf surfaces. Older larvae chew holes in leaves. Pupation occurs on the leaf surface, and the pupal stage takes about 5 days to complete. In South Carolina, continual overlapping generations are produced into October.

Another common beetle associated with yellow water lily in the eastern U.S. is **false longhorn leaf beetle** (*Donacia piscatrix*). Damage is caused by the larvae, which are adapted to aquatic life. They feed on the underwater stems and petioles, deriving oxygen from a special spiracle on the end of the body that is inserted into the plant stems. Pupation also occurs in water. Adults are bronzy colored beetles, about ¼ inch long. One generation is produced annually.

 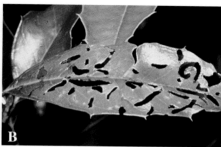

A. Feeding injury by cranberry rootworm adults. *J. Baker.* **B.** Feeding injury by cranberry rootworm adults. *J. Baker.*

Colorado Potato Beetle (*Leptinotarsa decemlineata*)

Hosts: Colorado potato beetle is most common and damaging to potato but also may be found on eggplant, nicotiana, petunia, and certain nightshade weeds.

Damage: Both the adult beetles and the larvae chew on foliage. Notching wounds along the leaf margin are more typical of adults, whereas larvae produce more ragged injuries and may soil foliage with excrement. Although plants can usually tolerate low levels of leaf loss (at least 25%), extensive and damaging defoliation occurs during outbreaks. Colorado potato beetle is considered the most important potato insect pest worldwide, being very damaging throughout much of Europe. Management is often complicated by high levels of pesticide resistance that have developed in many populations.

Distribution: Colorado potato beetle has spread dramatically over the past 150 years, and it is now generally found east of the Rockies, excluding some areas around the Gulf of Mexico and the Maritime Provinces. It is most damaging in the eastern and northcentral U.S.

Appearance: Adults are about ⅜ inch long, generally oval in shape and of convex body form. Alternating yellow and black stripes run along the back. Larvae are reddish or red-orange grubs with a dark head and some dark spotting. Colorado potato beetle produces masses of orange-yellow eggs, which are somewhat similar to those of lady beetles but larger and darker in color.

Other arthropods are sometimes confused with Colorado potato beetle. Certain blister beetles (p. 176) were sometimes known as old fashioned potato beetles because they were conspicuous on potato before Colorado potato beetle was present. Pillbugs (p. 502) are sometimes called potato bugs because of their habit of rolling in a ball. In some areas Jerusalem cricket (p. 58) is also called a potato bug.

Life History and Habits: Colorado potato beetles winter in the adult stage under cover near plantings infested the previous season. They are capable of flying over moderate distances and move back to fields and gardens in late spring as potatoes and other susceptible plants emerge. Eggs begin to be laid in late spring as potatoes first emerge. The orange-red larvae feed on leaves, originally in groups but later dispersing individually throughout the plant. After becoming full grown, they drop from the plant and pupate in the soil. In about 2 weeks, adult beetles emerge and feed on plants. A second generation is typically produced in southern areas of the range; one generation predominates in the north. After feeding for a few weeks, adults disperse to overwintering sheltering areas and remain dormant until the following season.

Related and Similar Leaf Beetles

In parts of the Midwest and High Plains a common insect that resembles Colorado potato beetle is **sunflower beetle** (*Zygogramma exclamationis*). Adults of both insects are very similar in appearance, although sunflower beetle is a bit smaller and its side stripes appear broken. Sunflower beetle larvae, which are pale green and grublike, feed on the leaves of sunflower and some related plants.

False potato beetle (*Leptinotarsa juncta*) is found over a broad area of the eastern U.S., from Maryland to eastern Texas. It feeds on horsenettle and other nightshade weeds.

A. Colorado potato beetle. *J. Capinera.* **B.** Damage by Colorado potato beetle. *W. Cranshaw.* **C.** Colorado potato beetle pupa. *W. Cranshaw.* **D.** Colorado potato beetle larvae at egg hatch. *W. Cranshaw.* **E.** Egg mass of Colorado potato beetle. *W. Cranshaw.* **F.** Colorado potato beetle larva. *W. Cranshaw.* **G.** Egg mass of Colorado potato beetle (larger) vs. twospotted lady beetle. *W. Cranshaw.* **H.** Sunflower beetles, mating pair. *W. Cranshaw.* **I.** Sunflower beetle adults and larva. *F. Peairs.* **J.** Colorado potato beetle laying eggs *K. Gray.* **K.** False potato beetle. *K. Gray.*

Asparagus Beetle (*Crioceris asparagi*)

Hosts: Asparagus.

Damage: Adult beetles chew pits in emerging spears, causing distortions of growth, and large numbers of the dark eggs may be laid on spears. Most injury, however, is caused by the sluglike larvae which chew the ferns, giving them a bleached appearance and reducing photosynthesis. Asparagus beetles are so abundant in some locations that their injuries can reduce subsequent yields and sometimes even kill plants. Moderate asparagus beetle injury, typical in regional gardens, is tolerated by plants with little or no effect.

Distribution: This insect of European origin is most common in the Midwest and in states along the Atlantic Coast. However, it can now be found in Colorado, California, and Oregon.

Appearance: The adult beetle is about ¼ inch long, of general metallic blue-black color. However, it is also marked with yellowish square spots and has some red along the margins of the wing cover and prothorax. Larvae are generally gray with a dark head and are rather sluglike in appearance.

Life History and Habits: Asparagus beetles overwinter in the adult stage around asparagus plantings. They become active in spring and fly to emerging spears and mate. The beetles chew on spears, and females lay upright, dark eggs on the plant. Eggs hatch in about 1 week, and the gray, grublike larvae feed on the ferns. The larvae become full grown in about 2 to 3 weeks and drop to the soil to pupate. Adults emerge and repeat the cycle. Two or three generations are completed in a season, with some larvae present into September.

Related Species

Spotted asparagus beetle (*Crioceris duodecimpunctata*) is often at least as common as asparagus beetle but is far less damaging to asparagus. The adult is a bright-orange beetle with black spots. However, larvae of this beetle develop in asparagus berries and do not damage the fern, causing little injury. Minor chewing on ferns and spears is done by adults.

A. Asparagus beetle, mating pair. *W. Cranshaw.* **B.** Asparagus beetle larvae. *W. Cranshaw.* **C.** Spotted asparagus beetle. *W. Cranshaw.* **D.** Asparagus beetle larvae. *W. Cranshaw.* **E.** Asparagus beetle eggs. *W. Cranshaw.* **F.** Damage to tip of spear by adult spotted asparagus beetle. *W. Cranshaw.* **G.** Asparagus beetle eggs. *K. Gray.*

Golden Tortoise Beetle (*Charidotella [= Metriona] bicolor*)
Mottled Tortoise Beetle (*Deloyala guttata*)
Striped Tortoise Beetle (*Agrioconota bivittata*)
Black-legged Tortoise Beetle (*Jonthonota nigripes*)
Argus Tortoise Beetle (*Chelymorpha cassidea*)

Hosts: Morning glory, sweetpotato, field bindweed, and related plants in the morning glory family (Convulvulaceae).

Damage: Adults and larvae feed on foliage, typically producing small holes in the leaf interior. Damage is usually insignificant, but the unusual appearance of the insects and the leaf riddling they produce may attract attention.

Distribution: Tortoise beetles are most common in the eastern U.S., particularly the southeast. Several species have ranges extending to the Rocky Mountains, Texas, and into Mexico.

Appearance: Adults are generally oval or squared, and most have metallic coloration, sometimes brilliant gold. They are sometimes mistaken for lady beetles and have been known as "gold bugs." Larvae are generally flattened, spiny, and vary in coloration from yellowish to reddish brown. Most carry cast skins and feces from the hind end, a habit sometimes lending them the name "peddlers."

Life History and Habits: Tortoise beetles winter as adults. During late spring and early summer they lay eggs, either singly or sometimes in small masses. Immature stages chew the underside of leaves, going through three larval stages. They pupate attached to the leaf, covered with fecal material and other debris collected during the larval stage. Adults feed for a brief period and then go into dormancy (diapause). With few exceptions one generation is produced per year.

Tortoise Beetles on Other Hosts

Eggplant tortoise beetle (*Gratiana pallidula*) is found throughout the eastern U.S., but is abundant only in the southern states. It often has spotted or striped markings. It makes small holes in the foliage of eggplant, potato, and various nightshade family weeds but does not cause serious injury. Larvae carry debris in a manner similar to that of other tortoise beetles.

Hemisphaerota cyanea is found in coastal areas of the southeastern U.S. to Texas where it feeds on foliage of Washington palms. It is dark gun-metal blue to purple and about 3/16 inch in length. The yellowish white larvae have conspicuous projections along the sides and cover themselves with fecal matter.

A. Tortoise beetle adult and larva. *W. Cranshaw.* **B.** Tortoise beetle with typical leaf-chewing injury. *W. Cranshaw.*
C. Tortoise beetles. *Courtesy Clemson University.* **D.** Tortoise beetle eggs. *W. Cranshaw.* **E.** Tortoise beetle larva. *W. Cranshaw.* **F.** Tortoise beetle pupa. *W. Cranshaw.* **G.** Tortoise beetle larva. *K. Gray.*

Case-Bearing Leaf Beetles

Sycamore leaf beetle (*Neochlamisus platani*) feeds on foliage of sycamore in both the adult and larval stages. River birch, hazel, and elm are additional, but infrequent, host plants. Eggs are laid singly on leaves and are covered by a bit of fecal material. Upon hatch the larvae feed on leaves and almost immediately begin constructing a case that covers the abdomen. This case is constructed primarily of frass the insect has produced mixed with some plant material, and it tapers at the tip. The larvae expand the case as they grow and feed on all of the leaf except for major veins. Pupation also occurs in the case, attached to the plant. Adults emerge in summer, feed for a period, and then move to winter shelter. Adults are small, bronze to reddish bronze beetles of irregular rounded body form, somewhat resembling a caterpillar dropping.

A related species, **blueberry casebeetle** (*N. cribripennis*), feeds on native lowland blueberry in eastern Canada and the northeastern U.S. It also has the larval habit of creating a case, which is somewhat bell shaped and covers the body.

Miscellaneous Leaf Beetles of Vegetable Crops

Red turnip beetle (*Entomoscelis americana*) can be a common vegetable garden pest in the northwestern U.S. and western Canada. In spring it feeds on most of the crucifers, including cabbage, broccoli, mustard, radish, watercress, and horseradish, and it can be damaging in both larval and adult stages. Larvae hatch from overwintered eggs and chew foliage, stems, and cotyledons of seedlings and young plants. Pupation occurs in the soil, and the adults may also feed on foliage for a brief period before undergoing a period of summer dormancy. Adults become active again in late summer, feed on foliage of crucifers, and lay eggs, which are the wintering stage.

Yellowmargined leaf beetle (*Microtheca ochroloma*) feeds on crucifers in some of the Gulf states. Both adults and larvae feed on foliage during spring. Only a single generation appears to be produced, with overwintered adults moving to plants in spring and laying eggs on the leaves. The life history of this introduced species is poorly understood in the U.S., but adults appear to go through a period of dormancy during the summer months.

Sweetpotato leaf beetle (*Typophorus nigritus*) occurs in most of the southeastern U.S. Adults feed on foliage of sweetpotato and morning glory, often in groups, and cause some localized defoliation. However, most damage to sweetpotato is produced by the larvae, which develop on the roots and stems. They may burrow deeply into the sweetpotato tubers or limit feeding to scarring of the surface. One generation is produced, with adults emerging from their overwintering pupal cells beginning in late May and early June.

Bean leaf beetle (*Ceratoma trifucata*) is common in the eastern U.S. It feeds on a wide variety of legumes and is most damaging to soybean but will damage garden beans, although is far less common than Mexican bean beetle (p. 202). It is particularly abundant on early-planted beans, and adults may cause serious defoliation of small plantings. Larvae develop on the roots of beans but apparently cause little injury. Two or three generations may occur annually.

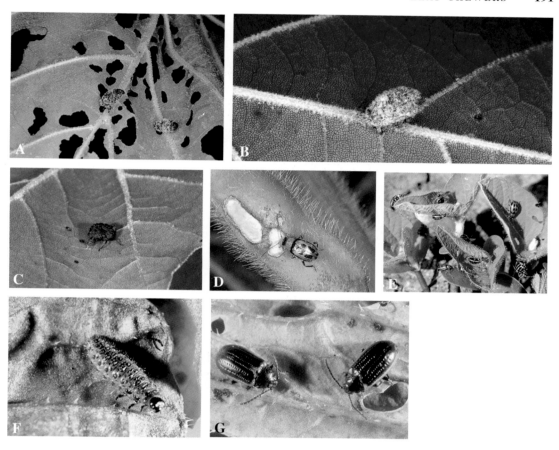

A. Sycamore leaf beetles feeding. *L. L. Hyche.* **B.** Sycamore leaf beetle larva. *L. L. Hyche.* **C.** Egg-laying by sycamore leaf beetle. *L. L. Hyche.* **D.** Bean leaf beetle feeding on pod. *M. E. Rice.* **E.** Bean leaf beetle on soybean. *M. E. Rice.* **F.** Yellowmargined leaf beetle larva. *J. Capinera.* **G.** Yellowmargined leaf beetle adults. *J. Capinera.*

Western Corn Rootworm (*Diabrotica virgifera virgifera*)

Hosts: Larvae develop solely on the roots of corn and a few related grasses. Adults are more general feeders of corn silk, various flowers (particularly of cucurbits), and foliage of a wide variety of plants.

Damage: Adult beetles feed on and chew off silks of corn. Although this damage is usually of little consequence, heavy infestations can occur in later plantings because beetles concentrate on these plants. Where silks are pruned severely during pollination, seed set can be poor. Beetles are also attracted to squash blossoms and can scar developing fruit of squash and melons. Larvae feed on corn roots and can weaken plants, causing them to fall over.

Distribution: Has expanded to currently cover a broad area west of the Rockies from Ontario to North Carolina. In Texas and Oklahoma a subspecies **Mexican corn rootworm** (*D. v. zeae*) occurs.

Appearance: A general yellow color and three dark stripes mark this species. However, the stripes are more indistinctly defined than in many similar-looking insects (e.g., striped cucumber beetle, three-lined potato beetle) and may coalesce. Adults are about ¼ inch in length.

Life History and Habits: Western corn rootworm beetles are present from late July through mid-September. Female beetles lay eggs during this time near the base of corn plants. Adults of both sexes may be found feeding on corn silks, tender corn leaves, and squash blossoms. Eggs hatch in June of the following year. The young wormlike larvae require corn roots to develop and quickly starve if corn is not replanted within a few feet of where eggs are laid. If corn roots are found, the larvae feed on them, sometimes causing severe root pruning. Pupation occurs in the soil during July, and adult beetles later emerge. There is one generation per year.

Related or Similar Species

Northern corn rootworm (*Diabrotica barberi*) is uniformly green and slightly smaller than western corn rootworm. Habits are similar, and this insect has spread eastward from its origin in Colorado and the Dakotas so that it is now found throughout the corn belt from Massachusetts to North Carolina.

Threelined potato beetle (*Lema trilinea*) is widely distributed in much of the U.S. Rarely seriously damaging, the grayish grublike larvae feed on various nightshade family plants, particularly tomatillo. Adults are generally yellow with some reddish markings and have distinct black stripes that give a close resemblance to striped cucumber beetle and western corn rootworm.

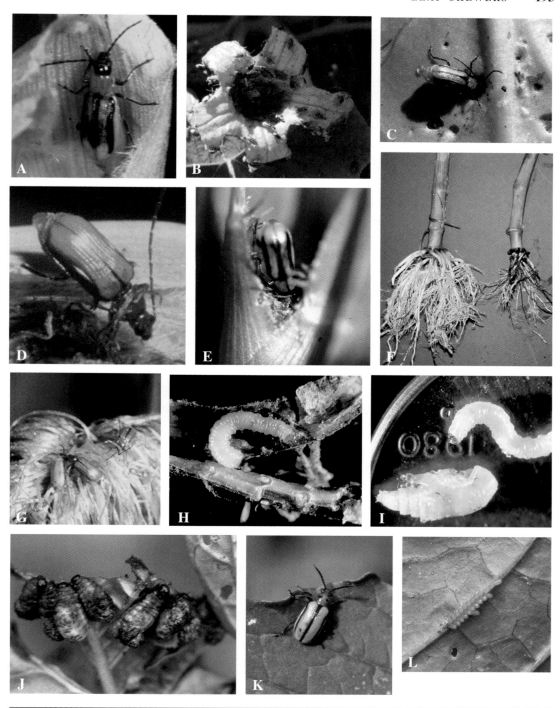

A. Western corn rootworm. *F. Peairs.* **B.** Western corn rootworm adults feeding at squash flower. *W. Cranshaw.*
C. Western corn rootworm feeding on cabbage leaf. *W. Cranshaw.* **D.** Mexican corn rootworm. *B. Drees.* **E.** Western
corn rootworm clipping corn silk. *W. Cranshaw.* **F.** Western corn rootworm root clipping. *F. Peairs.* **G.** Northern corn
rootworm. *W. Cranshaw.* **H.** Western corn rootworm larva in corn root. *J. Capinera.* **I.** Western corn rootworm larva
and pupa. *J. Capinera.* **J.** Threelined potato beetle larvae on tomatillo leaf. *W. Cranshaw.* **K.** Threelined potato beetle.
W. Cranshaw. **L.** Egg mass of threelined potato beetle. *W. Cranshaw.*

Striped Cucumber Beetle (*Acalymma vittata*)

Hosts: A wide variety of vegetables, although cucumber, melon, squash, and other cucurbits are preferred and most severely damaged.

Damage: Adult beetles feed on emergent seedlings and can retard development or even kill young plants. Later they may be found in large numbers in flowers of squash or melon and may chew pits in fruit. Larvae feed on the roots, causing little apparent injury, but may move into the rind of ripening melon fruit that rests on soil. Adult beetles can transmit a bacterium (*Erwinia tracheiphila*) that produces **bacterial wilt in cucurbits** and also transmits **cucumber mosaic virus**.

Distribution: Broadly distributed east of the Rockies. A closely related species, **western striped cucumber beetle** (*A. trivittatum*), is found in the Pacific states. The latter is yellowish orange with three black stripes and has a similar life history but is less often damaging.

Appearance: Adult beetles are about ⅕ inch long and bright yellow with three even, dark black stripes. The brighter yellow color, uniform width of the stripes, and presence of rows of minute indentations on the wing cover separate this insect from western corn rootworm, with which it is often confused.

Life History and Habits: Adult beetles spend winter under debris in the vicinity of gardens and fields. As temperatures warm in spring, they become active and feed on leaves and flowers (pollen) of several different trees and shrubs. When squash-family host plants emerge, the beetles move to these plants and chew seedlings. Eggs are laid in cracks around the base of the plants, and the hatching larvae feed on the roots for about a month. They then pupate in the soil, later emerging as adult beetles. There typically are two generations per season, but this may range from one to three depending on location and weather.

A. Striped cucumber beetle. *W. Cranshaw.* **B.** Mass of striped cucumber beetles. *W. Cranshaw.* **C.** Plants dying from infection with bacterial wilt. *R. Bessin.* **D.** Western striped cucumber beetles, mating pair. *K. Gray.* **E.** Striped cucumber beetle larvae on muskmelon rind. *W. Cranshaw.* **F.** Striped cucumber beetles and western corn rootworm adult (upper right) on ripe watermelon. *W. Cranshaw.*

Spotted Cucumber Beetle/Southern Corn Rootworm (*Diabrotica undecimpunctata howardi*)

Hosts: A wide range of plants, notably cucurbits and corn. Adults may be found in almost any type of flower.

Damage: Most damage is done by adults which chew on flowers, foliage, and rinds of ripening fruit. Larvae may tunnel roots and can stunt plants and sometimes may kill seedlings.

Distribution: East of the Rockies and ranges deep into Mexico. In the Pacific states a subspecies occurs known as **western spotted cucumber beetle** (*D. u. undecimpunctata*).

Appearance: Adults are yellowish or yellowish green and about ¼ inch long with 12 conspicuous black spots on the wings. The head is black. Larvae are pale colored and wormlike with a brown head.

Life History and Habits: In most areas, winter is usually spent in the adult stage in plant debris and particularly among plants that have not been completely killed by frosts. Spotted cucumber beetle may be active year-round in warmer climates, whereas in northern areas it may die out and infestations may result from migration from southern states during the growing season. Adults feed on pollen, corn silks, tender foliage, and other plant parts. Eggs are laid in soil cracks near seedlings of host plants in the spring, and larvae feed on roots for about 1 month. One to three generations may be produced during a growing season, but they overlap considerably and are difficult to distinguish.

Other Root-Damaging Leaf Beetles

Banded cucumber beetle (*Diabrotica balteata*) is originally from the southwestern U.S. and Mexico but has extended its range throughout the southern U.S. Adults feed on foliage and flowers of a wide range of vegetables. Larvae chew roots. Squash, melon, bean, and some crucifers are commonly damaged. Larval injury may also be severe in tubers of sweetpotato. The life history is similar to that of spotted cucumber beetle, and there can be nearly continual breeding in areas of warm climate. Also found feeding on squash in the southwestern U.S. is *Paranapiacaba trincincta*, a colorful leaf beetle with black and white spotting.

Grape colaspis (*Colaspis brunnea*) is a minor pest of corn and soybeans in many midwestern and eastern states. Adults cause minor injuries when they feed on leaves of various plants, particularly legumes such as bean and soybean. Grape, strawberry, apple, corn, okra, beet, and various weeds such as smartweed and dock are other adult host plants. However, most damage occurs from larval feeding on plant roots which can cause stunting. Grasses, corn, clover, alfalfa, and soybean—but not fruits and vegetables—are larval hosts. Grape colaspis overwinters as a partially grown larva in various stages. It resumes feeding in spring and pupates in the soil. Adults have usually emerged by mid- to late June and briefly feed before females begin to lay eggs. The eggs are laid in masses at the base of plants, and the larvae then move to the roots. One generation is produced annually.

[1] Coleoptera: Chrysomelidae

A. Spotted cucumber beetle, also known as southern corn rootworm, adult. *F. Peairs.* **B.** Damage to bean pod by spotted cucumber beetle. *K. Gray.* **C.** Damage to bean leaves by spotted cucumber beetle. *K. Gray.* **D.** *Paranapiacaba trincincta. W. Cranshaw.* **E.** Banded cucumber beetle. *F. Peairs.* **F.** Western spotted cucumber beetle. *K. Gray.*

FLEA BEETLES

Flea beetles are a subfamily (Alticinae)[1] of the leaf beetles. Several species are common pests of a wide range of vegetable and flower crops; a few are associated with trees and shrubs. Flea beetles are among the smallest of the leaf beetles, typically ⅟₁₅ to ⅙ inch. Characteristically they possess very large rear legs that enable them to jump, and the combination of small size and jumping ability lend them their name. Many flea beetles are uniformly metallic colored; others may have stripes or spots.

Adult flea beetles are usually the most damaging stage to plants. The beetles chew small pits, or shothole wounds, in leaves. Small plants may be killed or stunted by these wounds. Wounds may also damage crops grown for greens. Many flea beetles are specific in their habits, restricting feeding to certain plant families or genera. Some species, for example, feed only on potato, eggplant, and other members of the nightshade family (Solanaceae); others have a taste for broccoli, cabbage, and other mustard family crops (Brassicaceae).

Flea Beetles That Develop Belowground

Most flea beetle species develop below ground. Eggs are usually laid in soil cracks around the base of plants. The minute, wormlike larvae primarily feed on small roots, producing little damage. Pupation also occurs in the soil. A single generation is common with some species; others may have two to three generations per year. All winter in the adult stage under protective debris and move to host plants in spring.

Several flea beetles in the genus *Epitrix* are associated with nightshade family plants. They are among the smallest flea beetles (⅟₁₆ inch) and uniformly colored from black to dark brown. **Potato flea beetle** (*E. cucumeris*) is a common species east of the Rockies that chews small holes in the leaves of tomato, potato, and some other nightshade family plants. It is replaced in much of the western U.S. by **western potato flea beetle** (*E. subcrinita*). Less widely distributed but potentially more damaging is **tuber flea beetle** (*E. tuberis*), found from Colorado into the Pacific Northwest. Larvae produce shallow scars in potato tubers in the larval stage, and adults produce characteristic shotholes in leaves. **Tobacco flea beetle** (*E. hirtipennis*) commonly feeds on eggplant, tobacco, and potato. It has bronze coloration and is predominant in the southern half of the U.S. In much of the eastern states, eggplant is also a favored host of **eggplant flea beetle** (*E. fuscula*).

Cabbage family plants host several flea beetles in the genus *Phyllotreta*, some of which can be extremely damaging, particularly to seedlings. **Western black flea beetle** (*P. pusilla*) is a small, shiny black species that is injurious to a wide range of crucifers and throughout much of the western half of the northern U.S. and southern Canada. It has a considerably wider host range than other members of this genus and also is found on other vegetables such as beet, potato, and lettuce. **Crucifer flea beetle** (*P. cruciferae*) is an introduced species now widespread in Canada and the northern U.S. Adults are shiny metallic blue-black. A very similar species, though less damaging, is the native **cabbage flea beetle** (*P. albionica*). Other members of this genus are generally pale brown with dark striping of some pattern. These include **western striped flea beetle** (*P. ramosa*) in California, **horseradish flea beetle** (*P. armoraciae*), and **striped flea beetle** (*P. striolata*).

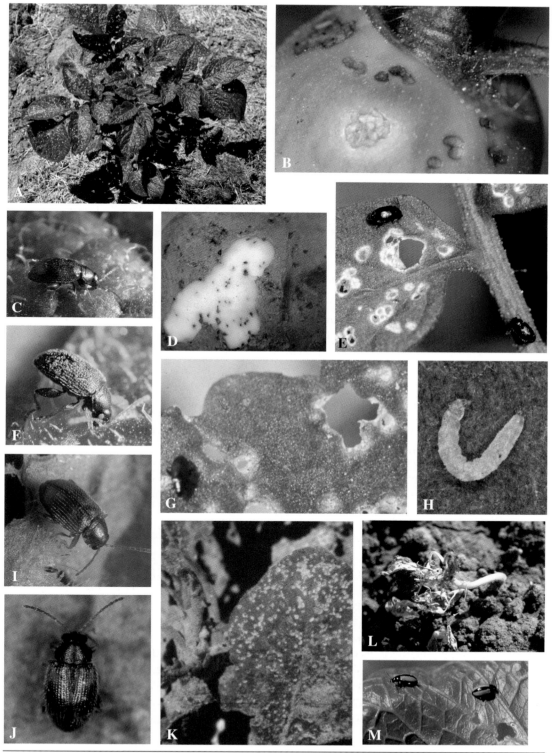

A. Potato flea beetle injury. *W. Cranshaw*. **B.** Potato flea beetle damage to tomato fruit. *W. Cranshaw*. **C.** Western potato flea beetle. *K. Gray*. **D.** Damage to potato by tuber flea beetle. *W. Cranshaw*. **E.** Potato flea beetle damage to tomato leaf. *W. Cranshaw*. **F.** Tuber flea beetle. *K. Gray*. **G.** Western black flea beetle. *W. Cranshaw*. **H.** Western black flea beetle larva. *W. Cranshaw*. **I.** Tobacco flea beetle. *K. Gray*. **J.** Tobacco flea beetle. *W. Cranshaw*. **K.** Tobacco flea beetle damage to eggplant. *W. Cranshaw*. **L.** Tomato transplant killed by potato flea beetles. *W. Cranshaw*. **M.** Horseradish flea beetles. *W. Cranshaw*.

Also among the smallest flea beetles are *Chaetocnema* species. Most feed strictly on grasses, and **corn flea beetle** (*C. pulicaria*) is an important species in parts of the Midwest where it may transmit the bacteria that produce the disease Stewart's wilt of corn. **Toothed flea beetle** (*C. denticulata*) also occurs in the midwestern and northeastern states on corn and other grasses. **Sweetpotato flea beetle** (*C. confinis*) is a common species, particularly in the southern U.S. where it develops on sweetpotato, dichondra, morning glory, and raspberry. In southern California **dichondra flea beetle** (*C. repens*) can be a pest where dichondra is grown as ground covers and lawns. Adults cut small crescent-shaped holes in leaves. More damage is done by larvae, which feed on roots and burrow into the crown of the plants, causing wilting and even death.

Striping is also found among flea beetles in the genus *Systena*, which tend to be slightly larger species (⅛ inch). **Palestriped flea beetle** (*S. blanda*) is not only one of the most widely distributed flea beetles of North America but has the broadest host range. It commonly damages squash family plants, bean, corn, sunflower, lettuce, potato, and many weeds. Closely resembling it is **elongate flea beetle** (*S. elongata*) which overlaps considerably in geographic range and host range. **Redheaded flea beetle** (*S. frontalis*) is common in the Midwest where it feeds on cabbage, bean, beet, corn, potato, forsythia, dogwood, and weeds such as smartweed. It is ⅙ inch long and black with a reddish yellow head.

Hop flea beetle (*Psylliodes punctulata*) occurs throughout the northern U.S. and southern Canada. It also can be found on a wide range of plants including cabbage, cucumber, hops, strawberry, tomato, and beet. Adults feed on the underside of leaves. Hop flea beetle is one of the first flea beetles to appear in spring. It produces a single generation annually, with adults emerging in August and moving to winter in sheltering debris.

Flea Beetles That Develop on Foliage

A few flea beetles, including some of the largest species, develop on foliage. Eggs are laid in masses on the leaves, and young larvae often feed gregariously, producing skeletonizing injuries typical of many other leaf beetles. Older larvae and adults chew larger holes in foliage.

Probably most commonly encountered is **spinach flea beetle** (*Disonycha xanthomelas*). It is one of the larger flea beetles (⅕ inch), with greenish black wing covers, a yellow thorax, and a black head. Although it occasionally chews spinach and beets, it is often most abundant on pigweed. Other *Disonycha* are striped or spotted and are associated with perennials such as willow and penstemon.

Shiny metallic flea beetles found on various trees and shrubs are in the genera *Macrohaltica* and *Altica*. **Grape flea beetle** (*Altica chalybea*) is found throughout the eastern U.S. on grape, Virginia creeper, apple, beech, elm, and plum. Buds are tunneled by adults of the first generation, causing the most damage. Later in the season leaves are skeletonized by larvae. *A. litigata* is an occasional leaf-chewing pest of crape myrtle and evening primrose in the southern states. Evening primrose and strawberry are hosts for **strawberry flea beetle** (*A. ignata*) in the eastern U.S., and willow is the host of *A. bimarginata* in the west. **Apple flea beetle** (*Altica foliacea*) is a metallic bright green or shiny blue species found throughout most of North America. Adults and larvae feed on the foliage of apple, crabapple, grape, evening primrose, willow, guara, rose, sedum, and fuschia. In the southwest, **steelblue grapevine flea beetle** (*H. torquata*) feeds on grape and evening primrose. **Alder flea beetle** (*Macrohaltica ambiens*) is a transcontinental species associated with alder.

Currant flea beetle (*Blepharida rhois*) is a rather large species common in northern areas east of the Rockies. Adults have striped patterning and a general shape similar to that of a small Colorado potato beetle. They develop on currant, sumac, and skunkbrush.

---

[1] Coleoptera: Chrysomelidae (Alticinae)

A. Palestriped flea beetle. *W. Cranshaw.* **B.** Redheaded flea beetle. *D. Shetlar.* **C.** *Disonycha alteranta. K. Gray.* **D.** Grape flea beetle adult. *J. Ogrodnik/NY Agricultural Experiment Station.* **E.** Grape flea beetle larva. *J. Ogrodnik/NY Agricultural Experiment Station.* **F.** Elongate flea beetle. *K. Gray.* **G.** Adult of *Altica bimarginata*, a western willow-feeding flea beetle. *K. Gray.* **H.** Alder flea beetle larvae and damage. *D. Leatherman.* **I.** Currant flea beetle. *W. Cranshaw.* **J.** Apple flea beetle. *W. Cranshaw.* **K.** Spinach flea beetle. *F. Peairs.*

MEXICAN BEAN BEETLE

Mexican bean beetle is a species of lady beetle, one of the few members of this important and beneficial family (Coccinellidae)[1] that develops feeding on plants rather than as a predator of insects.

Mexican Bean Beetle (*Epilachna varivestis*)

Hosts: Garden beans and field beans primarily; soybean and cowpea are less commonly damaged.

Damage: Mexican bean beetle is a plant-feeding lady beetle. Larvae feed on the underside of bean leaves in a typical skeletonizing manner, producing a lacy appearance. Adults primarily chew leaves but also may feed on green pods.

Distribution: Originally restricted to the southeastern U.S. and Mexico but has greatly extended its range and is now common in most areas east of the Rockies. It tends to be more abundant and damaging in southern areas of this range.

Appearance: Adults are a typical oval form, similar to that of other lady beetles, and slightly larger than most. General color ranges from nearly mustard yellow to copper, with those present late in the season often reddish brown. Each wing cover is marked with eight dark spots, arranged in three rows (3-3-2). Larvae are yellow or orange-yellow and quite spiny.

Life History and Habits: Mexican bean beetles winter in the adult stage in protected areas along the edges of plantings and emerge over an extended period in late spring. Females lay masses of yellow eggs on the lower leaf surface. The larvae feed for about 3 weeks, skeletonizing the lower surface of the leaf. When full grown they pupate underneath a leaf, often in small groups. One generation is typical in the western and northern states, but up to three may occur in the southeast. Greatest feeding and injury typically occur in late July and August.

Related Species

Squash beetle (*Epilachna borealis*) is a minor pest of squash family plants and is found in the eastern U.S., particularly in the Atlantic states. Adults and larvae chew foliage in a similar manner as the Mexican bean beetle but are rarely seriously damaging. Two generations annually occur in southern areas, one in the north.

[1] Coleoptera: Coccinellidae

A. Mexican bean beetle adult. *J. Capinera.* **B.** Mexican bean beetle laying eggs. *K. Gray.* **C.** Mexican bean beetle larvae. *J. Capinera.* **D.** Mexican bean beetle egg mass. *F. Peairs.* **E.** Mexican bean beetle pupa. *W. Cranshaw.* **F.** Squash beetle. *Courtesy Clemson University.* **G.** Mexican bean beetle damage to pole bean. *W. Cranshaw.* **H.** Mexican bean beetle feeding injury to leaves. *W. Cranshaw.*

CHAPTER FOUR

Leafminers

Some of the most discriminating feeders among the insects are the leafminers. These insects tunnel between the upper and lower leaf surfaces, feeding on the soft inner tissue and avoiding the tough epidermis. Immature stages of many different groups of insects share the leafmining habit, including the larvae of various flies, small moths, beetles, and sawflies. They are often classified by the pattern of the mine they create. Serpentine leaf mines meander across the leaf, gradually increasing in width as the insect grows. More common are various blotch leaf mines, which are an irregular but generally round form. One subgroup of these is the tentiform leaf mines, bulging blotchlike mines produced by moth larvae. Species that mine needles are known as needleminers.

LEAFMINING FLIES

Spinach Leafminer (*Pegomya hyoscyami*)[1]

Hosts: Spinach, chard, beet, lambsquarter, and related weeds.

Damage: The immature maggots tunnel through older leaves. The large, dark blotchy mines that are produced destroy the leaves for use as greens, although effects on plant growth appear to be minimal.

Distribution: Generally distributed except in the southern and southwestern U.S.

Appearance: The larvae are pale-colored, generally cylindrical maggots found in the leaf mines. Adults are small (ca. ⅕ to ⅓ inch) gray or grayish brown flies.

Life History and Habits: The insect overwinters in the soil as a pupa, emerging in midspring. The adult flies lay small masses of white eggs on the underside of older leaves. Upon hatching, the young maggots tunnel into the leaves, where they feed, typically for 2 to 3 weeks. When full grown, they cut through the leaf, drop to the ground, and pupate in the soil. Several generations may be completed during the season, but activity largely ceases in midsummer, with most damage occurring on the cooler sides of the growing season.

Note: **Beet leafminer** (*P. betae*) is now considered a separate species from spinach leafminer, although confusion remains on this point. Host range, life history, and other habits appear similar for both species.

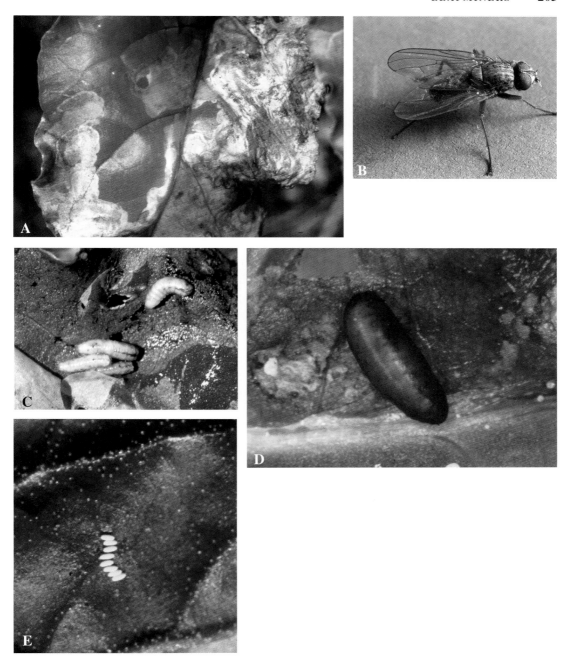

A. Spinach leafminer damage to beet. *W. Cranshaw.* **B.** Adult spinach leafminer. *K. Gray.* **C.** Spinach leafminer larvae exposed in mine. *W. Cranshaw.* **D.** Spinach leafminer pupa. *W. Cranshaw.* **E.** Spinach leafminer eggs. *W. Cranshaw.*

Vegetable (or Serpentine) Leafminer (*Liriomyza sativae*)[2]

Hosts: Many vegetables including bean, tomato, potato, onion, pepper, squash, and melon.

Damage: Larvae make thin, meandering serpentine mines. Puncture wounds are made by the ovipositor of the female during egg-laying or to produce fluid for feeding, and these may give the leaves a stippled appearance. Serious problems often are associated with insecticide use that adversely affects the many natural enemies that attack this insect.

Distribution: Predominately a problem in warmer areas of the southern U.S. but occasionally ranges northward into the Midwest.

Appearance: Adults are small (ca. $\frac{1}{15}$ inch) yellow and black flies. Larvae are pale, slightly greenish maggots found in mines.

Life History and Habits: Eggs are inserted into foliage, producing small puncture wounds. Larvae develop rapidly under warm temperatures and may complete development in under 2 weeks. Often they then cut the leaf surface, drop to the soil, and pupate; pupation occasionally occurs in the mined leaf. Numerous overlapping generations occur during the year.

Other Vegetable Leafminers

American serpentine leafminer (*Liriomyza trifolii*),[2] also known as **chrysanthemum leafminer**, is often mistaken for vegetable leafminer. It also has a wide range of hosts but is particularly damaging to flower crops, notably chrysanthemum. Primarily limited to warmer climates, it has spread widely among greenhouse crops. Problems are particularly severe following certain pesticide-use practices that devastate natural enemies. A closely related species of similar habit is **pea leafminer** (*L. huidobrensis*). Widely distributed in South and Central America, it is found in areas of the western U.S. **Cabbage leafminer** (*L. brassicae*) also is primarily a tropical species but may be common in the southern U.S. Cabbage, broccoli, mustard, and nasturtium are among the reported hosts.

Asparagus miner (*Ophiomyia simplex*)[2] is an introduced species that has spread through most of the East Coast states and is found in some areas of the Midwest. Larvae develop at the base of asparagus stems, mining the tissues. In large numbers they may girdle the stem, causing yellowing and dieback. More damage is thought to occur from incidental spread of Fusarium root-rotting fungi. Adults are tiny, shiny black flies about $\frac{1}{8}$ inch long.

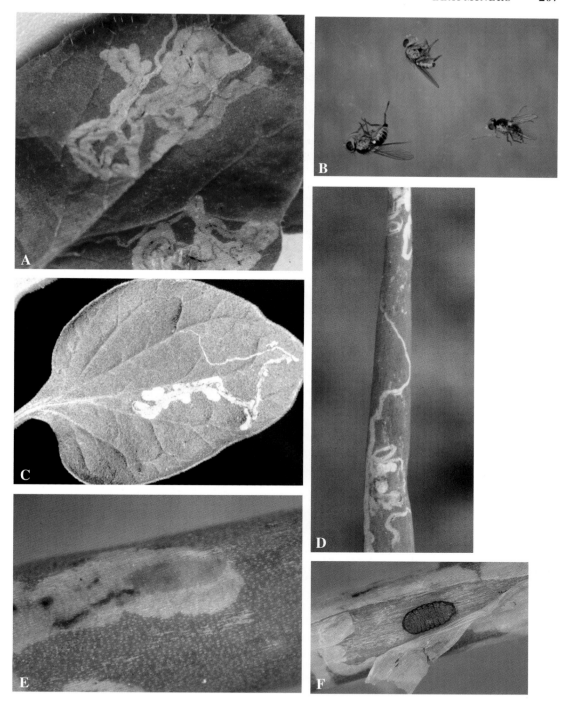

A. Vegetable leafminer on kale. *W. Cranshaw.* **B.** Adult vegetable leafminers. *W. Cranshaw.* **C.** Vegetable leafminer injury to tomato. *Courtesy Clemson University.* **D.** Vegetable leafminer tunneling of onion. *W. Cranshaw.* **E.** Vegetable leafminer larva in leaf mine of onion. *W. Cranshaw.* **F.** Vegetable leafminer pupa. *W. Cranshaw.*

Holly Leafminers (*Phytomyza ilicis, P. ililocola,* and others)[2]

Hosts: Various hollies (*Ilex* spp.), with each species having a specific associated leafminer.

Damage: Larvae make serpentine mines in foliage. Small dimples also occur when females insert their ovipositor to lay eggs or to produce oozing sap on which they feed.

Distribution: Primarily important in the eastern and southern U.S. where *Ilex* hosts occur. Some species are also present in the Pacific Northwest.

Appearance: Larvae are tiny, pale yellow maggots found in the mines. Adults are small gray flies.

Life History and Habits: The **native holly leafminer** (*P. ilicicola*) overwinters as a larva in the mine, pupating in early spring. Adults are present for a period of about 6 weeks, and females insert eggs in the underside of newly developing leaves. The larvae feed in the leaf, creating a gradually expanding mine that is blotchlike at the end. Much of the mining occurs during late fall and winter. Usually leafminers associated with deciduous holly have several generations per year, whereas those associated with evergreen hollies have a single generation.

Other Leafmining Flies of Ornamental Plants

Several species of leafminers in the genus *Phytomyza*[2] are associated with columbine. *P. aquilegiana* and *P. columbinae* produce blotchlike mines, whereas those of *P. aquilegivora* are more serpentine. *P. delphinivora* and other species develop in larkspur, delphinium, and aconite. Little is known about the biology of these species, but two generations normally appear to be produced annually. Chrysanthemum, marguerite, daisy, and several other composites may be hosts for *P. atricornis* or *P. chrysanthemi*. Blotch mines on many of the same hosts are also produced by *Amauromyza maculosa*,[2] a common species in Florida. Three to six larvae may commonly occur in each mine.

Small shotholes and leaf tatters in oak leaves may be due to wounds produced by **oak shothole leafminer** (*Agromyza viridula*).[2] The adult females produce puncture wounds with their sharp ovipositor in newly emergent leaves less than 2 inches expanded. This is done often to produce fluids on which the flies feed; eggs are sometimes inserted into leaves. The developing fly larva develops as a leaf miner, and the area drops from the leaf. As the leaves continue to expand, the holes produced by adult punctures and larval feeding continue to expand. One generation is normally produced annually.

Boxwood leafminer (*Monarthropalpus flavus*)[3] produces small blistered blotches in areas of the leaf where larvae feed. Most species of boxwood are affected, and this is often considered the most serious pest of this ornamental plant. This is an introduced insect, currently found in areas of New England and the mid-Atlantic states. Adults are tiny orange gnatlike flies that lay eggs in mid- to late spring. There is one generation per year.

Trunks and branches of several thin-barked woody plants may host **cambium miners** which make meandering tunnels just beneath the bark surface. Most such injuries are produced by larvae of small flies in the genus *Phytobia*,[2] although cambium mining may also occur from the activity of certain moths (*Marmara* spp.)[4] and beetles. Cambium mining injuries are cosmetic and produce no significant harm to affected plants. Similar shallow mining of the rind of citrus is produced by **citrus peelminer** (*M. salictella*) in the southwestern states.

[1] Diptera: Anthomyiidae; [2] Diptera: Agromyzidae; [3] Diptera: Cecidomyiidae; [4] Lepidoptera: Gracillariidae

A. Adult holly leafminer. *K. Gray.* **B.** Adult holly leafminer. *D. Shetlar.* **C.** Holly leafminer larva exposed from mine. *D. Shetlar.* **D.** Holly leafminer damage. *K. Gray.* **E.** Egg-laying scars produced by holly leafminer. *W. Cranshaw.* **F.** Columbine leafminer, exposed larva. *W. Cranshaw.* **G.** Columbine leafmine and oviposition punctures. *W. Cranshaw.* **H.** Boxwood leafminer injuries. *A. Antonelli.* **I.** Surface tunnels of citrus peelminer. *W. Cranshaw.* **J.** Boxwood leafminer adults. *J. Baker.* **K.** Boxwood leafminer larva. *Courtesy Clemson University.*

LEAFMINING SAWFLIES[1]

Birch Leafminer (*Fenusa pusilla*)

Hosts: Birch.

Damage: Larvae develop in leaves, creating large, dark blotch mines. After the insects exit, the mined areas wrinkle and turn light brown. Defoliation occurs on heavily damaged leaves. Stresses from repeated defoliation can increase risk of infestation by bronze birch borer.

Distribution: Birch leafminer is an introduced European species currently found in the northern half of the U.S. and southern Canada, east of the Rockies. It is particularly damaging in the Midwest.

Appearance: The mature larvae are ¼ inch long, slightly flattened, and yellowish white in color. They, and their dark droppings, are found in the mined leaf. Adults are black, thick-waisted wasps, about ¼ inch long.

Life History and Habits: Birch leafminer winters in the soil as a prepupae, pupating in spring as soils warm (April). Adults first appear in spring, coincident with when the first leaves are about half grown, and prefer to mate and oviposit on upper leaves in sunny areas. Small oviposition punctures are visible as dark spots, although eggs are not always laid. Larvae hatch and mine out the middle layers of the leaf; several mines may grow together to form one large blotch mine. After 2 to 3 weeks, the larvae cut exit holes, drop to the ground, and burrow into the soil to make a pupal chamber. After another 2 to 3 weeks, the second-generation adults emerge and the cycle repeats. Normally there are two generations per year, although if conditions are dry many of the first-generation wasps remain dormant and do not emerge until the second year. As attacks are limited to new foliage, subsequent generations are less damaging and develop primarily in the crown of the tree.

Other Leafmining Sawflies

European alder leafminer (*Fenusa dohrnii*) is a closely related species that produces blotch leafmines on alder. **Hawthorn leafminer** (*Profenusa canadensis*) produces blotchlike mines in the tips of leaves. *Crataegus* x *crusgalli* is most commonly damaged in Illinois, and three to four generations may occur.

Elm leafminer (*Kaliofenusa ulmi*) is primarily associated with English elm, American elm, and hybrids. Eggs are inserted in foliage in late spring. Early-stage larvae produce serpentine mines that gradually enlarge and turn blotchlike as they mature. One generation is produced annually.

Blackberry leafminer (*Metallus rubi*) mines the edges and tips of blackberry and dewberry, creating blotchlike mines. Two generations occur in Connecticut, with the first adults present in May and early June and second-generation adults present in August.

[1] Hymenoptera: Tenthredinidae

A. Birch leafminer injury. *W. Cranshaw.* **B.** Hawthorn leafminer injury. *S. Rachesky.* **C.** Elm leafminer larvae in blotch mines. *W. Cranshaw.* **D.** Elm leafminer adult. *W. Cranshaw.* **E.** Egg-laying wounds produced by elm leafminer. *W. Cranshaw.* **F.** Elm leafminer injury. *D. Leatherman.* **G.** Elm leafminer larva. *W. Cranshaw.*

LEAFMINING MOTHS

Spotted Tentiform Leafminer (*Phyllonorycter blancardella*)[1]

Hosts: Apple and crabapple.

Damage: Larvae make small (½ inch) mines close to the lower surface of the leaf. In high populations there can be reduction in fruit quality, which can contribute to premature fruit drop.

Distribution: Introduced from Europe. The range has expanded to include most of the midwestern and northeastern U.S. and eastern Canada.

Appearance: Adults are tiny moths with a wingspan of about ⅓ inch. The wings are patterned with gold, black, and white. Larvae are cream colored and flattened during early stages, developing a more typical caterpillar form and functional legs in later stages.

Life History and Habits: Adults emerge in spring at bud break, mate, and deposit their eggs on the young leaves as they appear. The young larvae enter leaves and feed on sap from cells they damage while feeding (sap-feeding stage). Older larvae chew small pits in the leaves, producing small translucent areas in them (tissue-feeding stage); they also spin silken threads across the mined tissues, and when the silk dries and shrinks, the area forms a raised ridge (tentiform leaf mine). By mid- to late June the larvae pupate in the mine. Just before adult emergence, the pupae wiggle halfway out of the mine and leave the pupal skin in this position. Second-generation adults appear in late June and early July. There are three generations per year, the last one spending the winter as a pupa in the fallen leaves.

Related Leafminers

In western orchards other *Phyllonorycter*[1] species predominate. **Western tentiform leafminer** (*P. elmaella*) develops in leaves of apple and cherry; **tentiform leafminer** (*P. mispilella*) feeds on apple, pear, and cherry. Some 17 species of rosaceous plants support **apple blotch leafminer** (*P. crataegella*), a species found in the northern U.S. and southern Canada. Habits of all these species are similar in most respects to those of spotted tentiform leafminer.

Numerous other *Phyllonorycter* species occur on other plants throughout North America. **Aspen blotch leafminer** (*P. tremuloidiella*) is often abundant on aspen in the northern U.S. and southern Canada. *P. salicifoliella* and *P. nipigon* make tentiform mines in the lower leaf surface of poplar and willow. **Maple leafminer** (*P. aceriella*) mines the upper leaf surface of red and sugar maples. Squarish mines are characteristic of *P. lucetiella* on basswood.

Cherry leafminer (*Nepticula slingerlandella*)[2] is currently an infrequent pest of cherry and plum but has had historical outbreaks in cherry orchards of the Great Lakes states. Adults emerge from overwintered pupae and lay eggs on the underside of leaves in June. The larvae tunnel under the upper epidermis, so their meandering mines are most visible from the top surface. Cherry leafminer caterpillars are about ⅛ inch when full grown and opaque greenish white. One generation is produced annually, with winter spent as a pupa in debris around the base of infested trees.

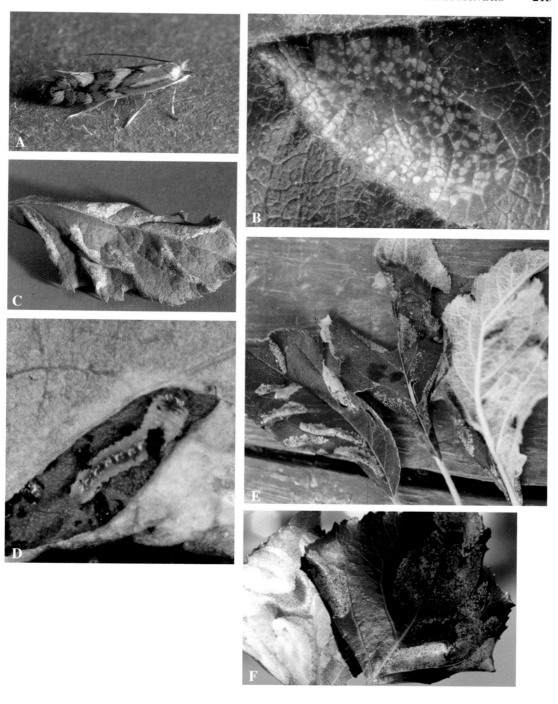

A. Apple blotch leafminer. *K. Gray.* **B.** Top view of leaf mine produced by spotted tentiform leafminer. *D. Shetlar.* **C.** Tentiform-type mines produced by apple blotch leafminer. *K. Gray.* **D.** Larva exposed from tentiform-type mine in cottonwood. *W. Cranshaw.* **E.** Tentiform leafminer injury to apple. *E. Nelson.* **F.** Tentiform leafminer injuries to cottonwood. *W. Cranshaw.*

Lilac Leafminer (*Caloptilia syringella*)[1]

Hosts: Lilac, privet. Rarely ash, euonymus.

Damage: Larvae first produce a blotch mine on the foliage, then tie and feed on the leaves. The ragged leaves and associated leafrolling can seriously detract from a plant's appearance.

Distribution: Primarily a western species found in northern states and southern Canada.

Appearance: Adults are small moths (ca. ½ inch long) that fold their wings tubelike over the body when at rest. The wings are generally gray with reddish brown patches, and there is some light striping across the body. Larvae are glossy green and found in mines or folded leaves. Younger larvae are more flattened than older larvae.

Life History and Habits: Lilac leafminer spends the winter as a pupa or full-grown larva in the mines of dropped leaves. The adult moths emerge in spring after leaves emerge and lay eggs in small groups on the leaves. Newly hatched larvae tunnel directly into the leaf from under the egg. As they develop and grow larger, they excavate a blotchlike mine, and tunneling by several larvae may coalesce. As the larvae become nearly mature, they leave the leaf mine and tie the edge of the leaf with silk. They continue to feed in the folded leaf and later pupate. There are probably two generations per season.

Related Species

Boxelder leafminer (*Caloptilia negundella*)[1] feeds on boxelder and causes injuries similar to those of lilac leafminer. There are two generations per year, and the life cycle is likely similar to that of lilac leafminer. **Azalea leafminer** (*C. azaleella*) is found commonly in the eastern and southeastern U.S. and incidentally in Pacific states. It is associated with low-growing azalea, and two generations are reported from North Carolina.

A. Adult lilac leafminer. *K. Gray.* **B.** Lilac leafminer damage. *W. Cranshaw.* **C.** Lilac leafminer eggs. *K. Gray.*
D. Lilac leafminer larva. *K. Gray.* **E.** Azalea leafminer adult. *K. Gray.* **F.** Lilac leafminer damage. *K. Gray.* **G.** Azalea leafminer damage. *K. Gray.* **H.** Azalea leafminer larva tying leaf. *K. Gray.*

Other Lepidopteran Leafminers

Aspen leafminer (*Phyllocnistis populiella*)[1] makes meandering mines just under the upper leaf surface of aspen and other *Populus* species. The mines are distinctively silvery with a dark line of excrement in the center.

Blotchy leafmines of oak in eastern North America are commonly produced by **oak leafminers** (*Cameraria* spp.).[1] Depending on the species, mines may be produced by a single larva or by larvae feeding in small groups. Several generations may be produced annually, with the overwintering generation in mines of dropped leaves.

In the Pacific states, leaves of hollyleaf cherry are commonly mined by larvae of **cherry leafminer** (*Paraleucoptera heinrichi*).[3] Full-grown larvae emerge from the mine, construct a white H-shaped tent of silk on the upper leaf surface, and pupate in this protective structure.

Throughout the continental U.S. and parts of southern Canada, **morningglory leafminer** (*Bedellia somnulentella*)[3] mines the leaves of sweetpotato, morning glory, and bindweed. Initial mines are serpentine and later enlarge to become blotchlike. Two generations are produced in the northern U.S.

Lyonetia leafminer (*Lyonetia speculella*)[3] has become increasingly common in the mid-Atlantic region since the 1980s. It produces small blotchy mines in young leaves of apple, plum, cherry, birch, and grape. Probably little damage is done since older leaves are not suitable hosts. Larvae are light green, and pupation occurs in a silken "hammock" on the undersurface of the leaf. Multiple generations occur during the year.

Larvae of **spruce needleminer** (*Endothenia albolineana*)[4] hollow out the base of spruce needles. Groups of needles are often cut and later webbed together in a small mass; often, several larvae may feed together. Infestation of large trees is usually confined to lower branches, but entire crowns of small trees may be infested and defoliated. Spruce needleminer is widespread through the northern half of the U.S. and southern Canada. Larvae are light greenish brown caterpillars with a dark head, about ⅜ inch long, and found associated with damaged needles.

Spruce needleminer spends the winter as a nearly full-grown larva in a cocoon constructed within mats of webbing and dead needles. It resumes feeding in early spring, becoming full grown in April or May. Adult moths emerge and lay eggs on the needles in late May and June. Eggs are laid in rows, on the underside of year-old needles. Larvae initially mine the interior of needles, and damaged needles are later cut off and bound to the twigs with webbing. Larvae feed throughout the summer, suspending feeding with the onset of cold weather. There is one generation per year.

Pine needle sheathminer (*Zelleria haimbachi*)[5] is primarily a western species but does occur in the Great Lakes states and Ontario. Larvae tunnel into the fascicle at the base of needles of several kinds of pines, including lodgepole, jack, ponderosa, and white. Individual larvae may destroy 6 to 10 bundles of needles in the course of development and may cause dieback of terminals in sustained outbreaks.

Larvae overwinter as miners in needles. After shoot elongation, they move to the new growth and tunnel into the base of needles. As they get older they form a silken tube outside the needles and cut them as they feed. Infested plants can be detected by drooping and faded needles hanging by the silk. The full-grown larvae are tan colored and about ½ inch. They pupate in late spring and early summer. Adults then lay eggs, and the newly hatched larvae then tunnel into needles to overwinter. One generation is produced annually.

A. Early-stage injury by spruce needleminer. Note webbing at base of dead needles. *D. Shetlar.* **B.** Spruce needleminer damage. *W. Cranshaw.* **C.** Pine needle sheathminer injury. *R. Childs.* **D.** Solitary oak blotch leafminer, larva exposed in mine. *J. Baker.* **E.** Solitary oak leafminer injury. *J. Baker.* **F.** Aspen leafminer larva and mines. *W. Cranshaw.*

Various species of *Argyresthia* are known as **arborvitae leafminers**[6] and mine the needles of arborvitae and cypress, causing tips to brown and die back. In most species, adults emerge in late spring and early summer. Eggs are laid in the tips of 1- or 2-year-old twigs, and the larvae tunnel under leaf scales. They feed as miners for the remainder of their lives and winter as partially grown larvae. Visible symptoms of damage usually appear in winter and are commonly mistaken for winterkill, although the presence of tunneling is diagnostic for arborvitae leafminers. Pupation occurs in spring, usually in the tunnels, although **cypress tipminer** (*A. cupressella*), a western species, exits and spins a cocoon on the foliage. Small holes indicate the emergence of *Argyresthia* adults or the exiting larvae.

Several *Coleotechnites*[7] species develop as needleminers of various conifers in western forests. Most important is **ponderosa pine needleminer** (*C. ponderosae*), which has produced several widespread outbreaks in the Rocky Mountain states. Adults lay eggs in August, usually in older, previously mined needles. After egg hatch, the larvae move to the new needles and bore near the tip. Larval development and feeding continue until the following spring, when pupation occurs. Other related species that may attract attention are *C. picealla*, which occasionally damages spruce, and *C. juniperella*, on junipers.

Shield bearers (*Coptodisca* spp.)[8] are tiny moths that develop as leafminers, producing small blotch-like mines. When feeding is completed, they cut a round section of leaf and fashion a small shielded case around themselves in which they pupate. Heavily infested plants may have numerous small holes, similar to those produced by a hole punch. **Resplendent shield bearer** (*C. splendoriferella*) is widespread in the U.S. and feeds on apple and cherry. **Madrone shield bearer** (*C. arbutiella*) is a common Pacific Coast species associated with madrone and manzanita.

Appleleaf trumpet leafminer (*Tischeria malifoliella*)[9] makes distinctive mines in apple, hawthorn, and crabapple. From the initial point of entry into the leaf, the mine expands to a large blotch, giving the appearance of a trumpet. Apple trumpet leafminer is a native species found in much of the northeastern quadrant of the U.S. and some areas of southeastern Canada.

[1] Lepidoptera: Gracillariidae; [2] Lepidoptera: Nepticulidae; [3] Lepidoptera: Lyonetiidae; [4] Lepidoptera: Tortricidae; [5] Lepidoptera: Yponomeutidae; [6] Lepidoptera: Argyresthiidae; [7] Lepidoptera: Gelechiidae; [8] Lepidoptera: Heliozelidae; [9] Lepidoptera: Tischeriidae

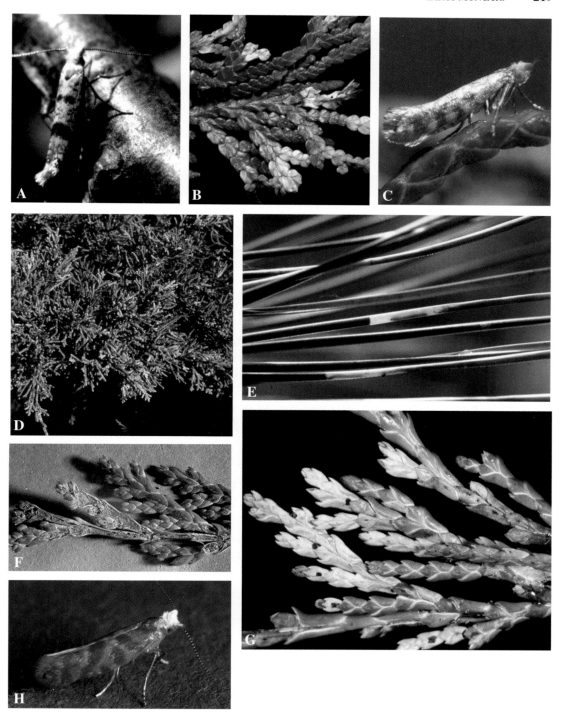

A. Adult arborvitae leafminer. *D. Shetlar.* **B.** Leaf mines produced by arborvitae leafminers. *D. Shetlar.* **C.** Adult cypress tipminer. *D. Shetlar.* **D.** Damage by cypress tipminer. *D. Shetlar.* **E.** Ponderosa pine needleminer larvae in needles. *R. Stevens.* **F.** Tunneling of terminals by cypress tipminer. *K. Gray.* **G.** Damage produced by cypress tipminer larvae. *J. R. Baker.* **H.** Cypress tipminer adult. *K. Gray.*

LEAFMINING BEETLES

Locust Leafminer (*Odontota dorsalis*)[1]

Hosts: Larvae develop in black locust and some other leguminous trees including false indigo and golden chain tree. Adults feed on a wider range of plants including oak, dogwood, elm, and hawthorn.

Damage: Larvae feed in the leaves, making irregular blotchlike mines. These mines, which during development may not be readily observed, can be seen most easily from the bottom. Adults feed on the underside of leaves and produce a skeletonizing injury.

Distribution: Most common in the mid-Atlantic area, extending into Ohio, but can be found from Alabama and Georgia north into southern Canada.

Appearance: Adults are moderate-sized beetles, about ¼ inch. They are primarily yellow or yellow orange with black patterning running down the center of the body and covering most of the hind end. The larvae, found in the leaf mines, are yellowish white, flattened, with dark appendages.

Life History and Habits: Locust leafminer overwinters as an adult, under fallen leaves and in other protective cover. It may feed on foliage of other trees, notably oak, before moving to black locust. Eggs are laid on the underside of leaves, and the larvae subsequently tunnel. They create a gradually expanding blotchlike mine, usually on the outer edge of leaves. Pupation occurs in the mine. In southern areas of the species' distribution, a second generation occurs.

Other Leafmining Beetles

Poplar blackmine beetle (*Zeugophora scutellaris*)[1] makes large, dark blotch mines in poplar and cottonwood. Adults feed on the surface of leaves, making meandering skeletonizing injuries. **Basswood leafminer** (*Baliosus ruber*)[1] occurs in much of eastern Canada and the U.S. where it makes blotch leafmines on basswood and several other deciduous trees. Both species have a single generation, with winter spent in the adult stage.

Yellow poplar weevil (*Odontopus calceatus*)[2] develops on magnolia, tuliptree, and sassafras in several midwestern and mid-Atlantic states. Primary damage is caused by larvae, which often feed as groups and produce large blotchlike leaf mines early in the season. Adults feed initially on buds, but as leaves expand they chew small bean-shaped areas in them. Chewing also occurs on the main veins and can cause tips of leaves to wilt. Eggs are inserted into pits chewed in the main veins of the leaf, and a dozen or more larvae may feed together. When feeding is completed, they pupate in spherical cocoons in the mined leaf. Adults that emerge in midsummer feed for a brief period and then move to winter shelter and go into dormancy. One generation is produced annually.

Another weevil that develops as a leafminer is **willow flea weevil** (*Rhynchaenus rufipes*). The adults are small (1/12 inch) black weevils with hind legs enlarged and adapted to jump. Overwintered adults move in spring to the buds and newly emergent leaves of hosts, which include willow, birch, elm, red maple, aspen, red oak, cherry, and serviceberry. They lay eggs on the underside of leaves, and the larvae develop as leafminers, pupating in the leaf. If infested plants are nearby, the adults may migrate in nuisance numbers into buildings during late summer. A related species, **apple flea weevil** (*R. pallicarnis*), has similar habits and develops on apple, quince, hawthorn, winged elm, and hazelnut. Both are most common in the midwestern and mid-Atlantic states.

[1] Coleoptera: Chrysomelidae; [2] Coleoptera: Curculionidae

A. Locust leafminer injury. *B. W. Kauffman.* **B.** Locust leafminer adults. *D. Shetlar.* **C.** Various life stages of locust leaf-miner—larva, pupa, adult. *E. B. Walker.* **D.** Typical mine produced by poplar blackmine beetle. *D. Leatherman.* **E.** Leaf mines produced by yellow poplar weevil larvae. *J. D. Solomon.* **F.** Locust leafminer larva in mined leaf. *D. Leatherman.* **G.** Adult feeding injuries produced by yellow poplar weevil. *L. L. Hyche.* **H.** Apple flea weevil adult. *D. Caldwell.* **I.** Apple flea weevil damage. *D. Caldwell.* **J.** Adult feeding injuries and early-stage blotch mine of poplar blackmine beetle. *W. Cranshaw.* **K.** Mating pair of willow flea weevils. *D. Shetlar.* **L.** Pupal cocoons produced by yellow poplar weevil. *L. L. Hyche.*

CHAPTER FIVE

Flower, Fruit, and Seed Feeders

FLOWER THRIPS

Note: Most thrips primarily damage leaves and are discussed separately on p. 386.

Western Flower Thrips (*Frankliniella occidentalis*)[1]

Hosts: A wide range of herbaceous plants including both broadleaves and grasses.

Damage: Scarring injury to flowers is the most common concern to gardeners. In the landscape, injuries are usually minor, but occasionally they may seriously blemish and/or distort flowers. Feeding injuries to vegetables typically involve slight scarring. Cloudy "pansy," or "halo," spots may be produced on fruit around egg-laying puncture wounds. Western flower thrips is also a highly efficient vector of viruses in the tospovirus group, which can produce the plant diseases **tomato spotted wilt**, **impatiens necrotic spot**, and **iris yellow fleck**.

Distribution: Formerly limited largely to western states but now found throughout most of North America. It is particularly common in the southern half of the U.S. where it can be a major pest of vegetable crops. Western flower thrips is one of the most important greenhouse pests throughout the continent.

Appearance: Difficult to distinguish from most common thrips on leaves and flowers without high magnification. Adults are about ¹⁄₁₆ inch, elongate, and range from yellow to brown. Nymphs are yellow.

Life History and Habits: Flower thrips are moderately cold hardy and likely survive winter outdoors in much of the southern half of the U.S. In warmest areas, and in greenhouses, reproduction may be continuous as long as conditions permit. Elsewhere flower thrips may winter under leaf debris or other protected sites. Adults feed on pollen in addition to plant sap.

Females insert eggs into emerging leaves, buds, and flowers. Eggs hatch in about 5 to 7 days, but this period can be extended considerably with cool temperatures. Subsequently there are two larval (nymphal) stages that actively feed and produce most of the physical plant injuries. It is during the larval stage that tomato spotted wilt may be acquired and later transmitted to healthy plants in the adult stage. Depending on temperature, the larval stages are normally completed in 1 to 2 weeks. Two nonfeeding stages (prepupa, pupa) then occur, which usually take place in soil. Another week or so is required for completion of these stages, after which the adult is present to repeat the cycle. Multiple generations occur outdoors, and breeding may be continuous in greenhouses. Mass movements frequently occur during summer following the decline of flowers and other alternate hosts.

Related Species

Flower thrips (*Frankliniella tritici*) is a native insect, primarily found in eastern North America. It has similar habits and hosts as western flower thrips but has been less important as a vector of tomato spotted wilt and impatiens necrotic spot viruses. **Tobacco thrips** (*F. fusca*) is common east of the Rockies and is particularly abundant in the southeastern U.S. It develops on grasses and many vegetables but is primarily a pest of field crops such as cotton, tobacco, alfalfa, and peanut. Tobacco thrips can also transmit tomato spotted wilt virus.

[1] Thysanoptera: Thripidae

A. Flower thrips scarring of carnation petals. *J. Capinera.* **B.** Pansy spot wound on pea pod surrounding flowers thrips egg-laying scar. *W. Cranshaw.* **C.** Ringspot symptoms of tomato spotted wilt on pepper leaf. *W. Cranshaw.* **D.** Ring spot symptoms on tomato fruit, characteristic of tomato spotted wilt. *W. Cranshaw.* **E.** Western flower thrips. *W. Cranshaw.* **F.** Flower thrips damage to blueberry flower. *J. A. Payne.*

TRUE BUGS THAT FEED ON FLOWERS, FRUITS, AND SEEDS

Tarnished Plant Bug (*Lygus lineolaris*)[1]

Hosts: Mostly herbaceous garden plants and weeds, particularly composites and legumes. Peach, apricot, and strawberry are among the fruit crops most commonly damaged.

Damage: Tarnished plant bug feeds on developing leaves, fruits, and flowers, killing the areas around the feeding site. This can cause abortion of young flowers, developing seeds, or fruit. Death of buds may lead to abnormally bushy growth. Older tissues may continue to grow but be deformed. Catface injuries to fruit are some of the more commonly observed distortions caused by tarnished plant bug feeding injury.

Distribution: Throughout North America.

Appearance: Adults are generally oval, about twice as long as wide, and about ¼ inch long. They are generally brown with some yellow and reddish markings. Color tends to darken with age. Nymphs are more rounded in form and usually yellowish green to dark green, often with dark spotting.

Life History and Habits: Winter is spent in the adult stage under the cover of piled leaves, bark cracks, or other sheltered sites. Adults emerge and become active in early spring, feeding on buds of trees and shrubs. Most then move to various weeds and other plants, and females insert eggs into the stems, leaves, and buds of these plants. The young hatch, feed, and develop on these plants, becoming full grown in about a month. Several generations are produced during the year.

Tarnished plant bug is an omnivore that also feeds on aphids and other small, soft-bodied insects, effecting some biological control of these pests that is considered beneficial.

A. Tarnished plant bug. *N. Demirel.* **B.** Tarnished plant bug nymph. *S. Bauer/USDA-ARS.* **C.** Tarnished plant bug. *S. Bauer/USDA-ARS.* **D.** *Lygus* plant bugs at egg hatch. *K. Gray.* **E.** *Lygus* plant bug eggs inserted into leaf. *K. Gray.* **F.** Spotting of cotton bolls from plant bug feeding injury. *B. Freeman.* **G.** Catfacing on peach caused by plant bug injury. *Courtesy Clemson University.* **H.** Tarnished plant bug injury to flowers. *W. Cranshaw.* **I.** Injury to cotton flower by tarnished plant bug. *B. Freeman.* **J.** Catfacing injuries to apple fruit. *W. Cranshaw.*

Related Species

Note: Most plant bugs primarily damage leaves and are discussed in a separate section on p. 374.

Thirty-four species of *Lygus* occur in North America, and most have similar life histories. Overwintering forms are adults. In northern areas, usually a single generation is produced, but as many as four or five can occur in the southern U.S. **Pale legume bug** (*L. elisus*) is a common and damaging species found west of the Mississippi. Summer forms are pale green, whereas the wintering adult form is slightly darker. Pale legume bug has a broad host range and, despite its name, is most commonly associated with cabbage family plants. **Western tarnished plant bug** (*L. hesperus*) is largely restricted to areas west of the Rockies. It is has a wide host range that includes vegetables, seed crops, alfalfa, and some fruit.

Campylomma bug (*Campylomma verbasci*),[1] also known as **mullein bug**, is found over a broad area of southern Canada and the northern U.S. It is sometimes considered a tree-fruit pest, particularly of apple; first-generation nymphs feed on developing fruit, causing abortion or corky warts to develop on the fruit surface. Later in the season, campylomma bug is considered beneficial to orchardists as a predator of aphids, mites, and pear psylla. Summer activity occurs primarily on various weeds, particularly common mullein. Adults are gray-brown, about $\frac{1}{10}$ inch. Nymphs are pale green and develop black spines on the legs. Winter in spent as eggs inserted in twigs of apple and pear.

The genus *Lopidea*[1] includes some relatively small (ca. $\frac{1}{6}$ inch), brightly colored plant bugs, often with predominately scarlet markings. **Phlox plant bug** (*L. davisi*) damages the buds and distorts the flowers of phlox in the midwestern U.S. Feeding by *L. confluenta* is associated with bud abortion on daylily and iris in the southern U.S.

[1] Hemiptera: Miridae

A. Pale legume bug. *W. Cranshaw.* **B.** Pale legume bug nymph. *N. Demirel.* **C.** Western tarnished plant bug. *N. Demirel.* **D.** Campylomma bug nymph. *J. Ogrodnik/NY Agricultural Experiment Station.* **E.** Campylomma bug injury to young apple. *E. Nelson.* **F.** Adult *Lopidea* sp. plant bug. *W. Cranshaw.*

STINK BUGS

Many stink bugs[1] are general feeders of plants and cause injuries primarily when they suck sap from buds, flowers, and developing fruits. Bud abortion, pitting of fruit or seeds, and other distortions commonly result from these stink bug injuries. Other stink bugs primarily restrict feeding to foliage and are discussed on p. 382. Stink bugs that are primarily predators of other insects are covered on p. 550.

Southern green stink bug (*Nezara viridula*) is found in the southeastern U.S. where it is considered an important pest of vegetables and field and orchard crops. Legumes and crucifers are particularly favored, but the host range is wide. Feeding on buds and blossoms causes them to wither and die. Feeding punctures of fruit cause deformed growth, and seeds may be shriveled. Adults are about ½ inch long and dull green. The young nymphs are pinkish but turn increasingly green with age. Development is usually completed in 65 to 70 days, and four generations are typically produced. The adults go dormant with decreasing day length.

Green stink bug (*Acrosternum hilare*) is broadly distributed throughout most of the U.S. and southern Canada. It is similar in appearance to southern green stink bug but is considered much less damaging. Hosts include most vegetables as well as many fruit trees. One or two generations are produced, depending on temperature and location.

Stink bugs of the genus *Chlorochroa* are primarily western in distribution. They are most commonly known to damage small grains but will feed on vegetables and certain flowers. Most are green, but some may be quite dark with purplish or reddish coloration. Common species associated with plant injuries include **Say's stink bug** (*C. sayi*), **Uhler stink bug** (*C. uhleri*), and **conchuela** (*C. ligata*).

Euschistus stink bugs are gray or brown and somewhat more angular in form. A few are minor pests of fruits and buds, including **brown stink bug** (*E. servus*), **consperse stink bug** (*E. conspersus*), and **onespotted stink bug** (*E. variolarius*).

Stink bugs of the genus *Thyanta* are generally green but may have colored markings, particularly a rosy border along the scutellum, behind the head. **Redshouldered stink bug** (*T. accerra*), *T. custator*, and *T. pallidovirens* are three of the more common species in yards and gardens, particularly east of the Rockies. Like many other stink bugs, they feed on fruit and seeds of a wide variety of plants but rarely cause significant injury.

Rough stink bugs (*Brochymena quadripustulata*, *B. pustula*) are dark brown or gray with a slightly scalloped body form. They blend in well with bark and most commonly are encountered on trees. Rough stink bugs are primarily predators of insects but sometimes feed on leaves.

---

[1] Hemiptera: Pentatomidae

A. *Thyanta custator. J. A. Payne.* **B.** Conchuela nymph. *K. Gray.* **C.** Conchuela. *K. Gray.* **D.** Say's stink bug. *K. Gray.*
E. Brown stink bug. *J. Capinera.* **F.** Eggs of Say's stink bug hatching. *K. Gray.* **G.** Consperse stink bug. *K. Gray.*
H. Onespotted stink bug. *K. Gray.* **I.** Southern green stink bug egg masses at egg hatch. *R. Smith.* **J.** Rough stink bug.
K. Gray. **K.** Southern green stink bug feeding injuries on cotton boll. *R. Smith.* **L.** Southern green stink bug. *Courtesy
Clemson University.* **M.** Redshouldered stink bugs. *W. Cranshaw.*

OTHER SEED-FEEDING BUGS

Boxelder Bug (*Boisea trivittata*)[1]

Hosts: Boxelder, caddo maple, sometimes silver maple.

Damage: Nymphs and adults usually feed on sap from seeds, flowers, and leaves but cause little damage to trees. Occasionally they feed on developing fruits, such as apples, and can produce puckered catface injuries to these plants. The major "damage" from these insects is their appearance in nuisance numbers on the windows and porches of homes in cooler months of the year. Their presence is most commonly noted on sunny days in fall and spring.

Distribution: Throughout North America, east of Nevada.

Appearance: Adult stages are brownish black, about ½ inch long, with three red lines on the head and a bright red abdomen beneath the wings. The nymphs are somewhat more oval in form and predominately red except where the black wing pads are developing.

Life History and Habits: Boxelder bugs overwinter in the adult stage in protected sites, often including homes. They emerge in midspring and lay groups of rusty red eggs near deposits of dropped seeds of boxelder, other maples, and occasionally ash. The first-generation nymphs feed on these seeds, various low-growing plants, and recently dead insects. They also may be cannibalistic, feeding on other nymphs that are in the process of molting. They become full grown in early summer.

A second generation occurs in late summer. Eggs are laid almost entirely on boxelder, particularly seeds produced by female trees. The nymphs often develop on these seeds into October if weather permits. After frosts, boxelder bugs move to winter shelter, during which time homes are invaded. Boxelder bugs can move hundreds of yards from boxelder trees.

Related and Similar Species

In the western states and British Columbia, **western boxelder bug** (*Boisea rubrolineata*)[1] is present but is not nearly as significant a nuisance pest as boxelder bug. Feeding on developing tree fruits causes pitting and catfacing injuries.

Goldenrain tree bug (*Jadera haematoloma*)[1] develops on the seeds of goldenrain tree and occasionally is a nuisance as it masses on homes in late summer. It is distributed primarily in the southeastern states but is found in other areas in association with its host.

A. Boxelder bugs on boxelder leaf. *W. Cranshaw.* **B.** Mass of boxelder bug nymphs and adults. *W. Cranshaw.*
C. Western boxelder bug. *W. Cranshaw.* **D.** Boxelder bug nymph. *F. Peairs.* **E.** Boxelder bug. *Courtesy Clemson University.* **F.** Western boxelder bug nymph. *K. Gray.* **G.** Goldenrain tree bug. *W. Cranshaw.* **H.** Boxelder bug mass on tree trunk. *J. D. Solomon.*

In the southeastern states, **hibiscus bug** (*Niesthrea louisianica*)[1] may be common on hibiscus and rose of Sharon. Eggs are laid in masses on leaves, and the young develop by feeding on buds and seeds. Little damage is produced, but hibiscus bugs may become sufficiently abundant to attract attention. Usually one and occasionally two generations are produced annually.

Another common black-and-red bug found in western North America and often mistaken for boxelder bug is **small milkweed bug** (*Lygaeus kalmii*).[2] It develops on seeds of a wide variety of plants, including many weeds, and is not considered a pest. A closely related species, *L. angustomariginatus*, is common in eastern North America.

The **leaffooted bugs** (Coreidae family)[3] are fairly large insects, often ¾ inch or larger, of rather bizarre appearance. Most are reddish brown to gray and have a distinct flattening on their long hind legs. **Western conifer seed bug** (*Leptoglossus occidentalis*) is common in the western U.S. and Canada and has substantially extended its range eastward to the Atlantic states. It develops on the flowers and seeds of pine, Douglas-fir, and other woody plants such as dogwood. It is a common nuisance invader of homes in fall, much in the manner of boxelder bug, but usually fails to survive winters in homes. A defensive odor of somewhat piney scent is often noted. **Leaffooted bug** (*L. phyllopus*) is common in the eastern half of the U.S. and is also found in southern California. Thistle is its most common host in Florida, and in Kansas it is common on yucca. It may also occur on tender shoots, buds, and fruits of a wide variety of plants and may incidently damage some fruit and nut crops. *L. clypealis* is a California species occasionally damaging to nut crops. **Leaffooted pine seed bug** (*L. corculus*) is commonly damaging to pine seeds in the southeastern U.S. *Euthochtha galeator* is another common leaffooted bug found feeding on buds, seeds, and terminal growth of various trees and shrubs in the eastern U.S. **Squash bug** (*Anasa tristis*) is a leaffooted bug that is a serious pest of cucurbits, feeding primarily on stems and leaves but also damaging fruit; it is discussed on p. 372.

[1] Hemiptera: Rhopalidae; [2] Hemiptera: Lygaeidae; [3] Hemiptera: Coreidae

A. Small milkweed bug. *K. Grays.* **B.** Adult of leaffooted bug *Leptoglossus oppositus. J. Capinera.* **C.** Western conifer bug on pine cone. *W. Cranshaw.* **D.** Leaffooted bug. *Courtesy Clemson University.* **E.** Leaffooted pine seed bug nymphs at egg hatch. *R. F. Billings.* **F.** Western conifer seed bug. *K. Gray.* **G.** Western conifer seed bug nymph. *K. Gray.* **H.** Leaffooted pine seed bug. *R. S. Cameron.*

FRUIT FLIES

The fruit flies (Tephritidae family) are a large group of flies that develop in fruits, stems, and leaves of plants. Adults have wings patterned with dark markings. Of the 290-odd North American species, only a few are seriously damaging to garden plants. Other flies that infest fruit include the gall flies (Cecidomyiidae) and the vinegar, or small fruit, flies (Drosophilidae). The latter are particularly common on overripe fruit and occasionally are household pests.

Apple Maggot (*Rhagoletis pomonella*)[1]

Hosts: Apple, pear, and large crabapples primarily. Late-season plum and cherry are infrequently infested. Hawthorn is an important wild host in some western states.

Damage: Most damage results when the young maggots tunnel fruit, producing meandering brown trails that hasten rot. Egg-laying by the adults involves small puncture wounds to the fruit surface that cause dimplelike distortions.

Distribution: Primarily in apple-growing areas east of the Great Plains but has become established throughout much of North America including isolated areas of the Pacific and Rocky Mountain states.

Appearance: Adults are picture-winged flies that have distinct black patterning on the wings. They are about ⅕ inch, generally black with a white spot on the back and a brown head. Larvae are cream-colored, legless maggots associated with the fruit. Pupae are pale yellowish brown, smooth, and somewhat seedlike.

Life History and Habits: During winter, apple maggot is in the pupal stage, buried shallowly in soil near previously infested trees. Adults emerge in early summer, and females first feed for about 2 weeks on honeydew and other fluids in the vicinity of fruit trees. They then move to apple and begin to lay eggs, which they insert singly under the skin of the fruit. Peak egg-laying tends to occur in mid- to late July. Eggs hatch within a week. Larvae feed in the fruit for 3 to 4 weeks before dropping to the soil to pupate. One generation is produced per year, with the pupae remaining dormant until the following season. Some pupae remain dormant through two winters.

Other Fruit-Infesting Flies

Cherry fruit fly (*Rhagoletis cingulata*), also known as **cherry maggot**, is an important pest of cherry in the northcentral and northeastern U.S. and adjacent areas of southern Canada. Apple is infrequently infested. Initial damage occurs when the adult female "stings" the cherry fruit with her ovipositor, producing small puncture wounds. Eggs are often laid in the punctures, and the immature maggots chew through the flesh of the fruit. Infested berries are misshapen, undersized, and mature rapidly.

Cherry fruit flies spend winter in the pupal stage around the base of previously infested trees. In late May, the flies begin to emerge and feed on fluids, including oozing sap from wounds made by fruit punctures. About 10 days are spent feeding before eggs begin to be laid. Females insert eggs under the skin of fruit for a period of 3 or 4 weeks. The immature maggots feed on the fruit, particularly the area around the pit. They become full grown in 2 to 3 weeks and drop to the ground to pupate. In most areas there is one generation per year.

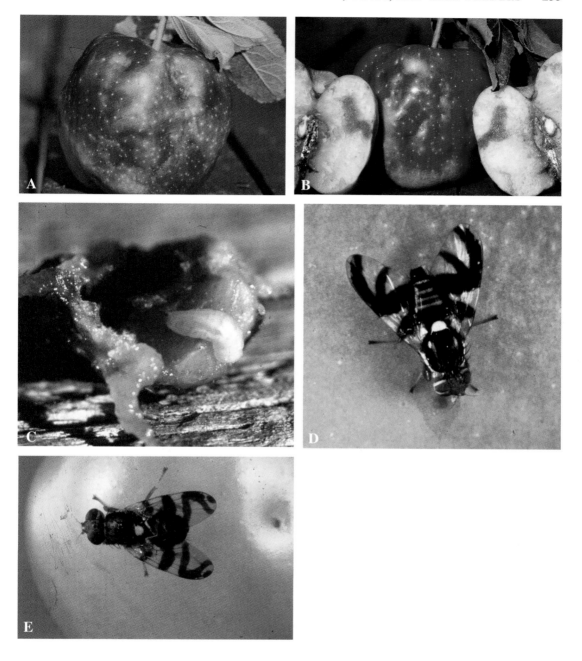

A. Exterior of apple fruit damaged by apple maggot. *W. Cranshaw.* **B.** Damage by larval tunnel of apple maggot. *W. Cranshaw.* **C.** Apple maggot larva in hawthorn fruit. *E. Nelson.* **D.** Apple maggot adult. *J. Ogrodnik/NY Agricultural Experiment Station.* **E.** Cherry fruit fly adult. *J. Ogrodnik/NY Agricultural Experiment Station.*

Black cherry fruit fly (*Rhagoletis fausta*) has a similar life history and often occurs with cherry fruit fly in orchards. Pin cherry is the common wild host. **Western cherry fruit fly** (*R. indifferens*) is found in most of the western states and British Columbia. Adults are present from June to August, most abundant often about the time of harvest. After eggs are laid in fruit, the larvae feed for about 10 days and then drop to the ground to pupate. In most areas this species limits damage to cherry, including wild types. However, strains have developed in some regions (e.g., Utah) that attack and tunnel into apple.

Walnut husk fly (*Rhagoletis completa*) is native to the southcentral U.S. but has become widespread throughout western North America. The maggots tunnel the flesh of walnut husks, which stains the nuts and reduces value. Uncommonly this species also develops in late-ripening varieties of peach.

Blueberry maggot (*Rhagoletis mendax*) is distributed throughout the eastern U.S. and Canada. Larvae develop in blueberry and huckleberry. This species is mostly a pest of commercial blueberry. In the southeastern U.S. adults emerge in late May and persist until late July, when their native host, deerberry, is fruiting. Females lay eggs singly in fruits, and larvae take about a month to develop. The pupae subsequently overwinter, sometimes for a second year before adults are produced.

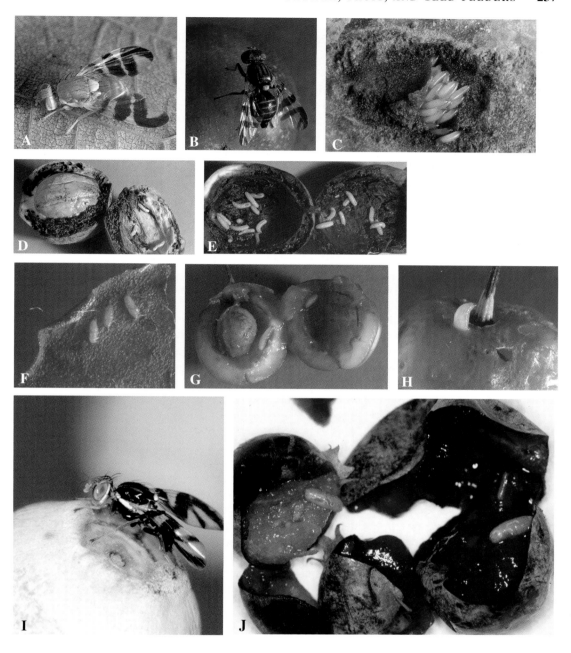

A. Adult of walnut husk fly. *K. Gray.* **B.** Adult of western cherry fruit fly. *K. Gray.* **C.** Eggs of walnut husk fly laid on black walnut. *K. Gray.* **D.** Damage to husk of black walnut by walnut husk fly. *K. Gray.* **E.** Walnut husk fly larvae in infested walnut. *K. Gray.* **F.** Eggs of western cherry fruit fly laid under skin of cherry. *K. Gray.* **G.** Western cherry fruit fly larvae in fruit. *K. Gray.* **H.** Western cherry fruit fly larva emerging from cherry fruit. *K. Gray.* **I.** Blueberry maggot adult. *J. A. Payne.* **J.** Blueberry maggot larvae and damage. *J. A. Payne.*

Adults of **currant fruit fly** (*Euphantra canadensis*)[1] are generally yellowish with bright green eyes. Larvae develop in red and white currants and gooseberries. Eggs are inserted into the developing berries, and the oviposition wounds usually develop a red spot. The larvae develop in the fruit, tunneling around the seeds, and become full grown about the time the fruit ripens. They then drop to the ground, dig into the soil, and pupate, which is the form in which they subsequently overwinter.

Pepper maggot (*Zonosemata electa*)[1] is found in much of eastern North America and is particularly common among the Atlantic seaboard states. Adults damage pepper fruit when inserting eggs, producing small dimpled wounds. Larvae feed on the flesh of the fruit core, producing brownish areas. Although widespread and fairly common, this species is rarely abundant and injuries are often overlooked. Only one generation is produced, and winter is spent as a pupa in the soil. Eggplant, tomatillo, and some wild nightshade weeds also host pepper maggot.

Vinegar (or Pomace or Small Fruit) Flies (*Drosophila* spp.)[2]

Hosts: Almost any overripe fruit or fermenting materials supporting yeast growth.

Damage: Vinegar flies are attracted to wounds on fruits and vegetables and to overripe fruit. They do not cause direct injury to growing plants but can become serious pests of harvested produce as tunneling by the tiny maggots hastens fruit rotting. The small flies also can be annoying in kitchens, around compost piles, and in worm beds where breeding conditions are favorable.

Distribution: Throughout North America, common.

Appearance: Adults are tiny flies, about $\frac{1}{10}$ inch. The general body color is often yellowish or light brown, sometimes gray, and the eyes are large and reddish.

Life History and Habits: Vinegar flies develop on the yeasts that grow on well-ripened fruit and around wounds of plants. Food residues in beverage containers or garbage cans also commonly support growth of yeasts and serve as breeding sites. Adults lay eggs in these areas, and the young maggots can become fully grown in less than a week. Prior to pupation, the larvae migrate away from the food source and attach themselves tightly to plant stems, container walls, or other dry areas. Individual adults live about 4 weeks, with females capable of laying a few dozen eggs daily. Breeding is continuous throughout the warm season, and numerous generations are produced, with peak populations developing in late summer and early fall. Outdoors vinegar flies go into dormancy during the cool season; indoors they may breed year-round.

A. Adult of currant fruit fly. *K. Gray.* **B.** Currant fruit fly larva in gooseberry fruit. *K. Gray.* **C.** Egg laying scar on gooseberry produced by currant fruit fly. *K. Gray.* **D.** Adult vinegar fly. *K. Gray.* **E.** Vinegar fly pupae. *K. Gray.* **F.** Vinegar fly larva. *K. Gray.* **G.** Larvae of pepper maggot. *R. Bessin.*

Rose Midge (*Dasineura rhodophaga*)[3]

Hosts: Rose, particularly hybrid tea types.

Damage: The small maggot stage of rose midge feeds by making small slashes in developing plant tissues to suck the sap. Developing flower buds are distorted by this injury or may be killed, resulting in "blind" shoots where no flower buds appear to form.

Distribution: Localized in many areas throughout North America.

Appearance: Adults are small, delicate flies, about ⅟₂₅ inch and brown with a reddish tinge. Larvae are tiny maggots, creamy white to pale red and found about the buds.

Life History and Habits: Rose midge overwinters in the pupal stage in the soil. The adult, an inconspicuous small fly, emerges in late spring, sometimes after the first crop of blossoms. Adults live only 1 or 2 days, but during this time the females lay numerous eggs under the sepals, in opening buds, and in elongating shoots. Hatching larvae slash plant tissues and feed on sap. Eggs hatch in a few days, and the larvae feed for about a week before dropping to the soil to pupate. The complete life cycle can take about 2 weeks, with numerous generations occurring in a growing season.

Other Gall Flies of Fruits and Flowers

Blueberry gall midge (*Dasineura oxycoccana*) infests blueberry and cranberry in the eastern U.S. and is particularly damaging to rabbiteye blueberry in the southeastern states. Larvae that develop in flower buds cause them to dry out and abort. The growing points on twigs may be destroyed, seriously reducing foliage growth. A generation can be completed in as little as 2 weeks, and multiple generations occur during the period of active growth of plants in late winter and spring.

Chokecherry gall midge (*Contarinia virginianae*)[3] distorts developing chokecherry fruits, causing them to enlarge and become hollow. Within this galled fruit the bright orange-red maggots develop and feed. Winter is spent in the pupal stage, around the base of previously infested chokecherries. Adults emerge in early spring, around the time of blossoming, and females lay eggs in the flowers. The larvae feed in the fruit until midsummer and then drop to the ground and pupate. There is one generation per year. A related species, **hemerocallis gall midge** (*C. quinquenotata*), has become established in parts of British Columbia. It is of European origin and distorts daylily flowers.

Several flies are associated with heads of sunflower. **Sunflower midge** (*Contarinia schulzi*) develop on buds and emerging flowers and can induce a gross clublike distortion of sunflower heads. Sunflower midge is particularly abundant in Minnesota, the Dakotas, and the Prairie Provinces where it is sometimes limiting to sunflower production. Feeding at the base of florets and minor damage to seeds are commonly produced by **sunflower seed maggot** (*Neotephritis finalis*).[1] Many other aster family plants may also be infested by sunflower seed maggot. Tunneling into the receptacle at the base of the florets may occur with *Gymnocarena diffusa*,[1] which often pupates at the base of the head.

[1] Diptera: Tephritidae; [2] Diptera: Drosophilidae; [3] Diptera: Cecidomyiidae

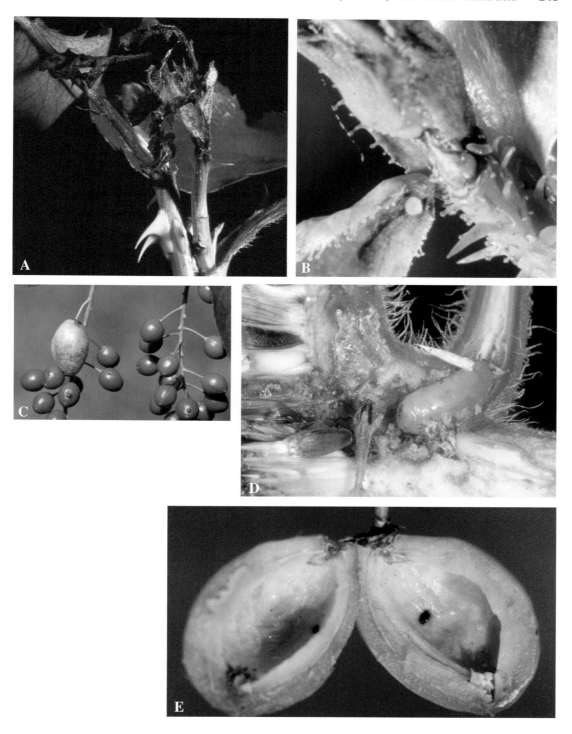

A. Rose midge damage to tips. *D. Shetlar*. **B.** Rose midge larva in tip of rose stem. *D. Shetlar*. **C.** Chokecherry fruit damaged by chokecherry gall midge. *W. Cranshaw*. **D.** Larva of *Gymnocarena diffusa* in base of sunflower. *F. Peairs*. **E.** Damaged chokecherry fruit, opened to expose larvae of chokecherry gall midge. *W. Cranshaw*.

YELLOWJACKETS AND HORNETS

Yellowjackets and hornets are members of the paper wasp family (Vespidae).[1] These are social insects that produce colonies, with nests constructed out of paper. Although all can sting, most paper wasps are valuable insects that feed on many garden pests, and they are discussed elsewhere (p. 556). Those that can damage plants or interfere substantially with gardening are discussed below.

Western Yellowjacket (*Vespula pensylvanica*)

Damage: Yellowjackets are rarely directly damaging to plants, although they can become problems when they forage on ripe fruit. Problems with stinging are most important, particularly as nests are often hidden and accidentally disturbed. Late in the season, serious nuisance problems occur as yellowjackets scavenge for meat and sweets. Western yellowjacket has omnivorous food habits and also feeds on many insects.

Distribution: Broadly distributed from the High Plains to the Pacific Coast.

Appearance: Adults are generally yellow with numerous black markings, including banding of the abdomen. They have a smooth body, without the numerous hairs found in bees.

Life History and Habits: The only stage surviving winters is a fertilized female, the potential queen. These females become active during warm days in spring and actively search for suitable sites to initiate a nest. Belowground hollows, notably abandoned rodent nests, are most commonly used. Other hollows such as found behind walls are also used. A queen subsequently begins to build nest cells of paper which she creates from chewed vegetable fibers, often obtained from weathered wood. As these cells are created, she begins to lay eggs into them and subsequently feeds the developing larvae meat she collects. Living and dead insects, dead earthworms, and carrion may be used for food.

The first yellowjackets reared are considerably smaller and are infertile female workers. These begin to take over the functions of nest-building and rearing young. Colony size increases exponentially during the summer and by early fall may include several or even thousands of individuals. Some larger rearing cells are built in which fertile females are produced. At this time males also begin to be produced and mating occurs outside the nests.

At the end of the season, rearing slows and colonies begin to break up. All workers and males die and only the fertilized females survive, which disperse to find shelter in various protected sites. The nests are abandoned and not reused.

A. Western yellowjacket. *K. Gray.* **B.** Immature stages of western yellowjacket exposed in paper comb nest. *K. Gray.* **C.** Western yellowjacket larva. *K. Gray.* **D.** Western yellowjacket eggs in comb. *K. Gray.* **E.** Excavated underground nest of western yellowjacket. *K. Gray.* **F.** Western yellowjacket pupa. *K. Gray.* **G.** Western yellowjacket queen. *W. Cranshaw.*

Other Yellowjackets and Hornets

Several other *Vespula* species occur in North America and have similar habits. **Eastern yellowjacket** (*V. maculifrons*) is common east of the Great Plains. **German yellowjacket** (*V. germanica*) is mostly restricted to the northeastern U.S. *V. flavipilosa* occurs in the Midwest and northeast and *V. squamosa* in the southeast. The latter occasionally produces colonies that survive a winter and may become very large. *V. vulgaris* broadly ranges across the northern U.S. and southern Canada.

European hornet (*Vespa crabro germana*) is a fairly recent introduction to the U.S. and is currently found in most of the Atlantic states and as far west as Ohio. It is a large insect and constructs its paper nests in a manner similar to yellowjackets—in hollows of trees or behind walls and in holes in the ground. It sometimes does considerable damage in late summer to certain trees and shrubs by chewing bark, which it uses to form its paper nest. Lilac, boxwood, birch, willow, mountain-ash, and poplar are among the plants most commonly damaged. Affected twigs and branches often wilt permanently and may die back following these injuries.

Baldfaced hornet (*Dolichovespula maculata*) and the closely related **aerial yellowjacket** (*D. arenaria*) produce large, aboveground paper nests in trees, dense shrubbery, and sheltered areas beneath overhanging roofs. Although these species are capable of stinging, their conspicuous nests greatly lessen the likelihood of accidental disturbance. Also, their diets consist almost entirely of live insects, and they do not scavenge as do many yellowjackets. Overall, baldfaced hornet can be very beneficial by assisting in the control of several garden pests.

[1] Hymenoptera: Vespidae

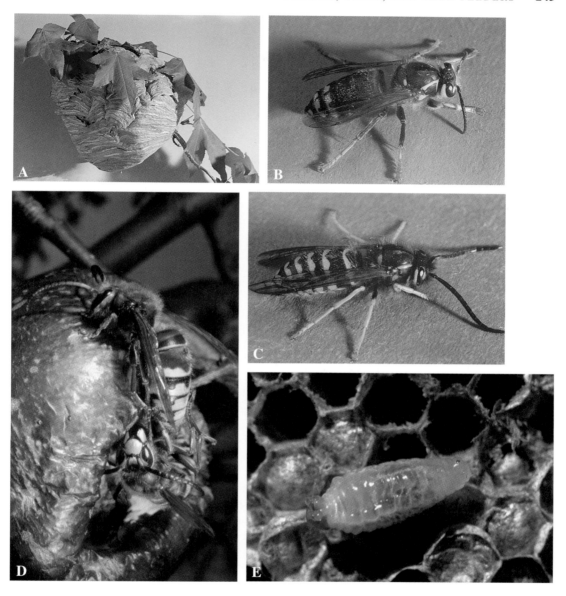

A. Baldfaced hornet nest. *K. Gray.* **B.** Baldfaced hornet. *K. Gray.* **C.** *Vespula vulgaris. K. Gray.* **D.** European hornet feeding on fruit. *D. Shetlar.* **E.** Baldfaced hornet larva exposed from comb. *W. Cranshaw.*

CATERPILLARS THAT DAMAGE FLOWERS, FRUITS, AND SEEDS

Codling Moth (*Cydia pomonella*)[1]

Hosts: Primarily apple and pear. Occasionally large-fruited crabapple, apricot, and peach.

Damage: Larvae tunnel into the fruit of apple, pear, and crabapple. (They are almost always the "worms" in wormy apples.) Less commonly they also damage other fruits, including apricot and peach. Codling moth is the single most important insect pest of tree fruits in North America.

Distribution: Throughout North America, common.

Appearance: Larvae are pale colored with a dark head and are found associated with the fruit. Adults are small (½ inch long) gray moths with coppery tipped forewings.

Life History and Habits: Codling moth larvae spend the winter inside a silken cocoon attached to rough bark or other protected locations around a tree. With warm spring weather they pupate, and the adult moths later begin to emerge around blossom time. The spring appearance of this stage may occur primarily over the course of 1 or 2 weeks but can be much more prolonged if weather is cool.

During periods when early evening temperatures are warm (above 60° F) and not windy, the moths lay small, white eggs on leaves. The larvae hatching from the eggs may feed first on the leaves but then migrate to the fruit, usually entering the calyx (flower) end. They tunnel the fruit, feeding primarily on the developing seeds. After about 3 to 4 weeks, the larvae become full grown, leave the fruit, and crawl or drop down the tree to spin a cocoon and prepare to pupate.

After about 2 weeks, most—but not all—of the pupae develop, producing a second generation of moths. The remaining moths stay dormant, emerging the following season. (For example, in western Colorado only about two-thirds of the larvae go on to produce a second generation, and fewer than half of their progeny go on to produce a third generation.) These moths lay eggs directly on the fruit, and damage by the larvae to fruit is greatest at this time. When full grown, the larvae emerge from the fruit and seek protected areas in which to pupate.

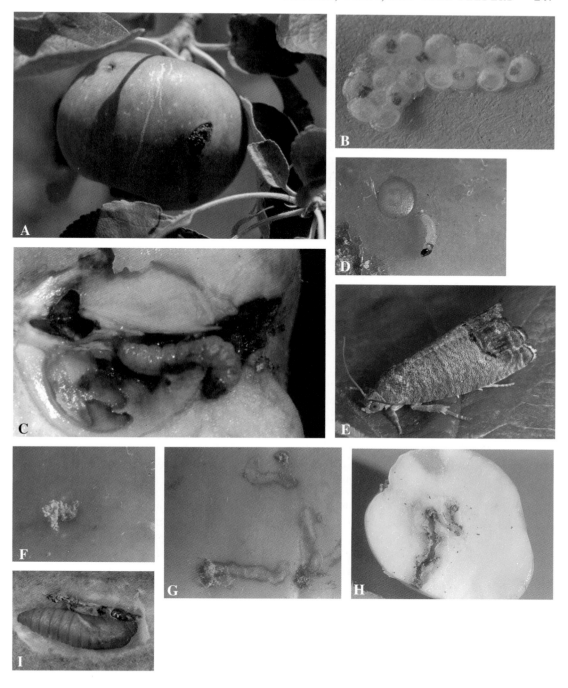

A. Codling moth–damaged apple. *W. Cranshaw.* **B.** Codling moth egg mass just before egg hatch, the "black head" stage. *K. Gray.* **C.** Codling moth caterpillar in apple. *W. Cranshaw.* **D.** Codling moth larva at egg hatch. *K. Gray.* **E.** Codling moth. *K. Gray.* **F.** Entry point into apple by codling moth larva. *K. Gray.* **G.** Surface tunnels on apple fruit by young codling moth larva. *K. Gray.* **H.** Fruit injury by larval tunneling of codling moth. *K. Gray.* **I.** Codling moth pupa under bark flap. *W. Cranshaw.*

Related Species

Hickory shuckworm (*Cydia caryana*), along with pecan weevil, is the most destructive insect pest of pecans in the U.S. It also may damage hickory nuts, the larvae feeding on the interior. Presently hickory shuckworm is found throughout eastern North America in association with its host, but its range has extended westward into New Mexico.

The overwintering stage is a late-instar larva in the old shucks of nuts. It pupates in the shuck in late winter or early spring. First-generation adults begin to emerge in early spring and continue over a few months. Eggs are laid around galls of the pecan phylloxera (p. 412) or in young nuts. A creamy white gelatin material is deposited to seal the eggs. Larvae complete development in nuts or galls, and 4 to 5 generations per year may be produced. Full-grown larvae are about ½ inch, creamy white with a reddish brown head and black spots on the abdomen.

Filbertworm (*Cydia latiferreana*) is associated with almost all cultivated and wild nuts grown in North America and is particularly common in acorn and hazelnut. Winter is spent as a full-grown larva in a cocoon on or in the vicinity of the previously infested host. Pupation occurs in spring, and adults are present over an extended period from late June into October. Eggs are usually laid on leaves, but the larvae migrate to nuts and develop in them. Larval development usually takes less than 1 month, after which the larvae exit to search for a protected site where they spin a cocoon. One generation per year is normal, but egg-laying continues over a period of several weeks.

Pea moth (*Cydia nigracana*) is primarily a pest of dried pea in the northwestern states. Occasionally it also damages green peas where large numbers of dried peas are grown nearby. The overwintering caterpillars pupate in spring, and the adults are present about the time peas flower in later spring. Eggs are laid singly near the flowers, and the caterpillar immediately bores into the developing pods. Larvae feed on the developing seeds and may injure several pods, often leaving little external evidence of infestation. When full grown they move to the soil and form a shelter in which they spend the winter. One generation per year is normal in much of the range, but two may occur in more southern areas.

A. Larval damage to nut by hickory shuckworm. *H. C. Ellis.* **B.** Egg-laying points made by hickory shuckworm. *H. C. Ellis.* **C.** Hickory shuckworm larva and injury. *L. Tedders.* **D.** Adult of filbertworm. *K. Gray.* **E.** Damage to nut by filbertworm larva. *K. Gray.* **F.** Hickory shuckworm adult. *L. Tedders.* **G.** Hickory shuckworm pupa. *J. A. Payne.* **H.** Full-grown filbertworm larva in cocoon. *K. Gray.*

Oriental Fruit Moth (*Grapholita molesta*)[1]

Hosts: Peach, apricot, and nectarine are most seriously damaged, but plum, cherry, apple, pear, almond, and rose are other hosts.

Damage: Larval tunneling into twigs causes wilting terminals ("shoot strikes"), and two or three such injuries may be produced by an individual insect. Fruit is damaged as larvae feed randomly through the flesh, not consuming the seeds in the manner of codling moth. Fruit injuries also differ in that entry holes produced by Oriental fruit moth are often inconspicuous.

Distribution: An introduced species that is widespread in orchards in the eastern and southern U.S. It has spread to California and also occurs in isolated area of many western states.

Appearance: Adults are small grayish moths, about ⅖ inch, which fly just after sunset. Larvae are pink with a brown head, very similar in appearance to codling moth larvae.

Life History and Habits: Winter is spent as a mature diapausing larva in a cocoon on or around a previously infested tree. Adults begin to emerge about the time peach blossom buds begin to show pink, and flights from this first generation may extend for almost 2 months. Eggs are laid on newly emerged shoots, and larvae feed in twigs. A second generation occurs in late spring (California) or early summer (Michigan) and attacks both twigs and fruit. Fruit injuries also occur when larvae move from twigs that harden and become unsuitable. A third generation occurs as peaches begin to mature, and most fruit infestations occur at this time. A small fourth generation is sometimes produced in Michigan; five generations per year are normally produced in California.

Related Species

Cherry fruitworm (*Grapholita packardi*) damages blueberry, tart cherry, apple, and peach throughout the northern two-thirds of the U.S. and Canada. Hawthorn and rose are other wild hosts. Larvae develop in fruit, and individuals may damage several small fruits before becoming mature. They then migrate to nearby canes, stubs of pruned twigs, pithy weeds, or other protected sites and burrow to produce a winter shelter. Winter is spent as full-grown larvae in cocoons, and pupation occurs in spring. Moths fly and lay eggs over a period of a month during the period when young fruits are present. One generation is produced annually.

Lesser appleworm (*Grapholita prunivora*) is a minor pest of apple and also occurs on cherry and plum. Primary damage to apple occurs when larvae tunnel shallowly under the fruit skin. Twigs are also tunneled. Two generations per year are reported from Michigan.

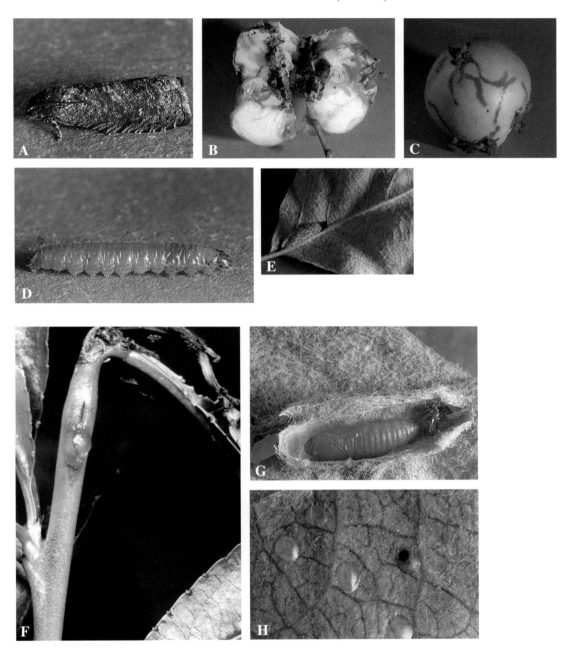

A. Oriental fruit moth. *K. Gray.* **B.** Damage by oriental fruit moth. *K. Gray.* **C.** Surface tunneling by oriental fruit moth larvae. *K. Gray.* **D.** Oriental fruit moth larva. *K. Gray.* **E.** Oriental fruit moth pupa attached to leaf. *K. Gray.* **F.** Shoot strike produced by oriental fruit moth tunneling. *Courtesy Clemson University.* **G.** Oriental fruit moth pupa. *K. Gray.* **H.** Oriental fruit moth eggs. *K. Gray.*

Miscellaneous Species

Grape berry moth (*Endopiza viteana*)[1] is an eastern species that develops on grape. The spring generation of larvae is most damaging as larvae may web together a cluster of flower buds and consume most of it. Tender shoots and newly set berries may also be eaten. Summer-generation larvae develop in the berries and may feed on two or three berries while developing. Two generations are produced annually, with winter spent as pupae.

Caterpillars of **navel orangeworm** (*Amyelois transitella*)[2] develop in a wide range of fruits and nuts. This species is particularly damaging to fig and almond in southern California. Eggs are laid in fissures of fruit and in cracks of nuts after hulls begin to split. Larvae are cream colored to slightly pinkish with a reddish brown head capsule.

Pecan nut casebearer (*Acrobasis nuxvorella*)[2] is found throughout areas where pecans are grown, from Florida to southern New Mexico. Larvae feed on and destroy developing nutlets, sometimes causing serious injury to orchards. Overwintered larvae feed and later pupate in shoots in early spring. The dark gray adult moths are first present around late May/early June and lay eggs near the calyx of nutlets shortly after pollination. Newly hatched larvae feed first on buds and may cause flowers to abort. They later bore into the base of developing nutlets, sometimes destroying an entire cluster. Conspicuous dark frass is produced as they feed and readily indicates infested nut clusters. Larvae feed for about 4 to 5 weeks and pupate in the nut. Adults emerge in July and lay eggs. Larvae from this second generation feed primarily on pecan shucks, causing little damage. Third-generation larvae feed little, moving to wintering shelter on twigs where they form a protective cocoon (hibernaculum).

Cranberry fruitworm (*Acrobasis vaccinii*)[2] is an important pest of blueberry in the eastern U.S. Adults are active when green berries are present, and eggs are laid around the blossom end of the fruit. The larvae usually enter the fruit around the stem. As many as eight berries may be consumed in the course of development. Berries are often loosely webbed together, and conspicuous brown frass is kicked out of the fruit as the larvae feed. Larvae are mostly green caterpillars with some brownish red coloration on the back. They have a dark head and are about ⅝ inch when full grown. The larvae then move to the soil and construct a cocoon among surface debris or shallowly in soil. They pupate in late winter. One generation is produced annually. Cranberry and huckleberry are other hosts for cranberry fruitworm. A related species is **destructive prune worm** (*A. tricolorella*), also known as **mineola moth**. It produces similar injuries to cherry and plum in most cherry-producing areas but is considered an infrequent and minor pest. The overwintering stage is a partially grown larva that moves to feed on buds in midspring.

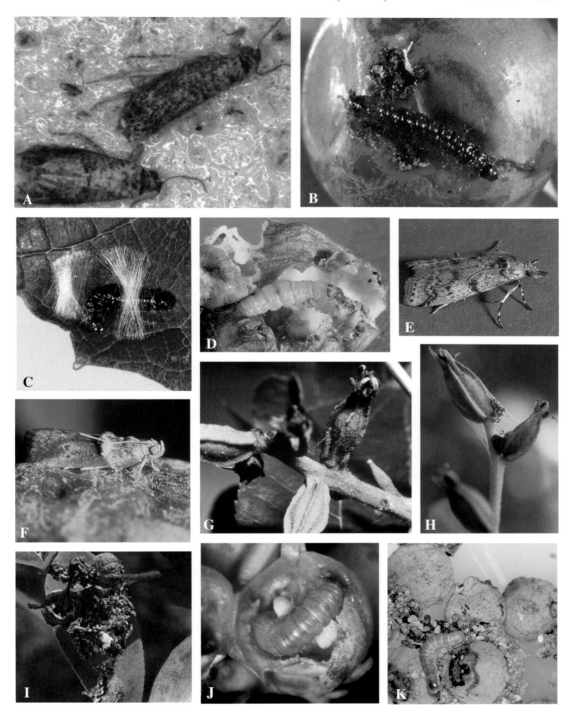

A. Adult grape berry moths caught in pheromone trap. *W. Cranshaw.* **B.** Grape berry moth larva and injury. *J. Ogrodnik/NY Agricultural Experiment Station.* **C.** Grape berry moth larva in leaf shelter. *J. Ogrodnik/NY Agricultural Experiment Station.* **D.** Navel orangeworm larva. *K. Gray.* **E.** Navel orangeworm adult. *K. Gray.* **F.** Pecan nut casebearer adult. *L. Tedders.* **G.** Pecan nut casebearer larva. *L. Tedders.* **H.** Damage by pecan nut casebearer. *H. C. Ellis.* **I.** Cranberry fruitworm injury to blueberry cluster. *F. Hale.* **J.** Cranberry fruitworm feeding in berry. *F. Hale.* **K.** Cranberry fruitworm damage to blueberry. *J. A. Payne.*

The genus *Dioryctria*[2] contains several species, collectively known as **coneworms**, that are most commonly observed feeding on conifer cones. In the southeastern states, west to parts of Texas, **southern pine coneworm** (*D. amatella*) is common in pine cones. The young larvae overwinter on the bark and move to the young cones and shoots in late spring. Cankers produced by rust fungi are also commonly colonized. In the northern half of the U.S. and southern Canada, **fir coneworm** (*D. abietivorella*) develops in Douglas-fir, fir, pine, and spruce. In cones it leaves a clean, pitch-free exit hole. It does considerable feeding on other parts of the plant, including buds, shoots, and even the trunk, in a manner similar to that of twig- and trunk-boring members of the genus (p. 440 and p. 470). Among the other species that develop predominantly in cones are **spruce coneworm** (*D. reniculelloides*) in spruce and fir, **blister coneworm** (*D. clarioralis*) on several southern pines, and **webbing coneworm** (*D. disclusa*) on various pines in eastern North America.

Sunflower moth (*Homoeosoma electellum*)[2] is common in the southern and central U.S., developing in flower heads of sunflower, coneflower, zinnia, and related plants. The overwintering larvae are fairly sensitive to cold and usually fail to survive winters above about 40° N latitude. The adults are highly migratory, however, and flights from the southcentral states may colonize areas into Canada and the northeastern states. Adults are usually present in the Midwest and High Plains states by late June or early July and lay eggs on flower heads. Larvae feed on florets and then on the developing seeds, consuming or damaging numerous seeds. They also cover heads with a fine silk which, mixed with plant debris and frass, gives them an unattractive appearance. The caterpillars are quite distinctive, being purplish or reddish brown with light stripes running the length of the body.

Banded sunflower moth (*Cochylis hospes*)[3] is common in the northern Great Plains but can be found from northern Texas east to North Carolina. Newly hatched larvae are white with a dark head, but body color changes throughout larval development and can vary from pink or yellow to purple or green at maturity. Females lay eggs in the base of flowers in late July, and larvae first feed on the florets. They later partially consume several seeds before moving to the soil and creating an overwintering cell in which they spend the winter. Pupation occurs the following June. The adult moths are straw colored with a wingspan of about ½ inch.

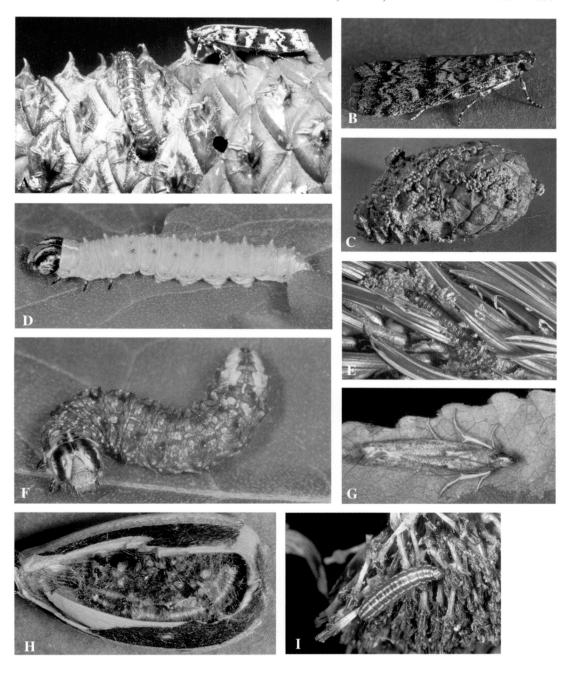

A. Southern pine coneworm larva and adult. *R. S. Cameron.* **B.** Fir coneworm adult. *K. Gray.* **C.** Typical cone-feeding damage by fir coneworm. *K. Gray.* **D.** Banded sunflower moth, light form. *F. Peairs.* **E.** Fir coneworm larva. *K. Gray.* **F.** Banded sunflower moth, dark form. *F. Peairs.* **G.** Sunflower moth. *F. Peairs.* **H.** Sunflower moth larva in seed. *F. Peairs.* **I.** Sunflower moth larva in sunflower head. *F. Peairs.*

Larvae of **artichoke plume moth** (*Platypilia carduidactyla*)[4] develop in the heads of various thistles. This is the most important insect pest of globe artichoke in California, but it also occurs throughout much of North America. Adults are small yellowish brown moths with unusual wings—the forewing is very narrow and clefted, and the hindwing consists of three long lobes. Wings are usually held perpendicular to the body when at rest and have a span of about 1 inch. The adults lay eggs singly among leaf hairs. The young larvae usually feed in small groups on tender foliage, often producing some webbing. Older larvae tend to tunnel plant parts, including buds. When full grown they pupate as a fairly unique form that is somewhat hairy and hangs from the tip of the abdomen. The complete life cycle takes about 100 days to complete. Two generations per year are reported from Minnesota, three from California. A related species is **snapdragon plume moth** (*P. antirrhina*) which develops in the buds, seed pods, and stems of snapdragon.

Cotton square borer (*Strymon melinus*)[5] develops on various legumes and plants in the mallow family (e.g., okra, cotton, hibiscus). Early-stage caterpillars feed on leaves, causing little injury. Older larvae may do some tunneling into pods of bean, okra, and other plants but are rarely abundant in gardens. Cotton square borer occurs throughout the U.S. and southern Canada but is only abundant in the southern U.S. The adult is an attractive butterfly known as **gray hairstreak**. Winter is spent in the chrysalis, with adults emerging in spring when host plants become available. Eggs are laid singly in plants. Young larvae feed on leaves, and older larvae concentrate more on reproductive tissues. Pupation occurs in a yellow or brown chrysalis marked with black spots. Two generations per year normally occur in the northern part of range and up to four in the south.

A. Artichoke plume moth larva in damaged bud. *J. K. Clark/UC Statewide IPM Program.* **B.** Artichoke plume moth. *K. Gray.* **C.** Damage by snapdragon plume moth. *K. Gray.* **D.** Cotton square borer larva and damaged bud. *R. Smith.* **E.** Snapdragon plume moth larva. *K. Gray.* **F.** Stem boring by snapdragon plume moth larva. *K. Gray.* **G.** Cotton square borer, larva of gray hairstreak. *J. Capinera.*

Tobacco (or Geranium) Budworm (*Heliothis virescens*)[6]

Hosts: A wide range. Although solanaceous plants such as petunia, nicotiana, and tobacco are particularly favored, tobacco budworm also feeds on geranium, ageratum, chrysanthemum, snapdragon, strawflower, rose, and many other flowering plants. It is rarely a vegetable pest, unlike the corn earworm it resembles.

Damage: Feeding injuries are concentrated on flower buds, the caterpillars favoring the reproductive tissues. Small larvae may restrict feeding to bud tunneling; later stages may consume entire buds and chew petals. Foliage is rarely damaged, but tunneling of leaf buds may occur. Reduced flower production ("loss of color") and ragged flowers result from tobacco budworm injuries.

Distribution: This insect is most damaging in areas of the southern U.S., as hard freezing temperatures can kill overwintering pupae. Mild winter conditions and some migration by the adult moths can allow significant infestations in more northern areas, however.

Appearance: Tobacco budworm is a moderate-sized insect, and caterpillars can reach 1½ inches when full grown. Color can be highly variable and is related in part to diet. Caterpillars may be nearly black to pale brown, with green and reddish forms also common. Banding may be present and prominent in darker caterpillars but indistinct in others. The presence of tiny "microspines" on some segments of the abdomen is used to separate this insect from the closely related corn earworm (tomato fruitworm/cotton bollworm).

The adult moth is a typical "cutworm" form with a wingspan of about 1½ inches. The general color is pale green, and the forewing is marked with four light and slightly wavy bands. Pupae, which are found in the soil, are spindle shaped and about ¾ inch long, typical of other cutworms.

Life History and Habits: Tobacco budworm overwinters as a pupa in an earthen cell buried a few inches beneath the soil surface. In spring, adults emerge and are active in the early evening. After mating, females glue eggs singly onto flower buds and leaves. The young caterpillars emerge and feed on buds, flowers, and, rarely, leaves. They become full grown in about 3 weeks, causing extensive injury. They then drop to the soil and pupate. In northern areas two generations per season are usually produced, with the highest caterpillar populations often occurring in August and early September. Four to five generations occur in the southern states.

A. Adult of the tobacco budworm. *W. Cranshaw.* **B.** Geranium bud tunneled by tobacco budworm. *W. Cranshaw.* **C.** Tobacco budworm eggs on geranium. *W. Cranshaw.* **D.** Tobacco budworm feeding on cluster of geranium buds. *W. Cranshaw.* **E.** Tobacco budworm tunneling geranium. *W. Cranshaw.* **F.** Tobacco budworm feeding in petunia flower. *W. Cranshaw.* **G.** Tobacco budworm damage to petunia. *W. Cranshaw.* **H.** Midstage larva of tobacco budworm. *Courtesy Clemson University.*

Corn Earworm/Tomato Fruitworm/Cotton Bollworm (*Helicoverpa zea*)[6]

Hosts: A wide range including many vegetables, field crops, fruits, flowers, and weeds. Corn, tomato, pepper, cotton, sorghum, and lettuce are among the crops most seriously damaged.

Damage: Larvae tunnel into ear tips of sweet corn, bore into various fruiting vegetables, and feed on leaves of lettuce and other vegetables. Corn earworm is considered one of the most destructive insects in the U.S., attacking many of the most important field and vegetable crops.

Distribution: Throughout North America except extreme northern areas. Where freezing winter temperatures prevent wintering, annual migrations originating from the southern U.S. and Mexico allow corn earworm to recolonize during summer and early fall.

Appearance: Young larvae are pale colored but darken as they get older. A range in color may be present from pale green to pink or even black. Adult moths are typical cutworm form, with light brown wings that often have a dark spot in the center.

Life History and Habits: Corn earworm is a tropical/subtropical species, and in parts of the southern U.S. development may be continuous. Winter temperatures limit survival in much of North America, and the species often dies out each year. (In the Midwest, Interstate 70 is often considered to be about the dividing line, south of which corn earworm regularly successfully survives winter conditions.) In the northern U.S. and Canada, infestations arise from annual migrations of the adult moths from the southern U.S. and Mexico. Migration flights typically begin in June, but with favorable weather additional migrations can occur through the growing season.

Moths fly at night, feeding on nectar and laying eggs singly on suitable host plants. On sweet corn, eggs are laid on green silks; on tomato and pepper, they are usually laid on the new leaves near flowers of developing fruit. Once corn earworm has migrated into an area, damage tends to be somewhat cyclical, as peak numbers of eggs tend to be laid during the period around a full moon.

Eggs hatch in about 2 to 5 days, and the young caterpillars begin to tunnel into the plants. Corn earworm caterpillars usually feed for about 4 weeks before becoming full grown. Older larvae become highly cannibalistic, and it is fairly uncommon to find more than one in a single corn ear. When full grown, they drop from the plant, construct a small cell in the soil, and pupate. Adults emerge in 10 to 14 days and produce the next generation.

A. Small group of eggs of corn earworm laid on cotton leaf. *B. Freeman.* **B.** Corn earworm pupa. *K. Gray.* **C.** Adult corn earworm. *W. Cranshaw.* **D.** Corn earworm adult visiting flower. *J. Lopez/USDA-ARS.* **E.** Corn earworm (cotton bollworm) feeding on cotton boll. *R. Smith.* **F.** Corn earworm larva in sunflower. *Courtesy University of Georgia Archives.* **G.** Corn earworm (tomato fruitworm) tunneling green tomato. *Courtesy Clemson University.* **H.** Tomato fruitworm and injury. *W. Cranshaw.* **I.** Corn earworm in ear tip. *W. Cranshaw.* **J.** Young corn earworm. *W. Cranshaw.* **K.** Corn earworm larvae, showing differences in coloration. *W. Cranshaw.*

Speckled Green Fruitworm (*Orthosia hibisci*)[6]

Hosts: A wide range of deciduous trees and shrubs including rose, apple, pear, cherry, peach, plum, crabapple, apricot, hawthorn, poplar, maple, willow, and white birch.

Damage: The caterpillars feed primarily on foliage and cause little injury. Damage occurs most often when developing fruits are present and are incidentally chewed. This often causes fruit drop. Fruits with small injuries often continue to grow but become misshapen and develop a corky area around the old chewing wound. This damage is similar to that produced by some leafroller caterpillars. Rosebuds may also be chewed in spring.

Distribution: Generally throughout southern Canada and the northern half of the U.S. but particularly abundant in eastern areas.

Appearance: Caterpillars have a green head and body, speckled with white spots. Indistinct white stripes run along the sides and back. Adult moths are nearly uniform gray with a wingspan of about 1½ inches.

Life History and Habits: Speckled green fruitworm is a climbing cutworm. It spends the winter underground in the pupal stage. Adults are among the first moths to emerge, in March or April, and females lay eggs singly or in small groups near plant buds. The caterpillars feed on the new leaves and remain on the tree throughout their development. If fruits are present, they may also chew these. By early June the larvae become full grown and drop from the plant. They often wander a short distance, then dig a few inches into the soil and pupate. One generation is produced per year.

Other Green Fruitworms

Caterpillars of several other species of climbing cutworms occasionally are associated with trees in mid- to early spring. **Green fruitworm** (*Lithophane antennata*)[6] is found throughout North America but is particularly abundant in the Midwest and northeastern states. It also is active early in the season, with moths emerging to lay eggs in late winter and spring when evening temperatures persist above about 50° F for a few hours. Eggs are laid singly or in small masses, and the larvae feed on opening buds, leaves, and young fruit. Other species include **pyramidal fruitworm** (*Amphipyra pyramidoides*),[6] **fourlined fruitworm** (*Himella intractata*),[6] and **yellowstriped fruitworm** (*Lithophane unimoda*). Injury is similar, and several species may be present concurrently. Life cycles vary somewhat, with *Lithophane* species overwintering as adult moths and pyramidal fruitworm as eggs.

A. Adult of speckled green fruitworm. *Courtesy Pacific Agri-Food Research Centre.* **B.** Speckled green fruitworm. *Courtesy Pacific Agri-Food Research Centre.* **C.** Pyramidal fruitworm. *W. Cranshaw.* **D.** Speckled green fruitworm damage to pear. *W. Cranshaw.* **E.** Green fruitworm feeding on apple. *R. Bessin.* **F.** Cankerworm and green fruitworm feeding on rose foliage. *D. Shetlar.* **G.** Fourlined fruitworm. *W. Cranshaw.*

Pickleworm (*Diaphania nitidalis*)[2]

Hosts: Summer and winter squash are most commonly damaged. Cucumber, cantaloupe, and some pumpkins are other hosts.

Damage: Larvae tunnel buds, blossoms, and fruit.

Distribution: Pickleworm is restricted by winter weather to parts of southern Florida and Texas. However, northward migrations occur annually into the Carolinas.

Appearance: Pale in early stages, pickleworm caterpillars darken with age and may be somewhat greenish or pink (turning coppery before pupation) with a dark area behind the head. Full-grown caterpillars are about ½ inch. Adults are attractive moths with about a 1-inch wingspan. The wings are generally margined with a yellowish band, and there is a prominent tuft on the hind end of the body.

Life History and Habits: Eggs are laid in small groups on buds, flowers, and new shoots. Larvae develop by feeding on the plant over a period of 2 to 3 weeks and then pupate in a thin cocoon tucked in folds of leaves or among crop debris. Adults usually disperse to weedy or woody areas where they spend the day and return to fields at night.

In the extreme southern U.S. where host plants are available year-round, activity may occur continuously. In Georgia and the Carolinas where hosts die out in winter and pickleworm fails to survive, there are typically two to four generations per year produced following the spring migration.

Related Insects

Melonworm (*Diaphania hyalinata*) is closely related to pickleworm and shares an almost identical host range and distribution in North America. Despite its name, it does not damage watermelon, and cantaloupe is not a favored host. Melonworm larvae are pale yellow-green and restrict feeding almost entirely to foliage. Direct fruit damage is limited to the fruit surface and produces scarring of the rind.

Limabean pod borer (*Etiella zinckenella*)[2] damages various legumes in the western states; it can also be found but is less damaging in some southeastern states. Lupine, lima bean, snap bean, cow pea, and milk vetch are among the more common hosts. Larvae destroy buds and blossoms and later tunnel into pods, destroying seeds and fouling pods with their excrement. The full-grown larvae are about ¾-inch long, tan or pinkish caterpillars with a yellow and black head. Limabean pod borer enters winter as a full-grown larva in diapause. It pupates in midwinter, and adults begin to emerge in early spring. Eggs are laid singly or in small groups, usually around flowers or at the base of pods. Larvae feed for more than a month and then enter the soil to pupate. About 2 months are required to complete the life cycle, and three to five generations are produced annually in southern California. The presence of wild lupine to support the initial generations has been important in the susceptibility of crops to later damage.

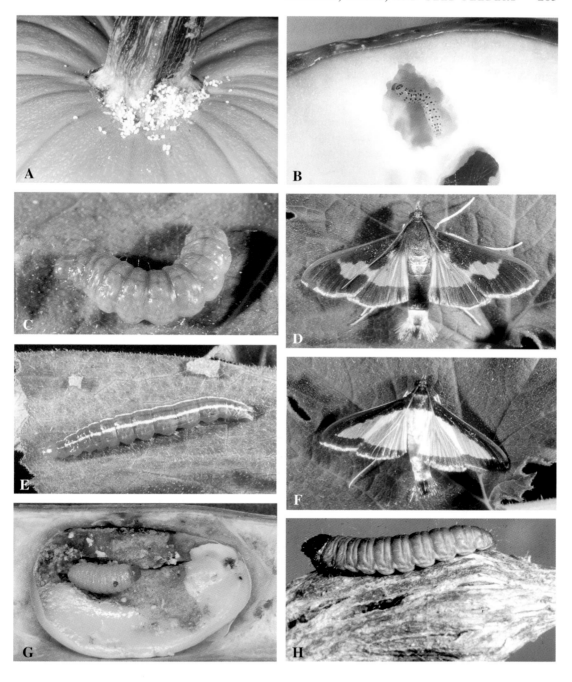

A. Fecal material extruded around entry point of pumpkin fruit, made by pickleworm larva. *J. Capinera.* **B.** Young pickleworm caterpillar in cucumber. *J. Capinera.* **C.** Mature pickleworm larva. *J. Capinera.* **D.** Pickleworm adult. *J. Capinera.* **E.** Melonworm larva. *J. Capinera.* **F.** Melonworm adult. *J. Capinera.* **G.** Limabean pod borer larva. *J. Capinera.* **H.** Limabean pod borer larva. *Courtesy Clemson University.*

Tomato pinworm (*Keiferia lycopersicella*)[7] occurs throughout warmer areas of the southwestern states. Tomato is the primary host, although some related plants such as eggplant, potato, and some nightshade weeds also host the insect. Eggs are laid in small clusters on the leaves, and young larvae mine leaves. Later they emerge and fold leaves, feeding as general defoliators. As the larvae get older, they darken from orange-brown to nearly purplish. Older larvae may tunnel fruit, causing most damage. Fruit injuries are concentrated around the stem end, but tunneling may extend to the core. Activity and reproduction may continue year-round if conditions permit. Seven to eight generations per year are commonly produced in southern California.

[1] Lepidoptera: Tortricidae; [2] Lepidoptera: Pyralidae; [3] Lepidoptera: Cochylidae; [4] Lepidoptera: Pterophoridae; [5] Lepidoptera: Lycaenidae; [6] Lepidoptera: Noctuidae; [7] Lepidoptera: Gelechiidae

FRUIT-INFESTING SAWFLIES

European apple sawfly (*Hoplocampa testudinea*)[1] is an introduced species found from New England south to West Virginia and west to Ontario. An isolated infestation also occurs on Vancouver Island, British Columbia. This species can be a serious pest of apple fruit and also damages crabapple.

Adults become active around the time apples begin to bloom and are present for about 2 weeks. Females lay eggs in the blossoms, and the newly hatched larvae feed on the surface of the young apples. These wounds may cause fruit to abort, but if fruit remains, injuries develop as spiral scars on the skin. After molting, later-stage larvae tunnel into the fruit and ultimately feed about the core. A large exit hole is produced from which reddish brown frass is continually expelled.

The larvae are pale brown with a dark head and very short appendages. They may feed on several fruits in a cluster before becoming full grown. They then drop to the ground and winter in a cocoon. Pupation occurs in spring, a few weeks before adults emerge.

Related Species

A few native *Hoplocampa* species, including *H. lacteipennis* and **cherry fruit sawfly** (*H. cookei*), damage wild and cultivated cherry. Cherry fruit sawfly is found in the Pacific Northwest where it also develops on plum.

[1] Hymenoptera: Tenthredinidae

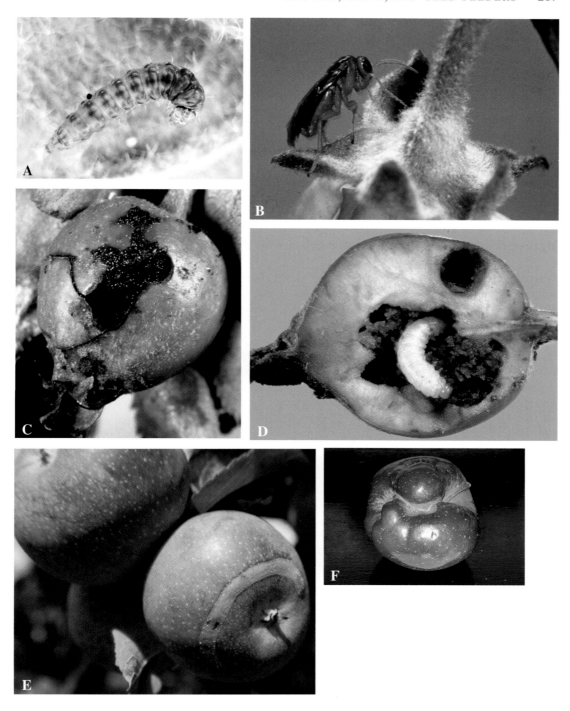

A. Tomato pinworm larva. *J. Capinera.* **B.** European apple sawfly. *J. Ogrodnik/NY Agricultural Experiment Station.*
C. European apple sawfly injury. *J. Ogrodnik/NY Agricultural Experiment Station.* **D.** European apple sawfly larva.
J. Ogrodnik/NY Agricultural Experiment Station. **E.** European apple sawfly injury. *J. Ogrodnik/NY Agricultural
Experiment Station.* **F.** European apple sawfly injury. *E. Day.*

FRUIT- AND FLOWER-INFESTING BEETLES

Japanese Beetle (*Popillia japonica*)[1]

Hosts: Adults feed on foliage of more than 300 species including rose, mountain-ash, willow, linden, elm, grape, Virginia creeper, bean, Japanese and Norway maples, birchs, pin oak, horse chestnut, rose of Sharon, sycamore, ornamental apple, plum, and cherry. Larvae develop on roots of various grasses.

Damage: Japanese beetle is one of the few beetles that is highly damaging in both the adult and larval stages. Adults feed on foliage and flower petals, producing skeletonizing injuries that cause leaves to appear lacelike. In high populations they may completely consume flower petals and more tender foliage. The larva, a type of white grub that feeds on grass roots (p. 526), is among the most damaging pests of turfgrass in the northeastern quadrant of the U.S.

Distribution: Originally introduced into New Jersey and now important in the northeastern U.S. and parts of southern Canada. This species ranges into Illinois and Iowa to the west and is found in parts of northern Alabama, northern Georgia, and South Carolina. Its range continues to expand, with localized infestations present in many other states.

Appearance: Adults are generally metallic green with bronze wing covers. A row of white hair brushes is present along each side. The overall form is broadly oval, and length ranges from about ⅓ to nearly ½ inch. Larvae are typical white grubs, C-shaped when at rest and a translucent creamy white. The accumulation of fecal matter in the hindgut may give a dark gray appearance to the posterior end.

Life History and Habits: Winter is spent in soil as a nearly full-grown grub that moves below frost line in winter. As soils warm, the grubs resume feeding on grass roots and pupate 1 to 3 feet below the surface, in a tamped earthen cell. Adults emerge in late June and early summer, feed on foliage, and mate, returning to lawn areas near sunset. The aggregation pheromones these insects produce combined with attractive odors produced by the food plants often result in large numbers feeding together.

Females lay eggs in small masses in soil cavities they excavate 2 to 4 inches deep. Most eggs are usually laid by early August, but some are laid into September. Over most of its range Japanese beetle has a 1-year life cycle, although it extends to 2 years in northern parts of the range.

A. Japanese beetle. *Courtesy Clemson University.* **B.** Japanese beetle larva. *D. Shetlar.* **C.** Japanese beetle grubs in lawn. *D. Herms.* **D.** Japanese beetles feeding at rose. *D. Herms.* **E.** Japanese beetles and feeding damage. *E. B. Walker.* **F.** Feeding damage by Japanese beetle. *J. D. Solomon.* **G.** Japanese beetles feeding on calla lily. *D. Shetlar.*

Other Scarab Beetles Common at Flowers

False Japanese beetle (*Strigoderma arboricola*),[1] sometimes known as spring rose beetle, occurs widely east of the Rockies and is particularly common in the midwestern U.S. The adult is very similar in appearance to Japanese beetle but is slightly duller colored and lacks the characteristic row of white tufts along the sides. Larvae feed on plant roots and are minor pests of potato, onion, grass, arborvitae, yew, and spruce. Adults are highly attracted to white and may cluster on white-petaled flowers during the brief period in early summer when they are active. False Japanese beetle is limited to areas of sandy soil and is known locally as "sandhill chafer" in parts of western Nebraska and eastern Colorado.

Adults of **rose chafer** (*Macrodactylus subspinosus*)[1] feed on leaves and particularly blossoms of a wide variety of plants, producing skeletonizing injuries. Rose and peony are highly preferred. Various berries, peach, cherry, amur cork tree, mountain-ash, grape, Virginia creeper, some birches, plum, cherry, and crabapple are other common hosts. Rose chafer contains a toxic heart poison, and birds can be poisoned by eating it.

Rose chafer is restricted to areas of the northeastern U.S. and eastern Canada where light, sandy soils are present. The larvae feed on roots of grasses and some weeds, apparently causing little injury. Adults emerge in June and live about a month. They are about ½ inch, more elongate than most scarab beetles, with gray or brown wings, a generally gray abdomen, and long orange legs. In the southwestern U.S. a related species is present, **western rose chafer** (*M. uniformis*), but it is rarely damaging.

Hoplia beetle (*Hoplia callipyge*),[1] also known as grapevine hoplia, is a minor pest of certain flowers and fruits in many western states. Injury to white and light-colored roses is most commonly reported, but flowers of ceanothus, calla lilly, California poppy, magnolia, lupine, and various legumes are also commonly fed on by adult beetles. Fruit clusters of grape are sometimes destroyed by this feeding, which usually occurs from mid-March through early May. Adults are about ¼ to ⅜ inch long and brownish or reddish brown with silvery scales on the back, providing a mottled appearance. Larvae feed on plant roots. One generation is produced annually. A related species in southwestern Canada that sometimes feed on flowers and small fruits is *H. modesta*. *H. oregona* has similar habits in the Pacific Northwest.

Bumble flower beetle (*Euphoria inda*)[1] is a moderately large, fuzzy scarab beetle. Adults are sometimes observed, often in small masses, at ooze from plant wounds and on fermenting fruit. Occasionally they damage flowers including daylily, large thistles, and strawflower. Larvae develop in decaying organic matter, preferring animal manures, and may be common in compost piles. (Container-grown plants using fresh compost sometimes are infested by bumble flower beetle larvae, which may incidentally chew on roots.) Bumble flower beetle is found throughout most of the area east of the Rocky Mountains. It overlaps in range with *E. sepulchralis*, which is restricted to eastern states. *E. kerni* feeds at garden flowers in Texas.

[1] Coleoptera: Scarabeaidae

A. False Japanese beetle. *W. Cranshaw.* **B.** Rose chafer. *J. Capinera.* **C.** *Hoplia modesta. Courtesy Pacific Agri-Food Research Centre.* **D.** Bumble flower beetles damaging cornflower. *W. Cranshaw.* **E.** *Hoplia oregona. K. Gray.* **F.** Bumble flower beetles feeding at bacterial ooze on willow. *D. Leatherman.* **G.** Bumble flower beetle larvae in horse manure compost. *W. Cranshaw.* **H.** Rose chafer feeding on rose hips. *Courtesy Clemson University.*

SAP BEETLES AND OTHER FRUIT-DAMAGING BEETLES

Sap beetles (Nitidulidae family) are common around fermenting fruit, oozing wounds of plants, and areas of decaying vegetation. Most do not cause any direct injuries to fruit or vegetables but are attracted to overripe fruit and can be a nuisance. Some species also may be involved in movement of bacteria and fungi, notably spores of *Cerataocystis fagacearum*, the causal organism of **oak wilt**. Approximately 180 sap beetle species occur in North America. Most are oval to nearly quadrate in form and have distinctly clubbed antennae. Several species in the fruitworm beetle family (Byturidae) also damage fruits.

Dusky Sap Beetle (*Carpophilus lugubris*)[1]

Hosts: Maturing sweet corn, most overripe fruits and vegetables, and trees infected with various bacteria and fungi.

Damage: Unlike most sap beetles, dusky sap beetle can directly injure intact sweet corn ears. Larvae chew on the developing kernels, although there is rarely any external evidence of infestation. Dusky sap beetle has been involved in moving spores of the oak wilt pathogen to wounds of healthy trees.

Distribution: Throughout most of North America, common.

Appearance: Adults are about ⅛ inch and dull dark gray with short wing covers. Larvae are pale colored, slightly flattened, with a brown head and a dark area on the hind segment.

Life History and Habits: Overwintered adults and pupae may be found in piles of discarded fruit, partially buried vegetable debris, or under the bark of trees with oozing wounds. Adults are active on warm days in early spring. At this time they feed and begin to lay eggs around decaying vegetation and on sap or bacterial ooze from damaged trees. Larvae can complete development in as little as 3 weeks, and pupation occurs in the soil. Two to three generations are probably produced in most years. Beetles are attracted to sweet corn shortly after pollen begins to be shed, at about the time that corn silk first begins to turn brown. Dusky sap beetle adults are present from early spring through November, with peak numbers often in late spring and midsummer.

A. Dusky sap beetle larvae in ear tip. *W. Cranshaw.* **B.** Dusky sap beetle larva. *R. Bessin.* **C.** Dusky sap beetle. *R. Bessin.* **D.** Dusky sap beetle. *K. Gray.* **E.** Symptoms of oak wilt. *Courtesy Minnesota Dept. Natural Resources.* **F.** Symptoms of oak wilt. *R. F. Billings.*

Other Sap Beetles

Fourspotted sap beetle (*Glischrochilus quadrisignatus*)[1] is common in the northern U.S. and southern Canada. It is sometimes known as picnic beetle because it often is attracted quickly and in nuisance numbers to ripe fruit, pickled vegetables, and fermented beverages during outdoor dining. It also commonly visits damaged or overripe fruits and vegetables, and it may chew on the silk of sweet corn and readily invade cavities made by corn earworm and European corn borer. Adults are about ¼ inch and shiny black with four orange-red spots. *G. fasciatus,* another common species, resembles fourspotted sap beetle but lacks the distinctive spotting.

Strawberry sap beetle (*Stelidota geminata*)[1] is a common pest of strawberry in the eastern U.S. It may aggregate in large numbers on ripening fruit, where the beetles feed and lay eggs. They can be important nuisance problems, particularly in pick-your-own operations. Adults are small (ca. ⅛ inch), mottled brown beetles. Strawberry sap beetle has a more restricted host range than many other sap beetles and is only damaging to strawberry. Two generations are typically produced annually.

Other Fruit-Damaging Beetles

Raspberry fruitworms (*Byturus* spp.)[2] are common insects associated with raspberry and loganberry throughout the northern U.S. and southern Canada. Primary damage is done by larvae, which tunnel into the receptacles at the base of the berries. These injuries directly damage many berries and cause them to drop. Contamination of berries by the larvae is also a concern. The larvae are distinctive in having two rows of light-colored, stiff hairs on the back.

Adults of **eastern raspberry fruitworm** (*B. rubi*) emerge in late April or early May, about the time leaves first emerge. They feed on the midrib of the unfolding leaves, which results in ragged, elongate holes. They then may feed on the unopened flower buds and can destroy an entire bud cluster and further damage leaves in a skeletonizing manner. Eggs are laid on or sometimes in unopened blossom buds. The larvae then bore into the developing fruit. When full grown, the larvae drop from the plant and pupate in the soil. One generation is produced per year. The life history is likely similar for **western raspberry fruitworm** (*B. bakeri*), common in western areas, and for *B. unicolor,* found in many areas of Canada.

[1] Coleoptera: Nitidulidae; [2] Coleoptera: Byturidae

A. Fourspotted sap beetle. *K. Gray.* **B.** Western raspberry fruitworm adult. *K. Gray.* **C.** Fourspotted sap beetles at wounded plant stem. *S. Rachesky.* **D.** Western raspberry fruitworm in raspberry fruit. *K. Gray.* **E.** Western raspberry fruitworm in raspberry fruit. *K. Gray.*

FRUIT, FLOWER, AND SEED WEEVILS

The weevils, or snout beetles, are the largest family (Curculionidae)[1] of insects, with more than 40,000 species described worldwide. Adults of all are marked with an elongated "snout," at the end of which are chewing mouthparts. This is usually used to chew into plants, and larval stages of many species develop inside seeds, fruits, and flower buds.

Many of the weevils that develop on seeds or fruit are known as curculios, a reference to the family name. Other weevils develop as borers of stems (p. 450) or as root feeders (p. 532), and a few develop on foliage (p. 220). Weevil larvae are legless with a distinct head and cannot be easily distinguished from bark beetle larvae.

Plum Curculio (*Conotrachelus nenuphar*)

Hosts: Plum, apple, and apricot are most seriously damaged, but peach, nectarine, quince, cherry, pear, hawthorn, wild plum, and native crabapple are also hosts.

Damage: Feeding and egg-laying wounds by adults produce scarring and distortion of developing fruit, often inducing premature fruit drop. Wounds may provide entry for brown rot fungus. Larvae tunnel fruit of plum, peach, and apricot.

Distribution: Generally distributed over the eastern and midwestern states and eastern Canada. Localized infestations occur in parts of Utah, the Pacific Northwest, eastern Texas, and Oklahoma.

Appearance: Adults are generally gray to black snout beetles, about ¼ inch, with light gray and brown mottling. The wing covers are rough with two prominent humps and two smaller ones. Larvae, found in fruit, are legless, creamy white grubs with a dark head; they are about ⅜ inch when full-size.

Life History and Habits: Adult weevils winter under covering debris in the vicinity of previously infested trees. They begin to move to trees when average spring temperatures exceed 55 to 60° F for 3 to 4 days, and migration continues for a month or more. When small fruits become available, females chew a small pit and insert eggs. They then make a crescent-shaped cut below the egg pocket, leaving a small flap of dead skin on the surface of the fruit.

Eggs hatch in about 1 week, and larvae feed in the fruit for about 3 weeks. On some fruit, such as apple, larvae survive poorly, apparently crushed by growing tissues. Larvae that develop successfully cut their way out and drop to the soil. They dig and produce a small earthen cell where they pupate. Adults emerge in 4 to 6 weeks. In most of its range, plum curculio has only one generation per year, and adults feed on maturing apples before moving to hibernation sites. Two generations are reported in Oklahoma and Texas.

A. Plum curculio adult. *D. Shetlar.* **B.** Plum curculio adult. *Courtesy Clemson University.* **C.** Egg-laying scars by plum curculio. *W. Hantsbarger.* **D.** Plum curculio emerging from blueberry. *J. A. Payne.* **E.** Plum curculio larva in fruit. *Courtesy Clemson University.*

Rose Curculio (*Merhynchites bicolor*)

Hosts: Rose, particularly wild rose.

Damage: Rose curculio damages roses by making feeding punctures in flower buds, resulting in ragged flowers. During periods when buds are not common, feeding occurs on the tips of shoots, killing or distorting the shoots. A "bent neck" condition of rose, similar to that which rose midge may produce (p. 240), can be caused by rose curculio feeding wounds to developing stems.

Distribution: Generally throughout the U.S. and southern Canada.

Appearance: Adults are about ⅕ inch with a pronounced dark-colored "beak," which is longer on the males. In most areas the wing covers, thorax, and head are reddish and the remainder of the body black. In many western states, however, this species may have metallic green or blue-green coloration.

Life History and Habits: Adults become active in late spring and lay eggs in developing flowers. The larval (grub) stage feeds on the reproductive parts of the flower. Blossoms on the plant, including those clipped off by a gardener, are suitable for the insect to develop. When full grown, the grubs fall to the soil and form an underground cell, pupating the following spring. There is one generation per year.

Other Seed-, Fruit-, and Flower-Damaging Weevils

Plum gouger (*Coccotorus scutellaris*) feeds on hard types of plum. Adult weevils make numerous feeding punctures, many of which result in a flow of clear ooze, in the developing fruit. Eggs are laid in some of the punctures, and the larvae develop in the pit. This species apparently spends the winter as an adult in the pit. Removal of damaged fruit usually helps control this species.

Apple curculio (*Anthonomus quadrigibbus*) is found in the midwestern and eastern U.S. and eastern Canada. Damage to apple is infrequent, mostly resulting from feeding punctures that heal as sunken areas on the fruit. Larvae cannot develop in growing apple fruit, only in early-season dropped fruit. Development most commonly occurs in other hosts—amelanchier, hawthorn, and wild crabapple.

Cherry curculio (*Anthonomus consors*) is a minor pest of sour cherry in the Rocky Mountain region. Adults chew small holes in the base of flowers and cause abortion of developing fruit. The skin of older fruit is pitted by this injury. Eggs are inserted into fruit, and larvae tunnel the fruit, ultimately feeding on the pit. One generation is produced per year.

Grape curculio (*Craponius inaequalis*) develops in the berries of grape grown in the southeastern states. Adults emerge in mid-June in Georgia and first feed on foliage, producing zigzag chewing wounds on leaves and petioles. They also puncture fruit to feed and lay eggs.

A. Reddish phase of the rose curculio. *K. Gray.* **B.** Adult rose curculio. *W. Cranshaw.* **C.** Dark-phase rose curculio. *K. Gray.* **D.** Rose petals damaged following rose curculio bud feeding. *W. Cranshaw.* **E.** Cherry curculio on cherry fruit. *W. Cranshaw.* **F.** Pit damage caused by feeding of larval cherry curculio. *W. Cranshaw.* **G.** Cherry curculio resting on leaf. *W. Cranshaw.*

Sunflower headclipping weevil (*Haplorhynchites aeneus*) damages sunflower by cutting the stalk near the base of the head. The adults are shiny black weevils, about ⅓ inch, with a pronounced snout. The overwintered adults become active in early summer and feed on pollen. During egg-laying, females first make a series of punctures at the base of the flower head, which subsequently wilts and usually drops from the stem. Eggs are laid in the head and the larvae feed in it, becoming about ⅓-inch-long grubs when full grown. One generation is produced per year.

In the eastern states, **strawberry bud weevil** (*Anthonomus signatus*), also known as strawberry clipper, can damage strawberry, blackberry, and related caneberries. Adults emerge in spring as temperatures rise above 60° F and initially feed on buds of strawberry and redbud. Some later move to blackberry, raspberry, and dewberry as buds begin to swell on these plants. Small holes are chewed in the buds and an egg inserted. The female then cuts the stem just below the bud, which often drops from the plant. About 20 to 30 eggs are laid by each female, mostly in April and early May. The summer-generation adults appear in early summer and feed on pollen before moving to winter shelters. Strawberry bud weevil is a small (ca. ⅒ inch) reddish brown weevil.

Pepper weevil (*Anthonomous eugenii*) is a tropical species that occurs in parts of southern Texas, south Georgia, and Florida. Larvae tunnel the center of pepper fruit and feed on the seed mass. Adults are black weevils, about ⅛ inch with a sparse covering of tan to gray hairs. Breeding may be continuous throughout the year, with fruit of nightshade an alternate host.

Hollyhock weevil (*Apion longirostre*) feeds on the seeds, buds, and leaves of hollyhock. Small feeding punctures in emerging leaves and petals give the plant a ragged appearance. The larvae consume the seeds of the plant. Hollyhock weevils spend the winter in the adult stage, either in protected areas around hollyhock or in seeds. They move to hollyhock plants in late spring and feed by chewing small holes in the buds of the plants. During this time the weevils are commonly observed mating, the female being identifiable by an extremely long "beak." As flower buds form in June, the females chew deep pits in the buds and lay eggs. The grub stage of the insect feeds on the developing embryo of the seed. After feeding is completed, it pupates in the seed. Adults usually emerge in August and September, but some remain in the seeds, emerging the following spring. There is one generation per year.

In the northern Great Plains, two species of small weevils develop in the seeds of sunflower: **red sunflower weevil** (*Smicronyx fulvus*) and **gray sunflower seed weevil** (*S. sordidus*). Adults of red sunflower weevil move to the plants and first feed on the bracts of the developing head, then on pollen. When young seeds start to form, the weevils lay eggs inside them and the grubs consume much of the seed interior while developing. In late summer they drop to the ground and dig a small soil cell where they spend the winter in diapause. Pupation occurs the following year. Gray sunflower seed weevil is less damaging as it lays fewer eggs and lays them earlier, beginning in the early to mid-bud stages.

A. Adult sunflower headclipping weevil. *W. Cranshaw.* **B.** Mating pair of hollyhock weevils. *W. Cranshaw.*
C. Damaged head from sunflower head clipper. *W. Cranshaw.* **D.** Pepper weevil damage. *J. Capinera.* **E.** Adult pepper weevil. *J. Capinera.* **F.** Hollyhock weevil larvae in developing seeds. *K. Gray.* **G.** Hollyhock weevil pupa in seed. *K. Gray.* **H.** Hollyhock weevil, male. *K. Gray.* **I.** Hollyhock weevil, female. *K. Gray.* **J.** Gray sunflower seed weevil. *F. Peairs.* **K.** Sunflower seed weevil larva. *F. Peairs.*

About 30 species of **acorn** and **nut weevils** (*Curculio* spp.) develop in the seeds of oak and various nut trees. Adults are usually brown, about ¼ inch with a prominent snout, particularly on the female. The legless grubs develop in the nuts and are a favored food of squirrels. The most important species is **pecan weevil** (*C. caryae*), often the most serious pest of pecan grown in the southeastern quadrant of the U.S. Hickory is also a common host. Adults are active primarily from early August through September. Adults feeding on young nuts cause abortion. Most damage, however, is produced by the larvae.

Females lay small packets of two to four eggs into the developing nut, and the larvae subsequently consume much of the nut meat over the next month. When feeding is completed, they drop to the ground and dig a small cell in the soil where they remain for 1 or 2 years before pupating. During winter a mixture of adults and larvae may be found.

Other economically important species include **large chestnut weevil** (*Curculio caryatrypes*) and **small chestnut weevil** (*C. sayi*), both associated with chestnut, **hazelnut weevil** (*C. obtusus*), and **filbert weevil** (*C. occidentis*). **Hickory nut curculio** (*Conotrachelus hicoriae*) is common in acorns and hickory nuts. Nuts of black walnut grown east of the Great Plains are infested by **black walnut curculio** (*C. retentus*). Wounds produced by adults that chew into the developing nuts in spring are a common cause of June drop. Larvae develop in the seed.

[1] Coleoptera: Curculionidae

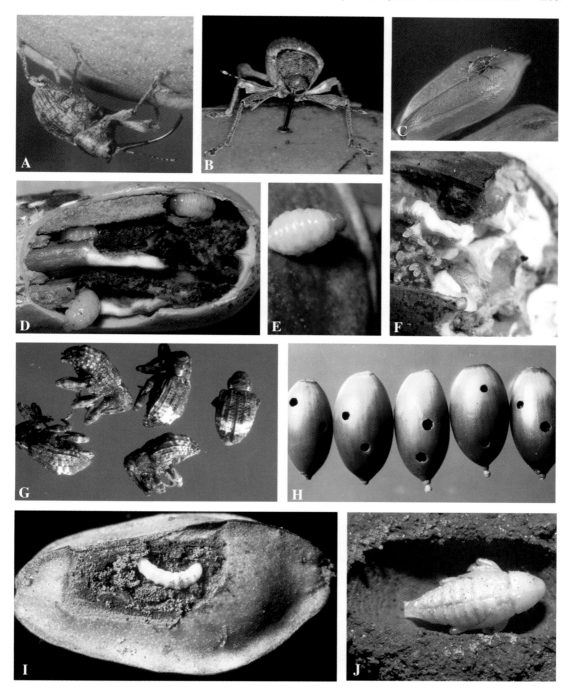

A. Pecan weevil. *Courtesy Clemson University.* **B.** Pecan weevil feeding. *J. A. Payne.* **C.** Female pecan weevil. *H. C. Ellis.* **D.** Pecan weevil larvae in pecan nut. *H. C. Ellis.* **E.** Pecan weevil larva emerging from nut. *L. Tedders.* **F.** Pecan weevil egg mass. *L. Tedders.* **G.** Hickory nut curculio adults. *J. D. Solomon.* **H.** Exit holes in acorns produced by hickory nut curculio. *J. D. Solomon.* **I.** Hickory nut curculio larva. *J. D. Solomon.* **J.** Pecan weevil pupa. *L. Tedders.*

CHAPTER SIX

Sap Suckers

WHITEFLIES

Whiteflies (Aleyrodidae family)[1] are primarily tropical or subtropical insects but occur widely in North America in association with houseplants and greenhouse crops. Adults are small (ca. 1/10 inch) insects typically covered with powdery whitish wax. Immature stages of whiteflies are scalelike, feeding on sap from plants and rarely moving after the first stage. Whiteflies possess a unique final development stage from which the adults emerge, sometimes termed a "pupa," which does not feed (see Figure 4).

Greenhouse Whitefly (*Trialeurodes vaporariorum*)

Hosts: Greenhouse whitefly has a wide host range and is known to develop on more than 250 ornamental and vegetable plants. Poinsettia, hibiscus, nicotiana, aster, calendula, cucumber, lantana, tomato, grape, ageratum, bean, and begonia are among the more commonly infested plants.

Damage: Greenhouse whitefly sucks sap from the plant, primarily from the phloem. Heavy infestations cause decline of plant vigor. Stunting, yellowing of foliage, and premature leaf drop are among the symptoms of injury. Infestations are also associated with production of honeydew excreted by the whitefly during feeding.

Distribution: Throughout North America, particularly in association with greenhouses and houseplants. Greenhouse whitefly cannot survive winter outdoors in areas with freezing winter temperatures but commonly is annually introduced into gardens on infested transplants.

Appearance: All of the immature stages of greenhouse whitefly are inconspicuous and easily overlooked. They are usually pale, almost translucent, in color and superficially resemble certain scale nymphs. Late-stage nymphs and the nonfeeding pupae may have numerous thin waxy threads along the sides of the body, giving them a somewhat spiny appearance. The spininess of the immature stages is variable and is affected by population density and the hairiness of the leaf surface. Adults have nearly pure white wings which are held broadly rooflike over the abdomen.

Life History and Habits: When conditions permit, eggs are laid on the plant surface and are a creamy yellow color before darkening after 24 hours. The great majority of eggs are laid on the newest leaves and in a semicircular pattern. Egg hatch typically occurs within 5 to 7 days, and the newly hatched nymphs move a short distance before flattening themselves against the leaf to feed. All remaining immature stages of greenhouse whitefly are immobile. There are three nymphal stages that feed on the plant, spaced at 2- to 4-day intervals, followed by a nonfeeding "pupal" stage lasting almost a week. Under highly favorable conditions, a generation of greenhouse whitefly can take as little as 3 to 4 weeks to complete. Each female is capable of laying 400 eggs over a period of up to 2 months, although usually far fewer eggs are produced.

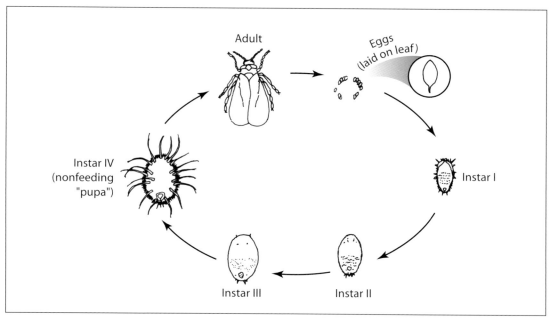

Figure 4. Typical life cycle of a whitefly. *Figure by L. Mannix.*

A. Adult greenhouse whitefly. *W. Cranshaw.* **B.** Greenhouse whitefly eggs, laid in characteristic semicircle. *K. Gray.* **C.** Greenhouse whitefly, recently emerged from nymphal skin, and nymph (upper right). *K. Gray.* **D.** Eggs and nymphal stages of greenhouse whitefly. *W. Cranshaw.* **E.** Greenhouse whitefly "pupae." Those that are dark are parasitized. *W. Cranshaw.* **F.** Greenhouse whitefly nymphs and exuvium. *K. Gray.* **G.** Greenhouse whitefly. *K. Gray.*

Other Whiteflies

Bandedwinged whitefly (*Trialeurodes abutilonea*) is a close relative of greenhouse whitefly but is rarely a pest. Adult bandedwinged whiteflies can be differentiated by the presence of two smoky gray, zigzag bands on the wings; pupae are distinguished by a dark band. Poinsettia, geranium, hibiscus, and petunia are the most common hosts in greenhouses. In southern states this species may breed outdoors on various weed hosts as well as on cotton and some ornamentals.

Silverleaf whitefly (*Bemisia argentifolii*) is a relatively newly introduced pest that has become established throughout much of the southwestern and southeastern U.S. It is also found in greenhouses. Sweetpotato whitefly biotype B and poinsettia whitefly are other names for this insect. It is generally similar in appearance to greenhouse whitefly but has a slightly more yellowish body. Adults tend to position their wings when at rest in a more tentlike manner over the body. The last instar (pupa) is the most distinguishing form, being teardrop shaped and much more flattened than that of greenhouse whitefly.

Silverfleaf whitefly has an extremely wide host range including poinsettia, hibiscus, chrysanthemum, tomato, pepper, squash, cucumber, cotton, bean, eggplant, cabbage, watermelon, broccoli, potato, and peanut. As with other whiteflies, adults and nymphs remove sap while feeding, causing reduction of plant vigor during heavy infestations. However, introduced saliva has some toxic effects, producing disorders such as silvering of squash foliage, yellowing of lettuce, and whitening of roots and stems of carrot and broccoli. Affected tomato also may show irregular ripening. Silverleaf whitefly can transmit plant viruses including those associated with tomato yellow leaf curl, tomato mottle, and bean golden mosaic.

There has been considerable debate as to whether silverleaf whitefly is a valid species or a biotype of **sweetpotato whitefly** (*Bemisia tabaci*). Sweetpotato whitefly is a serious pest of vegetable crops in many areas of the world, primarily because of its ability to vector many viruses. It was known to occur in the southern U.S. for more than a century but was not a serious pest. In the mid-1980s, however, silverleaf whitefly apparently became established and rapidly developed as a major pest. Furthermore, sweetpotato whitefly, which was present prior to the introduction of silverleaf whitefly, appears to have been entirely displaced by the latter and is no longer found in areas in the U.S. where it formerly occurred.

Mulberry whitefly (*Tetraleurodes mori*) is found throughout most of the U.S. although rarely as a pest. Common hosts include mahonia, hackberry, mountain laurel, sweetgum, maple, dogwood, sycamore, citrus, and mulberry. The last-stage nymph ("pupa") has an unusual and conspicuous appearance, being shiny black with a white fringe. Multiple overlapping generations are produced during the growing season, and the pupa is the overwintering stage. A species of similar appearance is **azalea whitefly** (*Pealius azalaeae*), an introduced species now found throughout the southeastern U.S. wherever azalea is grown. Rhododendrons may host **rhododendron whitefly** (*Dialeurodes chittendeni*).

A. Bandedwinged whiteflies. *R. Smith.* **B.** Silverleaf whitefly colony. *J. Capinera.* **C.** Bandedwinged whiteflies. *R. Smith.* **D.** Silverleaf whitefly. *S. Bauer/USDA-ARS.* **E.** Bandedwinged whitefly nymph. *W. Cranshaw.* **F.** Silverleaf whitefly nymphs with pupa in center. *J. Capinera.* **G.** Silverleaf whiteflies. *S. Bauer/USDA-ARS.* **H.** Mulberry whitefly nymphs and adult. *W. Cranshaw.* **I.** Rhododendron whitefly. *R. Childs.* **J.** Mulberry whitefly nymphs. *W. Cranshaw.*

Ash whitefly (*Siphonius phillyreae*) is a fairly recently introduced insect discovered in southern California in the late 1980s. It has since spread to New Mexico and Arizona and is also reported from North Carolina. Hosts include ash, mulberry, crabapple, flowering pear, serviceberry, western red bud, crape myrtle, tuliptree, lilac, pyracantha, and privet. Severe infestations, with associated problems of honeydew production and sooty mold, occurred shortly after its introduction. Establishment of the parasitic wasp *Encarsia inaron,* however, has since had a great effect on suppressing populations.

Citrus blackfly (*Aleurocanthus woglumi*) is an important whitefly associated with citrus in southern Florida. As it feeds it produces considerable amounts of honeydew which further promotes unattractive sooty molds. As in mulberry whitefly, the last-stage nymph is shiny black with a white wax fringe. Adults are slate blue, considerably darker than most common whiteflies. **Citrus whitefly** (*Dialeurodes citri*) is found throughout the southern U.S. It can be an important pest of citrus but develops on a wide range of hosts including ivy, gardenia, lilac, and privet. Development is continuous, with generations being completed in about 2 or 3 months during the growing season. Winter in the northern areas of the range is spent as late-stage nymphs on leaves. **Woolly whitefly** (*Aleurothrixus floccosus*) also develops on citrus, as well as eugenia. It is found in areas of southern California and Florida. Woolly whitefly became a serious pest following its accidental introduction around 1909 until several parasitic wasps were established that since have provided excellent biological control. As the name suggests, the body of the nymph is covered by long, loose waxy threads. **Giant whitefly** (*Aleurodicus dugesii*) is a recently introduced species currently found in southern California, Texas, and Florida. As the name indicates, it is substantially larger than other whitefly species. Giant whiteflies tend to reproduce on the same leaf on which they developed, causing clustering of colonies, and waxy filaments dislodged from the body may spread across the leaf surface. Furthermore, while egg-laying they make distinct waxy spirals on the underside of leaves. Giant whitefly has a wide host range of ornamental plants.

Iris whitefly (*Aleyrodes spiraeoides*) is reportedly common in California and sometimes injurious to iris and gladiolus. It has a wide host range including many vegetables, strawberry, and cotton. Adults have a slightly dark dot on each wing. Eggs are laid in distinct circles, and fine powdery wax is produced about the eggs and nymphs on the leaf.

[1] Homoptera: Aleyrodidae

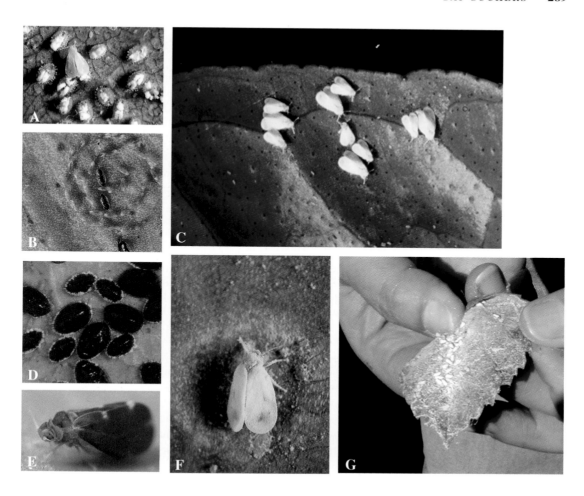

A. Ash whiteflies. *J. R. Baker.* **B.** Egg spiral produced by citrus blackfly. *Courtesy Florida Dept. Agriculture and Consumer Services/Div. Plant Industry.* **C.** Citrus whiteflies. *F. Peairs.* **D.** Citrus blackfly "pupae." *Courtesy Florida Dept. Agriculture and Consumer Services/Div. Plant Industry.* **E.** Citrus blackfly adult. *Courtesy Florida Dept. Agriculture and Consumer Services/Div. Plant Industry.* **F.** Iris whitefly. *J. K. Clark/UC Statewide IPM Program.* **G.** Giant whitefly. *S. Newman.*

PSYLLIDS

Psyllids (Psyllidae family)[1] are small insects, about ⅒ inch in length when full grown. Adults somewhat resemble miniature cicadas and are often referred to as jumping plant lice because of their ability to jump. Nymphs are flattened and somewhat scalelike in appearance, found attached usually to the underside of leaves.

Close to 200 species, several of foreign origin, occur in North America. Psyllids tend to be quite specific in their hosts, usually restricting their feeding to a single genus or family of plants. Damage may result from the removal of sap sucked from the plants, but psyllids often produce injury as a result of saliva injected during feeding. Distortions of leaf growth, production of galls (p. 414), and systemic effects on plant growth result from some of the species that possess particularly toxic saliva. At least one species, pear psylla, is also involved in transmitting plant pathogens.

Many psyllids excrete distinctive material as they feed. In some this takes the form of honeydew. Others may produce wax-covered pellets resembling granulated sugar, and others excrete large amounts of wax similar to that of "woolly" aphids and mealybugs.

Potato/Tomato Psyllid (*Bactericera [= Paratrioza] cockerelli*)

Hosts: Many solanaceous plants including eggplant, pepper, and certain nightshade. Only tomato and potato appear to sustain significant injury, however.

Damage: Saliva injected during feeding causes various disruptions of plant growth, collectively described as psyllid yellows. Slowed plant growth, leaf curling, and color changes are common results. Effects on potato tubers include reduced size, premature sprouting, and rough skin. Tomatoes damaged by this species produce small fruits that are soft and of poor quality.

Distribution: Texas, southern California, and areas of northern Mexico are most commonly infested during cool-season months. Dispersal through the High Plains and Rocky Mountain region occurs during summer.

Appearance: Mature adults are generally dark gray or black with distinct white bands and markings. These markings take a few days to develop, and newly emerged adults are pale colored. Nymphs are flattened and have a series of minute waxy projections surrounding the body. Young nymphs are pale brown or tan. Older nymphs become increasingly greenish and develop noticeable wing pads. Eggs are minute but are laid on a characteristic small stalk.

Life History and Habits: Potato/tomato psyllid is a migratory insect wintering in the extreme southwestern U.S. and Mexico. It annually migrates northward in late spring, when temperatures begin to get hot in the overwintering breeding areas. Females lay small yellow-orange eggs in small groups, usually on the underside of leaves. The resulting nymphs that hatch are flattened and somewhat scalelike. Nymphs rarely move and tend to concentrate on the underside of leaves in more shaded areas of the plant. After 3 to 4 weeks the adults emerge and repeat the cycle. During a season, three to four generations may be completed in a region. A reverse migration to southern areas is assumed to occur in early fall. Potato/tomato psyllid may breed continuously in greenhouses and has developed as a pest of greenhouse tomatoes.

A. Adult potato/tomato psyllid. *W. Cranshaw.* **B.** Small group of adult potato/tomato psyllids. *W. Cranshaw.* **C.** Psyllid yellows symptoms caused by potato/tomato psyllid. *W. Cranshaw.* **D.** Adult, nymphs, and eggs of potato/tomato psyllid. *W. Cranshaw.* **E.** Purpling of top growth resulting from potato/tomato psyllid injury to red potato variety. *W. Cranshaw.* **F.** Potato/tomato psyllid nymph. *W. Cranshaw.* **G.** Potato/tomato psyllid nymphs and characteristic sugar droppings. *W. Cranshaw.* **H.** Potato/tomato psyllid eggs. *W. Cranshaw.* **I.** Aerial tuber forming on stem of potato infested by potato/tomato psyllid. *W. Cranshaw.*

Pear Psylla (*Cacopsylla pyricola*)

Hosts: Restricted to fruit-producing pear. Species of ornamental pear do not appear to be susceptible to this insect.

Damage: Pear psylla feeds on the leaves of pear trees, excreting large amounts of honeydew that cover leaves and fruit and allow growth of sooty molds. High numbers of psyllids on trees can reduce plant vigor, cause necrotic spotting of leaves, and may even induce a condition known as psylla shock, resulting in leaf drop and suppressed growth from which it may take a plant several years to recover. In some areas pear psylla also is important in the spread of the bacteria (phytoplasma) that produce pear decline disease.

Distribution: Of European origin, pear psylla can be found wherever pear is grown. It is particularly damaging in the Pacific states and in the Northeast.

Appearance: Adults are dark reddish brown with clear wings. Young nymphs are pale yellowish but develop dark markings and wing pads as they get older. Nymphs are often covered with droplets of honeydew.

Life History and Habits: Pear psylla overwinters in the adult stage in protected areas (under bark, plant debris on soil, or other cover) in the vicinity of previously infested trees. It becomes active in late winter or early spring and moves to pear trees, laying yellow-orange eggs as pear buds begin to swell. The emerging nymphs then move to feed on the tender new growth.

As they feed, young pear psylla nymphs become covered with the honeydew droplets they excrete. During the final nymphal stage, conspicuous wing pads develop and the nymphs do not live in the honeydew. They then molt to the adult stage. Later generations lay eggs on the new leaves, often concentrating on sucker sprouts late in the season. Two to three generations are normally produced in a season. At the end of the year, dark-colored winter adult forms move to shelter.

A. Pear psylla adult. *K. Gray.* **B.** Pear psylla eggs on twigs. *K. Gray.* **C.** Pear psylla nymph in honeydew droplet. *E. Nelson.* **D.** Pear psylla nymph. *K. Gray.* **E.** Pear psylla leaf injury. *K. Gray.*

Other Psyllids

Perhaps the most important *Cacopsylla* species, aside from pear psylla, is **boxwood psyllid** (*C. buxi*). Common in the eastern U.S., this species can produce conspicuous leaf cupping distortion to American boxwood. Nymphs cover themselves with long threads of wax as they feed on the newly developing leaves in spring. One generation occurs per year, with adults laying overwintering eggs around bud scales in early summer.

Several other *Cacopsylla* species are associated with woody plants. **Apple sucker psyllid** (*C. mali*) feeds primarily on sprouts of fruit trees and causes little injury. **Boxelder psyllid** (*C. negundinis*) is found throughout the range of boxelder maple and is considered a minor pest, producing some honeydew and making modest leaf distortions. Related species occur on maple, birch, alder, cherry, and willow.

Redgum lerp psyllid (*Glycaspis brimblecomei*) became established in California in the late 1990s and has spread quickly. It is also known from Florida. In addition to causing feeding injuries and nuisance problems with excreted honeydew, it forms a conspicuous, conical wax cap (lerp) over the nymphs. **Bluegum psyllid** (*Ctenarytaina eucalptyi*) is also a recent introduction and has developed into an important pest of *Eucalyptus pulverulenta* grown to provide foliage in flower arrangements. *Blastopsylla occidentalis* occurs on eucalyptus in Florida.

In the eastern U.S., black-eyed Susan is commonly infested by a *Bactericerca* species (nr. *antennata*). It produces a purplish leaf blotching.

Acacia psyllid (*Acizzia uncatoides*) is a common species associated with acacia and silk tree, sometimes occurring in nuisance and/or damaging numbers.

---

[1] Homoptera: Psyllidae

A. Boxwood psyllid adult. *D. Shetlar.* **B.** Boxwood psyllid adult. *K. Gray.* **C.** Boxwood psyllids. *D. Shetlar.* **D.** Leaf cupping caused by boxwood psyllid feeding injury. *D. Herms.* **E.** Waxy covering (lerp) over redgum lerp psyllid nymphs. *J. K. Clark/UC Statewide IPM Program.*

APHIDS

More than 1,300 species of aphids (Aphididae family) occur in North America, including scores of species that are associated with and may be damaging to yard and garden plants. All are small, rarely exceeding $\frac{1}{12}$ inch, but they reproduce prolifically and may become extremely abundant. Furthermore, life cycles can be complex and typically involve several different forms that may also be associated with different groups of plants.

Normal reproduction of aphids is asexual. The presence of sexual forms (males, sexual females), if it occurs at all, is restricted to a single generation per year. Female aphids give live birth to daughter aphids throughout most of the growing season, and several dozen generations may be produced. Following three or four molts, the ultimate adult form may be either winged or wingless. Wingless adults predominate. Certain environmental conditions (e.g., overcrowding, day-length cues) stimulate production of winged forms.

Sexual reproduction precedes the production of overwintering eggs. These eggs are always laid on a perennial plant. Furthermore, aphid life cycles often involve alternation of host plants, so that overwintering eggs are laid on a different plant (called the primary host) than that on which the aphid is associated during the growing season (the secondary host). Winged males return to the winter host plant in late summer and early fall to mate with a special wingless female form, the oviparae, which subsequently lay eggs. This is the only time an egg is laid externally; eggs hatch in the mother when normal asexual reproduction occurs. The complete life cycle—involving summer forms, special sexual forms, overwintering eggs, and spring forms on the overwintering host plant—is known as a holocyclic life cycle (see Figure 5).

Overwintering eggs, and associated sexual forms, often are not present in warmer areas of North America, nor are they produced in greenhouses. These life cycles are termed anholocyclic.

Aphids feed by sucking sap from the phloem of plants and can cause several kinds of injuries. In high numbers there can be a decline in plant vigor. Aphids also excrete large amounts of watery honeydew, which may become a significant nuisance and allows for growth of associated sooty molds. Aphids feeding on new growth of some plants may cause leaf curling or discoloration. Also, aphids transmit many viruses.

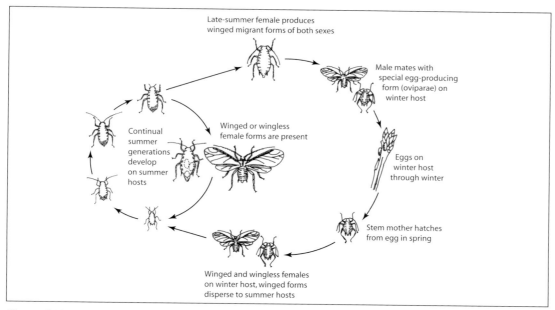

Figure 5. Typical holocyclic life cycle of an aphid. *Figure by L. Mannix.*

A. Eggs of an aphid (*Euceraphis* sp.) near birch bud. *K. Gray.* **B.** Needle twisting caused by balsam twig aphid. *D. Moorhead.* **C.** Leaf curling produced by honeysuckle witches' broom aphid. *W. Cranshaw.* **D.** Symptoms of bean common mosaic (left), a virus disease that can be spread by aphids. *W. Cranshaw.* **E.** Injury to spruce foliage by spruce aphid. *K. Gray.* **F.** Norway maple aphid colony with associated honeydew. *W. Cranshaw.*

Green Peach Aphid (*Myzus persicae*)

Hosts: Winter (primary) hosts include peach, apricot, and rarely, certain cherries and plums. Summer hosts include more than 200 species of herbaceous plants, many of them vegetables and ornamentals. Green peach aphid is also one of the most commonly damaging aphids of greenhouse crops.

Damage: On winter hosts (peach, apricot), spring generations can produce serious leaf curling. On vegetables, herbs, and other herbaceous plants colonized during the growing season, leaf curling is rare but high populations of aphids can cause stunting, wilting, and premature leaf drop. Green peach aphid is also an efficient vector of many plant viruses including potato virus Y, cucumber mosaic, plum pox, and bean common mosaic. Strains of green peach aphid that are highly resistant to many insecticides have become common in many areas.

Distribution: Throughout North America outdoors and as a common greenhouse pest.

Appearance: Nymphs and wingless adults are usually straw colored, sometimes pale green. Nymphs that will ultimately transform to winged forms may be pale orange or red. Winged females have a black head and dark patch on the abdomen.

Life History: Outdoors in cold climate areas, green peach aphid alternates between a primary winter host and various secondary summer hosts. On the primary host, winter is spent as eggs laid near buds of peach or apricot. Eggs hatch following bud break to produce wingless females (first generation). As these develop they subsequently give live birth, producing two or three generations on the winter host. In the last generation, winged forms are produced that abandon the winter host and migrate to herbaceous summer host plants.

On summer hosts, individual aphids may become mature within 2 weeks after birth. Under optimal conditions females may then daily produce two or more young for about 2 to 3 weeks. Most adults are wingless, but some winged forms occur, particularly when colonies become crowded. A dozen or more generations may be produced during the growing season. During late summer and early fall, new winged forms (males, fall migrant females) are produced which migrate to the *Prunus* winter hosts. Subsequently the overwintering eggs are laid.

In greenhouses and areas where warm temperatures occur throughout the year, the forms of green peach aphid associated with the *Prunus* winter hosts do not occur. Instead reproduction is continuous from females that give live birth without mating. Adults may be winged or wingless.

A. Green peach aphid damage to peach and dispersing aphids. *W. Cranshaw.* **B.** Green peach aphid stem mother and progeny curling peach leaves in early spring. *K. Gray.* **C.** Leaf curling on peach caused by green peach aphid infestation. *W. Cranshaw.* **D.** Winged and wingless adult forms of green peach aphid. *W. Cranshaw.* **E.** Green peach aphid on spinach leaf. *W. Cranshaw.* **F.** Immature green peach aphid prior to wing production. *K. Gray.*

Aphids in North America That Commonly Alternate between Primary (Winter) and Secondary (Summer) Host Plants[1]

Scientific Name	Common Name	Primary Host	Secondary Host
Anuraphis cardui	Thistle aphid	Apricot, plum	Thistle, chrysanthemum, etc.
Anuraphis helichrysi	Leafcurl plum aphid	Plum	Yarrow, chrysanthemum, clover, thistle, mallow, many other plants
Aphis citricola[2]	Spirea aphid	Spirea	Citrus, apple, pear
Aphis fabae	Bean aphid	Euonymus, viburnum	Bean, beet, cucumber, carrot, lettuce, etc.
Aphis gossypii[3]	Cotton/melon aphid	Catalpa, rose of Sharon	Many vegetables, flowers, subtropical/tropical shrubs
Aphis helianthi	Sunflower aphid	Dogwood	Sunflower, pigweed, four o'clock, ragweed
Aphis nasturtii	Buckthorn aphid	Buckthorn (*Rhamnus* spp.)	Potato, cucurbits, thistle, many garden flowers
Brachycaudus cardui	Thistle aphid	Plum	Thistle
Calopha graminis		Elm	Grass (roots)
Calopha ulmicola	Elm cockscomb aphid	American and red elm	Grass (roots)
Capitophorous elaeagni	Artichoke aphid	Russian olive	Globe artichoke, thistle
Cavariella aegopodii	Carrot-willow aphid	Willow	Carrot, parsley, dill, coriander
Ceruraphis eriophori		Viburnum	Sedge
Ceruraphis viburnicola	Snowball aphid	Snowball viburnum	Sedge
Cryptomyzus ribis	Currant aphid	Currant, gooseberry	Motherwort, marsh betony
Dysaphis plantaginea	Rosy apple aphid	Apple, pear	Narrow-leaved plantain
Eriosoma americanum	Woolly elm aphid	Elm	Amelanchier
Eriosoma crataegi	Woolly hawthorn aphid	Elm	Hawthorn
Eriosoma lanigerum	Woolly apple aphid	Elm	Apple, crabapple, mountain-ash, hawthorn
Eriosoma pyricola	Woolly pear aphid	Elm	Pear
Grylloprociphilus imbricator	Beech blight aphid	Beech	Cypress (on roots year-round)
Hyadaphis foeniculi	Honeysuckle aphid	Honeysuckle	Carrot, parsley, fennel, dill, celery
Hyalopterus pruni	Mealy plum aphid	Apricot, peach, plum	Phragmites
Hysteroneura setariae	Rusty plum aphid	Common plum	Numerous grasses, small grains
Macrosiphum euphorbiae	Potato aphid	Rose	Potato, tomato, many other garden plants
Metolophium dirhodum	Rose grass aphid	Rose	Grass, corn
Mordwilkoja vagabunda	Poplar vagabond aphid	*Populus* (*deltoides* group)	Loosestrife
Myzus cerasi	Black cherry aphid	Cherry	Wild crucifers, bedstraw
Myzus persicae	Green peach aphid	Peach, plum, apricot	Pepper, cabbage, potato, spinach, many other vegetable and ornamental plants
Nasonovia ribisnigri	Lettuce aphid	Currant, gooseberry	Lettuce, chicory, radicchio
Nearctaphis bakeri	Clover aphid	Hawthorn, quince, apple, pear	Clover, sweetclover
Nearctaphis crataegifoliae	Long-beaked clover aphid	Pyracantha, hawthorn, flowering quince	Red clover
Paraprociphilus tessallatus	Woolly alder aphid	Maple	Alder
Pemphigus bursarius	Lettuce root aphid	Poplar	Roots of lettuce, endive, chicory dandelion, sowthistle, some other weeds
Pemphigus populivenae	Sugarbeet root aphid	Narrow-leaved cottonwood	Roots of beet, many garden plants
Phorodon humuli	Hop aphid	Plum, apricot	Hops
Prociphilus americanus		Ash	Fir (roots)

A. Bean aphid colony. *K. Gray.* **B.** Thistle aphid colony. *K. Gray.* **C.** Leafcurl plum aphid. *K. Gray.* **D.** Currant damaged by currant aphid. *W. Cranshaw.* **E.** Potato aphid adult with young. *W. Cranshaw.* **F.** Rosy apple aphid colony. *K. Gray.* **G.** Carrot-willow aphids on dill. *W. Cranshaw.* **H.** Potato aphid colony around rosebud. *W. Cranshaw.* **I.** Mealy plum aphid colony. *W. Cranshaw.* **J.** Leaf curling of snowball viburnum by snowball aphid. *W. Cranshaw.* **K.** Leaf curling of snowball viburnum by snowball aphid. *W. Cranshaw.*

Scientific Name	Common Name	Primary Host	Secondary Host
Rhopalosiphum insertum	Apple grain aphid	Apple, pear, hawthorn	Small grains, grasses
Rhopalosiphum nymphaeae	Waterlily aphid	Apricot, almond, other *Prunus*	Waterlily, buttercup, Knotweed
Rhopalosiphum padi	Bird cherry-oat aphid	*Prunus* spp.	Corn, ryegrass, oat, other grasses
Thecabius populicondupli- folius	Folded-leaf poplar aphid	Cottonwood, poplar	Buttercup

[1] All species on this list commonly produce overwintering eggs (holocyclic life cycle).
[2] May be known as green citrus aphid when associated with citrus.
[3] In much of the southern half of U.S. and in greenhouses, reproduces continuously in normal asexual manner without use of alternate primary hosts.

Cotton/Melon Aphid (*Aphis gossypii*)

Hosts: A wide range that includes hundreds of plants. Among garden plants, cotton/melon aphid is particularly damaging to melon, cucumber, squash, and related vine crops. However, it is also commonly found on plants such as pepper, eggplant, spinach, asparagus, okra, hibiscus, crape myrtle, bougainvillea, pittosporum, and many tropical and subtropical shrubs. Cotton/melon aphid is also one of the most common aphid pests of greenhouse crops.

Damage: Sap feeding can cause wilting, yellowing, and in extreme cases, foliage death of older leaves. Infestation of new growth results in leaf curling. Cotton/melon aphid is often most important, however, because of its ability to readily transmit many viruses, including cucumber mosaic virus, watermelon mosaic virus 2, and zucchini yellow mosaic virus. Many populations of cotton/melon aphid have developed high levels of resistance to insecticides, further complicating management.

Distribution: Cosmopolitan and can occur throughout North America but is particularly damaging in the southern and southwestern U.S.

Appearance: Wingless females are about ⅟₁₆ inch and usually a mottled light green. They can vary, however, from pale yellow to dark green or almost blackish. A light coating of wax gives them a dull appearance. Winged adults have a black head and thorax, yellowish green abdomen, and light gray wings.

Life History and Habits: In the southern U.S. and in greenhouses, reproduction occurs continually as long as temperatures allow. Unlike most aphids, cotton/melon aphid thrives under warm conditions. Optimal temperatures are in the range of 70 to 80° F, and the life cycle may be completed in as little as 1 week. Females can produce about 70 to 80 young over a period of 2 to 3 weeks.

In northern areas, cotton/melon aphid may produce an overwintering egg that is laid on catalpa or rose of Sharon. When these eggs hatch in spring, there are usually two generations on the winter host before the species moves to vegetables, flowers, and other herbaceous plants. In the south and in greenhouses, eggs are not produced and continual generations occur year-round.

A. Cotton/melon aphid colony with cast skins. *W. Cranshaw.* **B.** Cotton/melon aphids. *D. Gilrein.* **C.** Black cherry aphids. *L. Mannix.* **D.** Cotton/melon aphids. *D. Gilrein.* **E.** Black cherry aphid colony. *W. Cranshaw.* **F.** Clover aphid colony. *K. Gray.*

Cabbage Aphid (*Brevicoryne brassicae*)

Hosts: Cabbage aphid feeds solely on crucifers and can be damaging to broccoli, cabbage, Brussels sprout, cauliflower, canola, and other plants in the mustard family (Brassicaceae).

Damage: Large numbers of cabbage aphids removing sap retard plant growth. Infestation of new growth distorts heads and produces severe leaf curls. The presence of cabbage aphid as a contaminant can be very important, particularly with Brussels sprout. Flowers and seed pods may produce poorly.

Distribution: Throughout North America.

Appearance: Mature females are grayish green with a dark head and dark cornicles. A double row of dark bars is present on the back, but the entire body is covered with fine powdery wax. Winged forms have a single row of dark dorsal bars and dark wing veins. Cabbage aphids are about ¹⁄₁₂ inch long. After molting, the powdery wax covering is absent, allowing markings to be visible. Wax is again produced shortly after the aphids resume feeding.

Life History and Habits: In southern areas, reproduction can be continual, with adult females giving live birth as long as temperatures permit. There are three nymphal stages followed by the adult form, and the complete life cycle can be completed in less then 2 weeks under optimal conditions. The great majority of adults are wingless unless host plants greatly deteriorate. They may live for about a month, during which time they can produce more than 80 young. Winged forms are weak fliers but readily infest nearby plantings. Relatively few young (ca. 6–10) are produced by winged stages.

In northern areas where winter conditions prevent continual reproduction, winter is spent as an egg, laid on a mustard-family plant. There is no alternation of host plants. Sexual forms are produced in September and October. Eggs are subsequently laid that hatch the following spring.

Aphids in North America That Do Not Commonly Alternate between Primary (Winter) and Secondary (Summer) Host Plants

Scientific Name	Common Name	Host
Species That Commonly Produce Overwintering Eggs (Holocyclic Life Cycle)		
Acyrthosiphon pisum	Pea aphid	Pea, alfalfa, clover, other legumes
Aphis ceanothi		Ceanothus
Aphis hederae	Ivy aphid	English ivy
Aphis middletoni	Erigeron root aphid	Aster, cornflower
Aphis pomi	Apple aphid	Apple, pear, quince, hawthorn
Aphis sedi		Sedum
Aulacorthum solani	Foxglove aphid	Numerous including foxglove, lettuce, potato, clover, bulbs
Brachycorynella asparagi	Asparagus aphid	Asparagus
Brevicoryne brassicae	Cabbage aphid	Brussels sprout, cabbage, other crucifers
Calaphis betulaecolens	Common birch aphid	Birch
Callaphis juglandis	Dusky-winged walnut aphid	Persian walnut
Callipterinella callipterus		European white birch
Chaitophorus populicola	Poplar leaf aphid	Poplar, cottonwood
Chaitophorus populifolii		Poplar, cottonwood
Chaitophorus viminalis	Small black and green willow aphid	Willow
Chromaphis juglandicola	Walnut aphid	Persian walnut
Cinara coloradensis	Black polished spruce aphid	Spruce
Cinara curvipes	Bowlegged fir aphid	Fir, Engelmann spruce
Cinara fornacula	Green spruce aphid	Spruce

A. Cabbage aphid colony. *W. Cranshaw.* **B.** Cabbage aphids infesting Brussels sprout. *W. Cranshaw.* **C.** Asparagus aphid. *W. Cranshaw.* **D.** Close-up of cabbage aphids on Brussels sprout. *W. Cranshaw.* **E.** Pea aphid adult with young. *K. Gray.* **F.** Cabbage aphid colony covering underside of cabbage leaf. *W. Cranshaw.* **G.** Tufting of asparagus fern caused by asparagus aphid. *W. Cranshaw.* **H.** Pea aphid colony on sweet pea. *W. Cranshaw.* **I.** Green apple aphid colony around bud. *W. Cranshaw.* **J.** Winged form of cabbage aphid and young. *K. Gray.* **K.** Apple aphids. *K. Gray.* **L.** Foxglove aphid colony. *K. Gray.*

Scientific Name	Common Name	Host
Cinara laricis	Larch aphid	Larch
Cinara sabiniae	Rocky Mountain juniper aphid	Juniper
Cinara strobi	White pine aphid	Eastern white pine
Drepanosiphum platanoides	Sycamore aphid	Sycamore
Hyadaphis tartaricae	Honeysuckle witches' broom aphid	Tartarian honeysuckle
Macrosiphoniella sanborni	Chrysanthemum aphid	Chrysanthemum
Macrosiphum rosae	Rose aphid	Rose
Melanocallis caryaefoliae	Black pecan aphid	Hickory, pecan
Mindarus abietus[1]	Balsam twig aphid	Fir, particularly balsam and Fraser fir
Monellia caryella	Blackmargined aphid	Hickory
Monelliopsis pecanis	Yellow pecan aphid	Pecan
Myzocallis alhambra	Dusky-winged oak aphid	Oak
Myzocallis coryli	Filbert aphid	Filbert, hazelnut
Periphyllus lyropictus	Norway maple aphid	Norway maple
Periphyllus negundinis	Boxelder aphid	Boxelder maple
Phyllaphis fagi	Woolly beech aphid	Beech
Prociphiulus fraxinifolii	Leafcurl ash aphid	Ash
Pterocomma smithiae	Black willow aphid	Willow, poplar
Shivaphis celti	Asian woolly hackberry aphid	Hackberry
Shizaphis graminum	Greenbug	Bluegrass, corn, small grains
Sitobion avenae	English grain aphid	Corn, small grains
Tinocallis kahawaluokalani	Crapemyrtle aphid	Crape myrtle
Tinocallis saltans		Siberian elm
Tinocallis ulmifolii	Elm leaf aphid	Elm, particularly American elm
Uroleucon ambrosiae	Brown ambrosia aphid	Lettuce, echinecea, rudbeckia, aster, yarrow, coreopsis, goldenrod, other flowers
Uroleucon pseudambrosiae		Lettuce, sowthistle, endive
Uroleucon rudbeckiae	Goldenglow aphid	Goldenglow, larkspur, delphinium
Utamphorphora crataegi	Fourspotted hawthorn aphid	Hawthorn

Species That Rarely or Never Produce Overwintering Eggs (Anholocyclic Life Cycle)

Aphis craccivora	Cowpea aphid	Legumes (cowpea, kidney bean, lima bean), asparagus, lettuce, carrot
Aphis nerii	Oleander aphid	Oleander, vinca, milkweed
Aulacorthum circumflexum	Crescentmarked lily aphid	Columbine, aster, lily, vinca, violet, cyclamen
Chaetosiphon fragaefolii	Strawberry aphid	Strawberry
Dysaphis tulipae	Tulip bulb aphid	Tulip, iris, gladiolus
Forda formicaria		Grass (roots)
Lipaphis pseudobrassicae	Turnip aphid	Many crucifers
Longistigma caryae[2]	Giant bark aphid	Oak, beech, nut trees
Myzus ascalonicus	Shallot aphid	Numerous, including alliums, dandelion, tulip, lettuce, strawberry
Rhopalosiphum maidis	Corn leaf aphid	Corn, small grains
Toxoptera aurantii	Black citrus aphid	Camellia, citrus, crape myrtle, ficus
Toxoptera citricidus	Brown citrus aphid	Citrus, ficus, camellia, gardenia
Tuberolachnus salignis	Giant willow aphid	Willow

[1] There is currently disagreement as to the scientific name of balsam twig aphid found in North America.
[2] Overwintering eggs may be produced in northern areas of range.

A. Dusky-winged walnut aphids. *K. Gray.* B. Green spruce aphid (*Cinara fornacula*). *K. Gray.* C. Colony of giant conifer aphids on pine. *D. Shetlar.* D. Honeysuckle witches' broom aphids. *W. Cranshaw.* E. Sycamore aphid nymph. *K. Gray.* F. Blackmargined aphid. *L. Tedders.* G. Poplar leaf aphid colony. *J. D. Solomon.* H. Black pecan aphid, winged adult. *L. Tedders.* I. Sycamore aphid colony. *K. Gray.* J. Damage produced by honeysuckle witches' broom aphid. *W. Cranshaw.* K. Spruce aphids. *K. Gray.*

A. Dusky-winged oak aphid colony. *W. Cranshaw.* **B.** Eggs of Norway maple aphid around buds. *K. Gray.* **C.** Black willow aphid colony on willow twig. *K. Gray.* **D.** Crapemyrtle aphids. *D. Caldwell.* **E.** Bright red form of brown ambrosia aphid on calendula. *W. Cranshaw.* **F.** Yellow pecan aphid. *H. C. Ellis.* **G.** Norway maple aphid colony. *W. Cranshaw.* **H.** Winged and wingless forms of elm leaf aphid. *W. Cranshaw.* **I.** Brown ambrosia aphid colony. *K. Gray.* **J.** English grain aphid colony. *K. Gray.*

A. Corn leaf aphid colony. *J. Capinera.* **B.** Oleander aphid colony with attending ant. *W. Cranshaw.* **C.** Colony of willow aphids (*Pterocomma*) on willow twig. *W. Cranshaw.* **D.** Turnip aphid colony. *J. Capinera.* **E.** Giant bark aphids on oak. *H. A. Pase III.* **F.** Giant willow aphid colony. *W. Cranshaw.* **G.** Black willow aphid colony on willow twig. *K. Gray.* **H.** Black citrus aphid colony. The white objects are eggs of a syrphid fly. *K. Gray.* **I.** Giant willow aphids. *W. Cranshaw.*

"WOOLLY" APHIDS

Some aphids cover their body with long waxy threads, an effective deterrent to many natural enemies. Most of these "woolly" aphids are in the subfamily Pemphaginae[1] and generally share life cycle similarities, including an affinity for developing on the roots of secondary (summer) hosts. Differences occur in the habits of the sexual form and the production of only a single overwintering egg. Leaf curling is often produced by forms that colonize foliage.

Woolly Apple Aphid (*Eriosoma lanigerum*)

Hosts: Apple, crabapple, hawthorn, mountain-ash, pyracantha, elm.

Damage: On apple, crabapple, and other summer hosts, woolly apple aphid colonizes roots, trunks, and branches, concentrating around previous wounds. Feeding interferes with normal wound healing and contributes to the production of knotlike growths. On roots, these may become pronounced swellings which can girdle and kill roots. On the primary (winter) elm host, infestations of emerging spring growth cause leaves to curl into closed, stunted clusters or rosettes at the twig tips.

Distribution: Throughout North America in association with its hosts.

Appearance: Dark purplish brown, but aboveground forms are densely covered with white wax. Forms produced belowground or in leaf curls are less densely covered than those colonizing trunks and branches.

Life History and Habits: In the complete life cycle there is both a winter host of elm and summer hosts of apple, crabapple, or mountain-ash. Eggs survive on the winter host, and the aphids emerge in spring, subsequently producing a curling on elm. After a few generations, winged forms are produced that disperse to apple and crabapple. On these hosts they produce a more densely woolly form that typically colonizes callous tissue surrounding previous wounds on trunks, branches, and larger roots. Multiple generations are present on this summer host. In early fall, winged forms return to elm. Mating occurs among sexual forms, and a single overwintering egg is laid by the mated female, near elm buds.

There may be variation in this life cycle in warmer areas, particularly where elm is not available as a winter host. Under these conditions woolly apple aphid may continually reproduce on roots or on trunks of trees.

Related Species

Other *Eriosoma* species winter on elm but have different summer hosts. **Woolly pear aphid** (*E. pyricola*) occasionally damages woody parts of pear in a manner similar to that of woolly apple aphid. **Woolly hawthorn aphid** (*E. crataegi*) is found on hawthorn and **woolly elm aphid** (*E. americanum*) on amelanchier in the summer. On elm, *E. americanum* produces a tight leaf curl in spring that is packed with aphids. **Woolly elm bark aphid** (*E. rileyi*) restricts its feeding to slippery and American elm, making purple leaf curls and then forming dense colonies on branches.

A. Woolly apple aphid colony on crabapple. *W. Cranshaw.* **B.** Woolly apple aphids. *K. Gray.* **C.** Woolly apple aphid. *K. Gray.* **D.** Root knot of apple caused by infestation of woolly apple aphid. *W. Hantsbarger.* **E.** Root damage by woolly apple aphid. *D. Caldwell.* **F.** Wingless nymph of woolly elm aphid. *K. Gray.* **G.** Winged form of woolly elm aphid. *K. Gray.* **H.** Woolly elm aphid colony in elm leaf. *K. Gray.* **I.** Woolly pear aphid colony. *K. Gray.* **J.** Woolly apple aphid colony on crabapple branch. *D. Leatherman.* **K.** Leaf curling and purpling of elm typical of woolly elm bark aphid. *K. Gray.* **L.** Leaf curling and purpling of elm typical of woolly elm bark aphid. *W. Cranshaw.*

Other "Woolly" Aphids

The genus *Pemphigus* includes several species that use various *Populus* as the primary (winter) host, on which they produce stem, leaf, or petiole galls. Summer forms develop on roots of beet, lettuce, and a variety of related cultivated and weed hosts. These species are discussed elsewhere as gall producers (p. 408) or as root feeders (p. 506).

Leafcurl ash aphid (*Prociphilus fraxinifolii*) develops on the expanding new growth of ash, creating tightly rolled and thickened leaves sometimes referred to as "pseudo-galls." Some associated distortion and twisting of twigs also occur, minor injuries in landscapes but significant to nurseries. The aphids are yellow-green with a brown head but are covered with white, waxy threads. Often they are found in curled ash leaves in dense mixtures of old cast skins and droplets of wax-coated honeydew. Leafcurl ash aphid is found throughout North America but is most common in western and some southern states.

Green and white ash are the sole hosts and winter is spent as colonies on the roots. Winged stages work their way through soil cracks and disperse to ash foliage shortly after bud break. Young aphids deposited on the emerging leaves are capable of inducing tight leaf curling. Numerous generations are subsequently produced on ash foliage and continue to distort new growth, creating large clumps of thickened, curled leaves. Colonies begin to decline as new growth ceases. In addition, natural enemies become more abundant. Winged stages that disperse back to the roots of ash are produced by midsummer, and the foliage-infesting phase of the insect passes.

Most other *Prociphilus* species alternate between a deciduous tree and a conifer as hosts. *P. americanus* produces injuries similar to leafcurl ash aphid in eastern North America during late spring but migrates to fir (*Abies* spp.) where summer generations occur on the roots. *P. caryae* alternate between amelanchier and pine as hosts. The related **woolly alder aphid** (*Paraprociphilus tessellatus*) is a conspicuous species associated with branches of alder during the summer months. It winters on silver maple and may produce slight leaf curling before migrating to alder.

Two common "woolly" aphids develop on beech. Colonies of **beech blight aphid** (*Grylloprociphilus imbricator*) develop on the foliage of beech in spring, later expanding to petioles and twigs. Migration to an alternate host, cypress, occurs in early summer. Roots are colonized on cypress, and year-round development can occur on this host. Those individuals that move back to beech produce sexual forms and overwintering eggs. **Woolly beech aphid** (*Phyllaphis fagi*) is a European species now widely distributed in North America. All stages occur on beech foliage, and the species is frequently abundant. Similarly, **Asian woolly hackberry aphid** (*Shivaphis celti*) is a recently introduced species that has spread throughout much of the southern U.S. and also is found in California. It produces conspicuous colonies on hackberry leaves, with pale bluish wax surrounding the developing insects.

[1] Homoptera: Aphididae

A. Leafcurl ash aphid colony. *W. Cranshaw.* **B.** Severe leaf curling of green ash by leafcurl ash aphid. *D. Leatherman.* **C.** Leafcurl ash aphid colony. *W. Cranshaw.* **D.** Woolly alder aphid on silver maple. *M. Merchant.* **E.** Asian woolly hackberry aphid, winged stage. *D. Cook.* **F.** Colony of woolly alder aphids. *D. Shetlar.* **G.** Beech blight aphid colony. *D. Shetlar.* **H.** Woolly beech aphid colony. *D. Shetlar.* **I.** Asian woolly hackberry aphids on hackberry leaf. *F. Hale.*

ADELGIDS

Adelgids[1] are a family of "woolly" aphids associated with conifers. Their life histories differ in some respects from those of "true" aphids, notably in that eggs are produced by all forms. Host alternation is common with many species, and some produce galls on the primary host (p. 410).

Hemlock Woolly Adelgid (*Adelges tsugae*)

Hosts: Hemlock, with Canada and Carolina hemlock most seriously damaged.

Damage: Hemlock woolly adelgid is native to Japan and China and since its accidental introduction in the 1950s has become the most serious insect pest of hemlock in the eastern U.S. The insects feed on sap from twigs and concurrently introduce saliva that is toxic to the plant. Foliage of infested plants yellows, and needles drop prematurely, particularly on interior areas of branches. Dieback of limbs is common, and trees have often been killed by this insect, particularly in New England.

Distribution: Generally distributed in areas east of the Appalachian Mountains, from South Carolina to Maine. Isolated infestations occur in parts of the Pacific Northwest and upper Midwest.

Appearance: Nearly black but often covered with white cottony wax. Newly hatched stages are tiny and dark reddish gray. Nymphs usually have a white fringe of wax around the body.

Life History and Habits: Winter is spent in the form of adults on twigs, with females beginning to lay eggs in late March. Eggs hatch in April, and this first generation is usually completed by early summer. A second generation follows and goes temporarily dormant during midsummer, resuming growth in fall.

Other Adelgids on Bark and Needles

Balsam woolly adelgid (*Adelges piceae*) is an introduced species now found in forests of both the northeastern and northwestern U.S. and areas of southern Canada. It is an important pest of balsam and Fraser fir, with large colonies developing on needles and bark of trunks, branches, and twigs. Infestations commonly result in distortions of twigs and small branches, usually following death of terminal buds. Two generations are produced annually, with winter spent as a first-stage nymph on the bark.

Various **woolly pine adelgids** (*Pineus* spp.) are associated with needles, twigs, branches, and trunks of pine. Individual insects are densely covered with whitish wax. Foliage of heavily attacked trees becomes yellowish, and growth is stunted. Needle and shoot feeding can cause shoots to droop and die. Species capable of developing dense colonies on trunks and branches are potentially most damaging. Perhaps the most important species in North America is **pine bark adelgid** (*P. strobi*) which colonizes the bark and needles of white, Austrian, and Scotch pine. All stages apparently occur on pine. Some other *Pineus* species alternate between pine and spruce.

[1] Homoptera: Adelgidae

A. Hemlock woolly adelgid colony. *D. Herms.* **B.** Hemlock woolly adelgid adults. *D. Shetlar.* **C.** Hemlock woolley adelgid nymphs. *J. A. Davidson.* **D.** Balsam woolly adelgid. *D. Shetlar.* **E.** Woolly pine adelgid eggs on pine needle. *J. W. Brewer.* **F.** Woolly pine adelgid on Austrian pine. *W. Cranshaw.* **G.** Pine bark adelgid colony on pine trunk. *R. S. Kelley.* **H.** Woolly pine adelgids on pine foliage. *W. Cranshaw.* **I.** Pine bark adelgid colony on bark. *A. Antonelli.*

MEALYBUGS

Mealybugs (Pseudococcidae family)[1] are soft-bodied insects that are covered with a fine, whitish wax. In addition, many species produce prominent egg sacks enclosed in cottony wax. Mealybugs are similar in appearance to some soft scales (pp. 338, 340), eriococcid scales (p. 324), and "woolly" aphids (p. 310). Approximately 280 species occur in North America, but relatively few are significant pests.

Note: Root-feeding mealybugs are discussed on p. 506.

Citrus Mealybug (*Planoccoccus citri*)

Hosts: Many plants grown in greenhouses are susceptible, as are several common plants used in interiorscapes such as ficus and philodendron. Coleus, fuschia, gardenia, apple, stone fruits (*Prunus* spp.), and rose are common hosts. Citrus mealybug is an important pest of citrus orchards, particularly grapefruit, where it tends to settle on the underside of fruit.

Damage: Citrus mealybug damages plants in several ways. Feeding injuries weaken the plant by removing sap, and the saliva introduced into plants causes systemic damage, particularly to new growth. Distorted growth and premature leaf drop are associated with infestations. The wax-covered bodies of the mealybugs and the honeydew they excrete degrade plant appearance. Citrus mealybug can produce large amounts of honeydew.

Distribution: Widespread in greenhouses and on indoor plants; outdoors restricted in the U.S. to extreme southern areas.

Appearance: Generally oval and marked by having 17 to 18 pairs of short wax filaments along the side of the body and no tail filaments. The body is fairly distinctly segmented. Citrus mealybug is about ⅛ inch when full grown. An indistinct single purplish stripe can often be observed along the back.

Life History and Habits: Eggs are produced by the adult females in a large egg sac (ovisac) which may contain up to 600 eggs. The eggs hatch after 7 to 10 days, and the young yellowish nymphs, known as crawlers, move about the plant seeking favorable sites for feeding. Terminal growth, cracks, and crotches are commonly areas where the crawlers settle. During development, females undergo two additional molts before becoming full grown. They maintain their legs throughout life but usually move little in later stages of development. However, they may move off plants and in greenhouses have been observed to lay eggs on benches, containers, and other nonplant surfaces. Off the plant, citrus mealybug may survive more than 2 weeks.

The rarely observed males undergo an additional (fourth) development stage which is nonfeeding and occurs in a small cocoon of loose wax. Adult males are much smaller than the females, have wings, and do not feed.

A generation of citrus mealybug can be completed in about 1 month under optimal conditions indoors. Two to three generations are produced annually outdoors in Florida.

A. Unknown mealybug with egg sac and young. *K. Gray.* **B.** Citrus mealybug eggs and crawlers. *W. Cranshaw.* **C.** Citrus mealybug nymphs. *W. Cranshaw.* **D.** Citrus mealybug on coleus. *W. Cranshaw.* **E.** Citrus mealybug with large egg sac. *W. Cranshaw.* **F.** Citrus mealybug with egg sac and nymphs. *W. Cranshaw.* **G.** Citrus mealybug. *W. Cranshaw.*

Longtailed Mealybug (*Pseudococcus longispinus*)

Hosts: A wide variety of plants including begonia, citrus, dracaena, gardenia, ivy, impatiens, philodendron, tomato, coleus, poinsettia, fig, fuschia, ferns, begonia, pyracantha, holly, yew, and rhododendron.

Damage: Longtailed mealybug feeds on the sap and in moderate numbers can induce leaf abscission. It also produces nuisance amounts of honeydew.

Distribution: Occurs outdoors in the southern states, as far north as Maryland. This mealybug is one of the most common and widely distributed insects associated with greenhouse/interiorscape plants.

Appearance: Oval, about ⅛ inch long, and covered with powdery wax. Longtailed mealybug lacks distinctive striping along the back but has numerous waxy filaments extending along the sides of the body. The presence of long threadlike tails, one pair of which may exceed the length of the body, is a distinguishing feature.

Life History and Habits: Longtailed mealybug produces eggs that hatch almost immediately once outside the mother, essentially in the form of live birth. The young may remain under the mother for a few days and are released into a loose, snowy white mass of wax the female produces which is conspicuous but much less developed than the ovisacs of some other species. The young feed on leaves and small branches, but females migrate to more protected sites when rearing young. (In orchards, large numbers of females have been trapped by providing corrugated cardboard bands into which they aggregate prior to producing young.)

Under optimal conditions, development may be completed in about 45 days, after which there is a fairly extended period during which eggs mature. Females produce young over a period of a month, but some 90% are typically laid in the first 10 days. Outdoors, typically two or three generations are completed annually.

Related Species

Comstock mealybug (*Pseudococcus comstocki*) is primarily found in the northeastern quarter of the U.S. and in parts of southern Canada, California, and Washington. Historically it has been a pest primarily of pear and other fruits such as apple and peach. Its host range is broad, however, and includes (but is not limited to) privet, mulberry, maple, hibiscus, catalpa, buckeye, pine, and yew. Young nymphs usually feed on leaves, whereas older stages tend to aggregate on twigs, often around nodes and scars. Two generations are annually produced. **Obscure mealybug** (*P. viburni*) is an important pest of ornamentals with a host range of more than 50 plant genera. It can occur on the upper roots as well as the aboveground portion of plants.

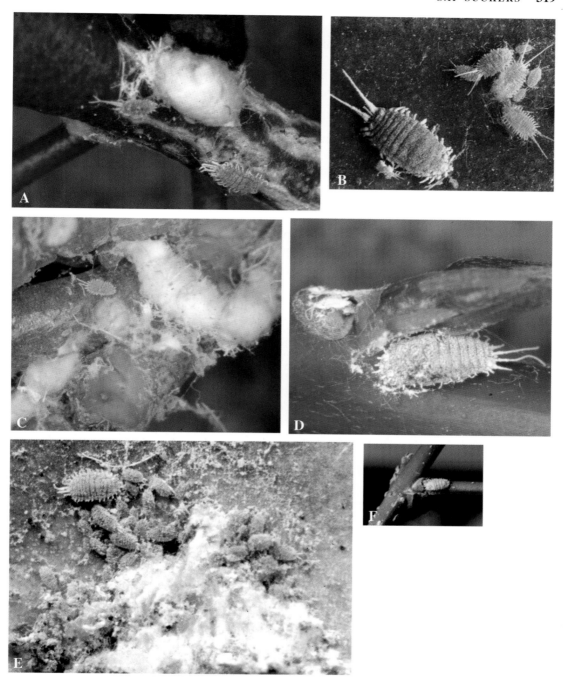

A. Longtailed mealybugs. *W. Cranshaw.* **B.** Longtailed mealybug. *K. Gray.* **C.** Longtailed mealybug nymph and eggs. *W. Cranshaw.* **D.** Longtailed mealybug. *W. Cranshaw.* **E.** Comstock mealybugs. *Courtesy Clemson University.* **F.** Obscure mealybug. *J. Baker.*

Hawthorn (or Two-Circuli) Mealybug (*Phenacoccus dearnessi*)

Hosts: Hawthorn primarily. Several other rosaceous plants, including pyracantha, mountain-ash, and amelanchier, are reported hosts.

Damage: Sap feeding can decrease plant vigor and result in twig dieback. Hawthorn mealybug produces large amounts of honeydew, and severe sooty mold develops following outbreaks.

Distribution: Probably generally distributed east of the Rockies but most often reported from midwestern states.

Appearance: Later stages of the insects, globular in form and with a red body finely covered with white wax, are conspicuous on twigs. Small but more elongate, pale reddish brown immature forms can be found on the bark of the trunk and larger branches during winter. Adult males are small, gnat-like, winged insects present in spring during the period of migration from branches to twigs.

Life History and Habits: Hawthorn mealybug spends the winter as a late-stage nymph on trunks and larger branches, packed in cracks on the bark. In spring, females move to twigs and continue to develop, becoming full grown in May or early June. Adult males remain on trunks until they subsequently transform to a winged adult stage which mates with the females.

After mating, the females swell greatly with hundreds of maturing eggs. The eggs hatch in the mother and crawlers emerge, although dispersal of the young nymphs is suspended during wet, cool weather. Peak production of nymphs occurs in late May and June but may extend into late summer. Only one generation per year is thought to be produced, although egg-producing females and egg hatch have been observed in late September, suggesting a small second generation.

Newly emerged nymphs feed on leaves for a brief period but later move to protected areas on twigs where they may remain through much of the summer. Populations often are again found in high numbers on leaves during late summer when the nymphs aggregate in leaf folds (domatia). Migration to overwintering areas on trunks generally occurs in September and October.

Related Species

Grape mealybug (*Phenacoccus maritimus*) is most commonly associated with pear, grape, and catalpa. Several other plants, including *Taxus*, honeylocust, and hackberry, are reported to be susceptible. The adult females are about 3/16 inch long and covered with a whitish wax. The life cycle is somewhat different than that of hawthorn mealybug, with overwintering stages being early-instar nymphs in or near the cottony egg sacs. In spring, most of these nymphs move to twigs and leaves where they feed and develop, becoming full grown in late June and July. This first, overwintered generation is usually little observed. Eggs are laid in early summer, and nymphs of the second generation develop in July and August. When full grown they move to older wood where the females again produce egg sacs. Egg production may continue until killing frosts.

A. Hawthorn mealybug, mature females swollen with eggs. *W. Cranshaw.* **B.** Hawthorn mealybug nymphs on leaves. *W. Cranshaw.* **C.** Hawthorn mealybug with crawlers. *W. Cranshaw.* **D.** Large colony of grape mealybug on catalpa. *W. Cranshaw.* **E.** Hawthorn mealybug female and winged male. *L. Mannix.* **F.** Grape mealybugs. *W. Cranshaw.*

Madeira mealybug (*Phenacoccus madeirensis*) and **Mexican mealybug** (*P. gossypii*) are two closely related species that are commonly confused. They can develop on a wide range of plants including aralia, chrysanthemum, English ivy, geranium, gynura, hollyhock, ixia, lantana, and poinsettia. They are subtropical species that can be found outdoors in the southern U.S. and are common greenhouse/interior plant pests throughout North America. Adult females are oval, about ⅛ inch, and somewhat bluish gray. There are three rows of short, waxy tufts along the back and short terminal filaments. Eggs are laid in a large elongate egg sac that may be twice the length of the female. As many as seven generations can be produced annually indoors. Mexican mealybug is sometimes found on the upper roots as well as on leaves, stems, and flowers.

Maple mealybug (*Phenacoccus acericola*) is found in the northeastern quadrant of the U.S. and areas of southeastern Canada. Nymphs develop on leaves and adults on twigs of maple, buckeye, basswood, and viburnum. They may be quite conspicuous but are rarely injurious. Two to three generations are produced annually. Females are yellow and lightly dusted with wax. **Apple mealybug** (*P. aceris*) is a European species found in the northeastern and northwestern states. It has a wide host range that primarily includes rosaceous trees and shrubs such as pyracantha, apple, cotoneaster, mulberry, and mountain-ash. Maple and basswood are other common hosts. This species overwinters as a second instar on twigs, and one generations is produced annually. The body of the adult is green but normally covered with fine powdery wax. Another recently introduced species is **Japanese mealybug** (*P. japonicus*) which is a pest of azalea in the mid-Atlantic states.

Miscellaneous Mealybugs

Taxus mealybug (*Dysmicoccus wistariae*) is a common species associated with *Taxus* in the northeast and midwest states. Occasionally it is also found on dogwood. It develops on stems and branches, clustering at forks, and can cause yellowing of plants. Taxus mealybug also produces large amounts of honeydew. Winter is typically spent as a nymph that resumes feeding in late May. Two or three generations may be produced annually in southern areas, one in the north.

Striped mealybug (*Ferrisia virgata*) is an introduced species found primarily in the eastern states. It has a gray body covered with white wax, except where two stripes on the abdomen distinctly mark this species. A pair of filaments on the tip of the abdomen is also present. Dogwood, hawthorn, azalea, holly, magnolia, apple, and mulberry are among the hosts. Two generations are produced, with winter spent as a nymph.

Cypress bark mealybug (*Ehrhornia cupressi*) is a serious pest of Monterey cypress and some related plants in the Pacific states. It often is are not observed because it develops protected beneath bark flakes. One generation is produced annually.

Noxious bamboo mealybug (*Antonina pretiosa*) develops at the nodes of *Bambusca* and *Phyllostachys* species of bamboo.

Pink hibiscus mealybug (*Maconellicoccus hirsutus*) has attracted considerable attention and concern since its discovery in south Florida in 2002. Despite its name, it has a wide host range including a variety of fruits and ornamentals and even certain vegetables. Adults are pinkish but covered with white wax. The eggs turn pinkish shortly after they are produced. As many as 15 generations can be produced annually, and pink hibiscus mealybug has the potential to become a serious pest throughout Florida and into southern Georgia.

[1] Homoptera: Pseudococcidae

A. Madeira mealybug. *L. Osborne.* **B.** Maple mealybug. *D. Caldwell.* **C.** Taxus mealybugs. *R. Childs.* **D.** Taxus mealybug. *R. Childs.* **E.** Striped mealybug colonies. *W. Ciesla.* **F.** Pink hibiscus mealybug. *L. Osborne.* **G.** Striped mealybug. *L. Osborne.* **H.** Striped mealybug. *J. Baker.*

ERIOCOCCIDS, OR FELTLIKE SCALES

The eriococcid scales (Eriococcidae family)[1] resemble mealybugs in most features but are not covered with as dense a waxy covering, nor do they produce egg sacs.

European Elm Scale (*Gossyparia spuria*)

Hosts: Elm, particularly American and rock elm.

Damage: Prolonged infestations weaken branches, often producing premature leaf yellowing (flagging) and leaf drop. Heavy infestations cause dieback of twigs and branches. European elm scale can cause serious nuisance problems because of honeydew production, with peak production in June and early July when the females mature.

Distribution: An introduced species now found throughout North America in association with its elm host.

Appearance: Mature females are broadly oval, swollen, and dark gray with a pronounced whitish fringe of wax around the edge of the body. Males are much smaller and produce an elongate white cocoon. Nymphs on leaves are yellowish brown with some whitish wax. European elm scale has reddish brown blood.

Life History and Habits: European elm scale spends the winter as second instar nymphs, packed into cracks on twigs and smaller branches. The nymphs are oval in general form and pale gray because of the light waxy cover of the body. In spring they resume development, and the females swell greatly. During late April and May, male scales may also begin emerging from small white cocoons and mate with the females. Males are not always produced, however, and this species can reproduce asexually.

Eggs hatch in the body of the female, and crawlers emerge over a period of several weeks, peaking between mid-June and mid-July. They move to leaves and settle on the leaf underside, the dark yellow nymphs almost always being found tucked next to main leaf veins. In late summer they migrate back to the twigs.

A. European elm scales, including cocoons produced by males. *W. Cranshaw.* **B.** Flagging caused by European elm scale infestation. *W. Cranshaw.* **C.** European elm scale nymphs and honeydew droplet. *W. Cranshaw.* **D.** European elm scale crawlers settled along leaf vein. *W. Cranshaw.* **E.** Coinfestation of European elm scale and European fruit lecanium. *W. Cranshaw.* **F.** Mature European elm scales with crawlers. *W. Cranshaw.* **G.** European elm scale colony, including numerous male cocoons. *W. Cranshaw.*

Other Eriococcid Scales

Beech scale (*Cryptococcus fagisuga*) is an introduced species that has contributed greatly to the death of beech trees in the northeastern U.S. and adjacent areas of Canada. It develops on trunks and branches of beech and covers itself with whitish wax. Primary damage occurs by weakening trees and producing wounds that allow a canker-producing fungus (*Nectria coccinea faginata*) to become established.

Other eriococcids that occur in North America include **oak eriococcin** (*Eriococcus quercus*), a native species that develops on new growth of oaks, found primarily in the southeastern states; **Norfolk Island pine eriococcin** (*E. araucariae*), an uncommon insect associated with Norfolk Island pine; **Gillette eriococcin** (*E. gillettei*), associated with juniper; and **azalea bark scale** (*E. azalae*), an introduced species that is spreading through the eastern U.S. in association with its hosts, primarily azalea and rhododendron.

[1] Homoptera: Eriococcidae

COCHINEAL SCALES

Cochineal scales (*Dactylopious* spp.)[1] develop on prickly pear and sometimes other cacti. They produce large, conspicuous cottony masses of wax that cover the mature female and eggs. First-stage nymphs (crawlers) feed for about 3 weeks before settling, after which they remain immobile. Males develop in a small cocoon during their later stages. Multiple overlapping generations are produced in warmer areas of the southwestern states and Florida, where *D. opuntiae* is present. Two generations are normal for *D. confusus* in the Rocky Mountain states. Cochineal scales have long been prized as a source of natural red dye, which is due to high levels of carminic acid in their blood. The Mexican species *D. coccus* is the species usually used commercially for this purpose.

[1] Homoptera: Dactylopiidae

A. Beech bark scale covering trunk. *D. Herms.* **B.** Azalea bark scales. *K. Gray.* **C.** Cankers produced incidental to beech bark scale infestation. *D. Herms.* **D.** Azalea bark scale with eggs. *K. Gray.* **E.** Azalea bark scale. *D. Shetlar.* **F.** Azalea bark scale. *A. Antonelli.* **G.** Cochineal scales on opuntia cactus. *W. Cranshaw.* **H.** Cochineal scales on opuntia cactus. *W. Cranshaw.*

SOFT SCALES

The soft scales (Coccidae)[1] make up one of the largest (ca. 1,000 North American species) and most important families of scale insects. Most are broadly oval in form and may swell to a large hemispherical form when eggs are maturing. Adult forms are usually attached to twigs and small branches. Immature stages often feed on leaves or needles, and most retain limited mobility through to the adult stage. Soft scales can be prolific, producing several hundred eggs. They feed on phloem sap and produce abundant amounts of honeydew.

Brown Soft Scale (*Coccus hesperidum*)

Hosts: Ficus and English ivy are among the most common hosts. However, a wide range of plants are potentially infested including agave, begonia, citrus, dizygotheca, euphorbia, gardenia, nerium, nephrolepis, peperomia, polystichum, schefflera, syngonium, vinca, and yucca.

Damage: Heavy infestations of twigs and leaves can cause wilting, premature leaf drop, and dieback. A more common problem, however, involves the abundant sticky honeydew the insect excretes, creating a serious nuisance.

Distribution: Throughout North America as a common houseplant pest. It may occur outdoors in extreme southern areas.

Appearance: Full-grown female scales (males are rare) are light brown, oval, and generally flattened in shape. Younger scales are yellowish brown with splotchy dark areas along the middle and sides.

Life History and Habits: Eggs hatch over an extended period, underneath the wax cover of the females. After crawling about the plant, the nymphs settle within a few days and begin to secrete a scale covering. They subsequently remain immobile for the rest of their life. Generations are produced continually, overlap, and require about 2 to 3 months to complete.

Related Species

Citricola scale (*Coccus pseudomagnoliarum*) is similar in appearance to brown soft scale but gets slightly larger and is grayish. Citrus, elm, hackberry, pomegranate, and walnut are common hosts in California. One generation is produced annually.

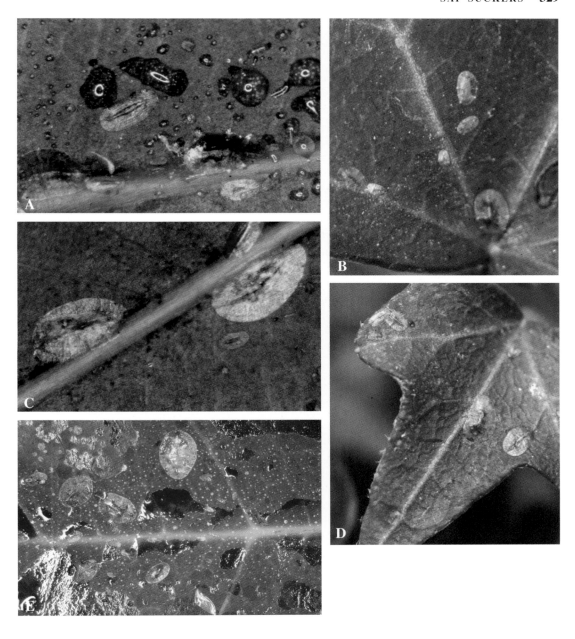

A. Brown soft scales. *W. Cranshaw.* **B.** Brown soft scales on ivy. *W. Cranshaw.* **C.** Brown soft scales. *W. Cranshaw.*
D. Brown soft scales. *W. Cranshaw.* **E.** Brown soft scales and honeydew. *W. Cranshaw.*

Hemispherical Scale (*Saisettia coffae*)

Hosts: Ferns, chlorophytum, and diszygotheca are favored hosts. Aphelandra, begonia, citrus, croton, cycas, euphorbia, ficus, gardenia, gynura, nephrolepsis, polystichum, and schefflera are among the many hosts.

Damage: The scales remove plant sap and can cause wilting and dieback of tender plant parts. Hemispherical scale produces less honeydew than does brown soft scale.

Distribution: Throughout North America as a common houseplant pest. It may occur outdoors in extreme southern areas.

Appearance: Hemispherical scale is slightly larger than brown soft scale, dark brown, and rounded (helmet shaped). Young adult females often have a series of ridges that form an H shape. Immature stages sometimes look like small warts.

Life History and Habits: Females can lay up to 600 or 700 eggs and then die. Eggs hatch underneath the scale covering, and the crawlers move over the plant in search of a feeding site. Shortly after feeding, they become immobile. Generations require 8 to 10 months to complete, but overlapping generations exist on interior plants, so all stages may be present.

Related Species

Black scale (*Saissetia oleae*) is similar in appearance to hemispherical scale but is dark brown to black. It occurs outdoors in the southern U.S. and is a common greenhouse/houseplant pest elsewhere. It has an extremely wide host range including ficus, citrus and other fruits, holly, pittosporum, rose, and peppertree.

Nigra scale (*Parasaissetia nigra*) has a wide host range but is reportedly most damaging to Japanese aralia, English ivy, English holly, oleander, orange-berry pittosporum, and hibiscus. Full-grown females are dark black and smoothly hemispherical, lacking the raised H-shaped hump of black scale. Nigra scale occurs outdoors in areas of California and Florida and is widespread elsewhere on houseplants.

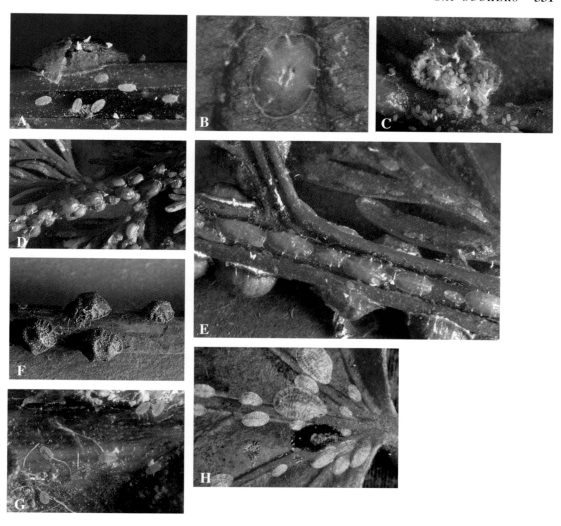

A. Hemispherical scale crawlers. *K. Gray.* **B.** Hemispherical scale. *W. Cranshaw.* **C.** Hemispherical scale with cover displaced to expose eggs. *K. Gray.* **D.** Hemispherical scales. *K. Gray.* **E.** Hemispherical scale nymphs. *K. Gray.* **F.** Black scales. *K. Gray.* **G.** Black scale crawlers. *K. Gray.* **H.** Nigra scales. *W. Cranshaw.*

European Fruit Lecanium (*Parthenolecanium corni*)

Hosts: A wide range including most fruit trees and many shade trees. Stone fruits (*Prunus* spp.), redbud, elm, maple, poplar, and willow are common hosts.

Damage: European fruit lecanium is a soft scale that feeds on the phloem of small branches. Under sustained outbreaks, it can cause decline and dieback, but often it is under a high level of natural control that largely prevents significant injury. European fruit lecanium is also capable of producing large amounts of honeydew, which can be a serious nuisance problem and favors the growth of sooty mold.

Distribution: Throughout North America, common. Despite its name, it is apparently native.

Appearance: Adult females swollen with eggs are generally hemispherical and often light to dark brown with mottling. Color and shape may alter depending on host, however.

Life History and Habits: Winter is spent on twigs as second instar nymphs that look like small, raised lumps, about ¼ inch in diameter. They continue growing in spring, molt to the adult stage, and develop rapidly. Most feeding, honeydew production, and injury occur at this time.

Males may be produced in midspring, and mating can occur at this time, but European fruit lecanium often reproduces asexually. In late May and June, females swell with maturing eggs. The eggs hatch underneath the body of the mother scale, and the crawlers move out continually for several weeks in midsummer during favorable weather. The mother scale then dies, having produced several hundred eggs. The newly hatched crawlers move to feed on leaves for the remainder of the growing season. Prior to leaf fall, the pale brown second instar scales return to twigs for winter.

Other Lecanium Scales

Fletcher scale (*Parthenolecanium fletcheri*) is associated with certain juniper, arborvitae, baldcypress, and yew. It is particularly abundant in the Midwest where it is an important pest of nurseries. Serious problems in landscape settings are infrequent. **European peach scale** (*P. persicae*) is generally distributed in North America and has a wide host range among deciduous trees and shrubs. Ornamentals including honeysuckle, grape, barberry, euonymus, and silk tree are most commonly infested. **Frosted scale** (*P. pruinosum*) is found in the Pacific states and has a host range and life history similar to that of European fruit lecanium. It is most commonly reported damaging walnut and stone fruits. **Oak lecanium** (*P. quercifex*) develops on oak, beech, sycamore, hickory, and a few other shade trees.

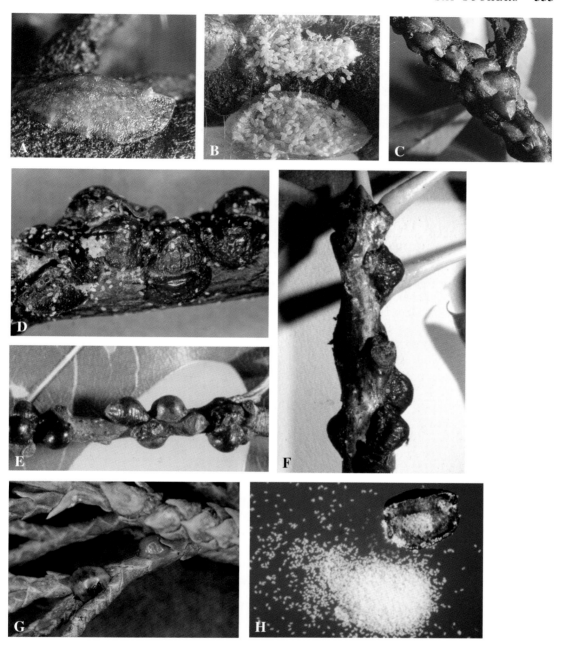

A. European fruit lecanium. *K. Gray.* **B.** European fruit lecanium, turned to expose eggs. *K. Gray.* **C.** European fruit lecanium colony. *K. Gray.* **D.** European fruit lecanium with crawlers and eggs. *W. Cranshaw.* **E.** European fruit lecanium. *D. Herms.* **F.** Oak lecanium. *J. A. Davidson.* **G.** Fletcher scales. *W. Cranshaw.* **H.** Eggs exposed from European fruit lecanium. *D. Herms.*

Magnolia scale (*Neolecanium cornuparvum*) is one of the largest and most conspicuous scales. It is primarily found on magnolia in the midwestern and mid-Atlantic states. High populations encrust branches, causing dieback, and it is a prolific producer of honeydew. Winter is spent as nymphs on 1- to 2-year-old twigs. The nymphs begin to molt to the adult stage in early to mid-May. The females subsequently begin to swell with eggs, and the newly hatched crawlers may be common from mid-July into early September. Adult females are almost ½ inch in diameter, irregularly shaped, and shiny light brown. Young adults are covered with fine wax, which tends to be lost about the time eggs start to hatch.

The native **terrapin scale** (*Mesolecanium nigrofasciatum*) is an occasional pest of blueberry and peach, although natural enemies usually suppress populations adequately. Maple and sycamore are other common hosts. The mature adults have a hemispherical cover with distinct radiating black bands. Winter is spent as a mated female on the twigs. Eggs hatch in the mother in spring, and the crawlers move to foliage where they feed during the summer. A reverse migration back to twigs occurs in fall.

Mature females of **calico scale** (*Eulecanium cerasorum*) are round, about ¼ inch in diameter, and mottled conspicuously with white and black. They occur in the Pacific states and have become established in Kentucky and some mid-Atlantic states. All stone fruits are hosts, as are many vines, crabapple, elm, pyracantha, honeylocust, maple, dogwood, and several other plants. Nymphs feed on leaves in summer and then move to twigs in fall. Females mature in late spring, with egg hatch and crawler activity most common in late June and July.

Wax scales (*Ceroplastes* spp.) are a large group of scales found in tropical areas worldwide. A few species develop outdoors in parts of the southern U.S., and they are sometimes moved elsewhere on indoor plants. This group of scales is notable in having a thick coating of whitish wax, often with pinkish or grayish tones. Unusual projections of the wax covering are common and characteristic of many species. Wax scales can excrete large amounts of honeydew.

With few exceptions, all stages of all wax scales occur on twigs and small branches, rarely on foliage. Females produce upwards of 1,000 eggs. Crawlers are typically reddish, and after settling they move little and secrete wax that often takes on an ornate form. Many young wax scales have a cameolike appearance, with the center surrounded by waxy projections. Mature females are more globular in appearance. Males do not occur in many species or are rarely produced. The number of generations produced outdoors varies with climate. For example Indian wax scale (*C. ceriferus*) may have two or three generations along the Gulf Coast but a single generation annually in northern areas of its range (Maryland).

Most wax scales have a wide host range. Blueberry, camellia, citrus, fig, eugenia, Chinese holly, jasmine, mulberry, pear, persimmon, plum, and quince are among the hosts of **Indian wax scale**. This species is also commonly referred to as Japanese wax scale and sometimes occurs on leaves, particularly the upper surfaces of holly leaves. **Florida wax scale** (*C. floridensis*) is most common on citrus, holly, laurus, nerium, schefflera, and psidium. **Barnacle scale** (*C. cirripediformis*) is found on gardenia, citrus, euonymus, and several other ornamental plants. Host plants of **red wax scale** (*C. rubens*) include citrus, gardenia, palms, persea, schefflera, aglaonema, and dieffenbachia. This species apparently is restricted to Florida. Citrus, holly, and dizygothela are hosts of **Chinese red scale** (*C. sinensis*).

A. Magnolia scale. *D. Herms.* **B.** Magnolia scales. *D. Shetlar.* **C.** Calico scales. *D. Shetlar.* **D.** Magnolia scale crawlers. *D. Herms.* **E.** Magnolia scales being tended by ants. *D. Shetlar.* **F.** Red wax scale. *Courtesy Florida Dept. Agriculture and Consumer Services/Div. Plant Industry.* **G.** Barnacle scales. *D. Shetlar.* **H.** Wax scales. *W. Cranshaw.* **I.** Indian wax scales, calico form. *J. R. Baker.* **J.** Indian wax scale crawler. *J. R. Baker.* **K.** Calico scale. *E. Day.* **L.** Indian wax scale. *J. A. Davidson.*

Striped Pine Scale (*Toumeyella pini*)

Hosts: Various pines, particularly Scotch pine.

Damage: Feeding stunts development of new growth and can induce premature needle drop. Heavy infestation may kill branches and severely detract from tree appearance. Striped pine scale produces abundant amounts of sticky honeydew, which attracts scavenging wasps in fall and promotes sooty mold growth.

Distribution: Widely distributed east of the Rockies, particularly in more northern areas.

Appearance: The adult female is hemispherical, about ¼ inch in diameter, and attached to twigs. General coloring is dark brown or black with reddish brown or cream-colored mottling. Males are smaller and more elongate and often develop on needles.

Life History and Habits: Striped pine scale spends the winter in the form of fertilized females on twigs. Feeding resumes in spring, at which time the insects become greatly enlarged with maturing eggs. Abundant amounts of sticky honeydew are produced at this time. Eggs may begin to hatch in the female beginning in late May or early June, and peak activity of crawlers occurs over about 1 month. Females usually settle at the base of needles, males on the needles. Adult males emerge to mate with the females in late summer.

Related and Similar Species

Pine tortoise scale (*Toumeyella parvicornis*) is also associated with pine. Its biology appears to be similar to that of striped pine scale, and it shares many hosts. Females are slightly smaller than striped pine scale and are more uniformly colored. **Irregular pine scale** (*T. pinicola*) is common on pine, particularly Monterey pine, in California. In the eastern U.S., **tuliptree scale** (*T. liriodendri*) is a common pest of yellow-poplar (tuliptree) and magnolia. Thinning of foliage, dieback of twigs, and serious honeydew problems may occur with this insect. Two generations per year appear to occur in southern areas of its range.

Spruce bud scale (*Physokermes piceae*) develops on the twigs of spruce, primarily infesting lower branches. The mature females are reddish brown and globular and closely resemble a bud scale in size and shape. Spruce bud scale spends the winter as small, first instar nymphs on needles of spruce. In midspring they resume activity and move to the twigs where they settle and feed. Females become full grown and swollen with eggs in June, and eggs hatch in late June and July. There is one generation per year.

A. Striped pine scale with crawlers. *W. Cranshaw.* **B.** Striped pine scale mature females. *W. Cranshaw.* **C.** Striped pine scale males on needles. *W. Cranshaw.* **D.** Spruce bud scales. *K. Gray.* **E.** Tuliptree scale with crawlers. *G. J. Lenhard.* **F.** Pine tortoise scales (left) and striped pine scales (right). *W. Cranshaw.* **G.** Tuliptree scales. *D. Shetlar.* **H.** Striped pine scale, flipped to expose emerging crawlers. *W. Cranshaw.* **I.** Spruce bud scales with eggs exposed. *K. Gray.* **J.** Tuliptree scales. *D. Shetlar.*

Cottony Maple Scale (*Pulvinaria innumerabilis*)

Hosts: Maple, honeylocust, hackberry, linden, and many other hardwoods.

Damage: Nymphs suck sap from leaves; late stages are found primarily on twigs and small branches. Large amounts of honeydew may be excreted by stages in late development.

Distribution: Generally throughout the U.S. and southern Canada.

Appearance: Cottony maple scale is one of the largest and most conspicuous of the soft scales. Adult females may swell to over ¼ inch in diameter when producing a large cottony egg sac. Nymphs are flattened, broadly oval, and translucent and are found on leaves. Overwintering females look like small dark warts. They subsequently swell dramatically as eggs mature.

Life History and Habits: Cottony maple scale spends the winter as mated adult females on twigs and branches. They resume feeding in spring and mature their eggs, which are contained in a large cottony egg sac somewhat resembling a small marshmallow. Eggs hatch from mid-June through July. The newly hatched crawlers settle on the underside of leaves, usually near the midrib. At the end of the season, tiny winged males emerge and mate with the females, which subsequently migrate to twigs.

Related Species

Cottony maple leaf scale (*Pulvinaria acericola*) develops on maple, dogwood, and holly in the eastern U.S. and southern Canada. Its life history differs a bit from that of cottony maple scale in that mature females migrate back to leaves in spring where they subsequently produce eggs. **Cottony camellia scale** (*P. floccifera*), sometimes known as cottony taxus scale, has a similar life history. It produces a long, narrow egg sac, and eggs hatch over an extended period of about 6 weeks. Holly, camellia, jasmine, and yew are among the more common hosts.

[1] Homoptera: Coccidae

A. Cottony maple scale nymphs on leaf. *W. Cranshaw.* **B.** Cottony maple scales with fully developed egg sacs. *W. Cranshaw.* **C.** Overwintering female cottony maple scales on twig. *D. Leatherman.* **D.** Cottony maple leaf scales. *D. Gilrein.* **E.** Cottony maple leaf scales. *D. Caldwell.* **F.** Cottony maple scales with fully developed egg sacs. *W. Cranshaw.* **G.** Cottony camellia scales. *K. Gray.* **H.** Cottony camellia scale nymphs. *K. Gray.* **I.** Cottony maple scale nymph on honeylocust leaflet. *W. Cranshaw.* **J.** Cottony camellia scales on holly. *E. Day.*

MARGARODID SCALES

The margarodid scales (Margarodidae family),[1] also known as the giant coccids, are primarily tropical and subtropical species, but about 40 species occur in North America. They typically produce eggs in a loose sac of cottony wax. Immature forms may look substantially different than adults.

Cottony Cushion Scale (*Icerya purchasi*)

Hosts: A wide range of trees and shrubs including citrus, maple, nut trees, pittosporum, nandina, Boston ivy, and several stone fruits (*Prunus* spp.).

Damage: Damage is primarily caused by removal of sap, which can produce premature yellowing and leaf and fruit drop. Cottony cushion scale also produces large amounts of sticky honeydew.

Distribution: A tropical/subtropical species accidentally introduced into North America. It is found in southern California, Arizona, the Gulf states, and north to Virginia. Greenhouse infestations may occur throughout North America.

Appearance: Adult females are about ¼ inch and mottled rusty red with black legs and antennae. They are usually covered with white wax and produce a conspicuous, fluted wax egg sac that may extend ⅜ inch.

Life History and Habits: Eggs are laid in the egg sac and hatch in 3 to 8 weeks depending on the season. All immature stages are capable of crawling about the plant, and they tend to be found first on leaves and twigs. Females nearing maturity often migrate to larger branches and trunks where they feed little if at all. The female produces eggs over about 2 weeks. An entire life cycle can be completed in about 2 to 3 months, longer with cool weather. In northern areas of the range only two or three generations are produced annually; many more can be produced in warmer areas or indoors.

Other Margarodid Scales

Sycamore scale (*Stomacoccus platani*) is an important pest of sycamore in southern California and Arizona. During its life cycle it moves between woody parts of the plant to leaves and back, a process repeated over three to five generations in a year. Twig dieback, leaf distortion, and yellowing are symptoms of heavy infestation.

Pinyon needle scale (*Matsucoccus acalyptus*) is an occasional pest of pinyon in the southwestern U.S. Feeding by adult females and nymphs causes needles to turn yellow and prematurely fall. The stage most commonly observed is the second instar nymph ("bean stage"), found attached to needles in early spring. Adult females that subsequently are produced are black, armored, mobile scales, about 1/16 inch long, that migrate to the trunk where they produce a cottony mass of eggs in spring.

[1] Homoptera: Margarodidae

A. Cottony cushion scales with crawler. *W. Cranshaw.* **B.** Pinyon needle scales. *W. Cranshaw.* **C.** Cottony cushion scale with crawlers. *W. Cranshaw.* **D.** Sycamore scale. *D. Caldwell.* **E.** Pinyon needle scales in "bean stage." *W. Cranshaw.* **F.** Pinyon needle scale–infested branch. *W. Cranshaw.* **G.** Cottony cushion scales. *Courtesy Clemson University.*

KERMES, PIT, AND FALSEPIT SCALES

Kermes scales (Kermesidae family)[1] are sometimes known as gall-like scales because of their large size and globose form. All are associated with oak. Winter is spent as first-stage nymphs on the bark of branches or trunks. These later move to new growth, completing development on twigs. Females swell greatly when producing eggs and become smooth and ball-like. Eggs of *Allokermes gillettei* hatch in October and early November, but life cycles of other species may differ in this feature. *Nanokermes pubescens* is a common eastern U.S. species whose eggs begin to hatch in July. Eggs of *A. kingi* are laid in summer but hatch in September. Most kermes scales cause little injury but may attract attention because of their large size. However, *A. gillettei* is important in Colorado where is produces serious twig dieback on pin oak; a gummy exudate commonly is produced at the feeding site.

Pit scales (Asterolecaniidae family)[2] feed on developing twigs, causing a sunken area to form around the insect. Most commonly damaging is **golden oak scale** (*Asterolecanium variolosum*) and related species that occur on oak (*A. quercicola*, *A. minus*), which can seriously reduce growth and cause branches to die prematurely. Mature females of golden oak scale are hemispherical and yellow-green to brown with a waxy fringe around the margin. They spend the winter as mature females that resume feeding in spring. Eggs hatch over a period of several months, with peak crawler activity in early summer. The crawlers do not move far from the mother scales, settling on first-year wood of twigs. One generation is produced per year.

Although pit scales on oak are most commonly encountered, some 29 pit scale species occur in North America, many associated with other plants. **Holly pit scale** (*Asterolecanium puteanum*) is found on various hollies in the eastern U.S. as far west as Texas. **Pitmaking pittosporum scale** (*A. arabidis*) is present on mock-orange, privet, and green ash in many of the states of the East and West Coasts. **Bamboo scale** (*A. bambusae*) is an introduced species that occasionally is found on bamboo but apparently causes little damage. Yucca is host for *A. agavis*. The pit scale with the widest host range is **oleander pit scale** (*A. pustulans*), which develops on many plants including fig, lantana, magnolia, oleander, bougainvillea, and mulberry.

The falsepit scales (Lecanodiaspididae family)[3] are represented by five species in North America, all in the genus *Lecanodiaspis*. **Common falsepit scale** (*L. prosopidis*) is typical. It lives on twigs and small branches of various deciduous trees and shrubs including ash, azalea, mulberry, and honeylocust. Feeding induces pits or welts to form, distorting the tree and contributing to dieback of branches and twigs. Full grown, this species appears rather domelike with a thick waxy white cover. Egg hatch and crawler activity occur around May.

[1] Homoptera: Kermesidae; [2] Homoptera: Asterolecaniidae; [3] Homoptera: Lecanodiaspididae

A. Kermes scale on pin oak. *W. Cranshaw.* **B.** Gumming reaction to kermes scale infestation on pin oak. *W. Cranshaw.* **C.** Immature kermes scales around bud. *W. Cranshaw.* **D.** Kermes scales on white oak. *J. D. Solomon.* **E.** Kermes scales on white oak. *W. Cranshaw.* **F.** *Allokermes gillettei* on pin oak. *W. Cranshaw.* **G.** Oak pit scale *Asterolecanium minus. K. Gray.* **H.** Oak pit scale *Asterolecanium minus. J. D. Solomon.* **I.** Oleander pit scales. *D. Shetlar.* **J.** Common falsepit scale on ash. *W. Cranshaw.* **K.** Golden oak scales. *W. Cranshaw.*

ARMORED SCALES

The armored, or "hard," scales (Diaspididae family) are small (½₀ to ⅛ inch) insects that secrete a hard waxy cover. Most are oval or somewhat elongate, in the case of the latter often similar to an oyster's shell. Much of what is visible is an expanded covering, known as the test, which covers the abdomen and later encloses the eggs. Foreparts of the body appear externally as a light brown or golden area, known as the exuvium, and may have bands reflecting different molts. The actual insect is found under the scale cover and lacks legs and is incapable of movement following the first molt, being completely enclosed by the cover. Only the mouthparts extend through the covering. A small slit develops on the underside of the covering to allow the crawlers to emerge following egg hatch.

Armored scales usually feed directly on plant cells rather than on sap from the phloem, the habit common to soft scales. Armored scales may kill areas of the plant where they feed, producing chlorotic spotting and twig dieback. They do not excrete honeydew. Approximately 200 species of armored scales are known to occur in North America, with additional new species often being accidentally introduced on infested plant materials.

Oystershell Scale (*Lepidosaphes ulmi*)

Hosts: A wide range of trees and shrubs. Aspen, ash, cotoneaster, dogwood, maple, willow, and lilac are among the most commonly damaged landscape plants. Apple and occasionally other fruit trees may be hosts.

Damage: Oystershell scale attaches itself to twigs, branches, and trunks. It sucks sap from adjacent cells, often killing tissue around the feeding site. Heavy infestations produce stunting, foliage yellowing, and bark cracking. Dieback of twigs and branches is a common result of oystershell scale injury, and infested trees are often so weakened they succumb to fungal cankers.

Distribution: Throughout North America but is most damaging in the northern U.S. and southern Canada.

Appearance: Light to dark brown, generally elongate and oyster shaped. On some hosts, the scale is covered with a fine powder of wax. Color may darken with age. The "lilac strain," common in some areas of eastern North America, is distinctly banded and usually darker brown.

Life History and Habits: Oystershell scale winters as whitish eggs underneath the scale covering of the mother. When eggs hatch in mid- to late spring, pale yellow crawlers move over the bark in search of sites where they can feed. If successfully established, the crawlers will molt in about a week, losing their legs but creating the protective wax cover. In most areas one generation per year is produced, with adults maturing in midsummer and producing the overwintering eggs. However, the lilac strain associated with maple and lilac in the mid-Atlantic region has two generations. Most oystershell scales present in North America do not produce males.

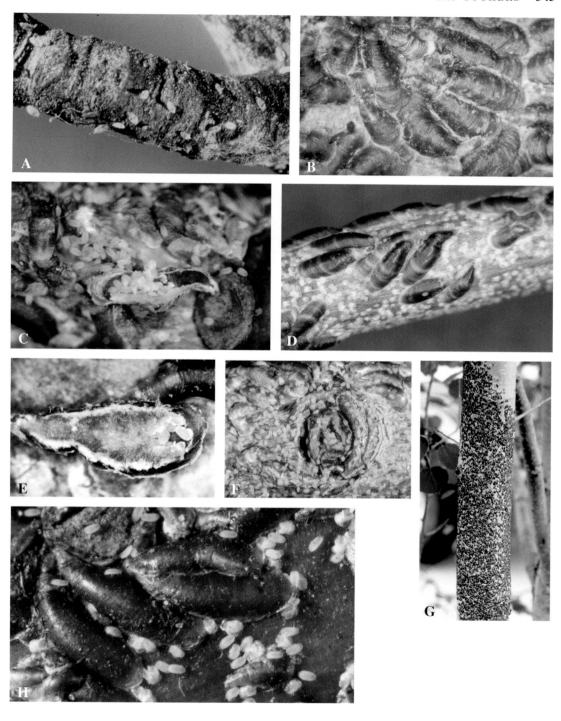

A. Magnolia scale crawlers. *D. Herms.* **B.** Oystershell scales. *W. Cranshaw.* **C.** Oystershell scale at egg hatch. *W. Cranshaw.* **D.** Oystershell scales with crawlers. *W. Cranshaw.* **E.** Oystershell scale cover, flipped to show underside with eggs. *W. Cranshaw.* **F.** Oystershell scale crawlers. *F. Peairs.* **G.** Oystershell scales covering aspen trunk. *W. Cranshaw.* **H.** Oystershell scales, lilac strain. *D. Gilrein.*

Related Species

Purple scale (*Lepidosaphes beckii*) is very similar in appearance to oystershell scale but is associated with citrus in parts of California and Florida. Three generations per year commonly occur in Florida. **Camellia scale** (*L. camelliae*) is widely distributed in the eastern half of the U.S., associated with camellia, holly (particularly Burford holly), privet, cleyeria, ternstroemia, and rhaphiolepsis. As many as four to five generations are reported in Georgia. **Winged euonymus scale** (*L. yanangicola*) develops on winged euonymus in some mid-Atlantic and midwestern states. **Maskell scale** (*L. pallida*) develops on cryptomeria and taxus. It is part of a species complex that includes **pine oystershell scale** (*L. pini*) on *Pinus thurnbergian* and *P. densiflora*, and **umbrella pine scale** (*L. sciadopitysi*) on sciadopitys. Two generations are commonly produced by Maskell scale, with crawlers appearing in June and August.

Pine Needle Scale (*Chionaspis pinifoliae*)

Hosts: A wide variety of conifers, particularly certain pines and spruce. Douglas-fir and hemlock are infrequent hosts in western states.

Damage: Pine needle scale feeds on needles, often producing some localized discoloration around the feeding site. In high numbers, it can produce premature needle shed and some dieback of branches.

Distribution: Generally distributed throughout North America but is most common in the northern half of the U.S. and in southern Canada.

Appearance: Adult females are almost pure white, elongated, and armored. They are slender and slightly yellow at the front end, widening at the rear. Males, when present, have a smaller, narrower scale cover. Crawler stages are light purple.

Life History and Habits: The life history varies in different parts of North America. In most areas, the primary overwintering stage is eggs, underneath the mother scale. In western North America, however, females may survive and produce eggs throughout winter and into early spring. Eggs usually hatch in midspring, often coincident with the peak bloom of common lilac. Crawlers settle within a few days of hatch and subsequently remain in place for the rest of their life.

In much of the eastern U.S. a second generation occurs, with eggs hatching in early summer and the adults maturing in early fall. (Small third generations have sometimes been observed.) Single-generation strains typically predominate in the west. Also, males are common in eastern areas but largely absent in western populations.

Related Species

Pineleaf scale (*Chionaspis heterophyllae*) is closely related to pine needle scale, nearly identical in form, and is associated with pine in the southeastern U.S. **Scurfy scale** (*C. furfura*) develops on trunks and branches of various deciduous trees and shrubs, with aspen, cottonwood, and willow among the most common hosts. Apple, hawthorn, mountain-ash, and *Prunus* species are less commonly infested. **Elm scurfy scale** (*C. americana*) is found in the eastern U.S. associated with certain deciduous trees and shrubs including elm, privet, and hackberry.

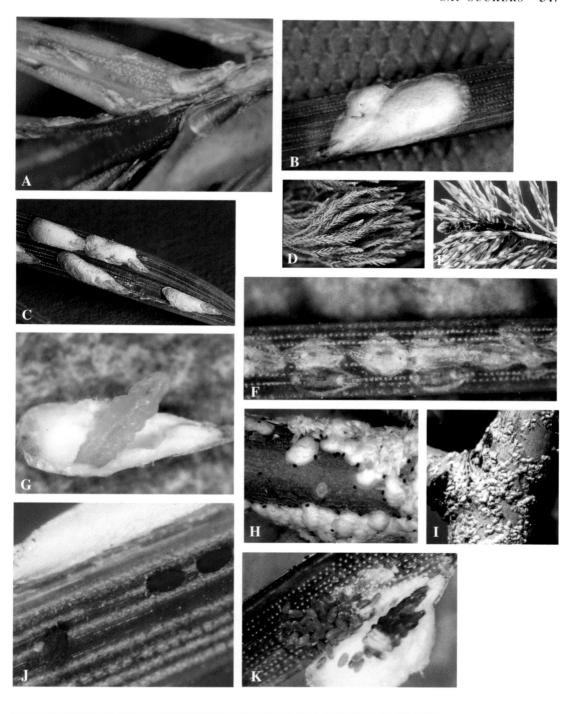

A. Maskell scales. *D. Gilrein.* **B.** Pine needle scales. *W. Cranshaw.* **C.** Pine needle scales. *K. Gray.* **D.** Maskell scale injury to cryptomeria. *D. Gilrein.* **E.** Pine needle scale. *D. Herms.* **F.** Pine needle scale nymphs. *W. Cranshaw.* **G.** Pine needle scale exposed from under cover. *W. Cranshaw.* **H.** Scurfy scale with crawlers. *W. Cranshaw.* **I.** Scurfy scale. *W. Cranshaw.* **J.** Pine needle scale crawlers. *D. Herms.* **K.** Pine needle scale female with eggs, exposed from cover. *W. Cranshaw.*

San Jose Scale (*Quadraspidiotus perniciosus*)

Hosts: Common hosts include apple, rose, pyracantha, cotoneaster, and crabapple, but many hardwood trees and shrubs, particularly in the rose family (Rosaceae), may be infested.

Damage: The scales feed on the sap of twigs and small branches, weakening and sometimes killing cells around the feeding site. A small reddish area often develops on the twigs around the feeding scale and extends internally to the xylem. Infested trees lose vigor with thinning and yellowing of foliage. Dieback of twigs and branches can occur during heavy outbreaks. San Jose scale also may infest fruit. Fruit becomes spotted around the feeding site of the scale.

Distribution: Throughout North America.

Appearance: First-stage nymphs ("white caps") are circular and dirty white. Later stages become gray brown and develop a more pronounced yellow "nipple" in the center. Coverings of the males are considerably smaller and elongate. The body of the female is yellow.

Life History and Habits: San Jose scale usually overwinters as second instar ("black cap") nymphs. They remain dormant until sap flows in the spring, then continue to feed and develop. By the end of April, adult forms are usually present. The adult males emerge from the scale cover as tiny, winged, gnatlike insects. They mate with the females which may subsequently produce eggs that hatch under the cover. The newly emerged crawlers move about the plant and usually settle to feed within the first 24 hours. During the growing season, San Jose scale develops and matures over a month or so and repeats the life cycle. Two generations are typical in northern areas, but near continual development in southern areas occurs, with up to five generations annually. As individual females can produce well over 100 eggs over a period of 6 weeks, generations soon overlap and all stages are present during much of the season.

Related Species

Walnut scale (*Quadraspidiotus juglansregiae*) is a common species associated with deciduous trees and shrubs including ash, birch, linden, maple, and ash. Despite its name, the only walnut (*Juglans*) species that hosts this insect is Persian walnut. Walnut scale is generally distributed throughout North America. It feeds on twigs, branches, and sometimes trunks, causing reduced vigor during heavy infestations with associated thinning and yellowing of foliage. Walnut scale is generally circular in form, similar in appearance to San Jose scale. It can be distinguish by having a more orange or orange-red body, and the top of the covering (exuvium) is sunken at the center.

Winter is spent as partially developed scales in the second instar, similar to San Jose scale. However, only one generation is produced annually, with eggs produced over an extended period by the overwintered females. Nymphs and eggs are present most of the summer.

Forbes scale (*Quadraspidiotus forbesi*) may occur on many kinds of fruit trees west of the Rockies but rarely is abundant. It can be distinguished from San Jose scale by having a raised reddish area in the center, versus the yellow "nipple" of San Jose scale. Only one generation a year is produced, with crawlers present in May and June.

A. San Jose scale crawlers. *K. Gray.* **B.** San Jose scales. *K. Gray.* **C.** San Jose scale fruit infestation. *K. Gray.* **D.** San Jose scales. *J. Capinera.* **E.** Walnut scales. *W. Cranshaw.* **F.** Walnut scales. *J. A. Davidson.*

Euonymus Scale (*Unaspis euonymi*)

Hosts: *Euonymus* species, particularly evergreen shrub varieties. There is a range of susceptibility, with spindle tree among the most susceptible. Pachysandra, holly, privet, and some boxwood are less common hosts.

Damage: Euonymus scale develops by sucking sap from cells of twigs and leaves. Yellowish or brown spots often are present at feeding sites, and infested leaves may drop prematurely. Heavily infested branches may be killed.

Distribution: Widely distributed in much of the U.S. in association with its hosts, being most damaging in part of the eastern and southwestern U.S.

Appearance: Males and females are present and look very different. Females are oystershell shaped, generally brown, and usually found on twigs. Male nymphs are fuzzy white, elongate, and most common on foliage.

Life History and Habits: Winter is spent as a mature, fertilized female that produces eggs in early spring. Orangish crawlers subsequently emerge over a period of few weeks, settle, and develop over the course of about a month. Adult males emerge and mate with females in early summer, followed by a second cycle of egg hatch and crawler dispersal in midsummer. Three generations per year may occur in southern areas of the range.

Other Armored Scales

Black pineleaf scale (*Nuclaspis californica*) is associated with pine and rarely spruce. It is generally dark, elliptical in form, and found on needles. Sometimes in mature scales the dark area is surrounded by white, creating a bull's-eye appearance. Outbreaks of black pineleaf scale often are reported to be associated with stressful growing conditions.

Elongate hemlock scale (*Fiornia externa*) is a serious pest of Canada and Carolina hemlock in many eastern states and contributes greatly to their decline. The covering of the adult female is elongate, parallel sided, and usually brown. Two generations are produced annually in the southern and mid-Atlantic states, one in the Northeast. Development is not well synchronized, however, so no distinct activity peaks occur and all stages may be present throughout the year. The related **tea scale** (*F. theae*) is an important landscape pest in the southeastern states, associated with camellia, Chinese and Japanese holly, tea plant, euonymus, ferns, bottlebrush, and dogwood.

Fern scale (*Pinnaspis aspidistrae*) develops on fronds of ferns and leaves of several indoor perennials including ficus, hibiscus, citrus, magnolia, liriope, and acacia. Mature females have a pear-shaped cover that is pale brown and about $\frac{1}{12}$ inch long. This species may survive outdoors on liriope as far north as Maryland, where it produces two generations per year.

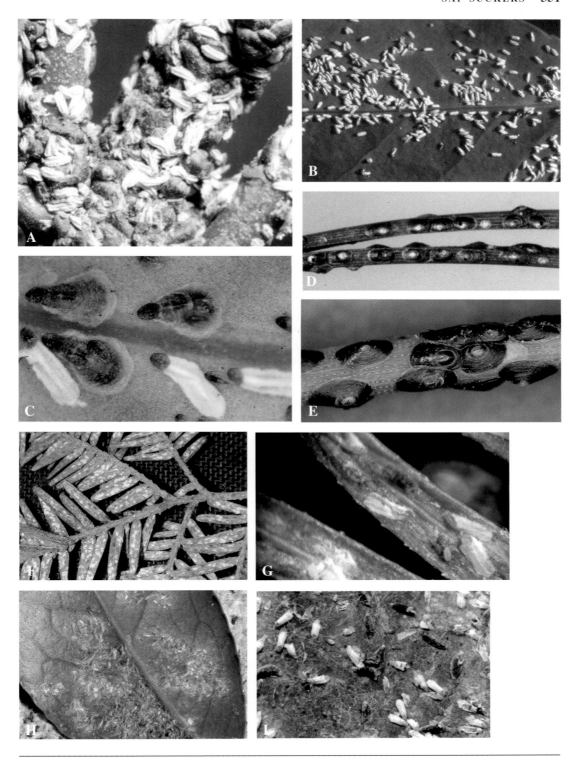

A. Euonymus scales. *Courtesy Clemson University.* **B.** Euonymus scales. *W. Cranshaw.* **C.** Euonymus scales. Females are brown, males white. *W. Cranshaw.* **D.** Black pineleaf scales. *D. Herms.* **E.** Black pineleaf scales. *W. Cranshaw.* **F.** Elongate hemlock scales. *E. Day.* **G.** Elongate hemlock scales. *E. Day.* **H.** Tea scales. *E. Day.* **I.** Tea scales. *Courtesy Clemson University.*

Juniper scale (*Carulaspis juniperi*) develops on juniper, cypress, incense cedar, false cypress, cryptomeria, and arborvitae. The scales suck sap from the needles, reducing vigor and production of new growth. Adult females are circular, about 1/10 inch in diameter, and look like creamy white dots on needles. Males are elongated but smaller. Heavily infested plants may look off-color and as if dusted with snow. Winter is spent as eggs, and one generation is produced annually. In the mid-Atlantic states and southern U.S. the closely related **minute cypress scale** (*C. minima*) is associated with ornamental cypress, arborvitae, and juniper.

Oleander scale (*Aspidiotus nerii*), also called ivy scale, may be the most common armored scale in California. It is found elsewhere primarily as a greenhouse pest. Citrus, sago palm, oleander, English ivy, and palm are common hosts. Females are circular, white to light brown, and moderately convex. Three to four generations can occur indoors per year. The related **cryptomeria scale** (*A. cryptomeriae*) is an introduced species well established in the mid-Atlantic states. It can be damaging to several conifer hosts including cryptomeria, eastern hemlock, cypress, and balsam fir. Winter is spent as a partially grown nymph (second instar), with egg hatch in late spring. A second generation occurs, with egg hatch in midsummer.

False oleander scale (*Pseudaulacaspis cockerelli*), also known as magnolia white scale and sometimes oleander scale, is found in the Gulf states and southern California. It can occur on more than 100 species including magnolia, bird-of-paradise, some palms, palmetto, English ivy, yew, and mango. Mature females have a pear-shaped shiny white cover and feed on foliage. Yellow chlorotic spots appear on the upper leaf surface around feeding sites.

California red scale (*Aonidiella aurantii*) affects many ornamental plants (acacia, boxwood, eugenia, euonymus, magnolia, mulberry, palm, podocarpus, privet, rose) and can be a serious pest of citrus. It is found outdoors in warmer areas of the southern U.S. and is a common greenhouse pest. Adult females are round, reddish orange, and have concentric rings on the cover. Young stages produce some cottony filaments of wax around their body; later stages form the more solid cover.

Latania scale (*Hemiberlesia lataniae*) is common in the Gulf states and present in southern California. It has a wide host range with palm and schefflera among the more common hosts. It is found on both leaves and twigs. The covering is gray-brown and broadly oval with an off-centered exuvium, giving it a tilted appearance. The closely related **greedy scale** (*H. rapax*) is similar in appearance. It gets its name from its wide host range which includes citrus, ivy, acacia, boxwood, cactus, ceanothus, fruit trees, holly, laurel, magnolia, palm, peppertree, pittosporum, pyracantha, and redbud.

Cycad aulacaspis scale (*Aulacaspis yasumatsui*), sometimes known as Asian cycad scale, is a recent introduction (1997) into Florida that is devastating to king and queen sago. Large populations build up quickly, with generation times of about 1 month, and heavily infested plants can be killed. Control is complicated by the occurrence of many individual scales on belowground parts of the plant. Efforts are being made to introduce natural enemies that control this insect well in is area of origin (southeast Asia).

A. Juniper scales. *W. Cranshaw.* **B.** Juniper scales. *W. Cranshaw.* **C.** Cryptomeria scales. *R. D. Lehman.* **D.** California red scale colony. *J. K. Clark/UC Statewide IPM Program.* **E.** Cycad heavily infested with cycad aulacaspis scale. *D. Caldwell.* **F.** Cycad aulacaspis scale with crawlers. *D. Caldwell.* **G.** False oleander scales. *D. Caldwell.* **H.** Oleander scales. *J. R. Baker.*

Miscellaneous Armored Scales and Their Common Hosts

Scientific Name	Common Name	Hosts
Abgrallaspis ithacae	Hemlock scale	Hemlock
Abgrallaspis townsendi	Townsend scale	Rhododendron, azalea
Aulacaspis rosae	Rose scale	Berry bushes, rose
Chrysomphalus aonidum	Florida red scale	Citrus, holly, palms, kentia, bird-of-paradise
Diaspidiotus aesculi	Buckeye scale	Alder, willow, walnut, fruit trees
Diaspidiotus ancylus	Putnam scale	Draceana, kentia, schefflera, palms
Diaspis boisduvalii	Boisduval scale	General feeder of many tropical plants but primarily a pest of orchids, yucca, palms
Diaspis echinocacti	Cactus scale	Various cacti, portulaca, jade plants
Dynaspidiotus britannicus	Holly scale	Holly
Furchadaspis zamiae	Cycad scale	Bird-of-paradise, cycads such as sago palm
Lopholeucaspis japonica	Japanese maple scale	Dogwood, zelkova, poncirus, other hardwoods
Melanaspis obscura	Obscure scale	Oak, particularly pin oak
Melanaspis tenebricosa	Gloomy scale	Silver and red maple
Odonaspis penicillata	Penicillate scale	Bamboo
Parlatoria oleae	Olive scale	Olive, deciduous fruit crops
Pseudaulacaspis pentagona	White peach scale	Privet, mulberry, catalpa, chinaberry, other ornamentals
Pseudaulacaspis prunicola	White prunicola scale	Stone fruits, privet, lilac

A. Rose scales. *D. Shetlar.* **B.** Cactus scales. *D. Shetlar.* **C.** Pinyon needle scale–infested branch. *W. Cranshaw.*
D. Boisduval scales. *D. Shetlar.* **E.** Holly scales. *K. Gray.* **F.** Gloomy scales. *J. A. Davidson.* **G.** Obscure scales. *J. D. Solomon.* **H.** White peach scale infestation. *E. Day.* **I.** Obscure scales. *J. A. Davidson.* **J.** White peach scale with cover removed. *K. Gray.* **K.** White peach scales. *K. Gray.* **L.** Putnam's scales. *Courtesy Florida Dept. Agriculture and Consumer Services/Div. Plant Industry.*

LEAFHOPPERS

Leafhoppers[1] are small insects, typically about ⅛ to ³⁄₁₆ inch in length, elongate and somewhat wedge shaped and tapering at the end. Eggs are inserted as small groups under the plant surface, usually in leaf veins or small twigs. The nymphs are active insects, usually moving readily when disturbed, often with a crablike walk. Adults are winged and fly readily, leaping from plants with their enlarged hind legs.

More than 2,500 species of leafhoppers are found in North America, and at least some may be associated with almost any plant except those with thick, waxy foliage. All feed on sap which they suck with stylet mouthparts from leaves and, less commonly, succulent stems. Damage to plants is variable as leafhoppers are often far less abundant than their distant relatives the aphids, but significant plant injury is rare. Most species feed on the phloem of plants, removing only modest amounts of sap and excreting some honeydew.

Several leafhoppers restrict feeding to the upper cell layers (mesophyll, parenchyma), producing white flecking wounds. These insects often excrete dark spots in the manner characteristic of other mesophyll-feeding insects such as lace bugs and some thrips and plant bugs. Some members of the genus *Empoasca* can injure the vascular system of plants, producing a condition known as hopperburn. One group of leafhoppers known as the "sharpshooters" feeds on the xylem fluids; they tend to be more elongated than other leafhoppers, with a prominent point at the front. They get their name from the habit of some species of flicking small droplets during excretion, which may be detectable as fine spray.

Some leafhoppers are important because of their ability to transmit plant pathogens that cause many diseases. These include viruses (curly top), phytoplasmas (aster yellows, ash yellows), and the xylem-limited bacteria (bacterial leaf scorch, Pierce's disease of grape).

Potato Leafhopper (*Empoasca fabae*)

Hosts: A wide variety of plants, particularly legumes such as bean and alfalfa. Potato, raspberry, and several trees, including maple, birch, and apple, are also common hosts.

Damage: Destruction of cells during feeding and injection of saliva toxic to plants disrupt the phloem and sap flow of plants. Photosynthesis is reduced and foliage discoloration is common, typically a yellowing. Symptoms are usually first evident at the leaf tip and may progressively cause tissues to be killed, resulting in a condition known as hopperburn. Severe leaf injury and even premature plant death are common on potato; more subtle leaf discoloration and curling are more characteristic on bean. On trees, reductions in shoot length result in stunting or swelling of twigs and may be accompanied by susceptibility to increased winter injury.

Distribution: Restricted to eastern North America, only infrequently being found as far west as Wyoming and Colorado.

Appearance: Pale green, about ⅛ inch, elongate, and gradually tapering to the hind end. Some pale spotting behind the head may be observed on close observation. The nymphs are lighter colored and highly active. They are found on leaf undersides and readily move sideways when disturbed.

A. Beet leafhopper. *K. Gray.* **B.** Beet leafhopper at egg hatch. *K. Gray.* **C.** Witches' broom growth characteristic of ash yellows. *J. Hartman.* **D.** Beet leafhopper nymph. *W. Cranshaw.* **E.** Young nymph of beet leafhopper. *K. Gray.* **F.** Symptoms of beet curly top in bean. *H. Schwartz.* **G.** Hopperburn symptoms on potato caused by potato leafhopper feeding injury. *W. Cranshaw.* **H.** Bacterial leaf scorch symptoms on northern pin oak. *J. Hartman.* **I.** Potato leafhopper injury to apple. *R. Bessin.* **J.** Potato leafhopper feeding injury to Japanese maple. *D. Herms.* **K.** Potato leafhopper nymph. *W. Cranshaw.* **L.** Potato leafhopper adult. *R. Bessin.*

Life History and Habits: Winter is spent in areas around the Gulf Coast where potato leafhoppers feed in alfalfa and various weeds. A northward migration occurs annually, and often suddenly, in May or early June. Alfalfa and bean are often early-season hosts, with potato increasingly favored later in the summer. Potato leafhopper may breed year-round in southern parts of its range but dies out in the north during winter.

Females insert eggs into veins on the underside of the leaf. The young nymphs are pale green and gradually darken with age, molting four times over the course of 2 to 3 weeks before reaching the adult form. Three to five generations per year typically are produced in the midwestern states.

Related Species

Several other less commonly damaging species of *Empoasca* leafhoppers, sometimes described as garden leafhoppers, occur throughout North America. All are similar in appearance to potato leafhopper and can be separated only by experts. Hopperburn-type symptoms have been observed on winter squash by *E. recurvata* in Colorado. However, the other species apparently feed primarily on the mesophyll and produce white flecking injuries to foliage. **Western potato leafhopper** (*E. abrupta*) and **intermountain leafhopper** (*E. filamenta*) are two western species that apparently produce white flecking injuries to potato and bean but do not induce hopperburn. **Southern garden leafhopper** (*E. solana*) may similarly damage potato, bean, and lettuce in southern states. White flecking of foliage is produced on apple by **apple leafhopper** (*E. maligna*).

Rose Leafhopper (*Edwardsiana rosae*)

Hosts: *Rosa* species and *Rubus* species are overwintering hosts. Dogwood, oak, elm, hawthorn, apple, poplar, maple, and oak are among the summer hosts.

Damage: Rose leafhoppers feed on the sap of mesophyll and produce white flecking wounds (stippling) on foliage. Damage occurs early in the season, after which time the insects disperse to summer hosts. Eggs are inserted into canes, and occasionally these wounds serve as entry courts for pathogens.

Distribution: Throughout North America in association with rose and bramble hosts.

Appearance: Rose leafhopper is pale yellow to creamy white in both the adult and nymphal stages. Early-stage nymphs have reddish eyes, but those of older nymphs and adults are white. Dark spotting on the nymphs can distinguish them from white apple leafhopper. One behavioral feature of the pale yellow nymphs is that, unlike most leafhoppers, they cannot move sideways.

Life History and Habits: Eggs survive winter inserted into stems of rose canes, and pimplelike swellings develop where eggs are laid. At egg hatch in early spring, nymphs move to foliage and feed on the leaf underside. All nymphal stages can usually be completed in 2 to 3 weeks. Individuals may remain on a single leaf the entire time, but rose leafhopper nymphs are quite active and readily move forward (but not sideways) when disturbed. The winged adults usually then disperse to alternate summer host plants, returning to rose in late summer for overwintering egg-laying. Eggs during the summer generations are laid into large veins and petioles of leaves. In addition to the first generation on rose, two additional generations are produced during the summer. In the Pacific Northwest, peak numbers of nymphs are usually observed in early June, late July/early August, and mid-September.

A. Leaf spotting of potato by western potato leafhopper. *W. Cranshaw.* B. *Empoasca recurvata* adult. *W. Cranshaw.* C. Rose leafhopper nymphs. *W. Cranshaw.* D. Hopperburn injury to pumpkin produced by *Empoasca recurvata. W. Cranshaw.* E. Intermountain leafhopper adult. *K. Gray.* F. Intermountain leafhopper nymph. *K. Gray.* G. Rose leafhopper nymph. *K. Gray.* H. Adult rose leafhopper. *K. Gray.* I. Intermountain leafhopper egg inserted in leaf. *K. Gray.* J. Rose leafhopper injury. *W. Cranshaw.* K. Stippling injuries to potato produced by feeding of western potato leafhopper. *W. Cranshaw.*

Other Mesophyll-Feeding Leafhoppers

Edwardsiana commisuralis is a common western species that produces injuries similar to rose leafhopper on dogwood and alder. *E. hippocastani* occurs on elm and *E. australis* on mountain-ash.

White apple leafhopper (*Typhlocyba pomaria*) is physically almost identical to rose leafhopper. It produces wounds around feeding sites that appear as whitish flecking (stippling) on leaves of apple, cherry, peach, prune, and hawthorn. Winter is spent as eggs inserted under the bark of twigs and small branches of these hosts. Nymphs are uniformly colored translucent white, occasionally yellow. Two generations typically are produced, but they overlap considerably and adults may be present from late May through October. White apple leafhopper is a major pest of apple orchards in much of North America, damaging plants by removing chlorophyll from leaves as it feeds and by excreting small dark droplets that may spot fruit.

Erythroneura leafhoppers also produce white flecking wounds. Larvae are cream colored or slightly yellow and have some spotting. **Western grape leafhopper** (*E. vulnerata*) is an important pest of grapes grown in the western states. Winter is spent in the adult stage under sheltering debris in the vicinity of previously infested plants. The adults emerge when spring temperatures reach the mid-60s and fly to the vines to feed shortly after the new growth emerges. After several weeks, the females begin egg-laying, inserting the egg just underneath the leaf surface; this appears as a small bubble when closely examined. Eggs hatch in 1 to 2 weeks, and the nymphs feed on the mesophyll of cells on the lower leaf surface. They become full grown in approximately 3 weeks. Depending on location, three to five generations may be produced annually and may overlap and be present on plants continuously, as long as foliage remains. In fall, the adults disperse to cover for wintering.

Related species have similar habits. Grape also hosts **variegated leafhopper** (*Erythroneura variabilis*) in southern California and **eastern grape leafhopper** (*E. comes*) in eastern states. **Virginiacreeper (ziczac) leafhopper** (*E. ziczac*) is common in the High Plains and Rocky Mountain region where it develops on grape, Virginia creeper, elm, and Boston ivy. **Threebanded leafhopper** (*E. tricincta*) may occur on grape, Virginia creeper, and apple in the east. *E. gleditsia* feeds on black locust, *Aesculus* species and hawthorn and *E. lawsoniana* feeds on sycamore.

Maple leafhopper (*Alebra albostriella*) produces stippling injuries on leaves of several trees and shrubs including various maples, American elm, basswood, oak, beech, hickory, hawthorn, and sumac. It produces one generation per year, with peak populations observed in late spring in the East and in midsummer in central California. It overwinters as eggs inserted into twigs.

A. Elm leaf injury caused by *Edwardsiana hippocastani*. *K. Gray.* **B.** Damage by white apple leafhopper. *W. Cranshaw.*
C. Leaf mottling from infestation of grape leafhopper. Green areas are where eggs were laid. *W. Cranshaw.* **D.** Grape
leafhopper eggs inserted into leaf. Brown eggs on right have been parasitized by a small wasp. *W. Cranshaw.* **E.** Ziczac
leafhopper nymphs and injury. *W. Cranshaw.* **F.** Grape leafhopper nymphs. *W. Cranshaw.* **G.** Grape leafhopper nymph.
W. Cranshaw. **H.** Grape leafhopper adult. *W. Cranshaw.* **I.** Leaf injury by ziczac leafhopper. *W. Cranshaw.*

Aster (or Sixspotted) Leafhopper (*Macrosteles quadrilineatus*)

Hosts: An extremely wide range of plants including small grains and turfgrasses, many vegetables, and flower crops.

Damage: Direct feeding effects are insignificant, producing minor spotting at most. However, aster leafhopper can transmit the phytoplasma that produces the eastern strain of aster yellows disease. Aster yellows is damaging to head lettuce, carrot, celery, cosmos, marigold, aster, and many other garden plants.

Distribution: Throughout most of North America but is most important in the Midwest and northeastern U.S. and much of southern Canada.

Appearance: Overall color of adults is usually grayish green. The presence of three pairs of dark markings on the head is the most distinguishing feature of this insect in separating it from other common leafhoppers.

Life History and Habits: Aster leafhopper survives poorly in areas of harsh winter temperatures but may survive as eggs as far north as New England and Manitoba if conditions are suitable. The primary wintering areas are along the Gulf of Mexico and the southern Great Plains. Winged adults are highly migratory, and large annual flights allow them to colonize a wide area each growing season, often moving on favorable winds in late May and early June. Spring grains are important hosts used after migrations, and populations may increase rapidly.

Eggs are laid in leaves and stems of plants and hatch in about a week. Nymphs pass through four stages over the course of 4 to 6 weeks. Adults can live for months. Two or four generations typically are produced during the growing season.

Leafhoppers that feed on plants infected with aster yellows acquire the causal phytoplasma. They cannot transmit the disease, however, until the phytoplasma has circulated in the leafhopper and moved to its salivary glands. This typically takes 10 days to 3 weeks, during which the phytoplasma reproduces in cells of the aster leafhopper. Once this period has passed, the leafhopper is capable of transmitting the disease organism for the rest of its life. Typically, somewhere between 1 and 5% of all leafhoppers carry the aster yellows phytoplasma in the Midwest during the growing season.

Other Aster Yellows Vectors

Several other leafhoppers are involved in transmitting the phytoplasma strains that produce aster yellows. In the far west and southeastern U.S., *Scaphytopius irroratus* is important in transmitting the western strain of this pathogen. *S. acutus* is a vector involved in transmission in the Northeast. Other vectors include **mountain leafhopper** (*Colladonus montanus*), **privet leafhopper** (*Fieberiella florii*), and *Ceratagallia abrupta*.

A. Twisting of head leaves from aster yellows infection of lettuce. *W. Cranshaw.* **B.** Witches' broom of top growth in carrot from aster yellows infection. *W. Cranshaw.* **C.** Distortion of flowers (phyllody) of cosmos from aster yellows infection. *W. Cranshaw.* **D.** Aster leafhopper. *K. Gray.* **E.** Aster leafhopper. *W. Cranshaw.* **F.** Witches' brooming of statice caused by aster yellows infection. *W. Cranshaw.* **G.** Gradation of aster yellows symptoms in carrot; advanced symptoms (left) and healthy plant (right). *W. Cranshaw.* **H.** *Scaphytopius acutus. K. Gray.* **I.** *Scaphytopius* sp. leafhopper. *J. A. Payne.* **J.** Mountain leafhopper nymph. *K. Gray.* **K.** Mountain leafhopper adult. *K. Gray.*

Miscellaneous Leafhoppers

Beet leafhopper (*Eutettix tenellus*) is the vector of the virus that causes beet curly top. This produces disease in several plants, notably pepper, tomato, beet, and bean. Damage by beet leafhopper feeding in the absence of the virus is insignificant. Beet leafhopper is originally of European origin but has become widely established in the western U.S., particularly the southwest. *E. strobi* is more widely distributed and commonly produces a very visible purplish spotting of beet leaves but causes little injury.

Honeylocust leafhopper (*Macropsis fumipennis*) is common on honeylocust and many other shade trees in much of North America. Feeding produces a slight flecking of the foliage, and it is a minor honeydew producer. The bright green nymphs are commonly confused with those of honeylocust plant bug, and early in the season both are present on foliage. At least two generations of honeylocust leafhopper are produced annually. *M. ocellata* is common on willow in the northeastern quadrant states, and *M. graminea* occurs on *Populus* species in the northern U.S. and Canada. **Plum leafhopper** (*M. trimaculata*) develops on stone fruits and is known to vector peach yellow leaf curl virus.

Privet leafhopper (*Fieberiella florii*) is a common species found primarily in western North America. It has a wide host range including stone fruits, privet, cotoneaster, currant, and spirea. It is among the most important leafhoppers involved in spreading plant diseases, acting as a vector for peach yellow leaf curl virus, western X-disease, and western aster yellows.

Whitebanded elm leafhopper (*Scaphoideus luteolus*) is important as the vector of the phytoplasma that produces elm phloem necrosis disease and because of direct injuries it can produce while feeding on elm leaves. The generally brown-colored nymphs are distinctive with a broad white band across the abdomen. One generation per year is produced, with winter spent as eggs inserted into twigs.

Candystripe leafhopper (*Graphocepahla coccinea*) is a gaudily colored leafhopper with alternating bands of magenta and green or blue. It is common on many garden flowers and caneberries but causes little injury. Egg scars on leaves of woody plant hosts may appear as small blisters on shrubs on which nymphs develop (e.g., rhododendron, laurel, azalea). The related **blue-green sharpshooter** (*G. atropunctata*) is more commonly associated with vines and woody plants. It is important in coastal areas of California in transmission of the bacteria that produces **Pierce's disease of grape**.

Pierce's disease, produced by infection with a strain of *Xylella fastidiosa*, has several other vectors in California. Of greatest concern is **glassywinged sharpshooter** (*Homalodisca coagulata*), a species that is highly mobile and feeds on a wide range of hosts, wild and cultivated. **Green sharpshooter** (*Draeculacephala minerva*) feeds primarily on grass, including many turfgrasses. **Redheaded sharpshooter** (*Carneocephala fulgida*) develops similarly on bermudagrass and is an uncommon vector. A closely related strain of *X. fastidiosa* produces the disease known as **bacterial leaf scorch** in areas of the eastern U.S. American elm, maple, mulberry, plum, oak, sycamore, sweetgum, and hackberry are among the plants that show symptoms, although the pathogen is also widespread in several turfgrasses and alfalfa. The specific leafhopper vectors are unknown. In the western U.S., strains of *X. fastidiosa* also produce diseases known as oleander leaf scorch and almond leaf scorch.

Many leafhoppers are associated with lawns and turfgrasses. None appear to cause much more than minor spotting and are not seriously damaging except during seedling establishment. Common species include **lawn leafhopper** (*Deltocephalus hospes*), **gray lawn leafhopper** (*Exitianus exitiosus*), **lesser lawn leafhopper** (*Graminella sonora*), **painted leafhopper** (*Endria inimica*), and **clover leafhopper** (*Aceratagallia sanguinolenta*). Several species in the genera *Deltoacephalus*, *Agallia*, *Forcipata*, *Latalus*, *Polyamia*, *Dikraneura*, and *Balclutha* may also be found on turfgrasses.

---

[1] Homoptera: Cicadellidae

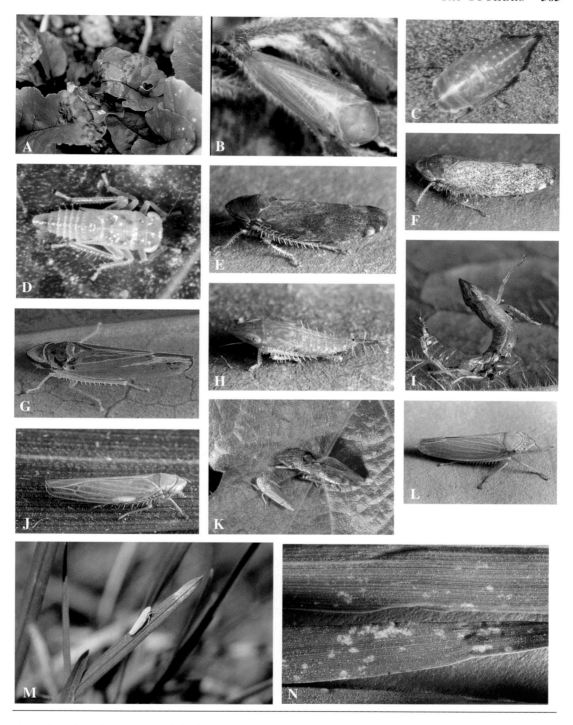

A. Leaf spotting of beet characteristic of *Eutettix strobi* feeding injury. *W. Cranshaw.* **B.** Honeylocust leafhopper adult. *W. Cranshaw.* **C.** Late instar of honeylocust leafhopper. *W. Cranshaw.* **D.** Early-stage nymph of honeylocust leafhopper. *W. Cranshaw.* **E.** Privet leafhopper adult, dark form. *K. Gray.* **F.** Privet leafhopper adult. *K. Gray.* **G.** *Graphocephala* sp., a "sharpshooter" leafhopper. *K. Gray.* **H.** Privet leafhopper nymph. *K. Gray.* **I.** Privet leafhopper nymph molting. *K. Gray.* **J.** *Dikraneura carneola*. *K. Gray.* **K.** Glassywinged sharpshooter (larger) compared to blue-green sharpshooter. *J. K. Clark/UC Statewide IPM Program.* **L.** *Draeculacephala crassicornis*. *K. Gray.* **M.** Leafhopper on turfgrass. *W. Cranshaw.* **N.** Leaf spotting caused by *Dikraneura carneola* feeding injury. *K. Gray.*

TREEHOPPERS

Treehoppers (Membracidae family)[1] are distinguished by a prominent enlargement of the segment behind the head (pronotum), which extends shieldlike over the head and much of the abdomen. This often is further enlarged to produce spiny or hornlike projections, leading to the term "thorn bugs" applied to some species. The nymphs often have spines running along the back. Treehoppers are infrequently encountered by gardeners. Most species have fairly innocuous habits, and the primary plant injuries occur during the course of laying eggs into twigs. The majority of treehoppers feed on trees and shrubs; a few feed on herbaceous plants such as Canada thistle and sunflower.

Buffalo Treehopper (*Stictocephala bisonia*)

Hosts: Apple, peach, ash, elm, and many other deciduous trees,

Damage: Buffalo treehopper injures plants when it inserts eggs into twigs. Small rows of scars appear on injured twigs which become scabby and may be sites for plant pathogens to become established.

Distribution: Throughout the U.S. and much of Canada; this is the most widely distributed and familiar North American treehopper.

Appearance: Generally triangular shaped with the sides of the front developed into small points, somewhat resembling a miniature bison. Buffalo treehopper is grassy green and about ⅜ inch long.

Life History and Habits: Buffalo treehopper overwinters in the egg stage, and eggs are inserted as small groups under the bark of twigs. The eggs hatch in late spring, and the nymphs usually feed on grasses and broadleaf weeds around the base of trees on which eggs were laid. They become full grown in late July or August, and females lay eggs from August until a killing frost occurs.

Other Treehoppers

Micrutalis calva is common on honeylocust and black locust but reportedly is not damaging. One of many treehopper species found on oaks, **oak treehopper** (*Platycotis vittata*) occurs widely throughout much of the U.S., developing on various oaks, birch, and chestnut. Feeding injuries are minor, but oviposition scars in twigs may attract attention. Large colonies of nymphs may be observed on twigs, often along with the mother. **Twomarked treehopper** (*Enchenopa binotata*) occurs commonly in many areas west of the Rockies, primarily in northern areas. Hoptree, nut trees, black locust, viburnum, redbud, bittersweet, and wisteria are among its reported hosts. As with other treehoppers, eggs are inserted into twigs but twomarked treehopper then covers these with a whitish frothy material which makes oviposition sites very conspicuous. The spiny nymphs aggregate to feed at tips of branches. **Threecornered alfalfa treehopper** (*Spissistilus festinus*) develops on legumes in the southern states and is particularly damaging to soybean. The primary injury is stem breakage, resulting from wounds produced by feeding and egg-laying. *Entylia carinata* feeds on several herbaceous perennial flowering plants, including dahlia and aster.

[1] Homoptera: Membracidae

A. Buffalo treehopper. *W. Cranshaw.* **B.** Treehopper *Micrutalis calva. W. Cranshaw.* **C.** Oak treehopper nymphs with adult (bottom). *L. Risley.* **D.** Egg-laying scars produced by buffalo treehopper. *W. Cranshaw.* **E.** Nymph of treehopper *Stictocepha bulbalus. K. Gray.* **F.** Twomarked treehopper and froth-covered eggs. *D. Caldwell.* **G.** Treehopper *Micrutalis calva. W. Cranshaw.* **H.** Threecornered and alfalfa treehoppers. *G. J. Lenhard.*

SPITTLEBUGS

Spittlebugs (Cercopidae family)[1] are closely related to the leafhoppers but tend to be somewhat broader in form. They are similarly small, with adults typically about ¼ inch when full grown. What is uniquely characteristic, however, is the spittle mass the nymphs produce after they begin to feed. This is produced from excess excreted fluids (spittlebugs suck sap from the xylem), combined with mucilaginous fluids into which air bubbles are introduced. The function of the spittle mass is thought to be to protect the nymphs from predators and/or from drying. The great majority of spittlebugs are associated with woody plants, but some feed on herbaceous plants for part of their life cycle.

Meadow Spittlebug (*Philaenus spumarius*)

Hosts: An extremely wide range of plants, including strawberry, various flowers, and legumes.

Damage: Little damage usually occurs from removal of sap from feeding, although some stunting of growth may occur. Significant damage to strawberry and alfalfa has been reported but is rare. The prominence and appearance of the spittle mass often attract attention and concern.

Distribution: Much of the U.S., excluding southwestern areas, but most common in the Northeast and Pacific Northwest.

Appearance: Adults are rarely observed but are about ¼ inch long, straw colored to dark brown. Nymphs are pale green and found in spittle masses.

Life History and Habits: Eggs are laid in small masses among crevices. Eggs hatch in spring, and the nymphs feed on stems, quickly producing a large frothy spittle mass. They become full grown in late spring, and the winged adults disperse to feed on a wide variety of plants through the summer. Eggs are laid in fall, and one generation is produced per year.

Twolined Spittlebug (*Prosapia bicincta*)

Hosts: Primarily warm-season grasses, particularly bermudagrass; also holly and, much less commonly, redbud and cherry.

Damage: Nymphs and adults feed on grass blades, removing sap. More significant effects seem to result from toxic effects of saliva which can cause leaf spotting and sometimes death of blades. Adults feeding on holly can produce leaf spotting and distortion.

A. Spittle masses of meadow spittlebug. *W. Cranshaw.* **B.** Twolined spittlebug adult. *Courtesy Clemson University.*
C. Meadow spittlebug adult. *K. Gray.* **D.** Meadow spittlebug nymph. *K. Gray.* **E.** Twolined spittlebug nymph. *D. Shetlar.*

Distribution: Much of the eastern half of the U.S., particularly common in the southeastern quadrant.

Appearance: Adults are broadly oval to wedge shaped, about ⅓ inch, and generally dark brown or black. Most have red or orange lines across the wings, although these may be absent. Legs and eyes are red as well. Nymphs, which are found in a spittle mass in the crown of the plant, generally resemble adults but lack wings and are creamy yellow.

Life History and Habits: Winter is spent in the egg stage among grass plants, and hatch occurs in late spring. The nymphs settle at the base of plants and begin to feed, subsequently producing a spittle mass. They repeatedly molt as they develop, becoming full grown in about a month. Adults may feed on nearby woody plants, notably holly, as well as grass. A second generation occurs in the southeastern U.S., one generation in more northern areas.

Other Spittlebugs

Numerous species of *Clastoptera* are found throughout North America. **Juniper spittlebug** (*C. juniperina*) is common on juniper and arborvitae in many western states. **Pecan spittlebug** (*C. achatina*) sometimes contributes to twig dieback in parts of the Midwest. **Alder spittlebug** (*C. obtusa*) feeds on various shrubs and trees, including hickory, birch, and alder. **Dogwood spittlebug** (*C. proteus*) is common on dogwood and *Vaccinium* in the Midwest. *Clastoptera* species that develop on Gambel oak are common in the Rocky Mountain region, with multiple nymphs present in spittle masses formed along the underside leaf vein.

Saratoga spittlebug (*Aphrophora saratogensis*) occurs in the eastern half of the U.S. where it develops on certain conifers, particularly red and jack pine. Nymphs develop on a wide variety of shrubs and herbaceous plants, notably sweetfern. Damage is produced by the adult stage as it feeds on shoots. Saliva that is toxic to the plant is injected, producing a pocket of damaged and dead tissue. Wilting beyond the feeding site may occur when the insects are abundant. **Western pine spittlebug** (*Aphrophora permutata*) is common in the northwestern states.

[1] Homoptera: Cercopidae

A. Juniper spittlebug adult. *W. Cranshaw.* **B.** Juniper spittlebug exposed from spittle mass. *W. Cranshaw.* **C.** Western pine spittlebug adult. *K. Gray.* **D.** Alder spittlebug adult. *K. Gray* **E.** Pecan spittlebug. *H. C. Ellis.* **F.** Oak spittlebugs. *W. Cranshaw.* **G.** Alder spittlebug nymphs. *K. Gray.* **H.** Saratoga spittlebug nymph. *K. Gray.* **I.** Saratoga spittlebug adult. *K. Gray.*

SQUASH BUG

Squash bug is the most notorious member of the leaffooted bug family (Coreidae).[1] All members of this family are moderate to large sized with a prominent head possessing piercing-sucking mouthparts, and most have a pronounced flattening of the hind legs. Most leaffooted bugs feed primarily on seeds and are discussed on p. 232.

Squash Bug (*Anasa tristus*)

Hosts: Winter types of squash, including pumpkin. Rarely, summer squash and melon are damaged.

Damage: Adults and nymphs suck sap from the stems and leaves, causing localized injuries that kill and collapse tissues. Initial symptoms are small yellow flecks on foliage that later turn brown. Later, foliage often wilts and dies beyond damaged areas. Feeding may occur on fruit, causing wounds that are readily colonized by rotting organisms. The wilting associated with squash bug is sometimes termed Anasa wilt of cucurbits.

Distribution: Generally distributed throughout the U.S., excluding the northwest, and southern Canada and extending south into Central America. This species is most common and damaging in southern areas.

Appearance: Adults are grayish brown and about $^{11}/_{16}$ inch in length. They lay distinctive shiny coppery red masses of eggs, and the newly hatched nymphs are pale green. Older nymphs are gray and develop wing pads that become increasingly prominent.

Life History and Habits: Squash bugs spend winter in the adult stage in protected sites around previously infested plantings. They become active and first appear and feed in June, shortly after plant emergence. At this time they mate, and females lay masses of eggs on leaf undersides and occasionally stems. After hatching, the nymphs feed together in groups, usually on the shaded undersides of the plant.

Only one generation per year is produced in the northern range of squash bug, but two or even three generations may be present in more southerly areas. Adults that develop late in the season do not lay eggs and leave the field for overwintering shelter.

Related Species

Horned squash bug (*Anasa armigera*) occurs in the southeastern U.S. as far west as Texas and occasionally damages plants in a manner similar to squash bug. Life histories apparently also are similar, but the two species differ markedly in appearance. Horned squash bug nymphs are white until the fifth instar, later turning variegated brown and yellow. Adults have a broad thorax with sharp angles.

Opuntia bug (*Chelinidea vittiger*)[1] develops on the pads of opuntia cacti. Overwintered adults move to opuntia in late spring and lay eggs in small masses. Nymphs feed on the plants and in high numbers may cause wilting. Two generations are produced annually. On cholla cacti the leaffootted bug *Narnia snowi*[1] is often common.

[1] Hemiptera: Coreidae

A. Squash bugs at egg hatch. *W. Cranshaw.* **B.** Squash bug egg mass. *W. Cranshaw.* **C.** Squash bug nymph. *K. Gray.*
D. Mating pair of squash bugs. *W. Cranshaw.* **E.** Squash bug nymphs. *W. Cranshaw.* **F.** Squash bugs on pumpkin fruit.
W. Cranshaw. **G.** Opuntia bugs on prickly pear. *W. Cranshaw.* **H.** Horned squash bug. *L. Tedders.* **I.** *Narnia snowi*,
leaffooted bug associated with cacti. *W. Cranshaw.*

PLANT BUGS

The plant bugs (Miridae)[1] are a large family of moderate-sized (ca. ¼ inch) insects. The great majority feed on plant sap, but a few are predators of other insects or omnivores. When feeding on plants, plant bugs use their mouthparts in a fairly destructive manner, known as lacerate-flush, which involves physically breaking many cells and flushing the feeding wound with digestive enzymes. This produces localized areas of dead cells. Feeding on developing leaves, buds, and flowers is common among plant bugs, resulting in secondary symptoms such as distortions and abortion. Plant bugs damaging to fruit and flowers are covered on p. 224.

Fourlined Plant Bug (*Poecilocapsus lineatus*)

Hosts: A wide range including shrubs such as currant and gooseberry, rose, amur maple, bluebeard, forsythia, azalea, dogwood, sumac, squash, cucumber, various flowers, and herbaceous plants,

Damage: Discrete white or dark spots originally are produced at feeding sites. These sites subsequently turn translucent and die as cells collapse, with symptoms sometimes appearing after the insects have left the plant. Injuries to new growth may cause wilting. Damage is concentrated on the upper areas of plants.

Distribution: Northeastern quadrant of the U.S. and adjacent areas of southern Canada.

Appearance: Adults are yellow, sometimes green, with four dark stripes and have an overall length of ¼ to ⅓ inch. Immature forms are bright red-orange with black dots on the thorax. The characteristic striping becomes apparent in later stages.

Life History and Habits: Winter is spent as eggs, laid in small clusters in slits of shoots. Nymphs hatch in mid- to late spring and develop over about a month. Adults usually appear in July and may be present for several weeks, mating and laying eggs. One generation is produced annually.

Garden Fleahopper (*Halticus bractatus*)

Hosts: A wide range of plants, with leaves of legumes preferred but also including garden vegetables such as pumpkin, squash, tomato, potato, beet, and pepper. This species is also found on many weeds.

Damage: Pale yellow spotting typically develops at feeding sites of garden leafhopper. Feeding can cause stunting and may kill seedlings. Dark fecal spots are produced that further detract from the appearance of infested plants.

Distribution: Eastern U.S., particularly southern areas.

A. Fourlined plant bug adult. *W. Cranshaw.* **B.** Garden fleahopper, adult female. *J. Capinera.* **C.** Watery necrotic spots at fourlined plant bug feeding sites on cucumber leaf. *W. Cranshaw.* **D.** Garden fleahopper, adult male. *J. Capinera.* **E.** Garden fleahopper leaf damage and spotting. *D. Shetlar.* **F.** Garden fleahopper nymph. *D. Shetlar.* **G.** Garden fleahopper and damage. *W. Cranshaw.*

Appearance: Adults are shiny black with yellowish legs and antennae. They are among the smallest of the plant bugs (ca. ¹⁄₁₂ inch) and have a generally rounded body form. The hind legs are greatly enlarged and allow adults to hop when disturbed, similar to flea beatles. Both short-winged and long-winged forms may be present. The nymphs are pale green and darken with age.

Life History and Habits: Garden fleahopper may winter as adults in extreme southern parts of its range but normally survives as eggs that were inserted into vegetation. Eggs hatch around April, and the nymphs develop over the course of a month. Numerous generations are produced (five reported in Virginia) which overlap considerably by midseason.

Other Leaf-Feeding Plant Bugs

Honeylocust plant bug (*Diaphnocoris chlorionis*) is a serious pest of honeylocust in much of the northern U.S. Nymphs feed on developing buds and leaves in May and June and often kill them. Older leaves may survive but show discoloration and deformation of developing foliage because of localized necrosis around feeding points. Heavy infestations may greatly retard foliage development in spring and have been associated with twig and branch dieback. One generation is produced annually, with overwintering eggs inserted into twigs in June and early July.

Ash plant bug (*Tropidosteptes amoenus*) produces whitish flecking wounds on leaves of ash (particularly green ash) in much of the U.S. and southern Canada. Emerging leaves that are damaged show distortion. Dark tarry spots of excrement are present around feeding sites on the leaf underside. Adults are light brown, about ³⁄₈ inch long, with heart-shaped markings on the plate behind the head (scutellum). The nymphs are more oval, shiny yellowish or reddish brown, and lack wings. Overwintering eggs are laid under loose bark, and nymphs usually hatch in late April and May. Most injury occurs during the period as nymphs approach maturity in late May. This generation of adults inserts eggs in the midribs of the leaves, and a second cycle of feeding occurs in July and August. Adults produced by this latter generation produce the overwintering eggs.

In eastern North America, *Tropidosteptes brooksi* may also cause spotting of ash leaves. This insect is greenish and presumably has a similar life history as ash plant bug. **Western ash plant bug** (*T. pacificus*) is the common species in the Pacific states. Adults are brown and the nymphs green with black spots. *T. illitus* is a yellow and brown or black species found in western states.

Plant bugs in the genus *Plagiognathus* cause leaf spotting, with damaged areas often dropping out. *P. punctatipes* is a common species associated with black walnut. **Sycamore plant bug** (*P. albatus*) develops on leaves of sycamore and planetree.

Yucca plant bug (*Halticotoma valida*) feeds on yucca foliage, producing white mottling marked with dark tarry spots of waste. It is found over the natural range of yucca and occurs in ornamental plantings as far north as Ohio and southern Pennsylvania. This is a small plant bug, about ³⁄₁₆ inch, with black wings and orange-red legs. Three to five generations per year can be produced in the Atlantic states.

[1] Hemiptera: Miridae

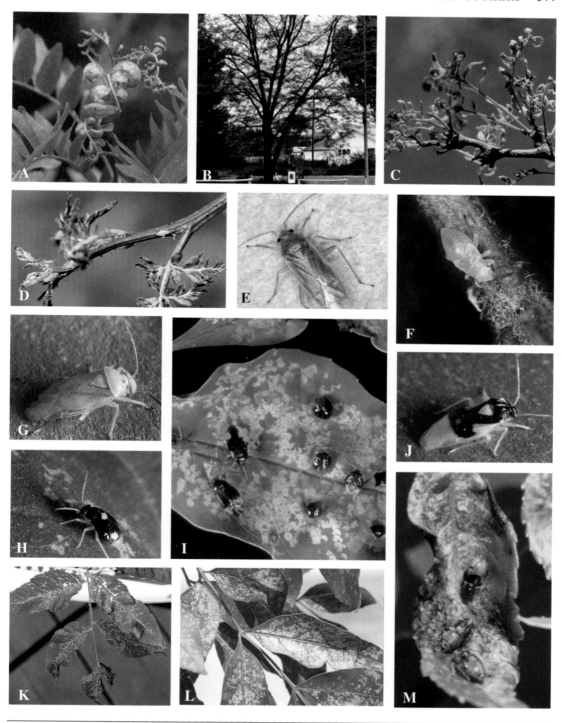

A. Honeylocust plant bug injury. *W. Cranshaw.* **B.** Thinned canopy caused by honeylocust plant bug injury. *W. Cranshaw.* **C.** Leaf injury produced by honeylocust plant bug. *W. Cranshaw.* **D.** Honeylocust plant bug nymphs on new growth. *W. Cranshaw.* **E.** Honeylocust plant bug adult. *W. Cranshaw.* **F.** Honeylocust plant bug nymph. *W. Cranshaw.* **G.** Adult western ash plant bug. *K. Gray.* **H.** Ash plant bug nymph. *K. Gray.* **I.** Adults and young nymphs of ash plant bug. *J. D. Solomon.* **J.** Ash plant bug adult. *K. Gray.* **K.** Plant bug injury to walnut. *W. Cranshaw.* **L.** Ash plant bug damage to expanded leaves. *D. Leatherman.* **M.** Ash plant bug nymphs and damage. *W. Cranshaw.*

CHINCH BUGS

Chinch bugs are members of the seed bug family (Lygaeidae)[1] that develop on grasses. Other members of this large family (ca. 290 species) feed on seeds, but few significantly damage any garden plants. One group of seed bugs, known as the big-eyed bugs (p. 554), are important predators of many insects.

Hairy Chinch Bug (*Blissus leucopterus hirtus*)

Hosts: Most turfgrass species, but perennial ryegrass and fine fescues are particularly damaged.

Damage: Chinch bug feeding apparently interferes with the ability of plants to transport water. Damage resembles that caused by drought and tends to occur in patches, with killed turfgrass appearing strawlike and failing to respond to watering. Problems are most severe following hot, dry conditions.

Distribution: Throughout the Midwest, northeastern U.S., and southeastern Canada.

Appearance: Adults are about ⅙ inch, gray-black, and covered with fine hairs. Wings are white with a dark spot in the middle. Forms of chinch bugs with short wings are common. Young nymphs have a bright orange abdomen which darkens to blue-black as they develop.

Life History and Habits: Hairy chinch bug winters in the adult stage, at the base of grass stems among the thatch. It becomes active when daytime temperatures begin to regularly reach 70° F. In southern areas, where two generations per year are produced, hairy chinch bugs usually begin laying eggs around mid-April. Egg-laying begins later but occurs over a longer period in northern areas. The eggs are laid in leaf sheaths or thatch, with peak egg laying in the New Jersey area approximately when white clover is in peak bloom. The nymphs feed for about 4 to 6 weeks and may occur in large masses in midsummer. The second generation usually peaks in late August and early September. It is rarely damaging, however, since natural enemies often are well established and cooler temperatures limit injury. The fungus *Beauveria bassiana* and the predatory big-eyed bugs (*Geocoris* spp.) are particularly important in biological control of hairy chinch bug.

Related Species

Southern chinch bug (*Blissus insularis*) is an important pest in the southeastern quadrant of the U.S. and locally important in parts of the southwest. It is very similar in appearance to hairy chinch bug, but their ranges do not overlap. Several warm-season grasses are hosts, but southern chinch bug is most damaging to St. Augustinegrass. Three or four generations are typically produced annually, with peak damage occurring with summer generations during hot, dry weather. Southern chinch bug is a highly migratory species that often walks considerable distances.

A. Hairy chinch bug damage to lawn. *D. Shetlar.* **B.** Hairy chinch bug. *D. Shetlar.* **C.** Hairy chinch bug mass in thatch. *D. Shetlar.* **D.** Short-winged and normal-winged forms of hairy chinch bug. *D. Shetlar.* **E.** Southern chinch bug damage to St. Augustinegrass. *D. Shetlar.* **F.** Southern chinch bugs. *D. Shetlar.*

Common chinch bug (*Blissus leucopterus leucopterus*) is generally distributed throughout the central U.S. It can be a serious pest of small grains, sorghum, and corn in the Midwest but rarely causes significant injury to turfgrass.

Buffalograss chinch bug (*Blissus occidus*) is a western species that has been reported damaging to buffalograss in the Central Plains. Overwintering populations consist primarily of short-winged forms. A mixture of long-winged and short-winged forms occurs during the summer. The general life history appears to be similar to that of hairy chinch bug.

False Chinch Bug (*Nysius raphanus*)

Hosts: Most garden plants can be damaged during outbreaks; crucifers and beet family plants are favored. Wild hosts include many weeds such as tansymustard, kochia, Russian thistle, and sagebrush.

Damage: False chinch bugs suck the sap from plants during feeding. The adults also commonly aggregate and occur in large numbers on individual plants, causing plants to wilt and die rapidly. Outbreaks are sporadic but can destroy plantings, particularly early in the year. Later in the season, aggregations tend to be greatest on developing seed heads. False chinch bugs are sometimes a nuisance pest of homes and buildings during hot summers when they may migrate into buildings.

Distribution: False chinch bugs are generally distributed throughout most of western North America but are particularly common in the High Plains and Intermountain regions.

Appearance: Adults are about ⅙ inch, winged, and slightly more elongate in form than *Blissus* chinch bugs. General coloration is mottled gray with the thorax and head somewhat darker. Nymphs are gray-brown and have some reddish or orange markings on the abdomen.

Life History and Habits: False chinch bugs spend the winter as nymphs or adults under protective debris near winter annual mustards which they use for hosts. They become active in early spring and move to developing mustards to feed. Adults lay eggs in loose soil or soil cracks around plants, and eggs hatch in about 4 days. Under summer conditions, the wingless, gray nymphs feed for about 3 weeks and then reach the adult stage. Adults live for several weeks, fly readily, and can disperse over wide areas. There is a strong tendency to aggregate, so large numbers may be present on individual plants. About three generations are usually produced, with peak numbers often appearing in July and early August.

Related Species

Two other *Nysius* species occasionally damage plants in western North America, *N. niger* and *N. angustatus*. Habits apparently are largely similar to those of false chinch bug.

[1] Hemiptera: Lygaeidae

A. Chinch bug mass on corn. *J. L. Hoerner.* **B.** Adult false chinch bug. *W. Cranshaw.* **C.** Mass of false chinch bugs. *W. Cranshaw.* **D.** False chinch bug nymphs. *W. Cranshaw.* **E.** Buffalograss chinch bug. *K. Gray.* **F.** Mass of false chinch bugs on flixweed seed head. *N. Demirel.* **G.** False chinch bug damage to lettuce. *W. Cranshaw.*

STINK BUGS

Stink bugs (Pentatomidae family)[1] are moderately large insects, about ½ inch long, with a characteristic, broad shield form. Most species produce a disagreeable odor when handled. Most are rather uniform green or brown, but some species do have bold patterning. Nymphs are generally similar in appearance to adults but tend to be more rounded in form and often have more distinct patterning. Stink bug eggs are laid in masses and are a unique form, barrel shaped and often with distinct spines around the top.

Stink bugs are primarily damaging to the fruiting parts of plants (p. 228). They feed with mouthparts designed to suck sap but also cause localized injury around the feeding site. This often appears as a somewhat cloudy area surrounding a central feeding puncture. Fruit may continue to grow but in a distorted manner, with indented areas developing at the feeding sites (catfacing). Young fruit may abort from stink bug damage. Seeds of legumes are sometimes killed or shrunken following pod feeding. With the notable exception of harlequin bug, these prominent insects are generally of incidental or minor importance to gardens.

Many stink bugs, such as **twospotted stink bug**, **Florida predatory stink bug**, and **spined soldier bug**, are beneficial predators of other insects (p. 550). A few others, such as **rough stink bugs**, may feed on both plants and insects.

Harlequin Bug (*Murgantia histrionica*)

Hosts: Various mustard family (Brassicaceae) plants. Cabbage and mustards grown for greens are most seriously damaged.

Damage: Harlequin bugs suck plant sap, and areas around the feeding site typically turn cloudy. When young tissues are fed on, growth develops in a distorted manner and may turn brown and die.

Distribution: Widely distributed throughout the southern U.S. Severe winters typically limit populations and subsequent damage in areas above about the 40th parallel.

Appearance: All stages of this insect are brightly patterned with red, white, and black. Adults are the typical broad form of a stink bug, about ⅜ inch in length. Nymphs have a more rounded shape with similar coloration.

Life History and Habits: Harlequin bugs usually survive winters only in the adult stage, hidden in protected sites such as under crop debris. The adults emerge from winter shelter in midspring and typically feed first on wild mustard and other weed hosts. By June or early July they may be found in gardens, feeding on cabbage, radish, or other crucifers. Females then lay egg masses which resemble rows of small black-and-white banded barrels on the leaves of these plants. The immature nymphs usually develop in the same plants where eggs were laid and feed for about 2 months before becoming full grown. If warm weather persists, three and sometimes four generations are produced annually.

[1] Hemiptera: Pentatomidae

A. Harlequin bug adult. *W. Cranshaw.* **B.** Harlequin bug adult. *W. Cranshaw.* **C.** Harlequin bug egg mass. *W. Cranshaw.* **D.** Harlequin bug nymphs and injury to cabbage leaf. *W. Cranshaw.*

LACE BUGS

The lace bugs (Tingidae family)[1] are relatively small insects (ca. ⅛ inch) with delicately sculptured wings that are held flat over the back. They feed on the underside of leaves, producing irregular white or yellow spotting that is evident on the upper leaf surface. Droplets of a varnishlike excrement also are deposited around feeding sites, assisting in diagnosis. More than 150 lace bug species occur in North America, with most damaging species found in the eastern U.S.

Members of the genus *Stephanitis* are associated with broad-leaved evergreens, and the injuries they produce are particularly conspicuous on these plants since they retain their foliage. These lace bug species winter as eggs, which are inserted into and/or cemented to leaves with a covering of crusty dark excrement. Eggs hatch in late spring, and there may be two generations.

Azalea lace bug (*S. pyrioides*) is the most damaging lace bug associated with landscape plants, producing severe injury to azalea foliage. It is particularly damaging in the southeastern and mid-Atlantic states where it is often considered a key pest of landscapes. It occurs over a broad area in the eastern U.S. where azalea is grown. **Rhododendron lace bug** (*S. rhododendri*) is common on rhododendron and mountain laurel along the East Coast. **Andromeda lace bug** (*S. takeyai*) develops on Japanese andromeda, with leucothoe, styrax, and willow as incidental hosts.

Corythuca is the largest and most diverse genus of lace bugs, and most of the 50-odd species in this genus develop on woody plants. All winter as adults under protective cover in the vicinity of previously infested plants. Eggs are laid in small groups inserted into leaf veins. Development typically takes about a month, and two generations are produced annually by most species.

Hawthorn lace bug (*C. cydoniae*) is probably the most damaging species in this group of lace bugs. It occurs throughout most of the U.S. and southern Canada and is associated with various roseaceous plants, particularly hawthorn, cotoneaster, amelanchier, quince, and pyracantha. Some differences in susceptibility to injury among different species and cultivars have been identified. Other commonly encountered lace bugs in this group include **oak lace bug** (*C. arcuata*) on various oaks; **birch lace bug** (*C. pallipes*) on birch, maple, and mountain-ash; **angulate tingid** (*C. angulata*) on ceanothus; **sycamore lace bug** (*C. ciliata*) on sycamore; **hackberry lace bug** (*C. celtidis*) on hackberry; **elm lace bug** (*C. ulmi*) on elm; **walnut lace bug** (*C. juglandis*) on walnut, butternut, and basswood; and various species on cherry and chokecherry.

A few species of lace bugs are also found on herbaceous plants. **Chrysanthemum lace bug** (*Corythuca marmorata*) occurs on goldenrod, aster, and chrysanthemum. **Distinct lace bug** (*C. distincta*) is known from bean, corn, and squash and is sometimes abundant on Canada thistle.

Eggplant lace bug (*Gargaphia solani*) is a minor pest of eggplant in parts of the central and southern U.S. This species has the unusual habit of the adult guarding the eggs and young nymphs. **Basswood lace bug** (*G. tilia*) is common on linden and basswood in the midwestern states.

Lantana lace bug (*Teleonemia scrupulosa*) is native to parts of Florida and Texas, occurring naturally southward into northern Chile. It develops on the underside of leaves of lantana and sage, producing the characteristic spotting typical of other lace bugs. Since lantana has become a noxious weed in some areas of the world where the plant was introduced, lantana lace bug has been introduced to assist in its control.

[1] Hemiptera: Tingidae

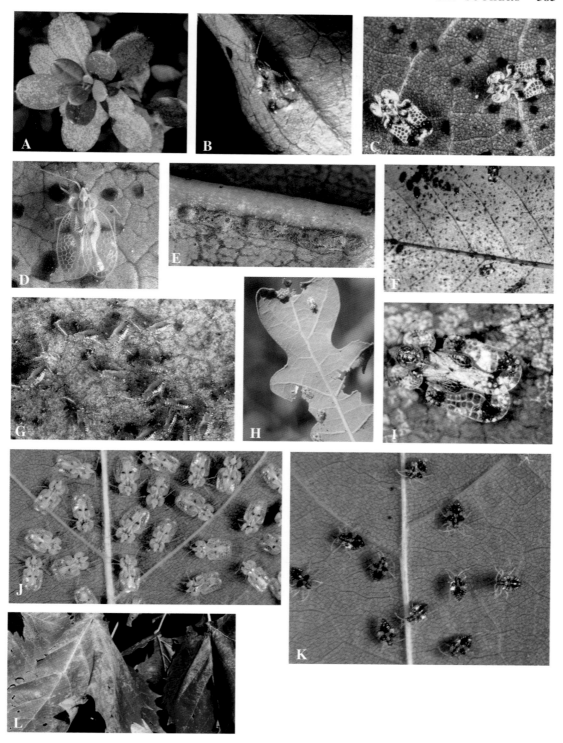

A. Leaf injury by azalea lace bug. *D. Shetlar.* **B.** Adult of azalea lace bug. *D. Shetlar.* **C.** Azalea lace bugs. *M. Ascerno.* **D.** Rhododendron lace bug adult. *K. Gray.* **E.** Eggs of rhododendron lace bug along leaf vein. *K. Gray.* **F.** Hawthorn lace bug damage to amelanchier. *D. Herms.* **G.** Rhododendron lace bug nymphs. *K. Gray.* **H.** Lace bugs on oak. *W. Cranshaw.* **I.** Adult birch lace bug. *E. B. Walker.* **J.** Sycamore lace bug adults. *J. D. Solomon.* **K.** Sycamore lace bug nymphs. *J. D. Solomon.* **L.** sycamore lace bug damage. *W. Cranshaw.*

THRIPS

Thrips are minute insects, rarely more than 1/16 inch, of elongate form. The order name, Thysanoptera, means "fringe wing," a reference to the unusual, highly fringed wings most adult thrips possess. Thrips also possess unusual mouthparts, with a single mandible that functions as a spike to puncture the leaf surface and a pair of finer stylets (maxillae) that penetrate interior cells. Thrips then suck the released fluids. Plant injuries typically appear as silvery scars marked with small varnish like fecal droppings.

The biology of thrips is unusual as well (see Figure 6). Eggs of most species are inserted into plants. Two active feeding stages (larvae) subsequently occur. These are followed by two inactive and non-feeding stages (prepupa and pupa) which usually take place in soil.

Note: The common name for insects of this order, thrips, is both singular and plural. Use of the word "thrip" in any context is incorrect. *Note:* Thrips that develop primarily in flowers, such as the flower thrips group, are discussed on p. 222. Predaceous thrips are discussed on p. 550.

Onion Thrips (*Thrips tabaci*)[1]

Hosts: An extremely wide range, with onion, cabbage, and bean among the most commonly damaged plants. Onion thrips is often the most common thrips found on leaves of vegetables and flowers.

Damage: During feeding, onion thrips puncture the leaf surface and remove cell sap. Damaged areas appear as light flecking wounds and silvery scars, often with dark fecal spots. Newly expanding leaves may curl when damaged, and some varieties of cabbage react to injuries by producing wartlike growths. Onion thrips may vector viruses in the tospovirus group, such as tomato spotted wilt virus, impatiens necrotic spot virus, and iris yellow spot virus.

Distribution: Throughout North America, common.

Appearance: Adults are usually yellowish or yellow-brown, tending to be darker with cooler weather. Larvae are creamy yellow.

Life History and Habits: Onion thrips overwinters in the adult stage throughout its range in protected sites and old plant materials. It may also be introduced into a field on infested transplants and is common on onion sets. Eggs are inserted into leaves and stems. They hatch in about 1 week, and 2 feeding wingless stages (larvae) occur on the plant, lasting about two weeks. These are followed by two nonfeeding stages (prepupa and pupa) which occur in the soil or in crevices on the plant. The winged adult stage commonly disperses throughout an area and may fly long distances aided by winds. Several generations occur annually, and all life stages may be present by early spring.

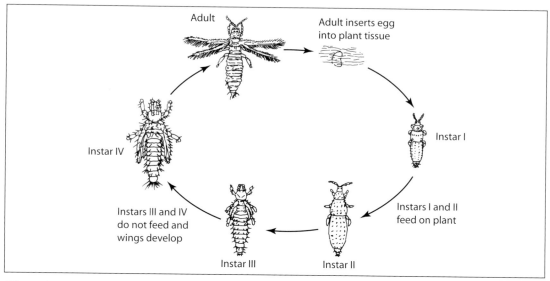

Figure 6. Typical life cycle of a thrips. *Figure by L. Mannix.*

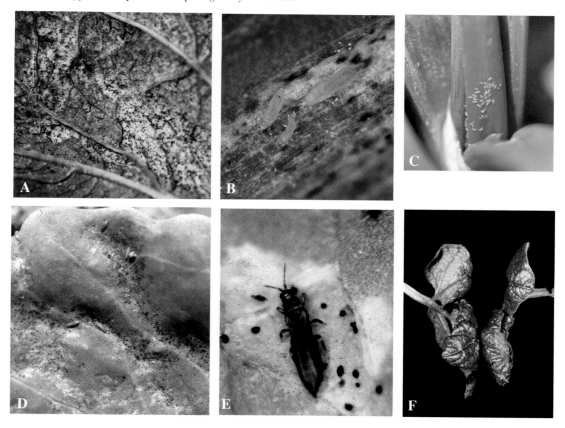

A. Leaf scarring and fecal spots of onion thrips. *W. Cranshaw.* **B.** Onion thrips nymphs. *W. Cranshaw.* **C.** Onion thrips at base of onion leaves. *W. Cranshaw.* **D.** Onion thrips and damage to cabbage. *W. Cranshaw.* **E.** Onion thrips adult. *W. Cranshaw.* **F.** Leaf curling from seedling damage of bean by onion thrips. *J. Capinera.*

Other Thrips Associated with Foliage

Gladiolus thrips (*Thrips simplex*) feeds on lily, iris, and gladiolus, although damage is restricted to the last. Feeding at the base of emerging leaves produces silvery scarring, which often later turns brown. Infestation of flowers produces serious scarring and often distortion. Heavy infestations can prevent flower production. Gladiolus thrips may also damage the corms in storage, causing them to become sticky and dark from plant sap at wounds. Infested corms produce poorly when replanted and are the primary source of new infestations, as gladiolus thrips fail to survive outdoors in most areas. Daylily is occasionally infested by **daylily thrips** (*T. hemerocallis*).

Melon thrips (*Thrips palmi*) is a tropical species that became established in southern Florida in the early 1990s. High populations develop on leaves, which become yellow or white and prematurely die. Melon, squash, tomato, pepper, and potato have been particularly damaged.

Introduced basswood thrips (*Thrips calcaratus*) is broadly distributed in the upper midwestern and northeastern U.S. It feeds on several hardwood trees, but American basswood is particularly susceptible and the only plant seriously damaged. Introduced basswood thrips has a single late-spring generation which appears on plants around bud break. A small amount of feeding at this time may cause basswood buds to die and drop. Eggs are laid in newly expanding leaves, and feeding may cause defoliation.

Pear thrips (*Taeniothrips inconsequens*)[1] is an introduced species now found throughout the northeastern quadrant of the U.S. and Pacific Coast states and provinces. It develops on several fruit trees and is of some concern to orchardists. However, it has been most damaging to sugar maple, causing leaf distortion and premature defoliation during outbreaks. Pear thrips has only one generation a year, with adults moving to trees in spring when sustained temperatures exceed 45 to 50° F. Eggs are laid in leaf veins, and larvae feed during spring, usually becoming full grown by June. They then drop, dig into the soil, and pupate.

Privet thrips (*Dendrothrips ornatus*)[1] produces foliage flecking on California and regal privet. Adults are generally brown with thin light bands on each of the abdominal segments. Multiple generations are produced beginning in late spring.

Toyon thrips (*Rhyncothrips ilex*)[1] develops on the new growth of Christmas berry, causing twisting and curling of foliage during spring. Adults are black and nymphs orangish. Only one generation is produced annually.

Iris thrips (*Iridothrips iridis*)[1] can be very damaging to Japanese iris, as feeding injuries scar leaves. Nymphs are white and thus can be distinguished from those of other thrips associated with iris.

A. Flower scarring caused by gladiolus thrips. *W. Cranshaw.* **B.** Pear thrips nymphs. *D. Shetlar.* **C.** Damage caused by basswood thrips injury. *Courtesy Minnesota Dept. Natural Resources.* **D.** Leaf scarring caused by gladiolus thrips. *W. Cranshaw.* **E.** Pear thrips damage to sugar maple. *R. S. Kelley.* **F.** Pear thrips adult. *E. B. Walker.* **G.** Pear thrips damage to maple. *D. Shetlar.* **H.** Damage by privet thrips. *D. Shetlar.*

Greenhouse thrips (*Heliothrips haemorrhoidalis*)[1] develops on the foliage of a wide variety of plants including avocado, viburnum, dogwood, azalea, grape, palms, orchids, avocado, philodendron, maple, magnolia, dahlia, ferns, and hibiscus. It is a common outdoor pest in southern California and Florida but is restricted to indoor plants in areas of temperate climate. Greenhouse thrips feed primarily on foliage, first on the lower surface and often later moving to the upper surface of shaded leaves. Damage typically appears as discolored areas between the lateral veins. Leaf distortion and dimpling of fruit also can occur. Small droplets of reddish fluid, later turning black, are excreted. Adult greenhouse thrips are fairly small (ca. ⅒₅ inch) and dark black with a silver sheen. Larvae are pale yellowish with red eyes.

Banded greenhouse thrips (*Hercinothrips femoralis*)[1] may also scar foliage of indoor-grown plants including African violet, chrysanthemum, fig, gardenia, jasmine, tomato, dieffenbachia, hoya, philodendron, rubber tree, and schefflera. Adults are generally brown with white patches on the forewing.

Grass thrips (*Anaphothrips obscurus*)[1] is common on many grasses, including turfgrasses. In the Rocky Mountain region, leaf-scarring injuries may contribute to early-season turf injury during periods of drought.

Cuban laurel thrips (*Gynaikothrips ficorum*)[2] is most commonly associated with *Ficus nitida* and *F. benjamani*, producing spotting and thickened leaf curls of new growth. Adults are jet black and lay eggs in large groups in the leaf curl. Nymphs are pale yellow.

[1] Thysanoptera: Thripidae; [2] Thysanoptera: Phlaeothripidae

A. Greenhouse thrips. *D. Caldwell.* **B.** Greenhouse thrips damage to croton. *D. Caldwell.* **C.** Cuban laurel thrips nymph and eggs. *W. Cranshaw.* **D.** Cuban laurel thrips adults and eggs. *D. Shetlar.* **E.** Damage to ficus by Cuban laurel thrips. *W. Cranshaw.* **F.** Cuban laurel thrips adult. *W. Cranshaw.* **G.** Banded greenhouse thrips. *J. R. Baker.* **H.** Banded greenhouse thrips nymphs. *J. R. Baker.* **I.** Grass thrips. *K. Gray.*

SPIDER MITES

Spider mites (Tetranychidae family) include the great majority of plant-feeding mites that cause serious injuries. Characteristic damage is caused as they feed by penetrating outer cell layers with their mouthparts (chelicerae) and sucking released plant fluids. This produces characteristic flecking or discoloration and decreases the vigor of plants.

Spider mite development typically involves five stages. The life cycle starts with eggs, which hatch to produce tiny, six-legged larvae. There follow two eight-legged immature stages (protonymph, deutonymph) and finally the adult. A resting stage, called the chrysalis, precedes each molt. Where both males and females occur, the males are somewhat smaller. Males may be only produced at some periods, and are unknown for some spider mites. Reproduction is asexual in their absence.

All spider mites are difficult to observe except with the use of a hand lens or other magnification. Many species are quite hard to distinguish, and the use of body color to separate species is unreliable.

Twospotted Spider Mite (*Tetranychus urticae*)[1]

Hosts: Rose, viburnum, euonymus, dogwood, pear, raspberry, bean, butterfly bush, marigold, impatiens, and hundreds of other plants. Twospotted spider mite has the widest host range of any spider mite in the world. It is also the most common mite pest of houseplants.

Damage: Pale flecks (stippling) may appear at feeding sites as a result of loss of cell contents. A more generalized bronzing or reddish discoloration often develops as infestations progress. Vigor of plants may be seriously reduced, and premature leaf drop often occurs on heavily infested plants. Visible webbing is produced when populations on plants are high. Many populations of twospotted spider mite show a high resistance to pesticides, often making management much more complex than for most other spider mites.

Distribution: Throughout North America. It is the most commonly damaging spider mite worldwide.

Appearance: Generally straw colored with a dark blotch along each side of the body. (*Note:* This character of having two dark spots is shared by several other mite species.) At the end of the season or at other times of colony stress, reddish orange forms develop, which indicate the mites are in a semidormant condition.

Life History and Habits: Twospotted spider mite is a warm-season species, its greatest activity occurring with warmer weather. Winter is spent as a semidormant adult female, usually under sheltering debris in the vicinity of previously infested host plants. A few may winter under bark cracks or other protected sites. Early spring feeding usually occurs on weeds and other herbaceous perennials. Much of the early-season feeding may occur at these sites before the mites move to shrubs and trees. Subsequent dispersal can also include being wind blown, as mites move to tips of foliage to be carried by air currents.

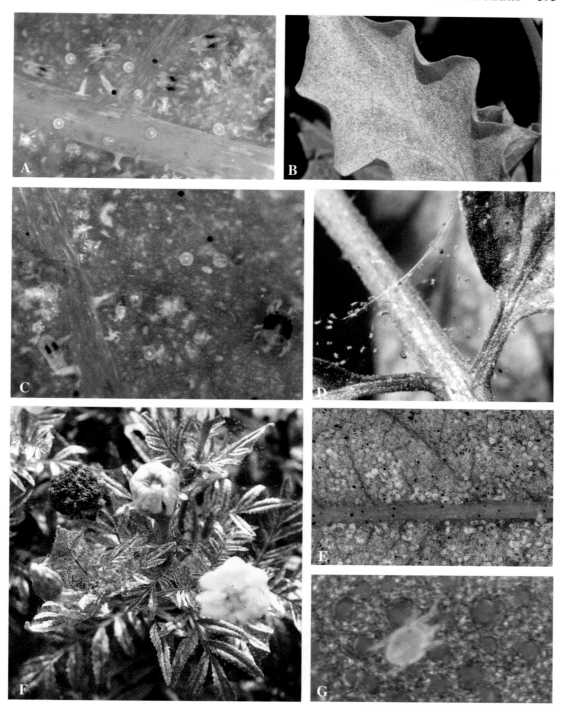

A. Twospotted spider mites and eggs. *W. Cranshaw.* **B.** Twospotted spider mite injury to eggplant. *W. Cranshaw.*
C. Twospotted spider mites, showing normal and orange diapausing coloration. *W. Cranshaw.* **D.** Twospotted spider mite and webbing. *Courtesy Clemson University.* **E.** Twospotted spider mites on heavily infested rose leaf. *W. Cranshaw.*
F. Twospotted spider mite injury and webbing of marigold. *W. Cranshaw.* **G.** Twospotted spider mite nymph. *W. Cranshaw.*

During the growing season, the life cycle of twospotted spider mite follows the pattern of life stages common to other spider mites (i.e., egg, larva, protonymph, deutonymph, adult). Under favorable conditions of warm temperature and low humidity, generations are completed in as few as 10 days. This can be greatly extended under cooler conditions. Adult females may lay five or more eggs per day over the course of 2 to 3 weeks.

Late in the growing season, twospotted spider mite populations produce males and females. Subsequently, less active nonfeeding females are produced. These females are orange-red and migrate to sheltered areas until more favorable conditions indicate the recurrence of host plants. Under protected conditions such as those found in greenhouses, however, twospotted spider mite can breed continually without the production of dormant forms.

Related Species

Carmine spider mite (*Tetranychus cinnabarinus*) is a closely related species of similar habit and appearance. It predominates over twospotted spider mite in the southern U.S. and often occurs in damaging outbreak numbers. **Fourspotted spider mite** (*T. canadensis*) is found in the eastern U.S. and Canada, feeding on shade trees such as elm, basswood, horsechestnut, and poplar. **McDaniel mite** (*T. mcdanieli*) is predominantly associated with fruit crops in the northern U.S. and southern Canada. Outbreaks are associated with prolonged hot, dry weather, and early symptoms include upward curling of the new growth.

European Red Mite (*Panonychus ulmi*)[1]

Hosts: Orchard trees are most seriously damaged, but many rosaceous plants including cherry-laurel, crabapple, hawthorn, mountain-ash, buckthorn, amelanchier, and pyracantha are also hosts.

Damage: Cells of the upper leaf surface are destroyed and cell contents removed, reducing photosynthesis. Bronzing is a typical reaction of European red mite infestation, and leaves may prematurely drop.

Distribution: Throughout most of North America but particularly abundant in the northern U.S. and southern Canada.

Appearance: Eggs are bright red and have a unique tiny stalk (stipe) arising from the center. Newly hatched larvae are orange-yellow but darken soon after feeding. Most stages are brick red, with some greenish coloration shortly after molt. The base of the hairs on the body (setae) is whitish.

Life History and Habits: Winter is spent as eggs on smaller branches and twigs, usually packed into areas of roughened bark and on the underside of branch forks. Eggs begin to hatch in late April or early May, around the time of tight cluster stage of apple. Most eggs hatch within a period of 10 days, and the larvae move to leaves, settling into leaf folds to feed. They go through a brief inactive stage, molt, and resume feeding. The adult stage is reached a few weeks after eggs hatch. Adults live for approximately 2 weeks and lay one to two dozen eggs. Up to seven generations per year are reported to occur in New York. On individual plants, numbers usually decline sharply because of reduced food quality after bronzing of leaves appears.

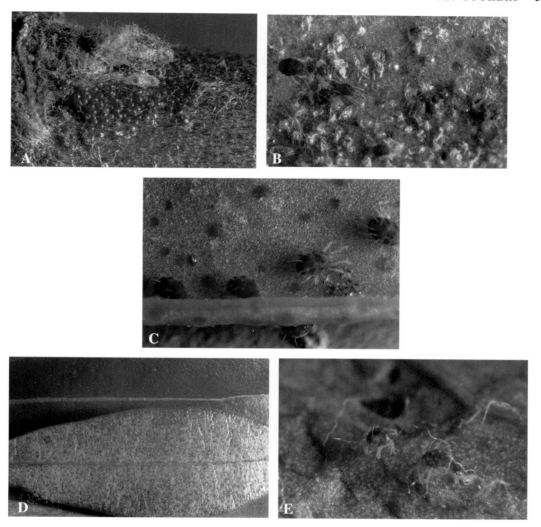

A. European red mite eggs. *K. Gray.* **B.** European red mites. *K. Gray.* **C.** European red mites. *K. Gray.* **D.** European red mite damage. *K. Gray.* **E.** European red mites. *K. Gray.*

Spruce Spider Mite (*Oligonychus ununguis*)[1]

Hosts: Most conifers, but injury is particularly common on spruce, arborvitae, hemlock, juniper, and Fraser fir grown for Christmas trees.

Damage: Sap is removed and tiny light-colored flecks are produced at feeding sites on needles. Infested trees become yellowish or grayish and may prematurely defoliate. Peak feeding injury occurs in late spring and fall, but symptoms of injury intensify during summer.

Distribution: Widespread and particularly common in the northern U.S. and Canada.

Appearance: Dark green (almost black) or dark red, depending on the season and/or host. (Newly hatched mites are light salmon to pale red.) There is only a single dark area that covers most of the abdomen which, along with the host plant, separates this species from twospotted spider mite. During heavy infestations, spruce spider mite may produce a fine netting of silk that can envelop the needles. Eggs have a small protrusion (stipe).

Life History and Habits: Spruce spider mite is a cool-season species, most active in spring and fall. It spends the winter in the egg stage, attached to the bark of branches, near the base of needles, and around buds. Eggs begin to hatch in midspring, and under optimal conditions a generation can be completed in 2 to 3 weeks. Feeding is originally concentrated on older needles of the plant interior; later, spruce spider mites move to newer growth.

Females lay about 30 to 40 eggs, tending to lay more at cooler temperatures. When temperatures consistently exceed 80° F, populations decline and many eggs go into dormancy (aestivation). As a result, populations usually peak by late spring. However, a few individual mites remain throughout summer in the cooler parts of the canopy. A resurgence of populations occurs in September and October. Six or more generations per year are reported from Pennsylvania.

Related Species

Southern red mite (*Oligonychus ilicis*) is the most important spider mite pest of broadleaf evergreens in the eastern U.S. Holly, camellia, and azalea are among the most commonly damaged ornamental hosts. This is also a cool-season species, most active in spring and fall with most individuals going dormant with high summer temperatures. Winter is spent as red eggs on the underside of foliage. The general color of nymphs and adults is dark reddish brown. No silk is produced by southern red mite.

Oak mite (*O. bicolor*) develops on oak, birch, chestnut, hickory, beech, and elm. It is a warm-season species that concentrates feeding on the upper leaf surface, producing leaf bronzing that is most severe in mid- to late summer. Oak mite is most commonly found in the Northeast and Midwest but has been found as far west as Arizona.

A. Spruce spider mite webbing. *D. Shetlar.* **B.** Spruce spider mite. *K. Gray.* **C.** Spruce spider mites. *D. Shetlar.* **D.** Spruce spider mite damage. *D. Herms.* **E.** Spruce spider mite needle injuries. *K. Gray.* **F.** Spruce spider mite damage and eggs. *E. B. Walker.* **G.** Southern red mites. *D. Shetlar.* **H.** Southern red mite damage to holly. *J. Baker.* **I.** Oak mites. *R. D. Lehman.*

Clover Mite (*Bryobia praetiosa*)[1]

Hosts: A wide variety of herbaceous plants including grasses, clover, and many weeds. Clover mites found on woody plants such as honeysuckle, ivy, elm, apple, and gooseberry are often considered subspecies or even different species.

Damage: Occasionally causes drying and death of turfgrass in spring, particularly in dry areas adjacent to buildings. However, problems are primarily due to the nuisance movement of clover mites into buildings, an extremely common occurrence during late winter and spring in much of North America.

Distribution: Throughout most of North America where cool winter conditions occur.

Appearance: Slightly larger than typical spider mite size and notable because it possesses very long front legs. Most are reddish or reddish green and the top of the abdomen is flattened. Silk is not produced by clover mites.

Life History and Habits: Clover mite is a cool-season species, most active in fall and spring. Most winter as eggs that may hatch during warm periods as early as February. They feed on plants, often producing meandering, silvery feeding tracks on the leaf surface. They may be full grown in a month or two depending on temperature. Adults migrate to nearby buildings, trees, and other upright surfaces to lay eggs. The most serious nuisance problems occur at this time as mites accidentally enter living areas.

A second generation may occur or, most commonly, eggs remain dormant through summer and hatch with the return of cool weather in early autumn. A fall generation is then produced but receives less attention. Activity ceases with very cool temperatures, with most surviving this period as eggs. A few adults may persist through winter.

Associated Turfgrass Species

Banks grass mite (*Oligonychus pratensis*)[1] limits feeding to grass and is found primarily in western North America. It can be very damaging to turfgrasses during late spring and early summer in droughty sites. Sweet corn is also occasionally damaged when mites feed on leaves and scar husks.

Brown wheat mite (*Petrobia latens*)[1] is primarily a pest of small grain crops in spring. It may occur in coinfestations with clover mite and Banks grass mite to damage turfgrasses in the western states during droughty conditions.

Another cool-season mite found on turfgrass is **winter grain mite** (*Panthaleus major*).[2] Eggs remain dormant throughout the warmer months and hatch as soil temperatures approach 50° F. This species may be active throughout the winter, feeding on grass blades during the night and clustering at the base of plants during the day. Outbreaks can kill grass in a manner that is often mistaken for winter kill. Winter grain mite is a bit larger than clover mite and brown wheat mite and possesses bright orange-red legs of uniform size.

[1] Acari: Tetranychidae; [2] Acari: Eupodidae

A. Clover mites and injury. *W. Cranshaw.* **B.** Clover mite molting. *J. Baker.* **C.** Clover mite. *K. Gray.* **D.** Clover mite, honeysuckle strain. *W. Cranshaw.* **E.** Clover mite eggs around base of twig. *W. Cranshaw.* **F.** Damage by coinfestation of clover mites and Banks grass mite. *W. Cranshaw.* **G.** Banks grass mites dispersing from grass blades. *W. Cranshaw.* **H.** Banks grass mite. *F. Peairs.* **I.** Sweet corn damaged by Banks grass mite. *W. Cranshaw.* **J.** Winter grain mites. *D. Shetlar.* **K.** Brown wheat mite. *F. Peairs.* **L.** Winter grain mite. *K. Gray.*

Other Spider Mites Associated with Landscape Plants

Scientific Name	Common Name	Host, Comments
Bryobia rubrioculus	Brown mite	Tree fruits; transcontinental
Eotetranychus carpini borealis	Yellow spider mite	Apple, pear; northwest states
Eotetranychus hicoriae	Pecan leaf scorch mite	Pecan, hickory, horsechestnut, oak; southeastern U.S.
Eotetranychus lewisi	Lewis spider mite	Citrus, poinsettia, ceanothus
Eotetranychus matthyssei	Elm spider mite	American and other elms
Eotetranychus populi		Poplar, willow
Eotetranychus querci		Pin oak
Eotetranychus tiliarium	Linden spider mite	Linden; occasionally sycamore, horsechestnut, hawthorn, willow
Eotetranychus weldoni		Poplar, willow
Eotetranychus willametti	Willamette mite	Grape, apple, pear, oak, elm, boxelder; West Coast
Eurytetranychus admes	Admes spider mite	Spruce, juniper, incense cedar
Eurytetranychus buxi	Boxwood spider mite	Boxwood; common and damaging
Oligonychus aceris	Maple spider mite	Maple; eastern North America
Oligonychus boudreauxi		Baldcypress; southern U.S.
Oligonychus milleri		Pine; southern half of U.S. to Pennsylvania
Oligonychus newcomeri		Tree fruits, related rosaceous plants
Oligonychus platani	Plantanus spider mite	Sycamore, oak; southwestern U.S.
Oligonychus subnudus	Ponderosa pine spider mite	Ponderosa pine; western U.S.
Oligonychus viridis		Hickory, pecan
Panonychus caglei	Raspberry red mite	Raspberry, blackberry, kudzu, bean, wild rose
Panonychus citri	Citrus red mite	Citrus
Platytetranychus libocedri		Arborvitae, cypress, tamarisk, juniper; southwestern and Rocky Mountain states
Platytetranychus multidigituli	Honeylocust spider mite	Honeylocust; transcontinental and commonly damaging; overwinters as orange-red female on branches and trunks
Platytetranychus thujae	Arborvitae spider mite	Juniper, cupressaceous conifers; eastern U.S.
Tetranychus humorous		Hickory, ash; southeastern U.S.
Tetranychus magnoliae		Magnolia; Gulf states
Tetranychus pacificus	Pacific spider mite	Tree fruits; Pacific Northwest
Tetranychus schoenei	Schoenei spider mite	Elm, black locust; eastern North America

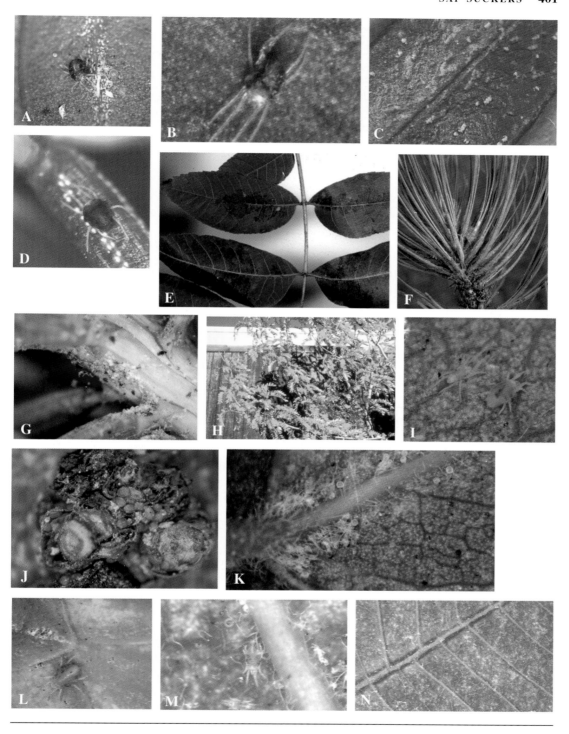

A. Boxwood spider mite and eggs. *R. D. Lehman.* **B.** Boxwood spider mite, male. *D. Shetlar.* **C.** Damage to upper leaf surface characteristic of boxwood spider mite. *R. D. Lehman.* **D.** Admes spider mite, female. *R. D. Lehman.* **E.** Pecan leaf scorch mite injury. *H. C. Ellis.* **F.** Ponderosa pine spider mite damage. *D. Leatherman.* **G.** Ponderosa pine spider mites at base of needles. *W. Cranshaw.* **H.** Yellowing of honeylocust caused by honeylocust spider mite. *W. Cranshaw.* **I.** Male and female honeylocust spider mites. *W. Cranshaw.* **J.** Overwintering females of honeylocust spider mite. *W. Cranshaw.* **K.** Honeylocust spider mite colony at base of leaflet. *W. Cranshaw.* **L.** Arborvitae spider mite. *R. D. Lehman.* **M.** Lewis spider mite. *R. D. Lehman.* **N.** Lewis spider mite damage to poinsettia. *R. D. Lehman.*

TARSONEMID MITES

The tarsonemid mites (Tarsonemidae family)[1] are extremely minute, often less than ⅟₈₀ inch. They are nearly colorless or may have a pale brown tint. Their life cycle differs in some details from that of spider mites, including the occurrence of a nonfeeding intermediate "pupal" stage that follows the larval stage. Development can be very rapid, with generation times completed in about 1 week.

Cyclamen Mite (*Phytonemus pallidus*)

Hosts: A wide range including scores of herbaceous plants. African violet, delphinium, and strawberry are among the plants most commonly reported damaged.

Damage: Stunting or twisting of new leaves and flowers are the most commonly observed symptoms. Leaves may look smaller and become more leathery than normal. Blackening and death of new growth, including flower abortion, may occur.

Distribution: Throughout North America.

Appearance: The pale yellow females are extremely small (250 microns) and require good magnification to be observed. Hind legs are reduced to threadlike structures.

Life History and Habits: Cyclamen mite can reproduce continually if temperature conditions are favorable. In areas of cold winter, it remains dormant and resumes activity in spring. Eggs are laid in small clusters in tight folds of young leaves and buds. An actively feeding larval stage may be completed in 3 to 4 days. The subsequent nonfeeding stage usually is completed in less than a week, after which adults are present. Females usually lay about 12 to 16 eggs over the course of a lifetime. Terminal growth is preferentially affected, and almost all activity occurs in protected sites of the plant such as unopened leaves of the crown, between tightly spaced young leaves, and in cuplike cavities of developing flower buds. Cyclamen mites feed on the upper leaf surface.

Related Species

Broad mite (*Polyphagotarsonemus latus*) develops on leaves of a wide variety of plants including begonia, impatiens, gerbera, ivy, dahlia, bean, schefflera, citrus, and pittosporum. It is restricted to greenhouses in temperate areas but occurs outdoors in warmer areas of the southern U.S. Broad mite is very similar in appearance to cyclamen mite and cannot be separated from it without high magnification. Unlike cyclamen mite, broad mite is almost always restricted to the underside of leaves and typically produces a bronzing. Infestations of some plants may produce sudden stunting, twisting, and crinkling of young leaves, often followed by the appearance of blisters or sudden dieback. This damage resembles herbicide injury and is often mistaken for it. Flower abortion may also occur. On citrus, broad mite can cause russeting of the fruit surface. The life cycle of broad mite can be completed in less than a week during favorable summer conditions. Males are smaller and faster than females.

[1] Acari: Tarsonemidae

A. Cyclamen mite damage. *D. Shetlar.* **B.** Cyclamen mite with eggs. *J. K. Clark/UC Statewide IPM Program.*
C. Cyclamen mite damage to African violet. *J. Baker.* **D.** Broad mite injury to begonia. *J. Baker.*

FALSE SPIDER MITES

False spider mites (Tenuipalpidae family)[1] have a flattened and somewhat elongate body. Most are orange to red and have short, stubby legs. Several species occur on plants, with those found on orchids and some trees and shrubs the most common. None produce silk.

Pentamerismus erythreus is found throughout North America and occurs on most conifers except pine. *P. taxi* is an eastern species found primarily on taxus. Both species can produce stippling and discoloration of foliage similar to that of spider mites, but injuries are considerably slower to develop.

Privet mite (*Brevipalpus obovatus*) is found on several woody plants but are most common on privet in the southeastern states. They cause bronzing or reddening of foliage and premature leaf drop. Privet foliage tends to turn yellowish bronze late in the summer as infestations are active from June through December. *B. oncidii*, *B. phoenicis*, *Tenuipalpus pacificus*, and *T. oarchidarum* are among those species associated with orchids.

[1] Acari: Tenuipalpidae

RUST MITES

These microscopic mites in the family Eriophyidae (or superfamily Eriophyoidea) most commonly attract attention when they have the habit of producing galls and other growths on plants (p. 430). However, the majority of species live on the surface of plants as "leaf vagrants." Some cause visible leaf injury, typically a "rust" or bronzing discoloration often associated with premature defoliation. Leaves may also be leathery textured. A few, notably pear rust mite and citrus rust mite, also develop on fruit and may discolor (russet) the skin surface.

Some eriophyid mites are involved in transmitting plant viruses. Wheat streak mosaic and rose rosette are two diseases that involve eriophyid mites as the vectors of the pathogen. It is thought that eriophyid mites may transmit several more diseases than are currently known, but the small size of the mites has made it difficult to research this.

Apple Rust Mite (*Aculus schlechtendali*)

Hosts: Apple, crabapple, and other *Malus*. Rarely pear.

Damage: Feeding involves removal of sap from surface cells of leaves, which can disrupt photosynthesis. Sustained high populations produce leaf-bronzing symptoms. Feeding on developing fruit may cause russeting of the skin. Normal populations are usually well tolerated by plants and can be beneficial by providing food for generalist predators of other pests found on the plants.

Distribution: Throughout North America in association with its hosts.

Appearance: Minute (less than 180 microns) and requires good magnification to observe. This mite is elongate, rather carrot shaped, and yellowish brown.

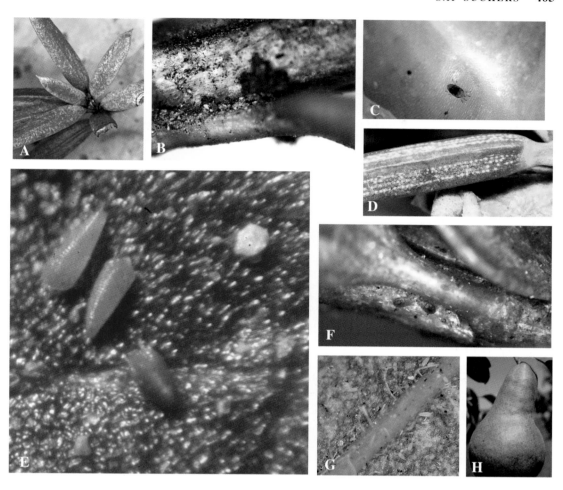

A. Damage by false spider mite *Pentamerismus taxi*. *R. D. Lehman.* **B.** *Pentamerismus taxi* adults and eggs. *R. D. Lehman.* **C.** Privet mite *Brevipalpus phoenicis*. *R. D. Lehman.* **D.** Rust mite eggs on spruce. *R. D. Lehman.* **E.** Rust mites. *E. Nelson.* **F.** False spider mite *Pentamarisus taxi*. *R. D. Lehman.* **G.** Honeylocust rust mites. *W. Cranshaw.* **H.** Fruit russeting by pear rust mite. *E. Nelson.*

Life History and Habits: Winter is spent as a special adult female form (deutogyne) in cracks and crevices of twigs and buds. These females resume activity with bud break, feed on emerging leaves, and lay eggs on the surface. There are two immature stages that feed and resemble miniature adults. Both males and summer-form females (protogynes) are produced at this time. During the growing season the entire life cycle can be completed in less than 2 weeks, and numerous generations are produced annually. In most areas populations peak in midsummer and decline as increasing numbers go into the dormant overwintering stage. In dry areas of very warm summer temperatures, peak numbers of apple rust mite occur in early summer and fall.

Some Rust Mites That Produce Bronzing Injuries to Foliage and Buds

Scientific Name	Common name	Host
Acalitus vaccinii	Blueberry bud mite	Highbush blueberry
Aculops gleditsiae	Honeylocust rust mite	Honeylocust
Aculops lycopersici	Tomato russet mite	Tomato
Aculops massalongoi	Lilac rust mite	Lilac
Aculus fockeui	Plum rust mite/peach silver mite	Cherry, plum, peach
Aculus ligustri	Privet rust mite	Privet
Aculus schlechtendali	Apple rust mite	Apple, crabapple, pear
Cosectacus camelliae	Camellia bud mite	Camellia
Epitrimerus pyri	Pear rust mite	Pear
Epitrimerus taxodii	Baldcypress rust mite	Baldcypress
Nalepella halourga	Spruce rust mite	Spruce
Nalepella octonema	Fir rust mite	Fraser fir
Nalepella tsugifoliae	Hemlock rust mite	Hemlock
Paraphytoptus chrysanthemi	Chrysanthemum rust mite	Chrysanthemum
Phyllocoptruta oleivora	Citrus rust mite	Citrus
Setoptus strobacus	White pine sheath mite	Eastern white pine

A. Rust mite injury to lilac. *W. Cranshaw.* **B.** Injury by honeylocust rust mite. *W. Cranshaw.* **C.** Blueberry bud mite damage. *J. A. Payne.* **D.** Injury by baldcypress rust mite. *D. Shetlar.*

Gall Makers

APHID GALLS

Although many species of "woolly" aphids[1] develop on stems, roots, and leaves (p. 310), a few induce distinctive growth changes in plants substantial enough to be categorized as galls. Most of these "woolly" aphids have complex life cycles that involve a primary winter host on which they produce galls and an alternate summer host. Most develop on the roots of the alternate host.

Petiolegall aphids (*Pemphigus* spp.) make a variety of galls on the stems, petioles, and leaves of cottonwood and poplar (*Populus*). **Poplar petiolegall aphid** (*P. populitransversus*) forms a spherical green gall with a transverse slit on the petiole of plains cottonwood; it is also a root aphid on cabbage family crops. *P. populicaulis* develops on eastern cottonwood, creating a gall that incorporates the lower edge of the leaf as well as the petiole. In summer it develops on the roots of various cabbage and aster family plants. *P. betae* develops on narrowleaf cottonwood or balsam poplar. **Sugarbeet root aphid** (*P. populivenae*) forms an elongated gall on the midvein of narrow-leaved cottonwood leaves. Alternately, the summer forms feed on the roots of beet and related garden plants, and they are sometimes serious pests of sugarbeet. **Lettuce root aphid** (*P. bursarius*) is an occasional pest of lettuce crops and also is known from lambsquarter and carrot. It produces a flasklike gall on the petioles of Lombardy poplar. **Poplar twiggall aphid** (*P. populiramulorum*) is another species in this gall-producing genus.

An enlarged, thickened, and twisted clump at the base of a developing leaf is typical of the distortion produced by **poplar vagabond aphid** (*Mordwilkoja vagabunda*) on aspen and certain cottonwoods. Galls tend to remain on trees and may not be visible until after normal leaf fall. Galling is concentrated on the upper third of the tree. Loosestrife is the alternate host for poplar vagabond aphid, which may winter as eggs either on buds of the cottonwood/aspen or on roots of loosestrife.

In the Pacific states, a common insect on manzanita is **manzanita leaf gall aphid** (*Tamalia coweni*), which produces thickened leaf curls that discolor. **Elm cockscomb gall aphid** (*Colopha ulmicola*) creates elongate, wrinkled swellings on the upper surface of leaves of American and red elms. The galls are reddish when newly formed but turn brown later in the season. By early summer the aphids leave the galls through a slit that develops on the underside and fly to the roots of grasses, their summer hosts. Late in the season different winged forms return to elm where they lay overwintering eggs around buds. *C. graminis* makes similar galls of elm leaves and also uses grasses as the alternate host.

Two interesting gall-making aphids are associated with witch-hazel. **Witch-hazel leaf gall aphid** (*Hormaphis hamamelidis*) makes curious conical galls on the upper leaf surface. Birch is the alternate host for this insect. **Spiny witch-hazel gall aphid** (*Hamamelistes spinosus*) makes a spiny oblong gall from the buds of witch-hazel in spring. The life cycle of this insect can be very complex. Winged forms ultimately emerge from a slit at the base and subsequently develop on leaves of the alternate host, birch. It may be an important leafcurler of birch.

[1] Homoptera: Aphididae

A. Winged petiolegall aphids emerging from gall. *K. Gray.* **B.** Flask-type gall of lettuce root aphid. *W. Cranshaw.*
C. *Pemphigus* gall on leaf midrib. *K. Gray.* **D.** Petiole gall. *D. Leatherman.* **E.** *Pemphigus* gall at base of petiole,
opened to expose aphids. *W. Cranshaw.* **F.** Stem galls on poplar produced by *Pemphigus* sp. *W. Cranshaw.* **G.** Leaf
galls produced by poplar petiogall aphid. *H. A. Pase III.* **H.** Gall produced by poplar vagabond aphid. *J. W. Brewer.*
I. Gall produced by poplar vagabond aphid. *W. Cranshaw.* **J.** Galls produced by manzanita leafgall aphids. *K. Gray.*
K. Elm cockscomb gall. *W. Cranshaw.* **L.** Witch-hazel leaf galls. *W. Cranshaw.* **M.** Spiny witch-hazel galls. *J. R. Baker.*

ADELGID GALLS

The adelgids (Adelgidae)[1] are the "woolly" aphids associated with pine, spruce, and other conifers (p. 314). Those that produce galls on plants have complex life cycles that usually involve alternate hosts. Galls are not produced on the alternate (summer) host.

Cooley Spruce Gall Adelgid (*Adelges cooleyi*)[1]

Hosts: Spruce, Douglas-fir.

Damage: On spruce, distinctive cucumber-shaped galls develop on the tips of new growth, which usually kill the terminal. On Douglas-fir, Cooley spruce gall adelgids are conspicuous "woolly" aphids that suck sap from needles. When infestations occur on developing needles, symptoms may include yellowing and twisting of needles.

Distribution: Throughout the northern U.S. and southern Canada where spruce and Douglas-fir co-occur. Cooley spruce gall adelgid is native to North America.

Appearance: Exposed stages are typical "woolly" aphids, covered completely with long white waxy thread. Stages found inside galls on spruce are greenish gray aphids covered with a fine powder of wax. Winged forms that migrate between host plants are dark green, almost black.

Life History and Habits: Cooley spruce gall adelgid has a life cycle involving several different forms that alternate between spruce and Douglas-fir. On spruce, winter is spent as a partially grown female on the underside of twigs. Females grow rapidly in spring, producing a large mass of several hundred eggs which hatch in synchrony with bud break. The newly hatched nymphs migrate to the base of newly expanding needles. Their feeding induces enlarged cavities to form, in which they develop. During late June and early July the nearly full-grown adelgids emerge through cracks in the drying galls, molt on the needles to winged adults, and migrate to Douglas-fir.

On Douglas-fir, the nymphs overwinter as partially developed nymphs on the needles. They continue to develop in spring, producing a large egg mass around early May. At egg hatch the nymphs move to tips of twigs to feed primarily on the current-season needles. They become full grown in July and produce a generation of adults that are a mixture of winged and wingless forms. The wingless forms remain on Douglas-fir and have a second generation. The winged forms fly to spruce and start the cycle on this host.

Related Insects

Eastern spruce gall adelgid (*Adelges abietis*) produces a pineapple-shaped gall on Norway spruce. A European species, it is widespread in eastern Canada and the northeastern U.S. Galls are not as large as those produced by Cooley spruce gall adelgid, and affected terminals often are not killed. All stages occur on Norway spruce, with winter spent as a partially grown female located near buds.

Some other species of *Adelges* cause galls on spruce. Other galls on spruce may be produced by adelgids in the genus *Pineus*. **Pine leaf adelgid** (*Pineus pinifoliae*) also makes galls in the terminal growth of spruce that resemble those of Cooley spruce gall adelgid but are of looser form. Galls remain green late in the season and are less conspicuous. Spruce is the primary (overwintering) host of this aphid, which infests pine during alternate stages of its life cycle.

[1] Homoptera: Adelgidae

A. Cooley spruce galls. *W. Cranshaw.* **B.** Winged adult Cooley spruce gall adelgids recently emerged from gall. *W. Cranshaw.* **C.** Cooley spruce gall adelgid on Douglas-fir. *W. Cranshaw.* **D.** Needle bending on Douglas-fir caused by infestation of Cooley spruce gall adelgid. *W. Cranshaw.* **E.** Cooley spruce gall adelgid with egg mass prior to bud break. *W. Cranshaw.* **F.** Eastern spruce gall. *W. Cranshaw.* **G.** Cooley spruce gall adelgid on spruce in early spring. *W. Cranshaw.* **H.** Cooley spruce gall adelgids inside gall. *W. Cranshaw.* **I.** Cooley spruce gall adelgid, swollen with eggs prior to bud break, on spruce. *W. Cranshaw.* **J.** Spruce galls produced by pine leaf adelgid. *W. Cranshaw.* **K.** Eastern spruce gall adelgid with eggs. *D. Herms.*

PHYLLOXERAN GALLS

The phylloxerans (Phylloxeridae family)[1] are closely related to the adelgids. Most produce galls on various deciduous trees and shrubs and have complex life cycles involving different forms.

Grape Phylloxera (*Daktulosphaira vitifoliae*)

Hosts: European grape vine (*Vitis vinifera*) and French-American hybrids.

Damage: In eastern North America the most common injuries are small, rounded leaf galls which can reduce photosynthesis and cause premature leaf drop. Greatest damage occurs when colonies develop on older roots. Dead areas develop around feeding sites, and knobby galls can develop on roots, which may girdle and kill the roots. Injury is most common on sandy soils.

Distribution: Eastern North America; locally important in California. Most abundant on sandy soils.

Appearance: Generally oval or pear shaped and about ⅟₂₅ inch when full grown. Coloration varies from yellow to olive green to brown or orange.

Life History and Habits: In the eastern U.S. the life cycle can be quite complex, with both leaves and roots colonized. Winter is spent either as eggs under the bark of canes or as young nymphs on the roots. Overwintered eggs hatch about the time of bud break, and the overwintered nymphs that are present feed on the tips. Tissues swell about the grape phylloxera and form a rounded gall on the underside of the leaf. After maturing, hundreds of eggs may be produced. The newly hatched crawlers disperse from the gall to tips and initiate new galls. Several generations may be produced in this manner. Some of the crawlers also colonize roots during the summer.

Roots are colonized by the insects working their way along soil cracks. Once they settle on roots, they may produce dense colonies that are a mixture of eggs, nymphs, and adults. Three to five generations may occur on the roots. At the end of the season, some work their way to the surface and produce winged forms and special sexual forms. The latter produce the overwintering eggs that are laid in crevices of the canes. In California, only root-infesting forms survive winter, as young nymphs.

Other Phylloxeran Gall Producers

At least 29 species of *Phylloxera* cause galls on pecan and hickory (*Carya* spp.). **Hickory leafstem gall phylloxera** (*P. caryaecaulis*) produces rounded galls early in the season on shoots and petioles of hickory. Overwintering eggs laid near buds hatch around mid- to late April to produce a "stem mother" that feeds on the swelling bud. This causes the rounded gall to form, and eggs are laid by the stem mother in the gall. After egg hatch, the crawlers move to the leaf underside to feed and develop. A sexual generation follows that results in production of the overwintering eggs. **Pecan leaf phylloxera** (*P. notabilis*) and **southern pecan leaf phylloxera** (*P. russellae*) are among those that commonly produce galls on pecan leaves in the southeastern states. **Pecan phylloxera** (*P. devastatrix*) is the most damaging species to pecan, producing galls on leaves, woody shoots, and spurs. Damage is done by the first-generation stem mother, which emerges from eggs and feeds on the expanding buds in spring.

[1] Homoptera: Phylloxeridae

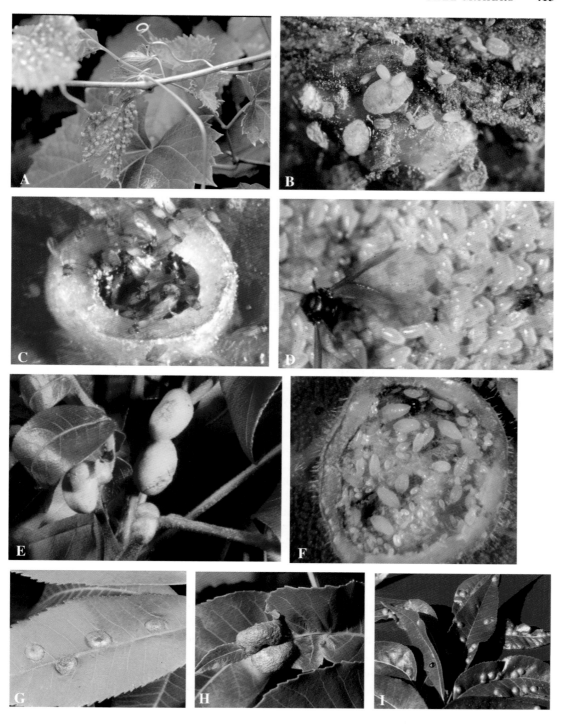

A. Grape phylloxera leaf galls. *R. Bessin.* **B.** Grape phylloxera colony associated with grape roots. *J. K. Clark/UC Statewide IPM Program.* **C.** Pecan leaf phylloxera gall. *D. Shetlar.* **D.** Pecan leaf phylloxera with eggs. *D. Shetlar.* **E.** Galls of pecan leaf phylloxera. *D. Shetlar.* **F.** Pecan leaf phylloxera in gall. *L. Tedders.* **G.** Pecan leaf phylloxera galls. *L. Tedders.* **H.** Pecan leaf phylloxera gall. *L. Tedders.* **I.** Pecan leaf phylloxera galls. *H. C. Ellis.*

PSYLLID GALLS

Psyllids (Psyllidae family),[1] also known as jumping plant lice, can produce a variety of effects on plants. Those species that remove excessive amounts of sap, cause simple leaf curling, or produce systemic effects on plant growth are discussed on p. 290. Many psyllids, however, induce highly distorted growth that is categorized as a gall.

Hackberry Nipplegall Maker (*Pachypsylla celtidismamma*)

Hosts: American and net-leaf hackberry.

Damage: Hackberry nipplegall maker produces prominent warty leaf galls, sometimes nearly covering the leaf. High levels of galling are usually restricted to only a few branches and do not produce much damage. This species is reported to be an important food for several insectivorous birds and for fox squirrels.

Distribution: Throughout North America in association with its host but more common east of the Rockies.

Appearance: Adults are a mottled light brown with wings held rooflike over the back. They jump and fly readily when disturbed. Immature stages are pale yellow, of generally rounded form, and are found in the gall.

Life History and Habits: Hackberry nipplegall makers overwinter as adults in protected areas. In spring, as the hackberry buds are expanding, the adults emerge and deposit eggs on the undersurfaces of the leaves. Eggs hatch, and young nymphs begin to feed on the leaf. An overgrowth that appears as a raised swelling on the lower leaf surface is induced by this feeding, ultimately producing the gall that covers the insect. The nymphs develop singly within the gall all summer, and adults emerge in late summer. There is one generation per year.

There can be a great difference in the number of galls produced on different leaves within the tree or between nearby trees. This is largely due to how synchronized the leaf development is when the adult psyllids are laying eggs and when eggs are hatching, since leaves are suitable hosts for only a brief period during their early development.

Related Species

At least six *Pachypsylla* species produce galls on hackberry and sugarberry (*Celtis* spp.). **Hackberry blistergall psyllid** (*P. celtidivescula*) is often the most abundant psyllid associated with hackberry. Galls are small, raised leaf swellings, much less conspicuous than the nipple galls. The life cycle of this species is similar to that of hackberry nipplegall maker. Blistergall psyllids are small enough to pass through most screens and sometimes enter nearby homes during fall and can be a nuisance. A similar gall, but with starlike projections on the leaf underside, is produced by **hackberry stargall psyllid** (*P. celtidisastericus*). **Hackberry petiolegall psyllid** (*P. venusta*) makes galls in the petioles of leaves, particularly in net-leaf hackberry. **Hackberry budgall psyllid** (*P. celtidisgemma*) produces an enlarged, spherical swelling of the bud tissues, killing the affected bud. Winter is spent in the gall. *P. celtidisinteneris* develops in small, inconspicuous twig swellings.

A. Hackberry nipplegalls. *W. Cranshaw.* **B.** Hackberry nipplegall maker adult. *W. Cranshaw.* **C.** Eggs of hackberry nipplegall maker on expanding leaf. *W. Cranshaw.* **D.** Hackberry leaf showing both nipplegalls and blistergalls. *W. Cranshaw.* **E.** Nymphs of hackberry nipplegall maker (left) and hackberry blistergall psyllid (right) exposed from galls. *W. Cranshaw.* **F.** Newly hatched hackberry blistergall psyllids settling around developing nipplegall. *W. Cranshaw.* **G.** Hackberry budgalls. *W. Cranshaw.* **H.** Nymph of hackberry budgall psyllid exposed in gall. *W. Cranshaw.* **I.** Hackberry blistergalls. *D. Leatherman.* **J.** Galls produced by hackberry petiolegall psyllid. *D. Leatherman.*

CHAPTER 7

Other Psyllids

Sumac is commonly host to various psyllids in the genus *Calophya*. None are considered significant pests. Since the 1990s, however, the related **peppertree psyllid** (*C. rubra*) has become established in southern California and is a significant pest of California pepper tree. Feeding by the orangish nymphs on succulent foliage results in the formation of prominent pitting. Natural enemies have been established that have helped reduce the incidence of damage by this insect.

Eugenia psyllid (*Trioza eugeniae*) induces small pits, which surround the scalelike nymphs, to form on new growth. Reproduction can occur throughout the year, with peak activity during periods of new plant growth. Other *Trioza* species cause leaf-curling distortions. **Red bay psyllid** (*T. magnoliae*) is common in southeastern states, producing thickened leaf curls and galls on various species of *Persea*, particularly redbay (*P. borbonia*). **Laurel psyllid** (*T. alacris*) induces thickened curling of leaf margins on Grecian laurel and produces nuisance amounts of honeydew. It is currently found in parts of California and New Jersey. Adults in the genus *Trioza* are generally similar in appearance to the potato/tomato psyllid (p. 290), with a generally dark color and banding. All are species of accidental introduction to North America.

Yaupon psyllid (*Gyropsylla ilicis*) is a common species in the southern U.S. where it produces thickened leaf curls on yaupon (*Ilex vomitoria*). Willow hosts numerous psyllids of the genus *Psylla*, some of which produce small raised swellings on foliage.

[1] Homoptera: Psyllidae

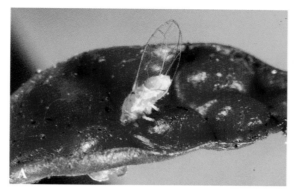

A. Adult eugenia psyllid. *D. Caldwell.* **B.** Galls produced by eugenia psyllid. *W. Cranshaw.* **C.** Red bay psyllid injury. *J. Baker.*

GALL-MAKING FLIES

Distortions of plant growth can be produced by numerous species of flies, the great majority of which are in the family Cecidomyiidae, the gall flies. Adults are inconspicuous midgelike flies, and the maggot-form larvae are found in the galls. Although some gall flies, such as rose midge (p. 240), cause modest leaf curls or dieback, most produce galls. These typically are in the form of abnormal swellings, thickenings, and/or stunting of foliage. Gall-making also occurs among a few flies in the families Agromyzidae (leafminer flies) and Tephritidae (fruit flies).

Honeylocust Podgall Midge (*Dasineura gleditschiae*)

Hosts: Honeylocust.

Damage: Larvae feed on developing leaves, causing the production of thickened podlike galls. The galls darken, dry, and drop a few weeks after adults emerge. This defoliation gives a thin appearance to the plant, particularly when most of the leaflets on a leaf are affected.

Distribution: Throughout North America in association with its host, honeylocust.

Appearance: Adults are delicate, tiny midges, generally black with a reddish abdomen. Larvae are cream-colored maggots found in the pod galls.

Life History and Habits: Honeylocust podgall midge spends the winter in the adult stage under protective cover around previously infested honeylocust plantings. The adults move to emerging honeylocust buds as they first start to break. Eggs are laid among the emerging leaves, and the larvae feed on the leaflets, causing them to curl and thicken into the characteristic pod gall. Larvae become full grown in about 3 to 4 weeks, and pupation occurs in the gall. As the adults emerge, the old pupal skin is often pulled partially out at the gall opening.

There are typically three generations per year, with populations usually declining by early July. Later infestations may extend for additional generations where sprout growth continues to be produced or in highly fertile, irrigated sites such as nurseries.

Other Gall-Making Flies

Dasineura pseudacaciae[1] induces young leaves of black locust to thicken and fold. Pouches develop in the main veins of red and sugar maples from developing larvae of **maple gouty veingall midge** (*D. communis*) in parts of the Midwest. **Pear leafcurling midge** (*D. pyri*) causes the new growth of pear to curl tightly and produce a reddish pod gall.

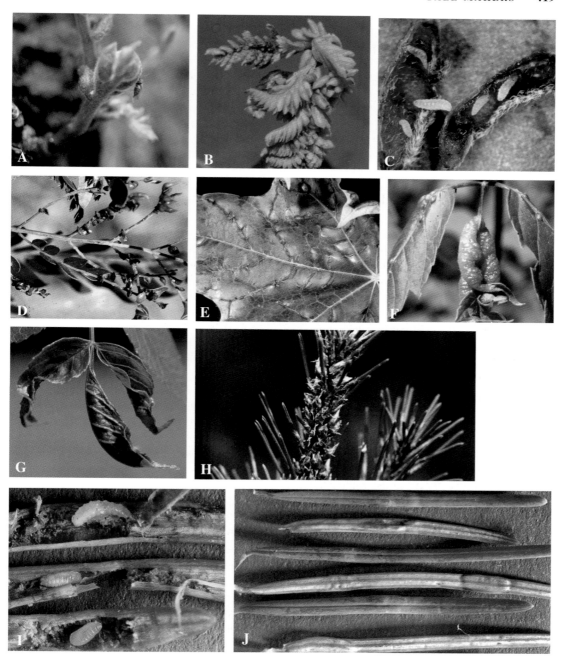

A. Honeylocust podgall midge adult. *W. Cranshaw.* **B.** Honeylocust podgalls. *W. Cranshaw.* **C.** Honeylocust podgall midge larvae exposed from gall. *W. Cranshaw.* **D.** Honeylocust podgalls, following adult emergence. *W. Cranshaw.* **E.** Gouty veingall on sugar maple. *E. B. Walker.* **F.** Gouty veingall of boxelder. *W. Cranshaw.* **G.** Ash midrib gall. *W. Cranshaw.* **H.** Stubby needlegalls. *W. Cranshaw.* **I.** Larvae of Douglas-fir needle midge. *K. Gray.* **J.** Needle swelling produced by Douglas-fir needle midge. *K. Gray.*

The genus *Continaria*[1] includes several species that produce thickened leaf foldings. **Gouty veingall midge** (*C. negundinis*) makes a prominent thickening along the midrib of boxelder maple, in which numerous pale larvae may be found. **Ash midrib gall midge** (*C. canadensis*) can produce a thickening along the midrib of ash leaves in late spring. **Linden wart gall** of basswood is produced by *C. verrucicola*. Leaves and developing seed pods of catalpa may be distorted by **catalpa midge** (*C. catalpae*). In the Rocky Mountain states, **stubby needlegall midge** (*C. coloradensis*) produces basal swellings and stunting of ponderosa pine needles. In the Pacific Northwest and Pennsylvania the **Douglas-fir needle midge** (*C. pseudotsugae*) is an important pest of Christmas tree plantings. Adults lay eggs in the newly expanding buds in spring, and the larvae develop in the base of needles. Infested needles yellow and then brown and drop prematurely. Winter is spent in the soil as a full-grown larva, which pupates the following March and April. One generation is produced annually.

Terminal growth of many native willows may be distorted by several flies in the genus *Rhabdophaga*.[1] **Willow conegall midge** (*R. strobiloides*) induces a conelike growth on the tips. A similar gall, more sharply drawn out, is produced by **willow beakedgall midge** (*R. rigidae*). Terminal distortions on red cedar and other junipers are commonly produced by **juniper tip midge** (*Oligotrophus betheli*)[1] in many midwestern and western states. Twisting and distortion of new growth on chrysanthemum may be due to injury by chrysanthemum gall midge (*Rhopalomyia chrysanthemi*).[1] Larvae feeding on buds may result in formation of cone-shaped galls.

Distortion and discoloration of rhododendron foliage can result from damage by **rhododendron gall midge** (*Clinodiplosis rhododendri*). Adults emerge from overwintering pupae and lay eggs on the young leaves emerging from the bud. Multiple generations are produced coinciding with the spring flush of growth, and peak damage typically is caused by the second and third generations. Pupation occurs in the soil.

A common gall of pinyon grown in ornamental plantings is **pinyon spindlegall midge** (*Pinyonia edulicola*).[1] It produces a basal swelling of new needles, in which as many as a dozen or more pale orange larvae develop. Needles turn brown and drop the following year. Basal swelling combined with needle stunting is produced by **pinyon stunt needlegall midge** (*Janetiella* sp.).

Grape tumid gallmaker (*Janetiella brevicauda*)[1] develops on wild and cultivated grapes in the northeastern U.S. and southeastern Canada. Round, succulent galls are produced on leaves, petioles, and flower clusters. Three generations are produced, with most injury caused by the first, which occurs as flower buds are present.

Ocellate gall midge (*Cecidomyia ocellaris*)[1] produces distinctive "eyespot" galls on red maple leaves. The galls are yellow margined with red and form on the upper surface of the leaf. *C. poculum* produces a cluster of pale or red saucerlike galls attached to a slender stalk on the underside of oak leaves. *C. pellex* produces reddish brown bullet-shaped galls on ash. Eyespotting of tuliptree leaves is produced by **eyespot gall midge** (*Thecodiplosis liriodendri*).[1]

A. Willow conegall. *W. Cranshaw.* **B.** Pinyon spindlegalls. *W. Cranshaw.* **C.** Larvae of pinyon spindlegall midge exposed in needle gall. *W. Cranshaw.* **D.** Willow beakedgalls. *D. Leatherman.* **E.** Maple eyespot galls. *D. Shetlar.* **F.** Pinyon stunt needlegalls. *W. Cranshaw.* **G.** Tuliptree eyespot galls. *L. Risley.* **H.** Grape tumid gallmaker. *J. Ogrodnik/NY Agricultural Experiment Station.* **I.** Pinyon spindlegall midge adults at emergence from needle. *W. Cranshaw.* **J.** Grape tumid gallmaker. *J. Ogrodnik/NY Agricultural Experiment Station.* **K.** Rhododendron gall midge injury. *D. Gilrein.*

Dogwood clubgall midge (*Resseliella clavula*)[1] is common in many midwestern and eastern states. It produces tubular or club-shaped swellings at the tip or along the stem. Twigs usually die back beyond these injuries. Females lay eggs on the emerging leaves at bud break, and wilted, deformed leaves are the first indication that buds are infested. One generation is produced annually, and the insect winters in the soil.

Poplar twiggall fly (*Hexomyza schineri*)[2] commonly produces smooth swellings on the new twigs of aspen and some poplars. These galls do not normally cause noticeable effects on tree growth, but the damaged areas continue to grow long after the insects are absent, ultimately producing knobby swellings on branches and trunks. This insect has become common in the Rocky Mountain region, and reports of damage in the Midwest suggest an expanding range.

Poplar twiggall fly overwinters in the gall as a full-grown, yellow-green maggot. Pupation occurs in late winter or early spring, in the gall. The majority of the pupae then drop to the ground. At the time the new growth is forming, the adult flies emerge from the pupae and become active. They are stout-bodied, shiny dark flies, about ⅙ inch long. During the day they can easily be found resting and sunning themselves on leaves. Females insert eggs into the growing twigs.

The developing larva is a greenish yellow maggot that grows slowly in the gall all summer. It is difficult to find until late summer and fall when it grows rapidly, filling a small cavity in the swollen area of the twig. Individual galls typically contain two to three larvae. There is one primary generation per year.

[1] Diptera: Cecidomyiidae; [2] Diptera: Agromyzidae

A. Dogwood clubgalls. *J. R. Baker.* **B.** Dogwood clubgall. *J. R. Baker.* **C.** Poplar twig galls. *W. Cranshaw.* **D.** Poplar twiggall fly larva in gall. *W. Cranshaw.* **E.** Poplar twiggall fly adult ovipositing in twig. *W. Cranshaw.* **F.** Poplar twiggall fly pupa emerging from gall. *W. Cranshaw.* **G.** Poplar twiggall fly and its primary parasitoid. *W. Cranshaw.*

GALL WASPS

Of all the insects that produce galls on woody plants, none are as numerous and diverse as the gall wasps (Cynipidae).[1] More than 600 North American species occur, and the great majority make elaborate, often bizarre galls on either oak or rose. All parts of the plants may support gall wasps—roots, branches, twigs, buds, flowers, acorns, and leaves. With few exceptions, these galls cause little if any significant damage to the plants and are primarily a curiosity. Some galls that develop on twigs and branches, however, can cause stunting and even some dieback.

Oak Gall Wasps

Most gall wasps on oak have life cycles that are relatively simple, typically involving an annual life cycle that produces one type of gall. In some species, however, the life cycles is very complex, sometimes extending over two or three seasons. Also, alternating forms of the insect and types of galls may be produced by a single species. As an example, **horned oak gall** (*Callirhytis cornigera*) forms conspicuous galls on the twigs of pin, scrub, and black oaks in eastern North America. These galls take two seasons to complete, and only females emerge from the twig galls. The subsequent generation produces swellings of the leaf veins. Both males and females develop in the leaf galls. Females lay eggs in twigs, initiating the twig-galling cycle.

Several other *Callirhytis* species develop on twigs. **Gouty oak gall** (*C. quercuspunctata*) is common on scarlet, pin, and black oaks in the northeast quadrant of the U.S. and southern Canada. It produces irregular swelling of the twigs, and galls commonly occur in groups, causing girdling. Gouty oak gall has an alternate form that makes small blisterlike galls on leaves. **Ribbed bud gall** (*C. quercusgemmaria*) makes conical, strongly ribbed galls on black oak. *C. crypta* makes a much more modest swelling on black oak twigs. *C. floridana* is a southeastern species that makes elongate swellings on branches close to the ground on Chapman, post, and sand post oaks.

Woody galls attached to twigs that are globular or nearly bullet shaped and pithy are sometimes referred to as bulletgalls. Galls produced by **oak rough bulletgall wasp** (*Disholcaspis quercusmamma*) can be common on twigs of swamp white and bur oak. The wasps emerge from old galls in late fall and lay eggs in the buds. There is little external evidence of infestation until early the following summer when dark green swellings emerge from the current-season twigs. These continue to swell through the summer, becoming knuckle sized by August. The galls darken and exude a honeydew-like material at this time which is attractive to many kinds of wasps. Inside the gall the wasp larva develops in a cell buried in the pith. Only a single wasp is produced in each gall. In California, a somewhat more rounded gall that similarly secretes honeydew is produced by *D. eldoradensis*, associated with valley and Oregon oak. Much smaller bulletlike galls are produced in dense clusters on twigs by **ridged bunch gall wasp** (*Callirhytis gemmaria*) on scrub, red, scarlet, and some other oaks.

Roly-poly galls are generally spherical and hollow, the larvae developing in a chamber that lies free in the center. Among those species that produce roly-poly galls are several *Andricus* species. Examples include **succulent oak gall wasp** (*A. palustris*), common in the northeastern U.S. on red oak; **California gallfly** (*A. californicus*), which makes globular galls on the twigs of valley, blue, scrub, and leather oaks; *A. pomiformis,* which makes apple-shaped galls on twigs of live oak; and **ant-like gallfly** (*A. lasius*), which makes rounded galls covered by filaments on live oak leaves.

A. Horned oak gall. *B. W. Kauffman.* **B.** Adults of horned oak gall wasp. *D. Shetlar.* **C.** Cross section of roly-poly gall, exposing chamber of developing larva. *J. H. Ghent.* **D.** Cross section of gouty oak gall. *G. J. Lenhard.* **E.** Adult of oak rough bulletgall wasp. *W. Cranshaw.* **F.** Adult of oak rough bulletgall wasp. *W. Cranshaw.* **G.** Oak rough bullet galls. *D. Leatherman.* **H.** Emerging new galls of oak rough bulletgall wasp. *W. Cranshaw.* **I.** Roly-poly type gall on oak. *Courtesy Clemson University.*

The production of dense hairs on the gall surface is particularly developed by **wool sower gall wasp** (*Callirhytis seminator*), which makes a densely cottony gall about the size of an oak apple gall (see below) on the petioles of white oak. The surface is whitish with brown spots. The larvae develop in a seedlike structure in the center of the gall. Short spiny hairs emerging from a globular leaf gall are produced by **hedgehog gall wasp** (*Acaraspis erinacei*) on white oak in eastern states. Stout spines are produced by **spined turban gall wasp** (*Antron douglasii*) on valley, blue, and California scrub oak in the western states.

One of the galls that attracts particular attention in the northwestern states and parts of the Midwest is produced by **jumping oak gall wasp** (*Neurotus saltatorius*). It makes seedlike galls on the leaves of oak, and the galls later drop from the leaf. The developing wasps in the fallen galls are active and cause the galls to jump about until they lodge in a protected crevice.

Perhaps the most spectacular of the oak galls are the **oak apples**, large parchment-covered galls derived from deformed leaves as they originate from the bud. The galls are large with spongy or fibrous material in the interior. In the center is a central chamber in which the gall wasp develops. **Large oak apple gall** (*Amphibolips confluenta*) forms galls on the leaves or petioles of red, black, scarlet, and some other oaks in the eastern U.S. The galls may be up to 2 inches in diameter and are dark greenish or brownish. This species produces two distinct generations, one with and the other without males. *Atrusca bella* produces pinkish brown oak apples on various oaks in the western states.

Rose Gall Wasps

Some 40 species of gall wasps, all in the genus *Diplolepis,* make galls on roses. All apparently reproduce asexually; males are unknown. A wide range of galls may be produced on almost all parts of the rose plant.

Roseroot gall wasp (*D. radicum*) is one of the most widespread rose gall wasps and one of the few that significantly damages plants. It produces hard, woody galls on the lower stems that can girdle canes. The galls are multicelled, and the wasps typically emerge from them in late winter. Roseroot gall wasp is found throughout the northern U.S. and southern Canada. Globular galls on stems are also produced by *D. fusiformis*, *D. tumidus*, and **globular rose gall wasp** (*D. globuloides*). Examples of stem galls of more elongate form are produced by **longrose gall wasp** (*D. dichlocera*) and by *D. politus*. Rounded, somewhat leafy galls on stems are produced by *D. tuberculatrix*.

Spines or hairs are common in many of the stem galls. **Spinyrose gall wasp** (*D. bicolor*) makes highly spined galls, usually in clusters, on twigs. *D. politus* makes highly spined, globular twig galls on wild rose. **Mossyrose gall wasp** (*D. rosae*) creates elaborate hairy growths, somewhat resembling sphagnum moss, on twigs. The developing young are found in chambers buried in the center of the gall. A smaller mossy-type gall is produced by *D. bassetti* in the western states.

Several other species gall rose leaves. Typically these galls are rounded, reddish, and spiny. *D. nebulosus* and **rose blister gall wasp** (*D. rosaefolii*) are examples of such species.

A. Wool sower gall. *E. Day.* **B.** Wool sower gall. *J. R. Baker.* **C.** Oak apple gall. *W. Cranshaw.* **D.** Cutaway of oak apple gall. *W. Cranshaw.* **E.** Gall of *Atrusca bella* opened to expose developing larva. *K. Gray.* **F.** Gall produced by gall wasp *Atrusca bella. K. Gray.* **G.** Oak apple gall. *J. D. Solomon.* **H.** Ball-type gall on rose leaf. *W. Cranshaw.* **I.** Stem galls on rose. *W. Cranshaw.* **J.** Gall of *Atrusca bella* opened to expose emerging adult. *K. Gray.*

Other Gall Wasps

A small number of gall wasps develop on other plants. *Diastrophus kincaidii* uses blackberry (*Rubus* spp.) as a host. It produces an irregularly shaped stem gall with multiple chambers. Gall wasps are also associated with amelanchier.

Gall-Making Sawflies

A few tenthredinid sawflies[2] make galls on woody plants, primarily willow. Twig and stem galls in willow are produced by *Euura* species. Adults emerge in spring, usually over a period of about 2 to 3 weeks. They insert eggs into developing stems, and the induced swellings develop rapidly. Larval feeding causes the gall to continue growing, and the pale yellow-green caterpillars feed for several months. Often multiple larvae occur in a single gall. Larvae of most species emerge from the gall in late summer and move to cover on the ground. Others may cut an emergence hole in late summer but remain in the gall to emerge later in spring. There is one generation per year.

Several *Pontania* species make leaf galls on willow. **Willow redgall sawfly** (*P. proxima*) is typical, producing a reddish bean-shaped swelling on the leaves of willow. The insect spends winter in soil or under protective debris. Adults emerge in spring and lay eggs in young, expanding leaves in late spring and early summer. The developing larvae feed on the soft tissues in the gall, later moving into firmer tissues to feed but remaining in the gall. When full grown, they drop to the ground and spin a cocoon. The related species *P. s-pomum* creates prominent rounded yellow or red swellings on willow leaves that develop in small clusters.

[1] Hymenoptera: Cynipidae; [2] Hymenoptera: Tenthredinidae

A. Mossyrose gall. *F. Peairs*. **B.** Mossyrose gall cut away to expose developing larvae. *K. Gray*. **C.** Developing larvae of mossyrose gall wasp in gall. *K. Gray*. **D.** Adult female of mossyrose gall wasp. *K. Gray*. **E.** Adult male of mossy-rose gall wasp. *K. Gray*. **F.** Gall produced by *Diastrophus kincaidii*, cut to expose larval chambers. *K. Gray*. **G.** Close-up of gall produced by *Diastrophus kincaidii*, showing developing larvae. *K. Gray*. **H.** Stem galls of willow produced by *Euura* sp. *W. Cranshaw*. **I.** *Pontania* sawfly adult. *K. Gray*. **J.** *Pontania* sawfly larva. *K. Gray*. **K.** Galls produced by *Pontania s-pomum*. *D. Leatherman*. **L.** Galls produced by willow redgall sawfly. *W. Cranshaw*.

ERIOPHYID MITE GALLS

Eriophyid mites (Eriophyidoidea superfamily) are microscopic mites that feed on plants (p. 404). Some produce abnormal plant growths—galls—and these are often distinctive. Scabby blisters on leaf surfaces in which the mites develop are produced by the "blistergall mites," whereas other species induce outgrowths of leaves in the form of small pouches or fingerlike projections. Overstimulation of plant hairs to produce feltlike patches, known as erinea (erineum in the singular), is a unique response of plants to feeding by an arthropod. Disorganized growths of buds or flower parts are also induced by infestation of some eriophyid mites.

Scientific Name[1]	Common Name (if proposed)	Host
Blister Mites[2]		
Eriophyes pyri	Pearleaf blister mite	Pear
Eriophyes mali	Appleleaf blister mite	Apple, crabapple
Eriophyes sorbi		Mountain-ash
Aceria erineus	Walnut blister mite	English walnut
Leaf-Curling Species		
Aceria caryae	Pecan leafroll mite	Pecan
Aculus lobulifera	Cottonwood leafcurl mite	Eastern cottonwood
Aculops fuschiae	Fuschia gall mite	Fuschia
Eriophyes tosichella	Wheat curl mite	Tulip and many lilies; wheat and many grasses
Pouchgall Species[2]		
Vasates quadripedes	Maple bladdergall mite	Maple
Colomerus vitis	Grape erineum mite	Grape
Eriophyes negundi	Boxelder erineum mite	Boxelder
Eriophyes chrondriphora		Ash
Eriophyes ulmi		American elm
Phyllocoptes didelphis		Aspen
Aculops tetanothrix		Willow
Aculops toxicophagus		Rhus
Phytoptus laevis	Alder beadgall mite	Alder
Fingergall Species		
Vasates aceriscrumena	Maple spindlegall mite	Sugar and silver maples
Eriophyes emarginatae		Plum, chokecherry, bitter cherry
Phytoptus cerasicrumena		Black cherry
Phytoptus tiliae		Basswood, linden
Aceria parulmi	Elm eriophyid mite	American elm

Continued

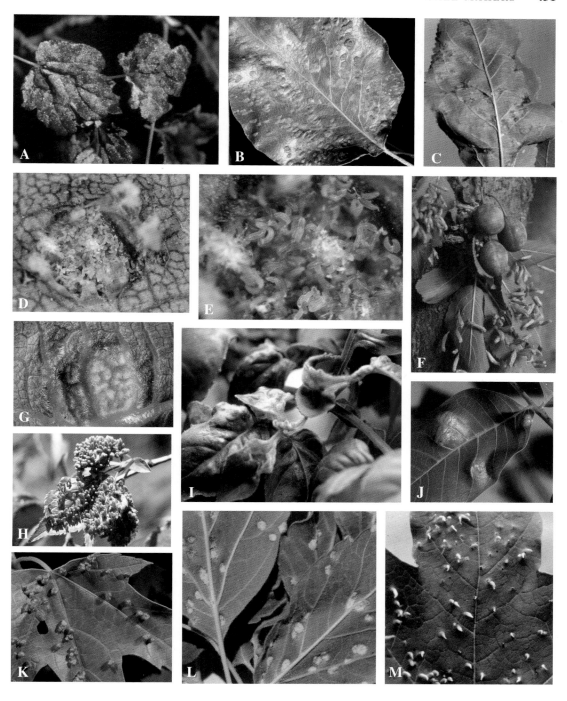

A. Erineum on Rocky Mountain maple. *D. Leatherman.* **B.** Pearleaf blister galls. *D. Shetlar.* **C.** Appleleaf blister galls. *W. Cranshaw.* **D.** Appleleaf blister gall opened to expose eriophyid mites within. *L. Mannix.* **E.** Eriophyid mites exposed from appleleaf blistergall. *L. Mannix.* **F.** Fingergalls of plum. *S. Rachesky.* **G.** Walnut blister mite injury. *K. Gray.* **H.** Fingergalls on chokecherry. *W. Cranshaw.* **I.** Leaf twisting caused by fuschia gall mite. *W. Cranshaw.* **J.** Walnut blister mite injury. *K. Gray.* **K.** Maple bladder galls. *D. Shetlar.* **L.** Erineum type gall on underside of boxelder. *W. Cranshaw.* **M.** Maple bladder galls. *W. Cranshaw.*

Scientific Name[1]	Common Name (if proposed)	Host
Erineum Producers		
Aceria aceris		Silver maple
Aceria modestus		Maple
Aceria elongatus		Sugar maple
Acalitus fagerinea		American beech
Colomerus vitis	Grape erineum mite	Grape
Eriophyes caulis	Black walnut petiolegall mite	Black walnut
Eriophyes calaceris	Western erineum mite	Rocky Mountain maple
Budgall Species		
Aceria parapopuli	Poplar budgall mite	Cottonwood, poplar
Aceria aloinis	Aloe mite	Aloe, *Haworthia*
Phytocoptella avellanae	Filbert bud mite	Filbert, hazelnut
Cecidophyopsis vermiformis		Filbert
Cecidophyopsis psilaspis	Taxus bud mite	Yew
Cecidophyopsis ribis	Currant bud mite	Black currant
Ceciophyes betulae		Birch
Acalitus vaccinii		Blueberry, huckleberry
Trisetacus pini	Pine bud mite	Pines
Trisetacus cupressi		Southern redcedar
Trisetacus campnodus		Pine
Trisetacus gemmavitians		Scotch pine
Trisetacus juniperinus		Juniper
Trisetacus quadrisetus	Juniper berry mite	Juniper, *Cedrus*
Trisetacus thujivagrans		Arborvitae
Witches' Brooming Species		
Eriophyes celtis	Hackberry witches' broom mite	Hackberry
Eriophyes cynodoniensis	Bermudagrass mite	Bermudagrass
Eriophyes slykhuisi	Buffalograss mite	Buffalograss
Eriophyes zoysiae	Zoysiagrass mite	Zoysiagrass
Flower-/Fruit-Distorting Species		
Eriophyes fraxiniflora	Ash flowergall mite	Green ash
Eriophyes neoessigi	Cottonwood catkingall mite	Cottonwood, poplar
Phytoptus paraspiraeae		Bridal-wreath spirea
Acalitus essigi	Redberry mite	Blackberry
Phyllocoptes gracilis	Dryberry mite	Raspberry
Aceria sheldoni	Citrus bud mite	Citrus

[1] Acari: Eriophyoidea
[2] Many pouchgalls and blistergalls intergrade with other forms, including several where erinea also are produced.

A. Erineum on maple leaf. *W. Cranshaw.* **B.** Taxus bud mites, close-up. *D. Gilrein.* **C.** Poplar budgalls. *W. Cranshaw.*
D. Taxus bud mite injury. *D. Gilrein.* **E.** Taxus bud gall. *D. Gilrein.* **F.** Hackberry witches' broom caused by eriophyid
mites and powdery mildew. *W. Cranshaw.* **G.** Pine eriophyid mite damage. *R. Byther.* **H.** Pine eriophyid mite damage.
R. Byther. **I.** Hackberry showing extensive infestation of hackberry witches' broom galls. *W. Cranshaw.* **J.** Witches'
broom from buffalograss mite. *W. Cranshaw.* **K.** Ash flower galls. *W. Cranshaw.* **L.** Distorted cottonwood catkin
galled by cottonwood catkingall mite. *W. Cranshaw.*

CHAPTER EIGHT

Stem and Twig Damagers

CICADAS

Cicadas[1] are the largest insects of the order Homoptera in North America. Distant relatives of the more diminutive spittlebugs, leafhoppers, and aphids, they develop by sucking sap from the roots of trees and shrubs. Cicadas require several years to complete their life cycle, which in some species has synchronized emergence. At least 75 species occur in North America; some taxonomists recognize significantly more species.

Periodical (or 17-Year) Cicada (*Magicicada septendecim*)

Hosts: A wide variety of deciduous trees and shrubs.

Damage: Injury results when females lay eggs, inserting them into twigs. This produces splintering wounds, which predispose breakage and allow entry of pathogens. Feeding injuries are minor. This species' spectacular periodic emergence attracts considerable attention and sometimes concern. Early European settlers incorrectly dubbed periodical cicadas "locusts"—a term appropriately applied only to certain migratory grasshoppers.

Distribution: Much of the northeastern quadrant of the U.S.

Appearance: Adults are 1¼ to 1¾ inches, generally dark, and may have some banding. Their eyes are conspicuously red, and the wings are nearly transparent with an orange tint.

Life History and Habits: Immature stages live on the roots of trees and shrubs, growing slowly. In the seventeenth year of their life they emerge from the soil, typically in late May and early June in the north, earlier in the south. They climb trees, buildings, and other upright surfaces. The nymphal skin is then shed, and adults shortly thereafter move to the trees. Adults do little feeding but may drink some sap from the twigs. Males produce a loud buzzing "song" to attract females, and mating occurs in the trees.

The females possess a bladelike ovipositor which is used to insert rows of eggs into twigs. Six to 10 weeks later, nymphs emerge from these eggs, drop to the ground, and dig into the soil to settle and feed on the roots. They remain belowground until emerging almost 17 years later.

Periodical cicada is a remarkable insect that has both a very extended life cycle and synchronized emergence. Twelve distinct broods exist in different regions through the eastern U.S. Each brood emerges every seventeenth year. The largest brood (Brood X) encompasses much of the northeastern U.S. and is next anticipated in 2004 and 2121.

A. Periodical cicada ovipositing in twig. *J. E. Appleby.* **B.** Periodical cicada eggs inserted into twig. *L. L. Hyche.* **C.** Mating pair of periodical cicadas. *D. Shetlar.* **D.** Egg-laying wounds produced by periodical cicada. *B. W. Kauffman.* **E.** Periodical cicada, front view. *L. L. Hyche.* **F.** Periodical cicada adults emerging from nymphal skin. *D. Shetlar.* **G.** Periodical cicada damage. *D. Herms.* **H.** Dead male periodical cicadas around base of tree following emergence. *L. L. Hyche.* **I.** Periodical cicada. *J. H. Ghent.* **J.** Periodical cicada damage. *L. L. Hyche.*

Other Cicadas

The **13-year cicada** (*Magicicada tredecim*) is the periodical cicada dominant in the southern U.S. Its habits and the injuries it inflicts are similar to those of 17-year cicada but its life cycle is completed in 13 years. Three distinct broods are recognized, which usually emerge in late April and May of their thirteenth year of development.

Dog-day cicadas (*Tibicen* spp.) are the largest cicadas in North America, but they are much less commonly observed than heard. Males make loud, droning buzzing calls during midsummer. They are found east of the Rockies. Dog-day cicadas are sometimes known as annual cicadas, as adults are present each season. Nymphs require 2 to 5 years to complete development, however, with overlapping generations allowing annual appearance. Oviposition injury by the females is usually minor.

In the western U.S., **Putnam's cicada** (*Platypedia putnami*) is common. Adults are present in late spring, and males make a subdued clicking call. Oviposition injury to maple, apple, crabapple, and some other trees occasionally occurs but is minor. Various *Okanagana* species of cicadas also occur in the western U.S., with at least one species reported to damage West Coast Christmas tree plantings.

[1] Homoptera: Cicadidae

A. Cast skin of dog-day cicada nymph. *W. Cranshaw.* **B.** Adult dog-day cicada, *Tibicen dorsata. W. Cranshaw.*
C. Putnam's cicada emerging from nymphal skin. *W. Cranshaw.* **D.** Dog-day cicada nymph. *W. Cranshaw.* **E.** Dog-day
cicada recently emerged from nymphal skin. *H. A. Pase III.* **F.** Twig break caused by egg laying wounds of Putnam's
cicada. *W. Cranshaw.* **G.** Putnam's cicada emerging from nymphal skin. *L. Bjostad.* **H.** Putnam's cicada emerging
from nymphal skin. *W. Cranshaw.* **I.** Dog-day cicada nymph recently emerged from soil. *L. L. Hyche.*
J. *Okanagana synodica. W. Cranshaw.* **K.** Putnam's cicadas. *W. Cranshaw.*

PINE TIP MOTHS

Several insects tunnel into the terminals of pine. Most important are those in the genus *Rhyacionia*,[1] of which approximately 22 species occur in North America.

Nantucket Pine Tip Moth (*Rhyacionia frustrana*)

Hosts: Most two- and three-needle pines are susceptible. Trees under 15 feet and growing in open sites are most severely attacked.

Damage: Larvae tunnel in developing shoots and can kill back terminals by as much as 8 inches. Some plant stunting and stem deformation ("crow's feet") can result from prolonged attack.

Distribution: New England to Florida, west to New Mexico and Arkansas. Nantucket pine tip moth has also been confirmed as established in southern California.

Appearance: Moths are small (wingspan ca. ½ inch), and the head, body, and appendages are covered with gray scales. The forewings are covered with reddish brown patches and have silver gray bands. Young larvae are cream colored with a black head. Mature larvae, which occur in tunneled terminal growth, are light brown to orange and about ⅜ inch.

Life History and Habits: Nantucket pine tip moth winters as a pupa in damaged terminals. It transforms to the adult form in early spring, and females lay eggs on shoots and needles, with egg-laying synchronized with the emergence of new growth. Eggs hatch in about 2 weeks, after which the young larvae mine needles, shoots, or buds. As they get older, they move to the axils of needles or buds and feed on buds and shoots. A small tent of silk covered with plant resin may be present at the site of injury. First symptoms of injury include some browning and dying of a few needles at the tips of branches, progressing to terminal dieback.

These larvae mature, pupate, and produce a second generation, with adults present 5 to 6 weeks after the first-generation adults. In warmer areas, a third generation of moths may be active and lay eggs in August. Occasionally even a fourth generation is reported.

Related Species

European pine shoot moth (*Rhyacionia buoliana*) is common in the northern U.S. and southern Canada, producing similar injuries to red, mugho, Scotch, Austrian, and some other pines. It has only one generation. **Southwestern pine tip moth** (*R. neomexicana*) is found in the High Plains and Rocky Mountain region. Austrian, ponderosa, and mugho pines are common hosts. Winter is spent in cocoons plastered to the base of trees, and adults emerge about the time new growth is emerging. **Western pine tip moth** (*R. bushnelli*) develops primarily on ponderosa pine but damages other pines, including Monterey pine since introduction of the insect into California. The species now occurs throughout most of the U.S. west of the Dakotas. One generation per year occurs in the northern area of the range, but two generations are reported from Nebraska, with flights in April–May and again in late June–July. Damage to ponderosa pine can be severe in areas with two generations.

[1] Lepidoptera: Tortricidae

A. Damage by Nantucket pine tip moth. *Courtesy Clemson University.* **B.** Nantucket pine tip moth injury. *D. Gilrein.* **C.** Nantucket pine tip moth. *D. Gilrein.* **D.** European pine shoot moth. *K. Gray.* **E.** Larva of European pine shoot moth. *K. Gray.* **F.** Pupa of European pine shoot moth. *K. Gray.* **G.** Injury to mugho pine produced by southwestern pine tip moth. *W. Cranshaw.* **H.** Pupal skin following European pine shoot moth emergence. *D. Shetlar.*

OTHER CONIFER-TIP-BORING MOTHS

Pinyon grown in Colorado and the southwestern U.S. is frequently damaged by **pinyon tip moth** (*Dioryctria albovittella*).[1] The overwintering stage is a first instar larva on the bark which resumes feeding in spring and enters unopened buds. Tunneling later extends into the pith of terminals, resulting in girdling wounds that cause terminals to die and break by mid-July. Cones are also sometimes tunneled.

Pinyon pitch nodulemaker (*Retinia arizonensis*)[1] also is a common tip moth in native pinyon stands but is often uncommon in cultivated plantings. It produces a large, characteristic purplish nodule, in which the larva can be found, at the wound site. Adults emerge in midsummer to lay eggs, and larvae initiate tunneling before fall dormancy. **Ponderosa pine tip moth** (*R. metallica*) attacks terminal growth of ponderosa pine in Nebraska, Colorado, and New Mexico. Although pitch forms at wounds, the large purplish pitch nodule does not form.

Northern pitch twig moth (*Petrova albicapitana*)[1] is found throughout Canada. Jack pine is its preferred host, although it is also found on Scotch, mugho, red, and lodgepole pines. Development is extended, requiring 2 years to complete.

Eastern pine shoot borer (*Eucosoma gloriola*)[2] is damaging to young conifers in northeastern North America. Larvae hollow out 6- to 8-inch tunnels in shoots, which then wilt and drop from the plant. These injuries stunt and distort growth of trees and are a particular problem in Christmas tree production. White and Scotch pine are most commonly damaged.

Winter is spent as a pupa in a cocoon among topsoil and debris under previously infested plants. The adults emerge in late April and May, during which time females lay eggs singly at the base of needles. The larvae bore into the shoot and tunnel downward. They are dirty white to gray with a yellowish brown head and a pale yellow area on the prothorax. A characteristic exit hole at the base of the tunnel is made, and the caterpillars drop to the ground to pupate. One generation is produced annually. Several other *Eucosoma* species cause similar injuries and have a similar life history. In the western states, **western pine shoot borer** (*E. sonomana*) is sometimes damaging to ponderosa and lodgepole pine.

Juniper twig girdler (*Periploca nigra*)[3] damages juniper, particularly Tam juniper, in the western U.S. Larvae are cream colored with a dark head and tunnel the twigs, causing them to die and conspicuously flag. Juniper twig girdler is common in parts of California, where it limits use of Tam juniper in landscapes.

[1] Lepidoptera: Pyralidae; [2] Lepidoptera: Oleuthreutidae; [3] Lepidoptera: Cosmopterigidae

A. Larva of pinyon tip moth in damaged terminal. *W. Cranshaw.* **B.** Injury to pinyon pine produced by pinyon tip moth. *W. Cranshaw.* **C.** Pinyon pitch nodulemaker. *D. Leatherman.* **D.** Pinyon pitch nodulemaker larva exposed in damaged terminal. *D. Leatherman.* **E.** Western pine shoot borer adult. *S. Tunnock.* **F.** Crooking caused by earlier damage by eastern pine shoot borer. *Courtesy Minnesota Dept. Natural Resources.* **G.** Pitch nodule produced in ponderosa pine by ponderosa pine tip moth. *D. Leatherman.* **H.** Western pine shoot borer exit hole. *S. Tunnock.* **I.** Northern pitch twig moth injury. *Courtesy Minnesota Dept. Natural Resources.* **J.** Western pine shoot borer larva in tunnel. *Courtesy USDA-FS Region 4 Archives Tunnock.*

STEM-BORING MOTHS OF DECIDUOUS TREES AND SHRUBS

Cottonwood twig borer (*Gypsonoma haimbachiana*)[1] tunnels into new shoots of cottonwood, causing tips to break. Branches of chronically infested trees develop a tufted appearance, and the dropped twigs may become a significant nuisance. The larvae are dirty gray caterpillars with a brown head and may be found associated with tunneled twigs.

The overwintering stage is usually a very young larva found in small pits in the bark, often near old leaf scars or tunneling wounds. Larvae resume activity in spring, boring into actively growing shoots and tunneling down the pith. When full grown (late May–early June), they emerge and crawl down the trunk, pupating in protected sites on trunks and branches. Adults emerge in about 8 to 10 days, and females typically lay eggs on the upper leaf surface. The young larvae first feed on the midrib or vein of leaves. Later they migrate to twig tips and begin tunneling. The twig-tunneling phase takes about a month to complete. Two or three generations are produced per year.

Boxelder twig borer (*Proteoteras willingana*)[1] can be commonly associated with boxelder maple in parts of the central U.S. and Prairie Provinces. Eggs are laid on leaves in midsummer, and the larvae feed on leaves until September. They subsequently bore into dormant buds where they spend the winter. In early spring they resume feeding and may damage several additional buds before they tunnel into a new shoot, which induces a local swelling. They drop to the ground to pupate around early June. Adults emerge about 3 weeks following pupation. The related **maple twig borer** (*P. aesculana*) produces similar injuries to twigs of silver maple. Twigs of black locust may be tunneled by **locust twig borer** (*Ecdytolopha insiticiana*).[1]

Peach twig borer (*Anarsia lineatella*)[2] develops in shoots and fruit of various stone fruit (*Prunus* spp.) trees and is particularly damaging to peach. Winter is spent as a partially grown caterpillar, protected in a small silk-covered cell on the bark of fruit trees. In early spring, the caterpillars become active, migrate to the twigs, and tunnel the buds and emerging terminal growth. The damaged new growth typically wilts and dies (flagging). The caterpillars then pupate in the tree and usually emerge as small grayish moths in May.

The emerged moths lay eggs on the twigs, small leaves, and developing fruits. The young caterpillars preferentially feed on terminal growth of twigs, later moving to fruits shortly after the pits start to harden. When full grown, these caterpillars pupate on the trunk and larger branches. Moths that emerge from this second generation lay eggs on fruit. Second-generation caterpillars restrict their feeding to the fruit, causing most crop injury. A third generation that causes little injury is produced in late summer.

Strawberry crownminer (*Monochroa fragariae*)[2] tunnels the crowns, buds, and young leaves of strawberry. It is primarily found in the Pacific Northwest, but isolated infestations occur elsewhere from movement of infested plants. Larvae, reddish with a dark head, are somewhat similar to those of peach twig borer.

A. Cottonwood twig borer in stem. *W. Cranshaw.* **B.** Peach twig borer in shoot. *K. Gray.* **C.** Injury produced by box-elder twig borer. *J. D. Solomon.* **D.** Peach twig borer adult. *K. Gray.* **E.** Fruit tunneling by peach twig borer. *Courtesy Clemson University.* **F.** Locust twig borer larva and injury. *J. D. Solomon.* **G.** Damage produced by larval tunneling of strawberry crownminer. *W. Cranshaw.*

Larvae of **ceanothus stem gall moth** (*Periploca ceanothiella*)[3] tunnel into stems of *Ceanothus*, primarily *C. griseus*. This produces shortening of terminal growth and induces spindle-shaped swellings on twigs. The insect is apparently widespread in association with its host but primarily damaging only in California.

The most common insect affecting terminal growth of black walnut is **walnut shoot moth** (*Acrobasis demotella*).[4] In early summer, moths are active and females lay eggs on the underside of leaves of walnut, hickory, and pecan. The larvae feed on the leaves for a brief period and then move to the twigs, where they spin a silken cover (hibernaculum) for winter. In spring, as buds begin to swell, they resume activity and tunnel buds. They later enter the expanding twigs, which kills the shoots.

European corn borer (*Ostrinia nubilalis*)[5] occurs widely over much of North America east of the Rockies and has an extremely wide host range. Larvae develop by tunneling into stems, fruit, and other parts of the plant, causing weakening and allowing introduction of plant pathogens that produce rots. European corn borer is a major pest of field corn, pepper, snap bean, chrysanthemum, dahlia, and several other ornamentals. Stems of seedling trees are also sometimes damaged by larvae.

Winter is spent as a full-grown larva in old plant debris. Pupation occurs in spring, and adults emerge in late spring and aggregate in dense grassy "action sites" for mating. Eggs are laid as masses on foliage. Early-stage larvae often tunnel into leaf veins, later moving into stalks or fruit as they get older. Pupation occurs in the plant, and there is usually a second generation in August. The biology is somewhat different in the extreme northern part of the range, along the U.S.-Canada border, where only one generation is produced. At least two strains of European corn borer occur, which differ in the sex attractants they produce.

[1] Lepidoptera: Tortricidae; [2] Lepidoptera: Gelechiidae; [3] Lepidoptera: Cosmopterigidae; [4] Lepidoptera: Pyralidae; [5] Lepidoptera: Crambidae

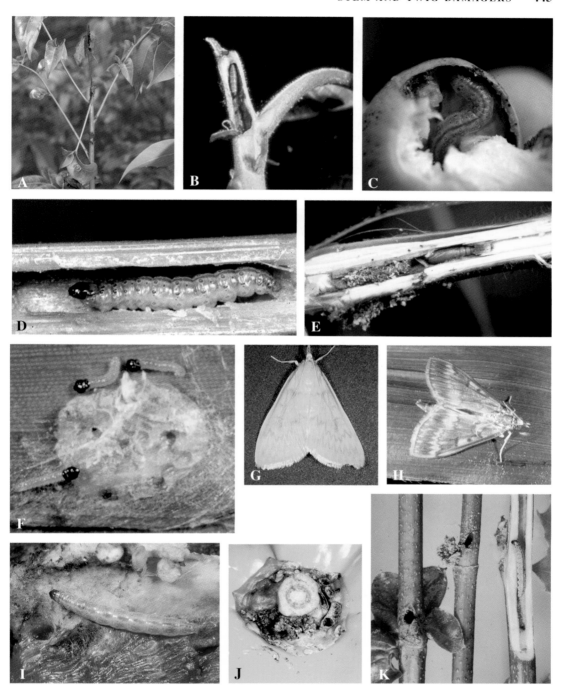

A. Walnut shoot moth injury. *R. L. Anderson.* **B.** Walnut shoot moth larva. *Courtesy Minnesota Dept. Natural Resources.*
C. European corn borer in cotton boll. *R. Smith.* **D.** European corn borer in corn stalk. *Courtesy Clemson University.*
E. European corn borer pupa in corn stalk. *R. Smith.* **F.** European corn borer larvae at egg hatch. *Courtesy University of Georgia.* **G.** Female European corn borer moth. *J. Capinera.* **H.** Male European corn borer moth. *J. Capinera.*
I. European corn borer larva in pepper fruit. *R. Bessin.* **J.** European corn borer larval entry wound in top of pepper fruit. *R. Bessin.* **K.** European corn borer tunneling of sycamore stems. *J. D. Solomon.*

STEM-BORING SAWFLIES

Rose Shoot (or Rose Stem-Boring) Sawfly (*Hartigia trimaculata*)[1]
Raspberry Horntail (*Hartigia cressoni*)[1]

Hosts: Rose, raspberry, blackberry, boysenberry.

Damage: Larvae tunnel the upper half of canes, causing wilting and often breakage beyond the point of injury.

Distribution: Rose shoot sawfly is widely distributed across North America east of the Rocky Mountains. Raspberry horntail is a western species found from California east to parts of Colorado and Montana.

Appearance: Adults, rarely observed, are elongate, ½-inch, black-and-yellow stingless wasps. The cream-colored larvae are found in the plant and have a distinct pale head capsule, distinguishing them from other borers found in canes.

Life History and Habits: Winter is spent as a full-grown larva in the old canes. The larvae pupate in spring, and adults emerge in April and May. Females insert eggs into succulent tissues at the tip of current-season growth. Upon hatching, the larvae enter the stem to feed, producing a spiraling girdle. Older larvae feed in the pith and occasionally are found in larger roots. Pupation occurs in the stem, and some pupae often transform to the adult stage and produce a second generation.

Other Sawfly Borers

Maple petiole borer[2] (*Caulocampus acericaulis*) is a common insect associated with sugar maple in much of the eastern U.S. Larvae burrow into leaf petioles, which subsequently break near the blade. This produces a noticeable shedding of leaves in late May and early June. Larvae pupate in the soil and have one generation per year, with adults laying eggs in late April and May.

Curled rose sawfly (*Allanthus cinctus*)[2] damages leaves and tunnels canes of rose in many midwestern and eastern states. The larvae are pastel green with numerous whitish spots and a yellow-orange head. They feed along the edge of leaves, curled and hidden largely on the undersides. Most damage occurs when they then tunnel into canes and excavate the pith to produce a cell for pupation. Two generations per year normally are produced.

[1] Hymenoptera: Cephidae; [2] Hymenoptera: Tenthredinidae

A. Maple petiole borer larva. *C. D. Pless.* **B.** Maple petiole borer damage. *C. D. Pless.* **C.** Rose shoot sawfly larva. *J. D. Solomon.* **D.** Rose shoot sawfly larva. *W. Cranshaw.* **E.** Adult rose shoot sawfly. *W. Cranshaw.* **F.** Tunneling of rose shoot sawfly larva in raspberry cane. *W. Cranshaw.* **G.** Wilting due to rose shoot sawfly injury. *W. Cranshaw.*

PITH-NESTING BEES AND WASPS

Small carpenter bees (*Ceratina* spp.)[1] attract attention because of their habit of nesting in the pith of various plants, including rose, sumac, and elder. (*Note:* Leafcutter bees, discussed on p. 70, also may share this habit.) Most are fairly small (ca. ¼ inch) dark bees with a slightly metallic sheen. The individual chambers cut into the pith are provisioned with pollen and nectar on which the larval bees develop. The nest-building activities of small carpenter bees usually cause little additional dieback of pruned canes.

Large carpenter bees (*Xylocopa* spp.)[1] are quite large, usually black or metallic dark green, and resemble bumble bees but lack hair on the abdomen. Large carpenter bees nest in dry wood and do not damage plants. However, they sometimes are considered pests of building timbers and can occur in many wooden garden structures. The males, which do not sting and are harmless, aggressively defend territories and will buzz humans.

Tunneling of plant stems can also be done by several hunting wasps.[2] In some areas, *Pemphredon* wasps are common inhabitants of stems of rose or other pithy plants. These hunt aphids or leafhoppers, which they paralyze and pack into excavated nest cells as food for the developing wasp larvae.

[1] Hymenoptera: Anthoporidae; [2] Hymenoptera: Sphecidae

A. Large carpenter bee. *J. Baker.* **B.** Small carpenter bee pupae. *J. Baker.* **C.** Small carpenter bee. *J. Baker.* **D.** Large carpenter bee. *J. A. Payne.* **E.** Entrance made into rose cane pith by *Pemphredon* wasp. *W. Cranshaw.* **F.** Small carpenter bee larvae in rose cane. *J. Baker.* **G.** Pollen plug in cell of small carpenter bee. *W. Cranshaw.* **H.** *Pemphredon* wasp exposed from nest cell in pith of ash. *W. Cranshaw.*

WEEVIL BORERS OF TERMINAL GROWTH

White Pine Weevil (*Pissodes strobi*)[1]

Hosts: White pine, spruce.

Damage: Larvae tunnel underneath the bark of the terminal. Girdling wounds cause the leader to suddenly wilt and die in early summer. Once the top leader is killed, some side branches change their growth habit and begin to grow upward to take the place of the killed leader. If successful, these new leaders form main trunks, and multiple main trunks occur above the damaged area. This changes the form of the tree from its normal tapering growth to one that is more densely bushy.

Appearance: Adults are small (ca. ¼ inch) snout beetles flecked with brown and white patches. Larvae are almost identical to those of bark beetles, resembling a grain of cooked white rice with a brown head.

Distribution: Widespread in the northern U.S. and southern Canada. Problems currently are reported expanding in Ohio and Colorado.

Life History and Habits: The insect overwinters in the adult stage, under leaf litter and in other protected areas. On warm, sunny afternoons in late spring, the weevils become active and fly to host trees. Feeding occurs on the cambium of main branches near the leader, and later the females may insert eggs into some of the feeding cavities. Small points of oozing pitch present on the main leader are indicators of this feeding and egg-laying activity.

Eggs hatch in 1 to 2 weeks, and the young grubs (larvae) tunnel downward underneath the bark. Damage increases as the insects grow—they feed for about 4 to 6 weeks—and wilting starts to become noticeable in June and July. When full grown, the larvae tunnel deeper into the stem and form a cocoon made of wood chips in which they pupate. In about 2 weeks, the adult beetles emerge through small holes chewed through the bark. The chip cocoons remain behind and are a useful means of diagnosing old white pine weevil injury.

Adult weevils feed on the needles, buds, and twigs of spruce for several weeks before going into a dormant condition for overwintering. Some minor chewing injury to buds may result if infestations are severe.

Related Species

Eastern pine weevil (*Pissodes nemorensis*), also known as **deodar weevil**, occurs in the southern states and damages true cedars (*Cedrus*) and some pines. Adults often are most damaging, causing branch tips and small branches to be killed by feeding punctures. Larvae develop under the bark and may girdle branches. **Northern pine weevil** (*P. approximatus*) is nearly identical and sometimes considered the same species. It has a northern distribution, and larvae develop in stumps and trunks of recently killed trees. Eggs are usually laid singly rather than in groups, often at the base of trees. This species is sometimes important on seedlings in pine plantations, where abundant amounts of freshly cut stumps allow numbers to increase.

[1] Coleoptera: Curculionidae

A. Adult white pine weevils feeding at white pine shoot. *D. Herms.* **B.** Characteristic wilting of terminal growth of spruce caused by white pine weevil damage. *J. Capinera.* **C.** White pine weevil larvae and chip cocoons under terminal of blue spruce. *W. Cranshaw.* **D.** Pupal chip cocoons produced by white pine weevil. *W. Cranshaw.* **E.** Pupal chip cocoons of white pine weevil. *D. Leatherman.* **F.** Death of white pine leader produced by white pine weevil. *W. Cranshaw.* **G.** Deodar weevil pupa. *G. J. Lenhard.* **H.** White pine weevil. *E. B. Walker.* **I.** Deodar weevil. *G. J. Lenhard.* **J.** Blue spruce terminal injured by white pine weevil. *D. Leatherman.* **K.** Deodar weevil full-grown larva in chip cocoon. *G. J. Lenhard.*

TWIG-FEEDING BEETLES

Beetles in several families (Scolytidae, Bostrichidae, Curculionidae, Cerambycidae) develop in the twigs of trees and shrubs.

Twig beetles (*Pityophthorus* spp., *Pityogenes* spp.)[1] develop in pine, spruce, true firs, and Douglas-fir. The larvae tunnel the inner bark, and girdling kills branches, tops, and small trunks. Damaged plants show distinctive flagging of terminal growth. In natural situations, these beetles function as pruners of shaded-out or broken twigs and branches. They also often serve as indicators of conditions that favor outbreaks of other, more damaging, bark beetles. In urban settings, they are major contributors to the death of recently transplanted or stressed pine.

Adults are tiny bark beetles, ½₂ to ⅙ inch long, generally dark brown. Adult emergence, flight, and attack activities occur throughout the warm months and may begin by mid-March following mild winters. The adults find suitable hosts and produce broods just under the bark. Attacks produce much tan or reddish sawdust but little pitch. The galleries made beneath the bark by adults and feeding larvae are generally star shaped and lightly etch the wood. Most species of twig beetles have two to four generations per year.

Oak bark beetles (*Pseudopityophthorus* spp.)[1] develop primarily in oak but may infest buckeye, beech, chestnut, hickory, birch, and maple. They are particularly common in the Pacific states and are not aggressive species, limiting attacks to trees that are under stress or recently killed. Oak bark beetles are also suspected of being among the insects that transmit the fungus involved in oak wilt. The adults are tiny reddish brown to black beetles and feed on buds, twig crotches, and leaf axils before constructing longitudinal egg galleries at the junction of the bark and sapwood. Two or more generations are produced annually.

Cedar bark beetles (*Phloeosinus* spp.)[1] develop in juniper, arborvitae, cypress, and cedar. Adults feed on small leaflets and may girdle small twigs, typically several inches back from the tip, causing flagging. Most damage is done as the developing larvae feed under the bark. If only certain branches are killed, this results in conspicuous flagging. Entire trees may be killed, particularly if there is a preexisting stress due to root rot or other injury which greatly increases susceptibility to these insects.

The gallery system made by cedar bark beetles has a central tunnel running parallel to the branch or trunk, with numerous side tunnels coming off it at right angles. The galleries are usually free of extensive sawdust. Larvae are minute, legless white grubs, found in their tunnels during active infestations. The adults are ⅛ inch long, reddish brown to black shiny beetles of typical oblong bark beetle form. The wing covers are marked by lengthwise rows of minute puncture marks. Twenty seven species are known from North America, primarily in the western U.S.

Common pine shoot beetle (*Tomicus piniperda*)[1] damages shoots of pine (Scotch, Austrian, eastern white, red, and jack) while in the adult stage. Adults emerge from furrows in bark and other protected sites on warm days in early spring and fly to newly cut stumps. The female excavates an egg gallery, mates, and lays eggs. The larvae develop under the bark in the stump and complete development in May or early June. Adults then fly to the crowns of living trees and initiate "maturation feeding." This involves boring into lateral shoots which are hollowed 1 to 4 inches and subsequently wilt and die. Several shoots may be damaged by an individual beetle. In late fall the beetles leave the shoot, dispersing to winter shelter. Common shoot beetle is currently found in most of the region surrounding the Great Lakes and in an area of northern New England where it is of most concern to Christmas tree plantations.

A. Tunnels produced by twig beetles. *D. Leatherman.* **B.** Tunnels produced by cedar bark beetles. *D. Shetlar.* **C.** Cedar bark beetle pupae in larval galleries. *D. Shetlar.* **D.** Flagging caused by common pine shoot beetle injury. *S. Passoa/USDA PPQ APHIS.* **E.** Common pine shoot beetle in tunnel of twig. *S. Passoa/USDA PPQ APHIS.* **F.** Common pine shoot beetle in tunnel of twig. *S. Passoa/USDA PPQ APHIS.* **G.** Common pine shoot beetle larval tunnels in trunk. *W. D. Ciesla.*

Adult damage to pine twigs also is the primary damage produced by **pales weevil** (*Hylobius pales*)[2] in the Midwest. This species chews small punctures in the twigs, and crystalized resin collects along the surface. These injuries often girdle the plant, causing small branches to die back. Damage is particularly important to seedlings, which can be killed. Pales weevils lay eggs in stumps of recently killed or cut trees in spring, and larvae mature by midsummer. Peak adult feeding occurs at this time. The presence of suitable cut stumps for larval development, as is found in Christmas tree farms, determines local importance of pales weevil. White, pitch, loblolly, and shortleaf pines are particularly favored, but juniper and other conifers may be damaged.

Adult feeding often is the most commonly observed damage by **pitcheating weevil** (*Pachylobius picivorus*).[2] Adults lay eggs in the soil around newly cut or dying pines, and the larvae develop on the roots. At night the adults fly to adjacent pines and feed on the inner bark of twigs, causing twig dieback. Larval damage to seedling trees occurs when new plantings occur near cut trees.

Larvae of **apple twig borer** (*Amphicerus bicaudatus*)[3] tunnel and girdle twigs of honeylocust, apple, grape, ash, and many other woody plants. This insect is a secondary pest in most situations, as larval attacks are restricted to parts of trees previously wounded or diseased and in decline. Adults that emerge in late summer may cut into healthy wood to feed and produce winter shelters. Adults are cylindrical-shaped, brown beetles about ¼ inch long. In spring they cut into the bark of twigs to lay eggs. The grublike larvae tunnel the twig as they develop, restricting feeding primarily to the pith and packing their tunnels with sawdust frass. Larvae feed throughout the summer, and most pupate in late fall in the larval tunnel. One generation is produced per season.

Hickory shoot curculio (*Conotrachelus aratus*)[2] develops in the new shoots of hickory and pecan in the eastern U.S. Adults move to trees about the time of bud break, and females make puncture wounds near the base of leaf axils. Eggs are laid in these punctures, and larvae tunnel into the shoots. They feed until midsummer and leave the plants to pupate in soil at the base of trees. Adults emerge in late summer, feed briefly, and move to sheltered spots for overwintering. The closely related **pecan shoot curculio** (*C. schoofi*) damages hickory and pecan in a similar manner. Egg punctures are made below the base of the leaf petioles, and adults feeding in spring on shoots and leaves often cause some leaf curling.

Shoots of grape and Virginia creeper may be damaged similarly in the Northeast and Midwest by **grape cane girdler** (*Ampeloglypter ater*).[2] The shiny black beetle, about ⅛ inch long, cuts a small hole in the cane and lays a single egg. It then chews a girdling cut both above and below where the egg was laid. The shoot subsequently wilts and often drops from the plant. The larva tunnels the shoot and completes its development in it, emerging as an adult in late summer. **Grape cane gallmaker** (*A. sesostris*) develops in a similar manner. Girdling cuts are not made, but a swelling occurs around the site where eggs are laid and shoots are weakened.

Potato stalk borer (*Trichobaris trinotata*)[2] develops in the stems of potato, eggplant, and related nightshade family weeds in many of the southeastern states. Winter is spent in the adult stage, usually in previously infested stems. The adults become active in late spring and chew pits in stems of new plants, laying eggs in some. Larvae hollow out the stems during late spring and early summer, sometimes excavating down to the roots. They are rather elongate, about ½ inch long when mature, and pale yellow. They pupate in a cell made of chewed bits of stalk and transform to adults during the latter half of the summer. Adults are about ⅕-inch-long snout beetles. Most of the body appears grayish because it is covered with fine hairs, and the head is black. The closely related tobacco stalk borer (*T. mucorea*) occasionally damages potato in southern California and Arizona.

A. Pales weevil. *R. S. Cameron.* **B.** Terminal injuries to pine produced by pales weevil. *D. Shetlar.* **C.** Pales weevil. *D. Shetlar.* **D.** Pales weevil (left) and white pine weevil (right). *G. J. Lenhard.* **E.** Pitcheating weevil. *R. L. Anderson.* **F.** Apple twig borer adult. *D. Leatherman.* **G.** Hickory shoot curculio adult. *L. Tedders.* **H.** Grape cane girdler larva. *J. Ogrodnik/NY Agricultural Experiment Station.* **I.** Hickory shoot curculio larva in stem. *J. D. Solomon.* **J.** Hickory shoot curculio larval injury. *L. Tedders.* **K.** Grape cane gallmaker adult. *J. Ogrodnik/NY Agricultural Experiment Station.* **L.** Grape cane girdler adult. *J. Ogrodnik/NY Agricultural Experiment Station.*

Sunflower stem weevil (*Cylindrocopturus adspersus*)[2] is the most important of the many insects that tunnel sunflower stalks in the central U.S. and Prairie Provinces. Adults are about ⅛-inch snout beetles, grayish brown with white spots on the back. They emerge from the soil in June and feed on plants, causing little observable injury. After a few weeks females begin to lay eggs, moving to the lower part of the stalk. Eggs are laid in small niches chewed in the stalk, with most eggs laid by mid-July. Newly hatched larvae tunnel into the stalk, ultimately doing most feeding in the pith. They work their way downward in the plant, and most pupate near the soil line. Feeding and the excavation of small chambers for the larvae to winter in cause weakening, which allows stalks to break.

Twig girdler (*Oncideres cingulata*)[4] produces conspicuous injury to several kinds of trees, although damage is peripheral and not serious to landscape trees. Adults neatly cut straight around the bark of small twigs (less than ⅜ inch in diameter) in September and October. Eggs are laid in the terminal, and larvae develop in the woody center of the plant. The life cycle is completed the following summer, with pupation in mid- to late summer. Hickory, pecan, elm, persimmon, and hackberry are among the most common hosts. Twig girdler is found primarily in the southeastern quadrant of the U.S., but occurs as far north as New England.

Flagging and twig breakage may also result from activity of **twig pruner** (*Elaphidionoides villosus*).[4] Larvae develop in the center of twigs, and at the base of their tunneling they girdle the twig, leaving only the bark. Injured twigs usually drop from the tree, and the larvae continue to develop in the twig. Adults emerge in late April and May. Elm, nut trees, flowering fruit trees, hackberry, maple, linden, honeylocust, and wisteria are among the host plants. A related species in Ontario and the northeastern U.S. is *E. parallelus*, associated with oak and hickory.

The genus *Oberea*[4] contains several species that develop in twigs and canes of woody plants. **Dogwood twig borer** (*O. tripunctata*) develops on viburnum, dogwood, azalea, apple, stone fruits, blueberry, and laurel over a broad area of the eastern U.S. Adults are elongate, yellowish tan beetles, about ½ inch long. Females make a series of punctures along the twig, about 3 to 6 inches from the tip, before laying eggs. The larvae originally tunnel between the punctures, then extend the feeding area by boring through the center of the twig. The life cycle is completed in 1 year in most areas, although it may take 2 years in the north. **Raspberry cane borer** (*O. bimaculata*) produces similar injuries to raspberry, blackberry, elm, hickory, dogwood, fruit trees, and rose in eastern North America. Other *Oberea* species include **sassafras borer** (*O. ruficollis*), **oak sprout oberea** (*O. gracilis*), **poplar twig borer** (*O. delongi*), **sumac stem borer** (*O. ocellata*), and **azalea stem borer** (*Oberea myops*).

[1] Coleoptera: Scolytidae; [2] Coleoptera: Curculionidae; [3] Coleoptera: Bostrichidae; [4] Coleoptera: Cerambycidae

A. Sunflower stem weevil larva. *F. Peairs.* **B.** Adult twig girdler and characteristic damage. *J. D. Solomon.* **C.** Twig pruner adult. *J. D. Solomon.* **D.** Twig girdler damage. *G. J. Lenhard.* **E.** Adult of poplar twig borer and feeding injuries to leaf veins. *J. D. Solomon.* **F.** Dogwood twig borer larva. *D. Shetlar.* **G.** Twig pruner damage. *J. D. Solomon.* **H.** Twig girdler damage. *H. A. Pase III.* **I.** Dogwood twig borer adult. *D. Shetlar.* **J.** Twig punctures produced by adult dogwood twig borer larva. *D. Shetlar.* **K.** Twig pruner larva in tunnel. *J. D. Solomon.* **L.** Larvae and tunneling by poplar twig borer. *J. D. Solomon.* **M.** Stem girdling by adult of sumac stem borer. *J. D. Solomon.*

TWIG-BORING FLIES

Pitch midges[1] develop in pits excavated in new twigs of pine and live in the exuded resin masses. **Gouty pitch midge** (*Cecidomyia resinicola*) causes swellings and malformation of the terminals and death of needles. Larvae are usually gregarious and found in the resin patches at wounds. *C. piniinopis* is often more damaging and occurs throughout the northern U.S. and southern Canada. Larvae develop in pits near the tips of various pines. Multiple injuries often cause girdling that causes tufts of needles to die. Winter is spent as a larva in the shoots and pupation occurs at the base of nearby needles in spring. Multiple generations may be produced.

Twig dieback of juniper grown in the Midwest can be produced by **juniper midge** (*Contarinia juniperina*).[1] Larvae tunnel into the twigs at the base of needles and produce girdling wounds. Damage begins in spring as overwintering larvae in the twigs resume feeding, and several generations may be completed annually. Junipers most commonly damaged include Andorra, blue rug, and *Juniperus chinensis*.

Among the many insects that tunnel stems of sunflower is **sunflower maggot** (*Strauzia longipennis*).[2] *Helichrysum* species may also be damaged. Heavily infested plants are weakened, and stems may break.

Raspberry cane maggot (*Pegomya rubivora*)[3] can be a common insect affecting raspberry and (rarely) rose and blackberry. Adults are about ¼-inch gray flies that lay eggs in spring on the tips of rapidly growing canes. The larvae tunnel into the pith of the cane and produce a girdling cut just underneath the bark. The tips rapidly wilt and die beyond this injury, often dropping from the plant. The larvae continue to tunnel downward, usually pupating in the lower part of the cane. One generation is produced annually, with winter spent in the pupal stage.

[1] Diptera: Cecidomyiidae; [2] Diptera: Tephritidae; [3] Diptera: Anthomyiidae

A. Pitch midge larvae in pine terminal. *J. W. Brewer.* **B.** Pitch midge larvae and pupae. *J. W. Brewer.* **C.** Pitch midge pupa. *K. Gray.* **D.** Pitch midge adult. *K. Gray.* **E.** Pitch midge eggs in pine terminal growth. *K. Gray.* **F.** Dieback of terminal caused by pitch midge feeding injuries. *K. Gray.* **G.** Pitch midge larvae. *K. Gray.* **H.** Pitch mass resulting from larval feeding of pitch midge. *K. Gray.* **I.** Sunflower maggot adult. *F. Peairs.*

CHAPTER NINE

Trunk and Branch Borers

HORNTAILS

The horntails (Siricidae family)[1] are large, thick-bodied wasps that develop as wood borers in recently killed and dying trees. Females are stingless but possess stout spinelike ovipositors used to insert eggs under bark. All horntails have a mutualistic association with wood-rotting fungi which are introduced during egg-laying and help provide food for the grublike young.

Pigeon Tremex (*Tremex columba*)

Hosts: Many hardwood trees including maple, beech, hickory, elm, oak, apple, pear, sycamore, and hackberry. Maple and beech are preferred.

Damage: Larvae develop as wood borers, creating meandering tunnels that can increase susceptibility to wind breakage. However, damage is confined to dead or dying wood. Adults may spread wood-rotting fungi. Their bizarre appearance often attracts attention.

Distribution: Throughout the U.S. and southern Canada, west to the Rockies. Isolated populations are reported from Arizona and southern California.

Appearance: Pigeon tremex is a large (1½ to 2 inches) thick-bodied wasp. Females have a spikelike, dark brown ovipositor. Males, which are smaller, lack the projection. Adults are generally brown and yellowish, with patterning varying among different races throughout the range.

Life History and Habits: Adults are most commonly present in late summer, searching and probing recently killed and declining trees for egg-laying sites. As they probe trees, they also introduce a white rot fungus, *Cerrina (= Daedalea) unicolor*, which rots and softens the wood for the developing larvae. Larvae feed for the next 8 to 9 months on the wood and fungi, creating tunnels that run through the heartwood. When full grown they create a pupal chamber just under the bark. The emerging adults cut through the bark, leaving a perfectly round exit hole. There is one generation per year over much of the range; the life cycle may take 2 years to complete in northern areas.

Other Horntails

Several other horntails occur in North America. The most abundant are *Sirex* species, blue-black wasps that develop in dead or dying conifers. Five species of *Urocerus,* which develop in recently killed fir and pine, also occur in North America. All horntails transmit white rot fungus and thus can be important pests of felled timber.

[1] Hymenoptera: Siricidae

A. Pigeon tremex tunnels. *J. D. Solomon.* **B.** Pigeon tremex horntail, male. *D. Shetlar.* **C.** Pigeon tremex ovipositing. *W. Cranshaw.* **D.** Circular exit holes of pigeon tremex and other horntails. *J. D. Solomon.* **E.** *Urocerus gigas* adult. *E. H. Holsten.* **F.** Horntail adult emerging from trunk. *D. Shetlar.* **G.** *Urocerus gigas* larva. *E. H. Holsten.* **H.** Pigeon tremex ovipositing. *W. Cranshaw.* **I.** Blue horntail. *K. Gray.*

CLEARWING BORERS

Clearwing borers (Sesiidae family)[1] are moderate-sized, day-flying moths that develop as borers, primarily in trees and shrubs. Appearance of the adults often mimics wasps or bees, and large areas of the forewings may be absent scales, hence the name "clearwing." Larvae are usually pale cream colored and found in the tunnels they gouge in trunks and stems. The presence along the abdomen of five pairs of small prolegs, each ending in a semicircular pattern of small hooks, can differentiate clearwing borers from borer larvae that are beetles (e.g., roundheaded borers, flatheaded borers).

Squash Vine Borer (*Melitta cucurbitae*)

Hosts: Summer squash and winter squash or pumpkin among *Cucurbita maxima*. Other squash family plants are infrequently damaged.

Damage: Larvae tunnel into stems at the base of the plant. Coarse yellowish frass occurs in the stems, and rotting organisms often invade. Affected plants frequently wilt and die.

Distribution: Primarily found in the U.S. east of the High Plains, including the southern U.S.

Appearance: Larvae are white with a brown head and wrinkled body and are found in the stems at the base of the plant. Adult moths are wasplike with metallic dark green forewings with a wingspan of about 1½ inches. The hindwings are transparent, and the legs are marked with feathery black and orange hairs.

Life History and Habits: Squash vine borer spends the winter in a cocoon in soil, either as a full-grown larva or pupa. Adults may begin to emerge in midspring and are usually present as host plants begin to become established in late spring. The moths are active daytime fliers and glue their small, dull red eggs to the base of the plant, at leaf axils, on the undersides of leaves, and on soil near the plant. Larvae bore into the base of the plant and feed for more than a month, migrating toward the base. When full grown they exit, burrow into the soil, and pupate in a dark brown cocoon mixed with soil. A second generation is common in the southern area of the range, with eggs laid during the latter half of summer.

Lilac/Ash (or Ash/Lilac) Borer (*Podosesia syringae*)

Hosts: Most ash species, particularly green and white ash. Lilac and privet are other reported hosts.

Damage: Larvae create rough gouging wounds under the bark and may riddle wood to a depth of about 2 inches. Injuries are concentrated in the lower 12 feet of the trunk and larger branches. Gnarled swellings form at areas of repeated attack, and sucker growth often increases. On smaller diameter branches, as are common on lilac and privet, larval injuries may girdle and kill main stems. On lilac, older stems are preferred over young stems.

Distribution: Native to North America, lilac/ash borer has extended its range to include most areas where ash is grown.

Appearance: Adults are mimics of paper wasps, quite similar in both size and color. The larvae are creamy white grubs with a small dark head. Prolegs on the abdomen are highly reduced, but small hooklike crochets are present at the tip of the prolegs, which allows separation from the roundheaded borers that are also associated with ash (p. 484).

A. Peachtree borer in base of tree. *E. Nelson.* **B.** Mating pair of currant borers. *W. Cranshaw.* **C.** Underside of peachtree borer, showing hooked crochets on base of prolegs. *W. Cranshaw.* **D.** Squash vine borer adult. *J. Capinera.* **E.** Squash vine borer larva. *W. Cranshaw.* **F.** Lilac/ash borer larvae in trunk. *D. Leatherman.* **G.** Wilting of squash vines caused by squash vine borer injury. *D. Shetlar.* **H.** Pupal skins of lilac/ash borer extruded from trunk. *D. Leatherman.* **I.** Mating pair of lilac/ash borers. *W. Cranshaw.*

Life History and Habits: Lilac/ash borer spends the winter as a partially grown larva in tunnels under the bark. It resumes feeding and larval development in early spring, pupating just under a thin cover of bark. The adults are brown and black clearwing borers that superficially resemble paper wasps in both size and color. Adult emergence may begin by early April during warm springs but usually is later and may extend for several weeks with cool overcast weather. Warm temperatures (above 60⁰ F) and sunny conditions appear critical for adult emergence, which takes place during morning. Frequently the old pupal skin is only partially extruded from the emergence hole and remains attached to the tree until it weathers. Adults are active for about 4 to 6 weeks after initial emergence, and females subsequently lay eggs on bark, typically near wounds or bark cracks. Eggs hatch in about 1½ weeks. Larvae tunnel into the cambium and phloem and may move an inch or more into the trunk, making irregular vertical galleries.

Related Species

Banded ash clearwing (*Podosesia aureocincta*) is a closely related species found in scattered areas of the eastern U.S. It is physically very similar in appearance to lilac/ash borer, differing in having two distinct bands on the abdomen. Banded ash clearwing produces similar feeding injuries but has a different life history, with adults emerging in late summer.

Peachtree (or Crown) Borer (*Synanthedon exitiosa*)

Hosts: Peach, cherry, plum, and most other *Prunus* species.

Damage: Larvae burrow into the base of trees, producing gouging wounds. Girdling injuries weaken and may kill trees, particularly smaller trees.

Distribution: Generally throughout North America.

Appearance: The adult male is bluish black with yellow bands on the body and has wings that are largely clear of scales except along the edge. Females have dusky-colored forewings and possess a broad orange band across the abdomen.

Life History and Habits: Adults emerge over an extended period that may range from late spring through early fall, but peak activity is typically during July and August. Females lay eggs on the bark of the lower trunk or on soil and weeds adjacent to it. Eggs hatch in about a week, and the larvae immediately burrow through the bark into the sapwood of the tree. Tunneling under the bark continues until late fall, with the insects mining down the trunk as cold weather approaches. With warmer weather, larvae resume feeding. Pupation occurs in a cocoon coated with excreted wood fragments, gum, and soil particles, usually just beneath the soil at the base of the trunk. Adults emerge in about 3 weeks.

Related Species

Lesser peachtree borer (*Synanthedon pictipes*) is found in much of eastern North America. It is particularly damaging to peach and plum, occasionally infesting other stone fruits. Unlike in peachtree borer, its larvae develop throughout the trunk and on larger scaffold branches, usually near previous wounds and cankers. Two generations are produced per year.

¹ Lepidoptera: Sesiidae

A. Banded ash clearwing adult. *D. Nielsen.* **B.** Frass kicked out of tunnels by banded ash clearwing borer larva. *D. Shetlar.* **C.** Peachtree borer damage at base of plum and old pupal cell. *W. Cranshaw.* **D.** Lesser peachtree borer adult. *D. Shetlar.* **E.** Peachtree borer eggs on bark. *K. Gray.* **F.** Mating pair of peachtree borers. *H. C. Ellis.* **G.** Peachtree borer damage at base of young tree. *J. D. Solomon.* **H.** Peachtree borer, male. *W. Cranshaw.* **I.** Peachtree borer female. *W. Cranshaw.* **J.** Peachtree borer larva. *Courtesy Clemson University.*

Some Common Clearwing Borers of North America

Scientific Name	Common Name	Host, Comments
Albuna fraxini	Virginiacreeper clearwing	Virginia creeper
Carmenta anthracipennis		Liatris. Eastern states
Carmenta corni		Aster. Eastern states
Paranthene asilipennis	Oak clearwing moth	Oak, particularly red oak. Occasionally ash and alder
Paranthene dollii	Cottonwood clearwing borer	Poplar, willow
Paranthene robiniae	Western poplar clearwing	Poplar, willow, birch. Western U.S. and Canada
Paranthene simulans	Red oak clearwing borer	Most oaks, American chestnut
Pennisetia marginata	Raspberry crown borer	Raspberry, blackberry, other *Rubus* spp.
Penstemonia clarkei		Penstemon. Western states
Sannia uroceriformis	Persimmon borer	Persimmon. Southeastern U.S.
Sesia apiformis	Hornet moth	Poplar, willow. Introduced; established in Northeast and California
Sesia tibialis	Cottonwood crown borer/ poplar clearwing/American hornet moth	Poplar, willow. Widely distributed in northern states and Canada
Synanthedon bibionipennis	Strawberry crown borer	Strawberry. Upper Midwest primarily
Synanthedon novaroensis	Douglas-fir pitch moth	Spruce, Douglas-fir, some pine. Pacific Coast region
Synanthedon pini	Pitch mass borer	White, Scotch, and mugho pine; occasionally spruce. Northeastern U.S. and southeastern Canada
Synanthedon pyri	Apple bark borer	Apple, hawthorn, pear
Synanthedon resplendens	Sycamore borer	Oak, sycamore, avocado, ceanothus. Southwest
Synanthedon rhododendri	Rhododendron borer	Rhododendron, less common on mountain laurel and azalea. Eastern states
Synanthedon scitula	Dogwood borer	Primarily dogwood and pecan. Many other deciduous trees and shrubs are occasional hosts. Throughout eastern U.S.
Synanthedon sequoiae	Sequoia pitch moth	Pine, particularly Monterey pine. Pacific states and British Columbia
Synanthedon tipuliformis	Currant borer	Currant, gooseberry
Synanthedon viburni	Viburnum clearwing borer	Viburnum. Widely distributed east of Rockies
Vitacea polistiformis	Grape root borer	Grape

A. Raspberry crown borer adult. *K. Gray.* **B.** Raspberry crown borer larva in base of plant. *K. Gray.* **C.** Sequoia pitch moth. *K. Gray.* **D.** Wound produced by sequoia pitch moth larva. *K. Gray.* **E.** Currant borer adult. *W. Cranshaw.* **F.** Currant borer larvae in stem. *K. Gray.* **G.** Male dogwood borer next to pupal skin. *D. Shetlar.* **H.** Mating pair of grape root borers. *R. Bessin.* **I.** Western poplar clearwing borer larva in stem. *J. D. Solomon.* **J.** Adult oak clearwing. *D. Shetlar.* **K.** Western poplar clearwing borer. *J. D. Solomon.* **L.** Adult rhododendron borer. *D. Shetlar.* **M.** Viburnum clearwing borer adult. *J. Capinera.* **N.** Strawberry crown borer adult. *K. Gray.* **O.** Larval tunneling injuries by rhododendron borer. *D. Shetlar.* **P.** Grape root borer larvae in base of plant. *H. C. Ellis.* **Q.** Strawberry crown borer larva. *K. Gray.* **R.** Dogwood borer larva and injury at base of trunk. *J. D. Solomon.* **S.** Pupal skin of currant borer extruded from stem. *K. Gray.* **T.** Raspberry crown borer larva in base of plant. *J. Capinera.*

CARPENTERWORMS

Carpenterworms (Cossidae family)[1] are caterpillars that develop as borers in various trees and shrubs. Some 45 species occur in North America, but only a few are considered significant pest species.

Carpenterworm (*Prionoxystus robiniae*)

Hosts: A wide host range of hardwoods, with oak, elm, ash, and poplar most consistently damaged.

Damage: Larvae excavate large cavelike galleries into the sapwood and heartwood of trunks and large branches. Heavily infested trees may break in high winds, and chronically infested trees appear gnarled and misshapen. Unlike in most other wood borers, the larvae maintain an exterior opening through which they continually expel sawdust. Large exit holes and flaking of bark occur along damaged areas of trees.

Distribution: Generally throughout the U.S. and southern Canada.

Appearance: The larvae are pinkish white caterpillars with a dark head and dark brown tubercles on the body. They are large, up to 3 inches long at maturity. Adults are large, heavy-bodied moths, somewhat resembling sphinx moths (p. 146). They have grayish forewings, mottled with black.

Life History and Habits: Carpenterworms winter as larvae in the tunnels produced in infested trees. Pupation occurs in spring, and adult moths appear around May. Often the purplish pupal case remains extruded from the exit hole until it has weathered. Eggs are laid in clusters in bark crevices or near wounds. After egg hatch the larvae bore directly into the phloem and cambium just under the bark. Early signs are small damp spots on the bark. They later extend tunnels into the sapwood and ultimately the heartwood. Typically they form a central cavity with side tunnels that may extend for several inches. Sawdust is regularly ejected and may conspicuously collect around the base of infested trees. Carpenterworm has a fairly long life cycle, ranging from 1 to 2 years in southern areas and 3 to 4 years in the north.

Other Carpenterworms

Leopard moth (*Zeuzera pyrina*), found in the northeastern states, nearly rivals carpenterworm in size. Young larvae tunnel twigs and small branches but leave when they get too large. External evidence of tunneling is obvious, with wood chips and excrement being pushed to the outside as the larvae feed. A wide range of hardwood trees are hosts. Development requires 2 years to complete. Eggs may be laid from late spring through September.

Pecan carpenterworm (*Cossula magnifica*) occurs in the southern states and appears to complete its life cycle in a single year. Pecan, oak, and hickory are hosts. As the caterpillars feed, they continually push sawdust from feeding sites. Eggs are laid in May and June. Affecting *Populus* species are two species, **poplar carpenterworm** (*Acossus centerensis*), which is primarily eastern, and **aspen carpenterworm** (*A. populi*), more broadly distributed throughout North America.

[1] Lepidoptera: Cossidae

A. Adult of carpenterworm. *D. Shetlar.* **B.** Carpenterworm larva. *W. Cranshaw.* **C.** Carpenterworm larva in trunk. *E. Nelson.* **D.** Pupa of carpenterworm. *D. Shetlar.* **E.** Carpenterworm in different life history stages. *G. J. Lenhard.* **F.** Carpenterworm galleries. *J. D. Solomon.* **G.** Aspen carpenterworm adult. *J. D. Solomon.* **H.** Leopard moth adult. *J. D. Solomon.* **I.** Pecan carpenterworm entrance hole with frass. *J. D. Solomon.* **J.** Pecan carpenterworm larva. *J. D. Solomon.* **K.** Pecan carpenterworm tunnels. *J. D. Solomon.*

PYRALID BORERS

A few pyralid moths (Pyralidae family),[1] including some serious woody plant borers, develop as borers in plants. Many others tunnel twigs and smaller branches (p. 438).

Zimmerman Pine Moth (*Dioryctria zimmermani*)

Hosts: Pine, particularly Scotch and Austrian pines.

Damage: Larvae tunnel under the bark, typically at crotches of branches. Branches may break or die directly from effects of the girdling. Infestations are commonly marked by dead and dying branches, often in the upper half of the tree. External symptoms of injury are popcorn-like pitch masses at the wound site.

Distribution: Most common in midwestern and Great Lakes states but is present from eastern Colorado to New England.

Appearance: The adults, rarely observed, are midsized moths with gray wings blended with red-brown and marked with zigzag lines. Larvae are generally dirty white caterpillars, occasionally with some pink or green coloration. They are found in characteristic popcorn-like masses of sap on trunks and branches.

Life History and Habits: Zimmerman pine moth has a 1-year life cycle. The insect overwinters as a very young caterpillar inside a small cocoon (hibernaculum) underneath scales of bark. In mid- to late April and May it again becomes active and tunnels into the tree. Tunneling typically occurs at pre-existing wounds or at the junction of the trunk and branch. (Rarely, tips may also be infested.) Initial tunneling may result in sawdust and pitch at the entry site, although these are difficult to detect in early stages. The larvae continue to feed into July and early August, at which time large amounts of pitch are produced. Prior to pupation they gouge out large areas under the bark, leaving a thin bark flap, and pupate just underneath this.

Adult moths are active primarily in late July and August. After mating, female moths lay eggs, often near wounds or previous masses of pitch. Eggs hatch in about a week and the larvae move immediately, without feeding, to protected sites on the bark where they overwinter in the hibernaculum.

Other Pyralid Borers

Dioryctria ponderosae, sometimes known as **pinyon pitch mass borer**, is found in the High Plains and Rocky Mountain regions of the U.S. Pinyon growing in overirrigated sites is most commonly damaged; ponderosa pine is also affected. Irregular wounds under the bark are produced, at which a creamy or slightly pinkish ooze mixes with frass.

American plum borer (*Euzophera semifuneralis*) is a minor pest of fruit trees, occasionally damaging various nut and shade trees. It is associated mostly with stressed trees or existing wounds, including poor pruning cuts. It is found primarily throughout the eastern U.S., but is known as far west as Arizona. Most tunneling occurs in the lower 4 feet of the trunk and almost always originates near previous wounds. The larvae are grayish green to grayish purple and pupate in a silken cocoon, often under bark flaps. In the upper Midwest, most eggs are laid in May.

Blue cactus borer (*Melitara dentata*) develops in prickly pear cactus in the western U.S. Larvae are vivid dark blue color caterpillars that tunnel into the cactus pad, producing large amounts of frass.

[1] Lepidoptera: Pyralidae

A. Trunk breakage caused by Zimmerman pine moth injury. *W. Cranshaw.* **B.** Zimmerman pine moth. *W. Cranshaw.* **C.** Zimmerman pine moth larva. *D. Shetlar.* **D.** Characteristic popcorn-like ooze at wound of Zimmerman pine moth. *W. Cranshaw.* **E.** Zimmerman pine moth pupa in branch. *D. Shetlar.* **F.** Pinyon pitch mass borer larva. *W. Cranshaw.* **G.** Pinyon pitch mass borer wound. *W. Cranshaw.* **H.** American plum borer larva in trunk. *J. D. Solomon.* **I.** American plum borer larva. *J. Ogrodnik/NY Agricultural Experiment Station.* **J.** Pinyon pitch mass borer wound. *W. Cranshaw.* **K.** Blue cactus borer larva. *J. Capinera.*

NOCTUID BORERS

The cutworm family (Noctuidae)[1] contains some species that develop as borers in plant stems. Others tunnel fruit (p. 262), and many others are important as cutworms (p. 134).

Iris Borer (*Macronocutua onusta*)

Hosts: Iris.

Damage: Larvae feed at the base of leaves and hollow out the rhizomes. Wound areas are frequently colonized by rots, and plants may be killed.

Distribution: Northeastern quadrant of the U.S. and southeastern Canada. May be locally distributed elsewhere through movement of infested plant material.

Appearance: Larvae are pale pink with a distinct brown head and may reach 1½ inches when full grown. The adults, rarely observed, are dull brown moths.

Life History and Habits: Winter is spent as eggs laid the previous season among old leaves or nearby crop debris. Larvae hatch in late spring and initially tunnel into emergent leaves, producing small pinholes and leaf mines. As they continue to develop, they move to the base of the leaf sheath, causing wilting and a bleeding symptom in the rhizome. They typically become full grown in midsummer and tunnel into the soil. Adults subsequently emerge and mate, and females may lay eggs in a series of small clusters.

Other Noctuid Borers

Elder shoot borer (*Achatodes zeae*) tunnels into the new canes of elderberry, particularly golden elder. The larvae are generally yellowish caterpillars with dark bands at the head end. Overwintering eggs, laid as masses around old canes, hatch when new shoots emerge, and larvae feed on unfolding leaves before tunneling shoots. Following larval development in the canes, pupation may occur in the damaged shoot but often occurs in the pithy center of dead, dry branches or on the ground. Adults emerge in July, and females lay eggs that remain dormant through winter.

Stalk borer (*Papaipema nebris*) is a native insect found primarily in the northeastern quadrant of the U.S. and southeastern Canada. Eggs are laid during summer on grasses and various weeds and hatch the following spring. Larvae develop as borers in stems of a wide variety of plants. Young caterpillars are distinctly marked with light stripes running along the generally brown or pinkish brown body; older larvae are more faded. There is one generation per year.

Two species with habits generally similar to those of stalk borer are **potato stem borer** (*Hydraecia micacea*) and **hop vine borer** (*H. immanis*). Both lay eggs among grasses in late summer, and eggs hatch in early spring. Larvae originally develop in grasses, later moving into nearby plants. Potato stem borer is a European native that has spread through much of eastern Canada and is known to damage corn, potato, raspberry, rhubarb, onion, and hops. Hop vine borer is more common in the northern U.S. and has a host range more limited to grasses (including corn) and hops. Larvae are whitish with pale reddish to purple stripes and can be distinguished by the head color: brown in hop vine borer, yellow in potato stem borer.

In the southeastern states, ranging to parts of Texas, **convict caterpillar** (*Xanthopastis timais*) develops on the rhizomes, bulbs, and foliage of various lilies. The adult form, known as **Spanish moth**, has a black body and wings patterned with black and yellow-orange on a rosy background. Eggs are laid in masses, and the larvae originally feed as a group on foliage. Multiple generations can be produced throughout the year when temperatures permit.

---

[1] Lepidoptera: Noctuidae

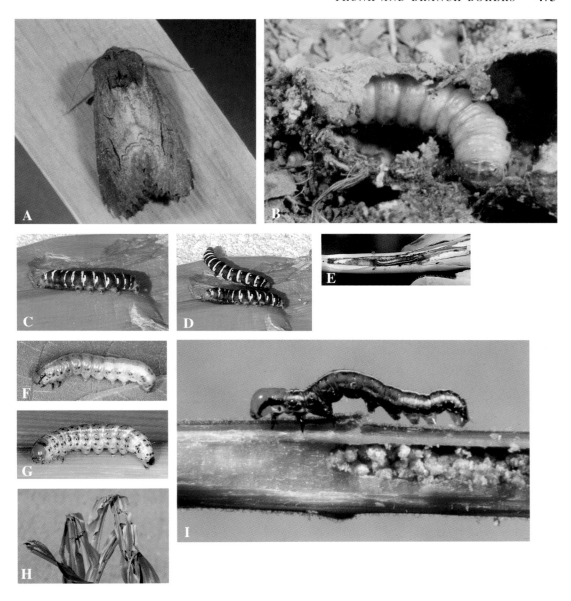

A. Iris borer, adult. *D. Shetlar.* **B.** Iris borer larva in base of iris. *D. Shetlar.* **C.** Convict caterpillar. *T. DelValle.*
D. Convict caterpillars. *T. DelValle.* **E.** Stalk borer in corn stalk. *M. E. Rice.* **F.** Late instar stalk borer. *M. E. Rice.*
G. Hop vine borer. *M. E. Rice.* **H.** Corn leaf injury resulting from stalk borer tunneling. *M. E. Rice.* **I.** Stalk borer
larva. *D. Shetlar.*

METALLIC WOOD BORERS/FLATHEADED BORERS

The metallic wood borers (Buprestidae family)[1] are elongate, slightly flattened beetles with a metallic sheen. Larvae are known as flathead borers because the first segment of the thorax (prothorax) is greatly enlarged. Legs are extremely reduced as the larvae tunnel under bark or in wood. Characteristic tunnels produced by most species are zigzag and filled with tightly packed, fine sawdust excrement. Almost all of the nearly 700 North American species develop in recently dead or dying trees and shrubs.

Bronze Birch Borer (*Agrilus anxius*)

Hosts: Birch; European white birch and Jacquemonti birch are particularly susceptible.

Damage: Larvae develop by tunneling the cambium layer, under the bark. Girdling injuries first cause limb dieback, with thinning of the crown an early symptom of infestation. Trees frequently are killed following sustained infestation. Birch grown in suboptimal sites, especially where periodic drought stress may occur, are most commonly infested.

Distribution: Throughout the range of birch in southern Canada and the northern half of the U.S.

Appearance: The adults are elongate, somewhat flattened beetles from ¼ to ⅓ inch long. Overall coloration is olive black with coppery reflections. The elongate larvae are creamy white with the first thoracic segment enlarged and flattened in a manner typical of flathead borers.

Life History and Habits: Adults emerge in late May or early June, cutting a D-shaped opening through the bark. They feed on leaves for 1 to 2 weeks before eggs mature. Females lay eggs in bark crevices, around curls of bark, or in other protected sites, primarily on the unshaded sides of trunks and branches. During the initial phases of attack, most egg-laying is concentrated in the upper crown on branches less than 1 inch in diameter. Larger branches and ultimately the trunk are attacked as infestations progress. Eggs hatch in about 2 weeks, and the larvae tunnel into the cambium where they spend most of their life, rarely moving into the xylem. Larval galleries often have a zigzag pattern and are packed with fine sawdust frass. Trees that overgrow these wounds with callous tissue may show evidence of tunneling as raised lumps, externally visible on bark. Mature larvae overwinter and pupate early in the spring. There is usually one generation per year; 2 years may be required in northern areas to complete the life cycle.

A. Metallic wood borer of genus *Buprestis*. *D. Leatherman*. **B.** Tracks of *Agrilus* flatheaded borer made under bark of aspen. *D. Leatherman*. **C.** Callousing on birch bark from response to wounding by bronze birch borer larval tunneling. *W. Cranshaw*. **D.** Bronze birch borer adult on trunk. *W. Cranshaw*. **E.** Tunnels produced by bronze birch borer larva. *K. Gray*. **F.** Crown thinning caused by bronze birch borer infestation. *W. Cranshaw*. **G.** Bronze birch borer. *W. Cranshaw*. **H.** Exit hole made by bronze birch borer. *W. Cranshaw*. **I.** Bronze birch borer pupa. *D. G. Nielsen*. **J.** Bronze birch borer pupa. *K. Gray*. **K.** Bronze birch borer larva and injury. *K. Gray*. **L.** Bronze birch borer larva. *K. Gray*.

Related Species

Approximately 25 species of *Agrilus* occur in North America. Adults are fairly small (¼ to ½ inch), elongate beetles and are a metallic bronze, green, or blue color. Larvae damage plants by making zigzag or spiraling tunnels under the bark. The life cycle is completed in a single year under normal conditions, with the nearly full-grown larva as the overwintering stage.

Twolined chestnut borer (*Agrilus bilineatus*), which develops in oak and chestnut, is particularly damaging to trees previously stressed by defoliation by gypsy moth or other causes. It is widely distributed over much of the eastern half of North America, south to Georgia. Adults emerge from trees in early June and intersperse feeding on leaves of the host and other hardwoods with egg-laying and mating. Adults are bluish black with a pale, rather indistinct stripe running the length of each wing cover.

Rose stem girdler (*Agrilus aureus*), also known as **bronze cane borer**, is an introduced species now found over a broad area of the northern U.S. extending westward into Utah. Raspberry, currant, and rose are the primary hosts. Larvae make spiraling tunnels under the bark, girdling canes and causing dieback. Adults may emerge by mid-May. Wing covers and pronotum are coppery overall, sometimes with a slight greenish tinge.

Rednecked cane borer (*Agrilus ruficollis*) develops in blackberry, raspberry, and dewberry in the eastern U.S. and Canada. External evidence of tunneling typically involves a longitudinal splitting of the bark and an irregular swelling of the cane. A metallic coppery, reddish, or brassy thorax and a black head mark this species.

Honeylocust borer (*Agrilus difficilis*) has become increasingly important with the extensive planting of its host, honeylocust, as a common street tree. Tunneling is usually restricted to larger branches and the trunk and is concentrated in areas of the tree affected by cankers or wounds. Honeylocust borer is known from New Jersey to Michigan, south to Georgia, and west to Texas and Colorado. Adults are metallic black with greenish or purplish tints. Adult beetles emerge over an extended time and have been observed from May through September.

Oak twig girdler (*Agrilus angelicus*) develops in the twigs and small branches of oak, particularly California live oak. It is found throughout California but is most commonly damaging in the south. Larvae have prominent constrictions between each segment. Adults are dark brownish copper. Two years are required to complete the life cycle.

Poplar, cottonwood, and aspen are hosts for **bronze poplar borer** (*Agrilus granulatus liragus*), **granulate poplar borer** (*A. g. granulatus*), and **western poplar agrilus** (*A. g. populi*), found in northern, southern, and western North America, respectively. **Common willow agrilus** (*A. politus*) is found in branches of maple and willow throughout North America. **Sinuate peartree borer** (*A. sinuatus*) is a European species now established in parts of the mid-Atlantic states where it damages pear. A newly identified species that has been seriously damaging to ash is **emerald ash borer** (*A. planipennis*), currently restricted to a small area of Ohio and to the Detroit area. Intensive efforts are being made to eradicate it.

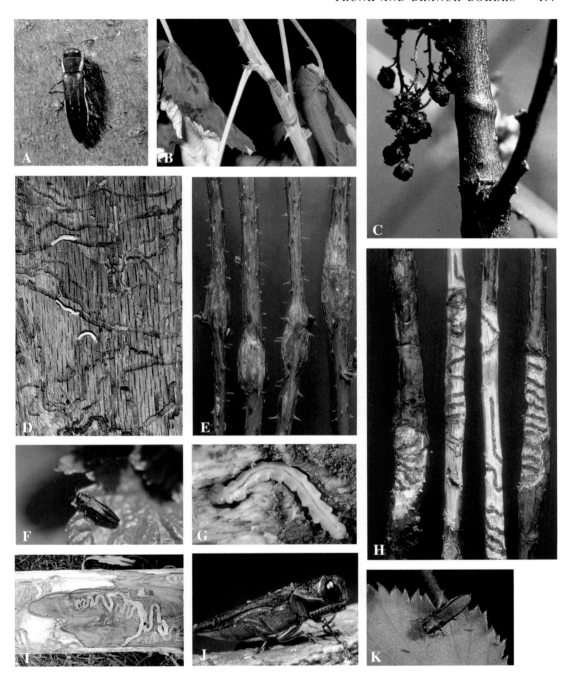

A. Twolined chestnut borer. *D. Shetlar.* **B.** Damage to raspberry cane by larval tunneling of rednecked cane borer. *R. Bessin.* **C.** Stem swelling at wound by bronze cane borer. *W. Cranshaw.* **D.** Galleries produced by twolined chestnut borer larvae. *J. D. Solomon.* **E.** Swellings of raspberry canes in response to injury by rednecked cane borer larvae. *J. D. Solomon.* **F.** Bronze cane borer adult. *W. Cranshaw.* **G.** Emerald ash borer larva. *D. Caeppert.* **H.** Galleries produced by rednecked cane borer in boysenberry canes. *J. D. Solomon.* **I.** Larval galleries produced by emerald ash borer. *D. Caeppert.* **J.** Emerald ash borer. *D. Caeppert.* **K.** Adult rednecked cane borer. *R. Bessin.*

Flatheaded Appletree Borer (*Chrysobothris femorata*)

Hosts: A wide range of food plants including most deciduous fruit, forest, and shade trees and shrubs. Maple and apple are among the more common hosts.

Damage: Larvae tunnel under the bark of trunks and larger branches, producing broad galleries that are tightly packed with fine sawdust frass. Areas of bark where injury has occurred often appear darkened, somewhat sunken, and may later split above the injury. On young trees, tunneling may girdle and kill the plant; tunnels are more restricted in area on established trees. Injuries are concentrated on the sunny side and most commonly occur on trees suffering from sunscald, wounds, or drought stress.

Distribution: Throughout the U.S. and southern Canada but common in the eastern and central states.

Appearance: Adults are dark olive-gray to brown metallic wood borers, about ½ inch long. Larvae are pale yellow, legless, with an enlarged prothorax.

Life History and Habits: Winter is spent as larvae under the bark. They complete development the following spring, cut a chamber into the sapwood, and pupate. Adults may begin emerging by mid-spring, but peak activity is from late May through June. The females may be observed searching the sun-exposed sides of trunks of host trees. Eggs are laid singly in bark cracks or near existing injuries, and over the course of a month about 100 eggs may be laid. Eggs hatch within 8 to 16 days, and the larvae chew through the bottom of the egg and begin to tunnel into the tree. Larval development can be rapid and gallery formation extensive in low-vigor trees. Development is retarded (and tunneling more restricted) in trees of high vigor. The larvae continue to feed for several months, becoming dormant during the cold season. There is one generation per year.

Related Species

Pacific flatheaded borer (*Chrysobothris mali*) predominates west of the Rockies, **flatheaded appletree borer** to the east. Biologies of the two species are similar. Pacific flatheaded borer is damaging to newly planted trees and shrubs and those damaged by sunscald.

Other Flatheaded Borers

Hemlock borer (*Melanophila fulvoguttata*) is associated with hemlock and, less commonly, other conifers in eastern North America. It is generally considered a secondary pest but can damage trees previously stressed by insects or other causes. Adults are black, elongate beetles, usually with three yellow spots on each wing cover. Adult activity occurs over an extended period, from May through August. Development of larvae in trees takes 1 or 2 years, with larvae produced from eggs laid later in summer having the more extended life history.

[1] Coleoptera: Buprestidae

A. Flatheaded appletree borer adult. *D. Shetlar.* **B.** Flatheaded appletree borer larva. *D. Shetlar.* **C.** Flatheaded appletree borer emerging from trunk. *D. Shetlar.* **D.** Flatheaded appletree borer emerging from trunk. *D. Shetlar.* **E.** Pacific flatheaded borer pupa. *K. Gray.* **F.** Adult Pacific flatheaded borer. *K. Gray.*

LONGHORNED BEETLES/ROUNDHEADED BORERS

The longhorned beetle family (Cerambycidae)[1] includes some of the most visually striking beetles. Most are fairly large, and the most massive of all North American insects are found in this group. Color can be variable, with some species dully colored brown or gray and others brightly colored. Very long antennae, sometimes exceeding the body length, are characteristic of most species. Larvae, known as roundheaded borers, develop by producing riddling tunnels through wood, producing oval galleries in cross section. Legs are highly reduced, and the body is relatively uniformly cylindrical, although slightly constricted at most segments. More than 900 species are known from North America, but very few seriously damage living trees. Most are associated only with nearly dead or recently killed trees and shrubs.

Locust Borer (*Megacyllene robiniae*)

Hosts: Black locust.

Damage: Larvae develop in trunks, causing deep tunneling that may riddle the plant and produce serious structural weakening.

Distribution: Expanding. It currently includes much of North America, excluding some Pacific states and southern Florida. Locust borer is common in black locust stands.

Appearance: The adult is a colorful, generally black beetle marked with yellow cross bands on the thorax and W-shaped bands on the wing covers. It is about ¾ inch in length with antennae nearly as long as the body. The larvae, about 1 inch long when full grown, are robust, cream-colored, legless grubs with a brown heads.

Life History and Habits: Adults are active in late summer and early fall, considerably later than most longhorned beetles. At this time they are commonly seen feeding on the pollen of goldenrod and other yellow flowers. Concurrently, eggs are deposited in cracks and crevices in the bark of host trees. Larvae hatch in late fall, bore into bark, and construct small hibernation cells for overwintering. They resume activity in the spring and tunnel extensively through heartwood. The larvae mature in the latter part of July. There is one generation per year.

Related Species

Some very attractive *Megacyllene* species commonly develop in recently killed trees. **Painted hickory borer** (*M. caryae*) occurs throughout the eastern U.S. and is associated with various nut trees, black locust, locust, mulberry, and ash. Acacia and mesquite host **mesquite borer** (*M. antennatus*) in the southwestern states. Although adults may be observed visiting flowers and emerging from firewood or recently cut lumber, they are not damaging to healthy trees.

A. Adult spotted pine sawyer. *D. Leatherman.* **B.** Locust borer on goldenrod. *R. L. Anderson.* **C.** Typical trunk riddling produced by roundheaded borer. *D. Leatherman.* **D.** Close-up of head of a roundheaded borer. *W. Cranshaw.* **E.** Painted hickory borer. *D. Shetlar.* **F.** Locust borer. *D. Leatherman.* **G.** Life stages of locust borer. *J. D. Solomon.* **H.** Locust borer larvae in trunk. *D. Leatherman.* **I.** Riddling of trunk caused by tunneling of locust borer. *D. Leatherman.*

Roundheaded Appletree Borer (*Saperda candida*)

Hosts: Trees and shrubs of the rose family, including apple, pear, quince, cotoneaster, hawthorn, mountain-ash, serviceberry, and crabapple.

Damage: Larvae tunnel the trunks at the base of trees and cause weakening that may lead to trees breaking near ground level. Adults chew on twigs and leaves, but this damage is usually minor. Round-headed appletree borer is the most important borer of apple orchards in the East and is particularly destructive to young trees.

Distribution: East of the Mississippi River, north of the hill areas of Georgia to Alabama.

Appearance: Adults are generally light brown with two prominent white stripes running along the back. Antennae are about the same length as the body, which is typically about ¾ to 1 inch. Larvae are yellowish white with a dark brown head and black jaws.

Life History and Habits: Most adults emerge over a period of 2 weeks, beginning in late April to June depending on location. They feed on the leaves of host trees for a few weeks, and then females begin to lay eggs. These are deposited singly into slits of the bark, almost always near the base of the tree. After egg hatch, the larvae feed in the sapwood and bark and then go dormant for the winter.

The larval period can be quite extended, sometimes requiring one or more additional seasons to complete. During this time the larvae enlarge their tunnels and extend them deeply into the trunk. Pupation occurs in late winter or early spring, in a chamber just below the surface. Adults begin to emerge a month or so after pupation occurs.

Related Species

Poplar borer (*Saperda calcarata*) develops primarily on aspen, but cottonwood and poplar are also hosts. Larvae develop under the bark and tunnel the sapwood, girdling trees. Early stages of attack are indicated by moist areas on the bark, often with some associated sawdust. Chronically infested trees exhibit a black varnishlike stain on the bark below points of borer attack. Stringy sawdust is pushed out of holes in the bark by the developing larvae and may pile around the base of trees. Poplar borer has an extended life cycle that likely requires 2 to 3 years to complete.

Poplar-gall saperda (*S. inornata*) induces swellings on the twigs of aspen, poplar, and willow. **Elm borer** (*S. tridentata*) develops in dead or weakened American elm, sometimes causing dieback of individual limbs. **Linden borer** (*S. vestia*) is sometimes an important pest of linden, particularly little-leaf linden, in the Midwest. **Alder borer** (*S. obliqua*) develops in alder and birch in the northern U.S. and Canada.

A. Roundheaded appletree borer. *J. Fengler.* **B.** Roundheaded appletree borer larva in trunk. *J. D. Solomon.* **C.** Frass pushed from tunnels of poplar borer larvae. *D. Leatherman.* **D.** Elm borer. *D. Shetlar.* **E.** Oozing on aspen trunk in response to tunneling injuries by poplar borer larvae. *D. Leatherman.* **F.** Various life stages of poplar borer. *J. D. Solomon.*

Other Longhorned Beetles

Redheaded ash borer (*Neoclytus acuminatus*) develops in ash, hackberry, several fruit trees, and other hardwoods. Most attacks occur on dying or recently killed trees, and they are common on firewood. Larval feeding can reduce the sapwood to a fine powder, and large oval-shaped holes may riddle the heartwood. Occasionally there is boring into twigs and branches. The adult beetles have a narrow brown body with a reddish head and thorax. They are about ⅝ inch long and have wing covers marked with four yellow transverse bands and long spindly legs. Redheaded ash borer is found in much of the continent east of the Rocky Mountains. **Banded ash borer** (*N. caprea*) is generally similar in appearance and habits. It is marked with yellow stripes on the wing covers and is slightly larger than redheaded ash borer. Biology is similar. *N. muricatulus* is associated with spruce and other conifers.

Eucalyptus longhorned borer (*Phoracantha semipunctata*) became established in California around 1984 and is now found attacking many eucalyptus species in the southern half of the state. Adults may lay eggs in small batches, and larvae originally feed just under the bark, often leaving visible dark streaks above tunnels. Older larvae penetrate the cambium, and tunnels ultimately may extend several feet. The adult beetle is about 1 inch long and shiny black or brown with a creamy zigzag band across the middle of the wing covers. Two or three generations, which overlap, may be produced annually.

Asian longhorned beetle (*Anoplophora glabripennis*) has been the source of considerable attention and concern since it was discovered in the New York City and Chicago areas in the late 1990s. Maple and poplar are preferred hosts, but a wide variety of hardwood trees are potential hosts. The larvae tunnel extensively in the trunk and branches, resulting in dieback and structural weakening. Most concern involves the species' apparent ability to damage healthy trees and difficulties in control, so a sustained effort is being made to eradicate it. The adult, sometimes known as starry sky beetle, is a large (1 to 1½ inches), coal black beetle with bright white markings and banded antennae, commonly mistaken for a pine sawyer. The species is native to Japan, Korea, and eastern China.

Cottonwood borer (*Plectodera scalator*) is a native species of similar size with dark checkered markings on a light-colored body. Willow, cottonwood, and poplar are hosts, and sometimes these are seriously riddled by larval tunneling. During heavy infestations, smaller trees may be severely weakened and break at the base. Adults are active in late spring or early summer and feed on tender young shoots. Eggs are then deposited in pits chewed in the bark at the tree base. Larvae hatch and feed in the phloem, progressing downward into larger roots during their first fall. They spend the second summer feeding in galleries at the tree base. The life cycle requires 2 years to complete.

Pole borer (*Parandra brunnea*), also known as **aberrant wood borer**, tunnels the heartwood of many hardwoods including willow, maple, elm, and poplar. It usually is associated with dead areas of wood but causes extensive riddling that can structurally weaken plants. As its name suggests, it is sometimes a problem in telephone poles and structural lumber. It is "aberrant" in appearance, lacking the long antennae characteristic of other longhorned beetles and possessing prominent jaws that make it appear somewhat like a predator. It is capable of breeding without emerging from the trunk.

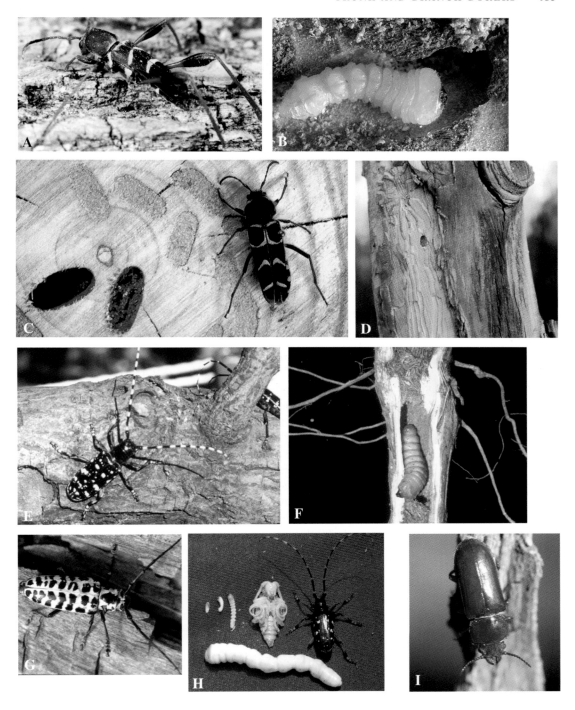

A. Redheaded ash borer adult. *G. J. Lenhard.* B. Redheaded ash borer larva. *K. Gray.* C. Banded ash borer adult. *J. D. Solomon.* D. Tunneling in trunk produced by eucalyptus longhorned borer. *D. Shetlar.* E. Asian longhorned beetle. *K. R. Law.* F. Cottonwood borer larva in base of tree. *J. D. Solomon.* G. Adult cottonwood borer. *W. Cranshaw.* H. Life history stages of Asian longhorned beetle. *K. R. Law.* I. Adult pole borer. *W. Cranshaw.*

Some of the largest insects of North America are found in the genus *Prionus* and are sometimes known as **giant root borers** or **tilehorned prionus**. Adults are dark brown to nearly black and typically range from 1½ to 2 inches in length. The antennae are prominent and in the males are particularly enlarged and characteristically serrated. Eggs are laid in soil at the base of trees, and the larve develop by tunneling roots of various hardwood trees, particularly oak and nut trees. Apparently healthy trees can be injured, and sometimes significant structural weakening is produced by the tunneling. Larval development is also quite extended, often requiring 3 or 4 years to complete. **Tilehorned prionus** (*P. imbricornis*) predominates in the eastern half of the U.S. Its range overlaps considerably with that of **broad-necked root borer** (*P. laticollis*). These are replaced in western North America by **California prionus** (*P. californicus*). Rivaling or exceeding these in size is **ponderous borer** (*Ergates spiculatus*) which develops on roots of Douglas-fir and pine in the western states.

Species in the genus *Callidium* develop in dead, dying, and seriously stressed conifers. Larvae sculpt tunnels just under the bark and often pack them with granulate frass. Boring activity is also commonly observed as the larvae expel sawdust from wood piles. **Blackhorned pine borer** (*C. antennatum*) commonly infests dead pines and sometimes those recently transplanted in poor sites. It is common in the Rocky Mountain region, throughout the southern states, and in most of the eastern U.S. and Canada. A closely related species is **blackhorned juniper borer** (*C. texanum*) which occurs in juniper. Adults of both species are shiny black or blue-black longhorned beetles.

Pine sawyers (*Monochamus* spp.) are widespread in North America, developing in recently dead and severely stressed pine, spruce, fir, and Douglas-fir. Adults are large beetles (about 1 inch long), black to brownish gray with white speckling, and have extremely long antennae one to three times the body length. Larvae bore extensively in sapwood and heartwood of dying and recently killed trees. Adults cause minor injury by feeding on needles and shoot bark. In the Midwest, pine sawyers are the primary vectors of **pine wilt nematode** (*Bursaphelenchus xylophilus*) which can produce pine wilt disease in susceptible pines. The nematode is introduced into feeding wounds of twigs made by the adult and is physically carried from tree to tree on the body of the beetles. This twig feeding also may cause flagging from girdling wounds. Common species include **whitespotted sawyer** (*Monochamus scutellatus*), **spotted pine sawyer** (*M. clamator*), and **southern pine sawyer** (*M. titillator*).

Larvae of **cactus longhorn** (*Moneilema armatum*) tunnel the pads of various cacti in the genera *Opuntia* and *Cylindropuntia*. They survive winter in a pupal cell they construct during late summer and early fall around the base of the cactus. Transformation to the pupal stage occurs in spring, and adults emerge in late spring and early summer. Adult beetles feed at night, typically eating young cactus pads or oozing sap. After mating, the females glue eggs to the cactus pad. The young larvae attempt to tunnel into the cactus, causing the plant to ooze sap at the wound. The larvae first feed in this ooze, later entering the plant. They feed throughout the summer and early fall. One generation is usually produced per year, but some of the later larvae may not emerge until the second season. Several other species of *Moneilema* occur in the southwestern U.S., all restricted to various cacti. *M. annulatum*, *M. appressum*, and *M. semipunctatum* generally resemble cactus longhorn but are somewhat smaller.

[1] Coleoptera: Cerambycidae

A. Adult *Prionus*. *J. D. Solomon*. **B.** California prionus, male. *K. Gray*. **C.** California prionus pupa. *K. Gray*. **D.** Adult ponderous borer, one of the largest longhorned beetles of North America. *D. Leatherman*. **E.** Blackhorned pine borer adult. *W. Cranshaw*. **F.** Sculpting typical of larval tunneling by *Callidium* spp. *W. Cranshaw*. **G.** Adult spotted pine sawyer. *W. Cranshaw*. **H.** *Monochamus carolinensis*, the primary vector of pine wilt. *J. E. Appleby*. **I.** Larval tunneling by *Callidium* larva in juniper. *W. Cranshaw*. **J.** Flagging caused by twig girdling by whitespotted sawyer. *R. S. Kelley*. **K.** Cactus longhorn. *W. Cranshaw*.

WEEVIL BORERS

A few weevils[1] develop as borers of trunks and larger stems of plants. Others feed in twigs (p. 452), on seeds and buds (p. 276), or on leaves and roots (p. 532).

Poplar and Willow Borer (*Cryptorhynchus lapathe*)

Hosts: Willow and, rarely, poplar.

Damage: Larvae tunnel into the lower trunk of trees. Infested trees may become malformed because of excessive sucker growth. Young willows may have bulblike swellings from borer attack and may break easily because of borer weakening.

Distribution: An introduced species now broadly distributed throughout southern Canada and the northern U.S.

Appearance: Larvae are cream-colored, legless, C-shaped grubs about ¼ inch long. At points of feeding, large amounts of moist sawdust are pushed from the entry holes. The adults are chunky snout weevils, about ⅜ inch long, and rough surfaced. They are primarily black except for the hind third of the wing covers which are gray, somewhat resembling a bird dropping.

Life History and Habits: Poplar and willow borer spends the winter as a partially grown larva in the sapwood. In the spring, the larvae grow and continue boring, pushing large amounts of fibrous frass through exit holes. Larvae pupate under the bark, beginning in May. Adults may be present from late May through mid-July. Eggs are deposited in small slits in the bark. There is one generation per year.

Other Trunk-Boring Weevils

Agave weevil (*Scyphophrus acupunctatus*) can be a serious pest of yucca and agave in the southern states. Adults make feeding punctures in young leaves. Most damage is produced by larval tunneling, which occurs primarily at the base of the flowering stalk, but it also can kill the growing point. Secondary infections with rotting organisms commonly occur following agave weevil damage, sometimes causing plants to collapse and die. Agave weevil is a large (ca. ½ to ¾ inch), black snout beetle. Larvae are creamy white, legless, and may be ¾ inch when full grown. The life cycle can be completed in less than 2 months, and up to four or five generations may be produced in more southern areas. A closely related species found in southern California is **yucca weevil** (*S. yuccae*).

Palmetto weevil (*Rhynchophorus cruentatus*) is the largest North America weevil and is present in many southern states from South Carolina to Texas. Adults may exceed 1 inch in length and have highly variable coloration, ranging from completely black to nearly all red. Adults are usually observed in late spring and early summer. The larvae develop as destructive borers of cabbage palm, occasionally damaging saw palmettos and some other palms. Infestations are often lethal as the larvae extensively tunnel the trunk and may kill the growing point. Serious rots usually develop around wounded areas. Adults usually lay eggs near existing wounds. Emergence holes made by the exiting adult may be the diameter of a quarter. Multiple generations can occur, with the life cycle taking about 3 months to complete under optimal conditions.

---

[1] Coleoptera: Curculionidae

A. Adult poplar and willow borer. *W. Cranshaw.* **B.** Poplar and willow borer larva. *K. Gray.* **C.** Poplar and willow borer larva in stem. *K. Gray.* **D.** Agave weevil. *D. Caldwell.* **E.** Poplar and willow borer damage to base of willow. *W. Cranshaw.* **F.** Poplar and willow borer eggs inserted into stem. *K. Gray.* **G.** Agave weevil larvae. *D. Caldwell.* **H.** Agave weevil damage. *A. D. Ali.* **I.** Palmetto weevil larva and pupa. *A. D. Ali.* **J.** Palmetto weevil. *A. D. Ali.*

BARK BEETLES

Bark beetles (Scolytidae family)[1] are fairly small beetles (ca. ¹⁄₁₆ to ¼ inch) that usually develop feeding on the cambium under the bark of trees. Adult beetles first cut distinctive galleries in which they mate and lay eggs. The legless, grublike larvae tunnel outward from these egg galleries.

Feeding by the insects under the bark can girdle the tree, although most beetles limit attack to damaged limbs or trees that are stressed or in decline; newly transplanted trees are particularly susceptible to attack. However, many bark beetles are associated with fungi that can also produce diseases in trees. These include fungi in the genera *Ophiostoma* and *Leptographium* involved in Dutch elm disease and blue stain of conifers.

Bark beetles that limit development to small branches and twigs are discussed on p. 450.

Shothole Borer (*Scolytus rugulosus*)

Hosts: Fruit trees (particularly *Prunus* spp.) and a few other hardwoods such as mountain-ash, English laurel, hawthorn, and in rare cases, elm. Most infestations involve overmature or damaged plum and cherry.

Damage: Shothole borer is the most common bark beetle affecting fruit trees. Larvae develop under the bark, producing typical girdling wounds that can weaken, and sometimes kill, the plant beyond the damaged area. Oozing gum often occurs on *Prunus* species where beetles enter the wood to lay eggs. When the adult beetles emerge through the bark, they chew small exit holes, the most commonly observed evidence of shothole borer activity.

Distribution: An accidentally introduced species now found in temperate areas throughout North America.

Appearance: Adults are small (¹⁄₁₀ inch), gray-black beetles.

Life History and Habits: Shothole borer spends the winter as a grublike larva under the bark or as a pupa in chambers cut into the sapwood. Adults begin to emerge and become active in late April or May but can subsequently be found throughout the growing season. After mating, the females seek out wounded or diseased trees and chew out a 1- to 2-inch-long egg gallery, generally parallel to the grain. Eggs are laid in little niches along the gallery, and larvae subsequently feed under the bark. Adults exit through the bark, leaving a characteristic exiting shothole. Two to three generations may occur, depending on climate, although these are indistinct and egg-laying may occur through much of the growing season.

Related Species

Hickory bark beetle (*Scolytus quadrispinosus*) attacks hickory, pecan, butternut, and walnut throughout much of the eastern U.S. and southeastern Canada. It is particularly damaging in southern areas of its distribution, where it is occasionally a serious forest pest. Some defoliation and leaf wilting may be present as newly emerged adults feed on twigs and leaf petioles. Egg-laying is limited to weakened trees. There is one generation per year in northern areas and two in the south.

A. Shothole borer adult. *K. Gray.* **B.** Shothole borer larvae. *K. Gray.* **C.** Shothole borers tunneling under bark. *K. Gray.* **D.** Shothole borer tunneling at bud. *K. Gray.* **E.** Sap oozing from wounds made by shothole borer tunneling. *D. Leatherman.* **F.** Hickory bark beetle tunnels. *J. D. Solomon.* **G.** Shothole borer exit holes. *Courtesy Clemson University.*

Smaller European Elm Bark Beetle (*Scolytus multistriatus*)

Hosts: Elm.

Damage: This is the primary insect involved in transmission of the fungus that produces Dutch elm disease (*Ophiostoma novo-ulmi*). Larvae develop under the bark and can cause girdling injuries but usually restrict attacks to injured limbs or dying trees. There is little damage in the absence of the fungus.

Distribution: Most of the U.S. where elm is grown, except in some far northern areas.

Appearance: This beetle is generally dark and about ⅛ inch long with reddish brown to reddish black wing covers. Its posterior end is concave and has a small projection, or spine, typical of the genus *Scolytus*.

Life History and Habits: Smaller European elm bark beetles overwinter in the larval stage, in galleries under the bark. Larvae mature in the spring and pupate. Adult beetles typically emerge around mid-May, although earlier emergence may occur. Beetles emerging from Dutch elm disease–infected trees may become contaminated with spores of *O. novo-ulmi*.

Dutch elm disease transmission by beetles occurs when the beetles subsequently fly to healthy elm trees and feed at the crotches of 2- to 3-year-old twigs. This period, known as maturation feeding, may last for several weeks, during which eggs mature. Adults then seek out diseased and weakened trees and construct egg galleries that run parallel to the wood grain. The larvae develop over the course of about 2 months, and adults emerge in mid- to late summer. Adults have a second round of twig-feeding and egg-laying, with the subsequent larval generation overwintering.

Other Elm Bark Beetles

Scolytus schevyrewi is a bark beetle of Asian origin first discovered in the U.S. in 2003 but appears already widely distributed through the Rocky Mountain region and perhaps elsewhere. Closely related to smaller European elm bark beetle, and with generally similar life history, *S. schevyrewi* has a considerably wider range of host plants, which include Russian olive, caragana, willow, and stone fruits in addition to elm.

Native elm bark beetle (*Hylurgopinus rufipes*) is an important vector of Dutch elm disease in areas of the upper Midwest, northeastern U.S., and adjacent areas of southern Canada where cold temperatures limit the smaller European elm bark beetle. Many winter as adults that construct special chambers in the lower trunk. Egg galleries run across the grain.

Ash Bark Beetles

Three *Hylesinus* species may damage green and white ash. **Eastern ash bark beetle** (*H. aculeatus*) and **Criddle's bark beetle** (*H. criddlei*) are generally distributed east of the Great Plains. **Western ash bark beetle** (*H. californicus*) is the most damaging species and is found throughout much of the western U.S. and Prairie Provinces.

Ash bark beetles may infest almost the entire tree, from finger-diameter branches to the main trunk. Injured limbs and heavily shaded branches in the interior of the tree are most commonly attacked. Adult beetles cut egg galleries under the bark across the grain, and these typically have two arms with a central chamber. Small ventilation holes appear above the egg galleries. These injuries and subsequent tunneling by the larvae girdle branches. The tunnels are almost invariably colonized by fungi that stain the wood a rich brown color around the feeding sites. Sap may ooze from wounds in twigs, staining the bark.

A. European elm bark beetle adult feeding on twig. *K. Gray.* **B.** Size of European elm bark beetles compared to paper clip. *W. Hantsbarger.* **C.** Vascular discoloration of debarked tree killed by Dutch elm disease. *D. Leatherman.* **D.** Vascular staining characteristic of Dutch elm disease infection. *R. S. Cameron.* **E.** Tunnels of European elm bark beetle. *D. Leatherman.* **F.** European elm bark beetle. *K. Gray.* **G.** *Scolytus schevyrewi. W. Cranshaw.* **H.** European elm bark beetle tunnels. *D. Leatherman.* **I.** Wilting of foliage symptomatic of Dutch elm disease. *Courtesy Minnesota Dept. Natural Resources.* **J.** Ash bark beetle tunnels under bark of trunk. *D. Leatherman.* **K.** Western ash bark beetle in egg gallery. *D. Leatherman.* **L.** Characteristic ventilation holes produced above egg galleries of ash bark beetles. *D. Leatherman.* **M.** Fungal staining at tunnels of ash bark beetle. *D. Leatherman.* **N.** Larval galleries of eastern ash bark beetle. *J. D. Solomon.*

Ash bark beetles overwinter either as late-instar larvae under the bark or as adults in niches cut into the green bark of the outer trunk and become active in early to mid-spring. The larvae feed under the bark, often extensively scoring into the sapwood. Those developing from spring eggs become full grown in late spring or early summer and pupate in the tunnels. Adults emerge from the branch and feed on green wood, causing little damage. There is evidence that a partial second generation is sometimes produced. These may not complete development and overwinter as larvae. Bark beetles that have reached the adult stage move to the trunks at the end of the season to cut hibernation chambers in which they winter.

Southern Pine Beetle and Relatives (*Dendroctonus* spp.)

Bark beetles in the genus *Dendroctonus* can be very damaging to conifers. They are typically small (ca. ⅛ inch) cylindrical beetles, dark brown or black. Thirteen species occur in North America, with many restricted to forest settings. Most *Dendroctonus* bark beetles can overcome tree defenses by mass attacks that are coordinated with chemical cues known as aggregation pheromones. Girdling of the tree results from egg galleries produced by the adults and larval tunnels under the bark. Many species also are associated with transmitting fungi that produce blue stain diseases which may contribute to tree death. Trees successfully attacked by *Dendroctonus* bark beetles typically show a fading of needles, progressing to a reddish brown color. These symptoms develop within a year after beetles begin to lay eggs and almost always are followed by the death of the tree.

Southern pine beetle (*D. frontalis*) is the most important forest insect in the southeastern U.S., with Kentucky being part of its northern range. It is most commonly found on shortleaf, loblolly, Virginia, and pitch pine and is usually restricted to trees older than 15 years but with a trunk diameter less than 6 inches. Adult beetles usually enter the trunk 6 to 20 feet above ground and chew curved or S-shaped egg galleries. Multiple generations are produced, and a single generation may be completed in as little as a month during favorable warm periods. Adults may be active much of the time from spring through fall.

Mountain pine beetle (*D. ponderosae*) is the most important bark beetle of western forests, particularly concentrated in the Rocky Mountains and Black Hills. It primarily attacks ponderosa, lodgepole, and limber pine; Scotch pine is occasionally damaged. Mature trees over 8 inches in diameter are most susceptible to attack. Mountain pine beetle has a 1-year life cycle, with adults active during early summer.

Two species of turpentine beetles are found in North America. **Red turpentine beetle** (*D. valens*) is the most widely distributed, occurring throughout the U.S. and southern Canada, excluding the southeastern and Gulf states, where **black turpentine beetle** (*D. tenebrans*) is found. Both species have similar habits and are among the largest bark beetles, with adults being ¼ to ⅜ inch long. They can develop in large-diameter pines and are particularly common in trees scorched near the base by fire or injured during construction. Turpentine beetle attacks are characteristically confined to the lower few feet of the trunk. Inner-bark feeding differs from that of most *Dendroctonus*, with larvae feeding as a group and excavating an irregular, round-edged patch under the bark. Trees can survive attack, but resultant weakening can make hosts more susceptible to other bark beetles.

In mountainous areas of the western states, forest species sometimes become serious pests of landscape plants. **Spruce beetle** (*D. rufipennis*) historically has had several widespread and sustained outbreaks on Colorado blue and Engelmann spruce in the Rocky Mountain states. Adults overwinter in small chambers cut into the base of the trunk and fly during June and early July, tending to attack more mature trees or those that are windthrown. Larvae take almost 2 years to complete development.

A. Oregon ash bark beetle. *K. Gray.* **B.** Eastern ash bark beetle adult. *J. D. Solomon.* **C.** Galleries produced by southern pine beetle. *L. L. Hyche.* **D.** Boring dust at base of pine infested with southern pine beetle. *G. J. Lenhard.* **E.** Mountain pine beetle "hits" and pitch flow at entry sites of trunk. *D. Leatherman.* **F.** Pitch masses produced by red turpentine beetle. *D. Leatherman.* **G.** Mountain pine beetle adults. *D. Leatherman.* **H.** Blue stain in bark-beetle-killed pine. *D. Leatherman.* **I.** Sawdust extruded from trunk "hits" by tunneling mountain pine beetle adults. *D. Leatherman.* **J.** Spruce bark beetle larvae. *E. H. Holsten.* **K.** Galleries produced by spruce beetle. *D. Leatherman.* **L.** Mountain pine beetle pupae in galleries with associated blue stain. *D. Leatherman.*

Ips (Engraver) Beetles

Ips beetles (*Ips* spp.), sometimes known as **pine engravers**, develop in most pines and spruce. At least one of the approximately two dozen *Ips* species that occur in North America likely is found wherever these hosts are found.

Ips beetles are less aggressive than *Dendroctonus* bark beetles, usually limiting attacks to trees that are seriously stressed by root injury, drought, disease, or defoliation. Attacks are less commonly lethal to trees and may be limited to large branches or, most commonly, the tops of trees. Trees killed by ips beetles show the uniform needle discoloration and death of *Dendroctonus* bark beetles. Blue stain fungi often, but not always, are introduced with ips beetles.

Adults are of typical size for bark beetles, ⅛ to ¼ inch long, and reddish brown to black. Characteristic is a pronounced cavity at the rear end lined with three to six pairs of toothlike spines.

Ips beetles have multiple generations, and adults may be active whenever temperatures allow. Unlike many other bark beetles, ips beetles are polygamous, with the initial tunneling produced by the male which cuts a cavity under the bark (nuptial chamber). Attracted females subsequently produce egg galleries, producing a characteristic pattern of Y- or H-shaped egg galleries. The egg galleries are free of sawdust; it is pushed out of the entrance hole by the scooped hind end of the beetles as they work. A yellowish or reddish brown boring dust in bark crevices or around the base of trees is indicative of ips beetle activity.

Some Important Ips Beetles of Landscape Conifers

Species	Host	Comments
Ips calligraphus	Pine	Largest ips beetle and known as **six-spined engraver**. Common throughout North America
Ips pini	Pine	Throughout North America and often the most common species affecting pine. Known as **pine engraver**
Ips avulus	Pine	Smallest ips beetle and known as **small southern pine engraver**. Occurs in a broad area of eastern U.S. south of Pennsylvania
Ips confusus	Pinyon, rarely other pines	Periodically kills pinyons over large areas
Ips hunteri	Spruce	An important species affecting Colorado blue spruce in Colorado and the southwest. Upper portions of tree are typically infested first. Known as the **spruce ips**

A. Ips beetle galleries with associated blue stain fungi. *D. Leatherman.* **B.** Characteristic galleries produced by ips beetles. *D. Leatherman.* **C.** Ips beetle galleries in ponderosa pine. *D. Leatherman.* **D.** *Ips avulus*–killed tree. *D. Moorhead.* **E.** Spruce ips larva. *W. Cranshaw.* **F.** Top dieback due to spruce ips infestation. *W. Cranshaw.*

Ambrosia Beetles

Ambrosia beetles develop differently from other bark beetles. All tunneling is done by the adult female which constructs a brood chamber in the sapwood or heartwood of trunks and branches. Small niches are often carved off a central chamber in which the larvae develop. Ambrosia beetles invariably carry into the brood chamber certain fungi (*Ambrosiella* spp.) with which they have a mutualistic relationship. The fungi colonize the wood, and the larvae feed on the fungi; larvae do no further tunneling. Damage by the native species of ambrosia beetles in the genera *Trypodendron, Xyleborus,* and *Xyleborinus* is usually minimal to living plants, as injuries are typically limited to nearly dead or recently felled trees. However, some introduced species in the genus *Xylosandrus* have significantly greater potential to damage trees and shrubs.

Asian ambrosia beetle (*Xylosandrus crassiusculus*) tunnels into the sapwood and heartwood of a wide range of trees and shrubs including various stone fruits (*Prunus* spp.), pecan, golden-rain tree, sweetgum, persimmon, Shumard oak, beech, Chinese elm, crape myrtle, and magnolia. Because of the site of tunneling, relatively little structural damage is done, but the activities of the beetle allow development of various canker-producing fungi. Subsequent disruption of sap flow by these fungi can seriously damage and sometimes kill plants. Furthermore, affected plants are conspicuous as wood particles produced by tunneling may project out of the trunk and branches as small sticks.

Asian ambrosia beetle is dark reddish brown and about 1/10 inch long. Since its original introduction into Florida, it has spread throughout much of the southeastern U.S., as far west as Texas. Adult flights are greatest during March and early April, and one generation is normally thought to occur. Adults are present throughout the year, however, and life cycles need more study.

Black stem borer (*Xylosandrus germanus*) is currently distributed widely through much of the eastern U.S., extending into parts of the Midwest and Texas. It has a wide host range of trees and shrubs, primarily broadleaf plants but also including some conifers. Tunneling causes wilting and dieback, particularly by contributing to the spread of cankers produced by Fusarium fungi. Adults emerge in March in southern areas of the range and in mid-May farther north. The females bore into sapwood, constructing a brood chamber with branching side tunnels. The fungus (*Ambrosiella hartigii*) is introduced and begins to grow in chambers at this time. Eggs are then laid, and larvae can develop in about 1 month. Pupation occurs in the gallery, as does mating. The males, which cannot fly, do not leave the rearing chamber, but females then disperse to produce new brood chambers. Two generations per year are normally produced.

Black twig borer (*Xylosandrus compactus*) is a tiny (ca. 1/16 inch) beetle occurring in the southeastern states. It is considered among the most aggressively damaging of the ambrosia beetles and develops in the twigs of various trees and shrubs, including oak, maple, hickory, magnolia, and willow. Females construct a ½ inch to 1½-inch tunnel as a brood chamber in the pith or wood of succulent twigs, and numerous females may nest in larger twigs. Pathogenic fungi, including *Fusarium solani*, are commonly introduced during entry, and twigs usually die beyond the point of the tunneling. Larvae can develop rapidly, with a generation completed in a little more than a month.

[1] Coleoptera: Scolytidae

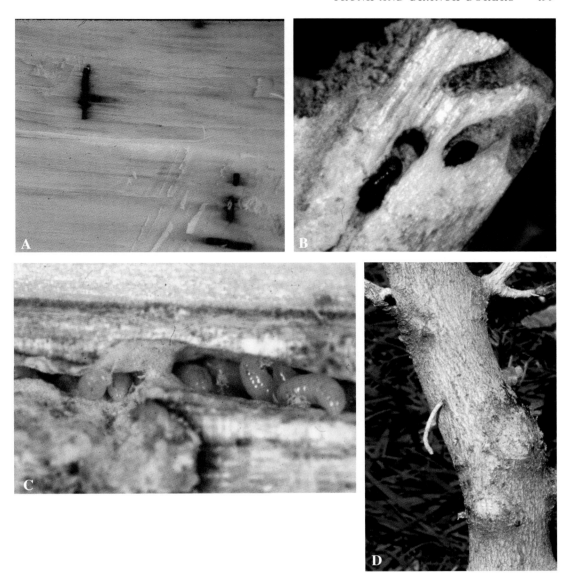

A. Fungal staining in ambrosia beetle galleries. *D. Leatherman.* **B.** Adult in galleries of ambrosia beetle *Xyleborus rubricollis. J. R. Baker.* **C.** Asian ambrosia beetle larvae in gallery. *J. Baker.* **D.** Frass tubes produced at entrance of egg chamber by Asian ambrosia beetle. *G. K. Douce.*

CHAPTER TEN

Root, Tuber, and Bulb Feeders

PILLBUG AND SOWBUGS

Some of the few crustaceans (subphylum Crustacea, class Malacostraca) adapted to life on land are those of the order Isopoda. Commonly encountered species in gardens include **pillbug** (*Armadillium vulgare*),[1] also known as roly-poly or potato bug, and the **sowbugs** (*Porcellio scaber*, *P. laevis*, *Onciscus asellus*).[2] Distant relatives of many familiar (and sometimes culinary) animals such as lobster, shrimp, and crab, the isopods share many physical features including seven pairs of legs, two pairs of antennae, and respiration through gills on the abdomen. The sowbugs possess a pair of tail-like appendages on the hind end. The absence of these, plus the ability to roll into a ball, distinguish pillbug ("roly-poly") from the sowbugs. All of the isopods commonly found in gardens of North America are introduced species of European origin. Their distributions have steadily expanded and include much of the continent.

Pillbug and sowbugs are general scavengers of plant matter. Their relatively weak chewing mouthparts restrict feeding to decayed or other soft matter. They do little damage to intact, healthy plant tissue. However, they are often found in association with plant tissues previously damaged by rots and may extend existing areas of damage.

Sowbugs and pillbug are rather long-lived but slow growing. Eggs and the newly hatched young remain inside the mother for several months, protected by the pouchlike marsupium. The young leave and undergo a series of molts as they develop. Young stages resemble the adults except for size. They become full grown after about 1 year. Most of the young fail to survive after leaving the mother, usually succumbing to excessive drying. However, surviving adults can live for 2 or more years. Pillbug and sowbugs usually feed at night, spending the day under cover. They can be seen during the day, however, particularly after rains or during overcast conditions.

[1] Isopoda: Armadillididae; [2] Ispoda: Oniscidae

A. Pillbugs. *W. Cranshaw.* **B.** Sowbug. *K. Gray.* **C.** Pillbug. *K. Gray.* **D.** Sowbug. *W. Cranshaw.* **E.** Pillbug, or "roly-poly." *W. Cranshaw.* **F.** Pillbug and sowbug. *W. Cranshaw.*

MILLIPEDES

Millipedes (class Diplopoda)[1] are most readily distinguished by the large number of legs they possess—two per body segment. Most millipedes have an elongate, wormlike form and chewing mouthparts. The species most commonly encountered (order Julida) are cylindrical, usually dark and hard, and have inconspicuous legs. Those in the order Polydesmida are more flattened with a maximum of about 20 segments and legs that are fairly prominent.

Millipedes feed on almost any plant matter in contact with the soil they inhabit. Their small mouthparts, however, usually limit them to decaying plant matter or plant materials that are very soft, such as mature fruit (e.g., ripe strawberries in contact with the soil). Occasionally, millipedes may damage tender vegetable seedlings and root crops such as carrots. The "small white worms" often found in such materials often prove on close inspection to be millipedes. Millipedes also sometimes attract attention when they make mass migrations, usually following wet weather. They may collect around building foundations or incidentally enter basement areas during these periods.

Most millipedes spend the winter as adults or nearly full-grown immatures. Eggs are laid in clusters in soil cracks or under moist, sheltering debris, usually between early spring and summer. Eggs hatch in a few weeks, and the immature stages are pale colored and wormlike. They grow slowly, increasing in size and number of body segments with each molt. As they get older, they increasingly resemble the adult form, becoming darker and thicker.

[1] Common orders: Julida, Polydesmida

SYMPHYLANS

The symphylans (class Symphyla) share many features with their relatives the millipedes and centipedes. They are quite small, however, rarely exceeding ⅓ inch, and thus may be mistaken for springtails. Symphylans possess a pair of legs on most, but not all, segments—typically there are 10 to 12 pairs on 15 body segments.

One species, **garden symphylan** (*Scutigerella immaculata*),[1] is a plant pest in parts of North America. Other names for it include garden symphylid, greenhouse centipede, and garden centipede. Although garden symphylan may occur over a wide area of North America (particularly much of the midwestern and Pacific northwestern U.S.), its occurrence is spotty and limited to areas with clay soils, particularly those high in organic matter. Garden symphylan can potentially damage a wide range of vegetables, small fruits, and flowers; grasses are little injured. Most serious damage occurs to belowground parts of plants, with flower bulbs, carrot, potato, radish, and beet being most severely damaged. Young roots may be killed, whereas those that are older may develop a gnarled appearance with corky tissues forming around wound sites.

Garden symphylan lays eggs in small masses from spring through summer. The young develop rapidly, becoming fully grown in about 2 months. All stages occur in soil, usually in the upper few inches. During hot, dry whether, however, individuals may migrate down a foot or more via soil cracks, earthworm burrows, and other soil channels. Adults remain dormant during cool weather but may be active in fall or even winter if mild conditions occur.

[1] Symphyla: Scutigerellidae

A. Millipedes. *W. Cranshaw.* **B.** Millipede. *W. Cranshaw.* **C.** Immature millipedes. *W. Cranshaw.* **D.** Young millipedes in strawberry fruit. *W. Cranshaw.* **E.** Millipede. *K. Gray.* **F.** Root injury by garden symphylan. *K. Gray.* **G.** Garden symphylan. *K. Gray.* **H.** Garden symphylan. *K. Gray.* **I.** Millipede. *K. Gray.*

SPRINGTAILS

Springtails[1] are small six-legged arthropods that are abundant in soils. They are often classified as insects, but many specialists consider them to be a separate subclass, Entognatha, within the class Hexapoda. Springtails are minute, typically about $\frac{1}{100}$ to $\frac{1}{25}$ inch. Most are of elongate form, although one common family has a globose appearance. Many of the common species are dully colored purplish gray or cream.

A unique tail-like structure (furcula) that hooks under the body is found on many springtails, particularly those that occur on the soil surface. When releaseed, this structure allows the springtail to make short jumps. Many springtails that restrict activities to the soil lack the ability to jump.

The great majority of springtail species feed on mold, bacteria, and other soil microbes. Rarely, some damage may be done to roots. The nuisance presence of springtails in potting soil of houseplants also sometimes raises concern. Springtails are sometimes a significant pest of high organic matter sites such as mushroom houses and worm beds.

Springtails have a simple metamorphosis, differing very little in form as they develop. Unlike insects, springtails may continually molt even after becoming sexually mature—as many as 50 times during their lifetime. They are common in environments of high humidity such as compost, rotting vegetation, and under stones. Those that feed on decaying plant matter and microbes are considered important in nutrient-cycling systems; others may be predators of nematodes and other springtails.

The ability to jump short distances is characteristic of many springtails that frequent the soil surface. Migrations into homes are sometimes observed, usually following heavy rains or irrigation that saturates soil. Masses of springtails are sometimes observed floating in rafts on the surface of still pools of water. In melting snows of late winter, the "snow flea" phenomenon is sometimes observed as springtails come to the surface, sprinkling it like "jumping dirt."

Springtails are abundant in soils of all but the harshest environments. Populations of almost 1.4 billion per acre have been estimated to occur in some environments. They can build up in very high numbers in lawns that are regularly watered and produce large amounts of organic matter.

[1] Collembola: Sminthuridae, Entomobyryidae, and Onychiuridae are common families

A. Springtail. *B. Drees.* **B.** Mass of springtails. *D. Shetlar.* **C.** Springtails. *W. Cranshaw.* **D.** Mass of springtails on water surface. *D. Shetlar.* **E.** Springtail. *K. Gray.* **F.** Globose springtail. *K. Gray.*

ROOT APHIDS AND OTHER SUCKING INSECTS

Various *Pemphigus* species[1] of aphids, sometimes known as **petiolegall aphids**, are root feeders during part of their life cycle. These winter as eggs on twigs of poplar and cottonwood and produce swellings on leaves, petioles, and stems of these plants in spring. (These gall-making species are discussed further on p. 408.) Winged stages fly from these winter hosts to feed on the roots of various plants during the summer, crawling to the roots via soil cracks. **Sugarbeet root aphid** (*P. populivenae*) is widespread in much of North America and produces colonies on the roots of lambsquarter, beet, and related plants in the summer. Severe wilting of sugarbeet occurs on susceptible varieties in the Dakotas and western states. **Lettuce root aphid** (*P. bursarius*) is sometimes important in California lettuce production. Both of these species have a fairly wide host range that includes several plants in the aster and beet families. Winged forms disperse from the summer hosts to seek their cottonwood/poplar winter hosts in late summer.

Many other aphids develop on roots and do not have an alternate woody plant winter host. **Western aster root aphid** (*Aphis armoraciae*)[1] occurs on roots of aster, dandelion, chicory, sunflower, horseradish, *Artemisia* and *Asclepias* species, and dock. The related **erigeron root aphid** (*A. middletoni*) is sometimes a pest of aster and cornflower. **Tulip bulb aphid** (*Dysaphis tulipae*)[1] is a common species found among the bulbs, roots, and stem bases of gladiolus, tulip, iris, carrot, celery, and waterhemlock. *Forda olivacea*[1] and related species develop on roots of various grasses including Kentucky bluegrass.

Mealybugs that develop on roots include several *Rhizoecus* species.[2] **Ground mealybug** (*R. falcifer*) develops on roots of many ornamental plants including anemone, chrysanthemum, gladiolus, and iris. It is about $\frac{1}{10}$ to $\frac{1}{8}$ inch long and has a fairly rounded and smooth body covered with fine web of slightly bluish wax. **Pritchard's ground mealybug** (*R. pritchardii*) is an important pest of African violet but also develops on roots of yarrow, manzanita, avens, and milkwort. High populations of either of these insects can cause wilting and decline of infested plants.

Miscanthus mealybug (*Miscanthiococcus miscanthi*)[2] develops at the base of the leaf sheaths of *Miscanthus,* producing dwarfing and poor growth. Roots also are commonly colonized. Three generations are produced per year in the central U.S., with winter spent as a fertilized adult female.

Rhodesgrass mealybug (*Antonina graminis*)[2] develops on various warm-season turfgrasses in the southern tier states. The removal of sap by the mealybugs stresses plants and is particularly injurious to bermudagrass that is under drought stress. This insect also produces considerable amounts of honeydew which can attract ants and wasps. Rhodesgrass mealybug is oval and about $\frac{1}{12}$ inch and is dark purplish brown but covered with whitish waxy filaments that yellow with age. It is usually found at the base of leaf sheaths. Multiple generations occur, with the life cycle being completed in about 2 months during the summer.

A. *Pemphigus* sp. aphid colony on rootball of aster. *W. Cranshaw.* **B.** Sugarbeet root aphid colony on quinoa roots. *W. Cranshaw.* **C.** Root-infesting aphids (*Forda* sp.) associated with Kentucky bluegrass. *W. Cranshaw.* **D.** Root-infesting aphid (*Forda* sp.) associated with Kentucky bluegrass. *W. Cranshaw.* **E.** Tulip bulb aphids. *D. Gilrein.* **F.** Rhodesgrass mealybugs. *D. Shetlar.* **G.** Tulipbulb aphids. *W. Cranshaw.* **H.** Ground mealybugs. *J. Baker.*

Ground pearls (*Margarodes meriodionalis*, *Eumargarodes laingi*)[3] are unusual scale insects that develop on the roots of centipedegrass, bermudagrass, zoysiagrass, and St. Augustinegrass. The ground pearls develop a globular shell, known as a cyst. This covering is about $\frac{1}{12}$ inch in diameter, hard and yellowish purple, and is attached to the roots, sometimes as deeply as 10 inches. In spring the adults emerge from the cyst and move to the surface where mating occurs. The female then lays small clusters of eggs shallowly in soil among the roots. The young scales move to feeding sites and begin to secrete the covering after they settle. Ground pearls occur throughout much of the southern U.S. and are particularly abundant in the southeastern and southwestern states. Severely infested grasses appear drought stressed, yellow, and may die.

Bermudagrass scale (*Odonaspis ruthae*)[4] is commonly associated with bermudagrass but is rarely damaging. It produces a circular or somewhat elongated white covering and concentrates around the nodes of plant stems. **Turfgrass scale** (*Lecanopsis formicarum*)[4] is a potential pest of red fescue and some other cool-season grasses. It is most visible in late spring and early summer when females produce a cottony egg sac at the base of stems and leaves. Turfgrass scale is a European species that has been found in eastern Canada. Early-stage nymphs (crawlers) are reddish, later stages more yellow.

[1] Homoptera: Aphididae; [2] Homoptera: Pseudococcidae; [3] Homoptera: Margarodidae; [4] Homoptera: Diaspididae

BULB MITES

Bulb mites (*Rhizoglyphus echinopus, R. robini*, *R. hyacinthi*, *R. engeli*)[1] are common throughout North America, although they are not thought to be native species. They feed primarily on decay fungi and are most commonly observed at existing plant wounds. However, they appear capable of greatly aggravating these injuries and of assisting in the growth and spread of decay organisms in plants. In high numbers, bulb mites also may damage the growing tips of bulbs, causing distortion. Bulbs of various flowers and vegetables have been recorded damaged, including lily, dahlia, tulip, hyacinth, freesia, gladiolus, onion, and garlic. Bulb mites can continue to develop on bulbs in storage.

Bulb mites are fairly "large" among mites (ca. $\frac{1}{30}$ inch), smooth bodied, and whitish to nearly translucent. They undergo an involved life cycle that may include five or six stages. Development may be continual as long as temperatures allow, and a generation may be completed in under a month under optimal conditions. Moderate temperatures, high humidity, and abundant food favor development. Dormant stages (hypopi) are produced when overcrowding occurs or the food supply degrades.

[1] Acari: Acaridae

A. Ground pearls. *D. Shetlar.* **B.** Bulb mites. *K. Gray.* **C.** Bulb mites. *K. Gray.*

TERMITES

Termites (order Isoptera) are well known for their ability to use the cellulose of wood as a food source. Because of this, these insects can seriously damage wood and related materials, causing billions of dollars of damage annually in North America alone. Direct injury to living plants is uncommon but does occur, particularly in dry soils. In addition, gardeners may encounter termites about the yard, associated with garden structures, woodpiles, and other sources where wood is in direct contact with the ground.

All termites are social insects that produce a colony containing hundreds to thousands of individuals of various specialized function (castes)—workers, soldiers, and reproductive forms, the last of which are winged. Colonies are usually initiated by a fertile female (queen) and male (king) following a mating flight. After pairing, they drop their wings and use their flight muscles for energy during colony initiation. Colony growth is slow during the first year or so but may increase rapidly once the colony is established.

Cellulose is the basic material in the diet and termites are essentially the only insects that can use this extremely common material. This is possible because of mutualistic microorganisms that establish in the digestive tract (protozoans, sometimes bacteria). These microbes, found nowhere else in nature, digest the cellulose and produce nutrients usable to termites.

Essentially all termites that cause serious injury in the U.S. are in the family Rhinotermitidae,[1] the subterranean termites. The most widespread and commonly encountered termites are in the genus *Reticulitermes*. Six *Reticulitermes* species occur in North America, of which **eastern subterranean termite** (*R. flavipes*), **western subterranean termite** (*R. hesperus*), **southeastern subterranean termite** (*R. virginicus*), and **arid-land subterranean termite** (*R. tibialis*) are most damaging, probably in that order.

When fully established, *Reticulitermes* colonies typically included 60,000 to 200,000 or more individuals which may forage over an area of about ⅓ acre. Damage to plants by subterranean termites is infrequent. They have been known to tunnel plant roots, particularly when soils become very dry. They also may invade the heartwood of trees, primarily dead wood in tree trunks, but can contribute to structural weakening.

Formosan subterranean termite (*Coptotermes formosanus*)[1] is a far more aggressively damaging species. It may nest in soil but also can make aboveground "carton" nests of mixed saliva, excrement, and soil. The nests may be located in buildings behind walls or under roofs but are also common in trees. In addition to causing extensive damage to buildings, this species also damages trees. More than 20 species of trees have been damaged in the New Orleans area alone, including oak, cypress, pine, elm, and maple.

Formosan termite colonies can become extremely large and include more than 7 million individuals. Typically about 10 to 15% are soldiers which can secrete a gluey defensive fluid from the head. As many as 70,000 winged reproductives have been recorded to emerge from a single colony during swarming flights, which take place in the evening in May and June. Winged stages are yellowish brown and ½ inch, larger than *Reticulitermes*.

Formosan subterranean termite is currently established in most of the Gulf states and in parts of Georgia and South Carolina. A spot infestation is present in southern California, and the species has long been established in Hawaii. Where established, it often displaces other termite species.

[1] Isoptera: Rhinotermitidae

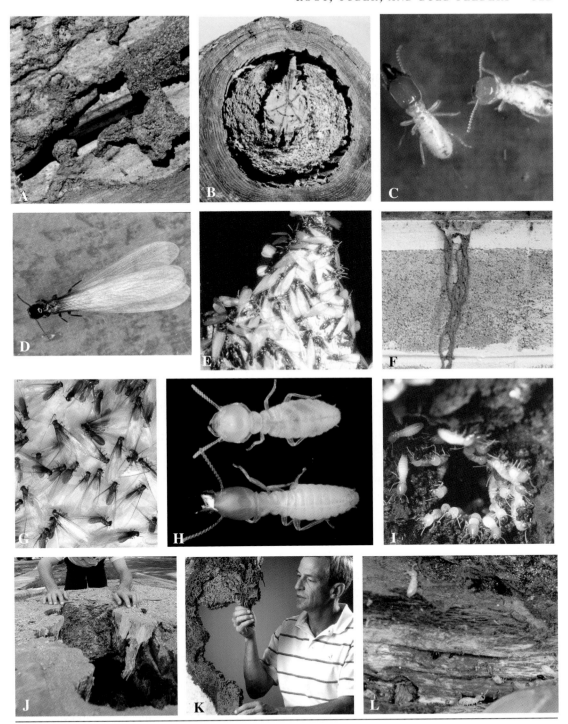

A. Damage and associated mud and feces around feeding area of subterranean termite. *W. Cranshaw.* **B.** Subterranean termite damage to telephone pole. *Courtesy USDA-FS Wood Products Lab.* **C.** Worker and soldier of arid-land subterranean termite. *W. Cranshaw.* **D.** Wing reproductive arid-land subterranean termite. *W. Cranshaw.* **E.** Winged forms of southeastern subterranean termite. *G. J. Lenhard.* **F.** Mud tubes produced by subterranean termites. *Courtesy USDA-FS Wood Products Lab.* **G.** Formosan subterranean termite winged reproductives. *S. Bauer/USDA-ARS.* **H.** Formosan subterranean termite worker (top) and soldier. *G. J. Lenhard.* **I.** Formosan subterranean termite workers. *S. Bauer/USDA-ARS.* **J.** Formosan subterranean termite nest in tree trunk. *S. Bauer/USDA-ARS.* **K.** Formosan subterranean termite carton nest. *S. Bauer/ USDA-ARS.* **L.** Subterranean termites in blueberry stem. *J. A. Payne.*

MOLE CRICKETS

Unlike almost all other members of the order Orthroptera, it is the fore legs rather than the hind legs that are highly developed in mole crickets.[1] This adaptation allows them to dig, and the great majority of mole cricket life history occurs belowground. Mole crickets are a small family, with seven North American species, including three introduced species that occur as pests in parts of the southern U.S.

Tawny Mole Cricket (*Scapteriscus vicinus*)

Hosts: Warm-season turfgrasses, particularly bermudagrass, St. Augustinegrass, and bahiagrass. Tawny mole cricket occasionally damages roots of vegetables and ornamentals.

Damage: Tawny mole cricket feeds on roots of grasses and causes serious pruning. Much damage also results incidentally from the physical effects of its tunneling, which can dislodge plants and cause roots to dry. This occurs most commonly in late summer when developing nymphs are most active.

Distribution: Southeastern U.S. This introduced insect is spreading in range, however, and a disjunct population is known from Arizona. Within these regions it is found only on sandy soils.

Appearance: Mole crickets are cylindrical in body form and about 1 to 1¼ inches long when full grown. Most are tan to golden brown with the area behind the head mottled. The prothorax is greatly extended, and the front legs are thickened and enlarged for digging. The hindwings of the adult extend shortly beyond the tip of the abdomen.

Life History and Habits: Most tawny mole crickets winter as adults. Mating occurs in spring, after which the females begin to excavate small chambers in the soil for egg-laying. Eggs are laid in groups and hatch in about 10 days. The nymphs subsequently leave the egg chamber and move to the surface to feed on plant matter and small insects. Most feeding occurs at night, with retreat to a burrow during the day. One generation is produced annually.

Adult mole crickets are capable of flight. Mating and dispersal flights are most common on warm spring nights, and the adults are strongly attracted to lights. Smaller flights may occur in the fall. During the mating period, mounds of soil may be thrown up around burrow entrances.

Other Mole Crickets

Southern mole cricket (*Scapteriscus borellii*) also is very damaging to turfgrasses in the southeastern states. It is primarily carnivorous, however, and damage results almost entirely from the effects of burrowing. The primary overwintering stage is a nearly full-grown nymph. Southern mole cricket is slightly more slender than tawny mole cricket and is grayish to reddish brown. It is quite an active insect, though it may readily play dead when disturbed. **Shortwinged mole cricket** (*S. abbreviatus*) presently occurs in southeastern Florida with a small disjunct population in Georgia. It damages turfgrasses in a manner similar to tawny mole cricket. The wing covers of the adults do not extend beyond the abdomen in this species.

[1] Orthoptera: Gryllotalpidae

A. Southern mole cricket. *B. Drees.* **B.** Mole crickets (right to left): northern mole cricket, shortwinged mole cricket, tawny mole cricket, southern mole cricket. *Courtesy University of Georgia.* **C.** Turfgrass damaged by mole crickets. *D. Shetlar.* **D.** Mole cricket damage. *Courtesy University of Georgia.* **E.** Shortwinged mole cricket. *J. Capinera.* **F.** Tawny mole cricket, female. *D. Shetlar.* **G.** Southern mole cricket, male. *D. Shetlar.* **H.** Mole cricket nymphs. *Courtesy University of Georgia.* **I.** Various life stages of tawny mole cricket. *D. Shetlar.*

ROOT MAGGOTS AND BULB FLIES

Larvae of several families of flies develop on belowground parts of plants. Most damaging are the various root maggots which develop by feeding on roots and germinating seeds of garden plants. Bulb flies are members of the flower fly family (Syrphidae), a group that includes many highly beneficial predators of aphids and other plant pests (p. 550). Those that develop on bulbs usually are fairly stout-bodied flies in the adult stage.

Cabbage Maggot (*Delia radicum*)[1]

Hosts: Most commonly grown crucifers (cabbage family), including rutabaga, broccoli, radish, cabbage, cauliflower, and Chinese cabbage.

Damage: The larvae feed on roots, which can stunt and sometimes kill developing plants. Root crops (turnip, rutabaga, radish) are directly damaged through scarring of the roots. During periods of extended dry weather, the damage may occur aboveground to the base of leaves.

Distribution: Generally throughout Canada and the northern half of the U.S.

Appearance: Adults are typical of this genus—moderate-sized (ca. ¼ inch), gray flies, somewhat resembling small house flies. Dark stripes are present on the thorax. Larvae are pale, rather plump maggots associated with roots of host plants. Pupae develop in a smooth, dark brown covering of rather seedlike form, known as a puparium.

Life History and Habits: Winter is spent in the pupal stage in soil. Adults emerge in mid- to late spring. Eggs are laid in masses, usually in soil cracks at the base of plants. Larvae develop over the course of 3 to 4 weeks, with a generation being completed in about 2 months. Two, and often three, generations occur per year, although injury tends to be greatest early in the season.

Other Root Maggots

Radish root maggot (*Delia planipalpis*) also develops on roots of crucifers, including radish, turnip, cabbage, Chinese cabbage, and various mustard-family weeds. It is western in distribution, found from Alaska to California.

Seedcorn maggot (*Delia platura*) is probably the most widespread of the root maggots found in North America. Larvae develop on seeds and seedlings, preventing successful emergence or wounding seedlings, particularly at the growing point. Damage is most common on warm-season plants with large seeds such as corn, bean, and melon. Cool weather and the presence of decaying organic matter are sometimes associated with greater injury. Seedcorn maggot also may be found as a secondary pest on plants that have been damaged by disease. Of very similar habit and commonly mistaken for seedcorn maggot is **bean seed maggot** (*D. florigela*), common in the northern U.S. and Canada west of the Rockies.

A. Adult cabbage maggot. *K. Gray.* **B.** Cabbage maggot damage to turnip. *K. Gray.* **C.** Seedcorn maggot adult. *K. Gray.* **D.** Cabbage maggot larvae in cabbage root. *Courtesy Clemson University.* **E.** Seedcorn maggot eggs. *K. Gray.* **F.** "Snakehead" symptom of bean, characteristic of seedcorn maggot damage. *W. Cranshaw.* **G.** Stem damage to bean seedling by seedcorn maggot. *K. Gray.* **H.** Bean seed damage by seedcorn maggot larvae. *K. Gray.*

Onion maggot (*Delia antiqua*) develops on roots of onion, garlic, leek, and many related plants. Larval tunneling can cause plants to wilt and die, either directly from injury or by facilitating rotting organisms. This species also readily invades decaying onions. It is widely distributed in the northern U.S. and southern Canada, particularly in areas where soils are high in organic matter.

Sugarbeet root maggot (*Tetanops myopaeformis*)[2] is an important pest of sugarbeet in the Great Plains and Rocky Mountain states. It is also sometimes a pest of summer-grown spinach and garden beet in the region. Larvae tunnel the roots and allow decay organisms to enter, causing wilting of the entire plant. One generation is produced annually, with the overwintering stage being full-grown larvae in soil. The emergence and activity of adults can be observed by the adults' tendency to aggregate on telephone poles and other prominent objects around previously infested fields.

Narcissus Bulb Fly (*Merodon equestis*)[3]

Hosts: Narcissus, daffodil, hyacinth, amaryllis, lily, tulip, and some other bulbs are occasionally infested.

Damage: Narcissus bulb fly tunnels into the base of bulbs, weakening or killing the plants and making the bulbs susceptible to rot.

Distribution: Generally distributed wherever narcissus and daffodil are grown.

Appearance: Larvae are plump, off-white, and markedly wrinkled maggots found in bulbs. Adults are hairy flies, similar in size and color to bumble bees.

Life History and Habits: This insect spends the winter as a large maggot inside the bulb. It pupates the following spring, and the adult fly emerges around mid- to late May, shortly after blooms have passed. Female flies lay eggs in soil cracks around the plant stems for a month or two after the flowers have died back. The newly hatched maggots crawl down the plant stem and tunnel into the base of the bulb. They continue to feed throughout the summer, becoming full grown in the fall.

Other Bulb Flies

Onion bulb fly (*Emerus strigatus*)[3] and **lesser bulb fly** (*E. tuberculatus*) are now found throughout North America. Larvae develop in association with bulb or root decay of narcissus, hyacinth, amaryllis, onion, shallot, and iris. Usually bulb flies are of secondary importance to plants, following existing decay, but they may extend wounding and increase injury. Adults are metallic flies, about ¼ inch, bronze or dark green with yellow banding on the abdomen. Larvae are dirty white, wrinkled, with a brown respiratory tube on the hind end.

A. Narcissus bulb fly adult. *W. Cranshaw.* **B.** Onion maggot eggs at base of plant. *K. Gray.* **C.** Narcissus bulb fly adult. *W. Cranshaw.* **D.** Onion maggot pupae. *K. Gray.* **E.** Narcissus bulb fly larvae and damage. *K. Gray.* **F.** Narcissus bulb fly larva in base of bulb. *W. Cranshaw.* **G.** Bulb tunneling by lesser bulb fly larva. *K. Gray.* **H.** Narcissus bulb fly larva. *K. Gray.* **I.** Onion bulb fly larva. *K. Gray.* **J.** Narcissus bulb fly pupa. *K. Gray.* **K.** Onion bulb fly adult. *K. Gray.*

Carrot Rust Fly (*Psila rosae*)[4]

Hosts: Primarily carrot. Occasionally celery, parsley, dill, coriander, celeriac, and fennel.

Damage: Larvae mine roots of carrot, particularly the lower third. Young plants may be killed. Older carrots sustain scarring, with burrows often a rusty red color. Wounds can promote rotting organisms.

Distribution: Scattered areas throughout the northern U.S. and southern Canada.

Appearance: The adult is a small (⅕ inch), thin-bodied black fly with yellowish legs and a reddish yellow head. Larvae are creamy white, of typical tapered maggot form.

Life History and Habits: Carrot rust flies winter in soil, usually as pupae but occasionally as larvae in roots. Adults emerge in late April to mid-May. Eggs are laid around the base of plants and hatch in 1 to 2 weeks depending on temperature. Pupation occurs in soil near infested plants. Feeding by larvae on the roots follows, after which there is a second generation, with adults laying eggs in late July and August. A small third, early-fall, generation is also reported in some areas.

European Crane Fly (*Tipula paludosa*)[5]

Hosts: Various grasses. Occasionally some vegetables, flowers, and strawberry.

Damage: Larvae chew roots and crowns of turfgrass and vegetable crops and disturb plants with their tunneling. Aboveground feeding may also occur at night. European crane fly is the most damaging turfgrass insect in the Pacific Northwest.

Distribution: Western Washington, Oregon, and parts of southwestern British Columbia; also parts of the Maritime Provinces. This is an introduced species, and its range has slowly spread since its introduction around 1965.

Appearance: Larvae are generally cylindrical, legless, and slightly tapered at either end. There is no distinct head capsule, but there are two dark spots on the hind end. Color is variable, from gray to greenish brown. The term "leatherjacket" is often applied to this larva and to those of related species. Adults somewhat resemble enormous mosquitoes but lack biting mouthparts and are harmless.

Life History and Habits: Winter is spent as partially grown larvae. They resume feeding in spring, during which they grow rapidly and produce most injury. During the day, feeding occurs belowground, but the larvae often migrate to feed on the surface during warm nights. They become full grown in early summer and pupate in soil burrows in August.

Adults emerge in late August and early September. Mating occurs immediately, and most eggs are laid within 1 to 2 days of emergence. The egg-laden females cannot fly and insert eggs into the upper layer of soil. High moisture conditions are essential for survival of eggs, which subsequently hatch in about 2 weeks. The insects grow rapidly during the fall, before slowing activity with the onset of cool weather.

A. Adult carrot rust fly. *K. Gray.* **B.** Tunneling by carrot rust fly larvae. *K. Gray.* **C.** European crane fly, female. *K. Gray.* **D.** European crane fly, male. *K. Gray.* **E.** Carrot root injury by carrot rust fly. *W. Cranshaw.* **F.** Leatherjacket, larva of European crane fly. *D. Shetlar.* **G.** European crane fly eggs. *K. Gray.* **H.** European crane fly pupa. *K. Gray.*

Related Species

A second species of turfgrass-damaging crane fly, *Tipula oleracea*, has recently been observed in parts of the Pacific Northwest. This species apparently has two generations per year, with adults present in both spring and fall.

The family of crane flies (Tipulidae) is the largest of all the flies, with more than 1,500 species in North America. With the exceptions above, none of the other species are considered to be plant pests in any manner. Larvae develop in moist areas where decaying organic matter is present. Adults are sometimes known as mosquito hawks or are mistaken for large mosquitoes. Neither characterization is warranted, as adult crane flies do not feed and are of innocuous habit.

March Flies

March flies[6] are common flies associated with moist habitats. They feed almost entirely on decaying plant matter and can be found in areas where plants have been injured by insects or diseases. Occasionally they do some chewing on roots of turfgrasses and other plants. Most of those associated with lawns and gardens are in the genera *Bibio* or *Dilophus*.

March flies primarily attract attention because of certain habits. The torpedo-shaped larvae are typically found feeding in large masses among plant roots and may cause concern because of their abundance. Adults emerge in spring, and some species occur in tremendous abundance. The somewhat notorious "lovebug" (*Plecia nearctica*) of the southeastern states causes periodic complaints when large numbers of mating flies, often in copula, are splattered by cars.

A. March fly (*Bibio* sp.) adult. *K. Gray.* **B.** March fly larva. *W. Cranshaw.* **C.** Mating pair of March flies (*Bibio* sp.) *D. Shetlar.* **D.** Mass of March fly larvae. *W. Cranshaw.*

Fungus Gnats (*Bradysia* spp., *Lycoriella* spp.)[7]

Hosts: Fungus gnats are associated with fungi in potting soil. They are also pests of mushroom houses.

Damage: Fungus gnats are primarily nuisance pests. The small, gnatlike adults emerge from the soil and may become bothersome, particularly in winter and early spring. The larvae may feed on roots and leaves lying on the soil surface. Fungus gnats can contribute to root diseases by wounding rootlets and moving pathogens in the soil.

Distribution: Throughout North America and common, indoors and outdoors.

Appearance: The adults are small (up to ⅛ inch), delicate dark flies somewhat resembling tiny mosquitoes. A single Y-shaped vein on the wings is useful for differentiating them from various other small flies. Fungus gnats are weak fliers and often run or make short skipping flights across soil and other surfaces. The larvae are wormlike, translucent with a dark head, and about ¼ inch when full grown.

Life History and Habits: Fungus gnats are associated with damp environments. Eggs are usually laid as clusters or strings in cracks of the soil surface. Immature stages (larvae) occur primarily within the top ½ inch of the soil and are rarely observed. Although larvae feed primarily on soil fungi, they also feed directly on root hairs and on leaves lying on the soil. Larval development typically requires 2 to 3 weeks to complete, and pupation occurs in the soil. The adult stage is brief, with females laying most eggs during a 3- to 5-day lifespan.

Fungus gnat larvae are very common insects in lawns, where they develop on decaying plant matter. Under some conditions, including high rainfall, mass migrations of the larvae may occur, which attract considerable attention.

Other Flies Associated with Indoor Plants

Very moist conditions supporting bacterial or algal growth may support other flies in greenhouses. **Shore flies** (*Scatella stagnalis* primarily)[8] are slightly larger than fungus gnats and somewhat heavier bodied with shorter legs. The light gray wings of shore flies are also marked with dark patterning. Shore flies feed on the algae that forms on the surface of potting mixes. They have not been associated with plant injuries but do produce dark "fly specks" which can soil containers and flowers on which the flies rest.

Moth flies (*Psychoda* spp.),[9] sometimes known as **drain flies**, may be present where stagnant water supports growth of bacterial slime in which the larvae develop. Moth flies also have been reported developing in compost or other high organic matter sites where there is sustained high moisture. The adults are tiny flies with wings covered with fine hairs, giving them the appearance of minute moths.

[1] Diptera: Anthomyiidae; [2] Diptera: Otitidae; [3] Diptera: Syrphidae; [4] Diptera: Psilidae; [5] Diptera: Tipulidae; [6] Diptera: Bibionidae; [7] Diptera: Sciaridae; [8] Diptera: Ephydridae; [9] Diptera: Psychodidae

A. Fungus gnat larvae. *W. Cranshaw.* **B.** Fungus gnat larva on potato slice. *W. Cranshaw.* **C.** Fungus gnat. *W. Cranshaw.* **D.** Fungus gnat on yellow sticky card. *W. Cranshaw.* **E.** Shore flies and associated fly specks. *W. Cranshaw.* **F.** Shore fly larva and pupa. *W. Cranshaw.* **G.** Adult fungus gnat. *K. Gray.* **H.** Adult moth fly, *Psychoda* sp. *K. Gray.*

WHITE GRUBS

Scarab beetles (Scarabaeidae family)[1] are one of the largest families of insects, including some 1,400 species in the U.S. and Canada. Adults are generally heavy-bodied insects that vary widely in size and are known by names such as May/June beetles or chafers. Larvae, known as white grubs, are pale-colored grubs that usually assume a C-shape when at rest. The overwhelming majority of them feed on fungi, animal manures, and other decaying organic matter. Many white grubs are important as macrodecomposers, essential in accelerating organic matter decomposition in the nutrient cycle. A few white grubs develop as plant pests, some of them serious. Those that are commonly observed feeding on leaves and flowers, such as Japanese beetle, are discussed on p. 268. Larvae of the common species of white grubs can be identified by the pattern of hairs on the tip of the abdomen (rastral pattern; see Figure 7).

Northern Masked Chafer (*Cyclocephala borealis*)

Hosts: Kentucky bluegrass, perennial ryegrass.

Damage: Larvae chew the roots of turfgrass, and these injuries may kill plants. The presence of the grubs in lawns also is attractive to various vertebrate predators, notably skunks, which dig up turfgrass while foraging.

Distribution: Much of North America and southern Canada, but an important turfgrass pest primarily in the northeast quadrant of this range.

Appearance: Adults are dark yellow to light brown, about ½ inch long, with dark brown markings around the head.

Life History and Habits: The adults emerge in late June and early July, flying at night, and are strongly attracted to lights. Unlike many scarabs, adults do not feed. Mated females tunnel 4 to 6 inches into soil and lay about 12 eggs. Soil moisture is critical to egg development; at optimum, eggs hatch in about 3 weeks. The larvae move to feed on roots and other organic matter near the soil surface. With cool temperatures they go deeper into the soil, returning to roots where they resume feeding in spring. Pupation occurs in late May and early June.

Related Species

Southern masked chafer (*Cyclocephala lurida*) is common from southern Pennsylvania to Nebraska and south. **Southwestern masked chafer** (*C. pasadaenae*) occurs from west Texas to southern California. **Western masked chafer** (*C. hirta*) occurs from central California to Colorado. The life history of these species is similar to that of northern masked chafer.

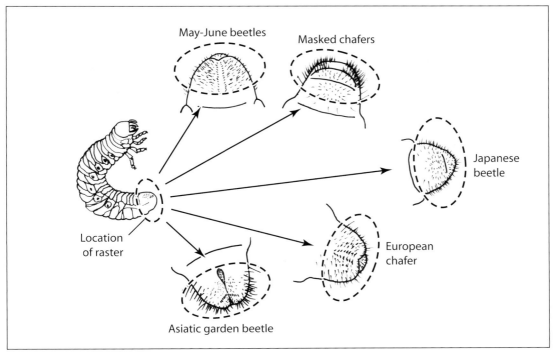

Figure 7. Rastral patterns of common turfgrass white grubs. *Figure by L. Mannix.*

A. Skunk diggings, for white grubs in lawn. *S. Rachesky.* **B.** White grub. *Courtesy University of Georgia Archives.*
C. Turfgrass injury by white grubs. *S. Rachesky.* **D.** Mixed infestation of Japanese beetle and chafer grubs. *D. Shetlar.*
E. Western masked chafer adults. *W. Cranshaw.* **F.** Western masked chafer larva and pupae. *W. Cranshaw.*

Other White Grubs Associated with Turfgrass

Japanese beetle (*Popillia japonica*) is among the most important of the turfgrass-damaging white grubs in many eastern and midwestern states and southeastern Canada. In the adult stage it is highly damaging to leaves and flowers of a wide range of ornamental, fruit, and vegetable plants. It is discussed separately on p. 268.

May/June Beetles (*Phyllophaga* spp.) are among the largest of the white grubs, typically about ¾ to 1 inch long and stout bodied. Adults are generally chocolate brown. More than 200 species occur in North America, with about 25 reported to damage turfgrasses. The adults are well-known insects that are observed careening around porch lights and bouncing off screens in May and June. The beetles feed on the foliage of various trees and shrubs at night, with oak a preferred host for many species. This damage is minor; the primary damage results from larval feeding on plant roots. Grasses are most commonly damaged, but larvae can seriously injure roots of young trees and shrubs grown in grassy areas.

In northern areas, most May/June beetles have an extended life cycle requiring 3 years to complete. With these species, eggs are laid in the soil in May or June, and a limited amount of feeding takes place by young larvae during the first season, before they migrate downward for winter. They return to feed on roots and grow rapidly during the second season, producing most damage at this time. In the third year there is some additional feeding before the insects pupate in a belowground chamber. They transform to adults in late summer and early fall, ready to emerge the following year.

Variations of May/June beetle life cycles occur, and in the southern U.S. many species complete development in a single season. *Phyllophaga crinita* is an important species in Texas with this habit. It commonly damages St. Augustine grass, bermudagrass, and buffalograss.

Tenlined June beetle (*Polyphylla decimlineata*) is slightly larger than May/June beetles and is strongly marked by a series of white bands that runs the length of the body. Larvae develop on the roots of grasses, shrubs, small fruits, and occasionally garden plants but rarely are sufficiently abundant to cause serious damage. The life history is similar to that of May/June beetles, with adults feeding on foliage and larvae requiring 2 or more years to complete development. The insects are attracted to lights and often attract attention because of their large size, overall coloration, and unusual antennae— also because they may audibly hiss when disturbed. Several other *Polyphylla* species (*P. hammondi*, *P. variolosa*, *P. comes*) are reported to occasionally damage turfgrass. These are of similar large size but have less distinct striping and are overall dark colored.

Black turfgrass ataenius (*Ataenius spretulus*) is a small (ca. ⅛ inch), black beetle, known as **black fairway beetle** in Canada. It is primarily a pest of golf course fairways, rarely injuring lawns. Adults of the spring generation sometimes attract attention as they fly during late afternoon and early evening. Larvae mature by early July, and a second generation is produced with peak feeding in late August and early September. Kentucky bluegrass and annual bluegrass are the common host plants.

Also damaging to fairways and sometime in coinfestation with black turfgrass ataenius is *Aphodius granarius*. It is similar in appearance to black turfgrass ataenius but slightly smaller. Like other members of its genus, it is primarily a scavenger of decaying plant matter and particularly animal manure. In the Rocky Mountain states, adults of *Aphodius ommissus ommissus* are occasionally noted to tunnel bentgrass golf course greens, particularly during mating swarms.

A. May/June beetle larvae and damage to tree roots. *J. D. Solomon.* **B.** May/June beetle. *J. Capinera.* **C.** Tenlined June beetle. *D. Leatherman.* **D.** Feeding group of *Polyphylla occidentalis. G. J. Lenhard.* **E.** Tenlined June beetle larva. *W. Cranshaw.* **F.** Adult May/June beetle *Phyllophaga crinita. D. Shetlar.* **G.** Black turfgrass ataenius larva and adults. *D. Shetlar.* **H.** Black turfgrass ataenius adult. *W. Cranshaw.* **I.** Mixed-age population of May/June beetle grubs. *W. Cranshaw.* **J.** Black turfgrass ataenius larvae. *W. Cranshaw.*

Oriental beetle (*Exomala orientalis*) is an introduced species currently found in New England and the mid-Atlantic states. The larvae often coexist with those of Japanese beetle (p. 268) and are very difficult to distinguish. In addition to turfgrass, larvae may damage roots of many nursery plants and small fruits, including plants grown in containers. Adults are about ⅒ inch, of broad form typical of scarab beetles. Coloration is highly variable, ranging from black to straw, with a wide range of patterned markings. Oriental beetles feed on flowers, notably daisy, but rarely cause much injury.

European chafer (*Rhizotrogus majalis*) is a relatively new species in North America that has spread to scattered locations from Connecticut to Michigan and parts of southern Canada. Larvae feed on the roots of grasses and also shrubs such as arborvitae. European chafer appears to supplant Japanese beetle (p. 268) at some turfgrass sites with sandier soils. Adults feed little but sometimes attract attention when spectacular mating swarms move to trees at dusk on warm evenings in mid-June. These large aggregations produce very little injury to trees, usually minor chewing along leaf margins. Later (late summer) the most serious damage to roots is produced by rapidly developing larvae. A 1-year life cycle predominates, but a small percent of European chafers have been observed to require 2 years to complete development.

Green fruit beetles (*Cotinus* spp.) are large (1¼ inches), brightly colored beetles. *C. nitidis* is a rather bizarre species found throughout the southeastern U.S., ranging north to New York and west into Texas. *C. mutabilis* is primarily found in the southwestern states. The larvae feed almost exclusively on dead or decaying organic matter. Occasionally they are associated with turfgrass and may cause minor injury through tunneling and production of small mounds, but they feed little on roots. At night the grubs crawl to the surface to feed, flip on their back, and crawl in a unique manner by contracting and expanding their body segments. The legs, which are relatively small, are not used for locomotion. The larvae winter as nearly full-grown grubs, resuming feeding in spring.

Adults are present and active mostly in July and August. They are metallic velvety green with yellow-orange margins and a shiny green underside. In flight they may make a buzzing sound like bumble bees. They may feed and damage various thin-skinned ripe fruits such as apricot, peach, nectarine, plum, grape, pear, blackberry, raspberry, apple, and fig.

A. Oriental beetle. *Courtesy Pacific Agri-Food Research Centre.* **B.** Three white grubs (left–right): Japanese beetle, European chafer, May/June beetle. *D. Caeppert.* **C.** European chafer adult. *D. Shetlar.* **D.** Shrub girdled by European chafer grubs. *D. Caeppert.* **E.** Green fruit beetle larva. *D. Shetlar.* **F.** Skunk damage, from digging for European chafer larvae. *D. Shetlar.* **G.** Green fruit beetle larva. *Courtesy Clemson University.* **H.** Green fruit beetle. *D. Shetlar.* **I.** Green fruit beetle. *D. Shetlar.*

White Grubs Associated with Garden Plants

Carrot beetle (*Ligyrus gibbosus*) is an occasional pest of root crops, producing gouging wounds. It is distributed throughout must of the southern and western U.S., from Texas and New Mexico east. Larvae are primarily grass feeders, and their presence in gardens is usually associated with previous grass or the presence of grassy weeds. Adults sometimes damage plants, however, as they burrow in soil and feed on the roots and taproot of plants such as sunflower, dahlia, potato, beet, and carrot. Carrot beetle winters as an adult in the soil, and there is one generation per year.

Asiatic garden beetle (*Maladera castanea*) is an introduced species now found throughout most of the Atlantic states from Massachusetts to South Carolina. Larvae feed fairly deeply in the soil, about 2 to 3 inches, and are considered less damaging to turfgrass than species that feed closer to the surface. Most commonly they are injurious to roots of flowers and vegetables and also develop on roots of many weeds. Adults emerge in late June and may be abundant in early summer, when they feed on the leaves of more than 100 kinds of trees, shrubs, flowers, and vegetables.

Rain beetles (*Pleocoma* spp.) occur in western North America. Larvae are very long-lived, sometimes requiring 9 to 13 years to complete development. They feed on the roots and base of the trunk of various trees and shrubs and can be particularly injurious to orchard crops. *P. crinita*, *P. minor*, and *P. oregonensis* are damaging in the Pacific Northwest.

Adults usually emerge in fall but also are active in spring. Only the males fly, and they seek females in their soil burrows, usually following rains. The mated female lays eggs throughout the following spring, in a spiraling pattern 10 to 30 inches deep in the soil. The larvae molt only once a year and may require a decade or more before they are ready to pupate. Because the females are flightless, rain beetles spread very slowly, but established populations can be difficult to control because of their unusual life history and deep burrowing habit.

¹ Coleoptera: Scarabaeidae

A. Carrot beetle adult. *K. Gray.* B. White grub and damage to sweetpotato. *Courtesy Clemson University.* C. Asiatic garden beetle. *D. Gilrein.* D. Asiatic garden beetle (left) compared to oriental beetle. *D. Gilrein.* E. Rain beetle. *K. Gray.* F. Rain beetle. *K. Gray.* G. Asiatic garden beetle. *R. Hiskes.*

ROOT WEEVILS

Several weevils[1] develop on the roots of woody and herbaceous perennial plants. Primary damage by many is from the larval root feeding. Adults feed aboveground on buds and leaves, however, sometimes causing serious injuries. On leaves, chewing injuries are characteristically notched from along the leaf margin. Adults of most root weevils, particularly those associated with ornamental plants, have fused wing covers and do not fly. Despite this, many species have spread widely in North America, primarily through the movement of infested plant materials.

Black Vine Weevil (*Otiorhynchus sulcatus*)

Hosts: A wide range that includes many shrubs. Hemlock, yew, rhododendron, euonymus, and other broadleaf evergreens are among those most seriously damaged.

Damage: Adult weevils feed on leaves at night, producing characteristic notching wounds along the leaf margin. When they are abundant, plants may be heavily defoliated. Larval stages feed on plant roots and can cause serious injury. In areas of the Pacific Northwest and Midwest, this is often considered to be the most important insect pest of nursery crops. The adults occasionally are minor nuisance invaders of homes in late summer and fall.

Distribution: Native to Europe, now generally found throughout the northern U.S. and southern Canada.

Appearance: The adults are dark gray or black snout beetles, about ⅓ inch long with wing covers marked with gold flecking.

Life History and Habits: Black vine weevil spends the winter usually as a larva, in the soil around the root zone of plants on which it feeds. Occasionally some adults may survive winters if they find suitable shelter, including areas in and around homes.

Larvae resume feeding in spring and can extensively damage roots in May and June. After becoming full grown they pupate in the soil, and adult weevils start to emerge in mid-June. The adults feed on the leaves of various plants during the night and cause characteristic notching wounds which somewhat resemble grasshopper injury. After about 2 weeks, the females begin to lay eggs around the base of plants. Eggs begin to hatch in midsummer, and the legless larvae feed on plant roots until cold weather temporarily stops development. One generation is produced per year.

A. Black vine weevil. *J. Capinera.* **B.** Black vine weevil. *K. Gray.* **C.** Black vine weevil larva. *K. Gray.* **D.** Notching injury to foliage characteristic of black vine weevil. *W. Cranshaw.* **E.** Black vine weevil larva and pupa. *D. Herms.* **F.** Root injury to container nursery stock by black vine weevil larvae. *D. Nielsen.*

Related Species

Strawberry root weevil (*Otiorhynchus ovatus*) and **rough strawberry root weevil** (*O. rugosostriatus*) are smaller but generally the same shape as black vine weevil. Although they have similar habits as black vine weevil, neither is as damaging to plants. However, strawberry root weevil much more frequently invades homes, particularly at higher elevations and during midsummer periods when hot, dry conditions persist. **Clay-colored weevil** (*O. singularis*) is smaller and considerably lighter than the above species. It occasionally is important because of bud-feeding damage to raspberry in the Pacific Northwest. Adults are active in spring and early fall, going dormant in midsummer.

Other Root Weevils

Larvae of **obscure root weevil** (*Sciopithes obscures*) feed on the roots of rhododendron and can be very damaging to nursery stock in the Pacific Northwest and northern California. Adults feed on the leaves, chewing notches along the leaf margin. Adults are about ¼ inch, brown with a single wavy brown line near the rear, and are present from August through October. The life cycle is similar to that of black vine weevil.

Woods weevil (*Nemocestes incomptus*), also known as raspberry bud weevil, is a common member of the root weevil complex associated with landscape plants in Washington and British Columbia. Most adults begin to emerge in late summer and may feed throughout the winter months as temperatures allow. Distinct generations do not occur, and all life stages may be present throughout the year. Adults are sooty dark brown, covered with small hairs, and about ⅓ inch. Another native forest species in the region is *Dyslobus granicollis*, which occasionally damages landscape plantings and strawberries. Like most root weevils, adults are flightless so damage usually only occurs in limited sites adjacent to woodlands. In New England, **polydrusus weevil** (*Polydrusus impressifrons*) chews buds and notches leaves of many deciduous trees and shrubs in late spring. Adults are pale metallic green and about ¼ inch long.

Arborvitae weevil (*Phyllobius intrusus*) is an introduced species found in the northeastern and mid-Atlantic states. Adults feed on the new growth of arborvitae, northern whitecedar, and eastern redcedar. Primary damage is caused by larval feeding on roots and bark at the base of plants. Winter is spent as pupae in the soil, and adults are present in late spring, during which time eggs are laid. Arborvitae weevil is a black snout beetle with shiny green scales on the wing covers. A related, also introduced, species is *P. oblongus*. Adults chew leaves of maple, elm, yellow birch, and serviceberry. It is known from New York west to Michigan.

A. Root injury by strawberry root weevil larvae. *K. Gray.* B. Strawberry root weevil. *K. Gray.* C. Adult strawberry root weevil. *D. Shetlar.* D. Strawberry root weevil larva. *K. Gray.* E. Asiatic oak weevil. *J. A. Payne.* F. Rough strawberry root weevil. *D. Shetlar.* G. Clay-colored weevil. *K. Gray.* H. Obscure root weevil. *K. Gray.* I. *Nemocestes* sp. adult. *K. Gray.* J. *Dyslobus granicollis* adult. *K. Gray.*

Asiatic oak weevil (*Cyrtepistomus castaneus*) feeds on leaves of a many woody plants including oak, beech, red maple, dogwood, willow, sycamore, redbud, persimmon, and viburnum. It has extended its range to Missouri from its original point of introduction in New Jersey. When abundant it may be a significant nuisance invader of homes.

Twobanded Japanese weevil (*Callirhopalis bifasciatus*) can cause extensive defoliation of many deciduous shrubs in the northeastern quadrant of the U.S. Adult feeding is typical of that of many other weevils, producing notched cuts that extend in from the leaf margin. Privet, azalea, forsythia, dogwood, holly, spirea, and ash are among the plants injured by adults. Larvae have been observed feeding on roots of forsythia and privet. One generation is produced annually, but all stages may be present throughout the year. Adults are about ¼ inch and light brown with two darker bands across the back.

Fuller rose beetle (*Asynonychus godmanni*) feeds on roots and foliage of a wide variety of ornamental plants and small fruits. Larvae girdle roots, but the most conspicuous damage is caused by adults, which make notching wounds on foliage and consume buds and blossoms. Unsightly dark fecal matter is left around feeding sites. Fuller rose beetle is found in most of the southern U.S. and in localized areas elsewhere, including parts of New York, New Jersey, Wisconsin, California, and Oregon. Adults are gray brown with a short snout and are about ¼ to ⅜ inch long.

Fuller rose beetle is flightless, and only females occur. Overwintered weevils crawl to nearby plants in spring and feed on leaves. Eggs are laid in small, sticky masses, usually in soil but also in bark crevices or between leaves. Larvae enter the soil and chew on roots. Pupation occurs near the soil surface. There are one to two generations per year, with peak numbers of adults in Florida found in early June and early September.

Diaprepes root weevil (*Diaprepes abbreviatus*) has developed into a serious pest in parts of the southern U.S. since its introduction into south Florida in 1964. Larvae develop on the roots of plants, and young plants may be completely girdled and killed directly. Often more important is that wounds allow development of root rots by Phytophthora fungi and other organisms. It is estimated to do approximately $70 million of damage annually in Florida alone and is also a key citrus pest in Texas. It has a wide host range of more than 270 species including citrus, other fruit crops, many woody ornamentals, and even some root crop vegetables. It is sometimes known as citrus root weevil or sugarcane root stalk borer weevil, reflecting its importance on these crops.

Adults may be present year-round in south Florida but are primarily active May through early November. Eggs are laid in clusters in leaves, and the newly hatched larvae subsequently drop to the ground and enter the soil. All subsequent larval development and pupation take place in the root zone. The life cycle is normally completed in 1 year, but this may be shorter in extreme southern areas. Although this species is a poor flier and disperses only short distances on its own power, it has been commonly moved about in infested soil.

A. Asiatic oak weevil adults. *J. D. Solomon.* **B.** Twobanded Japanese weevils on sweet pea. *D. Shetlar.* **C.** Twobanded Japanese weevil. *Courtesy University of Georgia.* **D.** Fuller rose beetle. *J. A. Davidson.* **E.** Fuller rose beetle. *J. A. Payne.* **F.** Diaprepes root weevil. *S. Bauer/USDA-ARS.*

Sweetpotato Weevil (*Cylas formicarius*)

Hosts: Sweetpotato, morning glory, and related plants.

Damage: The most serious injury occurs from tunneling of the tuber by larvae. These wounds allow rotting organisms to further destroy the crop and induce bitter tastes in affected tubers. Tunneling of vines can cause wilting as well. Sweetpotato weevil is the most important pest of sweetpotato.

Distribution: North Carolina south through the Gulf states and into parts of east Texas.

Appearance: The adult is slender, almost antlike, and about ¼ inch long with a long beak. It is generally blue black with a bright red prothorax and legs.

Life History and Habits: Females chew a small pit into the lower stem or roots and insert a single egg, plugging the cavity with their feces. The larvae chew through the stem, working their way to the "tuber." They feed for about 2 to 4 months depending on temperature, then pupate in a chamber they cut in the plant. The adults may feed on the tuber or on the underside of leaves. Capable of flight, they may migrate in a series of short flights up to a mile, usually during the night. As many as five to eight generations may be completed in a year. Development may occur throughout the year as long as temperatures and available food permit.

Other Vegetable Weevils

Carrot weevil (*Listronotus oregonensis*) can seriously damage carrot, parsley, dill, celery, and parsnip. Many related wild plants (Apiaceae family) also are hosts. Larvae tunnel and riddle the root. Young plants may be killed. Top growth wilts, and roots are inedible.

The adults are tannish gray, about ¼ inch long, and become active early in spring. Eggs are laid in cavities chewed into leaf petioles. The young grubs tunnel into the stalks and work their way downward into the roots. They become full grown in about 3 or 4 weeks and pupate nearby in the soil. Two to three generations are produced over much of the range, although only one generation may occur in cooler northern areas. Carrot weevil occurs in much of southern Canada and the northern U.S. west of the Rocky Mountains, ranging into northern Texas. Most damage has occurred in sites with high organic matter soils.

Vegetable weevil (*Listroderes difficilis*) also damages carrot as well as turnip, potato, and other root crops in the Gulf states. It also is reported as a pest of dichondra lawns in California. Feeding injury by larvae is more concentrated around the soil surface, causing stunting and defoliation as well as tunneling of larger roots. Adults are about ⅓ inch and dull grayish brown with a light V-shaped mark near the hind end. Vegetable weevil has only one generation a year, with peak adult activity and egg-laying occurring in late summer and early fall.

"Whitefringed beetle" is apparently a complex of three introduced *Naupactus* species that can be found in parts of the southern U.S. Adults are brownish gray snout beetles covered with fine hairs and sporting a pair of pale stripes along the thorax and sides of the abdomen. They can develop on a wide range of plants, with principal injury caused by the tunneling of larvae in roots and tubers. Sweetpotato is among the plants most seriously damaged. Whitefringed beetles are fairly long-lived; one generation per year is common, but development takes two seasons in northern areas of the range. Winter is spent as partially grown larvae, and eggs are usually laid in mid- to late summer.

---

[1] Coleoptera: Curculionidae

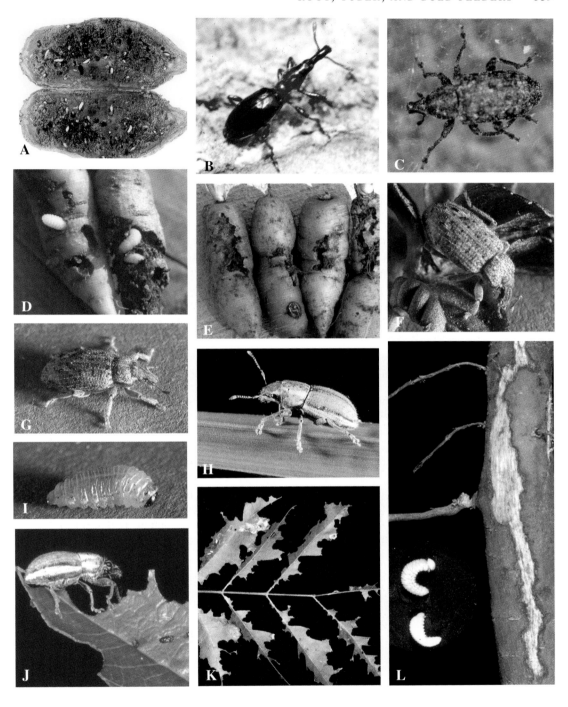

A. Sweetpotato weevil larval damage. *J. Capinera.* **B.** Adult sweetpotato weevil. *Courtesy Clemson University.* **C.** Adult carrot weevil. *W. Cranshaw.* **D.** Carrot weevil larvae in damaged carrot roots. *W. Cranshaw.* **E.** Damage by carrot weevil larvae. *W. Cranshaw.* **F.** Vegetable weevil adult. *K. Gray.* **G.** Vegetable weevil adult. *K. Gray.* **H.** Adult whitefringed beetle. *J. Capinera.* **I.** Vegetable weevil larva. *K. Gray.* **J.** Whitefringed beetle. *J. A. Payne.* **K.** Leaf-feeding injury by adult whitefringed beetles. *L. Tedders.* **L.** Larvae and associated root injury by whitefringed weevil. *J. D. Solomon.*

BILLBUGS

Billbugs[1] are weevils in the genus *Sphenophorus* that develop on grasses.

Bluegrass Billbug (*Sphenophorus parvulus*)

Hosts: Primarily Kentucky bluegrass; occasionally fescues and perennial ryegrass.

Damage: Young larvae develop in the crown of grasses, often killing the plant. Older larvae move into soil and chew roots. Peak injury occurs from late June to early August and is aggravated by moisture stress. Grass patches killed by billbug larvae often break at the crown of the plant and show evidence of tunneling and a characteristic sawdust excrement at the wound.

Distribution: Throughout the U.S., excluding south Florida, and parts of southern Canada.

Appearance: Adults are slate gray to black weevils with a body about 5/16 inch long. Larvae are plump, legless grubs with a dark brown head; they are found either in the plant crown or in the soil about the roots.

Life History and Habits: Bluegrass billbug winters in the adult stage either in the thatch of lawns or in adjacent areas under sheltering mulch or leaves. It typically begins to become active in mid- to early May, whenever soil temperatures reach about 65° F. Adults are often seen at this time crossing driveways and sidewalks—freezing or playing dead when disturbed.

Females chew small holes in the base of plant stems and insert eggs. The young develop in the plant, tunneling out the crown area and leaving behind a characteristic sawdustlike frass. As they outgrow the plant, they migrate to the soil and continue to feed on roots. Pupation occurs in the soil in early to middle summer. Adults are present in late summer, feed a bit on grass leaves, then move to wintering sites. Normally one generation is produced annually, although a small second generation has been noted in southern areas.

Other Billbugs

In much of the southeastern U.S., **hunting billbug** (*Sphenophorus venatus vestitus*) is an occasional pest of zoysiagrass and bermudagrass. Although its injuries and life cycle are generally similar to those of bluegrass billbug, it is less synchronized and most stages can be found throughout the year. This can also be said of **Denver billbug** (*S. cicatristriatus*), a pest of Kentucky bluegrass in parts of the Rocky Mountain region and northern High Plains. **Phoenix billbug** (*S. phoeniciensis*) is associated with zoysiagrass and bermudagrass in the southwestern U.S.

[1] Coleoptera: Curculionidae

A. Billbug-damaged crown area of turfgrass. *D. Shetlar.* B. Bluegrass billbug adult. *D. Shetlar.* C. Billbug larva in crown of grass plant. *K. Gray.* D. Hunting billbug. *D. Shetlar.* E. Denver billbug adult. *D. Shetlar.* F. Hunting billbug on lawn. *D. Shetlar.* G. Denver billbug on sidewalk. *W. Cranshaw.* H. Phoenix billbug. *D. Shetlar.* I. Denver billbug larvae. *W. Cranshaw.* J. Billbug larvae and damage. *W. Cranshaw.* K. Phoenix billbug. *D. Shetlar.*

WIREWORMS

Wireworms are the larval stage of click beetles.[1] Most wireworms are soil inhabiting and feed on roots of plants; some develop in decayed wood. The common name for the adults reflects their unusual ability to flip when laid on their back, often with an associated clicking sound. More than 880 species occur in North America, of which about two dozen may significantly damage crops.

Hosts: Roots and seeds of a wide variety of plants. Root crops, including potato, carrot, and sweetpotato, are often most seriously affected.

Damage: Larvae tunnel into germinating seeds, roots, and other belowground structures. Small plants may be killed. Riddling injuries degrade the quality of root crops.

Distribution: Wireworms can be found throughout North America, although some species tend to be of limited distribution. The genera *Ctenicerca* and *Limonius* are concentrated in the west, particularly the Pacific Northwest. *Conoderus* species are found mostly in the southeastern U.S.

Appearance: Larvae are elongate, somewhat hard bodied, and light brown. Adults are distinctive in having a greatly enlarged prothorax which is loosely jointed. This is structured to allow them to catapult by flexing the prothorax, sometimes producing an audible clicking noise. Most species are gray or brown, although there may be some patterning on the wing covers.

Life History and Habits: Life cycles vary among species and location. Most wireworms have relatively long life cycles that can extend several years, particularly if temperatures are cool. The exceptions are those in the genus *Conoderus,* found in the southeastern U.S., which may complete a generation within a year.

Adults are usually most abundant in mid- to late spring. Eggs are laid shallowly in soils. Some species prefer to lay eggs in grassy areas, whereas others are attracted to moist soil regardless of the nearby vegetation. The larvae are quite active and mobile in the soil. Pupation occurs in small cells constructed in soil.

[1] Coleoptera: Elateridae

A. Click beetle, adult of a wireworm. *R. Bessin.* **B.** Pacific coast wireworm. *K. Gray.* **C.** Click beetle, adult of a wireworm. *W. Cranshaw.* **D.** Wireworm. *K. Gray.* **E.** Wireworm larval damage to potato. *K. Gray.* **F.** Wireworm in potato. *W. Cranshaw.* **G.** Wireworm damage to potato tuber. *K. Gray.*

CHAPTER ELEVEN

Beneficial Garden Arthropods

PREDATORS

Several arthropods common to gardens develop as predators of other arthropods. In most, the immature stages are free-living hunters which move about to seek prey. During the course of their development, they consume many prey, often several dozen. Adult stages of predators may have similar habits, or they may feed instead on nectar, pollen, honeydew and similar materials.

Predators among the Hymenoptera, the ants and wasps, have a somewhat different habit. It is the adults—which collect insect prey to feed their developing young—that are the predatory stage. Their habits may be further modified by rearing of the young in a colony, as occurs with ants and the social wasps.

Lady Beetles (Lady Bugs, Ladybird Beetles)

Coleoptera: Coccinellidae

Lady beetles are the most familiar and widely recognized predators of garden pests. Almost 200 species can be found throughout North America, and with the exception of Mexican bean beetle and squash beetle, all are beneficial inhabitants of the garden. Adults of the great majority have a characteristic round or oval shape, are brightly colored, and often have bold patterning on the wing covers. Adult, and particularly larval, lady beetles may feed on large numbers of small, soft-bodied insects. Some species are generalists that feed on many kinds of insects, such as aphids and small caterpillars or beetles, and on insect eggs. Others have more specialized habits. For example, **twicestabbed lady beetle** (*Chilocorus stigmata*) feeds only on scales, and "**spider mite destroyers**" (*Stethorus* spp.) feed on mites. Adults of most species also feed on pollen, nectar, and honeydew, and the presence of such foods around the yard or garden may be important in maintaining these beneficial insects.

Most lady beetles lay eggs in masses of 5 to 30 orange-yellow eggs. The eggs are quite distinctive, although they somewhat resemble those produced by some leaf beetles (Chrysomelidae family, p. 178). Eggs are usually laid near colonies of insects that provide food for the lady beetles' larvae.

The larval stages of lady beetles look very different from the more familiar adults and often are overlooked or misidentified. Lady beetle larvae are elongated, usually dark colored, and flecked with orange or yellow. Some species may have fleshy spines, and a few are covered with white wax. Larvae are active hunters that can crawl rapidly over plants, searching for food. Most species can complete their larval stages in 2 or 3 weeks, after which they pupate attached to a plant or nearby object.

Most lady beetles survive winter as adults in sheltered locations. In some areas of the country, **convergent lady beetle** (*Hippodamia convergens*) migrates to higher elevations during its dormant periods and often aggregates in large numbers. These mass aggregations serve as the source of adult lady beetles sold by some nurseries. A fairly new species in North America is **multicolored Asian lady beetle** (*Harmonia axyridis*) which has a nuisance habit of moving into homes following autumn frosts.

A. Pink spotted lady beetle feeding on Colorado potato beetle eggs. *M. al-Doghairi.* **B.** Sevenspotted lady beetles. *F. Peairs.* **C.** Twicestabbed lady beetle. *L. Tedders.* **D.** Egg mass of lady beetle in colony of greenbug aphids. *F. Peairs.* **E.** Young lady beetle larva. *W. Cranshaw.* **F.** Lady beetle larvae at egg hatch. *W. Cranshaw.* **G.** Recently emerged adult lady beetle with pupa and pupal skins. *T. J. Weissling.* **H.** Larva of multicolored Asian lady beetle. *W. Cranshaw.* **I.** Lady beetle larvae, *Scymnus* sp., covered with wax. *W. Cranshaw.* **J.** Convergent lady beetle. *F. Peairs.* **K.** Spider mite destroyer lady beetle. *F. Peairs.* **L.** Adults of multicolored Asian lady beetle. *W. Cranshaw.* **M.** Massed lady beetles on tree trunk. *R. Simpson.*

Ground Beetles

Coleoptera: Carabidae

Ground beetles are common insects in gardens. Most are broadly oval in form with prominent forward-projecting jaws. They have hard wing covers that are typically dark but may have a metallic sheen. Adults can be very active and fast moving but usually spend days under the cover of leaf litter and other sheltering debris. Larvae are also predators and are usually active at the soil surface or tunnel in the upper soil.

Almost all ground beetles develop as predators and may feed on a wide variety of insects. As their name indicates, most restrict their activity to areas at or around the soil surface and are poor climbers. A few species, however, may occur on plants; these include the large, striking *Calosoma* species, known as "caterpillar hunters," which attack gypsy moth larvae and other caterpillars. *Bembidion* ground beetles can be important predators of insect eggs on leaves.

A group of insects now commonly classified with the ground beetles are the **tiger beetles**. These are extremely active and readily fly. Both adults and larvae are general predators of other insects, although larvae primarily hunt by ambush from soil tubes where they develop. Most tiger beetles are in the genus *Cicindela*.

Clerid Beetles

Coleoptera: Cleridae

Clerid, or checkered, beetles are usually brightly colored insects that are generally elongate in form and somewhat flattened. Several species are important predators of bark beetles and other wood-boring insects. Immature clerid beetles are commonly found in tunnels of bark beetles.

Soldier Beetles

Coleoptera: Cantharidae

Soldier beetles are elongate beetles with fairly soft wing covers, lending them the name "leather-winged beetles." Adults are usually patterned with yellow or orange and black markings. Some (*Cantharis* spp., *Podabrus* spp.) can be important predators of aphids, mealybugs, and other soft-bodied insects. The rarely observed larval stages develop in the soil where they feed on other arthropods. Larvae of the common **Pennsylvania leatherwing** (*Chauliognathus pennsylvanicus*) are reported to develop as predators of root maggot larvae in soil. Soldier beetles are most commonly observed on yellow flowers late in the season, feeding on pollen and often in copula (coupled during mating).

Rove Beetles

Coleoptera: Staphylinidae

Rove beetles are rather odd beetles, elongate in form with very short wing covers. They are general predators of insects found in soil. *Aleochara bilineata* is an important predator of root maggots; many other rove beetle species occur in gardens and around compost piles.

A. Ground beetle, *Pterostichus* sp. *W. Cranshaw.* **B.** Ground beetle, *Pasimachus* sp. *W. Cranshaw.* **C.** Ground beetle larva. *K. Gray.* **D.** Clerid beetle. *G. J. Lenhard.* **E.** Ground beetle, *Calosoma* sp. *K. Gray.* **F.** Tiger beetle. *K. Gray.* **G.** Soldier beetle, *Cantharis* sp. *K. Gray.* **H.** Soldier beetle. *W. Cranshaw.* **I.** Rove beetle. *K. Gray.* **J.** Rove beetle larva. *K. Gray.*

Fireflies, or Lightning Bugs

Coleoptera: Lampyridae

Most fireflies develop as predators of slugs, snails, and worms. Adults may also be predatory, feeding on scale crawlers, aphids, and similar small, soft-bodied insects.

Collops Beetles

Coleoptera: Melyridae

Collops beetles (*Collops* spp.) are moderately sized (⅕ to ⅓ inch), usually bluish black with red or orange markings. They may be found feeding on pollen at flowers but also eat insect larvae, aphids, and other small, soft-bodied insects. They can be common in fields but are infrequent in gardens.

Green Lacewings

Neuroptera: Chrysopidae

Several species of green lacewings, mostly in the genus *Chrysoperla,* commonly frequent yards and gardens. Adults are pale green or light brown with clear, highly veined wings that are held over the body at rest. These are delicate and attractive insects that feed primarily on nectar, pollen, and honeydew, although adults in the genus *Chrysopa* also feed on small insects. The females lay a distinctive stalked egg, approximately ½ inch high. Eggs may be laid in small groups or singly on leaves of plants throughout the yard.

Lacewing larvae emerge from the egg in about a week. Sometimes called "aphid lions," they are voracious predators capable of feeding on a wide range of insects, including small caterpillars, beetles, and aphids. In general shape and size, lacewing larvae are superficially similar to lady beetle larvae. However, immature lacewings usually are light brown and have a large pair of viciously hooked jaws projecting from the front of the head. A few larval lacewings cover their body with debris. Pupation occurs in a nearly spherical, pale-colored cocoon loosely attached to foliage.

Brown Lacewings

Neuroptera: Hemerobiidae

Brown lacewings are related to green lacewings and have generally similar habits, being predators of insects in both their adult and larval stages. Many are specialized predators, feeding primarily on "woolly" aphids and mealybugs. Brown lacewings are almost always associated with dense vegetation, including trees and shrubs.

Adult brown lacewings are somewhat smaller than adult green lacewings and have light brown wings. Mouthparts of the larvae are designed to pierce and capture prey but are a bit more pronounced than in green lacewings. Eggs of brown lacewings are not stalked.

Dustywings

Neuroptera: Coniopterygidae

Dustywings are small insects (ca. ⅛ inch) that develop as predators of aphids, scale insects, mites, and other small arthropods. The body of the adult insect is covered with fine powdery white wax; larvae are have a tapered form. Although easily overlooked, dustywings may be abundant on the trees and shrubs they frequent, especially conifers.

A. Firefly, *Lucidota* sp. *W. Cranshaw.* **B.** Firefly larva. *G. J. Lenhard.* **C.** Collops beetle feeding on insect larva. *K. Gray.* **D.** Green lacewing eggs. *W. Cranshaw.* **E.** Green lacewing at flower. *W. Cranshaw.* **F.** Green lacewing larva with looper prey. *K. Gray.* **G.** Brown lacewing feeding on rose aphid. *W. Cranshaw.* **H.** Green lacewing egg. *W. Cranshaw.* **I.** Green lacewing pupa. *W. Cranshaw.* **J.** Green lacewing larva. *W. Cranshaw.*

Syrphid Flies (Flower Flies, Hover Flies)

Diptera: Syrphidae

Syrphid flies are common, brightly colored flies. Typical markings are yellow or orange with black, and they may look very similar to bees or yellowjacket wasps. Syrphid flies are harmless to humans, however. The adults usually can be seen feeding at flowers.

It is the larval stage of a syrphid fly that is an insect predator. Variously colored, the tapered maggots crawl over foliage and can daily down dozens of aphids. Syrphid flies are particularly important in controlling aphid infestations early in the season and are capable of entering the tightly curled leaves some aphids produce. A tarry excrement produced by syrphid fly larvae is diagnostic of their activities.

A few species of syrphid flies, known as bulb flies, develop by feeding on and tunneling into plant tissues. Also common are **drone flies** (*Eristalis* spp.), excellent mimics of honey bees. In their larval form, known as a **rattailed maggot** because of the long breathing tube it possesses, drone flies develop in very moist soil or polluted water.

Predatory Midges

Diptera: Cecidomyiidae

Although most insects of the gall midge family Cecidomyiidae feed on plants and many produce galls or other distortions, a few prey on other insects. The larvae are tiny (ca. ¹⁄₁₀ inch) maggots, often orange or yellowish, and feed primarily on aphids. Some predatory midges in the genera *Aphidoletes* and *Feltiella* are sold to control insects in greenhouses.

Longlegged Flies

Diptera: Dolichopodidae

Longlegged flies are moderately small flies noted for their metallic sheen. Adult stages feed on small insects such as gnats and midges. Larvae also are predaceous, and some (*Medetera* spp.) live under bark and feed on bark beetle larvae.

Predatory Thrips

Thysanoptera

Many thrips, even some that occur as plant pests, may feed on mites, other thrips, and insect eggs. **Bandedwinged thrips** (Aeolothripidae family), which are fairly large thrips with black and white banding, are primarily predators. A species sold for biological control is **six-spotted thrips** (*Scolothrips sexmaculatus*), used to control spider mites.

Predatory Stink Bugs

Hemiptera: Pentatomidae

Although stink bugs include many species that feed on plants (p. 228), some are predators. All stink bugs are characterized by their distinctive shieldlike body and ability to produce an unpleasant odor when disturbed. Those that feed on insects are capable of subduing large prey such as caterpillars or beetle larvae, which they impale with piercing, sucking mouthparts. Among the predatory stink bugs more commonly found in gardens are **twospotted stink bug** (*Perillus bioculatus*), which specializes in beetle larvae such as Colorado potato beetle, and **spined soldier bug** (*Podisus maculiventris*), which primarily feeds on caterpillars.

A. Syrphid fly. *W. Cranshaw.* **B.** Syrphid fly. *W. Cranshaw.* **C.** Aphid predator midge (*Aphidoletes aphidimyza*) in aphid colony. *W. Cranshaw.* **D.** Predatory bandedwinged thrips. *W. Cranshaw.* **E.** Syrphid fly egg in spirea aphid colony. *W. Cranshaw.* **F.** Twospotted stink bug feeding on Colorado potato beetle larva. *J. Capinera.* **G.** Twospotted stink bug nymph feeding on Colorado potato beetle larva. *M. al-Doghairi.* **H.** Stink bug feeding on elm leaf beetle larva. *W. Cranshaw.* **I.** Spined soldier bug. *G. J. Lenhard.* **J.** Dolichopodid, or longlegged fly. *J. Capinera.* **K.** Spined soldier bug nymph. *G. J. Lenhard.*

Assassin Bugs

Hemiptera: Reduviidae

Assassin bugs are moderately large insects that can feed on fairly large prey such as insect larvae. Most assassin bugs are elongate in form, have a pronounced "snout" on the front which is the base for the stylet mouthparts, and are spiny. Despite their prodigious ability to dispatch most garden pests, they rarely become abundant since they in turn succumb to many natural enemies of their own. Common assassin bugs associated with gardens include **spined assassin bug** (*Sinea diadema*), **bee hunter** (*Api-omerus* spp.), and several elongate assassin bugs in the genus *Zelus*. Of even more dramatically slender form are the **thread-legged bugs** (*Emesaya* spp.).

Late in the season, **ambush bugs** (*Phymata* spp.) are commonly found on flowers. These are rather heavy-bodied assassin bugs with thick forelegs which are used to help capture flies, bees, and other insects that visit flowers. The ambush bugs' patterning and coloration blend well with the flowers on which they hide.

Damsel Bugs

Hemiptera: Nabidae

Damsel bugs are considerably smaller than assassin bugs (ca. ¼ inch) and usually dark yellow or pale brown. As in assassin bugs, the forelegs are slightly thickened to assist in holding prey. Damsel bugs develop as general predators of insect larvae, small soft-bodied insects, and insect eggs. They are most common in grassy fields.

Predatory Plant Bugs

Hemiptera: Miridae

The plant bug family includes several important species that can be seriously damaging to plants, such as tarnished plant bug, fourlined plant bug, and honeylocust plant bug. Many plant bugs are omnivorous, however, and frequently feed on insects and mites as well as plants. A few, notably in the genus *Deraeocoris*, are primarily predaceous and may be among the most important biological controls of spider mites, gall midges, and other shade-tree pests.

A. Assassin bug, *Rhynocoris* sp. *K. Gray.* B. Assassin bug. *W. Cranshaw.* C. Bee hunter assassin bug. *W. Cranshaw.* D. Nymph of assassin bug, *Zelus* sp. *W. Cranshaw.* E. Damsel bug nymph. *K. Gray.* F. Damsel bug, adult. *K. Gray.* G. Stilt bug, *Neides muticus*. *K. Gray.* H. Spined assassin bugs with prey. *K. Gray.* I. Predatory plant bug, *Deraeocoris* sp. *W. Cranshaw.* J. Ambush bug. *K. Gray.*

Big-eyed Bugs

Hemiptera: Lygaeidae

Most seed bugs (Lygaeidae) feed on seeds and foliage, with a few such as the chinch bugs and false chinch bugs occurring as significant plant pests. However, the members of one genus (*Geocoris*), known as the big-eyed bugs, develop as predators of caterpillars, spider mites, aphids, and many other insects. The large eyes that may extend over the prothorax are distinctive of this beneficial group of seed bugs.

Minute Pirate Bugs

Hemiptera: Anthocoridae

The smallest of the predatory "true" bugs commonly found in yards and gardens (typically about ¹⁄₁₆ inch), minute pirate bugs feed on smaller arthropods such as spider mites, thrips, and aphids and on insect eggs. The adults are distinctive with black and white markings; immature forms are generally a uniform straw color and about the size of their aphid prey.

Mantids

Mantodea: Mantidae

Mantids are familiar insects to gardeners. Large and statuesque, all develop as predators of other insects, which they capture with their distinct grasping forelegs. Mantids develop from eggs that are laid in masses and covered with a protective layer of dried foam, giving them the appearance of a packing peanut. Immature forms resemble the adults but lack wings.

The most common mantid in much of the U.S. is **European mantid** (*Mantis religiosa*), also known as praying mantid. Both brown and green forms occur, the latter being more common. A bull's-eye marking on the inside of the foreleg is characteristic. Also common locally may be **Chinese mantid** (*Tenodera aridifolia sinensis*), the mantid that has been widely distributed through sales of egg masses by garden centers and nursery catalogs. Chinese mantid is a large species that is generally brown with green and yellow striping along the sides of the wings. Native mantids common in some regions include **Carolina mantid** (*Stagmomantis carolina*) and **California mantid** (*S. californica*).

Earwigs

Dermaptera: Forficulidae, Labiduridae

Although **European earwig** (*Forficula auricularia*; p. 62) is often considered a plant pest as well as a common nuisance, it is an omnivore that feeds on a wide variety of materials, including many insects. Many other earwigs are primarily predaceous, including **striped earwig** (*Labidura riparia*) of the southwestern U.S. and **spine-tailed earwigs** (*Doru* spp.).

A. Big-eyed bug adult. *K. Gray.* **B.** Minute pirate bug adult. *W. Cranshaw.* **C.** Big-eyed bug nymph feeding on aphid prey. *K. Gray.* **D.** Egg case of European mantid. *W. Cranshaw.* **E.** Minute pirate bug nymph. *K. Gray.* **F.** Brown phase of European mantid. *W. Cranshaw.* **G.** Green phase of European mantid with grasshopper prey. *W. Cranshaw.* **H.** European mantid nymph. *W. Cranshaw.* **I.** Ringlegged earwig. *J. Capinera.* **J.** Egg sac of Chinese mantid offered for sale. *W. Cranshaw.* **K.** Chinese mantid feeding on grasshopper prey. *R. L. Anderson.*

Predatory Ants

Hymenoptera: Formicidae

A wide variety of habits exist among the hundreds of ant species found in North America. Some are considered pests because they occur in nuisance numbers in homes, nest in wood, or damage plants (p. 64). Effects on garden pests are mixed. Many are important predators of insect pests, particularly in sites such as turfgrass. Many sweet-loving ants, however, collect honeydew as an important part of their diet. These often protect honeydew-producing insects (e.g., aphids, soft scales) from predators such as lady beetles and disrupt biological control. Fire ants (*Solenopsis* spp.) may devastate populations of all manner of insects that occur in the vicinity of nests. Many of the common field ants (*Formica* spp.) and carpenter ants (*Camponotus* spp.) both feed on insects and collect honeydew.

Paper Wasps

Hymenoptera: Vespidae

Paper wasps annually make open-celled paper nests that are not covered with a papery envelope. They are usually located hanging from eaves, ceilings of outbuildings, or sometimes in aboveground hollows. The great majority of the species found in North America are in the genus *Polistes*. In addition to the native species is a recently introduced species, *Polistes dominulus,* the **European paper wasp**, now widely established in North America. In areas of western North America **yellowlegged paper wasp** (*Mischocyttarus flavitarsis*) may be common.

All of the paper wasps feed their young living insects. They are commonly seen searching plants for caterpillars, beetle larvae, and other suitable prey, which are then chewed and fed to the grublike larvae in the nest. Paper wasps are valuable in the biological control of many pest insects in yards and gardens. They can sting and aggressively defend the nest.

Hornets and Yellowjackets

Hymenoptera: Vespidae

Baldfaced hornet (*Dolichovespula maculata*) and **aerial yellowjacket** (*D. arenaria*) produce large aerial nests covered with a papery shell. These nests are produced annually, started by a single fertilized female (queen) in late spring and then abandoned at the end of the season. Both of these insects rear their young strictly on a diet of living insects, particularly caterpillars. Although they sting if the nest is disturbed, these insects are largely beneficial to gardeners because of their importance as biological control agents of pests.

Of far more mixed effects are the activities of **yellowjackets** (*Vespula* spp.). These also make paper nests, but they are located belowground or behind walls. Although some yellowjackets feed some living insects to their young, their diet primarily includes dead insects and earthworms and other carrion. They also forage on sweet materials, particularly late in the season, and can be serious nuisance pests. As they neither provide much biological control nor pollinate plants, as do the bees with which they are often confused, yellowjackets are usually considered undesirable around the garden. They are discussed further on p. 242.

A. Field ant tending boxelder aphids. *F. Peairs.* **B.** Field ant carrying sawfly prey. *L. L. Hyche.* **C.** Paper wasp *Polistes dominulus. W. Cranshaw.* **D.** Early-season nest of paper wasp. *W. Cranshaw.* **E.** *Polistes dominulus* with larvae. *W. Cranshaw.* **F.** Paper wasp returning to nest with chewed caterpillar prey. *H. E. Evans.* **G.** Western yellowjacket. *K. Gray.*

Potter Wasps

Hymenoptera: Vespidae (Eumeninae)

Potter wasps are related to yellowjackets and paper wasps but do not produce colonies. Most species, notably those in the genus *Eumenes*, produce nest cells in the form of clay pots which they provision with paralyzed caterpillars and beetle larvae. A single wasp larva develops in each nest cell. Potter wasps are nonaggressive and rarely sting.

Hunting Wasps

Hymenoptera: Sphecidae

Hunting wasps are solitary wasps and do not produce a colony as the social wasps (paper wasps, yellowjackets, hornets) do. Instead, working alone, females construct the entire nest and do all of the foraging needed to feed their young. Depending on the species, some hunting wasps make nests in soil in the form of underground chambers. Others excavate tunnels in the pith of plants. A few, notably the **mud daubers** (*Sceliphron* spp.), which capture spider prey, create nest cells out of mud.

When a female hunting wasp finds the proper insect, it paralyzes it with its stinger and carries it off to the nest. An egg is laid on the paralyzed prey, and the young hunting wasp grub feeds on it over the next several weeks.

Females begin to search for prey after the nest site has been established. Each species specializes in the kind of insect it accepts. For example, some take solely katydids and related grasshoppers, some hunt certain weevils, and others specialize in hairless caterpillars. Some of the smaller hunting wasps collect leafhoppers or aphids, for example the *Pemphredon* species. The largest hunting wasps are the **cicada killers** (*Sphecius* spp.), which capture dog-day cicadas and take them to large underground nests that the female wasp excavates.

Despite their often fearsome appearance, hunting wasps rarely sting and do not contain the potent venom of social wasps.

A. Nest cells made by potter wasp. *W. Cranshaw.* **B.** *Ammophila* wasp stinging caterpillar prey. *H. E. Evans.*
C. *Ammophila* wasp carrying paralyzed cherry sphinx caterpillar prey. *W. Cranshaw.* **D.** Hunting sand wasp (*Bembix*
sp.) digging nest. *H. E. Evans.* **E.** Mud dauber building nest. *H. E. Evans.* **F.** Cicada killer wasp. *G. J. Lenhard.*
G. Mud dauber adult, *Sceliphron caementarium.* *K. Gray.* **H.** Cicada killer wasp with dog-day cicada prey. *H. E. Evans.*

Crab Spiders

Araneae: Thomisidae

Crab spiders are usually distinguished by the front two pairs of legs being particularly elongated. Most have a fairly bulbous abdomen, and all hunt primarily by ambush, waiting on leaves and flowers for prey to approach. Many have coloration that allows them to blend well with their background.

Jumping Spiders

Araneae: Salticidae

Jumping spiders are some of the most active hunters, and as their name indicates they are capable of short (less than 1 inch) jumps. Most are brightly colored, and they have large eyes that allow them to track prey well. *Phidippus* species are particularly common in gardens.

Wolf Spiders

Araneae: Lycosidae

Wolf spiders are active hunters, primarily nocturnal, that do not use webbing to capture prey. Activity is usually restricted to crawling on the soil surface, and they rarely climb plants. Most wolf spiders are gray, brown, or nearly black, and some get quite large. A curious habit is that the female carries the egg sac attached to her hind spinnerets, and the newly hatched spiderlings spend a brief period carried on her back.

Dysderid Spiders

Araneae: dysderidae

Dysderid spiders are found in moist habitats where their primary prey—sowbugs and pillbugs—are abundant. These "roly-poly hunters" possess large jaws which, combined with their reddish coloration, often attract attention.

Orb-web Spiders

Araneae: Araneaidae

Orb-web spiders are well recognized as the masters of web spinning, with many producing beautifully patterned concentric webs in late summer and early fall. Perhaps the best recognized are the argiope spiders which make large webs, usually with a zigzag stripe of webbing (stabilimentum) running down the center, among vegetation. **Banded argiope** (*Argiope trifasciata*) is more common in western North America, **yellow and black argiope** (*A. aurantia*) in the east. Many webspinning spiders found in gardens are in the genus *Araneus*. In the southeastern U.S. **golden silk spider** (*Nephila clavipes*) attracts attention with the large webs it produces in open areas among trees and large shrubs. Orb-web spiders of the genus *Micrathena*, found commonly in some areas of the southern U.S., have unusual shapes with prominent spines.

Lynx Spiders

Araneae: Oxyopidae

Lynx spiders hide among vegetation and ambush passing insects. They have an elongate body and many long hairs (setae) on their legs. A common species in the southeastern U.S. is **green lynx spider** (*Peucetia viridans*).

A. Adult male crab spider on back of female. *W. Cranshaw.* **B.** Head of a jumping spider showing large eyes. *W. Cranshaw.* **C.** Wolf spider. *W. Cranshaw.* **D.** *Misumena* sp. crab spider with prey. *K. Gray.* **E.** Roly-poly hunter, a dys-derid spider. *W. Cranshaw.* **F.** Jumping spider, *Phidippus* sp. *W. Cranshaw.* **G.** Black and yellow argiope. *K. Gray.* **H.** Green lynx spider with egg sac. *H. A. Pase III.* **I.** Jumping spider, *Phidippus* sp. *W. Cranshaw.* **J.** Banded argiope. *W. Cranshaw.*

Funnel Spiders

Araneae: Agelenidae

Funnel spiders, including the common "grass spiders," make distinct funnel-shaped webs. The larger area of the web is sheetlike and is produced in tall grass, dense shrubbery, and other sites. These webs are most commonly observed in late summer and early fall, particularly after a dew. At one end of the sheet is a tunnel in which the spider retreats, emerging to capture prey that disturb the web. Grass spiders in the genera *Tegenaria* and *Agelenopsis* are common invaders of homes in late summer and fall.

Daddylonglegs, or Harvestmen

Opiliones: Phalangida

Daddylonglegs are distant relatives of spiders and are classed in their own order, Opiliones. More than 200 species occur in North America, many of which are of European origin. *Leiobunum* species and *Phalangium opilio* are usually the daddylonglegs most commonly encountered in gardens.

Like other arachnids, daddylonglegs have four pairs of legs. However, the legs are extremely long—proportionately longer and more conspicuous than on any other animal. Males, although somewhat smaller bodied than females, have particularly long legs. The body is generally globular and lacks distinct body regions, although the abdomen is clearly segmented. Two small eyes are mounted on tubercules of the head. The jaws (chelicerae) are designed to tear apart food so it can be mixed with digestive fluids. Unlike spiders, daddylonglegs do not possess poison glands, although their purported toxicity is a widespread (worldwide) urban legend. They also have no glands to produce silk.

Daddylonglegs are generalists in their feeding habits. They may consume small, soft-bodied insects, slugs, and mites and are considered to be beneficial in a garden. They also scavenge dead insects, spiders, or earthworms. Some may also feed on plant juices.

Predatory Mites

Acari: Phytoseiidae, Bdellidae, Camerobiidae, Trombiculidae, and others

Many types of mites prey on plant-feeding spider mites. Typically, predatory mites are pear shaped and have shinier bodies than do spider mites. They are also more active and can usually be detected by being considerably faster moving than their prey. Most predatory mites are generalist predators and may feed on eriophyid mites, thrips, and insect eggs. Pollen is also important in the diet of some predatory mites. Predatory mites can often provide good control of spider mites but tend to require higher humidities than do spider mites. They are often susceptible to insecticides.

A rather unusual group of predatory mites is the **velvet mites**. These live in or on the soil, and young stages of many are parasites of insects. (Young stages of some in this family, Trombiculidae, are parasites of other animals and are known as chiggers.) Adults are general predators that primarily feed on insect eggs. Their reddish color, often bright red, attracts attention.

Centipedes

Class Chilopoda

All centipedes develop as predators of other arthropods. They are rarely abundant enough to have much effect on pest populations but feed on a wide variety of potential pests that spend their lives in the ground or on the soil surface. The most common centipedes found in yards and gardens are the **stone centipedes** (Lithobiomorpha order) which are usually about 1 inch long and possess 15 pairs of legs.

A. Male funnel spider. *W. Cranshaw.* **B.** Stone centipede. *W. Cranshaw.* **C.** Daddylonglegs. *W. Cranshaw.* **D.** Giant velvet mite. *K. Gray.* **E.** Funnel web spider. *W. Cranshaw.* **F.** A predatory mite (*Anastis* sp.) with aphid prey. *K. Gray.* **G.** Predator mite with spider mite prey. *W. Cranshaw.*

PARASITES

Many wasps and some flies develop as parasites. In these species, the adult females seek a host insect for their young. They then lay their eggs in or on this host, which the developing young consume. Life cycles of these parasites and their hosts are closely synchronized, and the larvae may not kill their host for a long period, maintaining themselves on a diet of nonvital tissues. Ultimately, however, they are lethal to the host. (*Note:* The correct term for insects that kill their host is *parasitoid. Insect parasite*, however, has more general usage and is used in this book, although it is not technically correct.)

Most parasitic larvae develop inside their host and are not observed. (A few, notably in the wasp family Eulophidae, have stages that feed on the outside of the host.) However, larvae of many parasites emerge from the host when feeding is completed and pupate on the outside, where they can be observed. Adult parasites usually feed on nectar, pollen, and honeydew; a few feed on the blood of host insects, which they puncture with their ovipositor.

Tachinid Flies

Diptera: Tachinidae

The tachinid flies are a large (ca. 1,300 North American species) and important family of parasitic flies. All develop as internal parasites of other insects, including many caterpillars, beetles, true bugs, earwigs, and grasshoppers that are garden pests. Typical species somewhat resemble house flies but tend to have more stout, bristly hairs on the abdomen. Females usually parasitize host insects by gluing an egg to the body, often near the head. Some tachinid flies, however, insert larvae directly into the host insect, and others lay tiny eggs on foliage that hatch when ingested.

Parasitic Wasps

Hymenoptera

Numerous families of wasps include species that are parasites of insects and other arthropods. Collectively they are known as the Parasitic Hymenoptera.

Tiphiid wasps (Tiphiidae family) are mostly parasites of white grub larvae. Adult wasps can be fairly large and may superficially resemble yellowjackets or other hunting wasps. *Myzinum* and *Tiphia* are the two most common genera in North America.

Ichneumon wasps (Ichneumonidae family) are often fairly large, slender wasps. Antennae are quite long, and the females usually possess a long and conspicuous ovipositor. Ichneumon wasps are most commonly encountered as parasites of caterpillars. Beetles and other wasps are other hosts. Common genera include *Hyposoter*, *Diadegma*, *Ophion*, and *Exochus*. The largest ichneumon wasps are those in the genus *Megarhyssa*, which are parasites of horntail larvae, a type of wood-boring wasp. These **giant ichneumon wasps** may be 3 inches long, including the long tail-like ovipositor used to penetrate wood. The Ichneumonidae family is one of the largest of any insect group, with 3,300 described species in North America.

Braconid wasps (Braconidae family) are also a large and important family of wasps, with more than 1,900 North American species. In overall body form they often resemble ichneumon wasps but are usually much smaller. *Bracon*, *Chelonus*, *Leiophron*, *Macrocentrus*, and *Opius* are common genera. The white or yellowish pupae of *Cotesia* species, which are spun on or adjacent to their caterpillar host, are among the most commonly observed stages of any parasitic wasp.

A. Tachinid fly parasite of Colorado potato beetle. *J. Capinera.* **B.** Tachinid fly parasite of false chinch bug. *W. Cranshaw.* **C.** Eggs of tachinid fly laid near head of tent caterpillar host. *K. Gray.* **D.** Cocoons of pupae of *Cotesia* sp. parasitic wasp and imported cabbageworm host. *W. Cranshaw.* **E.** Larva of tachinid fly emerging from tent caterpillar host. *K. Gray.* **F.** Tiphiid wasp (*Myzinum* sp.) parasite of white grubs. *B. Drees.* **G.** Ichneumon wasp *Itoplectis con-quistor. G. J. Lenhard.* **H.** Pupal cocoons of parasitic wasp attached to buck moth host. *W. Cranshaw.* **I.** Pupa of tachinid fly near killed host. *K. Gray.* **J.** *Cotesia* sp. larvae emerging from imported cabbageworm host. *J. Capinera.* **K.** Giant ichneumon wasp laying eggs into horntail-infested tree. *W. Cranshaw.* **L.** Giant ichneumon wasp on stump. *D. Leatherman.*

Pteromalid wasps (Pteromalidae family) include species that are important parasites of sawflies. Another group are those that develop on larvae and pupae of various filth breeding flies; some are sold commercially as "fly predators" or "fly parasites" to control nuisance flies around livestock operations. *Pteromalus*, *Perilampus*, *Spalangia*, and *Nasonia* are among the genera of pteromalid wasps that are most important for biological control of pest species.

Aphid parasites (Aphidiidae family) are among the most ubiquitous of the parasitic wasps, found almost invariably among aphid colonies. As the wasp develops within the aphid, the host typically swells and becomes lighter in color and affixed to the leaf. Aphids killed in this manner are often referred to as "aphid mummies." A circular hole cut by the emerging wasp also is characteristic. Among the more common genera of aphid wasps are *Trioxys*, *Diaeretiella*, *Lysiphlebus*, and *Aphidius*.

Encyrtid wasps (Encyrtidae family) are small wasps, about $\frac{1}{12}$ inch, that develop internally in eggs, larvae, or pupae of certain insects. The genera *Anagyrus*, *Leptomastix,* and *Metaphycus* include species that are important natural enemies of some of the most common mealybugs and soft scales. An unusual species is *Copidosoma truncatellum*, which lays its eggs in the eggs of cutworms, loopers, and other caterpillars. The species is polyembryonic, and numerous larvae—sometimes more than 1,000—develop from the few eggs originally laid. The larvae of this wasp develop throughout the larval life of the caterpillar host, killing it as it prepares to pupate.

Within the encyrtids are the **aphelinid wasps** (Aphelininae subfamily), which include many important species that attack insects in the order Homoptera. Several *Encarsia* species are important parasites of whiteflies and cause the host nymph to turn black when parasitized. *Aphelinus* is a genus that includes important parasites of aphids, which also characteristically turn black when parasitized. *Coccophagus* and *Aphytis* include many of the parasites most important in control of scale insects.

Chalcid wasps (Chalcididae family) are for the most part internal parasites of caterpillars, although some develop in fly larvae. They are distinguished by having an enlarge femur on the hind legs. *Brachymeria* is the most common and widespread chalcid wasp genus in North America.

Eulophid wasps (Eulophidae family) are very small (typically ca. $\frac{1}{25}$ inch), and many develop as external parasites of their hosts. Some of the most conspicuous are *Euplectrus* species, which develop on the body of several kinds of caterpillars. Others are parasites of scales, psyllids, and flies, including many of the leafmining flies. Some eulophids are egg parasites of beetles.

The smallest parasitic wasps—and smallest insects known—are those that develop as internal parasites of insect eggs. The ***Trichogramma*** **wasps** (Trichogrammatidae family) are well known as parasites of caterpillar eggs and are widely available for sale for biological control. Even more minute are the **fairy flies** (Mymaridae family), which include the genus *Anagrus*, important in managing leafhoppers.

Pelecinid wasps (Pelecinidae family) have only one North American species, *Pelecinus polyturator*, a large black wasp of unusual appearance. The abdomen is extremely elongated, extending $1\frac{1}{2}$ inches. Larvae are parasites of June beetle white grubs in soil, and adults of the wasp are present in mid- to late summer.

A. Peteromalid wasp laying egg in sawfly pupa. *A. T. Drooz.* **B.** Trichogramma ovipositing in earworm egg. *J. K. Clark/UC Statewide IPM Program.* **C.** Larvae of parasitic wasp exposed in aphid host. *W. Cranshaw.* **D.** *Diaeretiella rapae* parasitizing aphid host. *F. Peairs.* **E.** Adults of aphidiid wasp *Diaeretiella rapae* and aphid host mummies. *W. Cranshaw.* **F.** Parasitic wasp *Lysiphlebus testacipes* laying egg into aphid host. *K. Gray.* **G.** Green peach aphids parasitized by *Aphelinus* sp. wasp. *W. Cranshaw.* **H.** Army cutworm larva packed with pupae of a polyembryonic encryrtid parasite. *J. Capinera.* **I.** Larvae of an ectoparasitic eulophid wasp on fall webworm host. *F. Peairs.* **J.** *Aphelinus* wasp ovipositing in aphid host. *K. Gray.* **K.** Bronze birch borer and chalcid parasite. *W. Cranshaw.* **L.** Chalcid wasp. *K. Gray.*

PATHOGENS

Although it is infrequently observed, arthropods often suffer from infection by pathogens, many of which produce lethal diseases. Certain kinds of fungi, bacteria, protozoa, and viruses all can kill arthropods, and many are important in their management.

Viruses

Viruses are most commonly found among caterpillars and sawflies. One particularly gruesome group of these viruses—nuclear polyhedrosis viruses, or NPVs—cause wilt diseases. Caterpillars and sawflies infected by these viruses are killed rapidly, their virus-filled bodies hanging limply by the prolegs. At the slightest touch, the insects rupture, spilling the virus particles onto leaves below them to infect other insects. Wilt diseases are important biological controls of several caterpillars, including cabbage looper, gypsy moth, and Douglas-fir tussock moth. Other types of viruses, such as one that affects codling moth, act much more slowly. These other viruses may produce only modest external symptoms such as a chalky color of the infected individual and/or a general listlessness.

Bacteria

Like some of the viruses, bacteria usually show little external evidence of infection. Many bacteria attack the digestive system of insects, which causes the insects to develop slowly. Some bacteria reproduce in the blood and cause blood poisoning. Infection of Japanese beetle and certain other grubs by milky spore bacteria (*Bacillus popilliae*) causes infected individuals to turn creamy white, grow poorly, and often die. *Bacillus thuringiensis* (Bt) is the best-known bacterium that produces insect disease, and it is commonly used as a microbial insecticide. Several strains exist each of which affects only certain types of insects that ingest the bacteria or the toxic protein crystal it produces. Currently, the most commonly available strains affect either caterpillars (*kurstaki, aizawi* strains), leaf beetles (*tenebrionis/san diego* strain), or larvae of mosquitoes, fungus gnats, and related flies (*israelensis* strain).

Fungi

Fungi produce some of the more spectacular diseases of insects and mites. A wide variety of species succumb to fungus disease around the yard and garden. Fungus-killed insects and mites become stiff and, when conditions are right, covered with a white, light green, or pink 'fuzz'—the spores of the fungus. One of the most commonly encountered fungus diseases of insects is *Entomophthora muscae* which infects various root maggot flies. Infected flies die stuck to the tops of plants and at other high points around the garden. *Entomophaga maimaiga* is a fairly recently introduced fungus that produces devastating outbreaks in gypsy moth when spring moisture conditions are optimal. *Beauveria bassiana* is a common disease of many insects and is also currently marketed for insect control in yards, gardens, and greenhouses. Some commercial development has also occurred with *Metarhizium anisopliae*, which infects many kinds of insects that live in soil.

Protozoa

Protozoa tend to cause debilitating infections in insects. Effects are often subtle, such as reduced feeding, activity, or reproduction. Immature stages are usually much more susceptible to protozoan infections, and survival can be reduced. Spruce budworms and grasshoppers are among the insect groups that are common hosts of protozoa. *Nosema locustae* preparations can infect developing grasshoppers and are sometimes used for grasshopper control.

A. Gypsy moth larva killed by infection with nuclear polyhedrosis virus. *D. Shetlar.* **B.** Alfalfa webworms killed by *Bacillus thuringiensis. J. Capinera.* **C.** Gypsy moth killed by infection with *Entomophaga maimaiga. D. Shetlar.* **D.** European corn borer larva killed by *Beauveria bassiana. F. Peairs.* **E.** Billbug killed by infection with *Beauveria bassiana. K. Gray.* **F.** Fungus-killed root maggot fly. *W. Cranshaw.*

Nematodes

Many kinds of nematodes develop as parasites of insects. One large group is the mermithid nematodes which develop as internal parasites. They may develop slowly in their host, causing debilitating disease that ultimately is lethal. Mermithid nematodes are common in many beetles, mosquito larva, and some grasshoppers. The largest of the mermithid nematodes one might encounter in a garden is *Mermis nigrescens*, a parasite of grasshoppers that may be more than 3 inches long.

Other nematodes are better described as entomopathogenic nematodes because of their involvement with bacteria. These nematodes always carry with them bacteria in the genus *Xenorhabdus,* with which there is mutual interdependence. The nematodes actively penetrate the body of some insect host, either through natural openings (mouth, spiracles, anus) or by cutting through the exoskeleton. They release the bacteria upon penetration, and the bacteria then grow rapidly in the blood (hemolymph) of the insect, killing it within a few days. The nematodes develop on the "soup" of bacteria and degraded insect tissue.

Two genera of entomopathogenic nematodes have been developed as biological controls for insect pests. Various *Steinernema* species are used to manage insects, including certain caterpillars, fungus gnats, and mole crickets. *Heterorhabditis* species tend to be more effective for control of larvae of white grubs and root weevils in soil. The latter is capable of direct penetration through the exoskeleton of its host.

Horsehair Worms

Another group of large wormlike parasites that affect insects are the horsehair worms. These are placed in a separate phylum (Nematomorpha) from the nematodes and are thicker and darker than *Mermis nigrescens*, the nematode parasite of grasshoppers. Horsehair worms have a wider host range and can affect many insects—various crickets and beetles perhaps most commonly. Several species in the genus *Gordius* may come to the attention of gardeners, particularly near water sources. Eggs of horsehair worms are laid in water, and infection of insects occurs when they ingest the young larvae while drinking. After the horseworm has developed, infected insects ultimately move to water where the mature parasites emerge. Their occurrence in animal watering troughs is the basis for the common name horsehair worm.

A. Nematode *Mermis nigrescens* and its grasshopper host. *J. Capinera.* **B.** Nematode, *Mermis nigrescens*, parasite of grasshoppers. *W. Cranshaw.* **C.** Horsehair worm emerging from ground beetle host. *W. Cranshaw.*

POLLINATORS

Also present in gardens are numerous pollinating insects. Of particular importance are bees, insects that rear their young on nectar and pollen and efficiently pollinate flowers as they forage. Although some of the most familiar bees are social insects that establish a colony, most bees have a solitary habit of rearing young.

Honey Bee
Hymenoptera: Apidae

Honey bee (*Apis mellifera*) is a social insect that produces a colony with distinct castes. The overwhelming majority of the colony comprises infertile females, known as workers. A single fertile female queen and a relatively small number of males (drones) make up the rest of the colony. The colony is perennial, surviving over the winter intact with the bees clustering together. Division of the colony occurs through swarming, when the old queen and about half of the workers leave en masse to establish a new hive. Swarming events usually occur on warm sunny days in late spring.

Honey bee is an introduced insect brought over early during European colonization. It is an excellent pollinator of many crops and is particularly important for pollinating tree fruits. Honey bees also produce large amounts of honey which are used as an energy source, and the excess is collected by beekeepers. Honey bees construct nest cells of wax, and beeswax is also an important commercial product.

Honey bees are nonaggressive and rarely sting unless their hive is disturbed or they are accidentally trapped or handled. (The great majority of "bee stings" result from the activity of very different insects, yellowjacket wasps.) The stinger of the workers is barbed and is pulled out in the act of stinging, resulting in the bee's death.

Bumble Bees
Hymenoptera: Apidae

Bumble bees (*Bombus* spp.) are large, fuzzy bees brightly colored black with yellow and/or orange. Like honey bees, they are social insects that produce a colony, usually in an abandoned rodent or bird nest where there is insulating material they use to surround the nest. Bumble bee colonies are abandoned at the end of the year, however, and only large, fertilized queens survive the winter. The queen establishes a new colony in spring, conducting all chores of foraging, hive construction, and rearing. The first workers produced are usually quite small, but they assist the queen as the the colony develops. As the colony grows, worker size tends to increase and some reproductive forms (queens, males) are produced toward the end of the season.

Bumble bees are native insects, with close to 50 species in North America. Many are important pollinators, and they have a unique method of acquiring pollen from some plants, known as buzz pollination, which shakes pollen from some kinds of flowers. Bumble bees are used extensively to pollinate greenhouse-grown tomatoes. Bumble bees sting readily in defense of their hive; the sting can be painful, but the stinger is not left behind.

A. Bumble bee at flower. *W. Cranshaw*. B. Interior of bumble bee nest showing cells used for rearing and food storage. *K. Gray*. C. Adult bumble bee. *K. Gray*. D. Honey bee swarm. *W. Cranshaw*. E. Honey bees on frame from colony. *W. Cranshaw*. F. Honey bee. *W. Cranshaw*. G. Honey bee with pollen load. *K. Gray*.

Leafcutter Bees

Hymenoptera: Megachilidae

Leafcutter bees are solitary bees that do not produce colonies. Nesting is done alone by the female, which emerges in late spring. Overwintering occurs as a larva in the nest cells. Nests usually are excavated out of soft, rotten wood or the pith of plants but can also occur in existing holes of the proper size, including holes in clay banks or stone walls. Some leafcutter bees are semidomesticated and can be managed by providing them with predrilled "bee boards."

As the name indicates, many leafcutter bees (*Megachile* spp.) cut leaves which are used in constructing nest cells. The leafcutter bees known as **mason bees** (*Osmia* spp.) similarly nest in existing or newly excavated hollows. They line their cells with mud, however, and do not cut leaf fragments. Leafcutter bees have an annual life cycle, with one generation produced per year. Winter is spent as a full-grown larva in the cell. The larvae pupate in spring and emerge in early summer. They are further discussed on p. 70.

Ground-Nesting Bees

Hymenoptera: Andrenidae, Anthoporidae, Halictidae

There are many other bees that are native and occur around yards and gardens. All are solitary insects, with females individually producing nests. Three of the most common groups are the **digger** and **carpenter bees** (Anthoporidae family), **sweat bees** (Halictidae family), and **acute-tongued burrowing bees** (Andrenidae family). Nests of all are constructed by digging in soil. Excavated tunnels branch and are lined with waxy or shellaclike material. Some species reuse tunnels in subsequent generations, and favorable breeding sites may host hundreds of individual nests. As in all bees, the nests are provisioned with pollen and nectar. In some species, their association with the host plant is highly specialized; *Xenoglossa* species, for example, solely visits cucurbits.

Females of ground-nesting bees can sting but are nonaggressive and rarely do. The stinger is not barbed and is only slightly painful. Occasional problems with sweat bees do occur, primarily related to their habit of visiting moisture, including sweat. This may cause them to sting if they become trapped after they alight to lap perspiration. Males of some species, notably the wood boring carpenter bees (*Xylocopa* spp.), aggressively buzz anything that approaches nesting areas, but this is pure bluff as they lack a stinger and are harmless.

A. Leafcutter bee visiting flower. *W. Cranshaw.* B. Sweat bee. *W. Cranshaw.* C. Sweat bees. *W. Cranshaw.*
D. *Xenoglossa* sp., a digger bee associated with squash flowers. *W. Cranshaw.* E. Digger bees at water. *W. Cranshaw.*
F. Digger bee colony. *H. E. Evans.* G. Orchard mason bee (*Osmia*). *K. Gray.*

Appendix of Host Plant Genera and Associated Insects and Mites

Abelmoschus (Okra)

Leaf chewers: banded cucumber beetle, Japanese beetle, gray hairstreak, corn earworm, redheaded flea beetle, southern armyworm, yellowstriped armyworm, okra caterpillar, vegetable leafminer
Flower, bud chewers: red imported fire ant, Japanese beetle, gray hairstreak, corn earworm
Sucking insects, foliage: green peach aphid, cotton/melon aphid, silverleaf whitefly, greenhouse whitefly, garden fleahopper
Sucking insects, flowers: brown stink bug, green stink bug, southern green stink bug
Mites: twospotted spider mite

Abies (Fir, balsam fir)

Leaf chewers: Douglas-fir tussock moth, whitemarked tussock moth, western spruce budworm, spruce budworm, hemlock looper, filament bearer, bagworm
Scales: hemlock scale, elongate hemlock scale, pine needle scale
Other sucking insects: pine spittlebug, Saratoga spittlebug, balsam twig aphid, balsam woolly adelgid, woolly pine adelgids, bowlegged fir aphid, *Prociphilus americanus*
Mites: *Nalepella octonema*, spruce spider mite
Borers, bark beetles: whitespotted sawyer, *Urocerus* horntails, red turpentine beetle

Abutilon (Flowering maple)

Chewing insects: okra caterpillar, Fuller rose beetle
Sucking insects: greenhouse whitefly, potato aphid, cotton/melon aphid, cowpea aphid, black citrus aphid, green peach aphid, cottony camellia scale

Acacia

Scales: fern scale, California red scale, greedy scale, oleander pit scale
Other sucking insects: acacia psyllid, western flower thrips
Leaf chewers: omnivorous looper, orange tortrix, puss caterpillar

Acer (Maple, boxelder)

Leaf chewers: bagworm, yellownecked caterpillar, cecropia moth, polyphemus moth, greenstriped mapleworm, orangehumped mapleworm, redhumped oakworm, saddled prominent, luna moth, imperial moth, puss caterpillar, io moth, hag moth, hackberry leaf slug, linden looper, spring cankerworm, fall cankerworm, Bruce spanworm, filament bearer, fall webworm, whitemarked tussock moth, hickory tussock moth, American dagger moth, forest tent caterpillar, maple leafcutter, maple trumpet skeletonizer, fruittree leafroller, boxelder leafroller, threelined leafroller, Japanese beetle, Asiatic garden beetle, twobanded Japanese weevil, *Phyllobius oblongus*, boxelder leafminer, maple leafminer
Scales: calico scale, terrapin scale, cottony maple scale, cottony maple leaf scale, cottony cushion scale, Putnam's scale, gloomy scale, walnut scale, oystershell scale, European fruit lecanium, Indian wax scale
Other sucking insects: rose leafhopper, potato leafhopper, maple leafhopper, boxelder psyllid, birch lace bug, fourlined plant bug, boxelder bug, western boxelder bug, pear thrips, boxelder aphid, Norway maple aphid, woolly alder aphid, mulberry whitefly, maple mealybug, Comstock mealybug
Gall makers: maple bladdergall mite, maple spindlegall mite, *Eriophyes negundi, E. calacerus, Aceria modestus, A. elongatus*, gouty veingall midge, maple gouty veingall midge

Twig, petiole borers: maple petiole borer, boxelder twig borer, maple twig moth, black twig borer, twig pruner
Borers: flatheaded appletree borer, pole borer, American plum borer, leopard moth, carpenterworm, pigeon tremex
Seed feeders: boxelder bug, western boxelder bug

Achillea (Yarrow, milfoil)

Sucking insects, roots: Pritchard's mealybug, leafcurl plum aphid

Aesculus (Buckeye, horse chestnut)

Leaf chewers: whitemarked tussock moth, omnivorous looper, filament bearer, bagworm, Asiatic garden beetle, Japanese beetle, fruittree leafroller, filament bearer
Sucking insects: maple mealybug, Comstock mealybug, common falsepit scale, walnut scale, *Erythroneura gleditsia*
Mites: pecan leaf scorch mite

African violet (see *Saintpaulia*)

Agave

Weevils: agave weevil, yucca weevil
Other sucking insects: agave plant bug
Scales: brown soft scale, oleander scale, California red scale

Ageratum (Flossflower)

Leaf, flower chewers: tobacco budworm, greenhouse leaftier
Sucking insects: greenhouse whitefly, leafcurl plum aphid
Mites: cyclamen mite, broad mite

Aglaonema (Chinese evergreen)

Scales: red wax scale

Agrostis (Bentgrass)

Leaf chewers: sod webworms, black cutworm, variegated cutworm, armyworm, fiery skipper
Sucking insects, mites: winter grain mite, hairy chinch bug
Root feeders: southern mole cricket, tawny mole cricket, black turfgrass ataenius, European chafer, Japanese beetle, hunting billbug

Ailanthus (Tree-of-heaven)

Leaf chewers: Fall webworm, pale tussock moth, whitemarked tussock moth, ailanthus webworm

Ajuga

Mites: twospotted spider mite

Albizia (Mimosa, silk tree)

Leaf chewers: mimosa webworm, whitemarked tussock moth, blister beetles
Scales: European peach scale
Sucking insects: acacia psyllid

Alcea (Hollyhock)

Leaf chewers: hollyhock weevil, hollyhock sawfly, hollyhock leaf skeletonizer, painted lady, European earwig, okra caterpillar, cabbage looper, bertha armyworm, Japanese beetle
Flower, seed chewers: hollyhock weevil, Japanese beetle
Sucking insects: Mexican mealybug, buckthorn aphid, black and red stink bug
Borers: European corn borer

Alder (see *Alnus*)

Allium (Onion, leek, garlic, ornamental allium)

Leaf chewers: banded cucumber beetle, saltmarsh caterpillar, beet armyworm, American serpentine leafminer, pea leafminer
Sucking insects: onion thrips, western flower thrips, tobacco thrips, shallot aphid
Bulb feeders: onion maggot, seedcorn maggot, onion bulb fly, bulb mites

Almond (see *Prunus*)

Alnus (Alder)

Leaf chewers: alder flea beetle, Pacific willow leaf beetle, elm calligrapha, apple flea weevil, birch skeletonizer, pale tussock moth, spearmarked black moth, threelined leafroller, boxelder leafroller, cecropia moth, birch sawfly
Leafminers: European alder leafminer
Gall makers: *Phytoptus laevis*
Sucking insects: alder spittlebug, buckeye scale, woolly alder aphid
Borers: alder borer, oak clearwing

Aloe

Scales: brown soft scale, hemispherical scale, California red scale, oleander scale
Mites: aloe mite

Aluminum plant (see *Pilea*)

Amaryllis (see *Hippeastrum*)

Amelanchier (Serviceberry, shadbush)

Leaf chewers: western tent caterpillar, yellownecked caterpillar, Bruce spanworm, apple buccalatrix, lesser appleworm, pearslug, walkingstick, Japanese beetle, apple flea weevil
Sucking insects: ash whitefly, woolly elm aphid, *Prociphilus caryae*, hawthorn mealybug, hawthorn lace bug
Fruit chewers: apple curculio, lesser appleworm
Mites: European red mite
Borers: roundheaded appletree borer, lesser peachtree borer

Andromeda (see *Pieris*)

Anemone (Pasque flower, windflower)

Leaf chewers: greenhouse leaftier
Sucking insects: ground mealybug, foxglove aphid

Annual aster (see *Callistephus*)

Antirrhinum **(Snapdragon)**

Leaf chewers: greenhouse leaftier, cabbage looper
Flower, seed chewers: snapdragon plume moth, tobacco budworm, corn earworm
Sucking insects: cotton/melon aphid, western flower thrips
Mites: broad mite, cyclamen mite

Aphelandra **(Zebra plant)**

Sucking insects: hemispherical scale, brown soft scale, citrus mealybug

Apium **(Celery)**

Chewing insects: cabbage looper, celery looper, celery leaftier, beet armyworm
Leafminers: American serpentine leafminer, vegetable leafminer, pea leafminer
Sucking insects: green peach aphid, aster leafhopper, tarnished plant bug
Root chewers: carrot rust fly, carrot weevil

Apple (see *Malus*)

Apricot (see *Prunus*)

Aquilegia **(Columbine)**

Leaf chewers: columbine leafminers, columbine sawfly
Aphids: crescent-marked lily aphid, spirea aphid, cotton/melon aphid, bandedwinged whitefly
Mites: twospotted spider mite

Aralia **(*Fatsia*)**

Sucking insects, mites: Mexican mealybug, nigra scale, bean aphid, broad mite, twospotted spider mite

Araucaria **(Norfolk Island pine, monkey puzzle tree)**

Sucking insects, mites: Norfolk Island pine eriococcid, twospotted spider mite

Arborvitae (see *Thuja*)

Arbutus **(Bearberry, kinni Kinnick, madrone)**

Leaf chewers: madrone shield bearer

Arctostaphylos **(Manzanita)**

Sucking insects: Pritchard's mealybug, greenhouse whitefly, manzanita leafgall aphid, bean aphid
Leaf chewers: madrone shield bearer, western tussock moth

Armoracia **(Horseradish)**

Leaf chewers: horseradish flea beetle, crucifer flea beetle, diamondback moth
Root feeders: horseradish flea beetle, crucifer flea beetle, imported crucifer weevil, western aster root aphid

Arrowhead (see *Viburnum*)

Arrowhead plant (see *Syngonium*)

Asclepias (**Butterfly weed**)

Aphids: oleander aphid, cotton/melon aphid

Ash (see *Fraxinus*)

Asparagus

Sucking insects: asparagus aphid, green peach aphid, cotton/melon aphid, citrus mealybug, tarnished plant bug, garden fleahopper, black and red stink bug, onion thrips, bean thrips, western flower thrips
Leaf chewers: asparagus beetle, spotted asparagus beetle, variegated cutworm, redbacked cutworm, beet armyworm, saltmarsh caterpillar, asparagus leafminer
Root feeders: garden symphylan

Asparagus fern (see *Asparagus*)

Aspen (see *Populus*)

Aspidistra

Scales: fern scale

Aster

Leaf chewers: soybean looper
Leafminers: *Amauromyza maculosa*, American serpentine leafminer
Sucking insects: crescent-marked lily aphid, brown ambrosia aphid, greenhouse whitefly, silverleaf whitefly, iris whitefly, aster leafhopper, chrysanthemum lace bug, *Entylia carniata*
Borers: *Carmenta corni*, European corn borer
Flower chewers: blister beetles, Japanese beetle, European earwig
Root feeders: black vine weevil, petiolegall aphids, erigeron root aphid, western aster root aphid

Astilbe

Leaf chewers: oriental beetle, saddleback caterpillar
Sucking insects: fourlined plant bug

Avocado (see *Persea*)

Azalea (see *Rhododendron*)

Bachelor's button (see *Centaurea*)

Bahiagrass (see *Paspalum*)

Baldcypress (see *Taxodium*)

Bamboo (Many genera)

Scales: pencillate scale, bamboo scale, hemispherical scale, cottony cushion scale
Mites: twospotted spider mite

Barbados lily (see *Hippeastrum*)

Barberry (see *Berberis*)

Basil (see *Ocimum*)

Basket flower (see *Centaurea*)

Basswood (see *Tilia*)

Bean (see *Phaseolus*)

Bearberry (see *Arctostaphylos*)

Beech (see *Fagus*)

Beefsteak plant (see *Iresine*)

Beet (see *Beta*)

Begonia

Leaf chewers: orange tortrix, variegated leafroller, soybean looper
Scales: brown soft scale, hemispherical scale, Florida red scale
Other sucking insects: citrus mealybug, longtailed mealybug, cotton/melon aphid, greenhouse white-fly, silverleaf whitefly, bandedwinged whitefly, greenhouse thrips
Mites: cyclamen mite, broad mite

Bellflower (see *Campanula*)

Bellis (English daisy)

Sucking insects: western flower thrips

Beloperone

Sucking insects: grape mealybug

Bentgrass (see *Agrostis*)

Berberis (Barberry)

Leaf chewers: barberry looper, barberry webworm, twobanded Japanese weevil
Sucking insects: barberry aphid, European peach scale, Indian wax scale

Bermudagrass (see *Cynodon*)

Beta (Beet)

Leaf chewers: banded cucumber beetle, redheaded flea beetle, hop flea beetle, spinach flea beetle, beet webworm, beet armyworm
Leafminers: Beet leafminer, spinach leafminer, American serpentine leafminer
Sucking insects, foliage: *Eutettix tenellus*, beet leafhopper, bean aphid, green peach aphid
Sucking insects, roots: sugarbeet root aphid

Betula (Birch)

Leaf chewers: dusky birch sawfly, birch sawfly, elm sawfly, *Trichiosoma triangulum*, elm sphinx, twinspot sphinx, spiny elm caterpillar/mourning cloak, eastern tiger swallowtail, cecropia moth, polyphemus moth, luna moth, redhumped oakworm, gypsy moth, *Acronicta leporina*, hickory tussock moth, whitemarked tussock moth, *Dasychira grisefacta*, fall webworm, forest tent caterpillar, gypsy moth, elm spanworm, apple and thorn skeletonizer, birch skeletonizer, *Ancylis discigerana*, *A. logiana*, Japanese beetle
Leafminers: birch leafminer
Borers: bronze birch borer, alder borer
Sucking insects: common birch aphid, *Callipterinella callipterus*, spiny witch-hazel gall aphid, birch lace bug, alder spittlebug, walnut scale, oystershell scale, potato leafhopper,

Birch (see *Betula*)

Bird-of-paradise (see *Strelitzia*)

Bittersweet (see *Celastrus*)

Black-eyed Susan (see *Rudbeckia*)

Black haw (see *Viburnum*)

Black locust (see *Robinia*)

Bloodleaf (see *Iresine*)

Bluebell of Scotland (see *Campanula*)

Blueberry (see *Vaccinium*)

Bluegrass (see *Poa*)

Boston ivy (see *Parthenocissus*)

Bougainvillea

Leaf chewers: leafcutter bees
Sucking insects, mites: cowpea aphid, cotton/melon aphid, oleander pit scale, hemispherical scale, twospotted spider mite

Boxelder (see *Acer*)

Boxwood (see *Buxus*)

Brassaia (Umbrella tree)

Sucking insects: Florida wax scale, red wax scale, brown soft scale, Putnam's scale, latania scale, citrus mealybug

Brassica (Cole crops: cabbage, broccoli, Brussels sprout, cauliflower, collard, mustard, etc.)

Leaf chewers: cabbage looper, alfalfa looper, cabbage webworm, diamondback moth, zebra caterpillar, imported cabbageworm, southern cabbageworm, purplebacked cabbageworm, cross-striped cab-

bageworm, beet armyworm, hop flea beetle, cabbage flea beetle, crucifer flea beetle, western black flea beetle, striped flea beetle, western striped flea beetle, palestriped flea beetle, red turnip beetle, yellowmargined beetle, cabbage leafminer, pea leafminer, milky garden slug
Sucking insects: cabbage aphid, turnip aphid, green peach aphid, silverleaf whitefly, greenhouse whitefly, onion thrips, harlequin bug, false chinch bug
Root chewers: cabbage maggot, radish root maggot, vegetable weevil, whitefringed beetle, European crane fly, milky garden slug

Bridalwreath (see *Spirea*)

Broccoli (see *Brassica*)

Brussels sprout (see *Brassica*)

Buchloe (Buffalograss)

Sucking insects/mites: buffalograss mite, buffalograss chinch bug
Root chewers: May/June beetles
Sucking insects, roots: buffalograss mealybugs

Buckeye (see *Aesculus*)

Buckthorn (see *Rhamnus*)

Buddleia (Butterfly bush)

Sucking insects, mites: black and red stink bug, fourlined plant bug, twospotted spider mite
Flower chewers: European earwig, Japanese beetle

Buffalograss (see *Buchloe*)

Bush red pepper (see *Capsicum*)

Busy Lizzie (see *Impatiens*)

Butterfly bush (see *Buddleia*)

Butterfly weed (see *Asclepias*)

Buxus (Boxwood)

Leaf chewers: boxwood leafminer, Asiatic garden beetle, brown garden snail
Scales: European fruit lecanium, California red scale, greedy scale, cottony camellia scale, Indian wax scale
Sucking insects: boxwood psyllid, Comstock mealybug, ground mealybug
Mites: boxwood spider mite

Cabbage (see *Brassica*)

Cactus (Many genera)

Scales: cactus scale, greedy scale, oleander scale, cactus eriococcin
Other sucking insects: cochineal, grape mealybug, ground mealybug, opuntia bug, *Narnia snowi*
Borers: cactus longhorn, blue cactus borer

Calendula (**Pot marigold**)

Leaf chewers: yellow woollybear, painted lady, greenhouse leaftier
Sucking insects: greenhouse whitefly, silverleaf whitefly, brown ambrosia aphid
Flower chewers: black blister beetle

Calla lily (**see** *Zantedeschia*)

Calliopsis (**see** *Coreopsis*)

Callistephus (**China aster**)

Leaf chewers: Asiatic garden beetle, Japanese beetle
Flower chewers: black blister beetle
Sucking insects: tarnished plant bug, potato aphid, aster leafhopper
Mites: twospotted spider mite

Camellia

Scales: hemispherical scale, Florida red scale, tea scale, cottony camellia scale, euonymus scale
Other sucking insects: cotton/melon aphid, citrus mealybug, longtailed mealybug, black citrus aphid, greenhouse whitefly
Leaf chewers: spotted cutworm, omnivorous looper, orange tortrix, Fuller rose beetle, black vine weevil, cranberry rootworm
Mites: southern red mite, citrus rust mite
Root chewers: black vine weevil, strawberry root weevil

Campanula (**Bellflower, bluebell of Scotland, Canterbury bell, harebell**)

Sucking insects, mites: twospotted spider mite, aster leafhopper, foxglove aphid

Candy tuft (**see** *Iberis*)

Canna

Sucking insects: citrus mealybug, latania scale
Leaf chewers: larger canna leafroller, lesser canna leafroller, saddleback caterpillar, yellow woollybear, Japanese beetle

Canterbury bells (**see** *Campanula*)

Cape jasmine (**see** *Gardenia*)

Capsicum (**Pepper**)

Leaf chewers: beet armyworm, yellowstriped armyworm, western yellowstriped armyworm, variegated cutworm, palestriped flea beetle, potato flea beetle, western potato flea beetle, American serpentine leafminer
Sucking insects, mites: green peach aphid, potato aphid, cotton/melon aphid, potato/tomato psyllid, tarnished plant bug, garden fleahopper, western flower thrips, onion thrips, broad mite
Fruit chewers: pepper maggot, pepper weevil, European corn borer, corn earworm, beet armyworm, tobacco budworm, variegated cutworm

Carnation (see *Dianthus*)

Carrot (see *Daucus*)

Carya (Hickory, pecan)

Leaf chewers: redhumped caterpillar, walnut caterpillar, unicorn caterpillar, false unicorn caterpillar, io moth, polyphemus moth, luna moth, hickory horned devil, pale tussock moth, hickory tussock moth, American dagger moth, fall webworm, bagworm, elm spanworm, butternut woollyworm, pecan cigar casebearer, Asiatic oak weevil, pecan casebearer, pecan leaf casebearer, pecan nut casebearer
Scales: walnut scale, oak lecanium, cottony cushion scale, obscure scale
Other sucking insects: hickory leaf stemgall phylloxera, black margined aphid, giant bark aphid, black pecan aphid, yellow pecan aphid, pecan spittlebug, *Phylloxera russellae*, *P. notabilis*, pecan phylloxera, maple leafhopper, twomarked treehopper, alder spittlebug, tobacco thrips, flower thrips, western flower thrips
Mites: *Oligonychus viridis*, oak mite, pecan leaf scorch mite, pecan leafroll mite
Borers, bark beetles: pigeon tremex, black twig borer, *Elaphidionoides parallelus*, twig girdler, twig pruner, pecan carpenterworm, painted hickory borer, banded ash borer, hickory bark beetle, apple twig borer, American plum borer
Seed feeders: hickory shuckworm, hickory nut curculio, pecan weevil, pecan nut casebearer

Caryopteris

Sucking insects: fourlined plant bug

Castanea (Chestnut)

Leaf chewers: gypsy moth, omnivorous looper, oak skeletonizer, Asiatic oak weevil, Japanese beetle
Borers: twolined chestnut borer, red oak clearwing borer, leopard moth
Seed feeders: large chestnut weevil, small chestnut weevil, filbertworm

Catalpa (Catawba, Indian bean)

Sucking insects: grape mealybug, Comstock mealybug, striped mealybug, common falsepit scale, white peach scale, cotton/melon aphid
Leaf chewers: catalpa sphinx, catalpa midge, Japanese beetle

Catawba (see *Catalpa*)

Cauliflower (see *Brassica*)

Ceanothus (Wild lilac)

Flower feeders: hoplia beetles
Leaf chewers: western tent caterpillar
Borers: sycamore borer, ceanothus stemgall moth
Sucking insects: angulate tingid, *Aphis ceanothi*, greenhouse whitefly, greedy scale

Celastrus (Bittersweet)

Scales: euonymus scale

Celery (see *Apium*)

Celtis **(Hackberry, sugarberry)**

Leaf chewers: fruittree leafroller, spiny elm caterpillar/mourning cloak, hackberry butterfly, fall cankerworm, puss caterpillar, hackberry leaf slug, ashgray blister beetle
Sucking insects: Asian woolly hackberry aphid, grape mealybug, striped mealybug, cottony maple scale, elm scurfy scale, Putnam's scale, hackberry lace bug, Forbes scale, walnut scale, European fruit lecanium
Gall makers: hackberry nipplegall maker, hackberry blistergall psyllid, hackberry petiolegall psyllid, hackberry stargall psyllid, hackberry budgall psyllid, *Pachypsylla celtidisintereris*, *Eriophyes celtis*
Borers: pigeon tremex, flatheaded appletree borer, redheaded ash borer, twig girdler, twig pruner, black stem borer

Centaurea **(Bachelor's button, basket flower, cornflower, dusty miller)**

Sucking insects: silverleaf whitefly, leafcurl plum aphid, aster leafhopper, erigeron root aphid, garden fleahopper

Centipedegrass (see *Eremochloa*)

Cercis **(Redbud, Judas tree)**

Leaf chewers: grape leaffolder, redbud leaffolder, whitemarked tussock moth, false unicorn caterpillar, stinging rose caterpillar, Asiatic oak weevil, hackberry leaf slug
Sucking insects: greedy scale, greenhouse whitefly, ash whitefly, twomarked treehopper

Chaenomeles **(Flowering quince)**

Leaf chewers: fruittree leafroller, leaf crumpler
Sucking insects: apple aphid, long-beaked clover aphid, apple grain aphid, grape mealybug, San Jose scale, tarnished plant bug, hawthorn lace bug

Chamaecyparis **(False cypress)**

Scales: juniper scale
Chewing insects: bagworm, imperial moth

Chamaedorea **(see Palms)**

Cherry (see *Prunus*)

Chestnut (see *Castanea*)

China aster (see *Callistephus*)

Chinese evergreen (see *Aglaonema*)

Chlorophytum **(Spider plant)**

Scales: hemispherical scale

Christmas berry (see *Heteromeles*)

Chrysalidocarpus (see Palms)

Chrysanthemum (Chrysanthemum, daisy, feverfew, marguerite, pyrethrum)

Leaf chewers: beet armyworm, cabbage looper, plantain looper, soybean looper, omnivorous leafroller, greenhouse leaftier, yellow woollybear, chrysanthemum leafminer, oriental beetle, Asiatic garden beetle, Fuller rose beetle
Leafminers: American serpentine leafminer, *Amauromyza maculosa*
Flower chewers: tobacco budworm, blister beetles, spotted cucumber beetle, rose chafer
Borers: European corn borer
Aphids: chrysanthemum aphid, cotton/melon aphid, green peach aphid, leafcurl plum aphid, foxglove aphid
Other sucking insects: western flower thrips, banded greenhouse thrips, greenhouse thrips, greenhouse whitefly, silverleaf whitefly, Mexican mealybug, hemispherical scale, chrysanthemum lace bug, fourlined lace bug, ground mealybug
Mites: twospotted spider mite, cyclamen mite, *Brevipalpus* sp.

Cineraria

Sucking insects: foxglove aphid, greenhouse whitefly, western flower thrips

Citrus (Orange, lemon, grapefruit, etc.)

Scales: Florida wax scale, red wax scale, Chinese wax scale, Indian wax scale, brown soft scale, citricola scale, black scale, nigra scale, hemispherical scale, barnacle scale, pyriform scale, oleander scale, Florida red scale, California red scale, tea scale, dictyospermum scale, cottony cushion scale, greedy scale, purple scale, fern scale
Other sucking insects: citrus mealybug, longtailed mealybug, cotton/melon aphid, black citrus aphid, brown citrus aphid, spirea aphid, cowpea aphid, woolly whitefly, citrus blackfly
Mites: citrus red mite, citrus rust mite, broad mite
Peelminers: citrus peelminer
Leaf chewers: orange tortrix, omnivorous looper, giant swallowtail, Texas leafcutting ant, brown garden snail

Clematis

Chewing insects: margined blister beetle, twobanded Japanese weevil
Sucking insects: garden fleahopper, green peach aphid

Codiaeum (Croton, Joseph's coat)

Sucking insects: brown soft scale, hemispherical scale, citrus mealybug, longtailed mealybug

Coleus

Sucking insects: citrus mealybug

Columbine (see *Aquilegia*)

Coneflower (see *Rudbeckia*)

Coral bells (see *Heuchera*)

Coreopsis (Calliopsis)

Leaf, flower chewers: coreopsis beetle, spotted cucumber beetle
Sucking insects: fourlined plant bug, potato aphid

Corn (see *Zea*)

Cornflower (see *Centaurea*)

Corn plant (see *Dracaena*)

Cornus (Dogwood)

Leaf chewers: polyphemus moth, cecropia moth, redhumped caterpillar, unicorn caterpillar, dogwood sawfly, twobanded Japanese weevil, Asiatic oak weevil, redheaded flea beetle
Scales: oystershell scale, tea scale, thorn scale, Forbes scale, cottony maple scale, cottony maple leaf scale, calico scale, gloomy scale, obscure scale, walnut scale, Japanese maple scale
Other sucking insects: fourlined plant bug, rose leafhopper, *Edwardsiana commisuralis*, sunflower aphid, mulberry whitefly, striped mealybug, taxus mealybug, alder spittlebug, basswood lace bug
Mites: twospotted spider mite
Twig feeders: dogwood clubgall midge, dogwood twig borer, raspberry cane borer, twig girdler
Borers: dogwood borer, Asian ambrosia beetle
Seed feeders: Western conifer seed bug

Corylus (Filbert)

Leaf chewers: Japanese beetle, fall webworm
Gall makers: filbert bud mite, *Cecidophyopsis vermiformis*
Sucking insects: filbert aphid
Seed feeders: filbertworm, filbert weevil

Cosmos

Sucking insects: aster leafhopper
Borers: European corn borer

Cotoneaster

Leaf chewers: pearslug, cotoneaster webworm, leaf crumpler
Scales: oystershell scale, San Jose scale
Other sucking insects: hawthorn lace bug, woolly apple aphid, apple mealybug, hawthorn mealybug, privet leafhopper
Mites: twospotted spider mite
Fruit, flower chewers: apple maggot, cotoneaster webworm
Borers: roundheaded appletree borer, sinuate pear tree borer

Cottonwood (see *Populus*)

Crabapple (see *Malus*)

Cranberry (see *Vaccinium*)

Cranberry bush (see *Viburnum*)

Crape myrtle (see *Lagerstroemia*)

Crassula **(Jade plant)**

Sucking insects: citrus mealybug, longtailed mealybug

Crataegus **(Hawthorn)**

Leaf chewers: pearslug, Japanese beetle, apple flea weevil, polyphemus moth, io moth, waved sphinx, unicorn caterpillar, yellownecked caterpillar, western tussock moth, fall webworm, western tent caterpillar, forest tent caterpillar, eastern tent caterpillar, pandemis leafroller, European leafroller, fall cankerworm, hawthorn leafminer, apple and thorn skeletonizer, apple buccalatrix, bagworm, leaf crumpler, speckled green fruitworm, eyespotted bud moth, lesser appleworm, appleleaf trumpet leafminer
Fruit chewers: apple maggot, apple curculio, speckled green fruitworm, eyespotted bud moth, lesser appleworm
Scales: San Jose scale, scurfy scale, terrapin scale, oystershell scale, Forbes scale
Other sucking insects: apple aphid, apple grain aphid, fourspotted hawthorn aphid, long-beaked clover aphid, woolly apple aphid, woolly hawthorn aphid, hawthorn mealybug, striped mealybug, white apple leafhopper, maple leafhopper, rose leafhopper, *Erythroneura gleditsia*, hawthorn lace bug
Mites: European red mite, linden spider mite
Borers, bark beetles: shothole borer, apple bark borer, flatheaded appletree borer, Pacific flatheaded borer, roundheaded appletree borer

Croton (see *Codiaeum*)

Crown of thorns (see *Euphorbia*)

Cryptomeria

Twig chewers: cypress weevil
Scales: juniper scale, Maskell scale, cryptomeria scale

Cucumber (see *Cucumis*)

Cucumis **(Cucumber, Melon)**

Leaf chewers: banded cucumber beetle, striped cucumber beetle, western striped cucumber beetle, spotted cucumber beetle, western corn rootworm, palestriped flea beetle, hop flea beetle, melonworm, pickleworm, southern armyworm, granulate cutworm
Leafminers: pea leafminer, American serpentine leafminer, vegetable leafminer
Sucking insects: tarnished plant bug, fourlined plant bug, cotton/melon aphid, greenhouse whitefly, silverleaf whitefly, onion thrips, melon thrips, western flower thrips
Mites: twospotted spider mite, broad mite
Seed feeders: seedcorn maggot
Fruit chewers: melonworm, pickleworm, striped cucumber beetle, fourspotted sap beetle, dusky sap beetle

Cucurbita **(Squash, Gourd, Pumpkin)**

Leaf chewers: banded cucumber beetle, striped cucumber beetle, western striped cucumber beetle, spotted cucumber beetle, western corn rootworm, northern corn rootworm, squash beetle, melonworm, pickleworm, beet armyworm, southern armyworm, granulate cutworm

Leafminers: pea leafminer, American serpentine leafminer, vegetable leafminer
Borers: squash vine borer
Seed feeders: seedcorn maggot
Sucking insects: squash bug, tarnished plant bug, cotton/melon aphid, *Empoasca recurvata*, potato leafhopper, onion thrips, melon thrips, western flower thrips
Mites: twospotted spider mite, broad mite
Fruit chewers: melonworm, pickleworm, striped cucumber beetle, fourspotted sap beetle, dusky sap beetle, beet armyworm

Cupressus (Cypress)

Leaf chewers: cypress tipminer, bagworm
Sucking insects, mites: cypress bark mealybug, juniper scale, minute juniper scale, *Platytetranychus libocedri*, beech blight aphid
Bark beetles: cedar bark beetles

Cycas (Sago palm)

Scales: hemispherical scale, oleander scale, cycad aulacaspis scale, cycad scale

Cyclamen (Shooting star)

Sucking insects: citrus mealybug, cotton/melon aphid, crescent-marked lily aphid, western flower thrips
Mites: cyclamen mite, broad mite

Cydonia (Quince)

Leaf chewers: pistol casebearer, cigar casebearer, fruittree leafroller, leaf crumpler, speckled green fruitworm, pearslug
Fruit chewers: codling moth, oriental fruit moth, plum curculio
Sucking insects: apple aphid, clover aphid, apple grain aphid, hawthorn mealybug, grape mealybug, San Jose scale, tarnished plant bug, hawthorn lace bug

Cynara (Globe artichoke, cardoon)

Leaf chewers: cabbage looper, painted lady, celery leaftier, differential grasshopper, spotted cucumber beetle
Bud chewers: artichoke plume moth, bumble flower beetle
Sucking insects: artichoke aphid, bean aphid, thistle aphid
Sucking insects, bud: southern green stink bug

Cynodon (Bermudagrass)

Leaf chewers: tropical sod webworm, armyworm, fall armyworm, fiery skipper, striped grassworms
Sucking insects/mites, leaves: bermudagrass mite, Banks grass mite, southern chinch bug, twolined spittlebug, rhodesgrass mealybug
Root chewers: southern mole cricket, tawny mole cricket, May/June beetles, hunting billbug, phoenician billbug
Sucking insects, roots: ground pearls

Daffodil (see *Narcissus*)

Dahlia

Leaf, flower chewers: oriental beetle, greenhouse leaftier, corn earworm, saddleback caterpillar, European earwig
Stem borers: European corn borer
Aphids: buckthorn aphid, leafcurl plum aphid, green peach aphid, bean aphid, foxglove aphid
Other sucking insects: greenhouse whitefly, silverleaf whitefly, *Entylia carniata*, potato leafhopper, citrus mealybug, greenhouse thrips, flower thrips, tarnished plant bug, fourlined plant bug
Mites: twospotted spider mite, broad mite, cyclamen mite, bulb mite

Daisy (see *Chrysanthemum*)

Daucus **(Carrot)**

Leaf chewers: alfalfa webworm, beet webworm, parsleyworm, anise swallowtail, celery leaftier, beet armyworm, palestriped flea beetle, American serpentine leafminer
Root chewers: carrot rust fly, carrot weevil, vegetable weevil
Sucking insects: carrot-willow aphid, coriander aphid, green peach aphid, cotton/melon aphid, honeysuckle aphid, aster leafhopper, tarnished plant bug, western tarnished plant bug, pale legume bug, garden fleahopper

Daylily (see *Hemerocallis*)

Delphinium **(Larkspur)**

Sucking insects: crescent-marked lily aphid, goldenglow aphid, aster leafhopper
Mites: cyclamen mite
Leaf chewers: Asiatic garden beetle, Japanese beetle, bertha armyworm, *Phytomyza delphinivora*

Deutzia

Sucking insects: bean aphid, cotton/melon aphid
Leaf chewers: twobanded Japanese weevil, lilac leafminer

Dianthus **(Carnation)**

Sucking insects: foxglove aphid, green peach aphid, bean aphid, western flower thrips
Mites: twospotted spider mite
Leaf, flower chewers: variegated cutworm, corn earworm, cabbage looper, obliquebanded leafroller, greenhouse leaftier

Dichondra

Leaf chewers: dichondra flea beetle

Dieffenbachia **(Dumb cane)**

Sucking insects: red wax scale, banded greenhouse thrips

Digitalis **(Foxglove)**

Sucking insects: foxglove aphid, crescent-marked lily aphid, longtailed mealybug
Leaf, flower chewers: Asiatic garden beetle, Japanese beetle

Diospyros (**Persimmon**)

Sucking insects: Indian wax scale, Comstock mealybug
Leaf chewers: hickory horned devil, luna moth, variable oakleaf caterpillar, redhumped caterpillar, puss caterpillar
Borers: persimmon borer, redheaded ash borer, twig girdler, Asian ambrosia beetle, apple twig borer

Dizygotheca (**False aralia**)

Scales: Chinese wax scale, brown soft scale, hemispherical scale, barnacle scale
Mites: twospotted spider mite

Dogwood (see *Cornus*)

Douglas-fir (see *Pseudotsuga*)

Dracaena (**Corn Plant**)

Sucking insects: Putnam's scale, citrus mealybug, longtailed mealybug

Dumb cane (see *Dieffenbachia*)

Dusty miller (see *Centaurea*)

Easter cactus (see Cactus)

Easter lily (see *Lilium*)

Eggplant (see *Solanum*)

Elaeagnus (**Russian olive, silverberry**)

Sucking insects: artichoke aphid, black citrus aphid, Comstock mealybug
Borers: redheaded ash borer, *Scolytus shevyrewi*

Elderberry (see *Sambucus*)

Elm (see *Ulmus*)

English daisy (see *Bellis*)

English ivy (see *Hedera*)

Eremochloa (**Centipedegrass**)

Leaf chewers: tropical sod webworm, armyworm
Sucking insects/mites, leaves: rhodesgrass mealybug, twolined spittlebug, southern chinch bug
Root chewers: tawny mole cricket, southern mole cricket, hunting billbug
Sucking insects, roots: ground pearls

Eucalyptus

Sucking insects: bluegum psyllid, red lerp psyllid, *Blastopsylla occidentalis*, cowpea aphid, giant whitefly, bandedwinged whitefly, woolly whitefly

Chewing insects: omnivorous looper, orange tortrix
Borers: eucalyptus longhorned borer, Pacific flatheaded borer

Eugenia

Scales: California red scale, Florida red scale, Indian wax scale
Other sucking insects: citrophilus mealybug, woolly whitefly, eugenia psyllid

Euonymus (Spindle tree, winter creeper)

Leaf chewers: bagworm, black vine weevil, lilac leafminer, twobanded Japanese weevil
Scales: euonymus scale, winged euonymus scale, California red scale, European peach scale, tea scale, common falsepit scale, Indian wax scale, cottony camellia scale, barnacle scale
Other sucking insects: bean aphid, ivy aphid
Mites: twospotted spider mite

Euphorbia (Crown of thorns, poinsettia, spurge)

Leaf chewers: soybean looper
Sucking insects: greenhouse whitefly, silverleaf whitefly, bandedwinged whitefly, Mexican mealybug, longtailed mealybug, brown soft scale, hemispherical scale, California red scale, black scale

Evening primrose (see *Oenothera*)

Fagus (Beech)

Leaf chewers: fall cankerworm, Bruce spanworm, redhumped oakworm, variable oakleaf caterpillar, saddled prominent, luna moth, polyphemus moth, Asiatic oak weevil
Borers: pigeon tremex, flatheaded appletree borer, leopard moth
Scales: oak lecanium, beech scale, oystershell scale
Other sucking insects: beech blight aphid, woolly beech aphid, giant bark aphid, maple leafhopper, *Macropsis graminea*
Mites: oak mite, *Acalitus fagerinea*

False aralia (see *Dizygotheca*)

Fatsia (see *Aralia*)

Felt plant (see *Kalanchoe*)

Fennel (see *Foeniculum*)

Ferns (Many genera; also see *Nephrolepis*)

Leaf chewers: Florida fern caterpillar, obliquebanded leafroller
Scales: fern scale, tea scale, hemispherical scale, brown soft scale
Other sucking insects: fern aphid, greenhouse thrips, onion thrips
Root feeders: black vine weevil

Fescue (see *Festuca*)

Festuca (Fescue)

Leaf chewers: sod webworms, armyworm, fall armyworm

Sucking insects/mites, leaves: winter grain mite, clover mite, Banks grass mite, hairy chinch bug, greenbug, rhodesgrass mealybug
Root chewers: masked chafers, European chafer, Japanese beetle, bluegrass billbug, hunting billbug, European crane fly, march flies

Feterbush (see *Leucothoe*)

Feverfew (see *Chrysanthemum*)

Ficus (Fig, rubber plant)

Scales: Florida wax scale, brown soft scale, hemispherical scale, nigra scale, black scale, oleander pit scale
Other sucking insects: citrus mealybug, black citrus aphid, banded greenhouse thrips, greenhouse thrips, Cuban laurel thrips

Fig (see *Ficus*)

Filbert (see *Corylus*)

Fine fescue (see *Festuca*)

Fir (see *Abies*)

Firethorn (see *Pyracantha*)

Flaming Katy (see *Kalanchoe*)

Flossflower (see *Ageratum*)

Flowering almond (see *Prunus*)

Flowering cherry (see *Prunus*)

Flowering onion (see *Allium*)

Flowering peach (see *Prunus*)

Flowering plum (see *Prunus*)

Flowering tobacco (see *Nicotiana*)

Foeniculum (Fennel)

Sucking insects: green peach aphid, honeysuckle aphid
Chewing insects: parsleyworm, anise swallowtail

Forsythia

Leaf chewers: redheaded flea beetle, twobanded Japanese weevil
Sucking insects: white peach scale, fourlined plant bug
Root chewers: twobanded Japanese weevil

Fortunella

Scales: hemispherical scale

Foxglove (see *Digitalis*)

Fragaria (Strawberry)

Leaf chewers: Fuller rose beetle, palestriped flea beetle, redheaded flea beetle, hop flea beetle, strawberry flea beetle, strawberry root beetle, redbanded leafroller, variegated leafroller, obliquebanded leafroller, sparganothis leafroller, strawberry leafroller, omnivorous leaftier, green fruitworms, European earwig, milky garden slug

Fruit chewers: strawberry sap beetle, fourspotted sap beetle, strawberry bud weevil, European earwig, green fruitworms, redbanded leafroller, variegated leafroller, obliquebanded leafroller, sparganothis leafroller, milky garden slug, millipedes

Sucking insects: meadow spittlebug, strawberry aphid, cotton/melon aphid, buckthorn aphid, tarnished plant bug, western flower thrips

Mites: cyclamen mite

Borers: strawberry crownminer, strawberry crown borer

Root feeders: strawberry root weevil, rough strawberry root weevil

Fraxinus (Ash)

Leaf chewers: brownheaded ash sawfly, blackheaded ash sawfly, *Trichiosoma triangulum*, spring cankerworm, fall cankerworm, elm spanworm, linden looper, forest tent caterpillar, fall webworm, fruittree leafroller, green fruitworm, great ash sphinx, twinspot sphinx, waved sphinx, promothea moth, cecropia moth, luna moth, polyphemus moth, western tiger swallowtail, eastern tiger swallowtail, walkingstick, twobanded Japanese weevil, leafcutter bees

Scales: oystershell scale, walnut scale, common falsepit scale, pitmaking pittosporum scale, European fruit lecanium, Putnam's scale, scurfy scale

Other sucking insects: western ash plant bug, ash plant bug, *Tropidosteptes brooksi*, *T. illitus*, sycamore lace bug, buffalo treehopper, leafcurl ash aphid, *Prociphilus americanus*, ash whitefly

Gall makers: ash flower gall mite, *Eriophyes chondriphora*, ash midrib gall midge, *Cecidomyia pellex*

Bark beetles: eastern ash bark beetle, western ash bark beetle, Criddle's bark beetle

Borers: lilac/ash borer, banded ash clearwing, oak clearwing, carpenterworm, leopard moth, emerald ash borer, redheaded ash borer, banded ash borer, flatheaded appletree borer, *Pemphredon* wasps

Freesia

Root feeders: bulb mite, tulip bulb aphid

Sucking insects: gladiolus thrips, crescent-marked lily aphid

Fuschia

Leaf, flower chewers: Japanese beetle, Fuller rose beetle, apple flea beetle

Scales: black scale, greedy scale, California red scale

Other sucking insects: western flower thrips, greenhouse thrips, citrus mealybug, greenhouse whitefly, bandedwinged whitefly, giant whitefly, iris whitefly

Mites: cyclamen mite, fuschia gall mite

Gaillardia

Leaf, flower chewers: Asiatic garden beetle, Japanese beetle, bumble flower beetle, *Amauromyza maculosa*

Sucking insects: fourlined plant bug, western flower thrips, onion thrips, aster leafhopper

Gardenia (Cape jasmine)

Scales: red wax scale, brown soft scale, hemispherical scale, barnacle scale
Other sucking insects: citrus mealybug, greenhouse whitefly, bandedwinged whitefly, citrus white-fly, longtailed mealybug, black citrus aphid, flower thrips, banded greenhouse thrips
Mites: twospotted spider mite
Flower chewers: tobacco budworm

Geranium (see *Pelargonium*)

Gerbera (Transvaal daisy)

Leafminers: American serpentine leafminer
Sucking insects, mites: silverleaf whitefly, greenhouse whitefly, western flower thrips, broad mite

Geum

Sucking insects: Pritchard's mealybug

Gingko

Sucking insects: grape mealybug
Leaf chewers: whitemarked tussock moth, fruittree leafroller, omnivorous looper

Gladiolus

Leaf chewers: bertha armyworm, corn earworm
Sucking insects, leaves and flowers: gladiolus thrips, tulip bulb aphid, cotton/melon aphid, iris whitefly, greenhouse whitefly, giant whitefly, grape mealybug, tarnished plant bug, fourlined plant bug
Sucking insects, bulbs: ground mealybug, bulb mite, gladiolus thrips
Borers of bulbs, stems: European corn borer, lesser bulb fly

Gleditsia (Honeylocust)

Leaf chewers: bagworm, mimosa webworm, fall cankerworm, fruittree leafroller, yellownecked cater-pillar, imperial moth, silverspotted skipper, ashgray blister beetle
Gall maker: honeylocust podgall midge
Scales: cottony maple scale, common falsepit scale, oystershell scale, California red scale
Other sucking insects: honeylocust plant bug, honeylocust leafhopper, *Micrutalis calva*, grape mealy-bug, Putnam's cicada, cowpea aphid
Mites: honeylocust spider mite, honeylocust rust mite
Borers: hickory borer, apple twig borer, twig pruner, honeylocust borer

Globe Artichoke (see *Cynara*)

Gloriosa daisy (see *Rudbeckia*)

Gloxinia (see *Sinningia*)

Golden-chain tree (see *Laburnum*)

Goldenglow (see *Rudbeckia*)

Goldenrain tree (see *Koelreuteria*)

Grape (see *Vitis*)

Green bean (see *Phaseolus*)

Gynura (Velvet plant, purple passion vine)

Sucking insects: hemispherical scale, Mexican mealybug

Gypsophila

Leaf chewers: American serpentine leafminer, snailcase bagworm, southern armyworm
Sucking insects: flower thrips, aster leafhopper

Hackberry (see *Celtis*)

Hamamelis (Witch-hazel)

Gall-makers: witch-hazel leafgall aphid, spiny witch-hazel gall aphid

Harebell (see *Campanula*)

Haworthia

Mites: aloe mite

Hawthorn (see *Crataegus*)

Hazelnut (see *Corylus*)

Heavenly bamboo (see Bamboo)

Hedera (English ivy)

Scales: brown soft scale, nigra scale, oleander scale, false oleander scale, greedy scale, cottony cushion scale, cottony camellia scale
Other sucking insects: citrus mealybug, grape mealybug, longtailed mealybug, Mexican mealybug, citrus whitefly, ivy aphid, bean aphid, green peach aphid
Mites: twospotted spider mite, broad mite, cyclamen mite
Leaf chewers: cabbage looper, omnivorous looper, puss caterpillar

Helianthus (Sunflower, Jerusalem artichoke)

Leaf chewers: variegated leafroller, painted lady, American lady, sunflower beetle, palestriped flea beetle, yellow woollybear, bertha armyworm, *Amauromyza maculosa*
Sucking insects: green peach aphid, buckthorn aphid, sunflower aphid
Stem borers: sunflower maggot, sunflower stem weevil
Head, seed-infesting insects: sunflower headclipping weevil, sunflower midge, sunflower seed maggot, sunflower moth, banded sunflower moth, gray sunflower weevil, red sunflower weevil
Root chewers: carrot beetle

Helichrysum (Strawflower)

Flower chewers: tobacco budworm, bumble flower beetle
Sucking insects: aster leafhopper

Hemerocallis (Daylily)

Leaf chewers: convict caterpillar, Japanese beetle
Flower chewers: Japanese beetle, bumble flower beetle, hemerocallis gall midge
Sucking insects, mites: daylily thrips, western flower thrips, *Lopidea confluenta*, twospotted spider mite

Hemlock (see *Tsuga*)

Heteromeles (Toyon, Christmas berry)

Leaf chewers: whitemarked tussock moth
Sucking insects: toyon thrips

Heuchera (Alumroot, coral bells)

Leaf, root chewers: black vine weevil, strawberry root weevil

Hibiscus (Rose of Sharon, Chinese hibiscus, cotton rose, rose mallow)

Leaf, flower chewers: gray hairstreak/cotton square borer, corn earworm, io moth, puss caterpillar, okra caterpillar, hibiscus sawfly, Japanese beetle, brown garden snail
Sucking insects: fern scale, black scale, California red scale, Comstock mealybug, pink hibiscus mealybug, cotton/melon aphid, cowpea aphid, silverleaf whitefly, greenhouse whitefly, bandedwinged whitefly, giant whitefly, greenhouse thrips, western flower thrips, hibiscus plant bug

Hickory (see *Carya*)

Hippeastrum (Amaryllis, Barbados lily)

Leaf, flower chewers: convict caterpillar, black blister beetle, spotted cutworm
Sucking insects: potato aphid, greenhouse thrips, gladiolus thrips, citrus mealybug, bulb mite
Root chewers: narcissus bulb fly

Holly (see *Ilex*)

Hollyhock (see *Alcea*)

Honeylocust (see *Gleditsia*)

Honeysuckle (see *Lonicera*)

Horseradish (see *Armoracia*)

Hosta

Leaf chewers: black vine weevil, oriental beetle, milky garden slug
Mites: twospotted spider mite

Howeia (see Palms)

Hoya

Sucking insects: citrus mealybug, longtailed mealybug, oleander aphid, banded greenhouse thrips

Hyacinth (see *Hyacinthus*)

Hyacinthus (Hyacinth)

Leaf chewers: yellow woollybear
Sucking insects: green peach aphid, bean aphid, foxglove aphid
Bulb feeders: bulb mite, lesser bulb fly

Hydrangea

Sucking insects, mites: greenhouse whitefly, silverleaf whitefly, giant whitefly, citrus mealybug, oystershell scale, cottony camellia scale, cotton/melon aphid, crescent-marked lily aphid, fourlined plant bug, boxelder bug, twospotted spider mite

Iberis (Candy tuft)

Leaf chewers: diamondback moth, western black flea beetle

Ilex (Holly, yaupon)

Leaf chewers: black vine weevil, twobanded Japanese weevil, blackheaded fireworm/holly bud moth, holly looper, fall webworm, holly leafminers
Scales: tea scale, holly pit scale, holly scale, cottony camellia scale, cottony maple leaf scale, Chinese red scale, Indian wax scale, Florida wax scale, black scale, nigra scale, greedy scale, walnut scale
Other sucking insects: black citrus aphid, striped mealybug, Comstock mealybug, twolined spittlebug, mulberry whitefly, yaupon psyllid
Mites: southern red mite
Borers: twig girdler, twig pruner
Root feeders: black vine weevil

Impatiens

Sucking insects: greenhouse whitefly, longtailed mealybug, tarnished plant bug, western flower thrips
Leaf, flower chewers: spotted cucumber beetle
Mites: cyclamen mite, broad mite, twospotted spider mite

Indian bean (see *Catalpa*)

Ipomoea (Sweetpotato, morning glory)

Leaf chewers: sweetpotato flea beetle, banded cucumber beetle, spotted cucumber beetle, palestriped flea beetle, Argus tortoise beetle, blacklegged tortoise beetle, golden tortoise beetle, mottled tortoise beetle, striped tortoise beetle, Asiatic garden beetle, southern armyworm, yellowstriped armyworm, beet armyworm, granulate cutworm, black cutworm, sweetpotato hornworm, morningglory leafminer, sweetpotato leafminer
Root chewers: sweetpotato weevil, whitefringed beetle, wireworms
Sucking insects: silverleaf whitefly, greenhouse whitefly, cotton/melon aphid, western potato leafhopper, potato leafhopper, garden fleahopper, fourlined plant bug

Iresine (Beefsteak plant, bloodleaf)

Scales: hemispherical scale

Iris

Sucking insects: iris whitefly, gladiolus thrips, iris thrips, *Lopidea confluenta*
Root feeders, chewers: lesser bulb fly, narcissus bulb fly, iris borer
Root feeders, sucking: ground mealybug, tulip bulb aphid, bulb mite

Ivy (see *Hedera*)

Ivy geranium (see *Pelargonium*)

Jade plant (see *Crassula*)

Jasmine (see *Jasminum*)

Jasminum (Jasmine)

Sucking insects: Indian wax scale, cottony camellia scale, banded greenhouse thrips
Mites: broad mite

Jerusalem artichoke (see *Helianthus*)

Jonquil (see *Narcissus*)

Joseph's coat (see *Codiaeum*)

Judas tree (see *Cercis*)

Juglans (Walnut)

Leaf chewers: walnut caterpillar, polyphemus moth, cecropia moth, fall webworm, hickory tussock moth, western tussock moth, hickory horned devil, luna moth
Scales: citricola scale, buckeye scale, walnut scale, oystershell scale
Other sucking insects: walnut aphid, dusky-winged walnut aphid, *Plagiognatus punctatipes*, twomarked treehopper, walnut lace bug
Mites: European red mite, walnut petiole gall mite, walnut blister mite
Borers, bark beetles: walnut shoot borer, pecan carpenterworm, hickory bark beetle
Seed feeders: walnut husk fly, black walnut curculio

Juniper (see *Juniperus*)

Juniperus (Juniper)

Needle chewers: juniper sawfly, silverspotted tiger moth, juniper webworm, cypress tip miner, *Coleotechnites juniperella*
Scales: juniper scale, minute juniper scale, Fletcher scale
Gall makers: juniper tip midge, juniper midge, *Trisetacus quadrisetus*, *T. juniperinus*
Other sucking insects: juniper spittlebug, Rocky Mountain juniper aphid, balsam twig aphid
Mites: spruce spider mite, *Platytetranychus libocedri*

Borers, bark beetles: juniper twig girdler, cedar bark beetles, blackhorned juniper borer
Root feeders: arborvitae weevil

Kalanchoe (Felt plant, flaming Katy, panda plant)

Sucking insects: citrus mealybug

Kalmia (Mountain laurel)

Leaf chewers: black vine weevil, azalea leafminer
Sucking insects: rhododendron lace bug, azalea bark scale, mulberry whitefly
Mites: southern red mite
Borers: rhododendron borer, azalea stem borer

Kentia

Scales: coconut scale, Florida red scale, dictyospermum scale, Putnam scale, greedy scale

Kentucky bluegrass (see *Poa*)

Kinnikinnick (see *Arctostaphylos*)

Koelreuteria (Goldenrain tree)

Sucking insects: white peach scale, goldenrain tree bug
Borers: Asian ambrosia beetle

Laburnum (Golden-chain)

Chewing insects: genista caterpillar, locust leafminer
Sucking insects: cowpea aphid, grape mealybug

Lactuca (Lettuce)

Leaf chewers: banded cucumber beetle, western corn rootworm, cabbage looper, alfalfa looper, celery looper, corn earworm, variegated cutworm, zebra caterpillar, beet armyworm, yellowstriped armyworm, western yellowstriped armyworm, saltmarsh caterpillar, celery leaftier, American serpentine leafminer, palestriped flea beetle, redheaded flea beetle, black slug, milky garden slug, spotted garden slug, brown garden snail
Sucking insects: lettuce aphid, potato aphid, pea aphid, green peach aphid, bean aphid, cabbage aphid, brown ambrosia aphid, *Uroleucon pseudambrosiae*, greenhouse whitefly, silverleaf whitefly, aster leafhopper, southern garden leafhopper, western flower thrips, tarnished plant bug, western tarnished plant bug, pale legume bug, false chinch bugs, garden fleahopper
Sucking insects, roots: lettuce root aphid

Lady's slipper (see Orchids)

Lagerstroemia (Crape myrtle)

Leaf chewers: Japanese beetle, genista caterpillar
Sucking insects: crapemyrtyle aphid, black citrus aphid, cotton/melon aphid, ash whitefly, citrus whitefly, hemispherical scale, Florida wax scale
Bark beetles: Asian ambrosia beetle

Lantana

Sucking insects: Mexican mealybug, hemispherical scale, oleander pit scale, western flower thrips, flower thrips
Mites: broad mite

Larch (see *Larix*)

Larix (Larch)

Needle chewers: bagworm, spruce budworm, eyespotted bud moth, whitemarked tussock moth, larch casebearer, redbanded leafroller, redheaded pine sawfly
Sucking insects: pine spittlebug, larch aphid
Wood borers, bark beetles: whitespotted sawyer, pales weevil, red turpentine beetle

Larkspur (see *Delphinium*)

Lathyrus (Sweet pea)

Leaf, flower chewers: cabbage looper, corn earworm, leafcutter bees
Sucking insects, mites: pea aphid, potato aphid, twospotted spider mite
Seed chewers: pea moth

Laurus (Sweet bay)

Sucking insects: Florida wax scale, brown soft scale, laurel psyllid
Chewing insects: eyespotted bud moth

Lavandula (Lavender)

Leaf chewers: orange tortrix, yellow woollybear
Sucking insects: silverleaf whitefly, greenhouse whitefly, fourlined plant bug

Lemon (see *Citrus*)

Lettuce (see *Lactuca*)

Leucothoe (Feterbush)

Sucking insects, mites: andromeda lace bug, southern red mite

Ligustrum (Privet)

Leaf chewers: lilac leafminer, cecropia moth, great ash sphinx, waved sphinx, European leafroller, leaf crumpler, fall webworm, leafcutter bees, black vine weevil, twobanded Japanese weevil
Scales: pitmaking pittosporum scale, elm scurfy scale, oystershell scale, white peach scale, California red scale, walnut scale
Other sucking insects: privet leafhopper, ash whitefly, citrus whitefly, privet thrips, Comstock mealybug, flower thrips
Mites: privet rust mite, privet mite
Borers: lilac/ash borer

Lilac (see *Syringa*)

Lilium (Lily)

Leaf chewers: Fuller rose beetle, saddleback caterpillar
Sucking insects: crescent-marked lily aphid, green peach aphid, cotton/melon aphid, foxglove aphid, greenhouse whitefly, hemispherical scale, gladiolus thrips
Bulb feeders: lesser bulb fly, narcissus bulb fly, bulb mites

Lily (see *Lilium*)

Lima bean (see *Phaseolus*)

Limonium (Statice)

Sucking insects: aster leafhopper

Linden (see *Tilia*)

Liquidambar (Sweetgum)

Leaf chewers: bagworm, fall webworm, forest tent caterpillar, luna moth, imperial moth, hickory horned devil
Sucking insects: mulberry whitefly
Mites: twospotted spider mite
Bark beetles: Asian ambrosia beetle

Liriodendron (Tuliptree)

Leaf chewers: yellow poplar weevil, eastern tiger swallowtail
Gall maker: eyespot gall midge
Sucking insects: tuliptree aphid, ash whitefly, tuliptree scale

Liriope

Leaf chewers: black vine weevil
Sucking insects: fern scale

Lobelia

Mites: twospotted spider mite

Lobularia (Sweet alyssum)

Leaf chewers: western black flea beetle, Japanese beetle
Sucking insects: harlequin bug

Locust (see *Robinia*)

Lolium (Ryegrass)

Leaf chewers: sod webworms, army cutworm, armyworm, bronzed cutworm, fall armyworm
Sucking insects/mites, leaves: winter grain mite, clover mite, Banks grass mite, brown wheat mite, hairy chinch bug, greenbug
Root chewers: black turfgrass ataenius, masked chafers, European chafer, Japanese beetle, bluegrass billbug, Denver billbug, European crane fly, march flies

London planetree (see *Plantanus*)

Lonicera (Honeysuckle)

Leaf chewers: hummingbird clearwing sphinx, snowberry clearwing, boxelder leafroller, oblique-banded leafroller, genista caterpillar
Sucking insects: honeysuckle witches' broom aphid, honeysuckle aphid, greenhouse whitefly, fourlined plant bug, hemispherical scale, European peach scale
Mites: clover mite

Lupinus (Lupines)

Leaf chewers: painted lady, blister beetles
Sucking insects: lupine aphid, silverleaf whitefly, greenhouse whitefly
Flower chewers: hoplia beetle, blister beetles

Lycopersicon (Tomato)

Leaf chewers: tomato hornworm, tobacco hornworm, beet armyworm, yellowstriped armyworm, southern armyworm, variegated cutworm, cabbage looper, potato flea beetle, western potato flea beetle, tobacco flea beetle, hop flea beetle, margined blister beetle, American serpentine leafminer, vegetable leafminer
Fruit chewers: corn earworm, beet armyworm, variegated cutworm, tomato pinworm, tobacco budworm, tomato hornworm, tobacco hornworm, green June beetle, vinegar/pomace flies
Sucking insects, leaves: potato/tomato psyllid, potato aphid, cotton/melon aphid, green peach aphid, beet leafhopper, banded greenhouse thrips, greenhouse whitefly
Sucking insects, fruit/flowers: green stink bug, southern green stink bug, onespotted stink bug, consperse stink bug, Say's stink bug, tarnished plant bug, western tarnished plant bug, garden fleahopper, western flower thrips, flower thrips
Mites: broad mite, tomato russet mite, twospotted spider mite

Lythrum

Leaf chewers: black vine weevil

Magnolia (Magnolia, cucumber tree, umbrella tree)

Leaf chewers: yellow poplar weevil, omnivorous looper, promothea moth, eastern tiger swallowtail, brown garden snail
Flower chewers: hoplia beetle
Scales: magnolia scale, oleander scale, common falsepit scale, fern scale, false oleander scale, California red scale, greedy scale, tuliptree scale, oleander pit scale, Indian wax scale
Other sucking insects: greenhouse thrips, tuliptree aphid, striped mealybug
Bark beetles: Asian ambrosia beetle, black twig borer

Mahonia (Grape holly)

Leaf chewers: barberry looper, barberry webworm
Sucking insects: mulberry whitefly, barberry aphid

Malus (Apple, crabapple)

Leaf chewers: redhumped caterpillar, yellownecked caterpillar, forest tent caterpillar, spring cankerworm, eastern tent caterpillar, western tent caterpillar, whitemarked tussock moth, hickory tussock moth, saddleback caterpillar, saddled prominent, cecropia moth, io moth, fall webworm, tufted apple bud moth, eyespotted bud moth, apple ermine moth, blackheaded fireworm, redbanded leafroller, fruittree leafroller, obliquebanded leafroller, European leafroller, variegated leafroller, apple pandemis, pistol casebearer, cigar casebearer, snailcase bagworm, leaf crumpler, apple and thorn skeletonizer, resplendent shield bearer, apple flea beetle, grape flea beetle, redheaded flea beetle, apple flea weevil, Japanese beetle

Leafminers: spotted tentiform leafminer, tentiform leafminer, western tentiform leafminer, lyonetia leafminer, appleleaf trumpet leafminer

Fruit, flower chewers: apple maggot, western cherry fruit fly, codling moth, oriental fruit moth, speckled green fruitworm, green fruitworm, spotted cutworm, lesser appleworm, cherry fruitworm, European earwig, tufted apple bud moth, eyespotted bud moth, apple ermine moth, blackheaded fireworm, redbanded leafroller, fruittree leafroller, obliquebanded leafroller, European leafroller, variegated leafroller, apple pandemis, European apple sawfly, plum curculio, apple curculio

Fruit, flower sucking insects: rosy apple aphid, western flower thrips, boxelder bug, western boxelder bug, consperse stink bug, green stink bug, redshouldered stink bug, Say's stink bug, onespotted stink bug, campylomma bug, tarnished plant bug

Scales: San Jose scale, Forbes scale, oystershell scale, European fruit lecanium, calico scale

Aphids: rosy apple aphid, apple aphid, spirea aphid, apple grain aphid, clover aphid, English grain aphid, woolly apple aphid

Other sucking insects: white apple leafhopper, apple leafhopper, rose leafhopper, maple leafhopper, hawthorn lace bug, apple sucker psyllid, ash whitefly, grape mealybug, apple mealybug, Comstock mealybug, periodical cicada, buffalo treehopper

Mites: appleleaf blister mite, apple rust mite, twospotted spider mite, McDaniel spider mite, European red mite, yellow spider mite, Pacific spider mite, brown mite

Oviposition injury, twigs: periodical cicada, buffalo treehopper

Bark beetles, borers: shothole borer, dogwood borer, apple bark borer, cherry bark tortrix, American plum borer, pigeon tremex, Pacific flatheaded borer, flatheaded appletree borer, redheaded ash borer, roundheaded appletree borer, apple twig borer

Root feeders: rain beetles, tenlined June beetle, roundheaded appletree borer

Malva

Sucking insects: silverleaf whitefly, greenhouse whitefly
Leaf chewers: hollyhock leaf skeletonizer, painted lady, west coast lady, okra caterpillar
Flower chewers: tobacco budworm

Mammillaria (see Cactus)

Manzanita (see *Arctostaphylos*)

Maple (see *Acer*)

Marguerite (see *Chrysanthemum*)

Marigold (see *Tagetes*)

Matthiola (Stock)

Leaf chewers: diamondback moth, cabbage looper, western black flea beetle

Melon (see *Cucumis*)

Milfoil (see *Achillea*)

Mimosa (see *Albizia*)

Miscanthus

Sucking insects: miscanthus mealybug

Mock orange (see *Philadelphus*)

Monkey puzzle tree (see *Araucaria*)

Morning glory (see *Ipomoea*)

Morus (**Mulberry**)

Leaf chewers: io moth, pale tussock moth, fall webworm
Scales: white peach scale, European fruit lecanium, cottony cushion scale, gloomy scale, Indian wax scale, common falsepit scale, California red scale, oleander pit scale
Other sucking insects: mulberry whitefly, ash whitefly, apple mealybug, Comstock mealybug, grape mealybug, striped mealybug, sycamore lace bug
Borers: carpenterworm, American plum borer, painted hickory borer

Moss rose (see *Portulaca*)

Moth orchid (see Orchids)

Mountain-ash (see *Sorbus*)

Mountain laurel (see *Kalmia*)

Mulberry (see *Morus*)

Mum (see *Chrysanthemum*)

Mustard (see *Brassica*)

Nandina (see Bamboo)

Narcissus (**Daffodil, jonquil**)

Leaf chewers: convict caterpillar
Bulb chewers: narcissus bulb fly, lesser bulb fly
Bulb feeders, sucking: tulip bulb aphid, bulb mite

Nasturtium (see *Tropaeolum*)

Nectarine (see *Prunus*)

Nephrolepis (**Fern**)

Scales: brown soft scale, hemispherical scale, fern scale
Mealybugs: obscure mealybug, longtailed mealybug
Caterpillars: Florida fern caterpillar

Nephytis (see *Syngonium*)

Nerium (Oleander)

Leaf chewers: oleander caterpillar, spotted oleander caterpillar
Scales: Florida wax scale, brown soft scale, hemispherical scale, nigra scale, black scale, oleander scale, cottony cushion scale, oleander pit scale, California red scale
Other sucking insects: longtailed mealybug, citrus mealybug, oleander aphid, bean aphid, root mealybug

New Guinea impatiens (see *Impatiens*)

Nicotiana (Flowering tobacco)

Leaf chewers: Colorado potato beetle, tobacco flea beetle, potato flea beetle
Flower chewers: tobacco budworm
Sucking insects: potato aphid

Norfolk Island pine (see *Araucaria*)

Nymphaea (Waterlily)

Leaf chewers: waterlily leaf beetle, China mark moth, waterlily leafcutter
Sucking insects: waterlily aphid

Oak (see *Quercus*)

Ocimum (Basil)

Leaf chewers: American serpentine leafminer, vegetable leafminer, painted lady
Sucking insects, mites: greenhouse whitefly, twospotted spider mite, carmine spider mite

Oenothera (Evening primrose)

Leaf chewers: apple flea beetle, strawberry flea beetle, steel-blue grapevine flea beetle, *Altica litigara*, whitelined sphinx, grape leaffolder
Flower chewers: false Japanese beetle
Sucking insects: western flower thrips

Okra (see *Abelmoschus*)

Oleander (see *Nerium*)

Onion (see *Allium*)

Opuntia (see Cactus)

Orange (see *Citrus*)

Orchids (Many genera)

Sucking insects: Boisduval scale, greenhouse thrips, crescent-marked lily aphid, cotton/melon aphid, giant whitefly, citrus mealybug

Root feeders: bulb mite
Mites: *Brevipalpus oncidii, Tenuipalpus pacificus, T. oarchidarum,* twospotted spider mite

Oregon grape holly (see *Mahonia*)

Ornamental cabbage (see *Brassica*)

Ornamental fig (see *Ficus*)

Ornamental kale (see *Brassica*)

Ornamental onion (see *Allium*)

Ornamental pepper (see *Capsicum*)

Pachysandra

Scales: oystershell scale, euonymus scale
Mites: twospotted spider mite

Paeonia (Peony)

Leaf chewers: black vine weevil, Japanese beetle, rose chafer
Flower associates: hoplia beetle, field ants, flower thrips

Painted daisy (see *Chrysanthemum*)

Palms (Many genera; also see *Cycas*)

Scales: red wax scale, oleander scale, false oleander scale, Florida red scale, California red scale, dictyospermum scale, Putnam's scale, Boisduval scale, latania scale, greedy scale
Leaf chewers: io moth
Sucking insects: greenhouse thrips

Panda plant (see *Kalanchoe*)

Pansy (see *Viola*)

Papaver (Poppy)

Sucking insects: longtailed mealybug
Leaf, flower chewers: bertha armyworm, hoplia beetle, false Japanese beetle

Parsley (see *Petroselinum*)

Parsnip (see *Pastinica*)

Parthenocissus (Boston ivy, Virginia creeper)

Leaf chewers: leafcutter bees, achemon sphinx, Virginiacreeper sphinx, whitelined sphinx, Virginiacreeper clearwing, Japanese beetle, grape flea beetle, yellow woollybear, eightspotted forester, grape leaffolder
Sucking insects: Virginiacreeper leafhopper, threebanded leafhopper, rusty plum aphid, grape mealybug, calico scale

Paspalum (**Bahiagrass**)

Leaf chewers: tropical sod webworm, armyworm, striped grassworms
Sucking insects: twolined spittlebug, southern chinch bug
Root feeders: southern mole cricket, tawny mole cricket

Pasqueflower (see *Anemone*)

Pastinica (**Parsnip**)

Leaf chewers: shorttailed swallowtail
Sucking insects, mites: green peach aphid, western aster root aphid, twospotted spider mite
Root chewers: carrot rust fly, carrot weevil

Pea (see *Pisum*)

Peach (see *Prunus*)

Pear (see *Pyrus*)

Pecan (see *Carya*)

Pelargonium (**Geranium**)

Leaf chewers: tobacco budworm, bertha armyworm, orange tortrix, obliquebanded leafroller, greenhouse leaftier, plantain looper, soybean looper, omnivorus looper
Flower, bud feeders: tobacco budworm
Sucking insects: fourlined plant bug, harlequin bug, green peach aphid, foxglove aphid, greenhouse whitefly, silverleaf whitefly, giant whitefly, bandedwinged whitefly, citrus mealybug, Mexican mealybug
Mites: cyclamen mite, Lewis spider mite
Root feeders: black vine weevil

Penstemon

Leaf chewers: *Disonycha* sp., Fuller rose beetle
Borers: penstemon clearwing
Sucking insects: foxglove aphid, crescent-marked lily aphid

Peony (see *Paeonia*)

Peperomia

Sucking insects, mites: brown soft scale, citrus mealybug, broad mite

Peppertree (see *Schinus*)

Perennial ryegrass (see *Lolium*)

Periwinkle (see *Vinca*)

Persea (**Red bay, avocado**)

Sucking insects: latania scale, hemispherical scale, red wax scale, California red scale, oleander pit scale, citrus mealybug, greenhouse whitefly, red bay psyllid, greenhouse thrips, cotton/melon aphid, grape mealybug

Leaf chewers: brown garden snail
Borers: sycamore borer

Persimmon (see *Diospyros*)

Petroselinum (Parsley)

Sucking insects: green peach aphid, carrot-willow aphid, coriander aphid
Leaf chewers: parsleyworm/black swallowtail, greenhouse leaftier, redheaded flea beetle
Root chewers: carrot weevil, carrot rust fly

Petunia

Leaf chewers: tobacco hornworm, tomato hornworm, bertha armyworm, yellow woollybear, oriental beetle, Asiatic garden beetle
Flower chewers: tobacco budworm, oriental beetle, Asiatic garden beetle
Sucking insects: potato aphid, bandedwinged whitefly, aster leafhopper, garden fleahopper, tarnished plant bug
Mites: cyclamen mite, twospotted spider mite

Phaseolus (Beans)

Leaf chewers: Mexican bean beetle, banded cucumber beetle, spotted cucumber beetle, striped cucumber beetle, bean leaf beetle, twobanded Japanese weevil, bean leafroller, corn earworm, armyworm, beet armyworm, zebra caterpillar, alfalfa looper, cabbage looper, soybean looper, saltmarsh caterpillar, yellow woollybear, Japanese beetle, palestriped flea beetle, redheaded flea beetle, American serpentine leafminer, milky garden slug
Pod, seed chewers: lima bean pod borer, gray hairstreak, European corn borer, European earwig
Root, seed feeders: seedcorn maggot, bean seed maggot, whitefringed beetle, vegetable weevil
Sucking insects/mites, foliage: bean thrips, melon thrips, onion thrips, western flower thrips, bean aphid, green peach aphid, cotton/melon aphid, cowpea aphid, potato leafhopper, southern garden leafhopper, western potato leafhopper, threecorned alfalfa treehopper, garden fleahopper, tarnished plant bug, pale western legume bug, beet leafhopper, silverleaf whitefly, greenhouse whitefly, Mexican mealybug, twospotted spider mite
Sucking insects, pods: brown stink bug, green stink bug, onespotted stink bug, Say's stink bug, southern green stink bug, tarnished plant bug, bean thrips, western flower thrips

Philadelphus (Mock orange)

Scales: pitmaking pittosporum scale

Philodendron

Sucking insects: citrus mealybug, longtailed mealybug, greenhouse whitefly, greenhouse thrips, banded greenhouse thrips

Phlox

Chewing insects: black vine weevil, oriental beetle, Asiatic garden beetle, black blister beetle, corn earworm, saddleback caterpillar
Sucking insects, mites: tarnished plant bug, fourlined plant bug, phlox plant bug, aster leafhopper, twospotted spider mite

Photinia

Sucking insects: toyon thrips, greenhouse thrips, European fruit lecanium, oystershell scale, San Jose scale
Leaf chewers: omnivorus looper, western tent caterpillar, cranberry rootworm

Phyllostachys (see Bamboo)

Picea (Spruce)

Needle chewers: Douglas-fir tussock moth, western spruce budworm, spruce budworm, spruce needleminer, *Cephalcia* spp., *Coleotechnites piceaella*
Scales: pine needle scale, black pineleaf scale, elongate hemlock scale, hemlock scale, spruce bud scale
Gall makers: Cooley spruce gall adelgid, eastern spruce gall adelgid, pine leaf adelgid
Other sucking insects: pine spittlebug, Saratoga spittlebug, green spruce aphid, spruce aphid, balsam twig aphid, black polished spruce aphid
Mites: spruce spider mite, *Eurytetranychus admes*, *Nalepella halourga*
Bark beetles: Spruce beetle, *Ips hunteri*
Borers: spotted pine sawyer, *Sirex* horntails, Douglas-fir pitch moth
Twig, terminal feeders: white pine weevil, northern pine weevil, twig beetles (*Pityophthorus*)

Pieris (Andromeda)

Sucking insects: andromeda plant bug, cottony maple leaf scale
Mites: twospotted spider mite, southern red mite

Pilea (Aluminum plant)

Scales: brown soft scale

Pine (see *Pinus*)

Pink (see *Dianthus*)

Pinus (Pine)

Needle chewers, conifer sawflies: European pine sawfly, redheaded pine sawfly, Swaine jack pine sawfly, *Neodiprion autumnalis*, white pine sawfly, blackheaded pine sawfly, pinyon sawfly, introduced pine sawfly, bull pine sawfly, webspinning sawflies, pine false webworm
Other needle chewers: tiger moth, pandora moth, pine budworm, jack pine budworm, pine needle sheath miner, pine tube moth, jack pine tube moth, pine webworm, ponderosa pine budworm, eastern pine looper, gypsy moth, imperial moth, Asiatic garden beetle
Needleminers: ponderosa pine needleminer, pinyon needleminer
Gall makers: pinyon spindlegall midge, pinyon stunt needlegall midge, stubby needlegall midge, *Trisetacus campnodus*, *T. gemmivitians*
Scales: pine needle scale, pine leaf scale, black pineleaf scale, pine oystershell scale, pine tortoise scale, striped pine scale, irregular pine scale, Monterey pine scale, pinyon needle scale
Other sucking insects: woolly pine aphids, pine bark adelgid, white pine aphid, Comstock mealybug, Saratoga spittlebug, *Aphrophora permutata*, cicadas
Mites: spruce spider mite, ponderosa pine spider mite, *Eutetranychus admes*, *Oligonychus milleri*
Twig, terminal feeders: southwestern pine tip moth, *Rhyacionia bushnelli*, Nantucket pine tip moth, ponderosa pitch nodulemaker, ponderosa pine tip moth, pinyon tip moth, pinyon pitch nodule moth, northern pitch twig moth, European pine shoot moth, eastern pine shoot borer, western pine shoot

borer, twig beetles (*Pityophthorus* spp., *Pityogenes* spp.), pales weevil, pitcheating weevil, common pine shoot beetle, white pine weevil, eastern pine weevil, northern pine weevil, pine root collar weevil, gouty pitch midge, pitch midges

Borers: pinyon pitch mass borer, Zimmerman pine moth, sequoia pitch moth, pitch mass borer, Douglas-fir pitch moth, southern pine sawyer, spotted pine sawyer, blackhorned pine borer, *Sirex* horntails, *Urocerus* horntails

Bark beetles: ips beetles, mountain pine beetle, southern pine beetle, red turpentine beetle, black turpentine beetle

Seed feeders: western conifer seed bug, leaffooted pine seed bug, coneworms (*Dioryctria* spp.)

Pisum (Pea)

Leaf chewers: cabbage looper, celery looper, speckled green fruitworm, American serpentine leafminer, pea leafminer

Sucking insects: pea aphid, green peach aphid

Seed, pod chewers: pea moth, stalk borer

Pittosporum

Scales: greedy scale, cottony cushion scale, black scale, nigra scale, pittosporum pitmaking scale, cottony camellia scale

Mites: privet mite

Planetree (see *Plantanus*)

Plantain lily (see *Hosta*)

Plantanus (Sycamore, Planetree)

Leaf chewers: bagworm, polyphemus moth, io moth, fall webworm, whitemarked tussock moth, sycamore tussock moth, pale tussock moth, stinging rose caterpillar, sycamore leaffolder, Japanese beetle, Asiatic oak weevil, sycamore leaf beetle

Scales: terrapin scale, oak lecanium, sycamore scale, walnut scale, Indian wax scale

Other sucking insects: mulberry whitefly, sycamore lace bug, sycamore aphid, cotton/melon aphid, spirea aphid, black citrus aphid

Mites: linden spider mite, plantanus spider mite

Borers: pigeon tremex, sycamore borer

Plum (see *Prunus*)

Poa (Bluegrass, Kentucky bluegrass)

Leaf chewers: sod webworms, armyworm, army cutworm, bronzed cutworm, fall armyworm

Sucking insects/mites, leaves: winter grain mite, clover mite, brown wheat mite, Banks grass mite, hairy chinch bug, greenbug

Root feeders: black turfgrass ataenius, northern masked chafer, southern masked chafer, European chafer, May/June beetles, Japanese beetle, oriental beetle, bluegrass billbug, Denver billbug, hunting billbug, European crane fly, march flies

Sucking insects, roots: *Forda* aphids

Podocarpus (Totara, yew pine)

Scales: California red scale

Poinsettia (see *Euphorbia*)

Polystichum

Scales: brown soft scale, hemispherical scale, fern scale
Other sucking insects: longtailed mealybug, greenhouse whitefly, silverleaf whitefly

Pomegranate (see *Punica*)

Poplar (see *Populus*)

Populus (**Aspen, cottonwood, poplars**)

Leaf chewers: western tent caterpillar, forest tent caterpillar, southwestern tent caterpillar, poplar tentmaker, cottonwood dagger moth, poplar dagger moth, gypsy moth, satin moth, *Dasychira grisefacta*, spearmarked black moth, large aspen tortrix, Nevada buck moth, redhumped caterpillar, spiny elm caterpillar/mourning cloak, fall webworm, twinspot sphinx, one-eyed sphinx, big poplar sphinx, Bruce spanworm, eastern tiger swallowtail, cottonwood leaf beetle, Pacific willow leaf beetle, poplar blackmine beetle, poplar leaffolding sawfly
Leafminers: poplar blackmine beetle, aspen leafminer, aspen blotch leafminer, *Phyllonorycter nipigon*, tentiform leafminer
Gall makers: poplar twiggall fly, poplar vagabond aphid, poplar petiole-gall aphid, poplar twiggall aphid, poplar leaf aphid, lettuce root aphid, sugarbeet root aphid, *Pemphigus betae*, poplar budgall mite, cottonwood catkingall mite, *Pyllocoptes didelphis*, cottonwood leafcurl mite
Scales: oystershell scale, walnut scale, scurfy scale
Other sucking insects: clear-winged aspen aphid, poplar leaf aphid, folded-leaf poplar aphid, rose leafhopper
Tip, terminal feeders: cottonwood twig borer, poplar twig borer, cicadas, grasshoppers
Borers: bronze poplar borer, granulate poplar borer, western poplar agrilus, poplar borer, poplar gall saperda, cottonwood borer, carpenterworm, aspen carpenterworm, poplar carpenterworm, leopard moth, American hornet moth, hornet moth, western poplar clearwing, cottonwood clearwing borer, poplar and willow borer

Portulaca (**Moss rose**)

Leaf chewers: whitelined sphinx, variegated fritillary
Sucking insects: cactus scale, bandedwinged whitefly

Pot marigold (see *Calendula*)

Primrose (see *Primula*)

Primula (**Primrose**)

Leaf chewers: Fuller rose beetle, apple flea beetle, steel-blue flea beetle
Sucking insects: cowpea aphid, foxglove aphid, green peach aphid, crescent-marked lily aphid, greenhouse whitefly
Mites: twospotted spider mite

Privet (see *Ligustrum*)

Prunus (**Stone fruits: almond, apricot, peach, plum, cherry, nectarine, etc.**)

Fruit chewers: plum curculio, plum gouger, cherry curculio, speckled green fruitworm, peach twig borer, eyespotted bud moth, oriental fruit moth, navel orangeworm, lesser appleworm, cherry fruitworm, mineola moth, cherry fruit sawfly, apple maggot, walnut husk fly, cherry fruit fly, western cherry fruit fly, black cherry fruit fly, chokecherry gall midge, European earwig, green fruit beetles

Leafminers: western tentiform leafminer, cherry leafminer (*Paraleucoptera heinrichi*), cherry leafminer (*Nepticula slingerlandella*)

Leafrollers: fruittree leafroller, apple pandemis, European leafroller, obliquebanded leafroller, red-banded leafroller, variegated leafroller, blackheaded fireworm

Other leaf chewers: western tent caterpillar, eastern tent caterpillar, plum webspinning sawfly, cherry webspinning sawfly, peach sawfly, chokecherry sawfly, pearslug, Japanese beetle, apple and thorn skeletonizer, pistol casebearer, resplendent shield bearer, promethea moth, saddleback caterpillar, stinging rose caterpillar, fall webworm, uglynest caterpillar, leaf crumpler, redhumped caterpillar, yellownecked caterpillar, twotailed swallowtail, eastern tiger swallowtail, Texas leafcutting ant, walkingstick, brown garden snail

Aphids: green peach aphid, leafcurl plum aphid, mealy plum aphid, rusty plum aphid, black cherry aphid, hop aphid, apple grain aphid, thistle aphid, waterlily aphid

Scales: calico scale, European fruit lecanium, terrapin scale, Indian wax scale, cottony cushion scale, San Jose scale, oystershell scale, Forbes scale

Other sucking insects: white apple leafhopper, rose leafhopper, plum leafhopper, privet leafhopper, buffalo treehopper, western flower thrips, pear thrips, boxelder bug, western boxelder bug, tarnished plant bug, *Corythuca* spp.

Mites: *Eriophyes emarginatae, Phytoptus cerasicramena*, plum rust mite/peach silver mite, twospotted spider mite, European red mite, brown mite

Borers, bark beetles: peachtree borer, lesser peachtree borer, American plum borer, cherry bark tortrix, Pacific flatheaded borer, redheaded ash borer, Asian ambrosia beetle, shothole borer

Root feeders: rain beetles, tenlined June beetle

Pseudotsuga (Douglas-fir)

Leaf chewers: western spruce budworm, Douglas-fir tussock moth, bagworm, Douglas-fir needle midge

Scales: elongate hemlock scale, fiorinia hemlock scale, pine needle scale

Other sucking insects: Cooley spruce gall adelgid

Borers: pine sawyers, Douglas-fir pitch moth, eastern pine shoot borer, pales weevil

Root feeders: tenlined June beetle, strawberry root weevil, cranberry girdler

Bark beetles: red turpentine beetle, Douglas-fir beetle

Seed feeders: western conifer seed bug

Pumpkin (see *Cucurbita*)

Punica (Pomegranate)

Sucking insects: hemispherical scale, citricola scale, cottony cushion scale, western flower thrips

Purple passion vine (see *Gynura*)

Pyracantha (Firethorn)

Leaf chewers: whitemarked tussock moth, western tussock moth, leaf crumpler, black vine weevil

Scales: San Jose scale, oystershell scale, calico scale, greedy scale, Indian wax scale

Other sucking insects: apple mealybug, hawthorn mealybug, Comstock mealybug, ash whitefly, hawthorn lace bug, apple aphid, long-beaked clover aphid

Mites: European red mite, southern red mite

Root feeders: black vine weevil

Pyrethrum (see *Chrysanthemum*)

Pyrus (Pear)

Fruit, flower chewers: codling moth, plum curculio, European earwig, apple maggot, eyespotted bud moth, speckled green fruitworm, green fruitworm, hoplia beetles

Leafrollers: apple pandemis, obliquebanded leafroller, fruittree leafroller, redbanded leafroller, European leafroller, omnivorous leaftier, eyespotted bud moth

Other leaf chewers: redhumped caterpillar, yellownecked caterpillar, forest tent caterpillar, eastern tent caterpillar, western tent caterpillar, fall webworm, saddleback caterpillar, speckled green fruitworm, green fruitworm, snailcase bagworm, leaf crumpler, pistol casebearer, apple flea beetle, palestriped flea beetle, pearslug, California pear sawfly, spotted tentiform leafminer, pear leafcurling midge

Fruit, flower sucking insects: western flower thrips, pear thrips, rosy apple aphid, consperse stink bug, green stink bug, redshouldered stink bug, Say's stink bug, onespotted stink bug, boxelder bug, western boxelder bug, campylomma bug, tarnished plant bug, pear rust mite

Aphids: rosy apple aphid, apple aphid, clover aphid, apple grain aphid, woolly pear aphid

Scales: Forbes scale, San Jose scale, oystershell scale, European fruit lecanium, Indian wax scale

Other sucking insects: pear psylla, grape mealybug, Comstock mealybug, obscure mealybug, ash whitefly, citrus whitefly, pear thrips, rose leafhopper

Mites: pearleaf blister mite, pear rust mite, twospotted spider mite, McDaniel spider mite, European red mite, brown mite

Oviposition injury, twigs: periodical cicada, buffalo treehopper

Borers, bark beetles: shothole borer, pigeon tremex, apple bark borer, Pacific flatheaded borer, flatheaded appletree borer, roundheaded appletree borer, redheaded ash borer, cherry bark tortrix

Root borers: roundheaded appletree borer, rain beetles, tenlined June beetle

Quercus (Oak)

Leaf chewers: gypsy moth, satin moth, western tussock moth, fall webworm, oak leafroller, threelined leafroller, eyespotted bud moth, orange tortrix, speckled green fruitworm, Sonoran tent caterpillar, Pacific tent caterpillar, forest tent caterpillar, waved sphinx, California oakworm, eastern buck moth, spiny oakworm, orangestriped oakworm, imperial moth, polyphemus moth, unicorn caterpillar, yellownecked caterpillar, redhumped caterpillar, redhumped oakworm, variable oakleaf caterpillar, io moth, stinging rose caterpillar, puss caterpillar, linden looper, elm spanworm, fall cankerworm, spring cankerworm, filament bearer, oak looper, bagworm, oak skeletonizer, oak ribbed skeletonizer, pin oak sawfly, scarlet oak sawfly, *Pamphilius phyllisae*, twobanded Japanese weevil, Asiatic oak weevil, Japanese beetle, walkingstick

Leafminers: oak leafminer, oak shothole miner

Gall makers: oak gall wasps, *Cecidomyia poculum*

Scales: kermes scales, golden oak scales, oak lecanium scale, obscure scale, oak eriococcin

Other sucking insects: giant bark aphid, western dusky-winged aphid, maple leafhopper, rose leafhopper, oak treehopper, oak lace bug

Mites: oak mite

Bark beetles: oak bark beetles, Asian ambrosia beetle, black twig borer

Borers: pigeon tremex, carpenterworm, leopard moth, sycamore clearwing, oak clearwing, red oak clearwing, twolined chestnut borer, oak sprout oberea, *Elaphidionoides parallelus*, painted hickory borer, redheaded ash borer

Seed feeders: hickory nut curculio, acorn and nut weevils, filbertworm

Quince (see *Cydonia*)

Radish (see *Raphanus*)

Ranunculus (Buttercup)

Sucking insects: waterlily aphid, folded-leaf poplar aphid, western flower thrips

Raphanus (Radish)

Leaf chewers: western black flea beetle, cabbage flea beetle, crucifer flea beetle, striped flea beetle, western striped flea beetle, hop flea beetle, diamondback moth, beet armyworm
Sucking insects: harlequin bug, false chinch bug, green peach aphid

Redbud (see *Cercis*)

Rhamnus (Buckthorn)

Leaf chewers: bagworm, Japanese beetle, western tent caterpillar
Sucking insects: buckthorn aphid, cotton/melon aphid
Borers: Pacific flatheaded borer

Rheum (Rhubarb)

Leaf chewers: red turnip beetle, hop flea beetle, potato flea beetle, Japanese beetle, spotted cutworm, variegated cutworm, European earwig, spotted cucumber beetle
Sucking insects: bean aphid, green peach aphid, potato aphid
Stem borers: potato stem borer, stalk borer

Rhododendron (Azalea, rhododendron)

Leaf chewers: black vine weevil, clay-colored weevil, twobanded Japanese weevil, strawberry root weevil, redheaded flea beetle, obliquebanded leafroller, variegated leafroller, io moth, azalea sawflies (*Amauronematus azalae*, *Nematus lipvskyi*), cranberry rootworm, azalea leafminer, luna moth, puss caterpillar
Scales: azalea bark scale, Indian wax scale, common falsepit scale, cottony camellia scale, Townsend scale
Other sucking insects: azalea lace bug, rhodendron lace bug, fourlined plant bug, striped mealybug, azalea bark scale, azalea whitefly, rhododendron whitefly, greenhouse whitefly, *Illinoia rhododendri*, candystriped leafhopper, green and red stink bug, greenhouse thrips
Mites: southern red mite, broad mite, cyclamen mite
Borers: rhododendron borer, azalea stem borer
Root feeders: black vine weevil, strawberry root weevil

Rhus (Sumac, skunkbrush, poison ivy)

Leaf chewers: sumac flea beetle, hickory horned devil
Stem borers: sumac stem borer
Sucking insects: *Calopsylla* spp., maple leafhopper, striped mealybug, western flower thrips, fourlined plant bug, oystershell scale
Gallmakers: *Aculops toxicophagus*

Ribes (Currant, gooseberry)

Mites: twospotted spider mite, clover mite, currant bud mite
Other sucking insects: fourlined plant bug, currant aphid, lettuce aphid, privet leafhopper

Scales: San Jose scale, forbes scale, walnut scale
Chewing insects: imported currantworm, currant spanworm, western tent caterpillar, fruittree leafroller, European leafroller, obliquebanded leafroller, speckled green fruitworm, redheaded flea beetle, sumac leaf beetle
Borers: currant borer, bronze cane borer
Fruit chewers: gooseberry maggot/currant fruit fly

Robinia (Locust, black locust)

Leaf chewers: redhumped caterpillar, io moth, silverspotted skipper, bagworm, walkingstick
Leafminers: locust leafminer
Sucking insects: twomarked treehopper, *Micrutalis calva*, *Erythroneura gleditsia*, cowpea aphid, latania scale, California red scale, *Plagiognathus politus*
Mites: Schoene spider mite
Gall makers: *Dasinerura pseudacaciae*
Borers: carpenterworm, locust borer, painted hickory borer, locust twig borer

Rosa (Rose)

Leaf chewers: roseslug, bristly roseslug, curled rose sawfly, leafcutter bees, western tent caterpillar, io moth, stinging rose caterpillar, saddleback caterpillar, hag moth, variegated leafroller, green fruitworm, fall cankerworm, Japanese beetle, oriental beetle, brown garden snail
Flower chewers: rose midge, rose curculio, European earwig, oriental fruit moth, tobacco budworm, speckled green fruitworm, green fruitworm, spotted cutworm, hoplia beetles
Gall makers: rose gall wasps
Scales: rose scale, black scale, California red scale
Sucking insects, flowers: western flower thrips, flower thrips
Other sucking insects: rose aphid, potato aphid, rose grass aphid, rose leafhopper, campylomma bug, fourlined plant bug
Mites: twospotted spider mite, European red mite
Cane borers: curled rose sawfly, leafcutter bees, hunting wasps, small carpenter bee, rose shoot sawfly, raspberry horntail, raspberry cane borer, bronze cane borer, European corn borer
Root feeders: tenlined June beetle

Rose (see *Rosa*)

Rose mallow (see *Hibiscus*)

Rose of Sharon (see *Hibiscus*)

Rose pincushion (see Cactus)

Rubber plant (see *Ficus*)

Rubus (Raspberry, blackberry, dewberry, etc.)

Leaf chewers: fruittree leafroller, redbanded leafroller, obliquebanded leafroller, apple pandemis, strawberry leafroller, Bruce spanworm, redhumped caterpillar, blackberry leafminer, raspberry sawfly, blackberry sawfly, redheaded flea beetle, Japanese beetle, woods weevil, clay-colored weevil, Texas leafcutting ant
Fruit chewers: raspberry fruitworms, fourspotted sap beetle, strawberry bud weevil, yellowjackets
Sucking insects: potato leafhopper, rose leafhopper, rose scale, fourlined plant bug, candystripe leafhopper

Mites: European red mite, raspberry red mite, twospotted spider mite, dryberry mite, redberry mite
Cane borers: rose shoot sawfly, raspberry horntail, raspberry cane borer, rednecked cane borer, bronze cane borer, raspberry cane maggot, tree crickets
Root feeders: raspberry crown borer, tenlined June beetle

Rudbeckia (Coneflower, black-eyed Susan, gloriosa daisy, goldenglow)

Sucking insects: fourlined plant bug, tarnished plant bug, greenhouse whitefly, silverleaf whitefly, goldenglow aphid, brown ambrosia aphid, aster leafhopper
Flower chewers: sunflower moth
Stem borers: European corn borer
Root feeders: bulb mite

Russian olive (see *Elaeagnus*)

Ryegrass (see *Lolium*)

Sage (see *Salvia*)

Sago palm (see *Cycas*)

Saintpaulia (African violet)

Sucking insects, leaves: citrus mealybug, Pritchard's mealybug, banded greenhouse thrips
Mites: broad mite, cyclamen mite
Root insects: fungus gnats, Pritchard's mealybug

Salix (Willow)

Leaf chewers: spiny elm caterpillar/mourning cloak, redhumped caterpillar, Nevada buck moth, cecropia moth, polyphemus moth, luna moth, io moth, speckled green fruitworm, western tent caterpillar, eastern tent caterpillar, gypsy moth, satin moth, *Dasychira grisefacta*, fall webworm, twinspot sphinx, one-eyed sphinx, big poplar sphinx, bagworm, poplar tentmaker, orange tortrix, sparganothis leafroller, Bruce spanworm, omnivorous looper, western tiger swallowtail, eastern tiger swallowtail, Asiatic oak weevil, imported willow leaf beetle, Pacific willow leaf beetle, elm calligrapha, *Chrysomela* spp., willow flea beetles (*Disonycha* spp.), willow sawfly, birch sawfly, elm sawfly, *Trichiosoma triangulum*, *T. viminalis*, poplar leaffolding sawfly
Leafminers: *Phyllonorycter nipigon*, *P. salicifoliella*, willow flea weevil
Gall makers: willow redgall sawfly, *Pontania s-pomum*, *Aculops tetanothrix*, willow stemgall sawflies (*Euura* spp.), willow conegall midge, willow beakedgall midge
Scales: oystershell scale, scurfy scale, buckeye scale
Other sucking insects: giant willow aphid, black willow aphid, western willow aphid, carrot-willow aphid, little green and yellow willow aphids, *Macropsis ocellata*
Mites: linden spider mite
Borers: black twig borer, poplar and willow borer, pole borer, flatheaded appletree borer, cottonwood borer, bronze poplar borer, granulate poplar borer, western poplar agrilus, common willow agrilus, *Scolytus shevyrewi*

Salvia (Sage)

Sucking insects, mites: twospotted spider mite, greenhouse whitefly
Chewing insects: Asiatic garden beetle

Sambucus (**Elderberry**)

Borers: elder shoot borer, currant borer
Sucking insects: green and red stink bug

Sassafras

Leaf chewers: Japanese beetle, promothea moth, hag moth
Scales: oystershell scale, San Jose scale

Scarlet sage (see *Salvia*)

Schefflera

Sucking insects: brown soft scale, latania scale, Putnam's scale, banded greenhouse thrips, giant whitefly

Schinus (**Brazilian peppertree, peppertree**)

Sucking insects: peppertree psyllid, greedy scale, black scale
Leaf chewers: omnivorous looper

Sciadopitys (**Umbrella pine**)

Sucking insects: umbrella pine scale

Sedum

Leaf chewers: black vine weevil, variegated fritillary
Sucking insects: sedum aphid, cotton/melon aphid, greedy scale

Serviceberry (see *Amelanchier*)

Shadbush (see *Amelanchier*)

Shasta daisy (see *Chrysanthemum*)

Shooting star (see *Cyclamen*)

Shrub althaea (see *Hibiscus*)

Silk tree (see *Albizia*)

Silverberry (see *Elaeagnus*)

Sinningia (**Gloxinia**)

Sucking insects, mites: greenhouse whitefly, western flower thrips, foxglove aphid, broad mite
Leaf, root chewers: black vine weevil

Skimmia

Sucking insects, mites: garden fleahopper, southern red mite

Snapdragon (see *Antirrhinum*)

Snowball bush (see *Viburnum*)

Solanum (Potato, eggplant, nightshades)

Leaf chewers: Colorado potato beetle, black blister beetle, potato flea beetle, western potato flea beetle, tuber flea beetle, tobacco flea beetle, eggplant flea beetle, palestriped flea beetle, hop flea beetle, eggplant tortoise beetle, beet armyworm, variegated cutworm, cabbage looper, American serpentine leafminer, vegetable leafminer
Sucking insects: potato/tomato psyllid, green peach aphid, potato aphid, foxglove aphid, bean aphid, crescent-marked lily aphid, cotton/melon aphid, potato leafhopper, intermountain potato leafhopper, western potato leafhopper, southern garden leafhopper, aster leafhopper, silverleaf whitefly, garden fleahopper, western tarnished plant bug, tarnished plant bug, false chinch bugs, southern green stink bug, melon thrips, onion thrips, western flower thrips
Mites: twospotted spider mite
Stem borers: potato stem borer, potato stalk borer, stalk borer, European corn borer
Tuber feeders: variegated cutworm, wireworms, seedcorn maggot, false Japanese beetle, May/June beetles, mole crickets, garden symphylan

Sorbus (Mountain-ash)

Leaf chewers: mountain-ash sawfly, pearslug, fall webworm, eastern tiger swallowtail, Japanese beetle
Scales: oystershell scale, scurfy scale, walnut scale, San Jose scale
Other sucking insects: hawthorn lace bug, birch lace bug, apple aphid, rosy apple aphid, woolly apple aphid, apple mealybug, hawthorn mealybug
Mites: European red mite, pearleaf blister mite, *Phytoptus sorbi*
Borers, bark beetles: flatheaded appletree borer, roundheaded appletree borer, shothole borer

Spider plant (see *Chlorophytum*)

Spinach (see *Spinacia*)

Spinacia (Spinach)

Sucking insects: green peach aphid, cotton/melon aphid
Root chewers: sugarbeet root maggot
Leaf chewers: beet armyworm, spinach leafminer, alfalfa webworm, hop flea beetle, spinach flea beetle

Spindle tree (see *Euonymus*)

Spirea (Spirea, bridal wreath)

Leaf chewers: twobanded Japanese weevil
Sucking insects: spirea aphid, privet leafhopper
Mites: *Phytoptus paraspiraeae*

Spruce (see *Picea*)

Squash (see *Cucurbita*)

Statice (see *Limonium*)

St. Augustinegrass (see *Stenotaphrum*)

Stenotaphrum (St. Augustinegrass)

Leaf chewers: tropical sod webworm, striped grassworms, armyworm, fiery skipper
Sucking insects/mites, leaves: Banks grass mite, rhodesgrass mealybug, southern chinch bug, twolined spittlebug
Root chewers: southern mole cricket, tawny mole cricket, May/June beetles, hunting billbug
Sucking insects, roots: ground pearls

Stock (see *Matthiola*)

Strawberry (see *Fragaria*)

Strawflower (see *Helichrysum*)

Strelitzia (Bird-of-paradise)

Flower chewers: tobacco budworm
Scales: Florida red scale, false oleander scale, greedy scale, cycad scale
Other sucking insects: citrus mealybug, longtailed mealybug, giant whitefly, iris whitefly

Styrax

Sucking insects: andromeda lace bug
Borers: Asian ambrosia beetle

Sumac (see *Rhus*)

Sunflower (see *Helianthus*)

Sweet alyssum (see *Lobularia*)

Sweet corn (see *Zea*)

Sweetgum (see *Liquidambar*)

Sweet pea (see *Lathyrus*)

Sweetpotato (see *Ipomoea*)

Sycamore (see *Plantanus*)

Syngonium (Arrowhead plant, nephytis)

Scales: brown soft scale

Syringa (Lilac)

Leaf chewers: cecropia moth, great ash sphinx, hummingbird clearwing, promothea moth, fall webworm, leafcutter bees, black vine weevil
Leafminers: lilac leafminer
Sucking insects: oystershell scale, ash whitefly, citrus whitefly
Mites: lilac rust mite

Borers: lilac/ash borer, leopard moth
Root chewers: black vine weevil, twobanded Japanese weevil

Tagetes (Marigold)

Leaf chewers: Japanese beetle, American serpentine leafminer
Flower chewers: tobacco budworm
Sucking insects: aster leafhopper, greenhouse whitefly, silverleaf whitefly, tarnished plant bug
Mites: twospotted spider mite, broad mite

Tall fescue (see *Festuca*)

Taxodium (Baldcypress)

Leaf chewers: bagworm, Japanese beetle
Twig borers: cypress weevil
Sucking insects, mites: baldcypress rust mite, *Scirtothrips taxodii*

Taxus (Yew)

Leaf chewers: black vine weevil
Sucking insects: Fletcher scale, false oleander scale, taxus mealybug, grape mealybug, Comstock mealybug
Mites: taxus bud mite
Root feeders: black vine weevil

Thorn (see *Crataegus*)

Thuja (Arborvitae, whitecedar)

Needle chewers: bagworm, arborvitae sawfly, arborvitae leafminers
Scales: juniper scale, minute juniper scale, Fletcher scale, Maskell scale
Other sucking insects: juniper spittlebug, spruce spider mite
Mites: *Pentamerismus taxi*, *Trisectus thujivagrans*, *Platytetranychus thujae*, twospotted spider mite, spruce spider mite
Borers, bark beetles: cedar bark beetles
Root feeders: arborvitae weevil

Tilia (Linden, basswood)

Leaf chewers: fruittree leafroller, sparganothis leafroller, linden looper, hemlock looper, spring cankerworm, fall cankerworm, elm spanworm, fall webworm, hickory tussock moth, gypsy moth, American dagger moth, redhumped oakworm, speckled green fruitworm, elm sphinx, eastern tiger swallowtail, polyphemus moth, variable oakleaf caterpillar, Japanese beetle, elm calligrapha
Leafminers: basswood leafminer, *Phyllonorycter lucetiella*
Gall makers: linden wartgall midge, *Phytoptus tiliae*
Scales: oystershell scale, walnut scale, cottony maple scale
Other sucking insects: basswood aphid, mulberry whitefly, maple leafhopper, alder spittlebug, maple mealybug, introduced basswood thrips, basswood lace bug, walnut lace bug
Mites: linden spider mite, *Phytoptus tiliae*
Borers: linden borer, American plum borer, twig pruner

Tomato (see *Lycopersicon*)

Totara (see *Podocarpus*)

Toyon (see *Heteromeles*)

Transvaal daisy (see *Gerbera*)

Tree-of-heaven (see *Ailanthus*)

Tropaeolum (Nasturtium)

Leaf chewers: western black flea beetle, corn earworm, cabbage looper
Flower insects: European earwig, corn earworm, western flower thrips
Sucking insects: buckthorn aphid, green peach aphid, foxglove aphid, bean aphid, greenhouse whitefly, giant whitefly, onion thrips
Mites: twospotted spider mite

Tsuga (Hemlock)

Needle chewers: hemlock sawfly, gypsy moth, spruce budworm, redbanded leafroller, filament bearer, hemlock looper, twobanded Japanese weevil, pales weevil
Scales: elongate hemlock scale, hemlock scale, pine needle scale, fiorinia hemlock scale
Other sucking insects: hemlock woolly adelgid
Mites: Hemlock rust mite, spruce spider mite
Root feeders: black vine weevil, strawberry root weevil, Asiatic garden beetle

Tulip (see *Tulipa*)

Tulipa (Tulips)

Sucking insects, leaves: citrus mealybug, crescent-marked lily aphid, bean aphid, potato aphid
Sucking insects/mites, bulbs: tulip bulb aphid, bulb mite

Tuliptree (see *Liriodendron*)

Turnip (see *Brassica*)

Ulmus (Elm)

Leaf chewers: elm leaf beetle, larger elm leaf beetle, elm calligrapha, grape flea beetle, apple flea weevil, Japanese beetle, *Phyllobius oblongus*, elm sawfly, elm leafminer, elm casebearer, bagworm, fruittree leafroller, forest tent caterpillar, redhumped caterpillar, unicorn caterpillar, false unicorn caterpillar, whitemarked tussock moth, gypsy moth, American dagger moth, fall cankerworm, spring cankerworm, elm spanworm, fall webworm, elm sphinx, twinspot sphinx, cecropia moth, io moth, redhumped oakworm, variable oakleaf caterpillar, puss caterpillar, spiny elm caterpillar/mourning cloak
Scales: European fruit lecanium, calico scale, citricola scale, Putnam's scale, European elm scale, elm scurfy scale, oystershell scale, walnut scale, Indian wax scale
Aphids: woolly apple aphid, woolly pear aphid, woolly elm aphid, woolly elm bark aphid, woolly hawthorn aphid, elm cockscomb gall aphid, *Calopha graminis*, elm leaf aphid, *Tinocallis saltans*
Other sucking insects: maple leafhopper, whitebanded elm leafhopper, buffalo treehopper, elm lace bug
Gall makers: elm cockscomb gall aphid, *Eriophyes ulmi*, *Aceria parulmi*
Mites: elm spider mite, Schoene spider mite, oak mite, clover mite, *Eriophyes ulmi*, *Aceria parulmi*

Borers: twig girdler, twig pruner, carpenterworm, leopard moth, pole borer, elm borer, flatheaded appletree borer, pigeon tremex
Bark beetles: smaller European elm bark beetle, *Scolytus shevyrewi*, native elm bark beetle, Asian ambrosia beetle, shothole borer

Umbrella pine (see *Sciadopitys*)

Umbrella tree (see *Brassaia* and *Magnolia*)

Vaccinium (Blueberry, cranberry, huckleberry)

Leaf chewers: rusty tussock moth, Bruce spanworm, blackheaded fireworm, oliquebanded leafroller, sparganothis leafroller, fall webworm, yellownecked caterpillar, cranberry rootworm, blueberry casebeetle, Japanese beetle
Fruit chewers: cranberry fruitworm, cherry fruitworm, brown fruitworm, blueberry maggot, blueberry gall midge
Sucking insects: alder spittlebug, terrapin scale, Florida wax scale
Mites: *Acalitus vaccinii*, blueberry bud mite

Verbena

Flower chewers: tobacco budworm
Sucking insects, mites: greenhouse whitefly, silverleaf whitefly, western flower thrips, broad mite, cyclamen mite, twospotted spider mite

Viburnum (Snowball bush, cranberry bush, arrowhead, black haw)

Leaf chewers: cecropia moth, viburnum leaf beetle, Asiatic garden beetle, Asiatic oak weevil
Sucking insects: snowball aphid, *Ceruraphis eriophori*, ivy aphid, bean aphid, maple mealybug, Comstock mealybug, twomarked treehopper, flower thrips
Mites: twospotted spider mite, broad mite
Borers: viburnum clearwing borer, dogwood borer

Vinca (Periwinkle)

Leaf, flower chewers: European earwig
Sucking insects: brown soft scale, citrus mealybug, oleander aphid, green peach aphid, crescent-marked lily aphid, silverleaf whitefly, aster leafhopper, flower thrips

Viola (Pansy, violet)

Leaf chewers: variegated fritillary, greenhouse leaftier, corn earworm, violet sawfly, snailcase bagworm
Sucking insects, mites: cotton/melon aphid, green peach aphid, crescent-marked lily aphid, buckthorn aphid, silverleaf whitefly, iris whitefly, twospotted spider mite

Violet (see *Viola*)

Virginia creeper (see *Parthenocissus*)

Vitis (Grape)

Scales: calico scale, European peach scale, European fruit lecanium, oystershell scale
Sucking insects: Virginiacreeper leafhopper, campylomma bug, western grape leafhopper, eastern grape leafhopper, variegated leafhopper, threebanded leafhopper, grape phylloxera, grape mealybug, obscure mealybug

Sucking insects, fruit: western flower thrips
Gall makers: grape tumid gallmaker, grape cane gallmaker, grape erineum mite
Leaf chewers: apple leaf beetle, grape flea beetle, Japanese beetle, rose chafer, leafcutter bees, grape sawfly, achemon sphinx, whitelined sphinx, Virginiacreeper sphinx, spotted cutworm, grapeleaf skeletonizer, western grapeleaf skeletonizer, eightspotted forester
Fruit chewers: redbanded leafroller, spotted cutworm, grape berry moth, grape curculio
Borers: grapevine root borer, apple twig borer, grape cane gallmaker, grape cane girdler
Mites: European red mite, *Colomerus vitis*, grape erineum mite

Walnut (see *Juglans*)

Waterlily (see *Nymphaea*)

Wild lilac (see *Ceanothus*)

Wild strawberry (see *Fragaria*)

Willow (see *Salix*)

Windflower (see *Anemone*)

Winter creeper (see *Euonymus*)

Wisteria

Leaf chewers: bean leafroller, silverspotted skipper
Sucking insects: cowpea aphid, twomarked treehopper, calico scale, Comstock mealybug
Mites: twospotted spider mite
Borers: twig pruner

Witch-hazel (see *Hamamelis*)

Yarrow (see *Achillea*)

Yaupon (see *Ilex*)

Yew (see *Taxus*)

Yew pine (see *Podocarpus*)

Yucca

Sucking insects: brown soft scale, Boisduval scale, oleander scale, *Asterolecanium agavis*, citrus mealybug, yucca plant bug, western flower thrips
Borers: yucca weevil, stalk borer

Zamia

Scales: oleander scale, hemispherical scale

Zantedeschia (Calla lily)

Bulb chewers: lesser bulb fly
Flower chewers: hoplia beetle, Japanese beetle

Zea (Corn, sweet corn)

Leaf chewers: western corn rootworm, banded cucumber beetle, northern corn rootworm, southern corn rootworm, corn flea beetle, toothed flea beetle, redheaded flea beetle, palestriped flea beetle, grape colaspis, Japanese beetle, Asiatic garden beetle, fall armyworm, armyworm, western bean cutworm, black cutworm
Ear chewers: corn earworm, western bean cutworm, fall armyworm, European corn borer, dusky sap beetle, fourspotted sap beetle, European earwig
Stalk borers: European corn borer, stalk borer, potato stem borer
Root chewers: western corn rootworm, northern corn rootworm, southern corn rootworm, seedcorn maggot, bean seed maggot, wireworms, whitefringed beetle
Sucking insects: corn leaf aphid, Banks grass mite, twospotted spider mite

Zebra plant (see *Aphelandra*)

Zelkova

Chewing insects: elm leaf beetle
Sucking insects: Japanese maple scale, calico scale

Zinnia

Leaf chewers: Japanese beetle, bertha armyworm, Asiatic garden beetle
Flower chewers: sunflower moth, European earwig, black blister beetle, Asiatic garden beetle, corn earworm
Stem borers: European corn borer
Sucking insects, mites: aster leafhopper, greenhouse whitefly, silverleaf whitefly, tarnished plant bug, buckthorn aphid, redbanded leafhopper, broad mite

Zoysia (Zoysiagrass)

Leaf chewers: tropical sod webworm, armyworm
Sucking insects/mites: zoysiagrass mite, hairy chinch bug, southern chinch bug
Root chewers: tawny mole cricket, southern mole cricket, hunting billbug, phoenician billbug
Sucking insects, roots: ground pearls

Zygocactus (see Cactus)

GLOSSARY

Abdomen Posterior of the three main body divisions in an insect; posterior of the two main body divisions in a mite, spider, or other arachnid.

Adelgid Family of "woolly" aphids (Adelgidae) that develop on conifers.

Aestivation Temporary dormancy induced by warm and/or dry conditions.

Alate With wings. Forms of aphids with wings in the adult stage are known as **alatae**.

Alternate host Plant required to complete the life cycle of an insect or fungus, other than the host plant that is primarily damaged. The habit of using an alternate host is common among certain groups of aphids and the rust fungi.

Annual Plant or fungal fruiting body that persists in an active, living state for only one season.

Apterous Without wings. Forms of aphids without wings in the adult stage are known as **apterae**.

Asexual Any type of reproduction not involving a union in which fertilization and meiosis occur.

Biennial Plant that takes two seasons to complete its life cycle. Growth during the first year is vegetative, and flowering structures are produced the second year.

Brambles Rose family plants of the genus *Rubus* that produce small fruit on prickly canes, including raspberries and blackberries. The term is often used interchangeably with **caneberries**.

Brassicas Cultivated plants in the genus *Brassica*, which includes broccoli, cabbage, cauliflower, Brussels sprout, mustard, collard, canola, and other plants.

Broadleaf Plant having broad leaves rather than needlelike or scalelike leaves. Most cultivated garden plants are broadleaved except grasses and conifers.

Bud break Time at which dormant buds begin expanding and opening.

Callus Mass of thin-walled undifferentiated cells that on plants often develops as the result of wounding.

Calyx Outer whorl of sepals that group together in a flower. On apple, the calyx end is at the tip of the fruit, opposite the stem end.

Cambium Layer of cells between the bark and wood that divides into phloem outward and xylem (wood) inward. If destroyed or exposed, the plant dies.

Caneberries Rose family plants of the genus *Rubus* that produce small fruit on prickly canes, including raspberries and blackberries. The term is often used interchangeably with **brambles**.

Caterpillar Larva of a butterfly, moth, or sawfly.

Catfacing Dimpling of fruit produced by injury during early development. It may result from feeding by various insects with sucking mouthparts, egg-laying wounds, or surface chewing of young fruit.

Chelicerae Pair of fang like appendages used by mites, spiders, and other arachnids to penetrate tissues. **Chelicera** is singular.

Chenopods Plants in the goosefoot, pigweed, or beet family of plants, Chenopodiaceae. Common chenopods include beet, spinach, lambsquarter, pigweed, and amaranth.

Chlorosis Yellowing of normally green tissue caused by chlorophyll destruction or failure of chlorophyll formation. Tissues that show chlorosis are described as being chlorotic.

Chrysalis Pupal stage of a butterfly. It is not covered with silk and often contains spines and patterned colors. **Chrysalid** is an alternatively accepted term; **chrysalids**, or **chrysalides**, is plural.

Cocoon Silken case in which the pupal stage of many insects is formed.

Cole crops Cultivated vegetables in the mustard family, Brassicaceae. This includes broccoli, cabbage, Brussels sprout, cauliflower, radish, turnip, and other plants. These are also sometimes known as **crucifers**.

Complete metamorphosis Pattern of metamorphosis exhibited by many insects (e.g., beetles, moths and butterflies, sawflies, flies) that involves eggs, followed by immature nymphs, a transition pupal stage, and finally adults. Adult and immature stages of insect that exhibit complete metamorphosis often have very different habits and appearances. Also called holometabolous metamorphosis.

Composites Plants in the sunflower family, Compositae (also known as the aster family and formerly called Asteraceae).

Conifer General term for cone-bearing plants; it includes pine, cypress, juniper, spruce, arborvitae, and yew.

Cornicle Tubular structure (paired) on the posterior of aphids through which alarm pheromones are released.

Crawler First stage after egg hatch of a scale or mealybug; it is the most dispersive form of the insect.

Crochets Hooks found on the tip of the prolegs of moth and butterfly larvae.

Crucifers Cultivated plants in the mustard family, Brassicaceae, formerly Cruciferae. This includes broccoli, cabbage, Brussels sprout, cauliflower, radish, turnip, and other plants. Also called **cole crops.**

Cucurbits Plants in the squash or gourd family, Cucurbitaceae. Cultivated plants include squash, pumpkin, cucumber, melon, and gourds.

Cuppressaceous conifers Plants in the cypress family, Cuppressaceae, which includes cypress, juniper, baldcypress, arbovitae, and other conifers with flattened or scalelike needles.

Cyst A stage encapsulated in a protective membrane. Cysts may be produced to allow an organism to survive during periods of adverse environmental conditions.

Deciduous Referring to a plant that annually sheds its leaves.

Defoliation Loss of leaves, as occurs in natural shedding or from the feeding activities of insects and other plant feeders.

Deutogyne Overwintering form of an adult female eriophyid mite.

Deutonymph Third and final immature stage of a mite or tick.

Diapause Period of dormancy many insects undergo to avoid adverse conditions (e.g., winter cold). Diapause is more involved than simple dormancy or hibernation and can only be terminated by certain stimuli such as day length or a prescribed length of exposure to cold.

Dieback Decline and dying of the upper or terminal growth of a plant.

Disease Any malfunctioning of host cells and tissues that results from continuous irritation by a pathogenic agent or environmental factor and leads to development of symptoms.

Disease cycle Chain of events involved in disease development, including the stages of development of the pathogen and the effect of the disease on the host.

Domatia Areas of dense plant hairs at the junction of leaf veins. A speculated function of these sites is to provide protection to predatory mites.

Dorsal Referring to the back or upper side.

Ectoparasitic Referring to a parasite that develops on the outside of its host.

Endoparasitic Referring to a parasite that develops inside its host.

Epidermis Outermost layer of cells of leaves, young stems, roots, flowers, fruits, and seeds. In insects the epidermis is the single, outermost layer of cells that secretes the cuticle.

Erineum A felty patch on a leaf surface, caused by a change in plant growth, or gall, where plant hairs are produced in great abundance. Many eriophyid mites cause such changes in leaf growth. **Erinea** is plural.

Eriophyids Mites in the superfamily Eriophyoidea, which have two pairs of legs, a generally elongate body form, are minute in size, and usually feed on plants.

Exoskeleton Skeletal structure formed on the external surface of an animal, as occurs with insects, mites, and other arthropods.

Exuvium Cast skin of an arthropod. The term does not exist in the singular and is also correct as **exuvia.**

Eyespots Prominent markings resembling eyes on the wings or body of certain insects.

Family Taxonomic subgroup of organisms within an order. For example, lady beetles and sap beetles are two families found in the order Coleoptera. Each family, in turn, is subdivided into genera. The scientific names of animal families end in the suffix *-dae.*

Fingergalls Abnormal growth forms in the shape of fingers, such as are produced by eriophyid mites on certain plants (e.g., wild plum, cherry).

Flagging Yellowing or wilting of foliage on a single branch.

Forewings Pair of wings closest to the head of an insect.

Frass Solid insect excrement, typically consisting of a mixture of chewed plant fragments.

Fundatrix Female aphid emerging from the overwintered egg that initiates colonies in spring.

Gall Abnormal growth of plant tissues, caused by the stimulus of an animal, microorganism, or wound.

Girdling Removal of tissue all around a stem or branch so that movement of water and nutrients is interrupted.

Gradual metamorphosis See **simple metamorphosis**.

Gregarious Living and feeding in groups.

Grub Immature form of many beetles.

Hemimetablous Referring to a type of simple metamorphosis found among some aquatic orders of insects (dragonflies, stoneflies, mayflies) where the winged adult is quite different in form from the aquatic nymph.

Herbaceous Referring to plants that lack woody tissues and annually die back.

Hibernaculum Tiny cocoon spun by first or second instar caterpillars for overwintering shelter. **Hibernaculae** is plural.

Hibernation Winter dormancy.

Honeydew Sugary, liquid excrement produced by certain aphids, scales, and other insects that feed in the phloem of plants.

Host Plant on which an insect or pathogen feeds; animal on which a parasite develops.

Hypopi Nonfeeding stage produced by some mites during development, often in response to adverse environmental factors.

In copula Act of being physically coupled during mating.

Injury Damage to a plant by an animal, physical, or chemical agent.

Inoculum Fungal spores, mycelium, bacterial cells, or viral particles that can initiate infections.

Instar Stage of an insect between periods when the skin is shed.

Internode Region between two adjacent nodes on a stem.

IPM—Integrated Pest Management Term applied to a philosophy of managing pests that has inherent to it proper identification of problems and assessment of potential injury before taking management actions. Management typically involves several approaches (e.g., biological, cultural, chemical) which are used in a complementary, integrated manner. Consideration is also given to environmental and social impacts of pest management activities.

June drop Natural shedding of fruit that occurs after fruit set. The term is usually applied to tree fruits, particularly apples.

Larva Immature form, between egg and pupa, of an insect with complete metamorphosis—i.e., caterpillar, maggot, or grub. Also the first immature stage of a mite or tick, which is six-legged. **Larvae** is plural.

Lateral Referring to the side. Used to describe markings on an insect.

Leafminer Insect that develops by feeding on internal leaf tissues which it chews as it mines the leaf. An insect that tunnels needles in a similar manner is called a **needleminer**.

Lenticel Small pore (natural opening) on a stem, tuber, root, or fruit through which carbon dioxide and other gases pass.

Lerp Wax-covered sugary excrement produced by some insects that suck sap, notably psyllids.

Lesion Localized, often sunken, area of diseased or disordered tissue; a wound.

Maggot Immature form of many true flies (Diptera).

Mandible Portion of the insect mouthpart that is usually prominent and highly hardened. In insects that chew, it is the primary structure used to cut and grind. In insects with sucking mouthparts, it penetrates tissues. Mandibles are paired in insects except in thrips, which have only one.

Marsupium Structure found in some animals in which immature stages continue development after birth.

Maxilla Portion of the insect mouthpart located immediately below the mandible. In insects that chew, it is used to manipulate food. The paired **maxillae** (plural) form the feeding tube for most insects that suck fluids.

Meconium Waste material excreted by an adult insect following emergence from the pupal stage.

Mesophyll Parenchyma cell tissues in a leaf or other part of the plant underneath the epidermis. Photosynthesis occurs in the mesophyll.

Metamorphosis Changes in form that take place during stages of animal development.

Mine To form a burrow or excavate a tunnel. Used to describe the activities of insects that live or feed in a leaf or needle.

Molt Shedding of the exoskeleton by an insect in the process of development.

Mosaic Symptom of certain viral diseases of plants, characterized by patches of normal color intermingled with patches that are light green or yellowish.

Mucus Viscous secretion used to protect tissues, primarily from drying.

Mutualistic Benefiting both species that are in some association.

Necrotic Dead and discolored.

Needle sheath Protective structure at the base of needles.

Neem Insecticidal materials (oils, azadirachtin) extracted from seeds of the neem tree (*Azadirachta indica*).

Nematode Generally microscopic, wormlike animals that live saprophytically in water or soil or as parasites of plants and animals.

Nightshade family The plant family Solanaceae.

Node Enlarged joint on a stem which is usually solid; site from which a leafy bud and branch arises.

Notching Angular, often nearly rectangular, cuts along a leaf edge, characteristic of insects such as root weevils.

Nymph Immature stage of an insect with simple metamorphosis (e.g., aphids, bugs, grasshoppers).

Omnivore Animal that feeds on a wide variety of materials, including animal products and plants.

Order Taxonomic subgroup of organisms found within a class. For example, beetles are an order of insects.

Osmeterium Fleshy Y-shaped gland extended by swallowtail larvae in response to disturbance. **Osmeteria** is plural.

Overwinter To spend the winter.

Oviparae Egg-producing form of an aphid, which appears at the end of the growing season.

Oviposition Process of laying an egg by an insect. **Oviposit** is the verb.

Ovipositor Egg-laying apparatus of a female insect.

Ovisac Large waxy sac into which eggs are laid by mealybugs, some soft scales, and related insects.

Parasite Organism that lives at the expense of another. (**Parasitoid** is often used to described parasitic insects that kill the host in which they develop.)

Parenchyma Thin-walled plant cells, capable of division, which make up much of a plant's tissues, exclusive of those that are involved primarily in structural support or nutrient transport. Photosynthesis and storage are functions of parenchyma cells.

Parthenogenesis Reproduction in which an unfertilized egg develops into an individual.

Pathogen Entity that can incite disease.

Paurometabolous Referring to insects that undergo simple, or gradual, metamorphosis, where the adult and immature stages have similar habits and transition in form is gradual, with the adults usually winged.

Perennial Plant or fungal fruiting body that persists in an active, living state for more than one growing season.

Petiole Leaf stem or stalk that attaches to a twig.

Pheromone Chemical used to communicate between members of the same species. For example, many female moths produce sex pheromones to attract mates.

Phloem Food-conducting tissue located in the bark of woody plants which consists of sieve tubes, companion cells, phloem parenchyma, and fibers.

Photoperiod Relative amount of time during the day that is light (or dark).

Phytoplasma Group of microorganisms, related to bacteria, that lack a cell wall and develop in the phloem tissues of plants.

Pitch Resinous material exuded by conifers, either naturally or in response to a wound.

Populus Genus of plants that includes poplar, cottonwood, and aspen.

Predator Animal that moves and hunts smaller animals.

Prepupae Period during the last larval stage, prior to pupation, when insects undergo changes in behavior and sometimes form.

Prey Animal that is hunted and killed for food.

Primocane Biennial cane of a caneberry, or bramble, in the first year of growth, before flowering occurs.

Proleg Fleshy leglike extensions of the abdomen found in the larval stages of sawflies and all moths and butterflies.

Pronotum Upper surface of the first segment of the thorax, located immediately behind the head.

Prothorax First segment of the thorax.

Protogyne Form of a female eriophyid mite that occurs during the growing season (vs. overwintering form).

Protonymph Second immature stage of a mite or tick.

Prunus Genus of plants known as stone fruits; it includes peach, plum, cherry, almond, and related plants.

Pupa Transitional stage, between larva and adult, of insects with complete metamorphosis.

Pyrethroids Synthetically manufactured insecticides that are chemically derived from the pyrethrins found in the pyrethrum daisy. Permethrin, bifenthrin, cyfluthrin, resmethrin, and esfenvalerate are common types of pyrethroid insecticides.

Pyrethrum Ground flowers of the daisy *Chrysanthemum cinaeriafolium*. They contain active insecticidal compounds known as **pyrethrins**, which are often extracted for use as garden insecticides.

Receptacle Enlarged tip of a flower on which the flower parts are borne. On raspberries and related plants, the receptacle is the elongated base to which the berry fruits attach.

Resin Sticky compound produced by plants, especially conifers.

Resistance Ability of an organism to exclude or overcome, completely or in some degree, the effect of a pathogen, insect, or other damaging factor.

Rosaceous plants Plants in the rose family, Rosaceae. This includes many commonly grown trees and shrubs including rose, stone fruits, apple and pear, mountain-ash, cotoneaster, pyracantha, brambles, amelanchier, and hawthorn.

Russeting Bronzy and somewhat thickened surface of a fruit or leaf induced by certain mites and by other causes.

Saprophyte Organism that feeds on dead organic matter, commonly causing its decay.

Sap wells Holes produced in plants by sapsuckers and other birds to produce a flow of sap on which they then feed. These are sometimes mistaken for the activity of wood-boring insects.

Sapwood Young, physiologically active zone of wood; outermost growth layers of xylem in woody plants that conducts water.

Scorch Damage to leaf margins resembling a burn, resulting from infection or unfavorable environmental conditions. Feeding of certain insects may cause scorch symptoms (e.g., hopperburn by *Empoasca* leafhoppers).

Scutellum Plate on the back of the middle segment of the thorax, often of triangular form. It is quite large and distinctive in insects such cicadas, stink bugs, and some beetles.

Secondary agent Any infection or infestation agent that results from a primary stress agent.

Serpentine Winding, twisting pattern, typically used to describe the shape of certain leaf mines.

Sexual Produced as a result of a union in which fertilization and meiosis occur.

Shepard's crook Type of injury in which newly produced plant shoots wilt and curl.

Shoot strike Terminal dieback of a plant caused by tunneling of some insect larvae.

Shotholes Small holes in leaves. These are most characteristics of flea beetles and some other insects that chew pits in the interior of leaves.

Simple metamorphosis Pattern of metamorphosis exhibited by many insects (e.g., true bugs, aphids, grasshoppers, earwigs) that involves eggs, followed by immature nymphs, and finally adults. Adult and immature stages usually feed in the same manner and are primarily differentiated by the adult features of sexual maturity and (usually) wings. Also called **gradual metamorphosis**. Insects with this life cycle are also referred to as being **paurometabolous**.

Skeletonize Feeding pattern of certain leaf-feeding insects that avoid feeding on larger veins of the leaf, producing a lacy "skeleton" of the leaf.

Solanaceous Referring to a member of the nightshade family of plants, Solanaceae. This includes many cultivated plants, among them petunia, potato, tomato, pepper, nightshade, and nicotiana.

Solitary Living along, not in groups.

Sooty mold Dark, typically black fungus growing on insect honeydew.

sp. Species in the singular; **spp.** refers to two or more species

Spiderling Newly hatched spider.

Spinnerets External structures used to spin silk. These occur at the tip of the abdomen in spiders and near the mouth in caterpillars.

Spinosad Insecticide derived from exudates of the soil microorganism *Saccharopolyspora spinosa*. The active compounds are known as spinosyns.

Spiracle Opening in the body through which arthropods breathe.

Spore Reproductive unit of fungi, consisting of one or more cells. It is analogous to the seed of green plants.

Stabilimentum Thick band of silk, often laid in a zigzag pattern, produced in the center of webs by some orb-weaving spiders.

Stippling Small, white flecking injuries on foliage produced by certain insects (some leafhoppers, lacebugs) and spider mites, resulting from removal of plant sap.

Stone fruits Plants that produce a fleshy fruit with a pit and that are found in the genus *Prunus*. They include cherry, apricot, peach, and plum.

Stylet When applied to insects, a reference to mouthparts designed to penetrate and suck fluids. In Hemiptera and Homoptera, the stylet bundle consists of paired mandibles and maxillae that are extremely elongate and fine.

Subfamily Subgrouping of organisms that occur in a single family but share features different from another subgrouping in the same family. The scientific names of animal subfamilies end in the suffix *-inae*.

Superfamily Grouping of several families of an organism within an order that share features different from another grouping of families in the same order. The scientific names of animal superfamilies end in the suffix *-oidea*.

Susceptible Lacking the inherent ability to resist disease or pesticides.

Symbiont Organism living together with another, larger, dissimilar organism.

Symptom External and internal reactions or alterations of a plant as a result of a infestation by insects, pathogens, other outside agents, or environmental conditions.

Systemic Spreading internally throughout the plant body; said of a pathogen or chemical.

Systemic insecticide An insecticide is capable of moving internally through a plant. Systemic insecticides may be sprayed on leaves, applied to soil, or injected and move from the point of application. Acephate and imidacloprid are examples of systemic insecticides.

Tent Protective shelter constructed of silk, spun by certain caterpillars.

Terminal growth Typically refers to new growth or buds at the end of a branch or twig.

Test Waxy covering (exuvium) produced by a scale insect.

Thorax Middle area of an insect body, where the legs and wings are attached. It is subdivided into three body segments, the **prothorax**, mesothorax, and metathorax.

Toxin Poisonous secretion produced by a living organism.

Tubercles Rounded protuberances found on many insects, particularly caterpillars.

Vector Living organism (i.e., insect, bird, higher animal, etc.) able to carry and transmit a pathogen.

Ventral Referring to the underside of the body.

Virus Submicroscopic obligate parasite consisting of nucleic acid and protein.

Windowpaning Chewing of leaves such that all of the tissues are removed except one layer of the epidermis, producing a translucent "window."

Wingspan Measurement between tips of the extended forewings of an insect.

Witches' broom Broomlike growth or massed proliferation caused by the dense clustering of branches of woody plants.

"Woolly" aphids Aphids that produce large amounts of wax in the form of strands that cover the body. They are most commonly found in the subfamily Pemphiginae. The closely related pine and spruce aphids (Adelgidae) are often also considered "woolly" aphids.

Xylem The complex supporting and water- and mineral-conducting tissue of vascular plants that makes up the sapwood and heartwood.

Selected References

WOODY PLANT AND ORNAMENTAL INSECTS

Baker, J. R., ed. 1978. *Insects and Related Pests of Flowers and Foliage Plants: Some Important and Potential Pests in North Carolina.* North Carolina Agricultural Extension Publication AG-136. Raleigh, N.C.: North Carolina State University.

Baker, J. R., ed. 1984. *Insects and Related Pests of Shrubs: Some Important, Common and Potential Pests in the Southeastern States.* North Carolina Agricultural Extension Publication AG-189. Raleigh, N.C.: North Carolina State University.

Byther, R., C. Foss, A. Antonelli, R. Maleike, and V. Bobbitt. 1996. *Landscape Plant Problems: A Pictorial Diagnostic Manual.* Pullman, Wash.: Washington State University Cooperative Extension.

Cranshaw, W. S., D. A. Leatherman, W. R. Jacobi, and L. Mannix. 2000. *Insects and Diseases of Woody Plants of the Central Rockies.* Colorado State University Cooperative Extension Publication 506A. Fort Collins, Colo.: Colorado State University.

Dreistadt, S. H., J. K. Clark, and M. L. Flint. *Pests of Landscape Trees and Shrubs: An Integrated Pest Management Guide.* 1994. University of California Statewide Integrated Pest Management Program Publication 3359. Oakland, Calif.: ANR Communication Services.

Drooz, A. T., ed. 1985. *Insects of Eastern Forests.* USDA-FS Miscellaneous Publication no. 1426. Washington, D.C.: U.S. Dept. of Agriculture.

Furniss, R. L., and V. M. Carolin. 1977. *Western Forest Insects.* USDA-FS Miscellaneous Publication no. 1339. Washington, D.C.: U.S. Dept. of Agriculture.

Gill, S., D. L. Clement, and E. Dutky. 1999. *Pests and Diseases of Herbaceous Perennials: The Biological Approach.* Batavia, Ill.: Ball Publishing.

Ives, W.G.H., and H. R. Wong. 1988. *Tree and Shrub Insects of the Prairie Provinces.* National Forestry Centre Information Report NOR-X-292. Georgetown, Ont.: UNIpresses.

Johnson, W. T., and H. H. Lyon. 1991. *Insects That Feed on Trees and Shrubs.* Ithaca, N.Y.: Cornell University Press.

Keifer, H. H., E. W. Baker, T. Kono, M. Delfinado, and W. E. Styer. 1982. *An Illustrated Guide to Plant Abnormalities Caused by Eriophyid Mites in North America.* USDA Agriculture Handbook no. 573. Washington, D.C.: U.S. Dept. of Agriculture.

Solomon, J. D. 1995. *Guide to Insect Borers in North American Broadleaf Trees and Shrubs.* USDA-FS Agricultural Handbook no. 706. Washington, D.C.: USDA Forest Service.

FRUIT INSECTS

Beers, E. H., J. F. Brunner, M. J. Willet, and G. M. Warner. 1993. *Orchard Pest Management: A Resource Book for the Pacific Northwest.* Yakima, Wash.: Good Fruit Grower.

Howitt, A. H. 1993. *Common Tree Fruit Pests.* North Central Regional Extension Publication no. 63. East Lansing, Mich.: Michigan State University Extension.

University of California Statewide IPM Program Publications. ANR Communication Services, 6701 San Pablo Avenue, Oakland, CA 94608-1239; www.ipm.ucdavis.edu/IPMRPROJECT.
Grape Pest Management. 2d ed. 1992.
Integrated Pest Management for Apples and Pears. 2d. ed. 1999.
Integrated Pest Management for Stone Fruits. 1999.
Integrated Pest Management for Strawberries. 1994.

VEGETABLE INSECTS

Capinera, J. L. 2001. *Handbook of Vegetable Insects.* New York: Academic Press.

Foster, R., and B. Flood, eds. 1995. *Vegetable Insect Management with Emphasis on the Midwest.* Willoughby, Ohio: Meister Publishing.

Howard, R. J., J. A. Garland, and W. L. Seaman, eds. 1994. *Diseases and Pests of Vegetable Crops in Canada: An Illustrated Compendium.* Ottawa: Canadian Phytopathological Society/Entomological Society of Canada.

Metcalf, R. L., and R. A. Metcalf. 1993. *Destructive and Useful Insects: Their Habits and Control.* 5th ed. New York: McGraw-Hill.

Sorensen, K. A., and J. R. Baker, eds. 1983. *Insects and Related Pests of Vegetables: Some Important, Common and Potential Pests in the Southeastern States.* North Carolina Agricultural Extension Publication AG-295. Raleigh, N.C.: North Carolina State University.

University of California Statewide IPM Program Publications. ANR Communication Services, 6701 San Pablo Avenue, Oakland, CA 94608-1239; www.ipm.ucdavis.edu/IPMPROJECT.

    Integrated Pest Management for Cole Crops and Lettuce. 1986.

    Integrated Pest Management for Potatoes in the Western United States. 1992.

    Integrated Pest Management for Tomatoes. 4th ed. 1998.

    Pests of the Garden and Small Farm: A Grower's Guide to Using Less Pesticide. 2d ed. 1998.

TURFGRASS INSECTS

Brandenburg, R. L., and M. G. Villani. 1995. *Handbook of Turfgrass Insect Pests.* Lanham, Md.: Entomological Society of America.

Cranshaw, W. S., and C. Ward. 1996. *Turfgrass Insects of Colorado and Northern New Mexico.* Colorado State University Cooperative Extension Publication 560A. Fort Collins, Colo.: Colorado State University.

Potter, D. A. 1998. *Destructive Turfgrass Insects: Biology, Diagnosis and Control.* Chelsea, Mich.: Ann Arbor Press.

Vittum, P. J., M. G. Villani, and H. Tashiro. 1999. *Turfgrass Insects of the United States and Canada.* 2d ed. Ithaca, N.Y.: Cornell University Press.

Watschke, T. L., P. H. Dernoeden, and D. J. Shetlar. 1995. *Managing Turfgrass Pests.* Boca Raton, Fl.: CRC Press.

BIOLOGICAL CONTROL ORGANISMS

Flint, M. L., and S. H. Dreistadt. 1998. *Natural Enemies Handbook: The Illustrated Guide to Biological Pest Control.* University of California Statewide Integrated Pest Management Program Publication 3386. Oakland, Calif.: ANR Communication Services.

Hoffman, M. P., and A. C. Frodsham. 1993. *Natural Enemies of Vegetable Insect Pests.* Ithaca, N.Y.: Cornell University Cooperative Extension.

GENERAL REFERENCES

Anonymous. 1976. *Hortus Third: A Concise Dictionary of Plants Cultivated in the United States and Canada.* New York: Macmillan Co.

Arnett, R. H., Jr. 1993. *American Insects: A Handbook of the Insects of America North of Mexico.* Gainesville, Fla.: Sandhill Crane Press.

Blackman, R. L., and V. F. Eastop. 1994. *Aphids on the World's Trees: An Identification and Information Guide.* Wallingford, U.K.: CAB International.

Blackman, R. L., and V. F. Eastop. 2000. *Aphids on the World's Crops: An Identification and Information Guide.* 2d ed. New York: John Wiley and Sons.

Borror, D. J., C. A. Triplehorn, and N. F. Johnson. 1989. *An Introduction to the Study of Insects.* Fort Worth, Tex.: Saunders College Publishing.

Drees, B. M., and J. A. Jackman. 1998. *A Field Guide to Common Texas Insects.* Houston, Tex.: Gulf Publishing.

Essig, E. O. 1929. *Insects of Western North America.* New York: Macmillan Co.

Evans, H. E. 1993. *Life on a Little Known Planet.* New York: Lyons and Burford.

Felt, E. P. 1965. *Plant Galls and Gall Makers.* New York: Hafner Publishing.

Jeppson, L. R., H. H. Keifer, and E. W. Baker. 1975. *Mites Injurious to Economic Plants.* Berkeley, Calif.: University of California Press.

Stoetzel, M. B. 1989. *Common Names of Insects and Related Organisms.* Lanham, Md.: Entomological Society of America.

Westcott, C. 1964. *The Gardener's Bug Book.* New York: Doubleday & Company.

White, S. C., and G. A. Salsbury. 2000. *Insects in Kansas.* 3d. ed. Kansas Department of Agriculture Publication S-131. Topeka, Kans.: Kansas Dept. of Agriculture.

Index

13-year cicada, 436
17-year cicada, 436
17-year locust, 436

aberrant wood borer, 484
Abgrallaspis ithacae, 354
Abgrallaspis townsendi, 354
acacia psyllid, 294
Acalitus essigi, 432
Acalitus fagerinea, 432
Acalitus vaccinii, 406, 432
Acalymma trivittatum, 194
Acalymma vittata, 194
Acantholyda erythrocephala, 108
Acaraspis erinacei, 426
Aceratagallia sanguinolenta, 364
Aceria aceris, 432
Aceria aloinis, 432
Aceria caryae, 430
Aceria elongatus, 432
Aceria erineus, 430
Aceria modestus, 432
Aceria parapopuli, 432
Aceria parulmi, 430
Aceria sheldoni, 432
Achatodes zeae, 472
achemon sphinx, 148
Achyra rantalis, 90
Acizzia uncatoides, 294
acorn and nut weevils, 282
Acossus centerensis, 468
Acossus populi, 468
acrea moth, 126
Acrobasis demotella, 444
Acrobasis indigenella, 164
Acrobasis juglandis, 162
Acrobasis nuxvorella, 252
Acrobasis tricolorella, 252
Acrobasis vaccinii, 252
Acronicta americana, 124
Acronicta leporina, 124
Acronicta lepusculina, 124
Acrosternum hilare, 228
Actias luna, 154
Aculops fuschiae, 430
Aculops gleditsiae, 406
Aculops lycopersici, 406
Aculops massalongoi, 406
Aculops tetanothrix, 439
Aculops toxicophagus, 430
Aculus fockeui, 406
Aculus ligustri, 406
Aculus lobulifera, 430
Aculus schlechtendali, 404, 406
acute-tongued burrowing bees, 574
Acyrthosiphon pisum, 304

Adelges abietis, 410
Adelges cooleyi, 410
Adelges piceae, 314
Adelges tsugae, 314
adelgids, 314, 410
Admes spider mite, 400
aerial yellowjacket, 244, 556
agave weevil, 488
Agelenopsis species, 562
Agrilus angelicus, 476
Agrilus anxius, 474
Agrilus aurichalceus, 476
Agrilus bilineatus, 476
Agrilus difficilis, 476
Agrilus granulatus granulatus, 476
Agrilus granulatus liragus, 476
Agrilus granulatus populi, 476
Agrilus planipennis, 476
Agrilus politus, 476
Agrilus ruficollis, 476
Agrilus sinuatus, 476
Agrioconota bivittata, 188
Agriphila ruricolella, 92
Agriphila vulgivagella, 92
Agrius cingulata, 148
Agromyza viridula, 208
Agrotis ipsilon, 140
Agrotis subterranea, 140
ailanthus webworm, 88
Albuna fraxini, 466
alder bead gall mite, 430
alder borer, 482
alder flea beetle, 200
alder spittlebug, 370
Alebra albostriella, 360
Aleochara bilineata, 546
Aleurocanthus woglumi, 288
Aleurodicus dugesii, 288
Aleurothrixus floccosus, 288
Aleyrodes spiraeoides, 288
alfalfa caterpillar, 166
alfalfa leafcutter bee, 70
alfalfa looper, 144
alfalfa webworm, 90
Allanthus cinctus, 446
Allokermes gillettei, 342
Allokermes kingi, 342
aloe mite, 432
Alsophila pometaria, 128
Altica chalybea, 200
Altica foliaceae, 200
Altica ignata, 200
Altica litigata, 200
Alypia octomaculata, 142
Amauromyza maculosa, 208
Amauronematus azalae, 76

ambrosia beetles, 498
ambush bugs, 552
American dagger moth, 124
American hornet moth, 466
American lady, 172
American lotus borer, 102
American plum borer, 470
American serpentine leafminer, 206
Ametastegia pallipes, 80
Ampeloglypter ater, 454
Ampeloglypter sesostris, 454
Amphibolips confluenta, 426
Amphicerus bicaudatus, 454
Amphipyra pyramidoides, 262
Amyelois transitella, 252
Anabrus simplex, 58
Anagrapha falcifera, 144
Anagrus species, 566
Anagyrus species, 566
Anaphothrips obscurus, 390
Anarsia lineatella, 442
Anasa armigera, 372
Anasa tristis, 232, 372
Ancylis comptana fragariae, 100
Ancylis discigerana, 100
Ancylis logiana, 100
Ancylis platanana, 100
Andricus californicus, 424
Andricus lasius, 424
Andricus palustris, 424
Andricus pomiformis, 424
andromeda lace bug, 384
angulate tingid, 384
anise swallowtail, 170
Anisomorpha buprestoides, 60
Anisota senatoria, 156
Anisota stigma, 156
annual cicadas, 436
Anomis erosa, 142
Anoplophora glabripennis, 484
Antheraea polyphemus, 156
Anthonomous eugenii, 280
Anthonomus consors, 278
Anthonomus quadrigibbus, 278
Anthonomus signatus, 280
ant-like gallfly, 424
Antonina graminis, 506
Antonina pretiosa, 322
Antron douglasii, 426
ants, 8, 45–46, 64–69, 566
Anuraphis cardui, 300,
Anuraphis helichrysi, 300
Aonidiella aurantii, 352
aphelinid wasps, 566
aphid galls, 408
aphid lions, 548

aphid mummies, 566
aphid parasites, 566
Aphidius species, 566
Aphidoletes species, 550
aphids, 10, 36–37, 296–313, 408, 506
Aphis armoraciae, 506
Aphis ceanothi, 304
Aphis citricola, 300
Aphis craccivora, 306
Aphis fabae, 300, 302
Aphis gossypii, 300–304
Aphis hederae, 304
Aphis helianthi, 300
Aphis middletoni, 304, 506
Aphis nasturtii, 300
Aphis nerii, 306
Aphis pomi, 304
Aphis sedi, 304
Aphodius granarius, 526
Aphodius ommissus ommissus, 526
Aphrophora permutata, 370
Aphrophora saratogensis, 370
Aphytis species, 566
Apiomerus species, 552
Apion longirostre, 280
Apis mellifera, 572
apple and thorn skeletonizer, 110
apple aphid, 304
apple bark borer, 466
apple blotch leafminer, 212
apple bucculatrix, 110
apple curculio, 278
apple flea beetle, 200
apple flea weevil, 220
apple grain aphid, 300
apple leafhopper, 358
apple maggot, 31, 234
apple mealybug, 322
apple pandemis, 100
apple rust mite, 404, 406
apple sucker psyllid, 294
apple twig borer, 454
appleleaf blister mite, 430
appleleaf trumpet leafminer, 218
Apterona helix, 160
Araneus species, 560
arborvitae leafminers, 218
arborvitae sawfly, 74
arborvitae spider mite, 400
arborvitae weevil, 534
Archips argyrospila, 96
Archips cerasivorana, 88
Archips fervidanus, 96
Archips negundanus, 96
Archips rosanus, 96
Archips semiferana, 96
Arge pectoralis, 84
Argentine ant, 68
Argiope aurantia, 560
Argiope trifasciata, 560

argus tortoise beetle, 188
Argyotaenia velutinana, 98
Argyresthia cupressella, 218
Argyrotaenia citrana, 98
Argyrotaenia pinatubana, 98
Argyrotaenia tabulana, 98
arid-land subterranean termite, 510
Ariolimax species, 50
Arion ater, 50
Arion circumscriptus, 50
Arion subfuscus, 50
Armadillium vulgare, 500
armored scales, 38–39, 344–56
army cutworm, 138
armyworm, 138
armyworms, 134–41
arthropod features, 1
artichoke aphid, 300
artichoke plume moth, 256
ash bark beetles, 42, 492–95
ash flowergall mite, 432
ash midrib gall midge, 420
ash plant bug, 376
ash whitefly, 288
ash/lilac borer, 462–64
ashgray blister beetle, 176
Asian ambrosia beetle, 498
Asian cycad scale, 352
Asian gypsy moth, 116
Asian longhorned beetle, 484
Asian woolly hackberry aphid, 306, 312
Asiatic garden beetle, 530
Asiatic oak weevil, 536
asparagus aphid, 304
asparagus beetle, 186
asparagus miner, 206
aspen blotch leafminer, 212
aspen carpenterworm, 468
aspen leafminer, 214
Aspidiotus cryptomeriae, 352
Aspidiotus nerii, 352
asps, 158,
assassin bugs, 552
aster leafhopper, 362
aster yellows, 362
Asterocampa celtis, 174
Asterocampa clyton, 174
Asterolecanium agavis, 342
Asterolecanium arabidis, 342
Asterolecanium bambusae, 342
Asterolecanium minus, 342
Asterolecanium pustulans, 342
Asterolecanium puteanum, 342
Asterolecanium quercicola, 342
Asterolecanium variolosum, 342
Asynonychus godmanni, 536
Ataenius spretulus, 526
Athrips rancidella, 86
Atomacerca decepta, 84

Atta texana, 64
Atteva punctella, 88
Aulacaspis rosae, 354
Aulacaspis yasumatsui, 352
Aulacorthum circumflexum, 306
Aulacorthum solani, 304
Autographa californica, 144
Autographa precationis, 144
Automeris io, 156
azalea bark scale, 326
azalea caterpillar, 150
azalea lace bug, 384
azalea leafminer, 214
azalea sawflies, 76
azalea stem borer, 456
azalea whitefly, 286

Bacillus popilliae, 34, 568
Bacillus thuringiensis, 29, 30, 568
bacterial diseases of insects, 568
bacterial leaf scorch, 364
Bactericera cockerelli, 290
bagworm, 160
baldcypress rust mite, 406
baldfaced hornet, 244, 556
Baliosus ruber, 220
balsam twig aphid, 306
balsam woolly adelgid, 314
bamboo scale, 342
banana slugs, 50
banded argiope, 560
banded ash borer, 484
banded ash clearwing, 464
banded cucumber beetle, 196
banded greenhouse thrips, 390
banded slugs, 50
banded sunflower moth, 254
banded woollybear, 126
bandedwinged thrips, 550
bandedwinged whitefly, 286
Banks grass mite, 398
barberry looper, 130
barberry webworm, 88
bark beetles, 42, 452, 490–501
barnacle scale, 334
basswood lace bug, 384
basswood leafminer, 220
bean aphid, 300, 302
bean leaf beetle, 190
bean leafroller, 106
bean seed maggot, 43–44, 514
Beauveria bassiana, 30, 37, 568
Bedellia somnulentella, 216
bee hunter, 552
beech blight aphid, 300, 312
beech scale, 326
bees, 8, 70, 448, 572–75
beet armyworm, 136
beet curly top, 364
beet leafhopper, 364

beet leafminer, 204
beet webworm, 90
Bembidion species, 546
Bemisia argentifolii, 286
Bemisia tabaci, 286
bermudagrass mite, 432
bermudagrass scale, 508
bertha armyworm, 140
Bibio species, 520
big poplar sphinx, 148
big-eyed bugs, 554
billbugs, 540
birch lace bug, 384
birch leafminer, 210
birch sawfly, 84
birch skeletonizer, 110
bird cherry-oat aphid, 302
black blister beetle, 176
black carpenter ant, 68
black cherry aphid, 300
black cherry fruit fly, 236
black citrus aphid, 306
black cutworm, 140
black fairway beetle, 526
black imported fire ant, 66
black pecan aphid, 306
black pineleaf scale, 350
black polished spruce aphid, 304
black scale, 330
black slug, 50
black stem borer, 498
black swallowtail butterfly, 168
black turfgrass ataenius, 526
black turpentine beetle, 494
black twig borer, 498
black vine weevil, 532
black walnut curculio, 282
black walnut petiole gall mite, 432
black willow aphid, 306
blackberry leafminer, 210
blackberry sawfly, 108
blackheaded ash sawfly, 78
blackheaded fireworm, 98
blackheaded pine sawfly, 74
blackhorned juniper borer, 486
blackhorned pine borer, 486
black-legged tortoise beetle, 188
blackmargined aphid, 306
Blastopsylla occidentalis, 294
Blepharida rhois, 200
Blissus insularis, 380
Blissus leucopterus hirtus, 378
Blissus leucopterus leucopterus, 380
Blissus occidus, 380
blister beetles, 176
blister coneworm, 254
blue cactus borer, 470
blueberry bud mite, 406
blueberry casebeetle, 190
blueberry gall midge, 240

blueberry leafroller, 100
blueberry maggot, 236
bluegrass billbug, 540
bluegrass webworm, 92
blue-green sharpshooter, 364
bluegum psyllid, 294
Boisduval scale, 354
Boisea rubrolineata, 230
Boisea trivittata, 230
Bombus species, 572
bowlegged fir aphid, 304
boxelder aphid, 306
boxelder bug, 230
boxelder erineum mite, 430
boxelder leafminer, 214
boxelder leafroller, 96
boxelder psyllid, 294
boxelder twig borer, 442
boxwood leafminer, 208
boxwood psyllid, 294
boxwood spider mite, 400
Brachycaudus cardui, 300
Brachycorynella asparagi, 304
Brachymeria species, 566
Brachystola magna, 54
Bracon species, 564
braconid wasps, 564
Bradysia spp., 522
Brevicoryne brassicae, 304
Brevipalpus obovatus, 404
Brevipalpus oncidii, 404
Brevipalpus phonecius, 404
bristly roseslug, 82
broad mite, 402
broadnecked root borer, 486
broadwinged katydid, 58
Brochymena pustula, 228
Brochymena quadripustulata, 228
bronze birch borer, 474
bronze cane borer, 476
bronze poplar borer, 476
bronzed cutworm, 138
brown ambrosia aphid, 306
brown citrus aphid, 306
brown garden snail, 50
brown lacewings, 8, 548
brown mite, 400
brown soft scale, 328
brown stink bug, 228
brown wheat mite, 398
brownheaded ash sawfly, 78
Bruce spanworm, 130
brushfooted butterflies, 172–75
Bryobia praetiosa, 398
Bryobia rubrioculus, 400
Bt, 568
Buccalatrix ainsliella, 110
Buccalatrix thurnberiella, 110
Bucculatrix albertiella, 110
Bucculatrix canadensisella, 110

Bucculatrix pomifoliella, 110
buck moths, 156
buckeye scale, 354
buckthorn aphid, 300
buffalo treehopper, 366
buffalograss chinch bug, 380
buffalograss mite, 432
bulb flies, 43–44, 516
bulb mites, 508
Bulimula alternatus mariae, 50
bull pine sawfly, 74
bumble bees, 572
bumble flower beetle, 270
butternut woollyworm, 80
Byturus bakeri, 274
Byturus rubi, 274
Byturus unicolor, 274

cabbage aphid, 304
cabbage butterfly, 166
cabbage flea beetle, 198
cabbage leafminer, 206
cabbage looper, 144
cabbage maggot, 43–44, 514
cabbage webworm, 90
cabbage white, 166
cabbageworms, 28, 166
Cacopsylla buxi, 294
Cacopsylla mali, 294
Cacopsylla negundinis, 294
Cacopsylla pyricola, 292
cactus longhorn, 486
cactus scale, 354
Calaphis betulaecolens, 304
Calastega aceriella, 164
calico scale, 334
California gallfly, 424
California mantid, 554
California oakworm, 152
California orangedog, 170
California pear sawfly, 78
California red scale, 352
Californis prionus, 486
Caliroa cerasi, 82
Caliroa lineata, 82
Caliroa petiolata, 82
Caliroa quercuscoccineae, 82
Callaphis juglandis, 304
Callidium antennatum, 486
Callidium texanum, 486
Calligrapha bigsbayana, 180
Calligrapha californica coreopsivora, 182
Calligrapha scalaris, 180
Callipterinella callipterus, 304
Callirhopalis bifasciatus, 536
Callirhytis cornigera, 424
Callirhytis crypta, 424
Callirhytis floridana, 424
Callirhytis gemmaria, 424

Callirhytis quercusgemmaria, 424
Callirhytis quercuspunctata, 424
Callirhytis seminator, 426
Callopistria floridensis, 142
Callosamia promethea, 156
Calopha graminis, 300
Calopha ulmicola, 300
Calophya rubra, 416
Caloptilia azaleella, 214
Caloptilia negundella, 214
Caloptilia syringella, 214
Calosoma species, 546
Calpodes ethlius, 106
cambium miners, 208
camellia bud mite, 406
camellia scale, 346
Cameraria species, 216
Camnula pellucida, 54
camplyomma bug, 226
Camponotus floridanus, 68
Camponotus herculeanus, 68
Camponotus modoc, 68
Camponotus novaboracensis, 68
Camponotus pennsylvanicus, 68
Campylomma verbasci, 226
candystripe leafhopper, 364
cankerworms, 128
Cantharis species, 546
Capitophorous elaeagni, 300
Carmenta anthracipennis, 466
Carmenta corni, 466
carmine spider mite, 394
Carneocephala fulgida, 364
Carolina grasshopper, 54
Carolina mantid, 554
Carolina sphinx, 146
carpenter ants, 68, 566
carpenter bees, 448, 574
carpenterworm, 468
Carpophilus lugubris, 272
carrot beetle, 530
carrot rust fly, 43–44, 518
carrot weevil, 538
carrot-willow aphid, 300
Carulaspis juniperi, 352
Carulaspis minima, 352
casebearers, 162–65
case-bearing leaf beetles, 190
catalpa midge, 420
catalpa sphinx, 148
catawba worms, 148
caterpillar hunters, 546
Caulocampus acericaulis, 446
Cavariella aegopodii, 300
ceanothus stem gall moth, 444
Cecidomyia ocellaris, 420
Cecidomyia pellex, 420
Cecidomyia piniinopis, 458
Cecidomyia poculum, 420
Cecidomyia resinicola, 458

Cecidophyopsis psilaspis, 432
Cecidophyopsis ribis, 432
Cecidophyopsis vermiformis, 432
Ceciophyes betulae, 432
cecropia moth, 154
cedar bark beetles, 42, 452
celery leaftier, 90
celery looper, 144
centipedes, 562
Cephalcia species, 108
Ceratagallia abrupta, 362
Ceratina species, 448
Ceratoma trifucata, 190
Ceratomia amyntor, 148
Ceratomia catalpae, 148
Ceroplastes ceriferus, 334
Ceroplastes cirripediformis, 334
Ceroplastes floridensis, 334
Ceroplastes rubens, 334
Ceroplastes sinensis, 334
Ceruraphis eriophori, 300
Ceruraphis viburnicola, 300
Chaetocnema confinis, 200
Chaetocnema denticulata, 200
Chaetocnema pulicaria, 200
Chaetocnema repens, 200
Chaetosiphon fragaefolii, 306
chafers, 524, 528
Chaitophorus populicola, 304
Chaitophorus populifolii, 304
Chaitophorus viminalis, 304
chalcid wasps, 566
Charidotella bicolor, 188
Chauliognathus pennsylvanicus, 546
checkered beetles, 546
checkered white butterfly, 166
Chelinidea vittiger, 372
Chelonus species, 564
Chelymorpha cassidea, 188
cherry bark tortrix, 98
cherry curculio, 278
cherry fruit fly, 234
cherry fruit sawfly, 266
cherry fruitworm, 250
cherry leafminer, 212, 214
cherry maggot, 234
cherry slug, 82
cherry webspinning sawfly, 108
chiggers, 562
child of the earth, 58
Chilocorus stigmata, 544
China mark moth, 102
chinch bugs, 378
Chinese mantid, 554
Chinese red scale, 334
Chionaspis americana, 346
Chionaspis furfura, 346
Chionaspis heterophyllae, 346
Chionaspis pinifoliae, 346
Chlorochroa ligata, 228

Chlorochroa sayi, 228
Chlorochroa uhleri, 228
chokecherry gall midge, 240
chokecherry sawfly, 78
Choreutis pariana, 110
Choristoneura conflictana, 98
Choristoneura fumiferana, 104
Choristoneura lambertina, 104
Choristoneura occidentalis, 104
Choristoneura pinus, 104
Choristoneura rosaceana, 98
Chromaphis juglandicola, 306
chrysanthemum aphid, 306
chrysanthemum gall midge, 420
chrysanthemum lace bug, 384
chrysanthemum leafminer, 206
chrysanthemum rust mite, 406
Chrysobothris femorata, 478
Chrysobothris mali, 478
Chrysomela scripta, 180
Chrysomphalus aonidum, 354
Chrysopa species, 548
Chrysoperla species, 548
Chrysoteuchia topiaria, 94
cicada killers, 558
cicadas, 10, 436
cigar casebearer, 162
Cimbex americana, 84
Cinara coloradensis, 304
Cinara curvipes, 394
Cinara fornacula, 304
Cinara laricis, 306
Cinara sabiniae, 306
Cinara strobi, 306
Citheronia regalis, 154
citricola scale, 328
citrus blackfly, 288
citrus bud mite, 432
citrus mealybug, 316
citrus peelminer, 208
citrus red mite, 400
citrus rust mite, 406
citrus whitefly, 288
Cladius difformis, 82
Clastoptera achatina, 370
Clastoptera juniperina, 370
Clastoptera obtusa, 370
Clastoptera proteus, 370
clay-colored weevil, 534
clearwing borers, 462–67
clearwing moths, 148, 462–67
clearwinged grasshopper, 54
clerid beetles, 546
click beetles, 542
Clinodiplosis rhododendri, 420
Clostera inclusa, 152
clover aphid, 300
clover leafhopper, 364
clover mite, 398
Cnephasia longana, 100

Coccophagus species, 566
Coccotorus scutellaris, 278
Coccus hesperidum, 328
Coccus pseudomagnoliarum, 328
cochineal scales, 326
Cochylis hospes, 254
codling moth, 31, 246
Colaspis brunnea, 196
Coleophora laricella, 162
Coleophora laticornella, 162
Coleophora malivorella, 162
Coleophora serratella, 162
Coleophora ulmifoliella, 162
Coleotechnites juniperella, 218
Coleotechnites picealla, 218
Coleotechnites ponderosae, 218
Colias eurytheme, 166
Colias philodice, 166
Colladonus montanus, 362
collops beetles, 548
Colomerus vitis, 430, 432
Colopha graminis, 408
Colopha ulmicola, 408
Coloradia pandora, 156
Colorado potato beetle, 28–29, 184
columbine leafminers, 208
columbine sawfly, 78
common birch aphid, 304
common chinch bug, 380
common falsepit scale, 342
common pine shoot beetle, 452
common sawflies, 76–83
common sulfur, 166
common willow agrilus, 476
Comstock mealybug, 318
conchuela, 228
coneworms, 254
conifer sawflies, 72
Conoderus species, 542
Conotrachelus aratus, 454
Conotrachelus hicoriae, 282
Conotrachelus nenuphar, 276
Conotrachelus retentus, 282
Conotrachelus schoofi, 454
consperse stink bug, 228
Contarinia juniperina, 458
Contarinia quinquenotata, 240
Contarinia schulzi, 240
Contarinia virginianae, 240
Continaria canadensis, 420
Continaria catalpae, 420
Continaria coloradensis, 420
Continaria negundinis, 420
Continaria pseudotsugae, 420
Continaria verrucicola, 420
convergent lady beetle, 544
convict caterpillar, 472
Cooley spruce gall adelgid, 410
Copidosoma truncatellum, 566
Coptodisca arbutiella, 218

Coptodisca splendoriferella, 218
Coptotermes formosanus, 510
coreopsis beetle, 182
corn earworm, 33, 260
corn flea beetle, 200
corn leaf aphid, 306
corn root webworm, 92
corn rootworms, 192, 196
Coryphista meadii, 130
Corythuca angulata, 384
Corythuca arcuata, 384
Corythuca celtidis, 384
Corythuca ciliata, 384
Corythuca cydoniae, 384
Corythuca distincta, 384
Corythuca juglandis, 384
Corythuca marmorata, 384
Corythuca pallipes, 384
Corythuca ulmi, 384
Cosectacus camelliae, 406
Cossula magnifica, 468
Cotesia species, 564
Cotinus mutabilis, 528
Cotinus nitidis, 528
cotoneaster webworm, 86
cotton bollworm, 260
cotton square borer, 256
cotton/melon aphid, 300–304
cottonwood borer, 484
cottonwood catkingall mite, 432
cottonwood clearwing borer, 466
cottonwood crown borer, 466
cottonwood dagger moth, 124
cottonwood leaf beetle, 180
cottonwood leaf curl mite, 430
cottonwood twig borer, 442
cottony camellia scale, 338
cottony cushion scale, 340
cottony maple leaf scale, 338
cottony maple scale, 338
cottony taxus scale, 338
cowpea aphid, 306
crab spiders, 560
Crambus caliginosellus, 92
Crambus leachellus, 92
Crambus luteolellus, 92
Crambus praefectellus, 92
Crambus sperryellus, 92
cranberry fruitworm, 252
cranberry girdler, 94
cranberry leafroller, 100
cranberry rootworm, 182
crane flies, 518–21
crapemyrtle aphid, 306
Craponius inaequalis, 278
crescentmarked lily aphid, 306
Cressonia juglandis, 148
crickets, 10, 56
Criddle's bark beetle, 492
Crioceris asparagi, 186

Crioceris duodecimpunctata, 186
Croesus latitarsus, 78
cross-striped cabbageworm, 90
crown borer, 464
crucifer flea beetle, 198
Cryptococcus fagisuga, 326
cryptomeria scale, 352
Cryptomyzus ribis, 300
Cryptorhynchus lapathe, 488
Ctenarytaina eucalptyi, 294
Ctenicerca species, 542
Cuban laurel thrips, 390
Curculio caryae, 282
Curculio caryatrypes, 282
Curculio obtusus, 282
Curculio occidentis, 282
Curculio sayi, 282
curculios, 276–83
curled rose sawfly, 446
currant aphid, 300
currant borer, 466
currant bud mite, 432
currant flea beetle, 200
currant fruit fly, 238
currant sawfly, 76
currant spanworm, 130
cutworms, 28–29, 134–41, 258, 260, 262
cycad aulacaspis scale, 352
cycad scale, 354
cyclamen mite, 402
Cyclocephala borealis, 524
Cyclocephala hirta, 524
Cyclocephala lurida, 524
Cyclocephala pasadaenae, 524
Cydia caryana, 248
Cydia latiferreana, 248
Cydia nigracana, 248
Cydia pomonella, 246
Cylas formicarius, 538
Cylindrocopturus adspersus, 456
cypress bark mealybug, 322
cypress tipminer, 218
Cyrtepistomus castaneus, 536

Dactylopious coccus, 326
Dactylopious confusus, 326
daddylonglegs, 562
dagger moths, 120, 124
Daktulosphaira vitifoliae, 412
damsel bugs, 552
Danaus plexippus, 174
Darapsa myron, 148
darksided cutworm, 138
Dasineura communis, 418
Dasineura gleditschiae, 418
Dasineura oxycoccana, 240
Dasineura pseudacaciae, 418
Dasineura pyri, 418
Dasineura rhodophaga, 240

Dasychira grisefacta, 122
Dasychira vagans, 122
Datana integerrina, 150
Datana major, 150
Datana ministra, 150
daylily thrips, 388
decollate snail, 50
Delia antiqua, 516
Delia florigela, 514
Delia planipalpis, 514
Delia platura, 514
Delia radicum, 514
Deloyala guttata, 188
Deltocephalus hospes, 364
Dendroctonus frontalis, 494
Dendroctonus ponderosae, 494
Dendroctonus rufipennis, 494
Dendroctonus tenebrans, 494
Dendroctonus valens, 494
Dendrothrips ornatus, 388
Denver billbug, 542
deodar weevil, 450
Deraeocoris species, 552
Deroceras agreste, 48
Deroceras reticulatum, 48
Derocerus laeve, 48
Desmia funeralis, 100
destructive prune worm, 252
Diabrotica balteata, 196
Diabrotica barberi, 192
Diabrotica undecimpunctata, 196
Diabrotica virgifera virgifera, 192
Diabrotica virgifera zeae, 192
Diadegma species, 564
Diaeretiella species, 566
diagnosis, 6–23
Dialeurodes chittendeni, 286
Dialeurodes citri, 288
diamondback moth, 94
Diaphania hyalinata, 264
Diaphania nitidalis, 264
Diapheromera femorata, 60
Diapheromera velii, 60
Diaphnocoris chlorionis, 376
Diaprepes abbreviatus, 536
diaprepes root weevil, 536
Diaspidiotus aesculi, 354
Diaspidiotus ancylus, 354
Diaspis boisduvalii, 354
Diaspis echinocacti, 354
Diastrophus kincaidii, 428
Dichomeris marginella, 86
dichondra flea beetle, 200
differential grasshopper, 52
digger bees, 574
Dilophus species, 520
dingy cutworm, 140
Dioryctria abietivorella, 254
Dioryctria albovittella, 440
Dioryctria amatella, 254

Dioryctria clarioralis, 254
Dioryctria disclusa, 254
Dioryctria ponderosae, 470
Dioryctria reniculelloides, 254
Dioryctria zimmermani, 470
Diplolepis bassetti, 426
Diplolepis bicolor, 426
Diplolepis dichlocera, 426
Diplolepis fusiformis, 426
Diplolepis globuloides, 426
Diplolepis nebulosus, 426
Diplolepis politus, 426
Diplolepis radicum, 426
Diplolepis rosae, 426
Diplolepis rosaefolii, 426
Diplolepis tuberculatrix, 426
Diplolepis tumidus, 426
Diprion similis, 74
Disholcaspis eldoradensis, 424
Disholcaspis quercusmamma, 424
Disonycha xanthomelas, 200
distinct lace bug, 384
dog-day cicadas, 436
dogwood borer, 466
dogwood clubgall midge, 422
dogwood sawfly, 80
dogwood spittlebug, 370
dogwood twig borer, 456
Dolichovespula arenaria, 244, 556
Dolichovespula maculata, 244, 556
Donacia piscatrix, 182
Doru species, 62, 554
douglas-fir needle midge, 420
douglas-fir pitch moth, 466
douglas-fir tussock moth, 120
Draeculacephala minerva, 364
drain flies, 522
Drepanosiphum platanoides, 306
drone flies, 550
Drosophila species, 238
dryberry mite, 432
Dryocampa rubicunda, 156
dusky birch sawfly, 78
dusky sap beetle, 272
dusky-winged oak aphid, 306
dusky-winged walnut aphid, 304
dustywings, 550
Dutch elm disease, 492
Dynaspidiotus britannicus, 354
Dysaphis plantaginea, 300
Dysaphis tulipae, 306, 506
dysderid spiders, 560
Dyslobus granicollis, 534
Dysmicoccus wistariae, 322

Eacles imperialis, 156
earwigs, 10, 62, 566
eastern ash bark beetle, 492
eastern buck moth, 156

eastern grape leafhopper, 360
eastern lubber, 54
eastern pine looper, 132
eastern pine weevil, 450
eastern pineshoot borer, 440
eastern raspberry fruitworm, 274
eastern spruce gall adelgid, 410
eastern subterranean termite, 510
eastern tent caterpillar, 112
eastern tiger swallowtail, 170
eastern yellowjacket, 244
Ecdytolopha insiticiana, 442
Edwardsiana australis, 360
Edwardsiana commisuralis, 360
Edwardsiana hippocastani, 360
Edwardsiana rosae, 358
eggplant flea beetle, 198
eggplant lace bug, 384
eggplant tortoise beetle, 188
Ehrhornia cupressi, 322
eightspotted forester, 142
Elaphidionoides parallelus, 456
Elaphidionoides villosus, 456
elder shoot borer, 472
elegant sod webworm, 92
elm calligrapha, 180
elm casebearer, 162
elm cockscomb aphid, 300, 408
elm eriophyid mite, 430
elm lace bug, 384
elm leaf aphid, 306
elm leaf beetle, 28–29, 178
elm leafminer, 210
elm sawfly, 84
elm scurfy scale, 346
elm spanworm, 130
elm sphinx, 148
elm spider mite, 400
elongate flea beetle, 200
elongate hemlock scale, 350
emerald ash borer, 476
Emerus strigatus, 516
Emerus tuberculatus, 516
Emesaya species, 552
Empoasca abrupta, 358
Empoasca fabae, 356
Empoasca filamenta, 358
Empoasca maligna, 358
Empoasca recurvata, 358
Empoasca solana, 358
Empyreuma affinis, 124
Enarmonia formosana, 98
Encarsia inaron, 288
Encarsia species, 35, 566
Enchenopa binotata, 366
encyrtid wasps, 566
Endelomyia aethiops, 82
Endopiza viteana, 252
Endothenia albolineana, 216
Endria inimica, 364

English grain aphid, 306
Ennomos subsignaria, 130
entomopathogenic nematodes, 570
Entomophaga maimaiga, 568
Entomophthora muscae, 43–44, 568
Entomoscelis americana, 190
Entylia carinata, 366
Eotetranychus carpini borealis, 400
Eotetranychus hicoriae, 400
Eotetranychus lewisi, 400
Eotetranychus matthyssei, 400
Eotetranychus populi, 400
Eotetranychus querci, 400
Eotetranychus tiliarium, 400
Eotetranychus weldoni, 400
Eotetranychus willametti, 400
Epargyreus clarus, 106
Epicauta fabricii, 176
Epicauta lemniscata, 176
Epicauta maculata, 176
Epicauta pensylvanica, 176
Epicauta pestifera, 176
Epicauta vittata, 176
Epilachna borealis, 202
Epilachna varivestis, 202
Episimus argutanus, 100
Epitrimerus pyri, 406
Epitrimerus taxodii, 406
Epitrix cucumeris, 198
Epitrix fuscula, 198
Epitrix hirtipennis, 198
Epitrix subcrinita, 198
Epitrix tuberis, 198
Erannis tiliaria, 130
Ergates spiculatus, 486
erigeron root aphid, 304, 506
Eriocampa juglandis, 80
eriococcids, 324
Eriococcus araucariae, 326
Eriococcus azalae, 326
Eriococcus quercus, 326
Eriophyes calaceris, 432
Eriophyes caulis, 432
Eriophyes celtis, 432
Eriophyes chrondriphora, 430
Eriophyes cynodoniensis, 432
Eriophyes emarginatae, 430
Eriophyes fraxiniflora, 432
Eriophyes mali, 430
Eriophyes negundi, 430
Eriophyes neoessigi, 432
Eriophyes pyri, 430
Eriophyes slykhuisi, 432
Eriophyes sorbi, 430
Eriophyes ulmi, 430
Eriophyes zoysiae, 432
eriophyid mites, 404–8, 430–33
Eriosoma americanum, 300, 310
Eriosoma crataegi, 300, 310
Eriosoma lanigerum, 300, 310

Eriosoma pyricola, 300, 310
Eristalis species, 550
Erythraspides vitis, 80
Erythroneura comes, 360
Erythroneura gleditsia, 360
Erythroneura lawsoniana, 360
Erythroneura tricincta, 360
Erythroneura variabilis, 360
Erythroneura vulnerata, 360
Erythroneura ziczac, 360
Estigmene acrea, 126
Etiella zinckenella, 264
Euborellia annulipes, 62
eucalyptus longhorned borer, 484
Eucosoma gloriola, 440
Eucosoma sonomana, 440
eugenia psyllid, 416
Eulecanium cerasorum, 334
eulophid wasps, 566
Eumargarodes laingi, 508
Eumorpha achemon, 148
euonymus scale, 350
Euphantra canadensis, 238
Euphoria inda, 270
Euphoria kerni, 270
Euphoria sepulchralis, 270
Euplectrus species, 566
Euptoieta claudia, 174
European alder leafminer, 210
European apple sawfly, 266
European chafer, 528
European corn borer, 444
European crane fly, 518
European earwig, 62, 566
European elm scale, 324
European fruit lecanium, 332
European hornet, 244
European leafroller, 96
European mantid, 554
European paper wasp, 556
European peach scale, 332
European pine sawfly, 72
European pine shoot moth, 438
European red mite, 394
Eurytetranychus admes, 400
Eurytetranychus buxi, 400
Euschistus conspersus, 228
Euschistus servus, 228
Euschistus variolarius, 228
Eutettix strobi, 364
Eutettix tenellus, 364
Euthochtha galeator, 232
Euura species, 428
Euxoa auxiliaris, 138
Euxoa messoria, 138
Euxoa ochrogster, 138
Euzophera semifuneralis, 470
Evergestis pallidata, 90
Evergestis rimosalis, 90
excreta, 12–13

Exitianus exitiosus, 364
Exochus species, 564
Exomala orientalis, 528
eyespot gall midge, 420
eyespotted bud moth, 96

fall armyworm, 134
fall cankerworm, 128
fall field cricket, 56
fall webworm, 28, 118
false celery leaftier, 90
false chinch bug, 380
false Japanese beetle, 270
false longhorn leaf beetle, 182
false oleander scale, 352
false potato beetle, 184
false spider mites, 404
false unicorn caterpillar, 152
falsepit scales, 342
Fascista cercerisella, 100
Feltia jaculifera, 140
Feltia subgothica, 140
Feltiella species, 550
felt-like scales, 324
Fenusa dohrnii, 210
Fenusa pusilla, 210
fern scale, 350
Ferrisia virgata, 322
Fieberiella florii, 362, 364
field ants, 68, 556
field crickets, 56
fiery skipper, 106
filament bearer, 132
filbert aphid, 306
filbert bud mite, 432
filbert leafroller, 96
filbert weevil, 282
filbertworm, 248
Fiornia externa, 350
Fiornia theae, 350
fir coneworm, 254
fir rust mite, 406
fire ant, 66, 556
fireflies, 548
Fissicrambus mutabilis, 92
five-spotted hawk moth, 146
flannel moths, 158
flatheaded appletree borer, 478
flatheaded borers, 474–79
flea beetles, 30, 198–201
Fletcher scale, 332
Florida carpenter ant, 68
Florida fern caterpillar, 142
Florida red scale, 354
Florida wax scale, 334
flower flies, 550
flower thrips, 222
fly parasites, 566
fly predators, 566
folded-leaf poplar aphid, 302

Forbes scale, 348
Forda formicaria, 306
Forda olivacea, 506
forest tent caterpillar, 114
Forficula auricularia, 62
Formica species, 68, 556
Formosan subterranean termite, 510
fourlined fruitworm, 262
fourlined plant bug, 374
fourspotted hawthorn aphid, 306
fourspotted sap beetle, 274
fourspotted spider mite, 394
foxglove aphid, 304
Frankliniella fusca, 222
Frankliniella occidentalis, 222
Frankliniella tritici, 222
frosted scale, 332
fruit flies, 31, 234–39
fruittree leafroller, 96
Fuller rose beetle, 536
fungal diseases of insects, 568
fungus gnats, 522
funnel spiders, 562
Furchadaspis zamiae, 354
fuschia gall mite, 430

gall midges, 418–23
gall wasps, 424–29
galls, 41, 408–33
garden bagworm, 160
garden centipede, 502
garden fleahopper, 374–76
garden leafhoppers, 358
garden slug, 50
garden spiders, 560
garden symphylan, 502
garden webworm, 90
Gargaphia solani, 384
Gargaphia tilia, 384
genista caterpillar, 102
geometers, 128
geranium budworm, 258
German yellowjacket, 244
Geshna cannalis, 102
giant bark aphid, 306
giant coccids, 340
giant ichneumon wasps, 564
giant root borer, 486
giant silkworms, 154–57
giant swallowtail, 170
giant whitefly, 288
giant willow aphid, 306
gladiolus thrips, 39, 388
glassywinged sharpshooter, 364
Glischrochilus fasciatus, 274
Glischrochilus quadrisignatus, 274
globular rose gall wasp, 426
gloomy scale, 354
Glycaspis brimblecomei, 294
gold bugs, 188

golden oak scale, 342
golden silk spider, 560
golden tortoise beetle, 188
goldenglow aphid, 306
goldenrain tree bug, 230
Gordius species, 570
Gossyparia spuria, 324
gouty oak gall, 424
gouty pitch midge, 458
gouty veingall midge, 420
Graminella sonora, 364
granulate cutworm, 140
granulate poplar borer, 476
grape berry moth, 252
grape cane gallmaker, 454
grape cane girdler, 454
grape colaspis, 196
grape curculio, 278
grape erineum mite, 432
grape flea beetle, 200
grape leaffolder, 100
grape mealybug, 320
grape phylloxera, 412
grape root borer, 466
grape sawfly, 80
grape tumid gallmaker, 420
grapeleaf skeletonizer, 110
grapevine hoplia, 270
Graphocephala atropunctata, 364
Graphocephala coccinea, 364
Grapholita molesta, 250
Grapholita packardi, 250
Grapholita prunivora, 250
grass loopers, 132
grass spiders, 562
grass thrips, 390
grasshoppers, 10, 27, 52–55
Gratiana pallidula, 188
gray hairstreak, 256
gray lawn leafhopper, 364
gray sunflower weevil, 280
great ash sphinx, 148
great gray garden slug, 48
greedy scale, 352
green citrus aphid, 302
green fruit beetles, 528
green fruitworm, 262
green lacewings, 8, 548
green lynx spider, 560
green peach aphid, 298–300
green sharpshooter, 364
green spruce aphid, 304
green stink bug, 228
greenbug, 306
greenhouse centipede, 502
greenhouse leaftier, 90
greenhouse thrips, 390
greenhouse whitefly, 284
greenstriped mapleworm, 156
ground beetles, 546

ground mealybug, 506
ground nesting bees, 574
ground pearls, 508
Grylloprociphilus imbricator, 300, 312
Gryllus pennsylvanicus, 56
Gryllus rubens, 56
Gryllus veletis, 56
Gymnocarena diffusa, 240
Gynaikothrips ficorum, 390
Gypsonoma haimbachiana, 442
gypsy moth, 28, 116
Gyropsylla ilicis, 416

hackberry blistergall psyllid, 414
hackberry budgall psyllid, 414
hackberry butterfly, 174
hackberry lace bug, 384
hackberry leaf slug, 158
hackberry nipplegall maker, 414
hackberry petiolegall psyllid, 414
hackberry stargall psyllid, 414
hackberry witches' broom mite, 432
hag moth, 158
hairy chinch bug, 378
Haltica torquata, 200
Halticotoma valida, 376
Halticus bractatus, 374–76
Halysidota tessellaris, 124
Hamamelistes spinosus, 408
Haplorhynchites aeneus, 280
hard scales, 344–56
harlequin bug, 382
Harmonia axyridis, 544
Harrisina americana, 110
Harrisina brillans, 110
Hartigia cressoni, 446
Hartigia trimaculata, 446
harvester ants, 68
harvestmen, 562
hawk moths, 146
hawthorn lace bug, 384
hawthorn leafminer, 210
hawthorn mealybug, 320
hazelnut weevil, 282
hedgehog gall wasp, 426
Helicoverpa zea, 260
Heliothis virescens, 258
Heliothrips haemorrhoidalis, 390
Helix aspersa, 50
Hellula rogatalis, 90
Hemaris diffinis, 148
Hemaris thysbe, 148
hemerocallis gall midge, 240
Hemiberlesia lataniae, 352
Hemiberlesia rapax, 352
Hemileuca lucina, 156
Hemileuca maia, 156
Hemileuca nevadensis, 156
Hemisphaerota cyanea, 188
hemispherical scale, 330

hemlock borer, 478
hemlock looper, 132
hemlock rust mite, 406
hemlock sawfly, 74
hemlock scale, 354
hemlock woolly adelgid, 310
Hercinothrips femoralis, 390
Herpetogramma phaeopteralis, 92
Heterocampa guttivitta, 152
Heterocampa manteo, 152
Heterorhabditis species, 44, 45, 570
hexapod features, 4
Hexomyza schineri, 422
hibiscus bug, 232
hibiscus sawfly, 84
hickory bark beetle, 492
hickory horned devil, 154
hickory leafstem gall phylloxera, 412
hickory nut curculio, 282
hickory shoot curculio, 454
hickory shuckworm, 248
hickory tussock moth, 124
Himella intractata, 262
Hippodamia convergens, 544
holly bud moth, 98
holly leafminers, 208
holly looper, 130
holly pit scale, 342
holly scale, 354
hollyhock leaf skeletonizer, 110
hollyhock sawfly, 84
hollyhock weevil, 280
Homadaula anisocentra, 86
Homalodisca coagulata, 364
Homoeosoma electellum, 254
honey bee, 572
honeydew, 12
honeylocust borer, 476
honeylocust leafhopper, 364
honeylocust plant bug, 376
honeylocust podgall midge, 418
honeylocust rust mite, 405
honeylocust spider mite, 400
honeysuckle aphid, 300
hop aphid, 300
hop flea beetle, 200
hop vine borer, 472
hoplia beetle, 270
Hoplia callipyge, 270
Hoplia modesta, 270
Hoplia oregona, 270
Hoplocampa cookei, 266
Hoplocampa lacteipennis, 266
Hoplocampa testudinea, 266
Hormaphis hamamelidis, 408
horned oak gall, 424
horned spanworm, 132
horned squash bug, 372
hornet moth, 466
hornets, 242–45, 556

horntails, 446, 460
hornworms, 28, 146–49
horseradish flea beetle, 198
horshair worms, 570
hover flies, 550
hummingbird clearwing, 148
hummingbird moths, 146–49
hunting billbug, 542
hunting wasps, 558
Hyadaphis foeniculi, 300
Hyalophora cecropia, 154
Hyalopterus pruni, 300
Hydraecia immanis, 472
Hydraecia micacea, 472
Hylephila phyleus, 106
Hyles lineata, 148
Hylesinus aculeatus, 492
Hylesinus californicus, 492
Hylesinus criddlei, 492
Hylobius pales, 454
Hylurgopinus rufipes, 492
Hyphantria cunea, 118
Hyposoter species, 564
Hysteroneura setariae, 300

Icerya purchasi, 340
ichneumonid wasps, 564
imperial moth, 156
imported cabbageworm, 166
imported currantworm, 76
imported willow leaf beetle, 180
inchworms, 28, 128
Indian wax scale, 334
insect parasites, 564–67
insect pathogens, 568–71
intermountain leafhopper, 358
introduced basswood thrips, 388
introduced pine sawfly, 74
io moth, 156
Ips avulus, 496
Ips beetles, 496
Ips calligraphus, 496
Ips confusus, 496
Ips hunteri, 496
Ips pini, 496
Iridothrips iridis, 388
iris borer, 472,
iris thrips, 388
iris whitefly, 288
irregular pine scale, 336
Isabella moth, 126
Itame ribearia, 130
ivy aphid, 304
ivy scale, 352

jack pine budworm, 104
jack pine tube moth, 98
Jadera haematoloma, 230
Janetiella brevicauda, 420
Japanese beetle, 34, 268, 526

Japanese maple scale, 354
Japanese mealybug, 322
Japanese wax scale, 334
Jerusalem cricket, 58
Jonthonota nigripes, 188
jumping oak gall wasp, 426
jumping spiders, 560
June beetles, 526
juniper berry mite, 432
juniper midge, 458
juniper sawfly, 74
juniper scale, 352
juniper spittlebug, 370
juniper tip midge, 420
juniper twig girdler, 440
juniper webworm, 86

Kaliofenusa ulmi, 210
katydids, 10, 58
Keiferia lycopersicella, 266
kermes scales, 342

Labidura riparia, 554
lace bugs, 384
lacewings, 8, 548
lady beetles, 202, 544
lady bugs, 544
ladybird beetles, 544
Lambdina fiscellaria, 132
Lambdina pellucidaria, 132
Lambdina punctata, 132
lantana lacebug, 384
larch aphid, 396
larch casebearer, 162
large aspen tortrix, 98
large carpenter bees, 448, 574
large chestnut weevil, 282
large oak-apple gall, 426
larger canna leafroller, 106
larger elm leaf beetle, 178
larger sod webworm, 92
latania scale, 352
laurel psyllid, 416
lawn leafhopper, 364
Leach's crambus, 92
leaf beetles, 29–30, 178–203, 220–21
leaf crumpler, 164
leafcurl ash aphid, 306
leafcurl plum aphid, 300
leafcutter bees, 70, 448, 574
leaffooted bugs, 232
leaffooted pine seed bug, 232
leafhoppers, 10, 356–65
leafminers, 30, 204–21
leafrollers, 28, 96–103
Lecanodiaspis prosopidis, 342
Lecanopsis formicarum, 508
Leiobunum species, 562
Leiophron species, 564
Lema trilinea, 192

leopard moth, 468
Lepidosaphes beckii, 346
Lepidosaphes camelliae, 346
Lepidosaphes pallida, 346
Lepidosaphes pini, 346
Lepidosaphes sciadopitysi, 346
Lepidosaphes ulmi, 344
Lepidosaphes yanangicola, 346
Leptinotarsa decemlineata, 184
Leptinotarsa juncta, 184
Leptoglossus clypealis, 232
Leptoglossus corculus, 232
Leptoglossus occidentalis, 232
Leptoglossus phyllopus, 232
Leptomastix species, 566
lesser appleworm, 250
lesser bulb fly, 43–44, 516
lesser canna leafroller, 102
lesser lawn leafhopper, 364
lesser peachtree borer, 464
lettuce aphid, 300
lettuce root aphid, 300, 408, 506
Leucoma salicis, 122
Lewis spider mite, 400
lightning bugs, 548
Ligyrus gibbosus, 530
lilac leafminer, 214
lilac rust mite, 406
lilac/ash borer, 462–64
limabean pod borer, 264
Limax flavus, 48
Limax maximus, 48
Limenitis archippus, 174
Limonius species, 542
linden borer, 482
linden leaf beetle, 180
linden looper, 130
linden spider mite, 400
linden wart gall, 420
Linepithema humile, 68
Liriomyza brassicae, 206
Liriomyza huidobrensis, 206
Liriomyza sativae, 206
Liriomyza trifolii, 206
Listroderes difficilis, 538
Listronotus oregonensis, 538
Lithophane antennata, 262
Lithophane unimoda, 262
locust borer, 480
locust leafminer, 220
locust twig borer, 442
locust, 52–55, 436
long-beaked clover aphid, 300
longhorned beetles, 456, 480–87
Longistigma caryae, 306
longlegged flies, 550
longrose gall wasp, 426
longtail skipper, 106
longtailed mealybug, 318
loopers, 28, 130, 132, 144

Lophocampa argentata, 124
Lophocampa caryae, 124
Lophocampa harrisii, 124
Lopholeucaspis japonica, 354
Lopidea confluenta, 226
Lopidea davisi, 226
lovebugs, 520
Loxagrotis albicosta, 140
Loxostege cerealis, 90
Loxostege sticticalis, 90
luna moth, 154
Lycoriella spp., 522
Lygaeus angustomariginatus, 232
Lygaeus kalmii, 232
Lygus elisus, 226
Lygus hesperus, 226
Lygus lineolaris, 224
Lymantria dispar, 116
lynx spiders, 560
lyonetia leafminer, 216
Lyonetia speculella, 216
Lysiphlebus species, 566
Lytta species, 176

Maconellicoccus hirsutus, 322
Macremphytus tarsatus, 80
Macrocentrus species, 564
Macrodactylus subspinosus, 270
Macrodactylus uniformis, 270
Macrohaltica ambiens, 200
Macronocutua onusta, 472
Macropsis fumipennis, 364
Macropsis graminea, 364
Macropsis ocellata, 364
Macropsis trimaculata, 364
Macrosiphoniella sanborni, 306
Macrosiphum euphorbiae, 300
Macrosiphum rosae, 306
Macrosteles quadrilineatus, 362
Madeira mealybug, 322
madrone shield bearer, 218
Magicicada septendecim, 436
Magicicada tredecim, 436
magnolia scale, 334
magnolia white scale, 352
Malacosoma americanum, 112
Malacosoma californicum, 112
Malacosoma constrictum, 114
Malacosoma disstria, 114
Malacosoma incurvum, 114
Malacosoma tigris, 114
Maladera castanea, 530
Mamestra configurata, 140
Manduca quinquemaculata, 146
Manduca sexta, 146
mantids, 10, 554
Mantis religiosa, 554
manzanita leaf gall aphid, 408
maple bladder gall mite, 430
maple gouty veingall midge, 418

maple leafcutter, 164
maple leafhopper, 360
maple leafminer, 212
maple mealybug, 322
maple petiole borer, 446
maple spider mite, 400
maple spindlegall mite, 430
maple trumpet skeletonizer, 164
maple twig borer, 442
March flies, 520
Margarodes meriodionalis, 508
margarodid scales, 340
margined blister beetle, 176
Marmara salictella, 208
marsh slug, 48
Maskell scale, 346
mason bees, 574
Matsucoccus acalyptus, 340
May beetles, 526
McDaniel mite, 394
meadow spittlebug, 368
mealy plum aphid, 300
mealybugs, 37, 316–23, 506
measuring worms, 128
Medetera species, 550
Megachile rotunda, 70
Megachile species, 70
Megacyllene antennatus, 480
Megacyllene caryae, 480
Megacyllene robiniae, 480
Megalopyge opercularis, 158
Megarhyssa species, 564
Melanaspis obscura, 354
Melanaspis tenebricosa, 354
Melanchra picta, 142
Melanocallis caryaefoliae, 306
Melanophila fulvoguttata, 478
Melanoplus bivittatus, 52
Melanoplus differentialis, 52
Melanoplus femurrubrum, 52
Melanoplus sanguinipes, 52
Melitara dentata, 470
Melitta cucurbitae, 462
Meloe species, 176
melon aphid, 300–304
melon thrips, 388
melonworm, 264
Merhynchites bicolor, 278
Mermis nigrescens, 570
mermithid nematodes, 570
Merodon equestis, 516
mesquite borer, 480
mesquite stinger, 158
metallic wood borers, 42–43, 474–79
Metallus rubi, 210
metamorphosis, 2–4
Metaphycus species, 566
Metarhizium anisopliae, 30, 568
Metolophium dirhodum, 300

Mexican bean beetle, 28–29, 202, 544
Mexican corn rootworm, 192
Mexican mealybug, 322
Micrathena species, 560
Microcentrum rhombifolium, 58
Microcrambus elegans, 92
Microtheca ochroloma, 190
Micrutalis calva, 366
midget milky garden slug, 48
migratory grasshopper, 52
milky garden slug, 48
milky spore, 568
miller moth, 138
millipedes, 502
mimosa webworm, 86
Mindarus abietus, 306
mineola moth, 252
minute cypress scale, 352
minute pirate bugs, 554
Miscanthiococcus miscanthi, 506
miscanthus mealybug, 506
Mischocyttarus flavitarsis, 556
mites, 10, 40, 392–401, 404–8,
  430–33, 508, 562
Mocus latipes, 132
mole crickets, 512
monarch, 174
Monarthropalpus flavus, 208
Moneilema annulatum, 486
Moneilema appressum, 486
Moneilema armatum, 486
Moneilema semipunctatum, 486
Monellia caryella, 306
Monelliopsis pecanis, 306
Monocesta coryli, 178
Monochamus clamator, 486
Monochamus scutellatus, 486
Monochamus titillator, 486
Monochroa fragariae, 442
Monoctenus fulvus, 74
Monoctenus melliceps, 74
Monophadnoides geniculatus, 78
Mordwilkoja vagabunda, 300
Mordwilkoja vagabunda, 408
Mormon cricket, 58
morning glory prominent, 152
morningglory leafminer, 216
mossyrose gall wasp, 426
moth flies, 522
mottled tortoise beetle, 188
mountain leafhopper, 362
mountain pine beetle, 494
mountain-ash sawfly, 78
mourning cloak, 174
mud daubers, 558
mulberry whitefly, 286
mullein bug, 226
multicolored Asian lady beetle, 544
Murgantia histrionica, 382
Myzinum species, 564

Myzocallis alhambra, 306
Myzocallis coryli, 306
Myzus ascalonicus, 306
Myzus cerasi, 300
Myzus persicae, 298–300

Nalepella halourga, 406
Nalepella octonema, 406
Nalepella tsugifoliae, 406
Nanokermes pubescens, 342
Nantucket pine tip moth, 438
narcissus bulb fly, 43–44, 516
Narnia snowi, 372
Nasonia species, 566
Nasonovia ribisnigri, 300
native elm bark beetle, 492
native fire ant, 66
native holly leafminer, 208
Naupactus species, 538
navel orangeworm, 252
Nearctaphis bakeri, 300
Nearctaphis crataegifoliae, 300
needleminers, 204, 216–19
Nematocampa limbata, 132
Nematocampa resistaria, 132
nematode diseases of insect, 570
Nematus lipvskyi, 76
Nematus ribesii, 76
Nematus ventralis, 76
Nemocestes incomptus, 534
Neochlamisus cribripennis, 190
Neochlamisus platani, 190
Neoclytus acuminatus, 484
Neoclytus caprea, 484
Neoclytus muricatulus, 484
Neodiprion autumnalis, 74
Neodiprion edulicolis, 74
Neodiprion excitans, 74
Neodiprion lecontei, 72
Neodiprion pinetum, 74
Neodiprion sertifer, 72
Neodiprion swainei, 74
Neodiprion tsugae, 74
Neolecanium cornuparvum, 334
Neoptilia malvacearum, 84
Neotephritis finalis, 240
Nephelodes minians, 138
Nephila clavipes, 560
Nepticula slingerlandella, 212
Neurotoma fasciata, 108
Neurotoma inconspicua, 108
Neurotus saltatorius, 426
Nevada buck moth, 156
New England buck moth, 156
Nezara viridula, 228
Niesthrea louisianica, 232
nigra scale, 330
Norape ovina, 158
Norape tenera, 158
Norfolk Island pine eriococcin, 326

northern corn rootworm, 192
northern masked chafer, 524
northern pine weevil, 450
northern pitch twig moth, 440
Norway maple aphid, 306
Nosema locustae, 27, 568
noxious bamboo mealybug, 322
Nuclaspis californica, 350
Nymphalis antiopa, 174
Nymphuiella daeckealis, 102
Nysius angustatus, 380
Nysius niger, 380
Nysius raphanus, 380

oak apple galls, 426
oak bark beetles, 42, 452
oak clearwing moth, 466
oak eriococcin, 326
oak gall wasps, 424–29
oak lace bug, 384
oak leafminers, 216
oak leafroller, 96
oak lecanium, 332
oak looper, 132
oak mite, 396
oak ribbed skeletonizer, 110
oak shothole leafminer, 208
oak skeletonizer, 110
oak sprout oberea, 456
oak treehopper, 366
oak twig girdler, 476
oak webworm, 96
Oberea bimaculata, 456
Oberea delongi, 456
Oberea gracilis, 456
Oberea myops, 456
Oberea ocellata, 456
Oberea ruficollis, 456
Oberea tripunctata, 456
obliquebanded leafroller, 98
obscure mealybug, 318
obscure root weevil, 534
obscure scale, 354
ocellate gall midge, 420
Odonaspis ruthae, 508
Odonaspsis penicillata, 354
Odontopus calceatus, 220
Odontota dorsalis, 220
Oecanthus species, 56
Oechanthus fultoni, 56
oil beetles, 176
Okanagana species, 436
okra caterpillar, 142
oleander aphid, 306
oleander caterpillar, 124
oleander pit scale, 342
oleander scale, 352
Oligonychus aceris, 400
Oligonychus bicolor, 396
Oligonychus boudreauxi, 400

Oligonychus ilicis, 396
Oligonychus milleri, 400
Oligonychus newcomeri, 400
Oligonychus platani, 400
Oligonychus pratensis, 398
Oligonychus subnudus, 400
Oligonychus ununguis, 396
Oligonychus viridis, 400
Oligotrophus betheli, 420
olive scale, 354
omnivorous leafroller, 100
omnivorous leaftier, 100
omnivorous looper, 132
Omphalocerca dentosa, 88
Oncideres cingulata, 456
Onciscus asellus, 500
one-eyed sphinx, 148
onespotted stink bug, 228
onion bulb fly, 43–44, 516
onion maggot, 43–44, 516
onion thrips, 386
Operophtera bruceata, 130
Ophiomyia simplex, 206
Ophion species, 564
Opius species, 564
opuntia bug, 372
orange tortrix, 98
orangedog, 170
orangehumped mapleworm, 152
orangestriped oakworm, 156
orb-web spiders, 560
Orgyia pseudotsugata, 120
oriental beetle, 528
oriental fruit moth, 250
Orthosia hibisci, 262
Orygia antiqua, 122
Orygia leucostigma, 120
Orygia vetusta, 122
Osmia species, 574
Ostrinia nubilalis, 444
Ostrinia penitalis, 102
Otiorhynchus ovatus, 534
Otiorhynchus rugosostriatus, 534
Otiorhynchus singularis, 534
Otiorhynchus sulcatus, 532
oystershell scale, 344

Pachylobius picivorus, 454
Pachypsylla celtidisastericus, 414
Pachypsylla celtidisgemma, 414
Pachypsylla celtidisinteneris, 414
Pachypsylla celtidismamma, 414
Pachypsylla celtidivescula, 414
Pachypsylla venusta, 414
Pachysphinx occidentalis, 148
Pacific flathead borer, 478
Pacific spider mite, 400
Pacific tent caterpillar, 114
Pacific willow leaf beetle, 180
painted hickory borer, 480

painted lady, 172
painted leafhopper, 364
pale legume bug, 226
pale tussock moth, 124
Paleacrita vernata, 128
pales weevil, 454
palestriped flea beetle, 200
palmetto weevil, 488
Pamphilius dentatus, 108
Pamphilius persicus, 108
Pamphilius phyllisae, 108
Pandemis cerasana, 100
Pandemis limitata, 100
Pandemis pyrusana, 100
pandora moth, 156
Panonychus caglei, 400
Panonychus citri, 400
Panonychus ulmi, 394
pansyworm, 174
Panthaleus major, 398
Papaipema nebris, 472
paper wasps, 556
Papilio brevicauda, 170
Papilio cresphontes, 170
Papilio glaucus, 170
Papilio multicaudatus, 170
Papilio polyxenes, 168
Papilio rutulus, 170
Papilio zelicaon, 170
Paraclemensia acerifoliella, 164
Paraleucoptera heinrichi, 216
Paranapiacaba trincincta, 196
Parandra brunnea, 484
Paranthene asilipennis, 466
Paranthene dollii, 466
Paranthene robiniae, 466
Paranthene simulans, 466
Parapediasia teterrella, 92
Paraphytoptus chrysanthemi, 406
Paraprociphilus tessellatus, 312
Parasa indetermina, 158
Parasaissetia nigra, 330
parasites, 564–67
parasitic wasps, 564–67
parasitoids, 564–67
Paratrioza cockerelli, 290
Paria fragariae, 182
Parlatoria oleae, 354
parsleyworm, 168
Parthenolecanium corni, 332
Parthenolecanium fletcheri, 332
Parthenolecanium persicae, 332
Parthenolecanium pruinosum, 332
Parthenolecanium quercifex, 332
pavement ant, 68
pea aphid, 304
pea leafminer, 206
pea moth, 248
peach sawfly, 108
peach silver mite, 406

peach tree borer, 464
peach twig borer, 442
Pealius azaleae, 286
pear decline, 292
pear leafcurling midge, 418
pear psylla, 292
pear rust mite, 406
pear sawfly, 82
pear thrips, 388
pearleaf blister mite, 430
pearslug, 82
pecan carpenterworm, 468
pecan cigar casebearer, 162
pecan leaf casebearer, 162
pecan leaf phylloxera, 412
pecan leaf roll mite, 430
pecan leaf scorch mite, 400
pecan nut casebearer, 252
pecan phylloxera, 248, 412
pecan shoot curculio, 454
pecan spittlebug, 370
pecan weevil, 248, 282
Pediasia bonifatellus, 92
Pediasia trisecta, 92
Pegomya betae, 204
Pegomya rubivora, 458
Pegomyia hyoscyami, 204
pelecinid wasps, 566
Pelecinus polyturator, 566
Pemphigus betae, 408
Pemphigus bursarius, 300, 408, 506
Pemphigus populicaulis, 408
Pemphigus populiramulorum, 408
Pemphigus populitransversus, 408
Pemphigus populivenae, 300, 408, 506
Pemphredon wasps, 448, 558
penicillate scale, 354
Pennisetia marginata, 466
Pennsylvania leatherwing, 546
Penstemonia clarkei, 466
Pentamerismus erythreus, 404
Pentamerismus taxi, 404
pepper maggot, 238
pepper weevil, 280
peppertree psyllid, 416
Peridroma saucia, 134
Perilampus species, 566
Perillus bioculatus, 550
periodical cicada, 436
Periphyllus lyropictus, 306
Periphyllus negundinis, 306
Periploca ceanothiella, 444
Periploca nigra, 440
persimmon borer, 466
petiolegall aphids, 408, 506
Petrobia latens, 398
Petrova albicapitana, 440
Peucetia viridans, 560
Phalangium opilio, 562
Phenacoccus acericola, 322

Phenacoccus aceris, 322
Phenacoccus dearnessi, 320
Phenacoccus gossypii, 322
Phenacoccus japonicus, 322
Phenacoccus madeirensis, 322
Phenacoccus maritimus, 320
Phidippus species, 560
Philaenus spumarius, 368
Phloeosinus species, 452
phlox plant bug, 226
Phobetron pithecium, 158
Phoenix billbug, 542
Phoracantha semipunctata, 484
Phorodon humuli, 300
Phryganidia californica, 152
Phyllaphis fagi, 306, 312
Phyllobius intrusus, 534
Phyllobius oblongus, 534
Phyllocnistis populiella, 216
Phyllocolpa bozemani, 80
Phyllocoptes didelphis, 430
Phyllocoptes gracilis, 432
Phyllocoptruta oleivora, 406
Phyllonorycter aceriella, 212
Phyllonorycter blancardella, 212
Phyllonorycter crataegella, 212
Phyllonorycter lucetiella, 212
Phyllonorycter mispilella, 212
Phyllonorycter nipigon, 212
Phyllonorycter salicifoliella, 212
Phyllonorycter tremuloidiella, 212
Phyllophaga crinita, 526
Phyllornorycter elmaella, 212
Phyllotreta albionica, 198
Phyllotreta armoraciae, 198
Phyllotreta cruciferae, 198
Phyllotreta pusilla, 198
Phyllotreta ramosa, 198
Phyllotreta striolata, 198
Phylloxera caryaecaulis, 412
Phylloxera devastatrix, 412
Phylloxera notabilis, 412
Phylloxera russellae, 412
phylloxerans, 412
Phymata species, 552
Physokermes piceae, 336
Phytobia species, 208
Phytocoptella avellanae, 432
Phytomyza aquilegiae, 208
Phytomyza atricornis, 208
Phytomyza chrysanthemi, 208
Phytomyza delphinivora, 208
Phytomyza ilicis, 208
Phytomyza ililocola, 208
Phytomyza minuscula, 208
Phytonemus pallidus, 402
Phytoptus cerasicrumena, 430
Phytoptus laevis, 430
Phytoptus tiliae, 430
pickleworm, 264

picnic beetle, 274
Pierce's disease of grape, 364
Pieris rapae, 166
pigeon tremex, 460
Pikonema alaskensis, 74
pillbug, 500
pin oak sawfly, 82
pine bark adelgid, 314
pine bud mite, 432
pine budworm, 104
pine engraver, 496
pine false webworm, 108
pine leaf adelgid, 410
pine needle scale, 346
pine needle sheathminer, 216
pine oystershell scale, 346
pine sawyers, 486
pine tip moths, 41–42, 438–41
pine tortoise scale, 336
pine tube moth, 98
pine webworm, 88
pine wilt nematode, 486
pineleaf scale, 346
Pineus pinifoliae, 410
Pineus strobi, 314
pink hibiscus mealybug, 322
pink-spotted hawkmoth, 148
Pinnaspis aspidistrae, 350
pinyon needle scale, 340
pinyon pitch mass borer, 470
pinyon pitch nodulemaker, 440
pinyon sawfly, 74
pinyon spindlegall midge, 420
pinyon stunt needlegall midge, 420
pinyon tip moth, 440
Pinyonia edulicola, 420
Pissodes approximatus, 450
Pissodes nemorensis, 450
Pissodes strobi, 450
pistol casebearer, 162
pit scales, 342
pitch mass borer, 466
pitch midges, 458
pitcheating weevil, 454
pitmaking pittosporum scale, 342
Pityogenes species, 452
Pityophthorus species, 452
Plagiodera versicolor, 180
Plagiognathus albatus, 376
Plagiognathus punctatipes, 376
Planoccoccus citri, 316
plant bugs, 224–27, 374–77, 552
plant diseases vectored by insects, 24
plantain looper, 144
plantanus spider mite, 400
Platycotis vittata, 366
Platynota flavedana, 98
Platynota idaeusalis, 98
Platynota stultana, 100
Platypedia putnami, 436

Platypilia carduidactyla, 256
Platyptilia antirrhina, 256
Platytetranychus libocedri, 400
Platytetranychus multidigituli, 400
Platytetranychus thujae, 400
Plecia nearctica, 520
Plecoma minor, 530
Plecoma oregonensis, 530
Plectodera scalator, 484
Pleocoma crinita, 530
plum curculio, 276
plum gouger, 278
plum leafhopper, 364
plum rust mite, 406
plum webspinning sawfly, 108
Plutella xylostella, 94
Pococerca robustella, 88
Podabrus species, 546
Podisus maculiventris, 550
Podosesia aureocincta, 464
Podosesia syringae, 462–64
Poecilocapsus lineatus, 374
Pogonomyrmex species, 68
pole borer, 484
Polistes dominulus, 556
pollinators, 572–75
Polydrusus impressifrons, 534
polydrusus weevil, 534
Polygonia interrogationis, 174
Polyphagotarsonemus latus, 402
polyphemus moth, 156
Polyphylla comes, 526
Polyphylla decimlineata, 526
Polyphylla hammondi, 526
Polyphylla variolosa, 526
pomace flies, 238
ponderosa pine needleminer, 218
ponderosa pine spider mite, 400
ponderosa pine tip moth, 440
ponderous borer, 486
Pontania proxima, 428
Pontania s-pomum, 428
Pontia protodice, 166
Popillia japonica, 268, 526
poplar and willow borer, 488
poplar blackmine beetle, 220
poplar borer, 482
poplar budgall mite, 432
poplar carpenterworm, 468
poplar clearwing, 466
poplar dagger moth, 124
poplar leaf aphid, 304
poplar leaffolding sawfly, 80
poplar petiolegall aphid, 408
poplar tentmaker, 152
poplar twig borer, 456
poplar twiggall aphid, 408
poplar twiggall fly, 422
poplar vagabond aphid, 300, 408
poplar-gall saperda, 482

Porcellio laevis, 500
Porcellio scaber, 500
potato aphid, 300
potato bug, 58, 184, 500
potato flea beetle, 198
potato leafhopper, 358–58
potato psyllid, 290
potato stalk borer, 454
potato stem borer, 472
potter wasps, 558
prairie walkingstick, 60
praying mantids, 554
predatory ants, 556
predatory midges, 550
predatory mites, 40, 562
predatory plant bugs, 552
predatory thrips, 40, 550
Prionoxystus robiniae, 468
Prionus californicus, 486
Prionus imbricornis, 486
Prionus laticollis, 486
Pristophora abbreviata, 78
Pristophora aquiligae, 78
Pristophora geniculata, 78
Pristophora serrula, 78
Pritchard's ground mealybug, 506
privet leafhopper, 362, 364
privet mite, 404
privet rust mite, 406
privet thrips, 388
Prociphilus americanus, 300, 312
Prociphilus caryae, 312
Prochiulus fraxinifolii, 306, 312
Profenusa canadensis, 210
promethea moth, 156
prominent moths, 150–53
Prosapia bicincta, 368
Proteoteras aesculana, 442
Proteoteras willingana, 442
protozoan diseases, 568
Pryeria sinica, 110
Pseudaletia unipuncta, 138
Pseudaulacaspis cockerelli, 352
Pseudaulacaspis pentagona, 354
Pseudaulacaspis prunicola, 354
Pseudococcus comstocki, 318
Pseudococcus longispinus, 318
Pseudococcus viburni, 318
Pseudopityophthorus species, 452
Pseudoplusia includens, 144
Psila rosae, 518
Psychoda species, 522
psyllids, 10, 290–95, 414
Psylliodes punctulata, 200
Pterocomma smithiae, 306
pteromalid wasps, 566
Pteromalus species, 566
Pterophylla carnellifolia, 58
Pulvinaria acericola, 338
Pulvinaria floccifera, 338

Pulvinaria innumerabilis, 338
purple scale, 346
purplebacked cabbageworm, 90
puss caterpillar, 158
Putnam scale, 354
Putnam's cicada, 436
pyramidal fruitworm, 262
Pyrrhalta decora, 180
Pyrrhalta luteola, 178
Pyrrhalta viburni, 180
Pyrrharctia isabella, 126

Quadraspidiotus forbesi, 348
Quadraspidiotus perniciosus, 348
Quadrispidiotus juglansregiae, 348
question-mark, 174

radish root maggot, 43–44, 514
rain beetles, 530
raspberry cane borer, 456
raspberry cane maggot, 458
raspberry crown borer, 466
raspberry fruitworms, 274
raspberry horntail, 446
raspberry red mite, 400
raspberry sawfly, 78
rattailed maggot, 550
red admiral, 172
red bay psyllid, 416
red carpenter ant, 68
red imported fire ant, 66
red oak clearwing borer, 466
red sunflower beetle, 280
red turnip beetle, 190
red turpentine beetle, 494
red wax scale, 334
redbacked cutworm, 138
redbanded leafroller, 98
redberry mite, 432
redbud leaffolder, 100
redgum lerp psyllid, 294
redheaded ash borer, 484
redheaded flea beetle, 200
redheaded pine sawfly, 72
redheaded sharpshooter, 364
redhumped caterpillar, 152
redhumped oakworm, 152
redlegged grasshopper, 52
rednecked cane borer, 476
redshouldered stink bug, 228
resplendent shield bearer, 218
Resseliella clavula, 422
Reticulitermes flavipes, 510
Reticulitermes hesperus, 510
Reticulitermes tibialis, 510
Reticulitermes virginicus, 510
Retinia arizonensis, 440
Retinia metallica, 440
Rhabdophaga rigidae, 420
Rhabdophaga strobiloides, 420

Rhabdopterus picipes, 182
Rhagoletis cingulata, 234
Rhagoletis completa, 236
Rhagoletis fausta, 236
Rhagoletis indifferens, 236
Rhagoletis mendax, 236
Rhagoletis pomonella, 234
Rheumaptera hastata, 130
Rhizoecus falcifer, 506
Rhizoecus pritchardii, 506
Rhizoglyphus echinopus, 508
Rhizoglyphus engeli, 508
Rhizoglyphus hyacinthi, 508
Rhizoglyphus robini, 508
Rhizotrogus majalis, 528
rhodesgrass mealybug, 506
rhododendron borer, 466
rhododendron gall midge, 420
rhododendron lace bug, 384
rhododendron whitefly, 286
Rhopalomyia chrysanthemi, 420
Rhopalosiphum insertum, 302
Rhopalosiphum maidis, 306
Rhopalosiphum nymphaeae, 302
Rhopalosiphum padi, 302
Rhopobota naevana, 98
Rhyaciona frustrana, 438
Rhyacionia buoliana, 438
Rhyacionia bushnelli, 438
Rhyacionia neomexicana, 438
Rhynchaenus pallicarnis, 220
Rhynchaenus rufipes, 220
Rhynchophorus cruentatus, 488
Rhyncothrips ilex, 388
ribbed bud gall, 424
ridged bunch gall wasp, 424
ringlegged earwig, 62
Rocky Mountain juniper aphid, 306
roly-poly galls, 424
roly-poly hunters, 560
roly-poly, 500
Romalea guttata, 54
root aphids, 408, 506
root maggots, 43–44, 514–17
root weevils, 45, 532–39
rose aphid, 306
rose blister gall wasp, 426
rose chafer, 270
rose curculio, 278
rose grass aphid, 300
rose leafhopper, 358
rose midge, 240
rose scale, 354
rose shoot sawfly, 446
rose stem girdler, 476
rose stem-boring sawfly, 446
roseroot gall wasp, 426
roseslug, 82
rosy apple aphid, 300
rough bulletgall wasp, 424

rough stink bugs, 228
rough strawberry root weevil, 534
roundheaded appletree borer, 482
roundheaded borers, 456, 480–87
rove beetles, 546
royal moths, 154–57
Rumina decollata, 50
rust mites, 404–8
rusty plum aphid, 300
rusty tussock moth, 122

Sabulodes aegrotata, 132
Sabulodes caberata, 132
saddleback caterpillar, 158
saddled prominent, 152
Saisettia coffae, 330
Saissetia oleae, 330
saltmarsh caterpillar, 126
San Jose scale, 348
sandhill chafer, 270
sandwich-man caterpillar, 102
Sannia uroceriformis, 466
sap beetles, 272–75
Saperda calcarata, 482
Saperda candida, 482
Saperda inornata, 482
Saperda obliqua, 482
Saperda vestia, 482
Saratoga spittlebug, 370
sassafras borer, 456
satin moth, 122
sawflies, 8, 28, 72–85, 446
Say's stink bug, 228
scales, 10, 37–39, 324–55
Scaphoideus acutus, 362
Scaphoideus luteolus, 364
Scaphytopius irroratus, 362
Scapteriscus abbreviatus, 512
Scapteriscus borellii, 512
Scapteriscus vicinus, 512
scarab beetles, 268, 524–29
scarlet oak sawfly, 82
Scatella stagnalis, 522
Sceliphron species, 558
Schizura concinna, 152
Schizura ipomoeae, 152
Schizura unicornis, 152
Schoenei spider mite, 400
Sciopithes obscures, 534
Scolopendra species, 562
Scolothrips sexmaculatus, 550
Scolytus multistriatus, 492
Scolytus quadrispinosus, 492
Scolytus rugulosus, 490
Scolytus schevyrewi, 492
scurfy scale, 346
Scutigerella immaculata, 502
Scyphophorus acupunctatus, 488
Scyphophorus yuccae, 488
seed bugs, 378–81

seedcorn maggot, 43–44, 514
sequoia pitch moth, 466
serpentine leafminer, 206
Sesia apiformis, 466
Sesia tibialis, 466
Setoptus strobacus, 406
seventeen-year cicada, 436
seventeen-year locust, 436
shallot aphid, 306
shield bearers, 218
Shivaphis celti, 306, 312
Shizaphis graminum, 306
shore flies, 522
shortailed swallowtail, 170
short-winged mole cricket, 512
shothole borer, 490
Sibine stimulea, 158
silk, 12
silkworms, 154–57
silver-barred webworm, 92
silverleaf whitefly, 286
silverspotted skipper, 106
silverspotted tiger moth, 124
silver-striped webworm, 92
Sinea diadema, 552
sinuate peartree borer, 476
Siphonius phillyreae, 288
Sirex species, 460
Sitobion avenae, 306
six-spined engraver, 496
sixspotted leafhopper, 362
six-spotted thrips, 550
skeletonizers, 110
skippers, 106
slug caterpillars, 158
slug sawflies, 82
slugs, 26, 48–51
small black and green willow aphid, 304
small carpenter bees, 448
small chestnut weevil, 282
small fruit flies, 238
small milkweed bug, 232
small southern pine engraver, 496
smaller European elm bark beetle, 492
Smerinthus cerisyi, 148
Smerinthus jamaicensis, 148
Smicronyx fulvus, 280
Smicronyx sordidus, 280
snailcase bagworm, 160
snails, 26, 48
snapdragon plume moth, 256
snow flea, 504
snowball aphid, 300
snowberry clearwing, 148
snowy tree cricket, 56
sod webworm, 92–95
soft scales, 37–38, 328–39
soldier beetles, 546
Solenopsis geminata, 66

Solenopsis invicta, 66
Solenopsis richteri, 66
Solenopsis xyloni, 66
Sonoran tent caterpillar, 114
southeastern field cricket, 56
southeastern subterranean termite, 510
southern armyworm, 136
southern cabbageworm, 166
southern chinch bug, 380
southern corn rootworm, 196
southern fire ant, 66
southern garden leafhopper, 358
southern green stink bug, 228
southern masked chafer, 524
southern mole cricket, 512
southern pecan leaf phylloxera, 412
southern pine beetle, 494
southern pine coneworm, 254
southern pine sawyer, 486
southern red mite, 396
southwestern masked chafer, 524
southwestern pine tip moth, 438
southwestern tent caterpillar, 114
sowbugs, 500
soybean looper, 144
Spalangia species, 566
Spanish moth, 472
spanworms, 128, 130
sparganothis leafroller, 100
Sparganothis sulfureana, 100
spear-marked black moth, 130
speckled green fruitworm, 262
Sphecius species, 558
Sphenophorus cicatristriatus, 542
Sphenophorus parvulus, 540
Sphenophorus phoeniciensis, 542
Sphenophorus venatus vestitus, 542
Sphinx chersis, 148
sphinx moths, 146–49
spider mite destroyers, 40, 544
spider mites, 40, 392–401
Spilonota ocellana, 96
Spilosoma virginica, 126
spinach flea beetle, 200
spinach leafminer, 204
spined assassin bug, 552
spined soldier bug, 30, 550
spined turban gall wasp, 426
spine-tailed earwigs, 554
spiny elm caterpillar, 174
spiny oakworm, 156
spiny witch-hazel gall aphid, 408
spinyrose gall wasp, 426
spirea aphid, 300
Spissistilus festinus, 366
spittlebugs, 368–71
Spodoptera eridania, 136
Spodoptera exigua, 136
Spodoptera frugiperda, 134, 136
Spodoptera ornithogalli, 136

Spodoptera praefica, 136
spotted asparagus beetle, 186
spotted blister beetle, 176
spotted cucumber beetle, 196
spotted cutworm, 140
spotted garden slug, 48
spotted oleander caterpillar, 124
spotted pine sawyer, 486
spotted tentiform leafminer, 212
spring cankerworm, 128
spring field cricket, 56
spring rose beetle, 270
springtails, 10, 504
spruce beetle, 494
spruce bud scale, 336
spruce budworm, 104
spruce coneworm, 254
spruce ips, 496
spruce needleminer, 216
spruce rust mite, 406
spruce spider mite, 396
squash beetle, 202, 544
squash bug, 40, 232, 372
squash vine borer, 43, 462
Stagmomantis species, 554
stalk borer, 472
steel-blue grapevine flea beetle, 200
Steinernema species, 29, 39, 44, 570
Stelidota geminata, 274
Stenopelmatus fuscus, 58
Stephanitis pyrioides, 384
Stephanitis rhododendri, 384
Stephanitis takeyai, 384
Stethorus species, 544
Stictocephala bisonia, 366
stinging rose caterpillar, 158
stink bugs, 228–29, 382, 550
Stomacoccus platani, 340
stone centipedes, 562
Strauzia longipennis, 458
strawberry aphid, 306
strawberry bud weevil, 280
strawberry clipper, 280
strawberry crown borer, 466
strawberry crownminer, 442
strawberry flea beetle, 200
strawberry leafroller, 100
strawberry root weevil, 534
strawberry rootworm, 182
strawberry sap beetle, 274
Strigoderma arboricola, 270
striped blister beetle, 176
striped cucumber beetle, 194
striped earwig, 554
striped flea beetle, 198
striped grassworms, 132
striped mealybug, 322
striped pine scale, 336
striped sod webworm, 92
striped tortoise beetle, 188

Strymon melinus, 256
stubby needlegall midge, 420
succulent oak gall wasp, 424
sugar pine tortrix, 104
sugarbeet root aphid, 300, 408, 506
sugarbeet root maggot, 516
sulfurs, 166
sumac leafroller, 100
sumac stem borer, 456
sunflower aphid, 300
sunflower beetle, 184
sunflower headclipping weevil, 280
sunflower maggot, 458
sunflower midge, 240
sunflower moth, 254
sunflower seed maggot, 240
sunflower stem weevil, 456
Swaine jack pine sawfly, 74
swallowtails, 168–71
sweat bees, 574
sweetpotato flea beetle, 200
sweetpotato hornworm, 148
sweetpotato leaf beetle, 190
sweetpotato weevil, 538
sweetpotato whitefly, 286
sycamore aphid, 306
sycamore borer, 466
sycamore lace bug, 384
sycamore leaf beetle, 190
sycamore leaffolder, 100
sycamore plant bug, 376
sycamore scale, 340
sycamore tussock moth, 124
Symmersia canicosta, 152
Symmersia leucitys, 152
Synanthedon bibionipennis, 466
Synanthedon exitiosa, 464
Synanthedon novaroensis, 466
Synanthedon pictipes, 464
Synanthedon pini, 466
Synanthedon pyri, 466
Synanthedon resplendens, 466
Synanthedon rhododendri, 466
Synanthedon scitula, 466
Synanthedon sequoiae, 466
Synanthedon tipuliformis, 466
Synanthedon viburni, 466
Synclita obliteralis, 102
Syntomeida epilais, 124
syrphid flies, 516, 550
Systena blanda, 200
Systena elongata, 200
Systena frontalis, 200

tachinid flies, 564
Taeniothrips inconsequens, 388
Tamalia coweni, 408
tar spots, 12
tarnished plant bug, 224
tarsonemid mites, 402

tawny emperor, 174
tawny garden slug, 48
tawny mole cricket, 512
taxus bud mite, 432
taxus mealybug, 322
tea scale, 350
Tegenaria species, 562
Tehama bonifatella, 92
Teleonemia scrupulosa, 384
tenlined June beetle, 526
Tenodera aridifolia sinensis, 554
tent caterpillars, 28, 112–15
tentiform leafminer, 212
Tenuipalpus oarchidarum, 404
Tenuipalpus pacificus, 404
termites, 10, 510
terrapin scale, 334
Tetanops myopaeformis, 516
Tethida cordigera, 78
Tetraleurodes mori, 286
Tetramorium caespitum, 68
Tetranychus canadensis, 394
Tetranychus cinnabarinus, 394
Tetranychus humorous, 400
Tetranychus magnoliae, 400
Tetranychus mcdanieli, 394
Tetranychus pacificus, 400
Tetranychus schoenei, 400
Tetranychus urticae, 392–94
Texas leafcutting ant, 64
Thaumatopsis pexellus, 92
Thecabius populiconduplifolius, 302
Thecodiplosis liriodendri, 420
thirteen-year cicada, 436
thistle aphid, 300
thistle caterpillar, 172
thread-legged bugs, 552
threebanded leafhopper, 360
threecornered alfalfa treehopper, 366
threelined blister beetle, 176
threelined leafroller, 100
threelined potato beetle, 192
Thrips calcaratus, 388
Thrips hemerocallis, 388
Thrips palmi, 388
Thrips simplex, 388
Thrips tabaci, 386
thrips, 8, 39–40, 222–23, 386–89, 550
Thyanta accerra, 228
Thyanta custator, 228
Thyanta pallidovirens, 228
Thyridopteryx ephemeraeformis, 160
Thysanopyga intractata, 130
Tibicen species, 436
tiger beetles, 546
tiger moths, 120, 124
tiger swallowtails, 170
tilehorned prionus, 486
Tinocallis kahawaluokalani, 306
Tinocallis saltans, 306

Tinocallis ulmifolii, 306
tip moths, 41–42, 438–45
Tiphia species, 564
tiphiid wasps, 564
Tipula oleracea, 520
Tipula paludosa, 518
Tischeria malifoliella, 218
tobacco budworm, 33, 258
tobacco flea beetle, 198
tobacco hornworm, 146
tobacco thrips, 222
tomato fruitworm, 260
tomato hornworm, 146
tomato pinworm, 266
tomato psyllid, 290
tomato russet mite, 406
Tomicus piniperda, 452
Tomostethus multicinctus, 78
toothed flea beetle, 200
tortoise beetles, 188
Toumeyella liriodendri, 336
Toumeyella parvicornis, 336
Toumeyella pini, 336
Toumeyella pinicola, 336
Townsend scale, 354
Toxoptera aurantii, 306
Toxoptera citricidus, 306
toyon thrips, 388
tree crickets, 56
treehoppers, 366
Tremex columba, 460
Trialeurodes abutilonea, 286
Trialeurodes vaporariorum, 284
Trichiosoma triangulum, 84
Trichiosoma viminalis, 84
Trichobaris trinotata, 454
Trichogramma wasps, 28, 566
Trichoplusia ni, 144
Trioxys species, 566
Trioza alacris, 416
Trioza eugeniae, 416
Trioza magnoliae, 416
Trisetacus campnodus, 432
Trisetacus cupressi, 432
Trisetacus gemmavitians, 432
Trisetacus juniperinus, 432
Trisetacus pini, 432
Trisetacus quadrisetus, 432
Trisetacus thujivagrans, 432
tropical sod webworm, 92
Tropidosteptes amoenus, 376
Tropidosteptes brooksi, 376
Tropidosteptes illitus, 376
Tropidosteptes pacificus, 376
true armyworm, 138
true katydid, 58
tuber flea beetle, 198
Tuberolachnus salignis, 306
tufted apple bud moth, 98
tulip bulb aphid, 306, 506

tuliptree scale, 336
turfgrass scale, 508
turpentine beetles, 494
tussock moths, 28, 120–25
twicestabbed lady beetle, 544
twig beetles, 452
twig girdler, 456
twig pruner, 456
twinspot sphinx, 148
twobanded Japanese weevil, 536
two-circuli mealybug, 320
twolined chestnut borer, 476
twolined spittlebug, 368–70
twomarked treehopper, 366
twospotted spider mite, 392–94
twospotted stink bug, 550
twostriped grasshopper 52
twostriped walkingstick, 60
twotailed swallowtail, 170
Typhlocyba pomaria, 360
Typophorus nigritus, 190

Udea profundalis, 90
Udea rubigalis, 90
uglynest caterpillar, 88
Uhler stink bug, 228
umbrella pine scale, 346
Unaspis euonymi, 350
unicorn caterpillar, 152
Urbanus proteus, 106
Uresiphita reversalis, 102
Urocerus species, 460
Uroleucon ambrosiae, 306
Uroleucon pseudambrosiae, 306
Uroleucon rudbeckiae, 306
Utamphorphora crataegi, 306

vagabond crambus, 92
Vanessa annabella, 172
Vanessa atalanta, 172
Vanessa cardui, 172
Vanessa virginiensis, 172
variable oakleaf caterpillar, 152
variegated cutworm, 134
variegated fritillary, 174
variegated leafhopper, 360
variegated leafroller, 98
Vasates aceriscrumena, 430
Vasates quadripedes, 430
vegetable leafminer, 206
vegetable weevil, 538
velvet mites, 562
Vespa crabro germana, 244
Vespula flavipilosa, 244
Vespula germanica, 244
Vespula maculifrons, 244
Vespula pensylvanica, 242
Vespula squamosa, 244
Vespula vulgaris, 244
viburnum clearwing borer, 466

viburnum leaf beetle, 180
viceroy, 174
vinegar flies, 238
violet sawfly, 80
Virginiacreeper clearwing, 466
Virginiacreeper leafhopper, 360
Virginiacreeper sphinx, 148
virus diseases of insects, 568
Vitacea polistiformis, 466

walkingstick, 60
walnut aphid, 306
walnut blister mite, 430
walnut caterpillar, 150
walnut husk fly, 236
walnut lace bug, 384
walnut scale, 348
walnut shoot moth, 444
walnut sphinx, 148
wasps, 8, 424–29, 448, 556–59,
    564–67
waterlily aphid, 302
waterlily leaf beetle, 182
waterlily leaf cutter, 102
wax scales, 334
wax, 14
webbing coneworm, 254
web-spinning sawflies, 108
webworms, 86–92, 118–19
weevils, 35, 276–83, 220–21, 450, 454,
    488, 532–41
west coast lady, 172
western ash bark beetle, 492
western ash plant bug, 376
western aster root aphid, 506
western bean cutworm, 140
western black flea beetle, 198
western boxelder bug, 230
western cherry fruit fly, 236
western conifer seed bug, 232
western corn rootworm, 192
western erineum mite, 432
western flower thrips, 222
western grape leafhopper, 360
western grapeleaf skeletonizer, 110
western lawn moth, 92
western lubber, 54
western masked chafer, 524
western pine spittlebug, 370
western pine tip moth, 438
western pineshoot borer, 440
western poplar agrilus, 476
western poplar clearwing, 466
western potato flea beetle, 198
western potato leafhopper, 358
western raspberry fruitworm, 274
western rose chafer, 270
western sod webworm, 92
western spotted cucumber beetle, 196
western spruce budworm, 104

western striped cucumber beetle, 194
western striped flea beetle, 198
western subterranean termite, 510
western tarnished plant bug, 226
western tent caterpillar, 112
western tentiform leafminer, 212
western tiger swallowtail, 170
western tussock moth, 122
western yellowjacket, 242
western yellowstriped armyworm, 136
white apple leafhopper, 360
white flannel moth, 158
white grubs, 268, 524–29
white peach scale, 354
white pine aphid, 306
white pine sawfly, 74
white pine sheath mite, 406
white pine weevil, 42, 450
white prunicola scale, 354
whitebanded elm leafhopper, 364
whiteflies, 10, 35–36, 284–89
whitefringed beetle, 538
whitelined sphinx, 148
whitemarked tussock moth, 120
whites, 166
whitespotted sawyer, 486
Willamette mite, 400
willow beakedgall midge, 420
willow conegall midge, 420
willow flea weevil, 220

willow redgall sawfly, 428
willow sawfly, 76
wilt diseases, 568
winged euonymus scale, 346
winter grain mite, 398
wireworms, 542
witch-hazel leaf gall aphid, 408
wolf spiders, 560
wood borers, 42–43, 460–90
woods weevil, 534
wool sower gall wasp, 426
woolly alder aphid, 312
woolly aphids, 37, 300, 310–14, 506
woolly apple aphid, 300, 310
woolly beech aphid, 306, 312
woolly elm aphid, 300, 310
woolly hawthorn aphid, 300, 310
woolly pear aphid, 300, 310
woolly pine adelgids, 314
woolly whitefly, 288
woollybears, 126

Xanthogaleruca nymphaeae, 182
Xanthopastis timais, 472
Xenoglossa species, 574
Xestia adela, 140
Xestia dolosa, 140
Xylocopa species, 448
Xylosandrus compactus, 498
Xylosandrus crassiusculus, 498
Xylosandrus germanus, 498

yaupon psyllid, 416
yellow and black argiope, 560
yellow crambus, 92
yellow pecan aphid, 306
yellow poplar weevil, 220
yellow spider mite, 400
yellow woollybear, 126
yellowheaded spruce sawfly, 74
yellowjackets, 46–47, 242–45, 556
yellowlegged paper wasp, 556
yellowmargined leaf beetle, 190
yellownecked caterpillar, 150
yellowstriped armyworm, 136
yellowstriped fruitworm, 262
yucca plant bug, 376
yucca weevil, 488

Zadiprion townsendi, 74
zebra caterpillar, 142
Zelleria haimbachi, 216
Zelus species, 552
Zeugophora scutellaris, 220
Zeuzera pyrina, 468
ziczac leafhopper, 360
Zimmerman pine moth, 470
Zonosemata electa, 238
zoysiagrass mite, 432
Zygogramma exclamationis, 184